Adolescence

SECOND EDITION

Laurence Steinberg

Temple University

Advisory Editor
Urie Bronfenbrenner
Cornell University

McGraw-Hill Publishing Company
New York St. Louis San Francisco Auckland Bogotá Caracas
Hamburg Lisbon London Madrid Mexico Milan Montreal New Delhi
Oklahoma City Paris San Juan São Paulo Singapore Sydney
Tokyo Toronto

For Wendy
and Benjamin

Second Edition
9876543
ADOLESCENCE

Library of Congress Cataloging-in-Publication Data
Steinberg, Laurence D., 1952–
  Adolescence Laurence Steinberg—2nd ed.
  Includes bibliographies and index.
  ISBN 0-07-557076-9
  1. Adolescence. 2. Adolescent psychology. 3. Youth—United States—
Social conditions. 4. Personality. 5. Developmental psychology. I. Title.
HQ796.S826 1989   88-8389
305.2'35—dc19   CIP

Permissions Acknowledgments appear below and continue on page 466.

Chapter-opening photos

Introduction: Hazel Hankin / Stock, Boston; **Chapter 1:** Joel Gordon; **Chapter 2:** Susan Lapides / Design Conceptions; **Chapter 3:** Spencer C. Grant III / The Picture Cube; **Chapter 4:** Joel Gordon; **Chapter 5:** Suzanne Arms Wimberley / Jeroboam; **Chapter 6:** Paul Conklin / Monkmeyer; **Chapter 7:** Barbara Alper / Stock, Boston; **Chapter 8:** Peter Menzel; **Chapter 9:** Owen Franken / Stock, Boston; **Chapter 10:** Peter Vandermark / Stock, Boston; **Chapter 11:** Peter Vandermark / Stock, Boston; **Chapter 12:** Spencer Grant / The Picture Cube; **Chapter 13:** Michael O'Brien / Archive.

Cover Photo: Craig Aurness / Woodfin Camp & Associates.

Preface

The first time I was asked to teach a semester-long course in adolescent development, my graduate advisor—who at that time had been teaching adolescent development for ten years—took me aside. "Getting them to learn the stuff is easy," John said, smiling. "Unfortunately, you'll only have about three weeks to do it. It'll take you ten weeks just to get them to *unlearn* all the junk they're sure is true."

He was right. I would present study after study documenting that turmoil isn't the norm for most adolescents, that most teenagers have relatively good relationships with their parents, that adolescence isn't an inherently stressful period, and so on, and my students would nod diligently. But five minutes later someone would tell the class about his or her cousin Billy, who had either run away from home, attempted to set his parents' bedroom on fire, or refused to say a word to either his mother or his father for eight years.

As most instructors discover, teaching adolescent development is both exhilarating and exasperating. Every student comes into class an expert; for many of them, adolescence wasn't very long ago. No good instructor wants to squelch the interest and curiosity most students bring with them when they first come into a class. But no conscientious teacher wants to see students leave with little more than the preconceptions they came in with and an even firmer conviction that social scientists who study human development are out of touch with the "real" world.

Urie Bronfenbrenner once wrote that the science of child development had found itself caught between "a rock and a soft place"—between rigor and relevance. Teachers of adolescent development find themselves in the same boat. How do you present scientific research on adolescent development in way students find interesting, believable, relevant, and worth remembering when the term is over? I hope this book will help.

About the Second Edition

About the time of the publication of the first edition of *Adolescence*, the study of development during the second decade of the life cycle suddenly became a hot topic. New journals, devoted exclusively to the study of adolescence, began publication; established journals in the field of child and adolescent development became deluged with submissions; more and more well-trained scholars specializing in the study of adolescent development appeared on the scene. During the four years between the publication of the first and second editions of this text, our understanding of adolescent development expanded dramatically.

The second edition of this textbook reflects this new and more substantial knowledge base. Although the book's original organization has been retained, the material in each chapter has been significantly updated and revised. More than 300 new studies have been cited.

In some areas of inquiry, issues that were unresolved at the time of the first edition have been settled by newer and more definitive studies. In many cases, conclusions that had been tentatively accepted by the field in the early 1980s were abandoned in favor of more contemporary views. For instance, when the first edition went to press, most scholars conceived of various aspects of problem behavior—drug use, unprotected sex, delinquency, for example—as being more or less independent phenomena, and theorists went out of their way to treat these issues under separate headings. (In the first edition, these issues were discussed often as boxed inserts in separate chapters.) By the time this edition went to press, however, our theories of adolescent problem behavior had changed substantially, because the weight of the evidence began to indicate that the various problem behaviors associated with adolescence are indeed highly interrelated. New theories linking these problem areas to one another necessitated discussing them in a unified, coherent fashion. Accordingly, *Adolescence* was revised to reflect this change in perspective, and Chapter 13, "Psychosocial Problems in Adolescence," devoted entirely to psychosocial problems was added.

This new chapter presents fuller, more detailed, interrelated treatments of the several pressing psychosocial issues including extensive discussions of adolescent pregnancy and its consequences for both parent and child, teenage depression and suicide, juvenile crime and delinquency, and drug and alcohol use. Despite this organizational modification, these issues should still be understood in the light of what we know about normative adolescent development.

In yet other areas, our knowledge has expanded so dramatically that several altogether new sections were added to the text. In addition to the new chapter dealing exclusively with psychosocial problems, readers also will find expanded sections on early versus late physical maturation, hormonal influences on behavior, social cognition during adolescence, transformations in family relations, adaptation to the transition into secondary school, and influences on academic achievement. The expansion of knowledge during the past four years about adolescents from minority groups has permitted increased coverage of the ways in which the course of development during adolescence is affected by race and culture. These additions, corrections, and expansions are natural responses to the development of new knowledge in a dynamic and growing scientific field.

This edition of *Adolescence* also contains a new feature that runs throughout the text. Several of my colleagues who were kind enough to review the first edition as plans were being made for a revision suggested that questions concerning differences and similarities between the sexes be addressed more explicitly. As a consequence, I have added material to each chapter that considers in detail whether a particular pattern of adolescent development is different for boys and girls. I emphasize the word "whether" here, for in many instances the scientific evidence suggests that the similarities between the sexes are far more striking than the differences. Some of the topics I examine are whether there are sex differences in the impact of early pubertal maturation, in cognitive abilities, in rates of depression, in relations with mothers and fathers, and in the nature of the transition into adulthood.

Adolescent Development in Context

If there is a guiding theme to *Adolescence,* it is this: adolescent development cannot be understood apart from the context in which young people grow up. Identity crises, generation gaps, and peer pressure may be features of adolescent life in contemporary society, but their prevalence has more to do with the nature of our society than with the nature of adolescence as a period in the life cycle. In order to understand how adolescents develop in contemporary society, students need first to understand the world in which adolescents live and how that world affects their behavior and social relationships. I have therefore devoted a good deal of attention in this book to the contexts in which adolescents live—families, peer groups, schools, and work settings—to how these contexts are changing, and to how these changes are changing the nature of adolescence.

Organization

The overall organization of this book has not changed since the first edition. Specifically, the chapters on psychosocial development during adolescence are separate from those on the contexts of adolescence. In this way, the psychosocial concerns of adolescence—identity, autonomy, intimacy, sexuality, and achievement—are presented as central developmental concerns that surface across, and are affected by, different settings.

This book contains an introduction and thirteen chapters, which are grouped into three parts: the *fundamental biological, cognitive, and social changes of the period* (Part One); the *contexts of adolescence* (Part Two); and *psychosocial development during the adolescent years* (Part Three). The introduction presents a model for studying adolescence developed by John Hill that serves as the organizational framework for the text. I have found the framework to be extremely helpful in teaching adolescent development, and I highly recommend using it. However, if the model does not fit with your course outline or your own perspective on adolescence, it is possible to use the text without using the framework. Each chapter is self-contained, so it is not necessary to assign chapters in the sequence in which they are ordered in the text. However, if you choose to use the model presented in the introduction, it may be helpful to follow the text organization.

Theory and Methods

One of the things you will notice about *Adolescence* when you thumb through the contents is that the ubiquitous chapters on "theories of adolescence," and "research methods" are missing. The chapter titles are indeed missing, but the material isn't. After teaching adolescence for many years, I am convinced that students seldom remember a word of the chapters on theory and methods because the information in them is presented out of context. Therefore, although there is plenty of theory in this text, it is presented when it is most relevant, in a way that shows students how research and theory are related. At the beginning of the chapter on intimacy, for example, Sullivan's perspective on intimacy (and on psychosocial development in general) is presented, and then the relevant research is examined. Similarly, the research methods and tools employed in the study of

adolescence are discussed in the context of specific studies that illustrate the powers—or pitfalls—of certain strategies. My approach has been to blend theory, research, and practical applications in a way that shows students how the three depend on each other.

Acknowledgments

Revising a textbook at a time when so much new information is available is a challenge that requires much assistance. Over the years my students have suggested many ways in which the text might be improved, and I have learned a great deal from listening to them. I am especially grateful to three students in particular, Sudha Kaul, Nina Mounts, and Sarah Mulder, who ably tracked down much of the new research published in the four years between editions; and to several colleagues, including Joseph Adelson of the University of Michigan, Ann Arbor; Kim Dolgin of Ohio Wesleyan University; Thomas R. Sommerkamp of Central Missouri State University; and especially Larry Shelton of the University of Vermont, who carefully reviewed the first edition and suggested a variety of ways in which the text might be revised. I also wish to thank my colleagues at Random House, Mary Falcon, Barry Fetterolf, and Rochelle Diogenes, who helped develop the book; Sheila Friedling and Susan Friedman, who edited the manuscript and readied it for production; and John Lennard, Sandra Josephson, Safra Nimrod, Barbara Salz, and Juanita Brown, who worked on various phases of the production process. Finally, I am thankful to the many colleagues across the country who took the time to write during the past four years with comments and suggestions based on their firsthand experiences using *Adolescence* in the classroom.

Contents in Brief

Contents

Adolescent Development in Context

INTRODUCTION

PREVIEW

1. The study of adolescent development in contemporary society requires information from a variety of disciplines, including psychology, sociology, anthropology, history, biology, and education. Valuable contributions to the understanding of adolescence have been made by social and behavioral scientists working from a range of perspectives.

2. It is difficult to specify what the boundaries of adolescence are. Adolescence has a variety of beginnings and endings for each individual.

3. Development during adolescence is the result of an interplay among three fundamental forces—biological, cognitive, and social—and the context in which young people live. In order to understand how adolescents develop in contemporary society, we need to understand more about the ways in which society has changed and how these changes have affected young people.

4. The central psychosocial concerns during adolescence revolve around the same basic issues that surface repeatedly throughout the life cycle. But during adolescence, these concerns emerge in new forms and change in special and important ways

Imagine you are a member of the state legislature, considering a bill that has been submitted by the Subcommittee on Educational Policy. The bill would lower the age at which adolescents could voluntarily leave school from age 16 to age 14. In essence, it would eliminate compulsory high school in your state, making formal education after the age of 14 entirely optional and leaving the decision to attend high school to each young person.

Before voting, you have many opportunities to ask questions of a panel of experts assembled by the subcommittee. You have already begun to form an opinion, but you want to be sure about your decision because you realize that a change of this magnitude would not only affect the lives of thousands of teenagers, it would also have an impact on family life, on the state's work force, and on the state's systems of secondary and postsecondary education.

The floor is open for questions. You ask the subcommittee's chair why the majority of her group favors the change. You explain that you represent a district in one of the state's largest cities and you are worried that your constituents will feel that letting teenagers out of school early will only add to the growing youth unemployment problem.

The chair motions to one of the panel's legal experts to respond to your question. The lawyer replies that adolescents are old enough to make their own decisions about whether to continue their education and indicates that it may be unconstitutional to hold people in school if they don't want to be there. "Besides," he says, "what evidence is there that staying in high school helps people find jobs?" He passes the microphone to an anthropologist who specializes in the study of young people in other cultures. She cites examples of many societies in which young people marry, have children, and work by the time they are 14 years old. Another panel member, a historian, points out that as recently as seventy years ago in this country, most individuals left school before the age of 14.

Another historian, however, who has dissented from the panel's recommendation, interrupts the speaker. "Things are not the same in this country today as they were seventy years ago," she points out. "And things are certainly different here from what they are in societies in which people become adults at the age of 14. We have to make decisions about adolescents on the basis of the world they live in *today*, not the one they lived in seventy years ago."

You want to hear from some of the psychologists on the panel. "Are 14-year-olds emotionally ready to make important decisions about their futures?" you ask. "Are 16-year-olds more mature than 14-year-olds, or is there little difference between adolescents who are only two years apart?" The psychologists on the panel disagree with each other. One replies that she wonders whether even *16-year-olds* are capable of making important decisions about their futures: she vehemently opposes changing the age at which adolescents may leave school. In fact, she thinks the age should be *raised* to 18. The other psychologist, however, is less certain; he argues that it is hard to make generalizations about adolescents because individuals develop at such different rates. "Some 14-year-olds," he says, "are more mature than many 18-year olds. Shouldn't they be given the chance to choose what they want to do? Furthermore," he adds, "adolescents' parents undoubtedly will help their children make decisions about whether to stay in school. The 14-year-olds won't be facing the dilemma on their own."

After listening to the panel members speak about the bill, you realize that you have never thought much about adolescence before. It has always seemed natural that there is a period of time between childhood and adulthood when people are not quite children any more but not yet ready to live as adults. Isn't adolescence supposed to be a time when people have "identity crises," when they agonize over dates and popularity in school and argue with their parents about staying out late or doing their schoolwork? How could people with these concerns be capable of deciding something as important as whether or not to continue in school? You realize now, however, that generalizing about the na-

At the turn of the century, the majority of teenagers left school before the age of 14. Like many of their contemporaries, these adolescents were employed full-time in factories. (Culver Pictures)

ture of adolescence may be more difficult than you had thought.

A MULTIDISCIPLINARY APPROACH

What is the nature of adolescents' identity development in a changing world? How should society deal with problems of youth unemployment, teenage pregnancy, or juvenile delinquency? What is the best way to prepare young people for the roles of adulthood? Should parents change the way they treat their children when those children become teenagers? Should adolescents be required to obtain their parents' consent in order to receive contraceptives? When *should* adolescents be permitted to leave school legally?

Answering these questions requires a thorough understanding of adolescents' psychological development, and in this book we will examine how—and why—people's hopes and plans, their fears and anxieties, and their ques-

tions and concerns change as they grow into adulthood. But answering these difficult questions also requires knowledge of how individuals develop physically, how their relationships with parents and friends change, how young people as a group are viewed and treated by society, how adolescence in our society differs from adolescence in other cultures, and how the nature of adolescence itself has changed over the years. In other words, a complete understanding of adolescence in contemporary society depends on being familiar with biological, social, sociological, cultural, and historical perspectives on adolescence.

In this book, we look at adolescence from a *multidisciplinary* perspective—a perspective that draws on a variety of disciplines. Each provides a view of adolescence that helps, in its own way, to further our understanding of this period of the life cycle. We will look at contributions to the study of adolescence made by biologists, psychologists, educators, sociologists, historians, and anthropologists. The challenge ahead of us in this book is not to try to determine which perspective on adolescence is best, but to find ways in which to integrate contributions from different disciplines into a coherent and comprehensive viewpoint on the nature of adolescent development in contemporary society.

THE BOUNDARIES OF ADOLESCENCE

Let's begin with a fairly basic question. When does adolescence begin and end? Perhaps we can gain some insight into this question by examining the word itself.

The word *adolescence* is Latin in origin, derived from the verb *adolescere*, which means "to grow into adulthood." In all societies, adolescence is a time of growing up, of moving from the immaturity of childhood into the maturity of adulthood. Adolescence is a period of transitions: biological, psychological, social, economic. It is an exciting time of life. Individuals become interested in sex and become biologically capable of having children. They become wiser, more sophisticated, and better able to make their own decisions. Adolescents are permitted to work, to get married, and to vote. And eventually, adolescents are expected to be able to support themselves financially.

Development during adolescence involves a series of passages from immaturity into maturity. Some of these passages are long and some are short; some are smooth and others are rough. And not all of them occur at the same time.

The Boundaries of Adolescence

One problem that students of adolescence encounter early is a fundamental one: deciding when adolescence begins and ends, what the boundaries of the period are. Different theorists have proposed various markers, but there is little agreement on this issue.

Here are some examples of the ways in which adolescence has been distinguished from childhood and adulthood that we shall examine in this book. Which boundaries make the most sense to you?

	WHEN ADOLESCENCE BEGINS	WHEN ADOLESCENCE ENDS
Biological	Onset of puberty	Becoming capable of sexual reproduction
Emotional	Beginning of detachment from parents	Attainment of separate sense of identity
Cognitive	Emergence of more advanced reasoning abilities	Consolidation of advanced reasoning abilities
Interpersonal	Beginning of a shift in interest from parental to peer relations	Development of capacity for intimacy with peers
Social	Beginning of entrance into adult work roles, family roles, and citizen roles	Full attainment of adult status and privileges
Educational	Entrance into junior high school	Completion of formal schooling
Legal	Attainment of juvenile status	Attainment of majority status
Chronological	Attainment of designated age of adolescence (e.g., 13 years)	Attainment of designated age of adulthood (e.g., 20 years)
Cultural	Entrance into period of training for a ceremonial rite of passage	Completion of ceremonial rite of passage

Consequently, it is quite possible—and perhaps even likely—that an individual will mature in some respects before he or she matures in others. The various aspects of adolescence have different beginnings and different endings for every individual. Every young person is a child in some ways, an adolescent in other ways, and an adult in still others.

Early, Middle, and Late Adolescence

Although adolescence may span a ten-year period, most social scientists and practitioners recognize that so much psychological and social growth takes place during this decade, it makes more sense to view the adolescent years as composed of a series of phases than as one homogeneous stage. The 13-year-old whose interests center around video games and baseball, for example, has little in common with the 18-year-old who is contemplating marriage, worried about the draft, and beginning a career.

Social scientists who study adolescence usually differentiate among **early adolescence,** which covers the period from about age 11 through age 14, **middle adolescence,** from about age 15 through age 18, and **late adolescence** (or *youth,* as it is sometimes known), from about age 18 through age 21 (Kagan and Coles, 1972; Keniston, 1970; Lipsitz, 1977). These divisions, as you may have guessed, correspond to the way in which our society groups young people in educational institutions; they are the approximate ages that customarily mark attendance at middle or junior high school, high school, and college. In discussing development during adolescence, we will need to be sensitive not only to differences between adolescence and childhood, or between adolescence and adulthood, but to differences among the various phases of adolescence itself.

A FRAMEWORK FOR STUDYING ADOLESCENT DEVELOPMENT

In order to organize information from a variety of different perspectives, this book uses a frame-

Social scientists who study adolescence usually differentiate among three periods: *early adolescence* (approximately 11 through 14 years of age), *middle adolescence* (15 through 18 years), and *late adolescence* (18 through 21 years). (Left and center, David S. Strickler/The Picture Cube; right, Rick Smolan/Stock, Boston)

work that is based largely on a model suggested by psychologist John Hill (1983). The framework is organized around three basic components: the *fundamental changes* of adolescence, the *contexts* of adolescence, and the *psychosocial developments* of adolescence.

Part One: The Fundamental Changes of Adolescence

What, if anything, is distinctive about adolescence as a period in the life cycle? According to Hill, there are three features of adolescent development that give the period its special flavor and significance: (1) the onset of puberty, (2) the emergence of more advanced thinking abilities, and (3) the transition into new roles in society. We refer to these three sets of changes—biological, cognitive, and social—as the *fundamental changes of adolescence*. And they are changes that occur universally; virtually without exception, all adolescents in every society go through them.

Biological changes.   The chief elements of the biological changes of adolescence—which together are referred to as **puberty**—involve changes in the young person's physical appearance (including breast development in girls, the growth of facial hair in boys, and a dramatic increase in height for both sexes) and the attainment of reproductive capability—the ability to conceive children (Petersen and Taylor, 1980).

Chapter 1 describes the impact of puberty on the adolescent's psychological development and social relations. Puberty requires adaptation on the part of young people and those around them. The adolescent's self-image, for example, is jolted by marked changes in physical appearance. The body changes, the face changes, and not surprisingly, the way the adolescent feels about himself or herself changes. Relationships inside the family are transformed by the adolescent's greater need for privacy and by his or her interest in forming intimate relationships with peers. Girls may suddenly feel uncomfortable about being physically affectionate with their fathers, and boys with their mothers. And of

The development of more sophisticated thinking abilities is one of the most striking changes to take place during adolescence. (Elizabeth Hamlin/Stock, Boston)

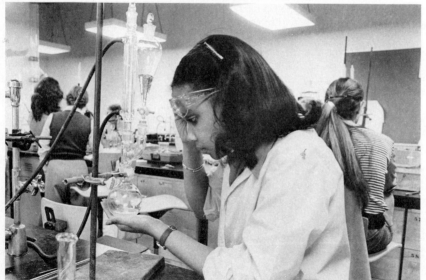

course, adolescents' friendships are altered by newly emerging sexual impulses and concerns.

Cognitive changes. The word *cognitive* is used to refer to the processes that underlie how people think about things. Memory and problem solving are both examples of cognitive processes. Changes in thinking abilities, which are dealt with in Chapter 2, constitute the second of the three fundamental changes of the adolescent period. The emergence of more sophisticated thinking abilities is one of the most striking changes to take place during adolescence. Compared with children, for example, adolescents are much better able to think about hypothetical situations (that is, things that have not yet happened but will, or things that may not happen but could) and are much better able to think about abstract concepts, such as friendship, democracy, or morality (Inhelder and Piaget, 1958).

The implications of these cognitive changes are also far-reaching. The ability to think more capably in hypothetical and abstract terms affects the way adolescents think about themselves, their relationships, and the world around them. We will see, for example, that teenagers' abilities to plan ahead, to argue with their parents, to solve chemistry problems, and to resolve moral dilemmas are all linked to changes in the way they think. For the first time, individuals become able to think in logical ways about what their lives will be like in the future, about their relationships with friends and family, and about politics, religion, and philosophy.

Social changes. All societies distinguish between individuals who are thought of as children and those who are seen as ready to become adults. Our society, for example, distinguishes between people who are "underage," or minors, and people who have reached the age of majority. It is not until adolescence that individuals are permitted to drive, purchase alcohol, and vote. Such changes in rights, privileges, and responsibilities—which are examined in Chapter 3—constitute the third set of fundamental

THE THREE FUNDAMENTAL CHANGES OF ADOLESCENCE

Biological Changes

Cognitive Changes

Social Changes

changes that occur at adolescence: social changes. In some cultures, the social changes of adolescence are marked by a formal ceremony— a **rite of passage.** In others, the transition is less clearly demarcated. Still, a change in social status is a universal feature of adolescence (Ford and Beach, 1951).

Society's redefinition provokes reconsideration of the young person's capabilities and competencies. As the young person's treatment by society changes, so do relationships around the home, at school, and in the peer group. Changes in social status also permit the young person to enter new roles and engage in new activities, such as marriage and work, which dramatically alter his or her self-image and relationships with others. The adolescent, on the verge of becoming an adult, has choices to consider that previously did not exist for him or her.

Part Two: The Contexts of Adolescence

Although all adolescents experience the biological, cognitive, and social changes of the period, the *effects* of these changes are not uniform for all young people. Puberty makes some adolescents feel attractive and self-assured, but it makes others feel ugly and self-conscious. Being able to think in hypothetical terms makes some youngsters thankful that they grew up with the parents they have, but it prompts others to run away in search of a better life. Reaching 18 years of age prompts some teenagers to enlist unhesitatingly in the army or apply for a marriage license, but for others, becoming an adult is frightening and unsettling.

If the fundamental changes of adolescence are universal, why are their effects so varied? Why aren't all individuals affected in the same ways by puberty, by changes in thinking, and by changes in social and legal status? The answer lies in the fact that the psychological impact of the biological, cognitive, and social changes of adolescence is shaped by the environment in which the changes take place (Bronfenbrenner, 1979). In other words, psychological development during adolescence is a product of the interplay between a set of three very basic and universal changes and the context in which these changes are experienced.

Consider, for example, two 14-year-old girls growing up in neighboring communities. When Alice went through puberty, around age 13, her parents responded by restricting her social life because they were afraid that Alice would become too involved with boys and neglect her schoolwork. Alice felt that her parents were being unfair and also foolish. She rarely had a chance to meet any boys she wanted to date, anyway. All the older boys went to the high school across town. Even though she was in the eighth grade, she was still going to school with fifth-graders. And she couldn't meet anyone through work, either. Her school would not issue work permits to any student under the age of 16.

Jennifer's adolescence was very different. For one thing, when she had her first period, her parents took her aside and discussed sex and pregnancy with her. They explained how different contraceptives worked and made an appointment for Jennifer to see a gynecologist in town in case she ever needed to discuss something with a doctor. Although she was still only 14 years old, Jennifer knew that she would begin dating soon, because in her community the junior and senior high schools had been combined into one large school, and the older boys frequently asked the younger girls out. In addition, since there was no prohibition at her school against young teenagers working, Jennifer decided to get a job; she knew she would need money to buy clothes if she was going to start dating.

Two teenage girls. Each goes through puberty, each grows intellectually, and each moves closer in age to becoming an adult. Yet each grows up under very different circumstances: in different families, in different schools, with different groups of peers, and under different work conditions. Both are adolescents, but their adolescent experiences are markedly different. And as a result, each girl's psychological development will follow a different course.

Alice's and Jennifer's worlds may seem quite different from one another. Yet the two girls share many things in common, at least in comparison to two girls growing up in different parts of the world or in different historical eras. Imagine how different your adolescence would have been if you had grown up without going to high school and had had to work full-time from the age of 12. Imagine how different it would have been to grow up 100 years ago—or how different it will be to grow up 100 years from today. And imagine how different adolescence is for a youngster whose family is very poor and for one whose family is very rich. Even siblings growing up within the same family have different growing-up experiences, depending on their birth order within the family and various other factors (Daniels et al., 1985). You can see that it is impossible to generalize about the nature of adolescence without taking into account the surroundings and circumstances in which young people grow up.

THE FOUR CONTEXTS OF ADOLESCENCE

Families

Peer Groups

Schools

The Workplace

For this reason, the second component of our framework is the *context of adolescence*. In modern societies, there are four main contexts that affect the development and behavior of young people: families, peer groups, schools, and work settings. The nature and structure of these contexts dramatically affect the way in which the fundamental changes of adolescence are experienced. To the extent that one adolescent's world differs from another's, the two young people will have very different experiences during the adolescent years.

Although young people growing up in modern America share some experiences with young people all over the world, their development is distinctively different from that of young people in other societies, because their families, peer groups, schools, and work settings are different. In other words, the contexts of adolescence are themselves shaped and defined by the larger society in which young people live. In this book, we shall be especially interested in how the contexts of adolescence have changed in Western society, and in the implications of these changes for adolescent development.

As in discussions of young people's psychological development, it is important when discussing families, peer groups, schools, and work settings to differentiate among the phases of adolescence. Take adolescent peer groups, for example. During early adolescence, peer groups are usually composed of teenagers of the same sex. During middle adolescence, peer groups become a context in which males and females interact. And during late adolescence, the large peer groups of earlier phases begin to disintegrate.

Let us now briefly survey how the contexts of adolescence have changed as society has changed.

Families. Frequent moves, high rates of divorce, increasing numbers of single-parent households, and more and more working mothers have become characteristic of family life in contemporary America (Parke, 1984). In Chapter 4, we look at these changes and try to assess how they are affecting young people's psychological development.

Peer groups.   Over the last 100 years, age-segregated peer groups—groups of people of the same age who spend most of their time together—have come to play an increasingly important role in the socialization and development of teenagers (Eisenstadt, 1956). But has the rise of peer groups been a positive or negative influence on young people's development? In Chapter 5, we discuss how peer groups are changing adolescence in contemporary America.

Schools.   Chapter 6 surveys schools as a context for adolescent development. Since the 1930s, Americans have turned more and more to schools as a setting to occupy, socialize, and educate adolescents (D. Tanner, 1972). Today, however, controversy about the purpose and nature of secondary education makes newspaper headlines and generates vehement debate (Boyer, 1983; Goodlad, 1984; Sizer, 1984). What role should schools play in the preparation of young people for adulthood? This is but one of the many difficult questions we will be examining.

The Workplace.   If you've been to a fast-food restaurant lately, you know that many of today's teenagers are working. But did you know that more adolescents are working now than at any other time in the last twenty-five years (Greenberger and Steinberg, 1986)? In Chapter 7, we look at the world of adolescent work and at how part-time jobs are affecting young people's psychological development and well-being.

Part Three: Psychosocial Development During Adolescence

Five sets of developmental concerns are paramount during adolescence: **identity; autonomy; intimacy; sexuality;** and **achievement.** These

The nature of adolescence is shaped by the context in which young people grow up. This young migrant worker's adolescence is likely to be very different from that of an affluent, suburban youth. (Peter Southwick/Stock, Boston)

five sets of *psychosocial issues,* as well as certain psychosocial problems that may arise at adolescence, constitute the third, and final, component of our framework. Theorists use the word ***psychosocial*** to describe aspects of development that are both psychological and social in nature. Sexuality, for instance, is a psychosocial issue because it involves psychological change (that is, changes in the individual's emotions, motivations, and behavior) as well as changes in the individual's social relations with others.

Of course, identity, autonomy, intimacy, sexuality, and achievement are not concerns that arise for the first time during the adolescent years; and psychological or social problems can and do occur during all periods of the life cycle. Nor do psychosocial concerns disappear when the adolescent becomes an adult. These five sets of issues are present throughout the entire life span, from infancy through late adulthood. They represent basic developmental challenges that all people face as they grow and change: discovering and understanding who they are as individuals (identity); establishing a healthy sense of independence (autonomy); forming close and caring relationships with other people

(intimacy); expressing sexual feelings and enjoying physical contact with others (sexuality); and being successful and competent members of society (achievement).

Although these are not new concerns to the adolescent, development in each of these areas takes a special turn during the adolescent years. Understanding how and why such psychosocial developments take place during adolescence is a special concern of social scientists interested in this age period. We know that individuals form close relationships before adolescence, for example, but why is it during adolescence that

THE PSYCHOSOCIAL ISSUES AND PROBLEMS OF ADOLESCENCE

Identity

Autonomy

Intimacy

Sexuality

Achievement

Psychosocial Problems

intimate relationships with opposite-sex age-mates first develop? We know that infants struggle with learning how to be independent, but why during adolescence do individuals need to be more on their own and make some decisions apart from their parents? We know that children fantasize about what they will be when they grow up, but why is it not until adolescence that these fantasies give way to serious concerns?

Part Three of this book (Chapters 8–13) discusses changes in each of the five psychosocial areas and examines several common psychosocial problems.

Identity.   Chapter 8 deals with changes in identity, self-esteem, and self-conceptions. At adolescence, a variety of important changes in the realm of identity occur. The adolescent may wonder who he or she really is and where he or she is headed (Erikson, 1968). Coming to terms

with these questions may involve a period of role experimentation—a time of trying on different personalities in an attempt to discover one's true self. The adolescent's quest for identity is a quest not only for a personal sense of self, but for recognition from others and from society that he or she is a special and unique individual.

Autonomy.   Adolescents' struggles to establish themselves as independent, self-governing individuals—in their own eyes and in the eyes of others—is a long and occasionally difficult process, not only for young people but for those around them, too. Chapter 9 focuses on three sorts of concerns that are of special importance to developing adolescents: becoming less emotionally dependent on parents, becoming able to make independent decisions, and establishing a

It is during adolescence that people first establish intimate relationships with opposite-sex age mates. Changes in the expression of intimacy as well as changes in the areas of identity, autonomy, sexuality, and achievement constitute the chief psychosocial developments of the period. (Susan Lapides/Design Conceptions)

A FRAMEWORK FOR STUDYING ADOLESCENT DEVELOPMENT

Fundamental Changes

Contexts

Psychosocial Issues and Problems

personal code of values and morals (Douvan and Adelson, 1966).

Intimacy. During adolescence, important changes take place in the individual's capacity to be intimate with others, especially with peers. As we shall see in Chapter 10, friendships emerge for the first time during adolescence that involve openness, honesty, loyalty, and exchanging confidences, rather than the mere sharing of activities and interests (Berndt, 1982). Dating takes on increased importance, and as a consequence, so does the capacity to form a relationship that is trusting and loving.

Sexuality. Sexual activity generally begins during the adolescent years. Becoming sexual is an important aspect of development during ad-

olescence—not only because it transforms the nature of relationships between adolescents and their peers but also because it raises for the young person a range of trying and difficult questions. Chapter 11 discusses these concerns, including efforts to incorporate sexuality into a still developing sense of self, the need to resolve questions about sexual values and morals, and coming to terms with the sorts of relationships into which one is prepared—or not prepared—to enter (Miller and Simon, 1980).

Achievement. In Chapter 12, we examine changes in individuals' educational and vocational behavior and plans. Important decisions—many with long-term consequences—about schooling and careers are made during adolescence. Many of these decisions depend on adolescents' achievement in school, on their evaluations of their own competencies and capabilities, on their aspirations and expectations for the future, and on the direction and advice they receive from parents, teachers, and friends (Spenner and Featherman, 1978).

Psychosocial problems. In Chapter 13, we look at four sets of problems typically associated with adolescence: teenage pregnancy, drug and alcohol use, delinquency, and depression. In each case, we examine the prevalence of the problem, the factors believed to contribute to its development, and approaches to prevention and intervention.

The illustration at left puts together the three pieces of the framework that we have been discussing: changes, contexts, and adolescent psychosocial development.

STEREOTYPES VERSUS SCIENTIFIC STUDY

One of the oldest debates in the study of adolescence is whether adolescence is an inherently stressful time for individuals. G. Stanley Hall, who is generally acknowledged as the father of the scientific study of adolescence, likened adolescence to the turbulent, transitional period in the evolution of the human species from savagery into civilization. "Adolescence is a new birth," Hall wrote. "Development is less gradual, suggestive of some ancient period of storm and stress" (1904, p. 6). Long before Hall, in the eighteenth century, French philosopher Jean-Jacques Rousseau had described adolescence by drawing an analogy to a violent storm: "As the roaring of the waves precedes the tempest, so the murmur of rising passions announces the tumultuous change. . . . Keep your hand upon the helm," he warned parents, "or all is lost" (Rousseau, 1762/1911, pp. 172–173).

Although neither Hall nor Rousseau had any scientific evidence that adolescence was any more stormy than childhood or adulthood, their portrayal of teenagers as passionate, fickle, and unpredictable individuals persists. For example, people still tend to think of adolescence as a difficult and stressful time. A 12-year-old girl once told the author that her mother had been telling her that she was going to go through a difficult time when she turned 14—as if some magical, internal alarm clock was set to trigger "storm and stress" on schedule.

The girl's mother wasn't alone in her view of adolescence, of course. Sometime this week, turn on the television and note how teenagers are depicted. If they are not portrayed as juvenile delinquents—the usual role in which they are cast—adolescents are depicted as sex-crazed idiots (if they are male), mindless schoolgirls (if they are female), or tormented lost souls, searching for their place in a strange, cruel world (if they aren't delinquent, sex-crazed, or mindless). Adolescents are one of the most stereotyped groups in American society, and as a consequence, they are one of the most misunderstood (Adelson, 1979). One recent study demonstrated that most of the undergraduates enrolled in an adolescent development course believed that adolescence was an inherently stressful period (Holmbeck and Hill, 1986). After completing the course, however, the students were less likely to endorse this view.

Many of our ideas about adolescence have been shaped by stereotyped portrayals of "troubled" youth in movies such as *Rebel Without a Cause*. Contrary to stereotypes, however, researchers have found that rebellion during adolescence is rare. (Culver Pictures)

One of the goals of this book is to provide you with a more realistic understanding of adolescent development in contemporary society. However, having a more realistic understanding of adolescence does not mean that one should gloss over or make light of the very real problems that some teenagers experience—problems such as alcoholism, dropping out of school, or family violence. Adolescence is stressful for some young people, and throughout this book, we will be asking why this is so and what can be done to make problems during adolescence less likely to occur.

In the following chapter, we examine the first of the three fundamental changes of the adolescent period—puberty.

Key Terms

achievement
autonomy
early adolescence
identity
intimacy
late adolescence

middle adolescence
psychosocial
puberty
rite of passage
sexuality

For Further Reading

ADELSON, J. (ED.). (1980). *Handbook of adolescent psychology.* New York: Wiley. This collection of articles by social scientists provides summaries of research on different aspects of adolescence and is an excellent source book.

HILL, J. (1983). Early adolescence: A research agenda. *Journal of Early Adolescence, 3,* 1–21. Psychologist John Hill discusses his framework for understanding adolescent development.

KENISTON, K. (1970). Youth: A "new" stage of life. *American Scholar, 39,* 631–641. In this article, Kenneth Keniston explains why late adolescents, or youths, must be distinguished from younger adolescents.

KETT, J. (1977). *Rites of passage: Adolescence in America, 1790 to the present.* New York: Basic Books. The history of adolescence in America, with an emphasis on how people's conception of this stage in the life cycle has changed.

LIPSITZ, J. (1977). *Growing up forgotten.* Lexington, Mass.: Lexington Books. A good source of information on the special problems of young adolescents. Lipsitz believes that social scientists and politicians have neglected this age group especially.

SPACKS, P. *The adolescent idea.* (1981). New York: Basic Books. A thorough examination of how writers, philosophers, and scientists have looked at adolescence over the years.

PART ONE

The Fundamental Changes of Adolescence

Puberty and Its Impact

CHAPTER 1

PREVIEW

1. One of the most dramatic aspects of development during adolescence is the set of biological changes that occur at puberty. The individual enters early adolescence with the physical appearance of a child and, within a few years, has the physical appearance of an adult.

2. The changes of puberty are set in motion by an elaborate process in the endocrine system. Although research has revealed that changes in hormonal levels affect physical growth and development, it is still not clear why puberty begins when it does or how the process comes to an end.

3. Barring extreme medical problems, all adolescents go through puberty. Yet despite the universality of biological change at adolescence, there are wide variations in its timing and tempo.

4. Not surprisingly, the marked changes in appearance characteristic of early adolescence have a profound impact on the young person's personality and interpersonal relationships. Researchers have focused on understanding how going through puberty affects the individual adolescent's behavior and psychological well-being and on the short- and long-term consequences of maturing early or late, relative to one's peers.

According to an old joke, there are only two things in life that one can be sure of—death and taxes. To this brief list one might add puberty—the physical changes of adolescence—for, of all the developments that take place during the second decade of life, the only truly inevitable one is physical maturation. Not all adolescents experience identity crises, rebel against their parents, or fall head over heels in love, but virtually all undergo the biological changes associated with maturation into adult reproductive capability. Indeed, the only exceptions to this developmental universal are individuals with severe physiological disorders or illnesses.

Puberty, however, is considerably affected by the context in which it occurs. Physical development is influenced by a host of environmental factors, and the timing and rate of pubertal growth varies across regions of the world, socioeconomic classes, ethnic groups, and historical eras. Today, in contemporary America, the average girl reaches menarche—the time of first menstruation—a little before her thirteenth birthday. (Age at menarche is a widely used indicator of the timing of puberty, although menarche does not indicate the *onset* of puberty. See pages 33, 36–40.) But among the Lumi people of New Guinea, the typical girl does not reach menarche until after 18 years of age (Eveleth and Tanner, 1976). Imagine how great a difference those five years make in transforming the nature of adolescence. Picture how different American high schools would be if sexual maturation did not occur until after graduation!

Physical and sexual maturation profoundly affect the way in which adolescents view themselves and the way in which they are viewed and treated by others. Yet the social environment exerts a tremendous impact on the meaning of puberty and on its psychological and social consequences. In some societies, pubertal maturation brings with it a series of complex initiation rites, which mark the passage of the young person into adulthood socially as well as physically. In other societies, recognition of the physical transformation from child into adult takes more subtle forms. Parents may merely remark that "our little boy has become a man" when they discover that he needs to shave. Early or late maturation may be cause for celebration or cause for concern, depending on what is admired or derogated in a given peer group at a given point in time. In the fifth grade, developing breasts may be a source of embarrassment; but in the ninth grade, it may be just as embarrassing *not* to have developed breasts.

In sum, even the most universal aspect of adolescence—puberty—is hardly universal in its impact on the young person. As is the case with all aspects of growth during the adolescent years, few generalizations can be made without consideration of the context in which development occurs. In this chapter, we examine just how and why the environment in which adolescents develop exerts its influence even on something as fundamental as puberty.

PUBERTY: AN OVERVIEW

Puberty derives from the Latin word *pubertas*, which means "adult." Technically, the term refers to the period during which an individual becomes capable of sexual reproduction, that is, it denotes the series of biological changes leading up to reproductive capability. More broadly speaking, however, *puberty* is used as a collective term to refer to all the physical changes that occur in the growing girl or boy as the individual passes from childhood into adulthood.

The following are the five chief physical manifestations of puberty (Marshall, 1978):

1. A *rapid acceleration in growth*, resulting in dramatic increases in both height and weight.

2. The further *development of the gonads*, or sex glands, which are the testes in males and the ovaries in females.

3. The *development of secondary sex characteristics*, which involve changes in the genitals and breasts, and the growth of pubic,

facial, and axillary (body) hair, and the further development of the sex organs.

4. *Changes in body composition,* specifically, in the quantity and distribution of fat and muscle.

5. *Changes in the circulatory and respiratory systems,* which lead to increased strength and tolerance for exercise.

Each of these sets of changes is the result of developments in the endocrine and central nervous systems, many of which begin several years before the external signs of puberty are evident.

ONSET AND TERMINATION

Only recently have scientists begun to understand the mechanism by which the physical changes of adolescence are set in motion and then ended. In the past, puberty was viewed chiefly as a series of changes that occurred rather suddenly during early adolescence. Puberty may appear to be rather sudden, judging from its external signs, but in fact it is "part of a gradual process that begins at conception. . . . [It is] the final, most rapid phase of the development of mature reproductive capacity" (Petersen and Taylor, 1980, p. 131). You may be surprised to learn that no new hormones are produced and no new bodily systems develop at puberty. Rather, some hormones that have been present since birth increase, and others decrease. Together, these endocrinological changes have dramatic effects on the young person's body.

The Endocrine System

Discussion of the onset of puberty requires a basic understanding of human endocrinology. The **endocrine system** produces, circulates, and regulates levels of hormones in the body. Hormones are highly specialized substances secreted by one or more endocrine glands. Glands are organs that stimulate particular parts of the body to respond in specific ways. Just as hormones are specialized to carry "messages" to particular cells in the body, so are the body's cells designed to receive hormonal messages selectively. For example, one of the many effects of the hormone adrenaline, secreted by the adrenal gland, is to stimulate the heart to increase its activity. The heart responds to adrenaline but not to all other hormones.

The endocrine system receives its instructions to increase or decrease circulating levels of particular hormones from the central nervous system, chiefly, the brain. When one perceives danger, for example, the brain transmits a signal to the endocrine system that results in increased adrenaline secretion. The higher level of adrenaline stimulates the heart to beat more actively, rapidly pumping blood and readying one for a fast response to any danger. When adrenaline levels reach an adequate point, the brain receives a message to this effect and instructs the endocrine system either to decrease adrenaline secretion (if the danger has passed) or maintain secretion levels as they are.

This type of **feedback loop,** through which hormonal levels are continuously monitored and adjusted, is structured somewhat like a thermostat. Hormonal levels are "set" at a certain point, just as you might set a thermostat at a certain temperature. By setting your room's thermostat at 60°F, you are instructing your heating system to go into action when the temperature falls below this level (or your air conditioning system to click on when the temperature rises above this level). Similarly, when a particular hormonal level in your body dips below the endocrine system's **set point** for that hormone, secretion of the hormone increases; when the level reaches the set point, secretion temporarily stops. And, as is the case with a room thermostat, the setting level for a particular hormone can be adjusted up or down, depending on environmental or internal bodily conditions.

A feedback loop of this sort figures very importantly at the time of the onset of puberty.

The development of secondary sex characteristics, such as the growth of facial hair, is the result of developments in the endocrine system. Many hormonal changes begin long before the external signs of puberty are evident. (Christine Carey)

Although the entire endocrine system is involved in the pubertal process, our discussion here of hormonal processes at puberty is limited to the glands, hormones, and pathways that are most important: (1) the **pituitary gland,** which controls hormonal levels in general; (2) the **hypothalamus,** the part of the lower brain stem that controls the pituitary gland; and (3) the glands that secrete the main hormones of interest in the study of puberty—the **thyroid,** the **adrenal cortex,** and the gonads (in males, the **testes** and in females, the **ovaries**).

Long before early adolescence—in fact, during infancy—a feedback loop develops involving the hypothalamus, the pituitary, and the gonads (see Figure 1.1). The hypothalamus secretes substances called **luteinizing hormone-releasing factor,** or **LH-RF,** and **follicle-stimulating hormone-releasing factor,** or **FSH-RF.** These secretions stimulate the pituitary to release two hormones called **gonadotropins**—hormones that stimulate the gonads. These gonadotropins are **luteinizing hormone (LH)** and **follicle-stimulating hormone (FSH).** LH and FSH are extremely important, since they stimulate the release of the "sex"hormones—**androgens** and **estrogens.** Although one typically thinks of androgens as "male" hormones and estrogens as "female" hormones, both types of hormones are produced by each sex, and both are present in males and females at birth. During adolescence, however, the average male produces more androgens than estrogens, and the average female, more estrogens than androgens (Petersen and Taylor, 1980).

The hypothalamus responds to the levels of sex hormones circulating in the body. Your endocrine system is set to maintain certain levels of androgens and estrogens. When these levels fall below the set points, the hypothalamus releases LH-RF and FSH-RF, which stimulate the pituitary to release LH and FSH, which, in turn, stimulate the release of sex hormones by the gonads. When sex-hormone levels reach the set point, the hypothalamus reponds by inhibiting LH-RF and FSH-RF secretion.

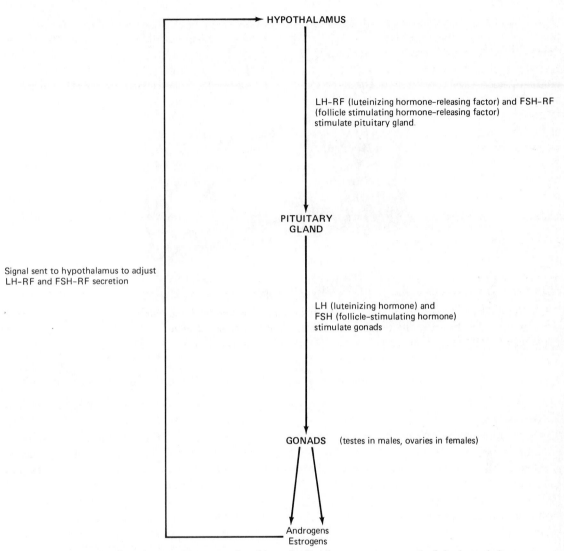

FIGURE 1.1   Levels of sex hormones are regulated by a feedback system composed of the hypothalamus, pituitary gland, and gonads. (Grumbach et al., 1974)

Endocrinological Changes at Puberty

During infancy, the set point for sex hormones is fixed so that very low levels of sex hormones will be maintained. But at puberty, there is a change in this feedback system. The hypothalamus appears to lose a certain degree of sensitivity to the sex hormones, and consequently, it takes higher and higher levels of these sub-

stances to trigger the hypothalamus to inhibit LH-RF and FSH-RF secretion. It is as if a thermostat that had previously been set at 60°F were now set at 80°F and required a lot more fuel to reach the set point. Before adolescence, the hypothalamus responds to very low levels of sex hormones by inhibiting LH-RF and FSH-RF secretion, thereby maintaining sex hormones at this low level. Right before puberty, the hypothalamus begins to lose sensitivity to the sex hormones and, consequently, permits levels of these hormones to rise. As far as is known, this gradually decreasing sensitivity of the hypothalamus to sex hormones is the chief mechanism in initiating the onset of puberty. But the cause of this change in hypothalamic sensitivity is not well understood (Grumbach, Roth, Kaplan, and Kelch, 1974). Studies do show, however, that the onset of puberty is affected by the adolescent's psychological and physical health. Stress, excessive exercise, and excessive thinness can all delay the onset of puberty (Frisch, 1983; McClintock, 1980).

In addition to the pituitary's release of gonadotropins—which stimulate the testes or ovaries to release androgens and estrogens—at puberty, the pituitary also secretes a hormone that acts on the thyroid (**thyroid-stimulating hormone,** or **TSH**), one that acts on the adrenal cortex (**adrenocorticotropic hormone,** or **ACTH**), and one that stimulates overall bodily growth (**growth hormone,** or **GH**). The release of these substances is also under the control of the hypothalamus. The thyroid and adrenal cortex, in turn, secrete hormones that cause various physical (somatic) changes to take place at puberty. The major pathways and hormonal mechanisms associated with physical development at puberty are diagrammed in Figure 1.2.

Far less is known about the mechanism through which the physical changes of puberty draw to a close. After a certain length of time, the endocrine system stabilizes levels of circulating sex hormones at an adult set point. It is not known, however, why this stabilization takes place when it does or what the physiological events leading up to the termination of puberty are (Petersen and Taylor, 1980).

FIGURE 1.2   The sequence of hormonal changes at puberty and their effects on the adolescent's body. (Shelton, 1974)

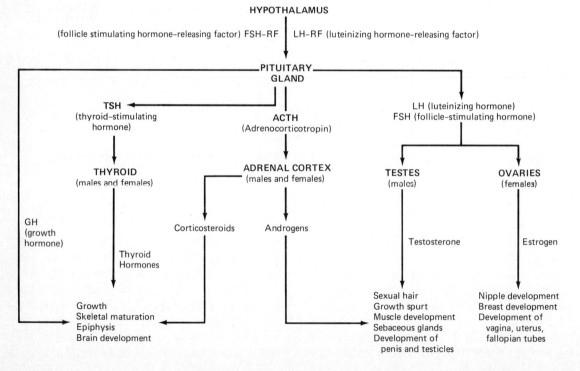

Nutritional Needs of Adolescents

According to most recent nutrition surveys in the United States, adolescent girls are one of the most poorly nourished groups in the nation. Typically cited causes of these nutritional problems are skipping meals, especially breakfast; frequently snacking on foods high in sugar; and erratic or fad dieting (Mounger, 1970). Nutrition is extremely important during adolescence because of the rapid acceleration in growth that takes place during this period. Inadequate nutrition can interfere with the growth process. Additionally, because nutritional needs increase during pregnancy, maintaining healthy eating habits is of critical importance for young women who eventually want families.

Nutrients most likely to be low in the dietary intake of adolescents, particularly girls, are calcium, iron, vitamin C, vitamin A, and the B complex vitamins. In a survey of adolescents conducted in Texas, for example, 80 percent of the teenagers surveyed received inadequate amounts of iron from their diets; 61 percent, inadequate amounts of protein; and over 30 percent, too little vitamin A and vitamin C. Over one-third received too few calories. More strikingly, about one-quarter of the youngsters received less than half of the recommended amounts of calcium, iron, and niacin; and well over 10 percent received too little vitamin A, vitamin C, thiamine, and riboflavin. Nutritional deficiencies were most severe among poorer youth; but even among the affluent, many teenagers' diets were lacking in the nutrients essential for growth during puberty (McGanity, 1976).

The following table shows the daily dietary allowances for early and middle adolescents recommended by the Food and Nutrition Board of the American Academy of Sciences:

		BOYS		GIRLS	
		11–14	*15–18*	*11–14*	*15–18*
Calories	(Kcal)	2,800	3,000	2,400	2,100
Protein	(g)	44	54	44	48
Vitamin A	(IU)	5,000	5,000	4,000	4,000
Vitamin D	(IU)	400	400	400	400
Vitamin E	(IU)	12	15	12	12
Ascorbic acid	(mg)	45	45	45	45
Folacin		0.4	0.4	0.4	0.4
Vitamin B_{12}	(µg)	3	3	3	3
Niacin	(mg)	18	20	16	14
Riboflavin	(mg)	1.5	1.5	1.3	1.5
Thiamin	(mg)	1.4	1.5	1.2	1.1
Vitamin B_6	(mg)	1.6	2.0	1.6	2.0
Calcium	(g)	1.2	1.2	1.2	1.2
Phosphorus	(g)	1.2	1.2	1.2	1.2
Iodine	(µg)	130	150	115	115
Iron	(mg)	18	18	18	18
Magnesium	(mg)	350	400	300	300
Zinc	(mg)	15	15	15	15

Source: J. Mueller, "Current Recommended Dietary Allowances for Adolescents," in J. McKigney and H. Munro (eds.), *Nutrient Requirements in Adolescence* (Cambridge, Mass.: MIT Press, 1976), pp. 137–144.

SOMATIC DEVELOPMENT

The effects of the endocrinological changes of puberty are remarkable. Consider the dramatic changes in physical appearance that occur during the short span of early adolescence. One enters puberty looking like a child and within four years or so has the physical appearance of a young adult. During this relatively brief period of time, the average individual grows nearly 12 inches taller, matures sexually, and develops an adult-proportioned body.

Changes in Stature and the Dimensions of the Body

The simultaneous release of growth hormone, thyroid hormones, and androgens stimulates rapid acceleration in height and weight. This dramatic increase in stature is referred to as the

adolescent growth spurt. What is most incredible about the adolescent growth spurt is not so much the absolute gain of height and weight that typically occurs, but the speed with which the increases take place. Think for a moment of how quickly very young children grow. At the time of **peak height velocity**—the time at which the adolescent is growing most rapidly—he or she is growing at the same rate as a toddler. For boys, peak height velocity averages about 4.1 inches (10.5 centimeters) per year; for girls, about 3.5 inches (9.0 centimeters) (J. Tanner, 1972).

Figure 1.3 shows just how remarkable the growth spurt is in terms of height. The graph on the left presents information on absolute height and indicates that, as you would expect, the average individual increases in height throughout infancy, childhood, and adolescence. As you can see, there is little gain in

FIGURE 1.3   Left: Height (in centimeters) at different ages for the average male and female youngster. Right: Gain in height per year (in centimeters) for the average male and female youngster. Note the adolescent growth spurt. (Adapted from Marshall, 1978)

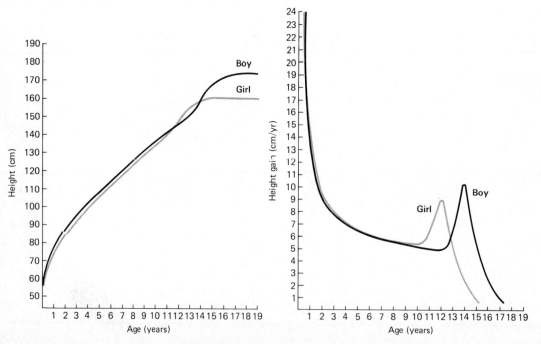

height after the age of 18. But look now at the right-hand graph, which shows the average increase in height *per year* over the same age span. Here you can see the acceleration in height at the time of peak height velocity.

Figure 1.3 also indicates quite clearly that the growth spurt occurs, on the average, about two years earlier among girls than among boys. In general, as you can see by comparing the two graphs, boys tend to be somewhat taller than girls before age 11, girls taller than boys between ages 11 and 13, and boys taller than girls from about age 14 on. You may remember what this state of affairs was like during fifth or sixth grades. Sex differences in height at this age can be a concern to many young adolescents when they begin socializing with members of the opposite sex, especially to tall, early-maturing girls and short, late-maturing boys.

As John Tanner, an authority on physical development during adolescence, points out, "practically all skeletal and muscular dimensions take part in the [growth] spurt, though not to an equal degree" (J. Tanner, 1972, p. 5). Much of the height gain is due to an increase in torso length, rather than leg length. The sequence in which various parts of the body grow is fairly regular. Extremities—the head, hands, and feet—are the first to accelerate in growth. Then follows accelerated growth in the arms and legs, followed by torso and shoulder growth. Consequently, "a boy stops growing out of his trousers (at least in length) a year before he stops growing out of his jackets" (J. Tanner, 1972,

During puberty there is a rapid acceleration in the adolescent's height and weight. Not all adolescents experience a growth spurt at the same age, however. (Janice Fullman/The Picture Cube)

p. 5). During puberty, the composition of the skeletal structure also changes, with bones becoming harder and more brittle. One of the markers of the end of puberty is the closing of the ends of the long bones in the body, which terminates growth in height.

Young adolescents often appear out of proportion physically—as if their noses or legs were growing faster than the rest of them. No, it's not an optical illusion. The parts of the body do not all grow at the same rate or at the same time during puberty. This phenomenon—referred to as **asynchronicity in growth**—can lead to an appearance of awkwardness or gawkiness in the young adolescent, who may be embarrassed by the unmatched accelerated growth of different parts of the body. It is probably little consolation for the young adolescent to be told that an aesthetic balance probably will be restored within a few years; nevertheless, this is what usually happens.

Generally, one's adult height is highly correlated (.67) with one's height before puberty—that is, the two are closely associated. (Correlations are statistics used by social scientists to indicate the strength of association between two measures. Correlations range from − 1.0 to 1.0, with higher numbers indicating very strong, positive associations.) Thus, most youngsters who were tall relative to their peers as children will be tall relative to their peers as adults (Petersen and Taylor, 1980). Adult height is only moderately correlated (.22) with the amount of height gained during the adolescent growth spurt, however.

The spurt in height at adolescence is accompanied by an increase in weight that results from an increase in both muscle and fat. However, there are important sex differences along these latter two dimensions. In both sexes, muscular development is rapid and closely parallels skeletal growth; but muscle tissue grows faster in boys than in girls (see Figure 1.4). Body fat increases for both sexes during puberty, but more so for females than for males, and at a somewhat faster rate for girls, especially during

the years just before puberty. For boys, there is actually a slight decline in body fat just before puberty. The end result of these sex differences in growth is that boys finish adolescence with a muscle-to-fat ratio of about 3:1, but the comparable ratio for girls is approximately 5:4. This has important implications for understanding why sex differences in strength and athletic ability often appear for the first time during adolescence. Before puberty, there are relatively few sex differences in muscle development and only slight sex differences in body fat.

Accompanying these gains in strength are increases in the size and capacity of the heart and lungs and, consequently, in exercise tolerance. In all these areas, the rate and magnitude of the gains favor males over females. By the end of puberty, boys are stronger, have "larger hearts and lungs relative to their size, a higher systolic blood pressure, a lower resting heart rate, a greater capacity for carrying oxygen to the blood, . . . a greater power for neutralizing the chemical products of muscular exercise, such as lactic acid," higher blood hemoglobin, and more red blood cells (Petersen and Taylor, 1980, p. 129).

It is tempting to attribute these sex differences purely to hormonal factors, because androgens, which increase during puberty in males at a much faster rate than in females, are closely linked to growth along these physical dimensions. But no studies have examined the role that sex differences in exercise patterns and diet may play. As Petersen and Taylor (1980) point out, there are strong social pressures on girls to curtail "masculine" activity—including some forms of exercise—at adolescence. Moreover, as noted earlier, adolescent girls' diets are generally less nutritionally adequate than those of boys. Both factors could result in sex differences in muscular development and exercise tolerance. At the very least, one would suspect that sex differences in physical maturation are influenced by a variety of factors, of which hormonal differences are but one part of an extremely complicated picture.

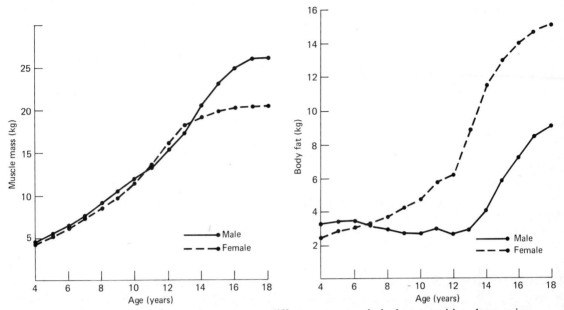

FIGURE 1.4 During preadolescence, important sex differences emerge in body composition that continue through adolescence. Figures reflect muscle and body fat for individuals of average height at each age. Note the changes in muscle mass (left) and body fat (right). (Adapted from Grumbach et al., 1974)

Sexual Maturation

Puberty brings with it a series of developments associated with sexual maturation. In both boys and girls, the development of the so-called **secondary sex characteristics** is an event that may be greeted with a certain degree of ambivalence—as we shall see.

Sexual maturation in boys. The sequence of developments in secondary sex characteristics among boys is fairly orderly (see Figure 1.5). Generally, the first stages of puberty involve growth of the testes and scrotum, accompanied by the first appearance of pubic hair. Approximately one year later, the growth spurt in height begins, accompanied by growth of the penis and further development of pubic hair—now of a coarser texture and darker color. The emergence of facial hair—first at the corners of the upper lip, next across the upper lip, then at the upper

parts of the cheeks and in the midline below the lower lip, and finally along the sides of the face and the lower border of the chin—and axillary (body) hair are relatively late developments in the pubertal process. The same is true for the deepening of the voice, which is gradual and generally does not occur until very late adolescence. During puberty, there are changes in the skin as well; the skin becomes rougher, especially around the upper arms and thighs, and there is increased development of sebaceous and apocrine sweat glands. These latter developments often give rise to acne, skin eruptions, and increased oiliness of the skin.

During puberty there are slight changes in the male breast—to the consternation and embarrassment of many boys. Breast development is largely influenced by the estrogen hormones. As noted earlier, both estrogens and androgens are present in both sexes and increase in both sexes at puberty—although in differing amounts.

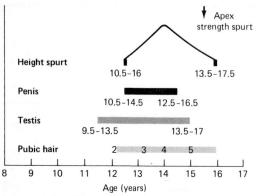

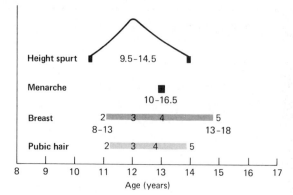

FIGURE 1.5   The sequence and approximate ages of the major changes at puberty for males. (Adapted from Tanner, 1972)

FIGURE 1.6   The sequence and approximate ages of the major changes at puberty for females. (Adapted from Tanner, 1972)

In the male adolescent, the areola (the area around the nipple) increases in size, and the nipple becomes more prominent. Some boys show a slight enlargement of the breast, although in the majority of cases this development is temporary.

Other, internal changes occur that are important elements of sexual maturation. At the time that the penis develops, the seminal vesicles, the prostate, and the bilbo-urethral glands also enlarge and develop. The first ejaculation of seminal fluid generally occurs about one year after the beginning of accelerated penis growth, although this is often culturally, rather than biologically, determined (J. Tanner, 1972).

Sexual maturation in girls.   The sequence of development of secondary sex characteristics among girls (shown in Figure 1.6) is somewhat less regular than it is among boys. Generally, the first sign of sexual maturation is the elevation of the breast—the emergence of the so-called breast bud. In about one-third of all adolescent girls, however, the appearance of pubic hair precedes breast development. The development of pubic hair follows a sequence similar to that in males—generally, from sparse, downy, light-colored hair to more dense, curled, coarse, darker

hair. Breast development often occurs concurrently and generally proceeds through several stages. In the bud stage, the areola widens and the breast and nipple are elevated as a small mound. In the middle stages, the areola and nipple become distinct from the breast and project beyond the breast contour. In the final stages, the areola is recessed to the contour of the breast, and only the nipple is elevated. The female breast undergoes these changes at puberty regardless of changes in breast size. For this reason, scientists who study puberty do not use changes in breast size as a measure of pubertal maturation. Changes in the shape and definition of the areola and nipple are far better indicators of sexual maturation among adolescent girls than is breast growth alone.

As is the case among boys, puberty brings important internal changes for the adolescent girl that are associated with the development of reproductive capacity. In girls, these changes involve development and growth of the uterus, vagina, and other aspects of the reproductive system. In addition, there is enlargement of the labia and clitoris.

As is apparent in Figure 1.6, the growth spurt is likely to occur during the early and middle stages of breast and pubic hair development. Menarche, the beginning of menstrua-

Nora Ephron's "A Few Words about Breasts"

For many adolescent girls, developing breasts later than their friends is a real cause for concern. Looking back, that concern may seem funny, but for many girls it was anything but funny at the time, as author Nora Ephron recalls:

I was about six months younger than everyone else in my class, and so for about six months after it began, for six months after my friends had begun to develop (that was the word we used, develop), I was not particularly worried. I would sit in the bathtub and look at my breasts and know that any day now, any second now, they would start growing like everyone else's. They didn't. "I want to buy a bra," I said to my mother one night. "What for?" she said. My mother was really hateful about bras, and by the time my third sister had gotten to the point where she was ready to want one, my mother had worked the whole business into a comedy routine. "Why not use a Band-Aid instead?" she would say. It was a source of great pride to my mother that she had never even had to wear a brassiere until she had her fourth child, and then only because her gynecologist made her. It was incomprehensible to me that anyone could ever be proud of something like that. It was the 1950s, for God's sake. Jane Russell. Cashmere sweaters. Couldn't my mother see that? "I am too old to wear an undershirt." Screaming. Weeping. Shouting. "Then don't wear an undershirt," said my mother. "But I want to buy a bra." "What for?"

I suppose that for most girls, breasts, brassieres, that entire thing, has more trauma, more to do with the coming of adolescence, with becoming a woman, than anything else. Certainly more than getting your period, although that, too, was traumatic, symbolic. But you could see breasts; they were there; they were visible. Whereas a girl could claim to have her period for months before she actually got it and nobody would ever know the difference.

I started with a 28 AA bra. I don't think they made them any smaller in those days, although I gather that now you can buy bras for five-year-olds that don't have any cups whatsoever in them; trainer bras they are called. My first brassiere came from Robinson's Department Store in Beverly Hills. I went there alone, shaking, positive they would look me over and smile and tell me to come back next year. An actual fitter took me into the dressing room and stood over me while I took off my blouse and tried the first one on. The little puffs stood out on my chest. "Lean over," said the fitter. (To this day, I am not sure what fitters in bra departments do except to tell you to lean over.) I leaned over, with the fleeting hope that my breasts would miraculously fall out of my body and into the puffs. Nothing.

"Don't worry about it," said my friend Libby some months later, when things had not improved. "You'll get them after you're married."

"What are you talking about?" I said.

"When you get married," Libby explained, "your husband will touch your breasts and rub them and kiss them and they'll grow."

That was the killer. Necking I could deal with. But it had never crossed by mind that a man was going to touch my breasts, that breasts had something to do with all that, petting, my God, they never mentioned petting in my little sex manual about the fertilization of the ovum. I became dizzy. For I knew instantly—as naive as I had been only a moment before—that only part of what she was saying was true: the touching, rubbing, kissing part, not the growing part. And I knew that no one would ever want to marry me. I had no breasts. I would never have breasts. . . .

Source: Nora Ephron, *Crazy Salad* (New York: Knopf, 1975), pp. 4–6.

tion, is a relatively late development. Hence it is incorrect to use menarche as a marker for the onset of puberty among girls. A great deal of pubertal development has taken place long before the adolescent girl begins to menstruate. Generally, full reproductive function does not occur until several years after menarche, and regular ovulation follows menarche by about two years (Hafetz, 1976).

TIMING AND TEMPO

You may have noted that, thus far, no mention has been made about the "normal" ages at which various pubertal changes are likely to take place. The truth is that the variations in the timing of puberty—the age at which puberty begins—and in the tempo of puberty—the rate at which ma-

turation occurs—are so great that it is misleading to talk even about "average" ages.

Variations in the Timing and Tempo of Puberty

The onset of puberty can occur as early as 8 years in girls and 9 1/2 in boys, or as late as 13 in girls and 13 1/2 in boys. In girls, the interval between the first sign of puberty and complete physical maturation can be as short as one and one-half years or as long as six years. In boys, the comparable interval ranges from about two years to five years (J. Tanner, 1972). Within a totally normal population of young adolescents, some individuals will have completed the entire sequence of pubertal changes before others have even begun. In more concrete terms, it is possible for an early-maturing, fast-maturing

FIGURE 1.7   These adolescent boys are the same chronological age but are at different stages of physical maturation. (Adapted from Shuttleworth, 1951; Copyright © The Society for Research in Child Development, Inc.)

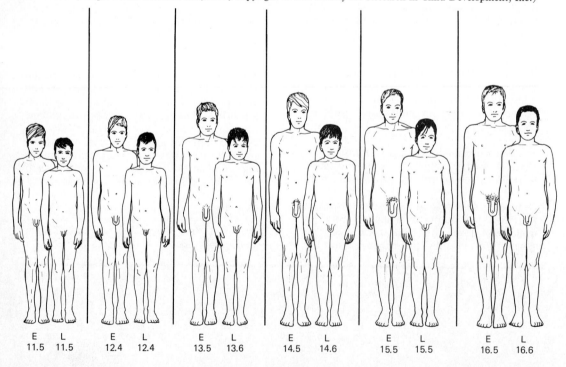

| E | L | E | L | E | L | E | L | E | L | E | L |
| 11.5 | 11.5 | 12.4 | 12.4 | 13.5 | 13.6 | 14.5 | 14.6 | 15.5 | 15.5 | 16.5 | 16.6 |

youngster to complete pubertal maturation by the age of 10 or 11—two years before a late-maturing youngster has even begun puberty, and *seven years* before a late-maturing, slow-maturing youngster has matured completely!

Individual differences in the timing and tempo of pubertal maturation are dramatically illustrated in Figures 1.7 and 1.8. In each picture, you see adolescents who are of the same chronological age but at obviously different stages of puberty. In each picture, however, the adolescents are within the "normal" range of pubertal development for their ages.

Figures 1.9 and 1.10 tell the same story in a somewhat different manner. In each figure, you see a series of pictures of two adolescents at 6-month intervals over the course of puberty. The pictures give some indication of the variations that are possible in the timing and rate of growth at puberty. Can you discern the timing

of the growth spurt in each of the yongsters' development?

There is no relation between the age at which puberty begins and the rate at which pubertal development proceeds. Furthermore, the timing of puberty has little to do with the ultimate adult stature or bodily dimensions of the individual. Late maturers, for example, attain the same average height as early maturers (Marshall, 1978).

Genetic and Environmental Influences on the Timing and Tempo of Puberty

What factors underlie the tremendous variations in the timing and tempo of puberty? Why do some individuals mature relatively early and others relatively late? One can point to both genetic and environmental factors.

Researchers who study variability in the on-

FIGURE 1.8   These adolescent girls are the same chronological age but are at different stages of physical maturation. (Adapted from Shuttleworth, 1951; Copyright © The Society for Research in Child Development, Inc.)

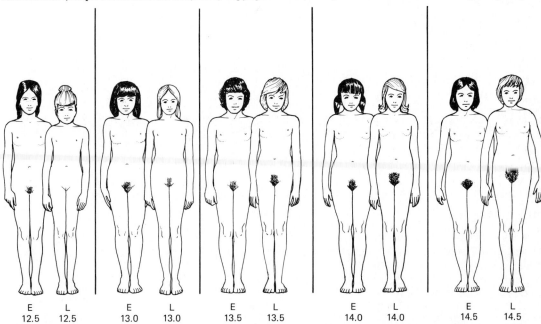

| E
12.5 | L
12.5 | E
13.0 | L
13.0 | E
13.5 | L
13.5 | E
14.0 | L
14.0 | E
14.5 | L
14.5 |

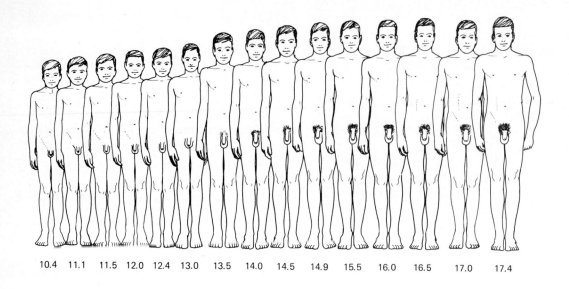

10.4   11.1   11.5   12.0   12.4   13.0   13.5   14.0   14.5   14.9   15.5   16.0   16.5   17.0   17.4

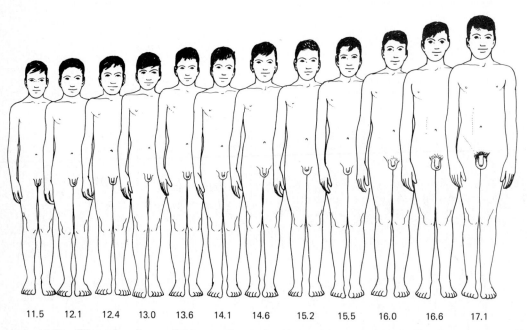

11.5   12.1   12.4   13.0   13.6   14.1   14.6   15.2   15.5   16.0   16.6   17.1

FIGURE 1.9   The pubertal growth history of an early-maturing and a late-maturing boy, based on photographs taken at 6-month intervals. (Adapted from Shuttleworth, 1951; Copyright © The Society for Research in Child Development, Inc.)

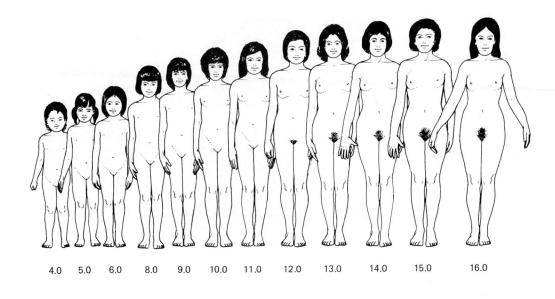

4.0   5.0   6.0   8.0   9.0   10.0   11.0   12.0   13.0   14.0   15.0   16.0

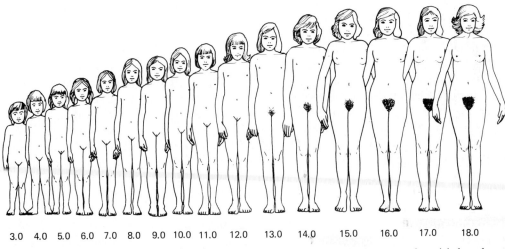

3.0 4.0 5.0 6.0 7.0 8.0 9.0 10.0 11.0 12.0 13.0 14.0 15.0 16.0 17.0 18.0

FIGURE 1.10   The pubertal growth history of an early-maturing and a late-maturing girl, based on photographs taken at 6-month intervals. (Adapted from Shuttleworth, 1951; Copyright © The Society for Research in Child Development, Inc.)

set and timing of puberty approach the issue in two ways. One strategy involves the study of differences among individuals (that is, studying why one individual matures earlier or faster than another). The other involves the study of differences among groups of adolescents (that is, studying why puberty occurs earlier or more rapidly in certain populations than in others). Let us first consider research on differences among individuals.

Individual differences in pubertal maturation. Differences in the timing and rate of puberty among individuals growing up in the same general environment are chiefly due to genetic factors. Comparisons between individuals who are genetically identical (identical twins) and individuals who are not reveal patterns of similarity in pubertal maturation indicating that the timing and tempo of an individual's pubertal maturation are largely inherited (Marshall, 1976).

Despite this powerful influence of genetic factors, the environment plays an important role. In all likelihood, every individual inherits a predisposition to develop at a certain rate and begin pubertal maturation at a certain time. But this predisposition is best thought of as an upper and lower age limit, rather than as a fixed absolute. Whether the genetic predisposition each person has to mature around a given age is actually realized, and when within the predisposed age boundaries he or she actually goes through puberty, are subject to the influence of the environment. In this respect, the timing and rate of pubertal maturation are the product of an interaction between nature—the genetic makeup—and nurture—the environmental conditions under which one has developed.

The two most important environmental influences on pubertal maturation are nutrition and health. Puberty occurs earlier among individuals who are better nourished throughout their prenatal, infant, and childhood years. Similarly, delayed puberty is more likely to occur among individuals with a history of protein and/or caloric deficiency. Chronic illness during childhood and adolescence is also associated

There is typically a great deal of variability in the timing and tempo of puberty within a group of adolescents of the same chronological age. Generally speaking, girls mature about two years earlier than boys. (Elizabeth Crews)

with delayed puberty, as is excessive exercise. For example, girls in ballet companies or in other rigorous training programs often mature later than their peers (Frisch, 1983). Generally speaking, then, after genetic factors, the most important influence on the timing of the onset of puberty is the overall physical well-being of the individual from conception through preadolescence (Marshall, 1976).

Group differences in pubertal maturation. Researchers typically study group differences in puberty by comparing average ages of menarche in different regions. It is extremely difficult to disentangle genetic influences from environmental ones, however, because regions are rarely equivalent on one set of factors but not the other. Suppose, for example, that you wanted to compare the timing of puberty in Asia with its timing in Europe. The average age at menarche in Japan is approximately 12.9 years, while in Norway it is about 13.2 years. But is the earlier maturation of Japanese youngsters due to genetic or environmental factors? It is difficult to say.

The few studies that have been able to separate genetic influences on population differences in pubertal maturation from environmental ones (by contrasting two groups who are genetically very different but whose environments are similar, for instance) have indicated that genetic factors play an extremely small role in determining population differences in pubertal maturation (Eveleth and Tanner, 1976). Thus differences among countries in the average rate and timing of puberty are likely to be due more to differences in their environments than to differences in their populations' gene pools.

The influence of the broader environment on the timing and tempo of puberty can be seen in more concrete terms by looking at three sorts of group comparisons: (1) comparisons of the average age of menarche across countries, (2) comparisons among socioeconomic groups within the same country, and (3) comparisons within the same population during different eras. (Although menarche does not signal the onset of puberty, researchers often use the average age of menarche when comparing the timing of puberty across different groups or regions.)

First, consider variations in the age of menarche across different regions of the world. Figure 1.11 presents median menarcheal ages throughout the world, across regions that vary considerably in typical dietary intake and health conditions. As you can see, the average age at menarche generally is lower in those countries where individuals are less likely to be malnourished and suffer from chronic disease. For example, in Western Europe and in the United States, the median menarcheal age ranges from about 12.5 years to 13.5 years. In Africa, however, the median menarcheal age ranges from about 14 years to 17 years. The range is much wider across the African continent be-

cause of the much greater variation in environmental conditions there. Interestingly, it was once believed that age at menarche was related to climate and that maturation occurred earlier in tropical regions. This is no longer thought to be the case (Eveleth and Tanner, 1976).

One strategy for disentangling genetic from environmental influences is to look at variations in pubertal timing *within* populations—where, presumably, genetic differences between subgroups are far smaller. Any differences in rates of maturation would then be more likely to be environmentally determined.

Figure 1.12 presents evidence bearing on this issue. When we look within a specific region, we find that, almost without exception, girls from affluent homes reach menarche before economically disadvantaged girls. In comparisons of affluent and poor youngsters from the United States, Hong Kong, Tunis, Baghdad, and South Africa, differences in the average menarcheal ages of economically advantaged and disadvantaged youngsters within each of these regions range from about 6 months to about 18 months. It is also the case that children from smaller families mature earlier than do children from larger families and urban youngsters earlier than rural youngsters. In all cases, these differences are probably due to health and nutritional differences before and during adolescence.

Finally, we can examine environmental influences on the timing of puberty by looking at changes in the average age of menarche over the past two centuries. Because nutritional conditions have improved during the past 150 years, we would expect to find a decline in the average age at menarche over time. This is indeed the case, as can be seen in Figure 1.13. Generally, "children have been getting larger and growing to maturity more rapidly" (Eveleth and Tanner, 1976, p. 260). This pattern, referred to as the **secular trend,** is attributable not only to improved nutrition but also to better sanitation and the control of infectious disease. In most European countries maturation has become earlier by about 3 to 4 months per decade. For example, in Norway 150 years ago, the average age of

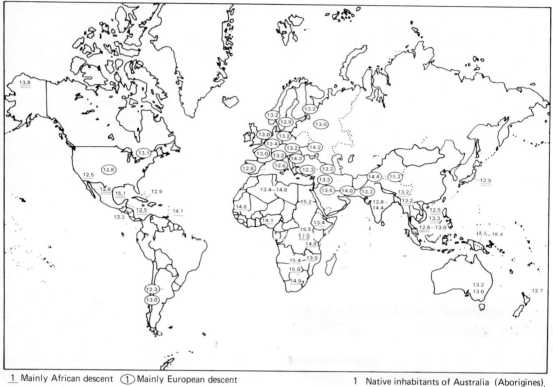

FIGURE 1.11   The average menarcheal age of adolescent girls varies in different regions of the world. (Adapted from Eveleth and Tanner, 1976)

menarche may have been about 17 years. Today, it is about 13 years. Similar declines have been observed over the same time period in other industralized nations and, more recently, in developing countries as well, although at least one writer has suggested that 100 years ago menarche may have occurred earlier than age 17 (Bullough, 1981).

The secular trend in pubertal maturation appears to be leveling off in most industrialized nations, however. This suggests that environmental conditions in these parts of the world have improved to the point where the average age of menarche is approaching its genetically bound lower limit. For example, no substantial changes in average menarcheal age have been reported during the past twenty-five years in Oslo, Norway, or London, England. You can lay to rest any fears you might have that children in future generations will go through puberty before they leave kindergarten. In all likelihood, the average age at menarche will not decline much below 12 years.

THE PSYCHOLOGICAL AND SOCIAL IMPACT OF PUBERTY

Researchers have generally taken two approaches to studying the psychological and social consequences of puberty. One approach is to look at individuals who are at various stages

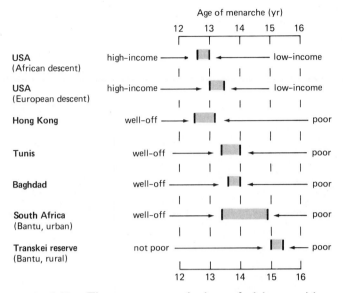

FIGURE 1.12   The average menarcheal age of adolescent girls varies across different social classes. (Eveleth and Tanner, 1976)

of puberty, either **cross-sectionally** (in which groups of individuals at different stages of puberty are compared) or **longitudinally** (in which the same individuals are tracked over time as they move through the different stages of puberty). Studies of this sort examine the *immediate impact* of puberty on the young person's psychological development and social relations. Researchers might ask, for example, whether youngsters' self-esteem is higher or lower during puberty than before or after.

A second approach compares the psychological development of early and late maturers. The focus of these studies is not so much on the absolute impact of puberty but on the effects of *differential timing* of the changes. Here, a typical question might be whether early maturers are more popular in the peer group than late maturers.

Each type of research has both strengths and limitations. The "immediate effects" strategy assumes that puberty is an important event for individual adolescents and those around them, regardless of when the onset of puberty

occurs. Research of this type has promoted understanding of the sorts of adaptational demands puberty places on the young person. Yet this research strategy ignores the fact that the meaning of puberty depends in part on its timing. For example, although all adolescents may revise their self-image during puberty, the nature and magnitude of the revision may be different for those who go through puberty early than for those who mature late. Because boys who mature early are bigger and stronger than their peers, puberty may make them feel more self-assured. But for late maturers who are simply catching up with their friends, pubertal changes may bring feelings of relief more than anything else.

In contrast, because the "differential timing" strategy takes into account the impact of early and late maturation, research of this type has led to an increased understanding of the importance of the relative timing of the pubertal changes. Yet, because this strategy tends to focus on extremes (that is, youngsters who mature very early and youngsters who mature very late),

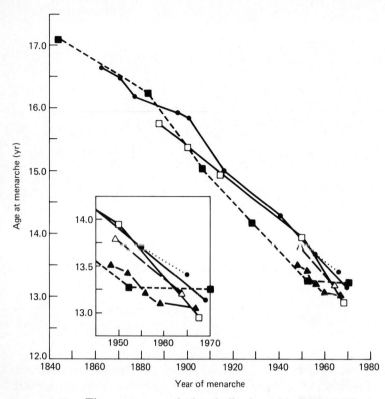

FIGURE 1.13   The age at menarche has declined considerably over the
past 150 years. This decline is known as the secular trend. (Adapted from
Eveleth and Tanner, 1976)

the research does not usually reveal very much
about the impact of puberty on the typical adolescent—one who is neither an early maturer
nor a late maturer but somewhere in the middle.
It is possible, of course, to examine *both* sets of
questions simultaneously, by studying early,
late, and on-time maturers over time.

In our discussion of the psychological and
social impact of puberty, we will focus, in turn,
on studies that approach the topic in each of
these ways. But first let us consider the cyclical,
or reciprocal, nature of puberty's impact.

Puberty's Impact: A Reciprocal Process

It is helpful to think of puberty's psychological
and social impact as occurring through a cycli-

cal, or reciprocal, process. Physical maturation
affects the adolescent's self-image and behavior,
and this in turn prompts changes in the behavior
of others. For example, a boy who has recently
gone through puberty may feel shy about his
changed body and seek more privacy at home
when he is dressing or bathing. He closes his
door more often and is more modest around his
parents than he used to be. If they are responsive
to his discomfort, his parents will change their
routines around the house. Before entering his
room, they will knock and wait to see if he is
dressed—something they did not have to do before.

The process works in the other direction as
well. The adolescent's changed physical appearance may elicit new sorts of behavior from peers,
parents, and others, and these new reactions

Youngsters went through puberty at a later age 100 years ago than they do today. The increasingly earlier maturation of young people is referred to as the *secular trend.* (The Bettmann Archive)

may prompt the adolescent to adjust his or her behavior and self-image. An adolescent girl who has recently matured physically may find herself suddenly receiving the attention of older boys who had not previously paid her much heed. In consequence, she will start to feel more attractive and confident. Moreover, she must now make decisions about how much time she wishes to devote to dating and how she should handle herself when out on a date.

Young people's reactions to the changes brought on by puberty, and others' reactions to them, are influenced by the broader social environment. Contemporary society's views of puberty and physical maturation are expressed through television commercials, newspaper and magazine advertisements, and depictions of young adolescents in films and other media. People cannot help but be influenced by these images, and the expectations they associate with puberty as well as the meaning they give it determine the reactions it brings out in them. Consider, for example, the treatment of menstruation in each of the advertisements reprinted on page 47. What sorts of reactions might each of the ads foster?

Let's now look at a sampling of studies that have examined the psychological and social consequences of puberty.

The Immediate Impact of Puberty

Studies of the psychological and social impact of puberty indicate that physical maturation, regardless of whether it occurs early or late, affects the adolescent's self-image, mood, and relationships with parents. The short-term consequences of puberty may be most taxing on the adolescent's family, however, and less significant for the adolescent's self-perceptions or mood (Simmons and Blyth, 1987; Steinberg, 1987a).

In a longitudinal study of changes in self-esteem during the early adolescent years, sociologist Roberta Simmons and her colleagues found that going through puberty may lead to modest declines in self-esteem among adolescent girls but only when accompanied by other changes that require adaptation on the part of the young person (Simmons, Blyth, Van Cleave, and Bush, 1979). Among the nearly 800 youngsters who were studied, those who showed the greatest declines in self-esteem between sixth and seventh grade were girls who began menstruating, began dating, and had to change schools all during the same year. (Boys did not show the same adverse effects of going through puberty, but we should remember that few boys are likely to begin puberty during the transition into junior high school.) This research suggests that puberty may be a potential *stressor* that has temporary adverse psychological consequences for girls when it is coupled with other changes that necessitate adjustment. By itself, however, puberty appears to have only modest effects on girls' and boys' self-image (Simmons and Blyth, 1987).

Although an adolescent's self-image could be expected to be changed during a time of dramatic physical development, it could also be the case that self-esteem or self-image is a reasonably stable characteristic, with long and sturdy roots reaching back to childhood. Finding that self-image is only modestly affected by puberty would not come as a surprise to those who believe that self-image, by adolescence, is fairly hard to shake and unlikely to be disrupted by puberty alone.

For this reason, some researchers have turned their attention to the impact of puberty on more transient states, such as mood. One reason for this choice is that adolescents are thought to be moodier, on average, than adults. One study (Csikszentmihalyi and Larson, 1984), in which adolescents' moods were monitored repeatedly by electronic pagers, for example, showed that adolescents' moods fluctuate during the course of the day more than the moods of adults (see Figure 1.14). Many adults assume that adolescent moodiness is directly related to the hormonal changes of puberty. The effect of hormones on mood is presumed to be negative— with pubertal hormones thought to make adolescents unpredictable, irritable, or unstable (Petersen, 1985). Is there any scientific evidence that the hormonal changes of puberty cause adolescents to be moody, or, for that matter, that these hormonal changes affect the adolescent's psychological functioning or behavior at all?

Recently, a number of studies have examined this question, but a clear answer has not yet been found. One team of investigators has found that high levels of a certain group of pubertal hormones, called **adrenal androgens,** may be related to sadness, aggression, and rebelliousness in adolescent boys (Susman et al., 1987) but that increases in levels of sex hormones, such as testosterone, may be related to better adjustment for male adolescents (Nottelmann, Susman, Inhoff-Germain, and Chrousos, 1987).

Another team of scientists has found that rapid increases in estrogen may be related to depression among early adolescent girls (Brooks-Gunn and Warren, 1987). In both cases, however, the researchers cautiously point out that the connection between hormones and mood is not strong and that we need to understand better how environmental and biological factors interact in influencing adolescents' mood and behavior. In addition, some researchers have pointed out that hormonal levels are themselves affected by experiences and that fluctuations in certain hormone levels could be caused by changes in mood and behavior, rather than the other way around (Brooks-Gunn and Warren, 1987; Steinberg, 1988). Nevertheless, the finding that rapid increases in estrogen may have negative effects on girls' mood, whereas rapid increases in testosterone may have positive effects on boys' mood, is especially intriguing, because this parallels some other findings on sex differences in the effects of early pubertal maturation. As you will see in the box on p. 52, studies indicate that early maturation may be advantageous for boys but problematic for girls.

If hormones do not seem solely responsible for adolescent moodiness, how can we account for the belief that adolescents are moodier than adults? Psychologists Mihaly Csikszentmihalyi and Reed Larson (1986), who monitored adolescents' moods and experiences over the course of several days, provide a partial explanation. These researchers had teenagers carry electronic pagers similar to the ones physicians carry, and they paged them periodically throughout the day. When the adolescents were paged, they filled out forms noting how they were feeling, what they were doing, where they were, and whom they were with. By looking at changes in mood across activities and settings, the researchers were able to determine the correlates of adolescent moodiness.

Their findings suggest that adolescent mood swings parallel their changes in activities. Over the course of a day, a teenager may shift from elation to boredom, back again to happiness, and then to anger. But this shifting appears to have more to do with shifts in activities—elated when seeing a girlfriend, bored in social studies class, happy when having lunch with his friends, and angry when assigned extra work at the fast-food restaurant—than with internal, biological changes. Adolescents may be moodier than adults because they change activities and contexts more often than adults do.

All in all, research on the immediate impact of puberty on individual psychological functioning has not indicated very strong effects. In contrast, research on the impact of puberty on *family relationships* has pointed to a more consistent pattern, namely, that puberty appears to increase distance between parents and children (Steinberg, 1987a). Several studies show that as youngsters mature from childhood toward the middle of puberty, distance between them and their parents increases and conflict intensifies, especially between the adolescent and his or her mother (Hill et al., 1985a, 1985b; Steinberg, 1987a, 1988). In one study, for example, triads of an adolescent boy and his mother and father were asked to discuss a series of decisions three times during a year, and their patterns of communication were charted alongside the sons' pubertal development (Steinberg, 1981). Shortly after the onset of puberty, conflict between the boys and their mothers began to intensify, reaching a peak sometime near the time of the boy's growth spurt. After this point, conflict began to subside somewhat. Other studies (for example, Steinberg, 1987a) indicate that although conflict may diminish after the adolescent growth spurt, adolescents and their parents do not immediately become as close as they were before the adolescents entered puberty.

Because this connection between pubertal maturation and parent-child distance is not affected by the age at which the adolescent goes through puberty—in other words, the pattern is seen among early as well as late maturers—it seems that something about puberty in particular may transform the parent-child bond. To date, we do not know whether this effect is due to the hormonal changes of puberty (perhaps increases in sex hormones make adolescents

more assertive toward their parents), to changes in the adolescent's physical appearance, or to changes in psychological functioning that in turn affect family relationships. One writer has pointed out that puberty increases distance between children and their parents in most species of monkeys and apes and that the pattern seen in human adolescents may have some evolutionary basis (Steinberg, 1987b).

Whatever the underlying mechanism, one way to interpret these studies is that puberty can upset psychological and social balances that are established during childhood, causing temporary periods of disruption or even distress. During childhood, for example, individuals develop a certain self-image that is suddenly shaken in early adolescence. It may take some time for them to integrate the changes brought about by puberty into their self-concept, and during this period of integration, their self-esteem and self-image may suffer.

Similarly, families develop patterns of relationships during a son's or daughter's childhood that are comfortable and workable, but they may find that puberty disrupts the patterns to which they have grown accustomed. They have developed a certain way of discussing things and a certain way of including the children in family discussions. But as the children go through puberty, they may want to be treated more like adults. They may want to have more of a say in family decisions. Consequently, families may experience a temporary period of conflict or tension when sons and daughters enter early adolescence. It may take some time for the individual and the family to achieve a new equilibrium that takes into account the changes brought on by puberty.

Puberty may have an effect on relationships in the peer group, too. One study of adolescents' *social networks*—the people they are most likely to see and spend time with—found that adolescents who were physically mature were less likely than their less developed peers to name adults as people who were important to them and more likely to name other adolescents (Garbarino, Burston, Raber, Russell, and Crouter,

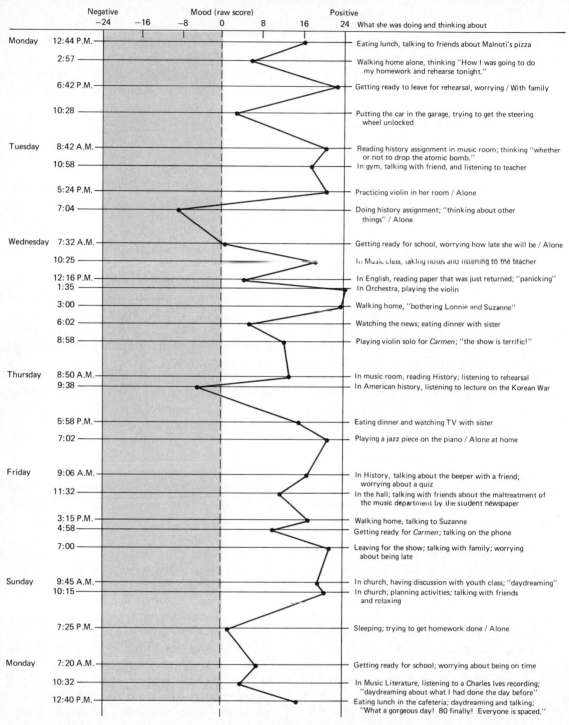

(A) The Week of Katherine Tennison

		Negative			Mood (raw score)			Positive	What she was doing and thinking about
		−24	−16	−8	0	8	16	24	

Monday	12:44 P.M.	Eating lunch, talking to friends about Malnoti's pizza
	2:57	Walking home alone, thinking "How I was going to do my homework and rehearse tonight."
	6:42 P.M.	Getting ready to leave for rehearsal, worrying / With family
	10:28	Putting the car in the garage, trying to get the steering wheel unlocked
Tuesday	8:42 A.M.	Reading history assignment in music room; thinking "whether or not to drop the atomic bomb."
	10:58	In gym, talking with friend, and listening to teacher
	5:24 P.M.	Practicing violin in her room / Alone
	7:04	Doing history assignment; "thinking about other things" / Alone
Wednesday	7:32 A.M.	Getting ready for school, worrying how late she will be / Alone
	10:25	In Music class, taking notes and listening to the teacher
	12:16 P.M.	In English, reading paper that was just returned; "panicking"
	1:35	In Orchestra, playing the violin
	3:00	Walking home, "bothering Lonnie and Suzanne"
	6:02	Watching the news; eating dinner with sister
	8:58	Playing violin solo for *Carmen*; "the show is terrific!"
Thursday	8:50 A.M.	In music room, reading History; listening to rehearsal
	9:38	In American history, listening to lecture on the Korean War
	5:58 P.M.	Eating dinner and watching TV with sister
	7:02	Playing a jazz piece on the piano / Alone at home
Friday	9:06 A.M.	In History, talking about the beeper with a friend; worrying about a quiz
	11:32	In the hall; talking with friends about the maltreatment of the music department by the student newspaper
	3:15 P.M.	Walking home, talking to Suzanne
	4:58	Getting ready for *Carmen*; talking on the phone
	7:00	Leaving for the show; talking with family; worrying about being late
Sunday	9:45 A.M.	In church, having discussion with youth class; "daydreaming"
	10:15	In church; planning activities; talking with friends and relaxing
	7:25 P.M.	Sleeping; trying to get homework done / Alone
Monday	7:20 A.M.	Getting ready for school; worrying about being on time
	10:32	In Music Literature, listening to a Charles Ives recording; "daydreaming about what I had done the day before"
	12:40 P.M.	Eating lunch in the cafeteria; daydreaming and talking; "What a gorgeous day! 80 finally! Everyone is spaced."

FIGURE 1.14(A and B)   Fluctuations in two adolescents' moods over the course of a week. (Csikszentmihalyi and Larson, 1984)

44

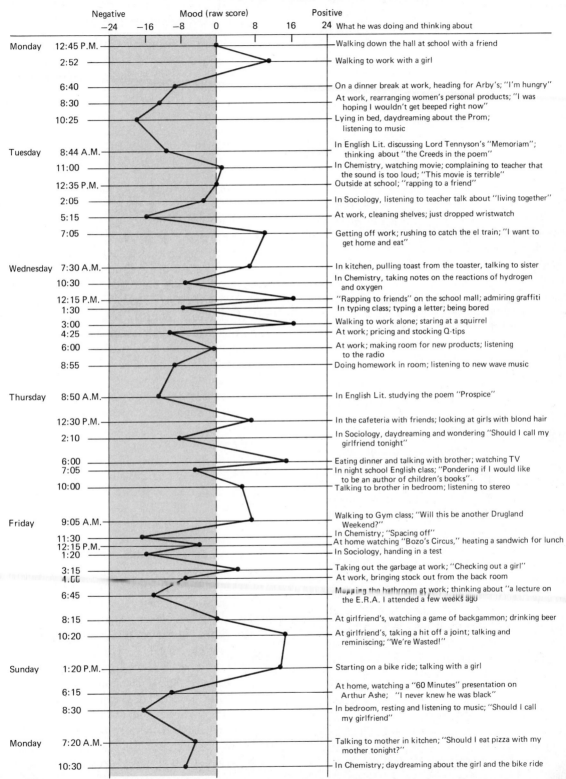

(B) The Week of Gregory Stone

	Negative	Mood (raw score)	Positive
	−24 −16 −8	0 8 16	24 What he was doing and thinking about

Monday 12:45 P.M. — Walking down the hall at school with a friend

2:52 — Walking to work with a girl

6:40 — On a dinner break at work, heading for Arby's; "I'm hungry"

8:30 — At work, rearranging women's personal products; "I was hoping I wouldn't get beeped right now"

10:25 — Lying in bed, daydreaming about the Prom; listening to music

Tuesday 8:44 A.M. — In English Lit. discussing Lord Tennyson's "Memoriam"; thinking about "the Creeds in the poem"

11:00 — In Chemistry, watching movie; complaining to teacher that the sound is too loud; "This movie is terrible"

12:35 P.M. — Outside at school; "rapping to a friend"

2:05 — In Sociology, listening to teacher talk about "living together"

5:15 — At work, cleaning shelves; just dropped wristwatch

7:05 — Getting off work; rushing to catch the el train; "I want to get home and eat"

Wednesday 7:30 A.M. — In kitchen, pulling toast from the toaster, talking to sister

10:30 — In Chemistry, taking notes on the reactions of hydrogen and oxygen

12:15 P.M. — "Rapping to friends" on the school mall; admiring graffiti

1:30 — In typing class; typing a letter; being bored

3:00 — Walking to work alone; staring at a squirrel

4:25 — At work; pricing and stocking Q-tips

6:00 — At work; making room for new products; listening to the radio

8:55 — Doing homework in room; listening to new wave music

Thursday 8:50 A.M. — In English Lit. studying the poem "Prospice"

12:30 P.M. — In the cafeteria with friends; looking at girls with blond hair

2:10 — In Sociology, daydreaming and wondering "Should I call my girlfriend tonight"

6:00 — Eating dinner and talking with brother; watching TV

7:05 — In night school English class; "Pondering if I would like to be an author of children's books"

10:00 — Talking to brother in bedroom; listening to stereo

Friday 9:05 A.M. — Walking to Gym class; "Will this be another Drugland Weekend?"

11:30 — In Chemistry; "Spacing off"

12:15 P.M. — At home watching "Bozo's Circus," heating a sandwich for lunch

1:20 — In Sociology, handing in a test

3:15 — Taking out the garbage at work; "Checking out a girl"

4:00 — At work, bringing stock out from the back room

6:45 — Mopping the bathroom at work; thinking about "a lecture on the E.R.A. I attended a few weeks ago

8:15 — At girlfriend's, watching a game of backgammon; drinking beer

10:20 — At girlfriend's, taking a hit off a joint; talking and reminiscing; "We're Wasted!"

Sunday 1:20 P.M. — Starting on a bike ride; talking with a girl

6:15 — At home, watching a "60 Minutes" presentation on Arthur Ashe; "I never knew he was black"

8:30 — In bedroom, resting and listening to music; "Should I call my girlfriend"

Monday 7:20 A.M. — Talking to mother in kitchen; "Should I eat pizza with my mother tonight?"

10:30 — In Chemistry; daydreaming about the girl and the bike ride

45

1978). This finding suggests that pubertal maturation may be an important influence in shifting adolescents' interests and energies toward the peer group. Boys and girls who are physically mature are more likely than less mature agemates to be involved in cross-sex activities such as having a boyfriend or girlfriend or going out on dates (Crockett and Dorn, 1987). Even within the boundaries of a small peer group, the pubertal status of the group's members has an effect. In groups of early adolescent boys as well as groups of early adolescent girls, those who are more physically mature are more likely to be assertive and dominant in interaction with their peers. They are most likely to boss other adolescents around, most likely to be listened to, and most likely to be looked up to as leaders (Savin-Williams, 1979).

The Impact of Menarche and First Ejaculation

Several studies have focused specifically on girls' attitudes toward and reactions to menarche and boys' reactions to their first ejaculation. The onset of menstruation is "not just one of a series of physiological events during puberty, but is also a sociocultural event . . . imbued with special meaning" (Brooks-Gunn and Ruble, 1979). Cultural beliefs concerning menarche and the specific information a young woman receives from parents, teachers, friends, and health practitioners all influence how she greets and experiences menarche (Brooks-Gunn and Ruble, 1982). Consider, for example, the different attitudes toward menstruation that each of the following parent's reactions might promote:

> "When I discovered it . . . [my mother] told me to come with her, and we went into the living room to tell my father. She just looked at me and then at him and said, 'Well, your little girl is a young lady now!' My dad gave me a hug and congratulated me and I felt grown up and proud that I was a lady at last." (Shipman, 1971, p. 331, cited in Brooks-Gunn and Ruble, 1979)

> "I had no information whatsoever, no hint that anything was going to happen to me. . . . I thought I was on the point of death from internal hemorrhage. . . . What did my highly educated mother do? She read me a furious lecture about what a bad, evil, immoral thing I was to start menstruating at the age of eleven! So young and so vile! Even after thirty years, I can feel the shock of hearing her condemn me for 'doing' something I had no idea occurred." (Weideger, 1976, p. 169, cited in Brooks-Gunn and Ruble, 1979)

In Western culture, many young women have developed a negative image of menstruation before reaching adolescence and enter puberty with ambivalent attitudes about menarche—a mixture of excitement and fear (Ruble and Brooks-Gunn, 1982). Recent studies, though, indicate that adolescent girls' attitudes toward menarche are less negative today than they appear to have been twenty years ago (Ruble and Brooks-Gunn, 1982; Greif and Ulman, 1982), a change that may be attributable to the more open and less mysterious presentation of information about menstruation in schools and in the media in recent years.

As is well known, the feelings one has before experiencing something for the first time influence the way one actually experiences it. If you are about to sit down to eat something you've never tried before, and everyone present tells you that the dish tastes awful, your judgment will probably confirm your expectation. But if you have been told that the same dish tastes wonderful, you are bound to like it more.

As it turns out, experiencing menstruation for the first time is analogous. One recent set of studies, by psychologists Diane Ruble and J. Brooks-Gunn, indicates that a strong negative bias toward menstruation before menarche may actually be associated with greater menstrual discomfort. Menstrual symptoms are reported to be more severe among women who expect menstruation to be uncomfortable, among girls whose mothers lead them to believe that menstruation will be an unpleasant or uncomfortable experience, and in cultures that label menstrua-

One sign that attitudes toward menstruation have changed in the last twenty-five years is that advertisements for tampons and sanitary napkins have become far more explicit and far less mysterious. As a consequence, adolescent girls receive very different messages about the meaning of maturation today from twenty or thirty years ago. Here are two excerpts from magazine advertisements for sanitary napkins—one from 1951, the other from 1982. (KOTEX® and LIGHTDAYS® are registered trademarks of Kimberly-Clark Corporation. These advertisements reprinted by permission. LIGHTDAYS® advertisement © 1982, KCC. All rights reserved.)

tion as an important event. In addition, girls who experience menarche early, relative to their peers, or who are otherwise unprepared for puberty report more negative reactions to the event (Brooks-Gunn and Ruble, 1979, 1982; Ruble and Brooks-Gunn, 1982).

Far less is known about boys' reactions to their first ejaculation, an experience that we might consider analogous to menarche in girls. Although most boys are not very well prepared for this event by their parents or other adults, first ejaculation does not appear to cause undue anxiety, embarrassment, or fear. It is interesting to note, however, that in contrast to girls, who generally tell their mothers shortly after they have begun menstruating and tell their girl-friends soon thereafter, boys do not discuss their first ejaculation with either parents or friends (Gaddis and Brooks-Gunn, 1985). The apparent secrecy surrounding this event may be due to the fact that the first ejaculation is actually more upsetting than boys are willing to admit or to the fact that it is perceived as relatively unimportant.

The Impact of Early or Late Maturation

Adolescents who mature relatively early or relatively late stand apart from their peers physically and may, as a consequence, elicit different sorts of reactions and expectations from those around them. Moreover, individual adolescents may be all too aware of whether they are early or late relative to their agemates, and their feelings about themselves are likely to be influenced by their comparisons. In short, early and late maturers may be treated differently by others, may view themselves differently, and may as a result behave differently.

Given the premium placed on appearing physically mature in our society, you might expect that it is advantageous to mature early. After all, as one writer notes, "Peers who appear to be older and more mature than their years are frequently the objects of admiration and envy" (Clausen, 1975, p. 26). Yet studies have shown that the issue is far more complicated than this. Early and late maturation have different consequences in the immediate present and in the long run, different consequences in different contexts, and, most important, different consequences for boys and girls.

Early versus late maturation among boys. The first studies to compare early- and late-maturing boys suggested that it was an advantage to mature earlier than one's peers. Drawing on data collected as part of the Oakland Growth Study (a longitudinal study begun earlier this century and continuing today), psychologist Mary Jones and her colleagues compared early- and late-maturing boys on a variety of psychological tests and measures of interpersonal relationships (Jones, 1957, 1965; Jones and Bayley, 1950; Mussen and Jones, 1957, 1958). They found that late maturers were seen by their peers as more childish and were less popular and less likely to have held leadership positions. On personality measures, late-maturing boys exhibited stronger feelings of inadequacy, higher needs for autonomy, more negative self-concepts, more childishness, less self-control, less responsibility, and less self-assurance.

Research conducted since these early studies has confirmed their findings, though with several modifications. With regard to self-image and popularity, early-maturing boys clearly have an advantage over their more slowly developing

During adolescence, late-maturing boys are less popular than early maturers. Late maturers are also less likely to hold positions of leadership and are perceived by their peers as more childish. (Elizabeth Crews)

peers (Petersen, 1985). With regard to *behavior*, however, early maturers may be more likely than their peers to get involved in problem or deviant activities, including truancy, minor delinquency, and problems at school (Duncan, Ritter, Dornbusch, Gross, and Carlsmith, 1985). One reasonable guess is that boys who are more physically mature develop friendships with older peers and that these friendships lead them into activities that are problematic for the younger boys.

With regard to *mood*, one interesting reanalysis of old data indicated that early-maturing boys may have more problems than research had indicated. Psychologist Harvey Peskin (1967) argued that researchers might have been confusing two different comparisons: early versus late maturers (the comparisons they were interested in) and postpubertal versus pubertal youngsters (a comparison they were making inadvertently). Perhaps, he reasoned, the apparently greater childishness and lower self-esteem of late-maturing boys found in the earlier studies were due not to their relatively late maturation but to the fact that they were still going through puberty at the time the personality measures were taken. It would be interesting, Peskin suggested, to see what the early-maturing youngsters were like *at the time they were going through puberty.*

Using personality data that had been collected during the Berkeley Guidance Study (a comparable longitudinal study conducted during the same era as the Oakland Growth Study), Peskin pursued the problem in the following way. He had access to information on a group of youngsters both before and during adolescence. Ignoring youngsters' chronological age, he compared groups of early- and late-maturing youngsters at points in time relative to the time of their pubertal onset. He took data gathered on the early maturers when they were one year before puberty and compared them with data gathered on the late maturers when they were also one year before puberty. Similarly, he compared early maturers while they were going through puberty with late maturers while they were going through puberty. And he compared early maturers when they were one year beyond the onset of puberty with late maturers when they were one year beyond puberty. His findings were surprising.

As you would expect, the groups were very similar when each was examined one year before pubertal onset. But at the time of pubertal onset and one year later as well, the late maturers showed significantly higher ratings on measures of

intellectual curiosity, exploratory behavior, social initiative, and activity level, whereas the early maturer[s] tended to avoid problem solving or new situations unless urged or helped. The early ma-

turer appeared to approach cognitive tasks cautiously and timidly, with a preference for rules, routines, and imitative action. Far from complacent or comfortable conformity, as the Oakland [Growth Study] findings in adulthood had suggested, it was the early maturer at pubertal onset who had experienced . . . more frequent and intense temper tantrums. (Livson and Peskin, 1980, p. 73).

Quite a turnaround of the initial findings!

Late maturers, Peskin argued, have the advantage of a longer preadolescent period, giving them more time to "prepare" psychologically for the onset of puberty. (You read earlier about the benefits of preparation for menarche.) Many theorists believe that the middle childhood and preadolescent years are extremely important periods for the development of coping skills—skills that prove valuable during adolescence and adulthood. Although puberty by no means marks the end of the growth of coping abilities, it does come as an abrupt interruption to the more relaxed preadolescent era. A later puberty, and hence a longer preadolescence, might allow for coping skills to develop more fully before adolescence. This may account in part for the apparently better coping skills demonstrated by late maturers—not only during puberty but as you will read, later, as adults.

Early versus late maturation in girls. The initial research on this issue, again conducted by researchers working on the Oakland Growth Study, suggested that in contrast to boys, early maturing girls were at a disadvantage—although the findings were far less consistent than they were in the studies of boys (Jones, 1949; Jones and Mussen, 1958). Briefly, early-maturing girls were found to be "less popular, less poised, less expressive, and more submissive, withdrawn, and unassured than [their] agemates" (Livson and Peskin, 1980, p. 71). Like the late-maturing boys, the early-maturing girl is out of step with her peers. And since girls mature about two years earlier than boys, the early-maturing girl is not only more physically advanced than her female peers but far more advanced than nearly all of her male classmates as well. In these studies, the late-maturing girls were more likely to be seen as attractive, sociable, and expressive.

As is the case for research on early- and late-maturing boys, recent research on girls has tended to corroborate the findings of the earlier studies, but we have learned a good deal more about the special plight of early-maturing girls in the ensuing years. In general, early-maturing girls have more self-image and emotional difficulties than do girls who mature on time or late (Aro and Taipale, 1987; Simmons and Blyth, 1987), a finding that has been confirmed in studies of girls in several Western countries. These difficulties seem to have a great deal to do with girls' feelings about their height and weight, because early maturers are, almost by definition, taller and heavier than their late-maturing peers (Petersen, 1988). In societies that define as physically attractive the thin, "leggy" woman, a late-maturing girl will look more like this image than an early-maturing girl will. Accordingly, during junior high school, early-maturing girls are more likely to be upset about the way they look than late-maturing or on-time girls.

Although early-maturing girls may have self-image difficulties, newer studies suggest that their popularity with peers is not necessarily jeopardized. Indeed, some studies indicate that early maturers are more popular than other girls, especially, as you would expect, when the index of popularity includes popularity with boys (Simmons, Blyth, and McKinney, 1983). Ironically, it may be in part because early maturers are more popular with boys that they report more emotional upset: At a very early age, pressure to date and, perhaps, to be involved in a sexual relationship, may take its toll on the adolescent girl's mental health. Consistent with this, one team of researchers (Blyth, Simmons, and Zakin, 1985) found that early-maturing girls in schools with older peers (for example, sixth-graders who were in a school that had seventh- and eighth-graders, too) were psychologically worse off than early-maturing girls who were in the highest grade in their school (for example,

sixth-graders who were in an elementary school).

Like their male counterparts, early-maturing girls are also more likely to become involved in deviant activities, including delinquency, drug and alcohol use, more likely to have school problems, and more likely to experience early sexual intercourse (Aro and Taipale, 1987; Magnusson, Statin and Allen, 1986). These problems appear to arise because early-maturing girls are more likely to spend time with older adolescents, especially older adolescent boys, who initiate them into activities that might otherwise be delayed (Magnusson et al., 1986). As you will read in a moment, although most of these behavioral differences disappear by the time the late-maturing girls have completed puberty, the earlier involvement of early-maturing girls in certain behaviors may have important long-term repercussions.

Long-term consequences.　Do the psychological and interpersonal differences between early and late maturers observed during adolescence persist into adulthood? Are early maturers likely to remain more popular and self-confident as adults, for example?

In order to answer these questions, a series of follow-up studies conducted some twenty-five years later looked at the adult personalities of males who had been studied during adolescence (Livson and Peskin, 1980). At age 38, the early maturers were more responsible, cooperative, self-controlled, and sociable. At first glance, it appeared as if the benefits of early maturation had carried over well into adulthood.

Yet the picture was not so clear-cut. By adulthood, some of the advantages had turned into disadvantages. True, the early maturers did appear more confident and responsible. But they had also grown up to be more conforming, conventional, and humorless. Their peers who had been late maturers remained somewhat more impulsive and assertive but turned out to be more insightful, more inventive, and more creatively playful. What had happened?

One interpretation is that because of their

more adultlike appearance, the early-maturing boys had been pushed into adult roles earlier than their peers. They were more likely to be asked to assume responsibility, take on leadership positions, and behave in a more "grown-up" manner. But this early press toward adulthood may have come too soon and stifled a certain amount of creativity and risk taking.

Have you gone to any gatherings of old high school classmates? Did you discover that some of the people whom you had remembered as extremely mature and socially successful during high school have turned out to be not all that interesting a few years after graduation? Perhaps too much leadership, responsibility, social success, and "maturity" during the high school years interferes with the sort of psychological development that makes for interesting and creative adults. As we shall see in a later chapter, many psychologists believe that adolescents may benefit in the long run from having an extended period of time during which they are *not* being pushed into adulthood.

Success and social status may come too easily and too early for early-maturing boys, leaving them with less need to develop creative or flexible solutions to life's problems and less time to experiment with new roles and identities. In contrast, late-maturing youngsters, experiencing more difficulty in achieving social standing and recognition because of their immature physical appearance, may be forced to develop more inventive means of problem solving and greater cognitive and social flexibility. In other words, the greater difficulty that late maturers face as early adolescents may lead to their developing coping skills that prove useful when they reach adulthood.

One study of the adult personalities of women who had been either early or late maturers suggests interesting parallels between the personality development of early-maturing girls and late-maturing boys (Peskin, 1973). Both sets of youngsters may have self-esteem problems during adolescence, but both appear to be somewhat more psychologically advanced than their peers during adulthood. Like the late-maturing

boys, early-maturing girls may be forced to develop coping skills during adolescence that have some long-term positive effects.

At the same time, however, more recent research indicates that the earlier involvement of early-maturing girls in problem behavior may adversely affect their long-term educational achievement. In one study of Swedish girls, for example, the researchers found that the school problems of early-maturing adolescent girls persisted, leading to the development of negative attitudes toward school and lower educational aspirations. In young adulthood, there were marked differences between the early- and late-maturing girls' levels of education; for example, the late-maturing girls were twice as likely as early-maturing girls to continue beyond the compulsory minimum number of years of high school (Magnusson et al., 1986).

Eating Disorders

Obesity. Because adolescence is a time of dramatic change in physical appearance, the young person's self-image is very much tied to his or her body image. Deviation from the "ideal" physique can lead to loss of self-esteem and other problems in the adolescent's self-image. In particular, being overweight can be a painful source of embarrassment to teenagers, who are unusually self-conscious about their appearance.

Although a variety of nutritional and behavioral factors can lead to weight gains during adolescence, gaining weight can sometimes result directly from the physical changes of puberty. Not only does the ratio of body fat to muscle increase markedly during puberty, but the body's **basal metabolism rate** also drops about 15 percent. The basal metabolism rate is the minimum amount of energy one uses when one is resting. One's weight is partly dependent on this ratio. Do you know people who seem to be able to eat as much as they want without gaining weight? Adolescents whose basal metabolism rate is high can eat more during the course of a day without gaining weight than their peers

The Sexes: The Effects of Early Maturation

Researchers are still trying to make sense of the complicated pattern of findings that emerges from comparisons of early and late maturers, but one fact is clear: Early maturation brings many more advantages for boys than it does for girls, and in many respects, it is actually a disadvantage for girls to go through puberty substantially earlier than their peers. Psychologists have offered several explanations for this sex difference. The explanations all are compatible, but they derive from very different premises.

One explanation might be termed the "deviance" hypothesis (Simmons and Blyth, 1987). Simply put, the notion is that youngsters who stand far apart from their peers—in physical appearance, for instance—will experience more psychological distress than adolescents who blend in more easily. Studies of adolescents who stand out physically in other ways—obese students or students who attend schools in which they are clearly in a racial minority—support the view that standing out too much can be an unfortunate disadvantage (Blyth et al., 1980; Simmons, Blyth, and McKinney, 1983). Because girls mature earlier than boys, on average, early-maturing girls mature much earlier than their male and female agemates. This presumably makes them stand out at a time when they would rather fit in and may make them more vulnerable. This explanation would also account for the lower self-esteem of late-maturing boys, who are "deviant" toward the other extreme.

A second explanation focuses on "developmental readiness." Here the notion is that psychological distress results when youngsters have experiences before they are psychologically "ready" for them (Simmons and Blyth, 1987). If puberty is a challenge that requires psychological adaptation by the adolescent, perhaps younger adolescents are less able to cope with the challenge than older ones. Because puberty occurs quite early among early-maturing girls (some may begin maturing at age 8 or 9 and experience menarche at age 10), it may tax their psychological resources. Early maturation among boys, because it occurs at a much later age, would

pose less of a problem. The **developmental readiness** hypothesis has been used to account for the finding that older (eighth-graders) youngsters fare better during the transition from elementary to secondary school than younger (sixth grade) ones do. This perspective also helps to account for the fact that in puberty, late-maturing boys seem more able to control their temper and their impulses (Peskin, 1967).

A final explanation concerns the cultural desirability of different body types (Petersen, 1988). Early maturation for girls means leaving behind the culturally admired state of thinness. As you read earlier, for girls, the ratio of fat to muscle increases dramatically at puberty. Many girls feel distressed when they mature because they gain weight, and early maturers experience this weight gain when most of their peers are still girlishly thin. One interesting study showed that in ballet companies—where thinness is even more important than in the culture at large—late maturers, who can retain the "ideal" shape much longer than earlier maturers, have fewer psychological problems than even on-time girls (Brooks-Gunn and Warren, 1985). Boys at puberty, in contrast, move from a culturally undesirable state for males—being short and scrawny—to a culturally admired one—being tall and muscular. Early maturers enjoy the special advantage of being tall and muscular before their peers and therefore are more likely to react well to puberty.

Whatever the explanation, the fact that early-maturing girls are at heightened risk for temporary psychological problems is an important fact for parents and school counselors to bear in mind. Unfortunately, as long as our culture overvalues thinness and encourages the view that women should be judged on the basis of their physical appearance rather than their abilities, values, or personality, the risks of early puberty will probably persist. Adults can help by being supportive, by helping the early-maturing girl to recognize her strengths and positive features—physical and nonphysical alike—and by preparing her for puberty before it takes place.

whose rate is low, because individuals with high metabolic rates naturally burn off more calories. Because basal metabolism normally decreases during adolescence, many individuals who are not overweight as children develop weight problems as teenagers. In fact, **obesity** is about three times more common during adolescence than during childhood (Paulsen, 1972). Often, a program of intense physical exercise combined with proper nutrition can help youngsters lose weight (Mayer, 1968).

Anorexia nervosa and bulimia.   In contemporary America, as the expression goes, one can never be too rich or too thin. Unfortunately, not everyone is genetically or metabolically meant to be as thin as fashion magazines tell people they should be. Some adolescents, especially young women, become so concerned about gaining weight that they take drastic—and dangerous—measures to remain thin. Some go on eating binges and then force themselves to vomit to avoid gaining weight, a pattern associated with an eating disorder called **bulimia.** In the more severe cases, young women suffering from an eating disorder called **anorexia nervosa** actually starve themselves in an effort to keep their weight down. Adolescents with these sorts of eating disorders have an extremely disturbed body image. They see themselves as overweight when they are actually underweight. Some anorectic youngsters may lose betwen 25 percent and 50 percent of their body weight. As you would expect, bulimia and anorexia, if untreated, lead to a variety of serious physical problems; in fact, nearly 20 percent of anorectic teenagers inadvertently starve themselves to death. Today, a variety of therapeutic approaches—including individual counseling, behavior modification, group therapy, and family therapy—are being employed successfully in the treatment of these eating disorders (Vigersky, 1977).

Several theories have been proposed to account for the onset of anorexia nervosa during adolescence. Some theorists have proposed that the eating disorder is related to the adolescent's attempts to assert her autonomy within an overly controlling family system (Bruch, 1973; Minuchin et al., 1978). Others have suggested possible links between anorexia and depression, noting that both disorders increase dramatically in prevalence during adolescence and that both are more likely to afflict females than males (Rutter and Garmezy, 1983).

Because anorexia nervosa and bulimia are ten times more common among adolescent and young adult women than among men of the same age, and because their onset coincides with adolescence and, consequently, with the bodily changes of puberty, it is likely that social forces are a main factor in the development of these eating disorders. Many adolescent women—even those without an eating disorder—develop excessive concerns about dieting. It is hard to imagine disorders like anorexia or bulimia outside a cultural context that emphasizes thinness, especially among women, and that encourages weight loss, through whatever means.

By way of comparison, it is interesting to note that at the turn of the century, a different illness was frequently seen in adolescent girls: **chlorosis,** which is a form of anemia. Although chlorosis is virtually unheard of today, during the early 1900s, it appeared regularly in physicians' writings about adolescent girls, according to social historian Joan Brumberg (1982). The disease was called chlorosis—the term comes from the Greek word meaning green—because these young women had a green tinge to their complexion.

Chlorotic girls complained of fatigue, listlessness, pallor, and depression. At the time, the medical establishment viewed chlorosis as an expected disorder of adolescence, having something to do with the onset of menstruation. As a consequence, the prevalence of the disorder was accepted with little question—chlorosis was something that the adolescent girl suffered from until her menstrual cycle became more regular. In retrospect, however, one clear reason for the prevalence of chlorosis among adolescent girls was that young women were discouraged from eating red meat. It was believed that eating meat accelerated sexual development and fueled the passions. In fact, an excessive amount of meat in a young woman's diet was believed to lead to nymphomania. In addition, as Brumberg points out, many young women avoided eating meat because they were concerned about staying slim. By encouraging young women to avoid red meat—a valuable source of protein, iron, and other nutrients—society had created an adolescent eating disorder.

Gradually, the medical establishment reached a better understanding of the physiology of normal menstruation, and by 1935, mention of the disorder had all but disappeared from the medical literature. The "green sickness" was no longer considered a normal part of adolescence; it was an eating disorder brought on in part by the social pressures of the era. Who knows? Fifty years from now, people may look back at the "epidemics" of anorexia and bulimia among today's young women and see these, too, as disorders peculiar to a particular era—one in which "thin was beautiful."

Just because cultural conditions contribute to the development of anorexia nervosa doesn't mean that individual characteristics do not play a role as well. It may be the case that cultural conditions predispose women more than men toward these eating disorders and that, within the population of adolescent women, those who have certain psychological traits (prone to depression, for example) or familial characteristics (overcontrolling parents, for example) may be more likely to develop problems. The onset of eating disorders, like so many aspects of adolescent development, cannot be understood apart from the context in which young people live.

Summary

Puberty is at once a biological, psychological, social, and cultural event. Because it is one of the few universals of adolescent development, puberty is given a great deal of prominence in theories of adolescence. Yet despite the fact that the biological changes of adolescence are universal in form, they are not universal in their consequences. The timing and tempo of puberty are affected partly by genetic factors and partly by the broader environment in which youngsters grow up. More significantly, the psychological and social impact of puberty on young people and those around them is dependent on the context in which maturation takes place.

Researchers have studied the immediate psychological and social impact of puberty as well as the differential consequences of early and late maturation. It now appears that puberty does not have dramatic effects on the adolescent's mood but can disrupt some of the psychological and interpersonal balances established during childhood and may require adaptation by the adolescent and those around him or her, especially the family. It is difficult to draw generalizations about the relative advantages and disadvantages of maturing early or late, however; the consequences differ for boys and for girls, the effects are different in the short term and in the long term, and the impact of early or late maturation varies across different social contexts. A growing body of research indicates, however, that standing too much apart from one's peers in physical appearance may have a temporary adverse impact on the young adolescent's self-image, especially for early-maturing girls.

Research on puberty and its impact has become increasingly sophisticated over the past two decades. It has moved away from the static comparisons of early and late maturers that dominated the field for many years. Today, social and biological scientists are looking more closely at the *processes* that underlie the psychosocial consequences of biological development. Research on puberty is beginning to bridge the gaps between biology, psychology, and sociology. As we look to the future, we can expect to find more longitudinal studies of physical development, more studies of hormonal fluctuations and their influence on adolescent behavior, and more studies of how contextual variations can shape the meaning of puberty and its impact on the developing person.

Many eating disorders, including obesity, anorexia nervosa, and bulimia, increase in prevalance during adolescence. This increase may be in part because puberty brings with it changes in metabolic function and in the ratio of body fat to muscle. Because anorexia and bulimia are so much more prevalent among females than males, it is important to consider the ways in which the culturally desired image of thinness among women has increased the prevalence of these problems.

Key Terms

adolescent growth spurt
adrenal androgens
adrenal cortex
adrenocorticotropic hormone (ACTH)
androgens
anorexia nervosa
asynchronicity in growth
basal metabolism rate
bulimia
chlorosis
cross-sectional design
developmental readiness
endocrine system
estrogens
feedback loop
follicle-stimulating hormone (FSH)
gonadotropins

growth hormone (GH)
hypothalamus
longitudinal design
luteinizing hormone (LH)
luteinizing hormone-releasing factor (LH-RF)
menarche
obesity
ovaries
peak height velocity
pituitary gland
secondary sex characteristics
secular trend
set point
testes
thyroid
thyroid-stimulating hormone (TSH)

For Further Reading

ADAMS, G., GULOTTA, T., AND MONTEMAYOR, R. (EDS.). (1988). *Advances in adolescent development* (Vol. 1). Beverly Hills: Sage. The first volume of this series, an annual collection of articles on research and theory, focuses on biological development during adolescence and its implications for psychological functioning.

BROOKS-GUNN, J. (1988). Antecedents and consequences of variations in girls' maturational timing. *Journal of Adolescent Health Care*, in press. An up-to-date review of research on the impact of early and late muturation on adolescent girls.

BROOKS-GUNN, J., PETERSEN, A., AND EICHORN, D. (EDS.). (1984). Time of maturation and psychosocial functioning in adolescence. *Journal of Youth and Adolescence*, 14 (3 and 4). A collection of recent articles on the impact of early and late maturation.

MARSHALL, W. Puberty. In F. Falkner and J. Tanner (Eds.), *Human growth* (Vol. 2). (1978). New York: Plenum Press. A good overview of the hormonal and somatic changes of puberty.

Cognitive Development

CHAPTER 2

PREVIEW

1. Changes in thinking constitute another set of fundamental developments that give adolescence many of its distinctive features. Changes in relationships, in the self-concept, and in values and plans during adolescence can all be traced, in part, to changes in the way young people think.

2. There are three chief ways in which adolescents' thinking differs from that of children: Adolescents are better at thinking about the world of the possible instead of limiting their thoughts to what is real; they are better at thinking through hypotheses; and they are better at thinking about abstract concepts.

3. Although we are able to specify the ways in which adolescents' thinking is superior to children's, we do not know why these changes take place at adolescence. Furthermore, theorists disagree about the basic processes that underlie cognitive development during adolescence.

4. Changes in thinking, of course, are not limited to scientific problem solving or performance on IQ tests. Adolescence is also a time of important changes in the way we think about other people, in the way we communicate with others, and in the way we make decisions about right and wrong.

Changes in cognition represent the second in a set of three fundamental changes that occur at adolescence—the others being the biological changes of puberty and the transition of the adolescent into new social roles. Like developments in the other two domains, the cognitive changes of adolescence have far-reaching implications for the young person's psychological development and social relations. Indeed, the expansion of thought during adolescence represents as significant an event and as important an influence on adolescents' development and behavior as puberty.

CHANGES IN COGNITION

Most people would agree that adolescents are "smarter" than children. Not only do teenagers *know* more than children—after all, the longer we live, the more opportunities we have to acquire new information—but adolescents actually *think* in ways that are more advanced, more efficient, and generally more effective. This can be seen in three chief ways. First, adolescents are better than children at thinking about possibilities. Second, they are better at thinking through hypotheses. And third, they are better at thinking about abstract things, including thinking about thinking itself (Keating, 1980). Let's look at each of these advantages in greater detail.

Thinking about Possibilities

The adolescent's thinking is less bound to concrete events than is that of the child. Children's thinking is oriented to the here and now—that is, to things and events that they can observe directly. But adolescents are able to consider what they observe against a backdrop of what is possible. Put another way, for the child, what is possible is what is real; for the adolescent, what is real is but one subset of what is possible. Children, for example, do not wonder, the way adolescents often do, about the ways in which

their personalities might change in the future or the ways in which their lives might be affected by different career choices. For the young child, you are who you are. But for the adolescent, who you are is just one possibility of who you could be.

This does not mean that the child is incapable of imagination or fantasy. Even young children have vivid and creative imaginations. Nor does it mean that children are unable to conceive of things being different from the way they observe them to be. Rather, the advantage that adolescents enjoy over children when it comes to thinking about possibilities is that adolescents are able to move easily between the specific and the abstract, to generate alternative possibilities and explanations *systematically*, and to compare what they actually observe with what they believe is possible.

We can illustrate this development by looking at two problems. How would you approach the following problem?

> Imagine four poker chips, one red, one blue, one yellow, and one green. Make as many different combinations of chips, of any number, as you can. Use the notations R, B, Y, and G to record your answers. (Adapted from Elkind, Barocas, and Rosenthal, 1968)

How did you tackle this problem? Did you need to use real poker chips to solve the problem? Probably not. In all likelihood, you used some sort of system, beginning perhaps with the case of zero chips (don't worry, a lot of people forget this one), then proceeding on to one-chip combinations (R, B, Y, G), two-chip combinations (RB, RY, RG, BY, BG, YG), three-chip combinations (RBY, RBG, RYG, BYG), and finally the single four-chip combination (RBYG). More important, you probably did not approach the problem haphazardly. You probably employed an abstract system for generating possibilities that you had in mind before being faced with the poker chip problem—a system that you can apply across a variety of similar tasks. Although preadolescent children might be able to solve the problem correctly—in the sense that they might, with luck, generate all the possible combinations—children are far less likely than teenagers to employ a systematic approach. Several studies of adolescents' and children's thinking abilities have reached this conclusion (Neimark, 1975).

Now let's look at this ability to consider possibilities systematically with a second problem:

> Figure 2.1 (page 62) shows a deck of twenty cards, each with a picture of a girl's face. Some of the girls have blond hair, and others have brown hair. Some have blue eyes, and others have brown eyes. What is the relationship (if any) between hair color and eye color in this series of pictures? (Adapted from Inhelder and Piaget, 1958)

What conclusion did you reach, and how did you reach it? You probably realized that hair color and eye color are strongly but not perfectly correlated. And in all likelihood, you began by mentally generating the four possible combinations of hair and eye color (brown/blue, brown/brown, blond/blue, blond/brown) and then sorting the cards into each of the four groups. By counting the number of cards in each group, you were able to reach a conclusion about the relationship between the two characteristics in question. You might not have even been aware that this was the approach you took. But what is most important, in this problem as well as in the previous one, is that you began with the *possible*—the possible combinations of poker chip colors and the possible combinations of hair and eye color—and moved from the possible to the real. This approach is far more likely to be employed by adolescents and adults than by children.

The adolescent's ability to reason systematically in terms of what is possible comes in handy in a variety of scientific and logical problem-solving situations. The study of mathematics in junior and senior high school (algebra,

geometry, and trigonometry), for instance, often requires that you begin with an abstract or theoretical formulation—for example, "the square of a right triangle's hypotenuse is equal to the sum of the squares of the other two sides" (the Pythagorean theorem). This theorem, after all, is a proposition about the possible rather than the real. It is a statement about *all possible* right triangles, not just triangles that we might actually observe. In mathematics, we learn how to apply these theorems to concrete examples (that is, real triangles). Scientific experimentation—in biology, chemistry, and physics—also involves the ability to generate possibilities systematically. In a chemistry experiment in which you are trying to identify an unknown substance by performing various tests, you must first be able to imagine alternative possibilities for the substance's identity in order to know what tests to conduct.

Even the strategies employed in such games as Twenty Questions differ markedly between children and adolescents. Adolescents generally eliminate broad categories ("Male or female?" "Living or dead?") and methodically narrow down the field of alternatives. Children are more likely to guess in very concrete ways from the beginning ("Is it George Washington?"), without using any system or plan (Flavell, 1977). That adolescents systematically narrow down the field of alternatives shows that they are more able than children to arrange categories in a hierarchy, with questions about more specific categories (male or female?) asked after questions about more general ones (animal or vegetable?).

The adolescent's use of this sort of thinking is not limited to scientific situations or games of logic. We see it in the types of arguments adolescents employ, in which they are more able than younger children to envision and therefore anticipate the possible responses of an opponent and to have handy a counterargument or a series of counterarguments (Clark and Delia, 1976). Many parents believe that their children become more argumentative during adolescence. What

FIGURE 2.1   According to these cards, what, if any, is the association between hair color and eye color?

probably happens is that their children become *better arguers*.

As we shall see in later chapters, the adolescent's ability to think in terms of the possible also influences the development of social, moral, and political reasoning. During adolescence, other people's points of view are not accepted unquestioningly but are evaluated against other theoretically possible beliefs. An adolescent might asks his mother for advice on how to

Delia Ephron's "How to Worry"

One of the more unfortunate outcomes of the adolescent's increased facility in thinking about possibilities is the potential to get lost in them—not just in thinking about them, but in worrying about them. Author Delia Ephron has devised an adolescent's guide, "How to Worry":

Worry that if you neck too much, you'll get mononucleosis.

Worry that if you masturbate, you'll get pimples.

Worry that if you masturbate, you'll get brain damage.

Worry that if you masturbate, you'll go blind.

Worry that in a long kiss, you'll have to breathe through your nose and your nose will be stopped up.

Worry that there's a right way to dress and you don't know it.

Worry that you won't like the food at other people's houses.

Worry that when you go to the bathroom, people will hear. Worry that the lock on the door doesn't work. Worry that someone will walk in.

If you are a girl, worry that your breasts are too round. Worry that your breasts are too pointed.

If you are a boy, worry that you will get breasts.

Source: Delia Ephron, *Teenage Romance, Or How to Die of Embarrassment* (New York: Viking, 1981), pp. 87–88.

---

handle a problem he is having with a friend and then ask someone else for a second opinion.

Thinking through Hypotheses

Thinking in hypothetical terms is another hallmark of adolescent cognition. The development of hypothetical thinking is most clearly evident in the following: (1) in the adolescent's ability to apply the "scientific method" in problem-solving situations (reasoning that systematically tests and then accepts or rejects hypotheses); (2) in the adolescent's facility in dealing with hypothetical situations, even if they are contrary to fact; and (3) in the adolescent's ability to reason through a series of "if-then" propositions. Undoubtedly, the ability to deal with hypothetical situations is closely linked to the adolescent's ability to deal with the possible instead of being limited to the concrete. In order to think hypothetically, you need to see beyond what is directly observable and reason in terms of what might be possible.

Consider the following "if-then" problem:

Read the following propositions, and answer "Yes," "No," or "Not enough information given," to each of the questions:

a. If this is Room 154, then this is a class in adolescent development. This is Room 154.
Is this a class in adolescent development?

b. If this is Room 154, then this is not a class in adolescent development. This is Room 154.
Is this a class in adolescent development?

d. If this is Room 154, then this is a class in adolescent development. This is not Room 154.
Is this a class in adolescent development? (Adapted from Shapiro and O'Brien; cited in Flavell, 1977, p. 112)

Most children are able to answer the first two questions correctly, responding yes to the first and no to the second. Each of these answers is a logically obvious conclusion. But preadolescents have trouble with the third question. As you can see, the third question cannot be an-

The advanced thinking abilities of adolescents allow them to employ more sophisticated and more effective reasoning strategies in a variety of situations. (Evan Johnson/Jeroboam)

swered solely on the basis of the information given. The class may or may not be a class in adolescent development. Adolescents and adults, who are much more facile in thinking through hypotheses, are more likely to answer the third question correctly.

The ability to think through hypotheses is an enormously powerful tool. Being able to plan ahead, being able to see the future consequences of an action, and being able to provide alternative explanations of events are all dependent on being able to hypothesize effectively. For example, consider the following:

> It takes brave pilots to fly airplanes in the Swiss Alps. One afternoon, a pilot was flying in the Alps and flew into a cable that was suspending a cable car traveling between two mountain peaks. The cable snapped, and many of the passengers in the car died in the ensuing crash.
>
> Was the pilot careless? Why? (Adapted from Peel, 1971)

Children generally answer yes or no, providing little logical support for reaching their conclusion. "Yes, he was careless because he hit the cable." "No, he wasn't careless because careless people aren't allowed to become pilots."

But adolescents are more likely to recognize that the answer to the question depends on other information—which is not given in the passage (Peel, 1971). Did the pilot know that the cable was there? What were the prevailing weather conditions? If the pilot saw the cable, did he make any attempt to avoid it? Adolescents' answers to the problem reflect their ability to think hypothetically. They are often phrased in "if-then" terms: "*If* the pilot knew the cable was there, *then* he should have made a special effort to fly above it." "*If* there was a lot of fog, *then* the pilot might not have been able to help flying into the cable."

Thinking in hypothetical terms also permits us to suspend our beliefs about something in order to argue in the abstract. Being capable of assuming a hypothetical stance is important when it comes to debating an issue, since doing so permits us to understand the logic behind the other person's argument, without necessarily agreeing with its conclusion. Playing devil's advocate, for example—that is, formulating a position contrary to what you really believe in order to challenge someone else's reasoning—requires the ability to think in hypothetical terms.

Of course, hypothetical thinking also has implications for the adolescent's social behavior. It helps the young person to take the perspective of others by enabling him or her to think through what someone else might be thinking or feeling, given that person's point of view. ("If I were in his shoes, then I would feel pretty angry.") Hypothetical thinking helps in formulating and arguing one's viewpoint, because it allows adolescents to think a step ahead of the opposition—a cognitive tool that comes in quite handy when dealing with parents. ("If they come back with 'You have to stay home and clean up the garbage,' then I'll remind them about the time they let Susan go out when she had chores to do.") And hypothetical thinking plays an important role in decision-making abilities, because it permits the young person to plan ahead and to foresee the consequences of choosing one alternative over another. ("If I choose to go out for the soccer team, then I am going to have to give up my part-time job.")

Thinking about Abstract Concepts

The appearance of more systematic, *abstract* thinking is the third notable aspect of cognitive development during adolescence. We noted earlier that children's thinking is more concrete and more bound to observable events and objects than is that of adolescents. This difference is clearly evident when we consider the ability to deal with abstract concepts—things that cannot be experienced directly through the senses.

One way in which facility with abstract thinking is apparent during adolescence is in the

Being able to think in hypothetical terms can be a powerful tool in situations that call for logical argument. (Joel Gordon)

ability to think about thoughts, a process sometimes referred to as **second-order thinking.** With increasing age, children become more capable of articulating the strategies they employ when attending to, memorizing, organizing, and recalling information. For example, in the poker-chip problem, an adolescent would not only be more likely than a child to use a systematic strategy for generating the different combinations but would also be better able to describe the strategy in abstract terms (for example, "First take the zero-chip combination, then the singles, then the doubles beginning with R, etc.") and to explain why and how the strategy works.

Adolescents also find it easier than children to comprehend the sorts of higher-order, abstract logic inherent in puns, proverbs, metaphors, and analogies. When presented with verbal analogies, children are more likely than adolescents to focus on concrete and familiar associations among the words than on the abstract, or conceptual, relations among them.

Consider the following analogy, for example:

Sun : Moon : : Asleep : ?
a. Star
b. Bed
c. Awake
d. Night

Instead of answering "awake"—which is the best answer of the four given above—children would be more likely to respond with "bed" or "night," since both of these words have stronger associations with the word *asleep.* It is generally not until early adolescence that individuals are able to discern the abstract principles underlying analogies—in the one above, the principle involves antonyms—and therefore solve them correctly (Sternberg and Nigro, 1980).

The adolescent's greater facility with second-order thinking also permits the application of advanced reasoning and logical processes to social and ideological matters. This is clearly seen in the adolescent's increased facility and interest in thinking about interpersonal relationships, politics, philosophy, religion, and morality—topics that involve such abstract concepts as friendship, faith, democracy, fairness, and honesty. The growth of social thinking—generally referred to as **social cognition**—during adolescence is directly related to the young person's improving ability to think abstractly. Later in this chapter, we will examine the ways in which social thinking improves in adolescence.

A final way in which abstract and second-order thinking are apparent during adolescence is in increased introspection, self-consciousness, and intellectualization. When we are introspective, after all, we are thinking about our own thoughts and emotions. When we are self-conscious, we are thinking about how others think about us. And when we intellectualize, we are turning relatively simple and concrete matters into complex and abstract ones. Introspection, self-consciousness, and intellectualization are all brought about by the adolescent's newfound ability to think about thinking. All three processes play an important role in the adolescent's psychological growth. As we shall see in Chapter 8, for example, these processes permit the sorts of self-examination and exploration that are important components of the young person's attempt to establish a coherent sense of identity.

Adolescent Egocentrism

As psychologist David Elkind (1978) points out, the intellectual advances of adolescence may occasionally result in problems for the young adolescent, particularly before he or she adjusts to having such powerful cognitive tools. Being able to introspect, for instance, may lead to periods of extreme self-absorption—a form of "adolescent egocentrism" (Elkind, 1967).

According to Elkind (1978), adolescent egocentrism results in three problems in thinking that help to explain some of the seemingly odd beliefs and behaviors of teenagers. The first, the **imaginary audience,** involves having such a heightened sense of self-consciousness that the teenager imagines that his or her behavior is the

Adolescent Self-Consciousness and the Imaginary Audience

One of the reasons for the young adolescent's increased self-consciousness is the expansion of cognitive abilities characteristic of early adolescence. For the first time, the adolescent is truly able to view himself or herself from the perspective of others. As psychologist David Elkind explains, this can sometimes lead to the creation of an "imaginary audience."

> Recently, I was having dinner alone at O'Hare Airport. During the course of the meal I happened to drop my knife, which made a horrible clang as it hit the floor. I was sure, at the moment, that everyone else in the restaurant heard the racket and was looking at me thinking, "What a klutz!" In fact, of course, few people heard it and even those who did, did not care. But at the moment, I was surrounded by an audience of my own making, an **imaginary audience**.
>
> Everyone has experienced similar moments. But what happens only occasionally in adults is characteristic of the young adolescent because of the formal operations which make it possible for young people to think about other people's thinking. This newfound ability to think about other people's thinking, however, is coupled with an inability to distinguish between what is of interest to others and what is of interest to the self. Since the young adolescent is preoccupied with his or her own self—all the physical and physiological changes going on—he or she assumes that everyone has the same concern. Young people believe that everyone in their vicinity is as preoccupied with their behavior and appearance as they are them-imaginary audience.
>
> The imaginary audience helps to account for the super-self-consciousness of the young adolescent. When you believe that everyone is watching and evaluating you, you become very self-conscious. In the lunchroom, on the bus going home, standing in front of the class, the young adolescent feels that he or she is at the center of everyone's attention. It is a different sort of self-consciousness than is experienced by children. The child is self-conscious about appearances, about clothes which are too big or the wrong style. But the young adolescent is more concerned about personal qualities, traits, physical features, and abilities which are unique to himself. Fantasies of singing before an audience, of making a touchdown before a cheering crowd, of playing a concerto in a concert hall are common imaginary audience fantasies in which the individual is the center of everyone's attention. . . . In general, imaginary audience behavior tends to decline with age, as young people come to recognize that each individual person has his or her own preoccupations. To be sure, all of us occasionally have imaginary audience reactions, but these are usually short-lived, as was my experience in the airport. Imaginary audience behavior in adults is a relic of early adolescence which all of us carry with us and to which we revert on occasion. But we need to recognize that it is pervasive in young adolescents and that it accounts for [their remarkable] self-consciousness.

Source: David Elkind, "Understanding the Young Adolescent," *Adolescence* 13 (1978): 127–134.

focus of everyone else's concern and attention (see box above). For example, a teenager who is going to a concert with 4,000 other people may worry about dressing the right way because "everybody will notice." Given the cognitive limitations of adolescent egocentrism, it is difficult indeed to persuade a young person that the "audience" is not all that concerned with his or her behavior or appearance.

The second problem described by Elkind is called the **personal fable.** The personal fable revolves around the adolescent's egocentric (and erroneous) belief that his or her experiences are unique. For instance, a young man whose relationship with a girlfriend had just broken up might tell his sympathetic mother that she could not possibly understand what it feels like to break up with someone—even though breaking up is something that most people have experienced plenty of times during their adolescent and adult years. Sometimes holding on to a personal fable can actually be quite dangerous, as in the case of a sexually active adolescent who believes that pregnancy simply won't happen to her or a careless driver who believes that he will defy the laws of nature by taking hairpin turns on a road at breakneck speed. Elkind points out that much of the risk-taking behavior engaged in by adolescents can be explained partly in terms of the personal fable.

Finally, Elkind has pointed out that the increased levels of intellectualization accompanying adolescent egocentrism may lead the adolescent to look for complicated solutions to problems when simple ones are sufficient—a phenomenon Elkind calls **pseudostupidity:**

> The obvious seem to elude them. In trying to find a sock or a shoe or a book, they ignore the obvious places and look in the esoteric ones. Simple decisions as to what dress or slacks to wear are overcomplicated by the inclusion of extraneous concerns such as why and by whom the clothes were bought in the first place. In school, young people often approach subjects at a much too complex level and fail, not because the tasks are too difficult, but because they are too simple. (Elkind, 1978, p. 129)

Although Elkind's ideas about adolescent egocentrism ring true, several researchers have found it difficult to confirm Elkind's prediction that the various manifestations of adolescent egocentrism, such as the imaginary audience or the personal fable, actually increase during early adolescence (Gray and Hudson, 1984; Riley, Adams, and Neilsen, 1984). If anything, it appears that individuals become *less* egocentric as they develop more sophisticated abstract-thinking abilities. One problem with these studies, as Elkind points out (1985), is that they rely on fairly simple questionnaires to assess rather complicated belief systems invoked in real-life situations. For example, it is easy to imagine that the same adolescent who worried about being seen by "everyone" at a rock concert might not appear so egocentric in his responses to a hypothetical dilemma posed in a questionnaire. This difference, of course, would raise doubts about whether adolescent egocentrism *is* an entirely cognitive phenomenon, since we would expect that cognitive deficiencies would show up in questionnaire assessments. It may be that Elkind is right about the increased prevalence of egocentrism during early adolescence but wrong about the processes that underlie it (Lapsley and Murphy, 1985).

THEORETICAL PERSPECTIVES

Although there is general agreement that adolescents' thinking is different and more advanced than children's in the ways we have just described, there is far less consensus about the processes underlying the cognitive differences between children and adolescents. Part of the lack of agreement stems from the different points of view theorists have taken toward the issue of cognitive development in general. Whereas some theorists have emphasized the *quantitative* aspects of intellectual growth, others have focused on *qualitative* changes in cognitive activity.

To what extent are the differences between a child's thinking and an adolescent's thinking differences in quantity, and to what extent are they differences in quality? In other words, do adolescents think in *different* ways from children, or do they employ the same basic cognitive processes used by children but with greater facility? Is the course of intellectual development between childhood and adolescence best depicted as a smooth, gradually increasing slope, or is a steplike picture, with a few abrupt and dramatic increases, more accurate? Theorists who take a *quantitative* perspective on cognitive development suggest that adolescent thinking is structurally similar to though more advanced than the thinking of children and that intellectual growth between these two eras is gradual and incremental. Theorists who take a *qualitative* perspective on cognitive development argue that adolescent thinking is structurally different from childhood thinking and that development occurs in a stagelike fashion.

In general, the distinction between changes in quantity and changes in quality is fraught with definitional problems. Take the perception of color, for instance (Keating, 1980). Suppose you were presented with a series of cards, each of a different color, and asked to sort colors that were "different" into separate piles. Like most people, you would probably agree that blue and green are qualitatively different colors—that is, that the difference in color between a green card and a blue card cannot be described merely in quantitative terms (that is, one color cannot be described as more "something" than the other). Yet if you were to take a blue card and a green card and separate them by a series of cards of various shades of blue-green arranged in a sequence from the most "bluish" blue-green to the most "greenish," the difference between green and blue would seem quantitative, not qualitative. The distinction between differences in quality and differences in quantity depends largely on how we go about measuring the phenomenon in question.

In many respects, the distinction between the quantitative and qualitative perspectives on cognitive development is an equally artificial one. Any conclusion we reach about the nature of cognitive change between childhood and adolescence is likely to be tainted by the way in which we go about studying youngsters' thinking. A study that assesses one youngster's performance repeatedly every few months, for example, will undoubtedly produce a smoother and less abrupt pattern of growth in intellectual abilities than a study that compares groups of 10-, 14-, and 18-year-olds. Because researchers working from different theoretical perspectives have posed different research questions, used different tasks to measure cognitive growth, and emphasized some aspects of cognitive activity more than others, their studies provide different but theoretically compatible pictures of mental development during adolescence. The three theoretical viewpoints that have been especially im-

portant are the **Piagetian**, the **psychometric**, and the **information-processing** perspectives. Each point of view provides valuable insights into why thinking changes during adolescence.

The Piagetian View of Cognitive Development

The **Piagetian**, or **cognitive-developmental**, view of intellectual development dominated the study of cognitive growth during adolescence until recently. Generally, theorists who take this point of view argued that cognitive development proceeds in a stagelike fashion, that adolescent thinking is qualitatively different from the type of thinking employed by children, and that during adolescence, individuals develop a special type of thinking that they use in a variety of situations.

Piaget and his theory of cognitive development. Before examining the Piagetian view of cognitive activity during adolescence, we need to look at Piaget's view of intellectual development in more general terms. Jean Piaget was a Swiss psychologist interested in **genetic epistemology**—the study of how knowledge develops. While administering intelligence tests to young children early in his career, Piaget became interested in the cognitive strategies that children use when trying to solve test problems. As opposed to other scientists employing intelligence tests, Piaget became more interested in *how* children reached the conclusions they did than in whether their answers were correct. Instead of simply asking questions and scoring the answers as correct or incorrect, Piaget would question children to find out the logic behind their answers. Through painstakingly careful observation of his own as well as other children, Piaget began to build his theory of intellectual development.

According to Piaget, cognitive development proceeds through four stages: the **sensorimotor** period (from birth until about age 2), the **preoperational period** (from about age 2 until about age 5), the period of **concrete operations** (from about age 6 until early adolescence) and, finally, the period of **formal operations** (from adolescence through adulthood). These stages are presented in Table 2.1. Each stage is characterized by a particular type of thinking, earlier stages of thinking being incorporated into new, more advanced, and more adaptive forms of reasoning. For example, Piaget believed that formal-operational thinking, which characterizes adolescent reasoning, is a more advanced and more effective way of dealing with the adolescent's world than is concrete-operational thinking. Although concrete-operational thinking is not replaced by formal-operational thinking at adolescence, formal-operational reasoning develops in adolescence on top of the concrete-operational foundation present during childhood.

Piaget stressed the adaptive nature of cognitive development: Advanced types of thinking develop as maturational gains and environmental demands combine to make old strategies less effective and new ones available. He conceptualized children's intellectual growth as moving from periods of cognitive equilibrium, during which their intellectual skills are adequate to meet the perceived demands of their environment; into periods of cognitive disequilibrium and eventual reorganization, during which new and more advanced skills emerge, extending previous skills; and back into periods of equilibrium, after the new skills have been consolidated. The biological maturation of the child,

for example, in combination with the new intellectual demands of entering school, may provoke the movement from preoperational thinking into the stage of concrete operations.

We sometimes move through stages of equilibrium and disequilibrium when we relearn how to do something that we already do well in order to be able to do it better. When a good tennis player changed her grip in an effort to become an *excellent* player, for example, her game actually deteriorated. She eventually adjusted to the new grip, and indeed, she became an excellent player. But it took her nearly two years to move from the "equilibrium" of the old grip (which worked well enough at the time), through a period of "disequilibrium" (when she was beginning to play with the new grip and was having difficulty using it consistently), into a new "equilibrium" (when the use of the new grip became habitual and her game reached a new level).

According to Piaget, transitions into higher stages of reasoning are most likely to occur at times when the child's biological readiness and the increasing complexity of environmental demands interact to bring about cognitive disequilibrium. Without biological readiness, environmental stimulation alone cannot bring about higher forms of thinking. Thus, for example, it is futile to try to teach a 3-month-old how to talk, because infants at this age are not biologically ready to acquire language. By the same token, biological readiness alone is not

TABLE 2.1   THE FOUR STAGES OF COGNITIVE DEVELOPMENT ACCORDING TO PIAGET

STAGE	APPROXIMATE AGES	CHIEF CHARACTERISTICS
Sensorimotor	Birth–2 years	Discovery of relationships between sensation and motor behavior
Preoperational	2–7 years	Use of symbols to represent objects internally, especially through language
Concrete operations	7–11 years	Mastery of logic and development of "rational" thinking
Formal operations	11 years +	Development of abstract and hypothetical reasoning

enough. Even at age 2, when most children are biologically capable of learning language, children who grow up in deprived environments, without adequate stimulation, will learn to speak much more slowly than children who are talked to and played with.

Given the emphasis that Piaget placed on the interaction between biological change and environmental stimulation in provoking intellectual growth, it comes as no surprise that early adolescence—a time of dramatic biological maturation and equally noteworthy changes in environmental demands—is viewed in Piagetian theory as an extremely important period in cognitive development.

The limits of concrete-operational thinking.

By the time children reach the end of the concrete-operational period, they have a wealth of cognitive tools with which to approach most of the day-to-day problems they typically encounter. They can evaluate whether statements presented to them are true or false, solve many types of logical problems, and make decisions on the basis of evidence presented to them. Actually, most of the tasks faced in one's everyday activities can be handled quite adequately with concrete-operational reasoning. What, then, are its limitations?

The chief limitation of concrete-operational thinking is that it is tied to events and phenomena in the concrete world (hence the term *concrete operations*)—the world that is directly observable. True, most of the problem-solving situations we encounter in daily living involve reasoning about the concrete world and can accordingly be tackled with concrete thinking. But some do not. In particular, concrete thinking is inadequate when it comes to reasoning about abstract concepts, about alternative courses of events, and about hypothetical situations.

The child whose thinking is limited to concrete operations finds it difficult to apply the same logical tools he or she so effectively employs in dealing with concrete phenomena to situations that are abstract, hypothetical, or not real but in the realm of possibility. If you show

Although children whose thinking is limited to concrete operations have the cognitive tools necessary to solve many day-to-day problems, they find it difficult to deal with situations that are abstract or hypothetical. (New York Times Magazine)

a child pictures of three people and ask her to line them up from shortest to tallest, she won't have any difficulty doing it correctly. But suppose you don't show her pictures but instead say, "John is taller than Ann, and Ann is taller than Bill. Is Bill taller than John?" She will probably have difficulty figuring out the answer.

Piaget believed that at the heart of formal-operational thinking was the use of an abstract system of **propositional logic**—a system based on theoretical, or formal, principles of logic (hence the term *formal operations*). Formal reasoning can be just as easily applied to hypothetical events as it can to real ones; is just as effective in dealing with abstract concepts as with concrete things; and is just as useful for thinking about alternatives to what really exists as it is for thinking about reality itself. Consider the significance of being able to understand the following example of propositional logic:

If A is true or B is true, then C is true.

This is a logical relationship that is encountered in all sorts of situations, ranging from scientific problem solving (for example, "If the solution turns blue or yellow, then it must contain the mineral copper") to understanding social relationships ("If Bob asks Susan out or if Judy calls me to do something this Friday night, then Bob and Judy must have broken up"). Once the *form* of the logic is understood—that *either* A or B is sufficient to demonstrate that C is true—it can be applied to all sorts of events—real as well as possible, concrete as well as abstract—merely by changing what A, B, and C stand for. While concrete operational thinkers are able to imagine alternative and hypothetical situations, they are unable to think about them in as systematic a way as formal operational thinkers can.

Just because adolescents can employ propositional logic, however, does not mean that they are always consciously aware of doing so. In the example given above, for instance, we would hardly expect that an adolescent who is trying to figure out whether two friends are still "going steady" consciously runs through the As, Bs, and Cs of propositional logic. But you do not have to be aware of using propositional logic to use it effectively. Piaget likened the use of formal operations by adolescents to the use of principles of harmony by musicians: Musicians do not have to be aware that they are playing according to a set of abstract rules of harmony to produce beautiful sounds.

The growth of formal-operational thinking. Piagetian theorists believe that the use of propositional logic—the foundation of formal-oper-

ational thinking—is the chief feature of adolescent thinking that differentiates it from the type of thinking employed by children. We noted before that adolescents' thinking can be distinguished from the thinking of children primarily in three respects—in thinking about possibilities, in thinking through hypotheses, and in thinking about abstract concepts. The connection between these three types of thinking and the development of formal operations is clear: In order to think about alternatives to what really exists, in order to think in hypothetical terms, and in order to systematically think about concepts that are not directly observable, you must have a system of reasoning that works just as well in abstract, imagined, and hypothetical situations as it does in concrete ones. The system of propositional logic provides the basis for precisely this sort of reasoning.

The development of formal thinking appears to take place in two steps. During the first step, characteristic of early adolescence, formal thinking is apparent, but it has a sort of "now you see it, now you don't" quality to it. Young adolescents may demonstrate formal thinking at some times but at others be able to think only in concrete terms; they may use formal operations on some tasks but not on others; they may reason formally under some but not all testing situations. Virtually all adolescents go through this period of "emergent formal operations" (Kuhn et al., 1977).

It is not until middle or even late adolescence that formal-operational thinking becomes consolidated and integrated into the individual's general approach to reasoning. Moreover, the attainment of "consolidated formal operations" is not universal. That is, although the initial appearance of formal thinking appears to be widespread among young adolescents, the final and complete development of formal reasoning is less common—according to some estimates, only about 60 percent of college students consistently demonstrate formal thinking on tests used to measure formal-operational thought (Neimark, 1975). It would seem, then, that the child is in a state of cognitive equilibrium during the late portion of the concrete-operational period and enters a period of disequilibrium and biological readiness during early adolescence—when formal-operational thinking appears in its rudimentary, emergent form. Subsequently, if levels of environmental stimulation are sufficient, formal-operational abilities are consolidated and permanently developed sometime during middle or late adolescence.

Under what conditions will formal-operational thinking become fully consolidated? Piaget suggested that formal operations are more likely to develop among adolescents encountering an environment that demands the use of formal-operational skills. Taking science courses, for example, that demand hypothetical reasoning might stimulate the growth of formal-operational abilities. He also felt that formal thinking is more likely to be employed in problem-solving situations with which the individual has some degree of familiarity. Some adolescents might be more likely to employ formal-operational reasoning in scientific problem solving, for example, while others might be more apt to use it in social situations. Some adolescents might be expected to use formal-operational thinking spontaneously, while others might require prompting.

Thus while all adolescents have the *potential* to develop formal-operational thinking, and most can and do demonstrate it from time to time, not all adolescents (or, for that matter, all adults) employ formal-operational thinking regularly and in a variety of situations. The extent to which consolidated formal-operational thinking appears depends on the environmental demands placed on adolescents as they develop and on the conditions under which their reasoning is assessed.

Research on the development of formal-operational thinking.
Researchers working from the Piagetian vantage point have employed a number of different tasks in assessing youngsters' ability to use formal-operational skills.

Two of these tasks have been discussed in this chapter: the poker chip problem and the hair and eye color problem. Generally, children and adolescents of different ages are tested on one or more tasks, and youngsters are categorized according to the extent to which they demonstrate formal reasoning. In a few studies, individuals have been assessed longitudinally, in efforts to see how formal thinking develops over time (Keating, 1980).

Researchers working in this area have asked three main questions. First, are there age differences (or changes over time) in performance on measures of formal operations that are consistent with Piaget's theoretical predictions? Second, does formal thinking develop in a stagelike fashion, as Piaget's theory suggests it does? And third, can the development of formal thinking be induced, and if so, is this more easily accomplished during adolescence than during childhood?

Age differences in formal thinking. Virtually every study of the development of formal-operational thinking has shown that older children perform better on tests designed to measure formal operations than do younger children and that individuals' performance on these tasks improves as they move from childhood into adolescence (Keating, 1980; Neimark, 1975). Although this pattern of results is consistent with Piaget's theory, it can be interpreted in a variety of ways. Generally speaking, performance on *all sorts* of cognitive tasks—not just those designed to measure formal operations—improves with age (Keating, 1980). It is therefore not clear whether age changes, or age differences, on measures of formal thinking genuinely reflect the development of propositional logic (as Piagetian theorists would claim) or merely reflect other important intellectual abilities not considered by Piaget to be defining features of adolescent thinking (for example, improvements in memory storage or retrieval). In other words, it is not necessary to propose the existence of a special or unique type of logic characteristic of adolescence in order to explain why adolescents outperform children on cognitive tests.

Formal operations as an adolescent "stage" of thinking.   A more critical test of Piaget's theory involves the examination of his claim that formal-operational thought represents a stage of thinking that does not appear until early adolescence, and this stage, once attained, is characteristic of an adolescent's thinking in general. Overall, research has not supported these claims. Although scientists have not observed children in everyday situations sufficiently to draw firm conclusions, studies of youngsters in test situations indicate that the development of formal thinking appears to be continuous and gradual, beginning in late childhood and continuing throughout adolescence—not stagelike, as Piagetian theorists have proposed. Second, when adolescents are given a series of different tasks, each designed to tap formal thinking,

their scores are not always consistent from one task to another (Keating, 1980). In other words, in contrast to Piaget's claim that, once attained, the "stage" of formal operations characterizes an individual's thinking across a range of different situations, many researchers find that formal thinking is actually quite situation-specific (Keating and Clark, 1980). These studies call into question the idea that there is a stage of thinking based on an underlying, advanced form of propositional logic which emerges at adolescence. If this were so, why would an adolescent employ the logic in some situations but not in others?

Can the development of formal-operational thinking be induced?   Although all adolescents do not necessarily demonstrate formal-operational thinking, studies suggest that all young people have the *potential* to think in this way, given the right degree of environmental stimu-

Piaget felt that encountering situations in the environment that demand formal-operational skills stimulates the development of formal-operational thinking in adolescents. Science classes may stimulate formal-operational thinking because they demand hypothetical reasoning. (Joseph Schuyler/Stock, Boston)

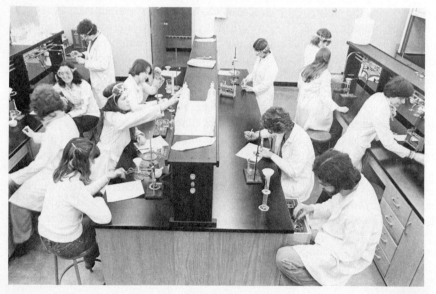

lation. Sufficient environmental stimulation may be especially necessary for the *consolidation* of formal-operational skills. Although most young adolescents exhibit a sort of transitory formal-operational thought—described earlier as "emergent formal operations" (Kuhn et al., 1977)—not all young adolescents receive the environmental challenge or demands for formal thinking needed to push them toward "consolidated" formal operations. Consequently, some youngsters slide back toward concrete thinking during middle adolescence and do not use formal-operational reasoning as adults.

Perhaps it is possible, however, to teach adolescents who appear nonformal in their thinking to employ formal operations. According to Piagetian theory, such teaching should be successful only after childhood, because preadolescent children presumably are not maturationally ready to make the transition from concrete to formal operations.

It is important to differentiate between *stimulating* the development of formal operations and *teaching* formal operational skills. The development of formal operations—at least in the sense that Piaget had in mind—ostensibly involves a major shift in the way the individual looks at the world. It is not simply a skill or set of skills that can be taught in the way spelling or algebra or history are taught. Therefore, when scientists attempt to stimulate the growth of formal operations, they do so by creating disequilibrium, or **cognitive conflict.**

Creating cognitive conflict is accomplished by presenting individuals with problems that they would have difficulty solving using concrete operations and then exposing them to formal-operational strategies. These are called the "demonstration" problems. Following the presentation of the demonstration problems, researchers measure the success of the intervention by presenting the individuals with *different* problems and examining whether they demonstrate an increased likelihood of using formal-operational strategies. This approach rules out the possibility that the intervention merely taught the youngsters how to solve the demonstration problems and shows whether the development of more general formal-operational abilities has actually been induced. For example, we might take a group of concrete-operational youngsters and present them with a scientific problem. After they had tried—and failed—to solve it, we could show them formal-operational strategies for solving the problem and let them practice these strategies. Following this intervention, we would then look at the students' solutions to other problems designed to assess formal operations, such as the poker chip problem.

Attempts to stimulate the development of formal-operational reasoning through this sort of intervention have been relatively successful, although, as one would expect, degrees of success have varied with the nature of the training program, the tasks used to measure success, and the age of the students receiving the training (Kuhn and Angelev, 1976; Kuhn, Ho, and Adams, 1979; Siegler, Liebert, and Liebert, 1973). Generally, the more intensive the stimulation, the more effective the intervention. Moreover, consistent with Piaget's theory, it appears easier to train adolescents than preadolescents in formal thinking and easier to train older adolescents than younger ones.

It does not appear *impossible*, however, to provoke formal thinking in preadolescents: Two teams of researchers (Danner and Day, 1977; Siegler, Liebert, and Liebert, 1973) found that formal-operational thinking could be elicited from children as young as 10 years old. These studies indicate that it is important to distinguish between the *spontaneous* demonstration of formal thinking and the demonstration of this level of thinking following an intervention designed to stimulate intellectual growth. The spontaneous demonstration of formal thinking is less likely and occurs later than the demonstration of formal thinking following a deliberate attempt to elicit it. Taken together, studies of intervention programs indicate that most, if not all, adolescents have the potential to think in formal-operational terms but that this potential may not be realized in certain environments.

Piaget's theory in perspective.   The Piagetian perspective on cognitive development during adolescence has stimulated a great deal of research on how young people think. Generally, the concept of formal operations as defined by Piaget and his followers appears to account for many of the changes in thinking observed during the adolescent years. Specifically, the theory of formal operations helps to explain why adolescents are better able than children to think about possibilities, to think through hypotheses, and to think about thoughts.

Where the Piagetian perspective on adolescent cognitive development appears to fall short is in its claim that cognitive development proceeds in a stagelike fashion and that the "stage" of formal operations is the stage of cognitive development characteristic of adolescence. Rather, research suggests that advanced reasoning capabilities (which may or may not be synonymous with what Piaget terms "formal operations") develop gradually and continuously from childhood through adolescence, probably in more of a quantitative fashion than was proposed by Piaget. Rather than talking about a "stage" of cognitive activity characteristic of adolescence, then, it appears to be more accurate to depict these advanced reasoning capabilities as skills that are employed by older children more often than younger ones, by some adolescents more often than other adolescents, and by individuals when they are in certain situations more often than when they are in other situations.

The Psychometric View of Cognitive Development

Compared to Piagetian theorists, *psychometricians* have taken a far more quantitative view of cognitive development during the adolescent years. The term *psychometric* refers to these researchers' concern with the *measurement* of mental functioning. Thus unlike Piaget, psychometricians have been more interested in *what* individuals know and are capable of doing than in how they come to know what they know.

The measurement of IQ.   The most widely used measures of what individuals know are intelligence, or IQ (for "intelligence quotient"), tests. A variety of such tests exists, including the Stanford-Binet, the Wechsler Intelligence Scale for Children (WISC), and the Wechsler Adult Intelligence Scale (WAIS). Although these three instruments contain different questions and yield somewhat different information about an individual's cognitive capabilities, for the purposes of our discussion, the similarities of the three measures far outweigh their differences. Our examination of adolescent cognitive development from the psychometric perspective will focus on the use of the Wechsler intelligence tests (the WISC and the WAIS), since these are the most commonly used instruments in the study of adolescent development.

The IQ test is one of the most widely used—and most widely misused—psychological instruments ever developed. Initially developed by the French psychologist Alfred Binet in 1905, the first intelligence test was devised in response to the French government's interest in better predicting which children would profit from formal schooling. Thus although Binet's test—and the many others that would be developed over the years—was designed to yield a measure of "intelligence," the test was devised with a very specific type of "intelligence" in mind: the type of intelligence it takes to succeed in formal educational institutions. Even the best IQ tests used today measure only a very specific type of intelligence.

An individual's performance on an IQ test is usually presented not as a raw score but as a relative score in comparison to the scores of other individuals of the same age and from approximately the same cohort (a *cohort* is a group of people born during the same historical era). Comparison scores are collected every so often, so that the comparison group for individuals taking the test at any given time is valid, representative, and up-to-date. The score of 100 is used to designate the midway point: An IQ score below 100 indicates a poorer test performance than half of the comparison group; a score above

Psychometricians study cognitive development through the use of standardized intelligence tests. Such tests are often administered to large numbers of individuals in group testings. (Arthur Grace/Stock, Boston)

100 indicates a better performance than half the comparison group. In other words, the higher an individual's IQ, the smaller the number of agemates who perform equally or better on the same test.

Although an individual's score on an intelligence test is often reported in terms of his or her overall IQ, intelligence tests are actually comprised of a series of tests, and it is usually possible to look at performance in different areas independently. The WISC and the WAIS, for example, each contain two groups of tests: *verbal* tests, which include measures of vocabulary, general information, comprehension, and arithmetic abilities; and *performance* tests, which include block design, mazes, picture completion, and picture arrangement. Generally, when intelligence testing is done for diagnostic or screening purposes, separate verbal and performance scores are reported. Such distinctions are useful in determining an individual's cognitive strengths and weaknesses.

Intelligence test performance in adolescence. Psychometric assessments of intellectual performance can be used to examine two seemingly similar but actually very different questions. First, how *stable* are IQ scores during adolescence? Second, do the sorts of mental abilities assessed via intelligence tests *improve* during adolescence?

It is easy to confuse these questions. At first glance, they seem to be asking the same thing. But consider this: Individuals' IQ scores remain remarkably stable during the adolescent years, yet during the same time period, their mental abilities improve dramatically. Although this might seem contradictory, it is not. Studies of stability examine changes in individuals' *relative* standing over time, whereas studies of change examine changes in individuals' *absolute* scores.

Take height, for example. As we saw in the previous chapter, children who are taller than their peers during middle childhood are likely to be taller than their peers during adulthood as well; children who are about average in height remain so throughout childhood and adulthood; and children who are shorter than their peers at one point in time are likely to be shorter than their peers later on. Height, therefore, is a very stable trait. But this does not mean that individuals don't grow between childhood and adolescence.

Like height, scores on intelligence tests are characterized by high stability and a good deal of change during childhood and adolescence. To the first question posed above—How stable are individuals' IQ scores during the adolescent years?—the answer, then, is very stable. Consider the pattern of correlations between an individual's intelligence test scores at various points during childhood and his or her score at age 18 (see Figure 2.2).

As you can see, from about age 1 to about age 5, intelligence test scores are not highly cor-

related with scores at age 18. Between ages 5 and 11, scores are moderately correlated with scores at age 18. From early adolescence on, however, scores are very highly correlated with scores at age 18. The pattern of correlations, then, indicates that intelligence test scores become increasingly stable during childhood and are remarkably stable during adolescence. To put it more concretely, youngsters who score higher than their peers on intelligence tests during early adolescence are likely to score higher throughout the adolescent years.

A 10-year-old whose score is average for his age would have an IQ of about 100. If his score was stable—that is, if he remained about average in comparison with his peers—his score would remain at about 100. Even if he became more intelligent over time, as any normal child would, his IQ score probably would not change very much, because the score would always reflect his performance *relative* to his peers. If his abilities increased at the same rate as his agemates', his relative standing would not change. In other words, when an individual's IQ scores are fairly stable, a graph of those scores over a period of time produces a relatively straight horizontal line.

For most individuals, this is indeed what happens. But a study by Robert McCall and his colleagues suggests that not everyone follows this pattern of high stability (McCall, Applebaum, and Hogarty, 1973). After graphing many individuals' IQ scores during childhood and adolescence, these researchers were able to identify five different patterns—some very stable but others very unstable. Their findings are shown in Figure 2.3. As expected, most individuals fell into cluster number 1—that is, their scores were extremely stable over the 17-year period. But many youngsters' scores fluctuated considerably. In fact, the scores of individuals in cluster number 4 changed by as much as 30 points over the course of adolescence! In others words, although *most* adolescents' IQ scores remain stable throughout adolescence, not all do.

We now turn our attention to our second question: In absolute terms, do mental abilities

FIGURE 2.2   Average correlations between individuals' intelligence test scores at various ages from 1 to 17 and their scores at age 18. By age 11, the correlation is over .90. (Adapted from Bayley, 1949)

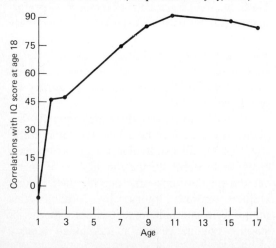

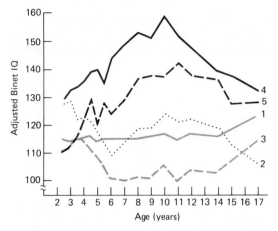

FIGURE 2.3   For some individuals, IQ scores fluctuate very little during childhood and adolescence. But for others, variations of 20 or 30 points occur. Here are five common patterns of change in IQ scores during childhood and adolescence. (Adapted from McCall et al., 1973)

interventions designed to stimulate intellectual development during adolescence.

The psychometric theory in perspective.   In comparison with the Piagetian viewpoint, the psychometric view of cognitive development has generated considerably less research on adolescence as a developmental period. Because psychometricians view cognitive development as gradual and quantitative, they have been less interested in focusing on particular periods in the life cycle as being special or different. Nevertheless, it is possible to look at the three types of intellectual advancement characteristic of adolescence—thinking about possibilities, thinking through hypotheses, and thinking about abstract concepts—from a psychometric point of view.

Given that both verbal and performance test scores increase between the ages of 12 and 17, one might argue that the adolescent's improved capabilities in hypothetical, deductive, and abstract thinking are merely reflections of gains in the sorts of abilities tapped by intelligence tests. For example, when faced with the problem of having to decide whether a pilot was careless for running into a suspension cable, adolescents may be better able to generate alternative explanations for the accident simply because they know more about planes, weather, flying, and so on. Along similar lines, improvements in the areas tapped by performance sub-

increase during adolescence? Figure 2.4 shows the growth of mental abilities as assessed by standardized tests. As you can see, abilities increase dramatically through childhood and adolescence, reaching a plateau sometime during early adulthood. Thus despite the fact that IQ scores remain stable during adolescence, individuals do become smarter as they get older—a fact that argues strongly in favor of educational

FIGURE 2.4   The growth of mental abilities from birth to age 36. (Adapted from Bayley, 1949)

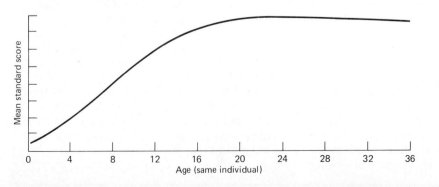

The Sexes: Are There Differences in Mental Abilities at Adolescence?

One very interesting finding to emerge from research on adolescents' intelligence test scores is that sex differences in certain mental abilities appear for the first time during adolescence. Although adolescent males and females do not show *overall* differences in IQ scores, adolescent girls outscore boys on measures of verbal ability, and boys outscore girls on measures of spatial ability and, to a lesser extent, on measures of mathematical skills. Before puberty, girls and boys score about the same on these measures (Maccoby and Jacklin, 1974).

As psychologist Anne Petersen (1979) points out, we do not know to what extent these differences are biologically based, socially based, or both. At present, three hypotheses have been offered for the emergence of sex differences in intellectual abilities at adolescence. As noted in the previous chapter, levels of androgens and estrogens change at puberty in different degrees for males and females. One possible explanation for the emergence of sex differences in mental abilities during early adolescence is that they are due to differential increases in sex hormones. There is some evidence, for example, that people with higher androgen levels—whether they are male or female—perform better on spatial ability tasks (Petersen, 1979).

A second possibility has to do with the different functions performed by the right and left hemispheres of the brain. Some theorists have hypothesized that males have a more strongly dominant right brain hemisphere than females, whereas the brains of females are more bilateral (that is, there is less dominance by one hemisphere over the other). Since it is thought that spatial and visual abilities are controlled by the right hemisphere of the brain, males would be expected to excel in activities controlled by these areas. But why would males have a stronger right hemisphere, and more important, why would their right hemispheric dominance not appear until adolescence?

One hypothesis is that the development of hemispheric dominance is curtailed by the onset of puberty (Waber, 1977). Since females mature about two years earlier than males, girls would have two fewer years to develop hemispheric dominance than boys. As a result, males would, on the average, outscore females in spatial abilities during but not before adolescence. This would also help to explain why late-maturing girls have better spatial abilities than early-maturing girls. At the present time, studies testing this possibility have not provided strong support for it, however. According to a recent comprehensive review, sex differences in cognitive abilities do not seem related to differences in the timing of puberty (Newcombe and Dubas, 1987).

Finally, it is possible that sex differences in mental abilities at adolescence are socially rather than biologically based. During elementary school, boys and girls take the same courses and therefore would be expected to develop similar intellectual strengths and weaknesses. But once young people are able to take elective courses, males and females may be led toward different educational paths by their guidance counselors, parents, and friends. Males, for example, are more likely to be encouraged to pursue coursework in math and science, and females are more likely to be steered away from classes in these areas (Fennema and Sherman, 1977). One study, for instance, demonstrated that individual differences in mathematical ability are more related to *attitudes* toward mathematics than to gender (Paulsen and Johnson, 1983). If sex-role expectations become more stereotyped after puberty, as some researchers have suggested (Hill and Lynch, 1983), this might explain why sex differences in mental abilities do not appear until adolescence.

Above all, though, it is clear that despite average differences between the sexes in verbal, spatial, and mathematical abilities, there is also a great deal of individual variation. As one scientist has pointed out, despite the consistency with which sex differences in certain intellectual abilities are reported, the *magnitude* of the differences is negligible (Hyde, 1981). Many males excel in verbal tasks and many females in spatial and mathematical ones, and the similarities between males and females overall are more striking than observed differences.

Some sex differences in mental abilities emerge for the first time in adolescence. Although boys, on average, outscore girls on tests of mathematical achievement, the magnitude of the difference is not very large. Many social scientists now believe that socialization, not biology, best explains why boys are more likely to excel in high-school math. (Jean-Claude Lejeune)

measure the same sorts of abilities (Keating, 1980). But the psychometric approach to cognitive development in adolescence does not assume a stagelike growth of intelligence; differences in thinking between adolescents and children are seen as differences in quantity, not quality.

At this point, you may well be wondering, "So what? Why does it matter whether cognitive development is quantitative or qualitative, as long as we can agree that *some* gains in thinking take place during adolescence?" Suppose you were asked by the supervisor of a school district to design a new science curriculum to be used in the fifth and eighth grades. It would be important to know whether scientific reasoning develops gradually or in stages in order to decide how best to approach the job. If, for example, you knew that scientific abilities develop in stages, you would want to take into account the fact that fifth-graders are likely to think in concrete-operational terms whereas the eighth-graders are likely to think in formal-operational terms. You might therefore suggest that very different approaches be taken with the two age groups. But if you knew that scientific reasoning develops gradually, you would be less concerned about abrupt changes in abilities between the fifth and eighth grades, and you might suggest trying similar approaches with the younger and older students.

scales of IQ tests, such as memory and spatial ability, might be reflected in advances in reasoning about abstract concepts and thinking through hypotheses. Simply being able to remember more information could in itself make someone a better problem solver.

Psychometric approaches to cognitive development provide as adequate an account of observed changes in thinking during adolescence as do Piagetian ones. Indeed, performance on measures of formal operations and on standardized intelligence tests are correlated with one another. In fact, some theorists believe that formal operations tests and standard IQ tests

The Information-Processing View of Cognitive Development

Although both the psychometric and the Piagetian approaches to adolescent cognitive development suggest that important changes in thinking processes take place between childhood and adulthood, neither perspective tells us very much about *what* it is that changes. If we are left only with the conclusion that cognitive growth between childhood and adolescence is due to changes in "logical reasoning abilities" or "general mental abilities," we have not moved a great deal closer to understanding which *spe-*

cific aspects of intellectual development during adolescence are the most important ones. Just what is it about the ways that adolescents think about things that makes them better problem solvers than children? This question has been the focus of researchers working from a relatively new theoretical vantage point: the information-processing perspective.

Ushered in, in part, as a result of advances in the study of information processing by computers—the study of "artificial intelligence"—the information-processing view of cognitive development has received increased attention during the last fifteen years. Researchers working in this tradition break down the thinking process into very small parts. They then attempt to specify which components are most essential to the particular type of reasoning under investigation and which components appear best able to explain differences in the thinking processes of people of different ages.

Information-processing researchers apply the same techniques to understanding human reasoning that computer scientists employ in writing programs. Many of you have had experience in working with computers. Suppose that you were asked to develop a computer program to solve the poker chip problem presented earlier in this chapter. A first step in the program might involve determining how many different colored chips are contained in the set. But as you know if you have ever written a computer program, this first step is actually quite complicated when broken down into discrete tasks. It involves (1) taking the first chip and perceiving what color it is, (2) storing this information in memory, (3) considering the second chip and deciding what color it is, (4) storing this information in memory, (5) retrieving the color of the first chip from memory, (6) retrieving the color of the second chip from memory, (7) comparing these two bits of information, (8) determining whether the colors are the same or different, and (9) storing the results of the comparison in memory. And these nine steps take us only as far as comparing the first two chips. Imagine how involved a program would

have to be in order to perform more complicated tasks!

It is possible to look at human information processing in much the same way. When broken down into its component processes, human thinking involves such "subprograms" as encoding information, retrieving information, comparing different pieces of information, and making decisions based on such comparisons. Obviously, deficiencies in any of these component functions will interfere with accurate problem solving. In the poker chip problem, for example, not perceiving the colors correctly will cause mistakes to be made. The ways in which component processes are combined also will affect the results. For example, if we try to compare the two chips' colors before storing the color of the first chip in memory, we will not be able to solve the problem.

Some arrangements of component processes are not only more accurate than others, they are more efficient. Suppose you have successfully determined that the first two poker chips you have examined are indeed different in color. What is your next step? Do you compare the third chip with both the first and second chips before moving on to the fourth chip, or do you compare the third with the first and then compare the fourth with the first? If you work this problem out, you will find that one approach is more efficient than the other.

Changes in information-processing abilities during adolescence. We do not know a great deal about the cognitive processes that may underlie differences between adolescents' and children's thinking. Yet we can speculate on a few types of information-processing changes characteristic of adolescence that might account for advances in thinking about possibilities, thinking through hypotheses, and thinking about abstract concepts.

A few studies point to four sets of gains that occur during adolescence: (1) advances in *memory* (Keating and Bobbitt, 1978); (2) advances in the ways in which various *cognitive processes are organized* (Sternberg and Nigro,

1980; Sternberg and Rifkin, 1979); (3) advances in *attentional abilities,* such as being able to divide one's attention between two sources of information (Schiff and Knopf, 1985); and (4) advances in individuals' use of *information-processing plans* (Pitt, 1976, cited in Keating, 1980).

As one example of research on information processing during adolescence, let's look at the work of psychologist Robert Sternberg, who has studied children's and adolescents' solutions to problems involving analogies (Sternberg, 1977; Sternberg and Nigro, 1980; Sternberg and Rifkin, 1979). Through a series of experiments in which different types of analogies were presented to third-graders, sixth-graders, ninth-graders, and college students, Sternberg and his colleagues examined age differences in the use and organization of cognitive processes. Overall, different strategies were employed by the third-

and sixth-graders, on the one hand, and by the ninth-graders and college students, on the other. The major difference between younger and older subjects concerned the incomplete nature of the younger ones' information processing. Although older and younger subjects appeared to use similar processes, the older ones employed them in a far more exhaustive fashion. For example, in determining the relation between pairs of terms, the third and sixth graders tended to curtail their information processing prematurely, before all possible relations had been considered.

Sternberg attributes this premature termination to information overload in memory. Because adolescents are able to hold more information in immediate memory than children can, they are more successful in the sorts of tasks (such as analogies) that require repeated comparisons between newly encoded information and information that has been stored previously.

The information-processing perspective on cognitive development draws an analogy between human reasoning abilities and information processing performed by computers. Recent studies have found that the development of more advanced thinking abilities during adolescence may be due to growth in memory capacity. (Donald Dietz/Stock, Boston)

Running out of "storage space" before all of the necessary information has been encoded will result in information-processing errors.

Memory capacity is just one of many components of information processing that helps to account for differences between adolescents' and children's thinking. The idea that adolescents are more planful—that is, that they are more likely to approach a problem with an appropriate information-processing plan in mind—would also help to explain why they have more advanced hypothetical and deductive reasoning abilities. Psychologist Ann Brown (1975), for example, has suggested that the use of mnemonic and other organizational strategies helps to account for differences in the performance of older and younger children on tasks requiring memory, and moreover, that older children are better able to judge *when* the use of such strategies is likely to be helpful and when it is not. She argues that a key difference between older and younger children is not so much in their information-processing capabilities as such but in their ability to *control* their information-processing strategies, using them selectively and appropriately. In the poker chip problem, for example, perhaps children are just as capable as adolescents of combining the chips systematically, but adolescents see more easily than children do that a systematic approach is better. Maybe the main difference in thinking between children and adolescents is that as we get older, we come to know which problem-solving strategies work best in different situations.

Thinking about abstract concepts and second-order thinking would also be simpler for an individual with a more efficient information-processing system. It may be the case, for example, that reasoning about abstract concepts requires that multiple levels of information processing be pursued simultaneously. Trying to figure out what someone thinks you think he thinks may demand very sophisticated information-processing skills. Such higher-order thinking might easily tax the memory capacity of a younger child but will not push the storage space of an adolescent to its limits.

The information-processing theory in perspective.   At this time, it is difficult to evaluate the contribution of information-processing approaches to the study of cognitive development during adolescence, because too few studies employing this approach have been carried out to permit one to draw any definitive conclusions. However, some studies have shown that formal-operational thinking is correlated with the use of more organized information-processing strategies (Wyatt and Geis, 1978). Other researchers have suggested that interventions designed to enhanced information-processing skills—by teaching new strategies for paying attention or remembering, for example—can help adolescents' school learning (Gagne, 1985).

Casting the cognitive differences between children and adolescents in terms of differences in their information-processing abilities appears to bring us closer to understanding *why* as well as *how* adolescents think in more advanced ways. Moreover, such an approach may shed light on the elusive question of *what* it is that develops when individuals become more intelligent problem solvers.

CHANGES IN SOCIAL COGNITION

Many of the examples of adolescent thinking we have looked at in this chapter have involved reasoning about scientific problems or physical objects. But the same sorts of gains in intellectual abilities observed in young people's thinking in these realms are apparent in their reasoning about social phenomena as well. **Social cognition** is the term used to refer to this sort of cognitive activity—thinking about people, thinking about social relationships, and thinking about social institutions.

Consider the following discussion between two young adolescent males overheard by psychologist Marvin Berkowitz (Berkowitz, 1985) on a public bus. Here we see how the advanced logical skills of adolescence are used by one teenager to "outrank" another:

A: You are a hornybird!

B: No. *You* are a hornybird!

A: You are the biggest hornybird I've ever seen.

B: You are the hornybird of hornybirds.

A: No, I'm not, you hornybird. You're such a hornybird I can't believe it.

B: You must be a hornybird because you don't have a girlfriend.

A: Your mother is my girlfriend.

B: Oh, big man! You'd be afraid to go near my mother.

A: Oh no I wouldn't.

B: Why don't you ask her out then? Because you're a hornybird, that's why!

A: I will so ask her out. Besides, you're the hornybird, not me. Hornybirds are always confused.

B: Right and you're confused if you think I am the hornybird, so that proves you are a hornybird, you hornybird.

A: Hornybirds always deny that they are hornybirds. That's a sure test of being a hornybird, and you said you're not a hornybird, so that makes you a hornybird.

B: Are you a hornybird?

A: I used to be a hornybird. I admit it, but I'm not anymore, you hornybird.

B: Ah, so you deny you are a hornybird. That makes you a hornybird.

A: I didn't deny it. I admitted I *used to be.* Only non-hornybirds can admit they used to be hornybirds.

B: Are you a hornybird now?

A: I used to be.

B: Are you a hornybird right now?

A: No.

B: Aha! That proves it! You are a hornybird. You said hornybirds always deny they are hornybirds and you just denied it, you hornybird.

A: But non-hornybirds can also deny it, and I am not a hornybird. But hornybirds are always accusing non-hornybirds of being hornybirds. Are you calling me a hornybird?

B: Yeah, but you . . .

A: No "buts." You are accusing me of being a hornybird, so that not only makes you a hornybird, hornybird, hornybird, but it proves that I am not a hornybird. Besides, I've seen that Elaine that you went out with. What a pig! (Berkowitz, 1985)

It is not difficult to imagine that adolescents' advanced abilities in thinking about possibilities, thinking through hypotheses, and thinking about abstract concepts make them more sophisticated when it comes to reasoning about social matters. Compared with those of children, adolescents' conceptions of interpersonal relationships are more mature, their understanding of human behavior is more advanced, their ideas about social institutions and organizations are more complex, and their ability to figure out what other people think is far more accurate. As we shall see in subsequent chapters, gains in the area of social cognition help to account for many of the psychosocial advances typically associated with adolescence—advances in the realms of identity, autonomy, intimacy, sexuality, and achievement.

Research on Social Cognition During Adolescence

Studies of social cognition during adolescence typically fall into three categories: studies of **impression formation,** which examine how individuals form and organize judgments about other people; studies of **role taking,** which examine how, and how accurately, individuals

Are Teenagers Taken in by Television Commercials?

According to national surveys, young adolescents watch television more than just about any other age group. Television viewing increases steadily from age 2 until age 5, then dips slightly (when children begin elementary school). From age 6 until age 12, however, television begins to occupy more and more of the child's day, reaching a peak of about 4 hours daily for 12-year-olds. During adolescence, television viewing declines; 20-year-olds watch about 3 hours of television each day (Comstock et al., 1978). To put the figure for 12-year-olds in more concrete terms, consider this fact: By age 12, American children spend more of their waking hours watching television than doing anything else, including going to school.

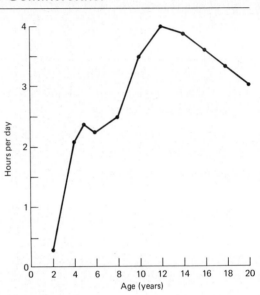

For many years, researchers have investigated the impact of television viewing on antisocial behavior, such as aggression, and on prosocial behavior, such as cooperation. Generally speaking, studies convincingly demonstrate that children can be taught almost *anything* from television. In other words, if television programs contain high amounts of violence, young viewers will be more inclined to behave aggressively. But if programs contain high amounts of cooperation and sharing, young viewers will be more likely to behave prosocially. Contrary to the idea that television is a uniformly bad influence on children, most studies show that its impact on positive behaviors can be just as powerful as its impact on negative behaviors (Comstock et al., 1978). There is no simple answer to the question of how TV affects children and adolescents. Its effects depend on what sorts of television programs youngsters watch.

Because of the powerful role played by television in the socialization of young peo-

---

make assessments about the thoughts and feelings of others; and studies of morality and **social conventions,** which examine individuals' conceptions of justice, social norms, and guidelines for social interaction. Although we discuss research on these subjects in detail in later chapters, it is important here to highlight and summarize the main findings in each of these areas of study and to look at the development of social cognition during adolescence in view of the intellectual gains characteristic of the period.

Impression formation. During preadolescence and adolescence, individuals' impressions of other people develop in five main directions, according to a summary of this body of research (Hill and Palmquist, 1978). First, impressions become progressively *more differentiated.* Adolescents are more likely than children to describe people—themselves as well as others—in more narrowly defined categories and with more differentiated attributes. Whereas children tend to use fairly global descriptors, such as gender and

ple, researchers in recent years have begun to study how children and adolescents are affected by television commercials. Do television commercials encourage children to eat sugar-coated cereals, buy needless toys and games, and develop insatiable cravings for junk food? Are youngsters taken in by the messages they see, or are they less gullible than advertisers think? Interestingly, there appear to be important changes in youngsters' susceptibility to television commercials around adolescence—changes that coincide with the expansion of cognitive abilities.

Several studies indicate, for example, that adolescents are far more likely than children to distrust television ads. In fact, by the time youngsters reach the sixth grade, they have a "global distrust" of television commercials in general. Teenagers realize the motives behind advertisements and are likely to characterize them as "stupid," "hypocritical," and "in bad taste." Only one-third of adolescents believe that "TV commercials tell the truth" (Comstock et al., 1978). Although teenagers, like adults, occasionally make purchasing decisions on the basis of television commercials, they do not appear to be taken in the way that children are.

The increasing distrust of television advertising during adolescence can be explained in terms of the changes in cognitive abilities discussed in this chapter. Because adolescents are able to see things from several perspectives, they are able to recognize that commercials are designed to sell products rather than provide objective information. The same commercial that a child may see as presenting the "truth" about a certain topic may be viewed by a more skeptical adolescent as presenting the truth from the advertiser's point of view. Teenagers recognize that there may be other sides to a product that an advertiser will not televise.

Although teenagers may be hard to convince through television commercials, it does not appear to curtail advertisers' efforts to reach them. The teen market accounts for a tremendous amount of advertising expenditures. And no wonder: Teenagers spend well over $50 billion each year—mostly on clothing and entertainment but including over $15 billion on food (Moschis, 1982). You can be sure that, for better or for worse, as a better understanding is reached of how cognitive processes change during adolescence, television advertisers will be using that knowledge to devise better and more irresistible commercials.

For further information:
A good source of information on teenagers and television is Action for Children's Television, a nonprofit organization concerned with television and young people. The organization is based in Newton, Massachusetts.

age, adolescents are more likely to describe people in terms of such things as interests and personality characteristics. A second trend in the development of impression formation is toward *less egocentric* impressions. Adolescents are more likely to be aware that their impressions of others are personal viewpoints and therefore subject to disagreement. They realize that impressions of others are subjective, not objective, and potentially tainted by one's own viewpoint.

Third, impressions of other people become *more abstract*—that is, they become less rooted in such concrete attributes as physical characteristics or personal possessions and more tied to such abstract things as attitudes and motives. Fourth, individuals come to make *greater use of inference* in their impressions of others. Compared with children, adolescents are more likely to interpret the feelings of others and infer the motives, beliefs, and feelings of others, even when specific information of this sort is not directly observable. Finally, adolescents' impressions of others are *more highly organized*. Adolescents are more likely than children, for example, to make judgments of others that link personality traits to the situations in which they are likely to be expressed ("She's impatient when she works with other people") and to reconcile apparently discrepant information about people into a more complex impression ("He's friendly toward girls but not at all toward boys").

Taken together, these developments in the realm of impression formation point toward the development and refinement during adolescence of an *implicit psychological theory* (Barenboim, 1981)—a theory of personality, motivation, and behavior. As we shall see in Chapter 10, the development of more advanced impression-formation skills has important implications for the development of intimate relationships.

Role-taking abilities.   Related to these gains in impression-formation abilities are considerable improvements in the adolescent's ability to view events from the perspective of others. According to Robert Selman (1976), who has studied the development of role-taking extensively, children become better able as they grow older to step back from their own point of view and see that others may view an event from a different, but equally valid, perspective. Not only are adolescents more capable of discerning another person's perspective on some issue or event, they are also better able to understand that person's perspective on their own perspective.

According to Selman, role-taking ability progresses through five stages. During early childhood (before the age of 6 or so), children easily confuse their own feelings with those of others. For instance, a 3-year-old who is feeling angry may believe that his father is angry, too, even if his father has not done anything to indicate anger. Selman calls this the *egocentric* stage. During the early elementary-school years, children come to realize that other people have their own thoughts and feelings, but they have

difficulty putting themselves in others' shoes. A second grader may know that gifts make people happy, but she may have difficulty understanding that a gift that would make *her* happy might not be equally satisfying to her brother. This is called the *subjective* stage. During the third stage in the development of role taking, the *reciprocal* stage (characteristic of the later elementary-school years), preadolescents can put themselves in others' shoes but do not yet see how the thoughts and feelings of one person may be related to the thoughts and feelings of another. One deficiency, for instance, is in what psychologists call **recursive thinking,** the type of thinking that involves, "I thought that you thought that I thought," and so on (Hill and Palmquist, 1978).

The transition into adolescence coincides with the progression into what Selman calls *mutual* role taking. During this stage, the young adolescent can be an objective third party and see how the thoughts or actions of one person can influence those of another. In thinking about two of her friends, for instance, an adolescent at this level would be able to look at their relationship and see how each person's behavior affects the other's. Finally, sometime during early adolescence, we see the development of role-taking that is *in-depth and societal* in orientation. The adolescent at this level understands that the perspectives people have on each other are complicated, often unconscious, and influenced by larger forces than individuals can control, including each person's position in society or within a social institution. For example, you are able to understand that your perspective on the instructor teaching your class is influenced not only by your own personality and the instructor's, but by forces inherent in the structural relationship of professor and student. Imagine, for example, trying to figure out why a professor might resist being overly friendly to students outside of class. Someone able to understand role taking at the societal level could see that the professor might be behaving this way not because she is an unfriendly person, but

Gains in role-taking abilities allow the adolescent to evaluate a speaker's words in terms of the speaker's perspective and vested interests. (Susan Lapides/Design Conceptions)

because a "role conflict" would surface between being an objective evaluator of students' work and being too chummy with students.

Older adolescents at the societal stage of role taking are able to realize that groups of individuals may share points of view that are related to other beliefs and attitudes—points of view that go along with membership in a group. By late adolescence, for example, individuals are able to complete questionnaires about social issues as they think other people in various social roles might (for example, "the average policeman," "the average philosopher"; [Yussen, 1976]). Ultimately, these gains in role-taking

abilities lead to improvements in communication, as the adolescent becomes more capable of formulating his or her arguments in terms that are more likely to be understood by someone whose opinion may be different.

One study (Clark and Delia, 1976), for example, looked at how good youngsters of different ages were at persuading other people to do something for them—convincing their parents to buy them a new stereo, for instance. The researchers found that adolescents were more likely to use reasoning that pointed out advantages to their parents ("If I have my own stereo in my room, you won't be bothered by my music.'') than reasoning that simply stated the case from their own point of view ("I really need to have my own stereo. All the other kids do."). A major shift in reasoning took place during early adolescence, coinciding with the transition into the stage of "mutual" role taking. Although one might think that parents might find dealing with a more persuasive teenager more difficult, studies suggest that when adolescents are able to take their parents' perspective in an argument, family communication becomes more effective and satisfying (Silverberg, 1986).

In addition, adolescents are much better able to see that people giving advice may have a vested interest in one perspective over another or that disagreements between individuals can be understood as emanating from differences in their initial assumptions or underlying interests. In Chapter 9, for example, we examine the way in which changes in role-taking abilities affect how adolescents decide whom to turn to for advice.

Conceptions of morality and social convention.

The realization that individuals' perspectives vary and that their opinions may differ as a result leads to changes in the ways that issues regarding morality and social convention are approached. Changes in moral reasoning during adolescence have been investigated extensively, and we examine this body of research in detail in Chapter 9. Briefly, during childhood, moral guidelines are seen as absolutes emanating from such authorities as parents or teachers; judgments of right and wrong are made according to concrete *rules*. During adolescence, however, such absolutes and rules come to be questioned, as the young person begins to see that moral standards are subjective and based on points of view that are subject to disagreement. Later in adolescence comes the emergence of reasoning that is based on such *moral principles* as equality, justice, or fairness—abstract guidelines that transcend concrete situations and can be applied across a variety of moral dilemmas (Kohlberg and Gilligan, 1972).

The development of individuals' understanding of social conventions—the social norms that guide day-to-day behavior—follows a similar course (Turiel, 1978). During middle childhood, social conventions—such as waiting in line to buy movie tickets—are seen as arbitrary and changeable, but adherence to them is not; compliance with such conventions is based on rules and on the dictates of authority. When you were 7 years old, you might not have seen why people had to wait in line to buy movie tickets, but when your mother told you to wait in line, you waited. By early adolescence, however, conventions are seen as arbitrary and changeable in both their origins and their enforcement; conventions are merely social expectations. As an adolescent, you began to realize that people wait in line because they are expected to, not because they are forced to. Indeed, young adolescents often see social conventions as *nothing but* social expectations and, consequently, as insufficient reason for compliance. You can probably imagine youngsters in their midteens saying something like this: "Why wait in a ticket line simply because other people are lined up? There isn't a *law* that forces you to wait in line, is there?"

Gradually, however, adolescents begin to see social conventions as means used by society to regulate people's behavior; conventions may be arbitrary, but we follow them because we all share an understanding of how people are expected to behave in various situations. In fact, high schoolers see conventions as so ingrained in the social system that individuals follow them partly out of habit. We wait in line for theater tickets not to comply with any "rule" but because it is something we are accustomed to doing.

Ultimately, individuals come to see that social conventions serve a function in coordinating interactions among people. Social norms and expectations are derived from and maintained by individuals' having a common perspective and agreeing that, in given situations, certain behaviors are more desirable than others, because such behaviors help society and its institutions to function more smoothly. Without the conven-

TABLE 2.2   DIFFERENCES BETWEEN PREADOLESCENT AND ADOLESCENT THINKING IN FIVE COGNITIVE AND SOCIAL COGNITIVE DOMAINS

DOMAIN	PREADOLESCENT THOUGHT	ADOLESCENT THOUGHT
Scientific (e.g., Piaget)	Limited to the concrete, the here and now; any hypothetical thinking likely to be unsystematic	Abstract, hypothetical, systematic consideration of alternatives and possibilities
Impressions of Others (e.g., Barenboim)	Global, egocentric, concrete, disorganized, and haphazard	Differentiated, objective, abstract, and organized into coherent whole
Role Taking (e.g., Selman)	Able to put self in other's shoes but difficulty seeing how one person's perspective affects another's	Able to take "third party" perspective (mutual) and to see the bigger, societal picture
Moral Reasoning (e.g., Kohlberg)	Morals are based on concrete rules handed down by authorities	Morals come out of agreements between people or out of abstract principles
Social Conventions (e.g., Turiel)	Conventions are based on the rules and dictates of authorities	Conventions are based on expectations or grow out of social norms

tion of waiting in line to buy movie tickets, the pushiest people would always get tickets first. The older adolescent can see that waiting in line doesn't only benefit the theater, it preserves everyone's right to a fair chance to buy tickets. In other words, we wait in line patiently because we all agree that it is better if tickets are distributed fairly.

Table 2.2 summarizes some of the important differences in cognitive and social cognitive abilities between preadolescents and adolescents.

Summary

Changes in cognition during adolescence are noteworthy and comprise one more set of fundamental changes that give the adolescent period many of its characteristic features. Thinking expands in three main directions during the adolescent years: in the ability to think about possibilities; in the ability to think through hypotheses; and in the ability to think about abstract concepts. The expansion of thought results in increased intellectual capability and helps to account for many of the psychosocial developments usually associated with this period of the life cycle. Changes in relationships, in the self-concept, and in values and plans during adolescence can all be traced in part to changes in the way young people think about things.

It is not clear exactly what adolescents are capable of doing intellectually that gives them an advantage over children. Piagetian theorists believe that a new type of logic emerges during adolescence. Psychometricians, however, feel that improvements in thinking at adolescence are due not to the emergence of any new capabilities but to the enhancement of existing capabilities. Still other theorists attribute the adolescent's improved thinking to gains in memory and other specific information-processing skills.

In the area of social cognition, thinking becomes more tied to abstract, rather than concrete, phenomena and to what is possible and hypothetical rather than to what is real. These shifts are necessary if the adolescent is to generate an implicit theory of personality that enables him or her to judge the behavior of others, to understand and coordinate the perspectives and points of view of others, and to see social conventions and moral guidelines as emanating from individuals' shared understanding rather than as the mindless dictates of authority.

Key Terms

cognitive conflict
cognitive-developmental (Piagetian)
concrete operations
formal operations
genetic epistemology
imaginary audience
impression formation
information processing
personal fable
preoperational period

propositional logic
pseudostupidity
psychometric
recursive thinking
role taking
second-order thinking
sensorimotor
social cognition
social conventions

For Further Reading

ELKIND, D. (1978). Understanding the young adolescent. *Adolescence 13*, 127–134. In this article, David Elkind explains how adolescents' social behavior can be understood in terms of their cognitive development.

FLAVELL, J. (1977). *Cognitive development*. Englewood Cliffs, N.J.: Prentice-Hall. A comprehensive discussion of cognitive development during childhood and adolescence.

HILL, J., AND PALMQUIST, W. (1978). Social cognition and social relations in early adolescence. *International Journal of Behavioural Development, 1*, 1–36. A review of research on the development of social-cognitive abilities during adolescence.

PIAGET, J. (1972). Intellectual evolution from adolescence to adulthood. *Human Development, 15*, 1–12. One of Piaget's own discussions of his theory of cognitive development during adolescence.

Transitions into Adulthood

CHAPTER 3

PREVIEW

1. In all societies, adolescence is a time for changes in individuals' social roles and status. Over the course of adolescence, young people cease to be seen as children and are given the rights, privileges, and responsibilities of adults.

2. The social redefinition of individuals at adolescence has important implications for their behavior and psychosocial development. As adolescents come to be seen as adults, they begin to act and see themselves differently and are treated differently by others.

3. Changes in the individual's legal, political, interpersonal, and economic status typically occur during adolescence. However, the transition of the adolescent into adulthood is structured differently in contemporary society than in traditional cultures or past eras. Generally speaking, the passage into adulthood is more difficult today than it was in the past.

4. Social scientists have suggested that many of the problems faced by young people in contemporary America are due to the nature of their transition into adult roles and responsibilities. Problems associated with poverty have made the transition into adulthood especially difficult for many minority youth.

Among the Thonga (an agrarian society in the southeastern region of Africa), at the time of her first menstruation, the adolescent girl goes to an older woman of her choosing and announces that she has come of age (Ford and Beach, 1951). At this point, a seclusion period of one month commences, and

> three or four girls, undergoing the initiation ceremony together, are shut up in a hut, and when they come out, must always wear over their face a veil consisting of a very dirty and greasy cloth. Every morning they are led to the pool, and their whole body is immersed in the water as far as the neck. Other initiated girls or women accompany them, singing obscene songs, and drive away with sticks any man who happens to be on the road, as no man is allowed to see a girl during this period. . . . When the cortege of women accompanying the initiated has returned home, the nubile girls are imprisoned in the hut. They are teased, pinched, scratched by the adoptive mothers or by other women; they must also listen to the licentious songs which are sung to them. . . . They are also instructed in sexual matters, and told that they must never reveal anything about the blood of the menses to a man. . . . At the end of the month the adoptive mother brings the girl home to her true mother. She also presents her with a pot of beer. A feast takes place on this occasion. (Junod, 1927, cited in Ford and Beach, 1951, p. 175)

Along with the biological changes of puberty and changes in thinking abilities, changes in social roles and status constitute yet another universal feature of development during adolescence. All societies differentiate among individuals on the basis of how old they are (although not all use chronological age as the defining criterion).

In all societies, adolescence is a period of social redefinition. Over the course of the adolescent years, the individual ceases to be viewed by society as a child and comes to be recognized as an adult. Although the specific elements of this social passage from childhood into adulthood vary considerably from one society to another, the presence during adolescence of some sort of recognition that the individual's status has changed—a **social redefinition** of the individual—is universal.

This social redefinition at adolescence is certainly less vivid and less ceremonial in contemporary America than it is among the Thonga. We do not seclude young people from the rest of society at the onset of puberty, nor, with the exception of certain religious ceremonies, do we generally mark the passage into adulthood with elaborate rituals. But just because the social transition into adulthood is less explicit in contemporary society than it is in many traditional cultures does not mean that the passage is any less significant. Indeed, some theorists have argued that the nature of adolescence is far more influenced by the way in which society defines the economic and social roles of young people than by the biological changes of puberty. Strong proponents of this view have even suggested that the concept of adolescence is entirely a social invention (Lapsley et al., 1985).

The study of social redefinition at adolescence provides an interesting vehicle through which we can compare adolescence across different cultures and historical epochs. While certain features of the social passage from childhood into adulthood are universal, considerable differences exist between the processes of social redefinition in contemporary society and in more traditional cultures. In examining some of these differences, you will come to understand better how the way in which society structures the transition of adolescents into adult roles influences the nature of psychosocial development during the period.

Because young people go through puberty earlier today than 100 years ago, and because they tend to stay in school longer, the adolescent period has been lengthened and the transition into adulthood prolonged. Today, young people are caught between the world of childhood and the world of adulthood for an extremely long time, with only a vague sense of when—and how—they become adults. Indeed, in the minds of many social scientists who study adolescence in modern society, the social passage of young people into adult roles is too long, too vague, and too rocky (National Commission on Youth, 1980; President's Science Advisory Committee, 1974).

SOCIAL REDEFINITION AND PSYCHOSOCIAL DEVELOPMENT

Like the biological and cognitive changes of adolescence, changes in social definition have important consequences for the young person's psychosocial development in the realms of identity, autonomy, intimacy, sexuality, and achievement. Indeed, from a sociological or cultural perspective, it is social redefinition at adolescence—rather than, for example, puberty as such—that has the most profound impact on the individual's development and behavior. In the realm of *identity*, for example, attainment of adult status may transform the young person's self-concept, causing him or her to feel more adultlike and to think more seriously about future work and family roles. Doing for the first time such things as reporting to work, going into a bar, or registering to vote all make us feel older and more mature. In turn, these new activities and opportunities may prompt self-evaluation and introspection. Looking for a job, for instance, may encourage an adolescent to think seriously for the first time about work interests and career goals.

Becoming an adult member of society, accompanied as it is by shifts in responsibility, independence, and freedom, also has an impact on the development of *autonomy*. In contrast to the child, the adolescent-turned-adult is permitted to make a wider range of decisions that may have serious long-term consequences. A young woman who has reached the drinking age, for example, must decide how she should handle this new privilege. Should she go along with the crowd and drink every weekend night, or should she follow her parents' example and abstain from drinking? And in return for the privileges that come with adult status, adolescents are expected to behave in a more responsible fashion.

Receiving a driver's license carries with it the obligation of driving safely. Thus the attainment of adult status provides chances for the young person to exercise autonomy as well as chances to develop a greater sense of independence.

Changes in social definition often bring with them changes in the sorts of relationships and interpersonal behaviors that are permitted and expected. Social redefinition at adolescence is therefore likely to raise new questions and concerns for the young person about *intimacy*—including, in particular, such matters as dating and marriage. Many parents prohibit their children from dating until they have reached an "appropriate" age. And not until the **age of majority** are individuals allowed to marry without first gaining their parents' permission. In certain societies, young people may even be *required* to marry on becoming adults. A marriage may have been arranged while they were children, and they will be expected to marry as soon as they have been initiated into adulthood.

Status changes at adolescence may also affect development in the domain of *sexuality*. In contemporary society, for example, laws governing sexual behavior (such as the definition of statutory rape) typically differentiate between individuals who have and have not attained adult status. By becoming an adult in a legal sense, the young person may be confronted with the need for new and different decisions about sexual activity. One problem currently facing society is whether sexually active individuals who have not yet attained adult *legal* status should be able to make independent decisions about such "adult" matters as abortion and contraception.

Finally, reaching adulthood often has important implications in the realm of *achievement*. For instance, in contemporary society, it is not until adult status is attained that one can enter the labor force as a full-time employee. Not until young people have reached a designated age are they permitted to leave school of their own volition. In less industrialized societies, becoming an adult typically entails entrance into the productive activities of the community. Taken to-

One privilege that accompanies the young person's transition into adult status in contemporary society is the right to vote. (Bob Daemmrich/The Image Works)

gether, these shifts are likely to prompt changes in the young person's skills, aspirations, and expectations.

CHANGES IN STATUS

"The most casual survey of the ways in which different societies have handled adolescence makes one fact inescapable," wrote anthropologist Ruth Benedict in her classic work, *Patterns of Culture*. "[E]ven in those cultures which have made the most of the trait, the age upon which they focus their attention varies over a great range of years. . . . The puberty they recognize is social, and the ceremonies are a recognition in some fashion or other of the child's new status of adulthood. . . . In order to understand [adolescence] . . . we need . . . to know what is identified in different cultures with the begin-

ning of adulthood and their methods of admitting to the new status" (Benedict, 1934, p. 25). Changes in social definition at adolescence typically involve a two-sided alteration in status. On the one hand, the adolescent is given certain privileges and rights that are typically reserved for the society's adult members. On the other hand, this increased power and freedom generally are accompanied by increased expectations for self-management, personal responsibility, and social participation.

We can find examples of this double shift in social status in all societies, across a variety of interpersonal, political, economic, and legal arenas.

Changes in Interpersonal Status

In many societies, individuals who have been recognized as adults are usually addressed with adult titles. They also are expected to maintain different sorts of social relationships with their parents, with the community's elders, and with young people whose status has not yet changed. On holidays such as Thanksgiving, for example, some large families set two tables: a big table for the adults and a smaller, "children's" table. When a young person is permitted to sit at the big table, it is a sign that he or she has reached a new position in the family. These interpersonal changes are typically accompanied by new interpersonal obligations—for example, being expected to take care of and set a proper example for the younger members of the family.

Changes in Political Status

With the attainment of adult status, the young person is often permitted more extensive participation in the community's decision making. Among the Navaho (Southwestern United States), for example, it is only following a formal initiation ceremony that adolescents are considered members of the Navaho People and permitted full participation in ceremonial life (Cohen, 1964). In contemporary America, attaining the age of majority brings the right to vote. But in return for this increased power usually come new obligations. Young adults are expected to serve their communities in cases of emergency or need. And training for warfare is often demanded of young men once they attain adult status (Benedict, 1934).

Changes in Economic Status

Attaining adult status also has important economic implications that again entail obligation as well as privilege. In some societies, only adults may own property and maintain control over their income (Miller, 1928). In many American states, for example, any income that a youngster earns before the age of 16 is technically the property of the young person's parents. In societies in which animals are raised for food and for trade, adolescents may have the right to use the family's animals in farm labor but may not be permitted to make decisions about buying and selling animals until they have been recognized as adults.

Entrance into certain work roles is also restricted to adults. In most industrialized societies, employment is regulated by child labor laws, and the attainment of a prescribed age is a prerequisite to employment in certain occupations. Among the Tikopia (Melanesia), one of the first privileges accorded boys when they reach adolescence is accompanying older males on fishing expeditions, as members of the crew (Fried and Fried, 1980). In most communities, however, once they have attained the economic status and rights of adults, young people are expected to contribute to the economic well-being of their community. They are depended on to participate in the community's productive activities and to carry out the labor expected of adults. In contemporary society, the young adult's economic responsibilities to the broader community may entail having to pay taxes for the first time.

Changes in Legal Status

In most societies, not until adult status is attained is the young person permitted to participate in a variety of activities that are typically reserved for adults. Gambling, purchasing alcoholic beverages, and driving are but three of the many privileges we reserve in America for individuals who have reached the legal age of adulthood. In many cultures, the eating of certain foods is restricted to individuals who have been admitted to adult society (Mead, 1928). Among the Jibaros (Ecuador), smoking tobacco is permitted only to those who have been initiated (Miller, 1928).

Once an adolescent is designated as an adult, however, he or she is also subject to a new set of laws and must expect to be treated differently by the legal institutions of the society from how he or she was treated as a child. In the United States, for example, crimes by young

The criminal activities of young adolescents are typically adjudicated in a separate juvenile justice system. Although many have called for harsher treatment of young offenders, it is difficult to know at what chronological age we should draw the line between individuals who should be treated as adults by the courts and those who should be viewed as children. (J. Berndt/Stock, Boston)

adolescents are generally adjudicated in a separate juvenile justice system, which operates under different rules and principles from the system that applies to adults. Having a separate justice system for juveniles has raised many complicated questions about the costs and benefits of treating adolescents differently from adults. On the one hand, adolescents have been viewed as less capable of controlling their own behavior. First offenses have been treated lightly, and judges have been prohibited from taking juvenile offenses into account when individuals are tried for crimes as adults. On the other hand, adolescents commit a disproportionate share of crimes, as you will read in Chapter 13. In reaction to this, the juvenile justice system has come under fierce attack, and many adults have called for the harsher treatment of young offenders. Unfortunately, development during the adolescent years is so rapid and so

variable that it is difficult to know at what chronological age a line should be drawn between legally viewing someone as an adult and viewing someone as a child (Gold and Petronio, 1980).

Many other issues surrounding the legal status of adolescents remain vague and confusing. For example, courts have ruled that teenagers have the right to seek abortion or obtain contraceptives without their parents' approval. But they also have upheld laws forbidding adolescents access to cigarettes or to magazines that, while vulgar, were not considered so obscene that they were outlawed among adults (Zimring, 1982). In general, legal decisions have tended to restrict the behavior of adolescents when the behavior in question is viewed as potentially damaging to the young person (buying cigarettes, for example) but have supported adolescent autonomy when the behavior is viewed as having potential benefit (using contraceptives).

TABLE 3.1   SOME CONSEQUENCES OF ATTAINING ADULT STATUS

	IN TRADITIONAL SOCIETIES	IN CONTEMPORARY SOCIETIES
Interpersonal	Addressed with "adult" title by other members of community	Permitted to sit with grownups for special occasions
Political	Permitted to participate in community decision making	Eligible to vote
Economic	Permitted to own property	Permitted to work
Legal	Permitted to consume certain foods	No longer dealt with in a separate juvenile justice system

THE PROCESS OF SOCIAL REDEFINITION

Social redefinition at adolescence is not a single event, but a series of events that may occur over a relatively long time. In contemporary America, the process of redefinition typically begins at the age of 15 or 16, when the young person is first permitted to drive, to work, and to leave school. But the social redefinition of the adolescent continues well into the young adult years in many parts of the country. Some privileges, such as voting, are not conferred until the age of 18, and others, such as purchasing alcoholic beverages, are not conferred until the age of 21, five or six years after the redefinition process begins. Even in societies that mark the social redefinition of the young person with a dramatic and elaborate **initiation ceremony,** the social transformation of the individual from a child into an adult may span many years, and the initiation ceremony may represent just one element of the transition. In fact, the initiation ceremony usually marks the beginning of a long period of training and preparation for adulthood rather than the adolescent's final passage into adult status (Cohen, 1964).

The specific nature of the initiation ceremony is often related to the economic and social organization of the adolescent's society. Psychologist Karen Paige (1983) has pointed out that virginity rituals—initiation ceremonies in which the virginity of the adolescent woman is tested to assure her chastity—are more prevalent in societies in which the economic system is strongly linked to land and other inheritable resources and in societies in which there are distinct social classes. The reason, she argues, is that the economic stakes are higher when marriage bargains are made in these societies, and therefore it becomes more important for a family to be able to "prove" that their daughter is a desirable bride. Although this practice may seem odd to you, consider the many lectures young women in our society get over the years on the importance of preserving their "reputation." Paige notes that concern about their daughters' premarital sexual behavior may be especially strong among middle-class parents, who, like their counterparts in stratified traditional societies, may have much to gain economically—or a good deal to lose—by their daughter's desirability in the marriage market.

In many cultures, the social redefinition of young people occurs in groups. That is, the young people of a community are grouped with peers of approximately the same age—a cohort—and move through the series of status transitions together. One of the results of such age-grouped social transitions is that very strong bonds are formed among youngsters who have shared certain rituals. In many American high

The boys of the Mandingo tribe are initiated in an elaborate group ritual. First, their courage is tested by a "ghost." Then they are circumcised in a group ceremony. Following the circumcision, they live together in a special hut, separated from the tribe, until they have completed their religious instruction. Group rituals often create lifelong bonds among the members of the group. (Arthur Tress/Photo Researchers)

schools, for example, attempts are made to create "class spirit" or "class unity" by fostering bonds among students who will be graduated together. On college campuses, fraternities and sororities may conduct group initiations that involve difficult or unpleasant tasks, and special ties may be forged between "brothers" or "sisters" who have pledged together. In the Soviet Union and China, youngsters' participation in age-grouped political organizations is strongly encouraged as a means of creating group cohesion.

In some societies, these group rituals are so elaborate that lifelong ties are forged among adolescents who go through them together. Among the Tikopia, for instance, superincision (a pro-

① sep. from parents
② accentuation of differences b/w males & females
③ passing down of information

cedure in which the top of the penis's foreskin is cut) is performed on a group of boys at one time in an elaborate ceremony preceded by much feasting and ceremony. The boys' parents all help in the preparation of food for the ceremony, and the food often fills several ovens. Throughout adolescence and adulthood, young men who underwent superincision together refer to their bond with one another, saying, "We had our ovens fired together" (Fried and Fried, 1980, p. 63).

Common Practices in the Process of Social Redefinition

Although the specific ceremonies and signs of social redefinition at adolescence vary from one culture to another, several general themes characterize the process in all societies. First, social redefinition usually entails the *real or symbolic separation of the young person from his or her parents.* In traditional societies, this may take the form of **extrusion:** During late childhood, children are expected to begin sleeping in households other than their own. Youngsters may spend the day with their parents, but they spend the night with friends of the family, with relatives, or in a separate residence reserved for preadolescent youngsters (Cohen, 1964). In America, during earlier times, it was customary for adolescents to leave home temporarily and live with other families in the community, either to learn specific occupational skills (i.e., as apprentices) or to work as domestic servants (Kett, 1977). Interestingly, the "placing out" of adolescents from their parents' home often coincided with puberty (Katz, 1975). In contemporary societies, the separation of adolescents from their parents takes somewhat different forms. They are sent to summer camps, to boarding schools, or, as is more common, to live at college.

A second aspect of social redefinition at adolescence entails the *accentuation of physical and social differences between males and females* (Ford and Beach, 1951). This accentuation of differences occurs partly because of the physical

changes of puberty and partly because adult work and family roles are generally highly sex-differentiated. Many societies separate males and females during religious ceremonies, have individuals begin wearing sex-specific articles of clothing (rather than clothing permissible for either gender), and keep males and females apart during initiation ceremonies. Some traditional societies employ a practice called **brother-sister avoidance:** After puberty, a brother and sister may not have any direct contact or interaction until one or both are married (Cohen, 1964).

The separation of males and females is not limited to social redefinition in traditional societies. In earlier times in America (and to a certain extent in many other industrialized societies today), males and females were separated during adolescence in educational institutions, either by excluding adolescent girls from secondary and higher education, grouping males and females in different schools or different classrooms, or having males and females follow different curricula. In present-day America, many of these practices have been discontinued, but some elements of accentuated sex-differentiation and sex-segregation during adolescence still exist: in residential arrangements, in styles of dress, in athletic activities, and in household chores (Hill and Lynch, 1983; Medrich, Roizen, Rubin, and Buckley, 1982; White and Brinkerhoff, 1981).

Third, social redefinition at adolescence typically entails the *passing on of cultural, historical, and practical information* from the adult generation to the newly inducted cohort of young people. This information may concern (1) matters thought to be important to adults but of limited utility to children (for example, information on the performance of certain tasks); (2) matters thought to be necessary for adults but unfit for children (for example, information regarding sex); or (3) matters concerning the history or rituals of the family or community. In traditional societies, initiates are often sent to some sort of "school" in which they are instructed in the productive activities of the community (hunting, fishing, farming). Following puberty, boys and girls receive instruction about sexual relations, moral behavior, and societal lore (Fried and Fried, 1980; Miller, 1928). In contemporary society, too, adolescence is a time of instruction in preparation for adulthood. Elementary school students, for example, are generally not taught a great deal about sexuality, work, or financial matters; such coursework is typically reserved for high school students. We also restrict entrance into certain "adult" activities (such as sexually explicit movies) until the adolescent is believed to be old enough to be exposed to them.

Because formal initiation ceremonies are neither very common nor very meaningful in modern society, students sometimes overlook important similarities between the processes of social redefinition in traditional and contemporary societies. Practices like extrusion, brother-sister avoidance, and superincision are alien and seem odd to us. But if we look beneath the surface, at the meaning and significance of each culture's practices, we find many common threads. In contemporary society, for example, our own form of "brother-sister avoidance" begins at puberty: Once adolescents have reached puberty, brothers and sisters are more likely to seek privacy from each other when dressing or bathing. And while we do not practice anything as "alien" as superincision, we do have our share of body rituals which often are not seen until adolescence and which might seem equally alien to someone unfamiliar with our society: the punching of holes in women's earlobes (ear piercing), the scraping of hair from men's faces (shaving), and the application of brightly colored paints to lips, eyes, and cheeks (putting on make-up)!

Variations in Social Redefinition Practices

Different societies recognize and orchestrate the passage into adult status at different times and in different ways. In this respect, although the presence of social redefinition in a general sense is a universal feature of adolescent development, there is considerable diversity in the nature of the transition. Examining social redefinition from cross-cultural and historical perspectives provides a valuable means of contrasting the nature of adolescence in different social contexts. Two very important dimensions along which societies differ in the process of social redefinition are in the explicitness, or *clarity*, of the transition and in the smoothness, or *continuity*, of the passage.

Variations in clarity. Initiation ceremonies are in many ways religious ceremonies. As such, they are most often employed in societies in which a shared religious belief unites the community and structures individuals' daily experiences. Formal initiation ceremonies therefore have never been prevalent in American society, largely because of the heterogeneity of the population and the general separation of religious experience from everyday affairs.

There are, however, factors other than the presence of formal rites of passage that determine how clear the transition into adult status is to the young person and society. One such factor concerns the extent to which various aspects of the status change occur at about the same time for an individual and during the same general time period for adolescents growing up together (Elder, 1980). When transitions into adult work, family, and citizenship roles occur close in time, and when most members of a cohort experience these transitions at about the same age, the passage into adulthood takes on greater clarity. If all young people were to graduate from high school, enter the labor force, and marry at the age of 18, this age would be an implicit boundary between adolescence and adulthood, even without a formal ceremony. But when different aspects of the passage occur at different times, and when adolescents growing up in a similar environment experience these transitions in different order and along different schedules, the boundary between adolescence and adulthood is made more cloudy.

The clarity of social redefinition in contemporary society. When did you become an adolescent? When did you (or when will you) become an adult? If you are like most individuals in contemporary society, your answers to these questions will not be clearcut. We have no formal ceremonies marking the transition from childhood into adolescence, nor do we have any to mark the passage from adolescence into adulthood. Although in many religions and social groups the young American adolescent may undergo an initiation ceremony of sorts—the confirmation, the bar mitzvah, and the "coming out" parties of debutantes are some examples—rarely does this rite have much significance outside the youngster's family, circle of friends, or religious community. School graduation ceremonies perhaps come the closest to universal rites of passage in contemporary society, but school graduation does not bring with it many meaningful or universal changes in social status, responsibilities, or privileges. As a result, social redefinition in contemporary society does not give the adolescent any clear indication of when his or her responsibilities and privileges as an adult begin.

Attaining adult status is essentially an individual matter in contemporary society, and the absence of clearcut and universal markers of the passage make the process confusing. It is often difficult for young people to tell when they have reached adulthood. In California, for example, the age for starting employment is 15; for leaving high school, 16; for attending restricted (R-rated) movies, 17; for voting, 18; and for drinking, 21. We have few universal markers of adulthood—adolescents are treated as adults at different times by different people in different contexts. A young person may be legally old enough to drive, but his parents may feel that 16 is too early and refuse to let him use the family car. Another may be treated like an adult at work, where she works side by side with people three times her age, but she may be treated like a child at home. A third may be viewed as an adult by her mother but as a child by her father. It is little wonder, in light of the mixed and sometimes contradictory expectations facing young people, that for many adolescents

Formal rites of passage from childhood into adolescence or from adolescence into adulthood are rare in contemporary society. Certain religious ceremonies, such as the Confirmation or the Bar Mitzvah (pictured here), are as close as we come to initiation rites in contemporary America. (Peter Southwick/ Stock, Boston)

the transition into adult roles is a difficult passage to navigate. According to social psychologist Kurt Lewin (1948), the adolescent in modern society is a *marginal man*, caught in a transitional space between childhood and adulthood.

It is not that contemporary society is entirely without rituals. We undoubtedly recognize that some life transitions benefit from being made dramatic and clear. We still use fairly elaborate marriage ceremonies, for example, which ritualize the passage from singlehood into married life; the giving away of the bride, the public exchange of vows, the use of wedding rings, and so forth. For immigrants who want to become American citizens, we have an extensive sort of initiation ceremony—including a test of American history and a public oath of loyalty—that formally marks the individual's transition into citizenship and all the rights and privileges that accompany this new status. Yet the passage from adolescence into adulthood, although itself an extremely important life transition, is not recognized in any formal way.

The clarity of social redefinition in traditional cultures. Unlike the case in contemporary society, social redefinition at adolescence is clearly recognized in most traditional cultures. Typically, the passage from childhood into adolescence is marked by a formal initiation ceremony, which publicly proclaims the young person's entrance into a new position in the community (Ford and Beach, 1951). For boys, such ceremonies may take place at the time of puberty, at the attainment of a designated chronological age, or at a time when the community decides that the individual is ready for the status change. For girls, initiation is more often linked to puberty and, in particular, to the onset of menstruation. In both cases, the initiation ceremony serves to ritualize the passing of the young person out of childhood and, if not directly into adulthood, into a period of training for it.

In many initiation ceremonies, the adolescent's physical appearance is changed, so that other members of the community can distinguish between initiated and uninitiated young people. For example, new types of clothing may be worn following initiation; or some sort of surgical operation or scarification (the intentional creation of scars on some part or parts of the body) may be performed to create a permanent means of marking the individual's adult status (see the accompanying box). In most traditional societies, there is no mistaking which individuals are adults and which still children.

In many traditional cultures, adolescent boys' initiation rites include some sort of operation on the youngster's penis. Among the Tikopia, for example, sometime following completion of his first fishing expedition, the young adolescent boy prepares for an elaborate superincision ceremony. The operation is performed by the boy's mother's brother (in many cultures,

maternal uncles play a special role in adolescent boys' upbringing). Following the operation, bark is applied to the wound as a bandage, and the boy exchanges his beads and ornaments and receives a new waistcloth. An elaborate meal and celebration follow. Later, the uncle will teach the boy how to care for his wounded penis. When the healing is completed, the boy is considered an adult: "He has entered Tikopian society and may participate fully in all adult activities" (Fried and Fried, 1980, p. 67).

The clarity of social redefinition in previous eras. Historical documents concerning life in early nineteenth-century America indicate that the transition into adulthood may actually have been then even more disorderly and cloudy than it is today. According to historian Joseph Kett (1977), many young people at that time moved back and forth between school, where they were viewed as children, and work, where they were viewed as adults. Moreover, timetables for the assumption of adult roles varied considerably from one individual to the next, because they were highly dependent on family and household needs rather than on generally accepted age patterns of school, family, and work transitions. An adolescent might have been working and living away from home, but if his family needed him— because, let's say, someone became ill—he would leave his job and move back in with his parents. During the middle of the nineteenth century, in fact, many young people were neither enrolled in school nor working, occupying a halfway stage that was not quite childhood but not quite adulthood (Katz, 1975). Descriptions of adolescent idleness during the era are strikingly reminiscent of descriptions of unemployed, out-of-school youth today. Indeed, concern about juvenile misbehavior was one factor that encouraged the development of public high schools.

One study comparing adolescents' transitions today with those of their counterparts 100 years ago indicates that the passage into adulthood may have been more prolonged as well as less clearly defined during the latter part of the

have a continuous transition into adult work roles. In contrast, children who do not have any work experience while they are growing up and who enter the labor force for the first time when they graduate from college have a discontinuous transition into adult work roles.

The continuity of the adolescent passage in contemporary society. Transitions into adulthood in contemporary society tend to be more discontinuous than in other cultural or historical contexts. Young people in general are given little preparation before their entrance into adult status in the roles they will be expected to fulfill. Rather, in contemporary society, we tend to exclude young people from the world of adults; we give them little direct training for adult life and then thrust them rather abruptly into total adult independence.

Consider three of the most important roles of adulthood that individuals are expected to carry out successfully—the roles of worker, parent, and citizen. In all three cases we find that adolescents in contemporary society receive little preparation for these positions. Young people are segregated from the workplace throughout most of their childhood and early adolescent years and receive little direct training in school relevant to the work roles they will likely find themselves in as adults. The transition into adult work roles, therefore, is fairly discontinuous for most young people in contemporary society.

The transition of young people into adult family roles is even more abrupt than is their transition into work roles. Prior to actually becoming a parent, young people have virtually no training in child rearing or other related matters. Families are relatively small today, and youngsters are likely to be close in age to their siblings; as a result, few opportunities exist for participating in child-care activities at home. Schools generally offer little if any instruction in family relationships and domestic activities, and because so much time is spent in school once children reach the age of 5 or so, youngsters are away from the home for most of the day and do not have an opportunity to assist or observe their parents in child-rearing responsibilities. And with childbirth generally taking place in hospitals rather than at home, few young people today have the opportunity of observing a younger sibling's birth.

Passage into adult citizenship and decision-making roles is also highly discontinuous in contemporary Western society. Adolescents are permitted few opportunities for independence and autonomy in school and are segregated from most of society's political institutions until they complete their formal education. Young people are permitted to vote once they turn 18 years old, but they have received little preparation for participation in government and community roles before this time.

Some fifty years ago, anthropologist Ruth Benedict (1934) pointed out that the degree of stress individuals experience at adolescence is related to the degree of continuity they experience in making the transition into adulthood; the more discontinuous the passage, the more stressful it is likely to be. Benedict's view suggests that adolescent turmoil, if it exists, is more likely due to environmental than biological factors. It is little surprise, then, that some young people today have difficulty in assuming adult roles and responsibilities. Instead of being gradually socialized into work, family, and citizenship positions, adolescents in modern society typically are segregated from activities in these arenas during most of their childhood and youth. Yet young people are supposed to be able to perform these roles capably on reaching the age of majority. With little preparation in meaningful work, adolescents are expected to find, get, and keep a job immediately after completing their schooling. With essentially no training for marriage or parenting, they are expected to form their own families, manage their own households, and raise their own children soon after they reach adulthood. And without any previous involvement in community activities, they are expected on reaching the age of majority to vote, pay taxes, and behave as responsible citizens.

Discontinuity may be exacerbated by rapid community growth and social change. Accord-

The Sexes: Similarities and Differences in the Transition into Adulthood

The transition from adolescence to adulthood is marked by several related changes in social roles. Among the most important events in this transition are the completion of formal schooling, entrance into the full-time labor force, marriage, and parenthood. One way to think about the transition into adulthood, therefore, is to think about the transition out of one role—that of student—and into three others—those of worker, spouse, and parent (Marini, 1984).

Because these four transitions do not occur simultaneously, it is interesting to ask how they might be related to one another over time. Do most individuals finish school before taking on a full-time job, or does entry into the world of work precede leaving school? How do transitions into family roles, such as spouse and parent, link up with nonfamily transitions? For instance, do individuals become "adults" in nonfamily roles (that is, by leaving school and entering the workforce) before or after they become adults with respect to family roles? Is one sequence more common than another?

Sociologist Margaret Marini has examined these questions by looking at the way in which role transitions during young adulthood are ordered in contemporary America.

Using data collected as a part of a longitudinal follow-up of individuals who had been high school students during the late 1950s (and who had participated in one of the most famous studies of adolescents ever conducted, *The Adolescent Society* [Coleman, 1961], which you will read about in Chapter 5), Marini was able to look at the relations among the role transitions out of school and into work, marriage, and parenthood. Although Marini found that about half of all males and females followed one particular sequence of role transitions, she also found several important differences between males' and females' patterns that have implications for understanding sex differences in educational and occupational attainment.

The most common sequence followed for both sexes was exit from school, followed by entrance into work, entrance into marriage, and then into parenthood, in that order. But half of all the individuals did not follow this "normative" path toward adulthood. One-fifth of the women and nearly one-third of the men had taken a full-time job before finishing school; some worked while in school, and others left school for a time and returned later. One-fifth of the women and nearly one-quarter of the men married

---

ing to one recent study, rapid industrialization and expansion may more negatively affect adolescents than adults, however. (Freudenberg, 1984). This researcher compared teenagers and adults living in a rapidly growing boomtown in the Rocky Mountains with their counterparts in three nearby communities. Although there were few differences among adults, the boomtown teenagers were more likely than other teenagers to feel alienated and dissatisfied. Interestingly, when asked, "What does it take to be accepted around here?" teenagers in the boomtown were

more likely than the others to mention good looks, money, having a car, and having parents in the "right" occupations. Teenagers in the other communities were more likely to say that it was important to be honest, friendly, confident, and genuine. One hypothesis is that the rapid expansion of the community was especially stressful for the teenagers, who, because of the influx of newcomers, were forced to cope with ever-changing cliques and crowds in school. Adults may have been buffered against some of the ill effects of expansion by well-established

before finishing school, and about one in ten men and women had married and become parents before their education was finished.

In general, the longer an individual stayed in school, the less likely he or she was to follow the expected sequence—primarily because longer schooling made it more likely that one of the other transitions would occur before education was completed. In other words, if you decide to go to graduate or professional school after college, you have a greater chance of spending some time as a married student or as a student-worker than you do if you stop at an undergraduate degree. As Marini points out, the findings counter the widely held belief that entering into work or family commitments before finishing school necessarily impedes educational attainment. As she notes, we need more research on the long-term occupational experiences of students who marry or work before completing school.

Why were men somewhat more likely than women to interrupt or combine their schooling with work or family commitments? Women who went on to higher levels of education were especially likely to delay taking on family roles. Apparently, men found it easier than women to become both spouse and parent while still in school. Marini suggests that women's traditional family roles— and, in particular, their greater involvement in domestic responsibilities—make it more difficult for them to move between student and nonstudent roles and make marriage and parenthood "less compatible with the continuation of education for women than for men" (Marini, 1984, p. 78). As she writes, "Although for men the continuation of education does not permit direct fulfillment of the traditional male role of provider, because of its future payoff for the well-being of the family, it is viewed as an investment in the family's future. Women's educational and occupational pursuits tend to be viewed as secondary to those of their husbands" (p. 78).

Because becoming a spouse and parent interrupt the process of educational attainment more for women than for men, it may be more important for women to delay taking on family roles until after they have finished school, or they risk compromising their careers. Indeed, in other articles, Marini has pointed out that the earlier transition into parenthood among women than men and its greater educational cost for women are main factors in the generally lower occupational attainment of women (Marini, 1978). Although it is *possible* for men and women to marry and become parents before they stop being students, the costs of deviating from the "normative" sequence are not equal for the two sexes.

social networks and longstanding friendships and sources of social support.

Not all industrialized societies, however, are characterized by the level of discontinuity in the socialization of young people typical of life in contemporary America and comparable Western nations. In China, for example, middle school students have been required to spend one month a year in workshops, working in such fields as electronics, agriculture, and construction. They also have been required to put in a period of time away from their school, working in other communities and sharing their knowledge with adults who may be less educated (Kessen, 1975). A deliberate attempt was made to use formal schooling as a means of easing young people into work roles deemed important by the larger society. In the Soviet Union as well as in China, young people are organized into a two-tiered political organization, with preadolescents and young adolescents grouped together in the Young Pioneers and with older youth (from about 15 through 25) in the Young Communist League. Such political participation provides a

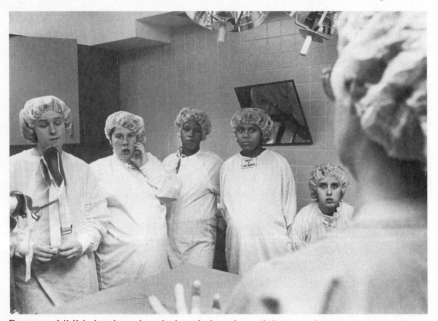

Because childbirth takes place in hospitals today, adolescents have no opportunity to observe a birth—which further adds to the discontinuous transition of adolescents into adult roles. These pregnant teenagers are receiving their first lesson on childbirth in a hospital maternity ward. (Polly Brown/Archive)

more continuous transition into the citizenship roles they will be expected to play as adults (Fried and Fried, 1980).

The continuity of the adolescent passage in traditional cultures. The high level of discontinuity found in contemporary America is not characteristic of adolescence in traditional societies. Consider the socialization of young people in Samoa, for example. From early childhood on, youngsters are involved in work tasks that have a meaningful connection to the work they will perform as adults. They are involved in the care of younger children, in the planting and harvesting of crops, and in the gathering and preparation of food. Their entrance into adult work roles is gradual and continuous, with work tasks graded to children's skills and intelligence. Young people are charged with the socialization

of their infant brothers and sisters, particularly during middle childhood, when they are not yet strong enough to make a substantial contribution to the community's fishing and farming activities. Gradually, young people are taught the fundamentals of weaving, boating, fishing, building, and farming. By the time they have reached late adolescence, Samoan youngsters are well trained in the tasks they will need to perform as adults (Mead, 1928).

Such continuity is generally the case in societies in which hunting, fishing, and farming are the chief work activities. As Margaret Mead (1928) has observed, the emphasis in these societies is on informal, **observational learning,** rather than on **didactic teaching.** Children are typically not isolated in separate educational institutions, and they accompany the adult members of their community in daily activities. Adolescents' preparation for adulthood, therefore, comes largely from observation and "hands-on" experience in the same tasks that they will continue to carry out as adults. Typically, boys learn the tasks performed by adult men, and girls those performed by adult women. Where work activities take adults out of the community, it is not uncommon for children to travel with their parents on work expeditions. Among the Boloki (Africa), boys accompany their fathers on trading journeys and in this way learn how to barter, negotiate, and exchange goods (Miller, 1928).

In virtually all aspects of life—not simply work activity—the socialization of young people in traditional societies is more continuous than it is in contemporary society. For example, whereas we tend to limit adolescents' knowledge of sexual matters, in many traditional societies no attempt is made to hide this knowledge from young people, particularly once they have reached puberty. Indeed, in many such cultures, explicit instruction in sex, pregnancy, and childbirth is included in the adolescent's initiation into adulthood. Among the Chewa (Africa), for instance, preadolescents are encouraged by their parents to build huts some distance from the village, and boys and girls play at being husband and wife (Ford and Beach, 1951). The onset of sexual activity during adolescence may be made more stressful in modern society by the discontinuous manner in which sexuality is treated (Mead, 1928). In contrast to life in many traditional societies (in which relatively few conflicts over sexuality are reported), young people in

In societies in which hunting, farming, and fishing are the primary work activities, young people often are taught the skills they will need as adult workers by accompanying—and observing—their elders in daily activities rather than by attending school. (Owen Franken/Stock, Boston)

contemporary society are discouraged from sexual experimentation before marriage and are given little or no information about sexual matters at all during their adolescent years.

The continuity of the adolescent passage in previous eras.   During earlier periods in American history, the transition into adult roles and responsibilities began at an earlier age and proceeded along a more continuous path than generally is the case today. This is especially true with regard to work. During the eighteenth century, of course, and well into the early part of the nineteenth century, when many families were engaged in farming, a good number of adolescents were expected to work on the family farm and learn the skills necessary to carry on the enterprise. Some youngsters, generally boys, accompanied their fathers on business trips, learning the trades of salesmanship and commerce (Kett, 1977)—a pattern reminiscent of that found in many traditional societies.

Many other young people left home relatively early—some as early as age 12—to work for nonfamilial adults in the community or in nearby villages (Katz, 1975; Kett, 1977). Even as recently as the mid-nineteenth century, it was common for young adolescents to work as apprentices, learning skills and trades in preparation for the work roles of adulthood; others left home temporarily to work as servants or to learn domestic skills. The average nineteenth-century youngster left school well before the age of 15 (Modell, Furstenberg, and Hershberg, 1976).

However, census data and historical documents—such as letters, diaries, and community histories—indicate that while adolescents of 100 years ago took on full-time employment earlier in life than they typically do today, they were likely to live at home with their parents for a longer period than is usual in contemporary society. That is, although the transition into work roles may have occurred earlier in the nineteenth century than in the twentieth century, this transition was made in the context of semi-independence rather than complete emancipation (Katz, 1975; Kett, 1977; Modell, Furstenberg, and

Hershberg, 1976). This semi-independent period—which for many young people spanned the decade from about ages 12 to 22, and even beyond—may have increased the degree of continuity of the passage into adulthood by providing a time during which young people could assume certain adult responsibilities gradually (Katz, 1975). The semi-independence characteristic of adolescence in the nineteenth century had largely disappeared by 1900 (Kett, 1977).

Socialization for family and citizenship roles may also have been more continuous in previous historical eras. Living at home during the late adolescent and early adult years, particularly in the larger families characteristic of households 100 years ago, contributed to the preparation of young people for future family life. It was common for the children in a family to span a wide age range, and remaining at home undoubtedly placed the older adolescent from time to time in child-rearing roles (President's Science Advisory Committee, 1974). As opposed to today's adolescents, who typically have little experience with infants, adolescents 100 years ago were more likely to have fed, dressed, and cared for their younger siblings. They were also expected to assist their parents in maintaining the household (Modell, Furstenberg, and Hershberg, 1976), and this experience probably made it easier for young people to manage when they eventually established a home separate from their parents. One recent study indicates that leaving one's parents' home earlier and living independently before marriage has encouraged young women to develop less traditional attitudes, values, and plans than their counterparts who live with their parents as young adults (Waite et al., 1986).

There is also some evidence that adolescents' participation in political and community affairs was greater during the nineteenth century than it typically is today. Historian Joseph Kett reports, for example, that adolescents often attended town meetings and public and political gatherings. One 16-year-old reports having passed "hour after hour in the village store, talking politics with adults" (Kett, 1977, p. 43).

The Great Depression.   Occasionally a specific event occurs that is so powerful it temporarily alters the nature of the adolescent passage and produces exceptions to general historical trends. One such event was the Great Depression of the early 1930s. Sociologist Glen Elder, Jr., has examined the impact of growing up during this era on adolescents' behavior and development (Elder, 1974), and many of his findings are relevant to the issue of continuity in the adolescent passage. Elder looked at the data collected during the Depression as part of a longitudinal study of individuals living in Oakland, California. The group Elder focused on was born between 1920 and 1921 and thus were preadolescents during the worst years of the Depression.

Elder found that youngsters whose families experienced economic hardship during these years were more likely to be involved in adult-like tasks at an earlier age than their more privileged peers. Boys, for example, were more likely to work and help support their families; girls were more likely to play a major role with household chores. And both boys and girls were more likely to marry and enter into full-time employment relatively early.

Thus some aspects of the semi-independent stage of adolescence that had become uncommon by 1930 may have reappeared during the Great Depression. For many youngsters growing up during this time period, the adolescent passage may have resembled that of an earlier era.

The emergence of the teenager.   You have read in this chapter that in most societies, adolescence is a transitional stage of the lifespan, during which young people are recognized as being in preparation for adulthood. Although such a period of preparation had long existed in non-industrialized societies, and although virtually all societies have always distinguished between young people and adults, scholars in this country have written that modern adolescence was "invented" during the Industrial Revolution of the nineteenth century (Bakan, 1972). It was invented because changes in the workplace required and permitted a longer transitional period than had been the case previously.

During the 1940s, though, adolescence was further transformed in ways that have continued to affect the transition into adulthood, even today. Observers of contemporary adolescent culture point to the "invention" during this era of the "teenager," as distinct from the "adolescent." The mass media had a great deal to do with this (Gilbert, 1985). Although the term *adolescent* first appeared in the *Reader's Guide to Periodical Literature* in 1919, the term *teenager* did not appear until 1943. The term *teenager* "referred to more than simply an individual whose age placed him or her somewhere between childhood and adulthood. It carried with it a sense of freedom, autonomy, and frivolousness; it connoted an individual who was not old enough to function as an adult member of society but who nonetheless was no longer under stringent parental control" (Greenberger and Steinberg, 1986, p. 77). As a result, teenagers may have the trappings and superficial appearance of adults—they wear designer clothes, cosmetics, and have easy access to money and what it can buy—but they lack the sense of responsibility of mature individuals. Many social commentators have suggested that this combination of freedom and irresponsibility has encouraged the development of *pseudomaturity*—the outward appearance of maturity without the accompanying psychological skills (Friedenberg, 1959; Greenberger and Steinberg, 1986; Reisman, 1950). According to these critics, the emergence of the teenager on the American scene has further complicated the transition into adulthood, because teenagers are encouraged to appear like adults but are *not* encouraged to develop genuine psychological maturity.

The Transition into Adulthood: "A Bridge Too Long"?

We do not know for certain whether the confusion and discontinuity characteristic of the passage into adulthood today impedes the adolescent's psychosocial development and respon-

The Great Depression temporarily altered the nature of the adolescent's passage into adult roles. Because of widespread economic hardship, adolescent boys were forced to leave school and enter the work force full-time at a relatively early age. Adolescent girls also left school early to assume adult responsibilities at home. (Culver Pictures)

sible assumption of adult roles. But many social scientists have speculated that these consequences may result. Identity development, to take one example, is probably made more difficult by the higher levels of confusion and inconsistency that surround the social passage into adulthood in modern society. Erik Erikson (1968) and other theorists view identity development during adolescence as the result of the interplay between the young person's growing self-awareness and society's changing view of him or her. It is not difficult to see, then, how an "identity crisis" might be intensified by not knowing whether one is an adult or a child or when the change in social definition takes place.

In recent years, observers of adolescence in America have suggested that the vagueness and discontinuity in the passage into adulthood have become so great that many youngsters are having problems negotiating the passage into adult roles (Hamburg, 1986; National Commission on Youth, 1980). One commission called the transition of adolescents into adulthood "a bridge too long" (National Commission on Youth, 1980). These observers point to problems many young people experience in developing a coherent sense of identity, establishing a healthy sense of autonomy, and making informed decisions about commitments to family and work. They note that the lack of clarity and continuity in the transition into adulthood may contribute to some of the problems faced by adolescents in contemporary society and as well to some of the problems faced by contemporary society in dealing with young people (Conger, 1977a). Many social scientists believe that our relatively high rates of divorce, family violence, youth unemployment, juvenile delinquency, and teenage alcoholism stem in part from the confusing and contradictory nature of the passage into adulthood in modern society (National Commission on Youth, 1980).

As David Hamburg, president of the Carnegie Corporation of New York, wrote recently:

> In the rapid world transformation of this century, preparation [for adulthood] increasingly involves readiness to cope with change itself. It is very difficult—not only for children but for parents as well—to anticipate the future circumstances of adulthood. . . . [T]here are now so many changes within a lifetime, so many requirements for learning and relearning, so many moving targets to hit, so many disruptions of fundamental social support systems. Furthermore, preparation for life, which is inherently perplexing and difficult, has become all the more stressful for those who cannot foresee a future at all, at least not a decent one. For those who lack any worthwhile perception of opportunity and hope, the task of preparing for adult life can be burdensome and disaster prone. (Hamburg, 1986, p. 13)

Special transitional problems of minority youth. No discussion of the transitional problems of young people in America today is complete without noting that youngsters from some minority groups—black, Hispanic-American, and American Indian youth, in particular—have more trouble negotiating the transition into adulthood than do their white and Asian-American counterparts. Youngsters from minority backgrounds make up a substantial and growing portion of the adolescent population in America. By the end of this century, about 15 percent of the youth population will be black and another 13 percent Hispanic. Approximately 4 percent of the youth population will be composed of Asian-American, Pacific Islander, and American

Indian youth. In other words, about one-third of the youth population in the year 2000 will be from minority groups (Wetzel, 1987; and see Figure 3.1).

Growing up in poverty may profoundly impair youngsters' ability to move easily between adolescence and adulthood. Poverty is associated with failure in school, unemployment, and out-of-wedlock pregnancy, all of which contribute to transition difficulties. Because minority youngsters are more likely than other teenagers to grow up in poverty, they are more likely than other youths to encounter transitional problems during middle and late adolescence (see Figure 3.2). As you will read in later chapters, school dropout rates are much higher among Hispanic and American Indian teenagers than other groups, and college enrollment is lower among black, Hispanic, and American Indian youth than other young people. Youth unemployment is much higher among black, Hispanic, and American Indian groups than other groups. Black and Hispanic youth are more likely to be victimized by crime than other young people. And rates of out-of-wedlock births are higher among black and Hispanic teenagers than among white teenagers (Wetzel, 1987). All of these factors disrupt the transition into adulthood by limiting individuals' economic and occupational success. Poverty impedes the transition to adulthood among *all* teenagers, regardless of race, of course, but because minority youth are more likely to grow up poor, they are more likely to have transition problems.

A variety of suggestions have been offered for making the transition into adulthood smoother for all young people, including restructuring secondary education, expanding work and volunteer opportunities, and increasing contact between adolescents and adults so that more observational learning can take place (Carnegie Commission on Policy Studies in Higher Education, 1979; National Commission on Youth, 1980; President's Science Advisory Committee, 1974). Some groups have called for expanded opportunities in the workplace as a

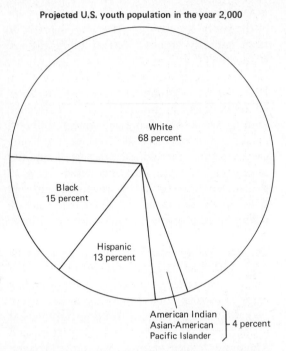

Projected U.S. youth population in the year 2,000

White
68 percent

Black
15 percent

Hispanic
13 percent

American Indian
Asian-American   } 4 percent
Pacific Islander

FIGURE 3.1   By the end of this century, youngsters from minority backgrounds will comprise about one-third of the U.S. adolescent population. (Wetzel, 1987)

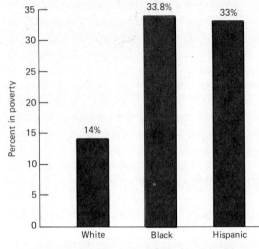

FIGURE 3.2   Poverty rates of 16–21-year-olds, 1985. (Wetzel, 1987)

way of making the high school years more of a "bridge" between adolescence and adulthood (Carnegie Council on Policy Studies in Higher Education, 1980). Other groups have suggested that adolescents be encouraged to spend time in voluntary, nonmilitary service activities—such as staffing day-care centers, working with the elderly, or cleaning up the environment—for a few years after high school graduation so that they can learn responsibility and adult roles (Committee for the Study of National Service,

1979). Still others have called for more extensive pregnancy and dropout prevention programs so that fewer young people enter adulthood at an economic disadvantage (Hayes, 1987).

Although these ideas have received a good deal of acceptance in theory, they have been hard to implement on a wide scale. It is difficult to structure the passage of adolescents into adulthood in today's world in a way that is similar to that found in traditional societies or previous eras.

As you read this book, give some thought to how adolescence ought to be structured. Should we have some sort of initiation ceremony that signifies when young people have become adults? Should we rethink the purpose of high school? What do you think is the best way to prepare adolescents for the responsibilities they will face as adults?

Summary

Changes in social definition, along with biological and cognitive changes, constitute the third set of universal transformations to take place

during the adolescent years. In all societies, adolescence is a time when individuals come to be recognized as adult members of society rather than as children. This social passage into adulthood—which involves changes in the individual's interpersonal, political, economic, and legal status—generally carries with it new rights and privileges as well as new expectations and obligations. The process of social redefinition has important consequences for the young person's psychosocial development, provoking changes in the domains of identity, autonomy, intimacy, sexuality, and achievement.

Although the specific elements of the transition into adulthood vary from one context to another, three general themes characterize social redefinition in all cultures: the real or symbolic separation of young people from their parents; the accentuation of differences between males and females; and the passing on of cultural, historical, or practical information deemed important for adulthood.

Examining adolescence in other cultures and other eras indicates just how much the social environment in which young people grow up affects their psychosocial development. The passage of adolescents into adulthood is far more difficult in modern society than in traditional cultures and past eras. In contemporary society, young people receive little direct preparation for adult roles prior to attaining adult status and move from a long period of extreme dependency into total emancipation over a very short period of time. Many observers believe that the confusing and discontinuous nature of the transition into adulthood is the cause of many problems for young people in contemporary society. In addition, the special problems associated with growing up in poverty have made the transition into adulthood particularly difficult for many minority youth.

As society has changed, the settings in which adolescents spend time—at home, with friends, in school, and at work—have been transformed profoundly. In the next portion of this book, we look at the contexts of adolescence, at why and how these contexts have changed, and at how these changes have affected young people.

We begin with a look at the changing American family.

Key Terms

age of majority
brother-sister avoidance
continuous transition
didactic teaching
discontinuous transition

extrusion
initiation
observational learning
social redefinition

For Further Reading

ENRIGHT, R, AND LAPSLEY, D. (EDS.). (1985). *Early adolescence throughout American history.* Complete issue of the *Journal of Early Adolescence,* 5. A collection of articles examining adolescence from colonial America until the present.

KETT, J. (1977). *Rites of passage: Adolescence in Amer-* *ica, 1790 to the present.* New York: Basic Books. An extensive discussion of how adolescence in America has changed over the last two centuries.

MEAD, M. (1928). *Coming of age in Samoa.* New York: Morrow. Margaret Mead's classic discussion of adolescence in the South Pacific and what we can learn about our own society by studying a more traditional one.

MODELL, J., FURSTENBERG, F., JR., AND HERSHBERG, T. (1976). Social change and the transition to adulthood in historical perspective. *Journal of Family History, 1,* 7–32. A comparison of the timing of adolescents' transitions into adulthood in nineteenth- and twentieth-century America.

NATIONAL COMMISSION ON YOUTH. (1980). *The transition of youth to adulthood: A bridge too long.* Boulder, Col.: Westview Press. One of the important "blue-ribbon" reports on the problems adolescents face in becoming adults and what society should do in response.

PART TWO

*The Contexts
of
Adolescence*

Families

CHAPTER 4

PREVIEW

1. American family life has undergone tremendous change during the past thirty years because of rising rates of divorce, single parenthood, and maternal employment. Nevertheless, one thing that has not changed is the important role that the family plays in adolescent development.

2. The concept of the "generation gap" is largely a myth. Contrary to stereotypes, adolescents and parents usually get along very well, share similar values, and see eye to eye on a range of important issues.

3. Families are systems that must adapt to the changing needs and capabilities of family members. Adolescence presents a challenge to most families—not only because of changes in the adolescent but because of changes in the adolescent's parents as well.

4. Not surprisingly, the way in which parents raise their youngsters has a tremendous impact on the children's psychosocial development. Generally speaking, adolescents who grow up in households in which parents are warm yet firm are happier, more self-reliant, and more socially capable than their peers. Adolescents do best in families that encourage both autonomy and closeness.

In the eyes of many, the American family by 1980 was on its way to becoming an endangered species, and children and adolescents were bearing the costs of the family's demise. According to some observers, the problems of young people—declining achievement test scores, increasing rates of alcohol and drug use, violence in the schools—were due to the progressive fragmentation of the family.

Others, less pessimistic, argued that the family was not dying but *changing*. They noted that although the family of the 1950s—two parents (with mother at home), three children, and a station wagon—might be disappearing, new forms of family life, commendable in their own right, were emerging. The family of the 1950s, these observers pointed out, was not very well suited for life in the 1980s, and there was little reason to lament its disappearance. Today, the debate continues: Is the family dying or simply changing?

There is no question that in America and in many comparably industrialized countries, the family has undergone a series of profound changes during the past quarter-century. Rising rates of divorce, increases in maternal employment, and accelerating geographic mobility all have dramatically altered the world in which children and adolescents grow up. But questions as to whether these changes have weakened the family's influence over young people or, in one way or another, have harmed young people are difficult to answer. Yes, the family has changed—but so has society. This chapter and the three that follow focus on the changing nature of adolescence in contemporary society. As you will see, it is not only the family that has changed.

Amidst all this talk of change, it is important to bear in mind two very fundamental points about young people and their families that have *not* changed very much at all. First, the family remains an extremely important influence on adolescent development. As an influence on the development of identity, autonomy, or achievement, for example, few forces are as significant as the young person's family. And

second, regardless of the family's structure or composition—one parent or two, natural or reconstituted, working mother or not—having positive and warm family relationships stands out as one of the most powerful predictors and correlates of healthy psychosocial growth during the adolescent years. In this chapter, we take a close look at families during adolescence and at why they exert such an important influence on development.

THE BROADER ECOLOGY OF THE FAMILY

The family does not exist in a social vacuum. As a consequence, it is impossible to discuss the changing nature of the family in America without putting these changes into broader perspective. Changing rates of divorce, single parenthood, and maternal employment during the past thirty years are not isolated trends but the results of a constellation of historical, economic, and ideological shifts that took place following World War II. Like the other contexts in which adolescents develop, the structure and nature of the family has changed as society has changed. Chief among the social transformations that have affected the contemporary family most profoundly have been changes in the world of work, changes in attitudes toward women's roles, changes in patterns of housing, and changes in individuals' values and priorities.

The Changing Nature of Work

Following World War II, the chief growth in the American labor force was concentrated in retail and service jobs. Many of these jobs were part-time, and most of the people who took them were women (Ginzberg, 1977). The trend toward increasing participation of women in the world of work was evident by 1950. Increasingly, women—many of whom had children—were drawn into the labor force, not so much by changing attitudes toward women's roles (the impact of the women's movement was not apparent until the late 1960s) but by a proliferation of jobs that were open to them. As a consequence, the familiar pattern of family life—the man as sole wage earner, the woman as housewife—became less prevalent as America moved into the 1960s (Bronfenbrenner, 1975).

The Women's Movement

It is crucial to distinguish between part-time and full-time employment in discussions of the impact of women's work on family life. As social scientists George Masnick and Mary Jo Bane (1980) point out, it is only when women's participation in the labor force becomes a full-time, permanent attachment to work that patterns of family life change in any dramatic way. Many women who were in the labor force part-time during the 1950s and 1960s structured their work hours in a way that altered patterns of family life very little. Many took jobs in which their work hours coincided with their children's school schedules, minimizing time conflicts between family and work commitments.

It was not until attitudes toward women's roles began to change that patterns of work among women were transformed in ways that had important consequences for patterns of family life, because it was not until the early 1970s that year-round, full-time employment—perhaps the best indicator of involvement in the labor force—became prevalent among women and, in particular, among women with school-aged children. A good deal of this increase in full-time work among American women was no doubt due to economic factors, but a major contributing force was the widespread and far-reaching impact of the women's movement. In the minds of many, in fact, the women's movement was the single most significant change of the 1970s (Conger, 1981).

Changing Patterns of Housing

A third trend that had an important impact on the family relates to changing patterns of housing. As increasing numbers of families moved from rural to urban areas during the first half of this century, and from urban to suburban areas during the 1950s and 1960s, nuclear families became increasingly isolated—from each other and from the extended family. Many families moved into single-family dwellings, cut off from neighbors and relatives. While the extended family household was never particularly popular in America, earlier in this century family members were more likely to live near one another, and extended family networks (if not households) played an important role in child rearing. Residential mobility was not very common. Now, in contrast, "half of all families in the United States move every five years" (Conger, 1981, p. 1475). In day-to-day terms, these changed patterns of housing have left the family

The phenomenal rise of the suburbs during the 1950s and 1960s resulted, in part, in the isolation of families from neighbors and relatives. Some experts believe that this isolation has left many families without adequate sources of support when they are under stress. (Bill Owens/Archive Pictures)

more detached from other people and other institutions that can provide support during times of emotional stress or material need.

Changing Values and Priorities

During the past twenty years, Americans' values and priorities have changed, and these changes have affected family life in profound ways. Two components of this value shift stand out. First, people became more preoccupied with themselves and their needs as individuals and less concerned about the needs of others. (Cynical observers labeled the 1970s the "me decade" [Wolfe, 1976].) Second, and related to this first shift, Americans became more tolerant of behavior that veered from socially determined norms and standards (Conger, 1981).

These shifts had both positive and negative elements. On the positive side, people became more concerned about such issues as nutrition, health, and exercise and more willing to pursue lifestyles that they felt were correct for them, rather than adhering to social standards that they felt were arbitrary and rigid. But on the negative side, the movement toward preoccupation with the self and away from adherence to social norms also smacked of selfishness and narcissism, of self-indulgence and idle pleasure seeking, of "doing one's own thing" without regard for the needs and well-being of others.

The impact of this value shift on family life was dramatic. One of the most important trends identified by demographers in their predictions of changes in household composition and family structure during the remainder of this century is the remarkable diversity that is coming to characterize American family life. At the simplest level, diminished concern with adherence to society's ideal pattern of behavior permitted individuals to pursue a wider variety of family forms than had been socially acceptable in the past. Self-fulfillment, rather than social obligation, became the driving force behind individuals' familial and marital decisions. Cohabitation, divorce, remarriage, single parenthood, reconstituted families, having children out of

wedlock—all of these lifestyles became more acceptable and more accepted (some, of course, more than others). The traditional nuclear family form not only became less prevalent, it also became less idealized as the morally correct way to live. In 1960, demographers observe, there was a "typical" family form in this country: a married couple with children and with the man as the sole full-time worker. Today, this structure is but one of many prevalent, and accepted, family forms (Masnick and Bane, 1980). In 1955, for example, nearly two-thirds of all households "consisted of a working father, a housewife mother, and two or more school age children" (Hodgkinson, 1985, p. 3). By 1985, the proportion had dropped to 7 percent.

THE CHANGING AMERICAN FAMILY

Just how dramatic have the changes in American family life been over the past thirty years? Consider three of the most important shifts: increases in the rate of divorce, increases in the number of single parents, and increases in the rate of mothers' employment. These shifts have transformed the nature of family life for many young people.

Changes in Family Structure

As you can see from Figure 4.1, the rate of divorce has been increasing since 1950 and has been rising steadily, and at times rapidly, since then. The divorce rate increased most dramatically after 1965 and peaked around 1980. By 1979, the divorce rate in the United States was the highest in the world (Hetherington, 1981). By 1980, fewer than two-thirds of all children under the age of 18 were living with both natural parents in their first marriage (Conger, 1981). When youngsters live with only one of their natural parents, either in single-parent or in two-parent households, it is nearly always with the mother; only about 10 percent of children whose parents have been divorced live with the father

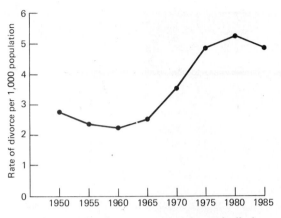

FIGURE 4.1   The divorce rate rose dramatically between 1960 and 1980 and has fallen slightly since then.

(Hetherington, 1981). We may hold on to images of what family life was like twenty years ago, but the fact is that today well over *half* of all people spend some time during childhood or adolescence living in an arrangement other than with both of their natural parents.

Nearly half of all individuals experience their parents' divorce or separation by the end of adolescence, and about half of this group experiences their parents' remarriage. Nearly another half of *these* youngsters experience a second divorce by their parents, because divorce rates are higher for second marriages than for first marriages. There are important racial differences in these patterns, however. Black youngsters are far more likely than white youngsters to experience parental divorce but far less likely to experience their parents' remarriage (Furstenberg et al., 1983). All in all, today's adolescents are far more likely to experience one or more family transitions—parents' separation, divorce, remarriage—than were adolescents in the recent past.

The trends concerning single parenthood are equally noteworthy. Although the majority of divorced adults remarry, the remarriage rate has lagged behind the divorce rate. Many children spend a good deal of time in a single-parent

family as a result. Because out-of-wedlock births have also been on the rise—the number of births outside of marriage *tripled* during the 1970s— many youngsters are born into single-parent families (Hetherington, 1981). Sixty percent of all individuals born during the 1980s will spend some time in a single-parent household before the end of adolescence; the average length of time spent by children in a single-parent household because of marital disruption is about six years (Hetherington, 1981).

The third trend worth noting concerns maternal employment. Figure 4.2 indicates that, among women with school-aged children, full-time employment has increased steadily since 1950, with the most dramatic increase occurring between 1965 and 1970 (Masnick and Bane, 1980). Today, about two-thirds of all married women with school-aged children are employed outside the home. And the rate, not surprisingly, is even higher among single mothers, over 80 percent of whom work.

The Adolescent's Family Today

Few adolescents live in the idealized—perhaps even romanticized—family structure that was common before 1960: the two-parent family with the father as the only wage earner. In fact, less than 25 percent of all adolescents live in this sort of arrangement. Today, nearly as many adolescents live in single-parent households, almost invariably with their mothers; and in most cases those mothers work. Of the young people living in two-parent families, a substantial number—close to 15 percent—live with only one of their natural parents (U.S. Bureau of the Census, 1980; 1981; 1982).

Living arrangements vary a great deal among the adolescent population, however. While the overall proportion of adolescents living in single-parent households is about 22 percent, this figure is considerably higher among economically disadvantaged and black youth than among more affluent, white, or Hispanic youth. Today, in fact, remarkable as it may seem, more black teenagers live in single-parent

More than half of all individuals born during the 1980s will spend a portion of childhood or adolescence in a single-parent household, typically for six or more years. (Jim Harrison/Stock, Boston)

than in two-parent households (see Figure 4.3 [U.S. Bureau of the Census, 1986]).

ADOLESCENT DEVELOPMENT AND THE CHANGING FAMILY

To what extent has the changed nature of the American family changed the nature of adolescent development? How do divorce, absent fathers, and working mothers affect adolescents' development?

Because the conditions under which divorce, father absence, and maternal employment take place vary tremendously from family to family, it is hard to generalize about their effects on adolescents. To some young people, divorce may bring a welcome end to family conflict and tension; to others, it may be extremely psychologically disruptive. Some young people living

with their mothers see their fathers more often than do their peers who live in homes where the father ostensibly is present. And while for some adolescents, having a working mother may mean curtailed family time and less contact with her, for others, a mother who is employed may provide an important role model and added opportunities to take on responsibility around the household. In other words, the variations *within* different family structures are likely to be more important than the differences *among* them.

Factors that Make a Difference

Five factors appear to influence the impact of changes in family structure on adolescent development: the levels of stress and the amount of support at the time of the change in family structure; the age of the child when the change takes place; the sex of the child; the amount of time

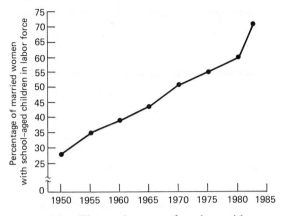

FIGURE 4.2   The employment of mothers with school-aged children has increased steadily since 1950.

that has elapsed since the change; and the par-

(6)

ents' response to the change.

Stress and support.   Changes in a family's structure—if the parents get divorced or if the mother decides to enter the labor force full-time, for example—are transitions that are not troublesome in and of themselves; but they have a *potential* to be stressful and problematic in the presence of other stresses and in the absence of supports for the child and for the family. For example, divorce is far more difficult for children who already have psychological problems or whose families have financial problems (Wallerstein and Kelley, 1974; Rutter, 1978). Supports outside the home—such as a teacher who cares about the child—can soften the effects of family stress on youngsters' mental health (Hetherington, 1981).

Similarly, mothers' employment does not affect all children in the same way. Children whose mothers are happily employed are much more likely to benefit from the experience than children whose mothers would prefer not to work or who have jobs they are unhappy with. When a mother is happy to be working, her youngster is more likely to develop self-reliance and independence and to be pleased that his or

her mother works (Hoffman, 1974). A mother who has to work because the family is under severe financial pressure gives a very different impression to her child from the mother who is happily and actively pursuing a fulfilling career.

The child's age.   It is crucial to distinguish between an event that takes place during early or middle childhood and one that does not take place until late childhood or adolescence (Wallerstein and Kelley, 1980). The impact of divorce or fathers' absence on children's development, for example, appears to be greatest if the event occurs during childhood (Biller, 1981). Children's capacity for coping with stress is greater when they are older. Moreover, resources and emotional support outside the family (for example, from friends) are more likely to be available to the older child than to the younger one. An adolescent who is upset about his parents' divorce can turn to friends for advice and sup-

FIGURE 4.3   The proportion of youngsters living in single-parent households varies a great deal across racial and ethnic groups.

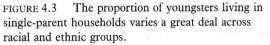

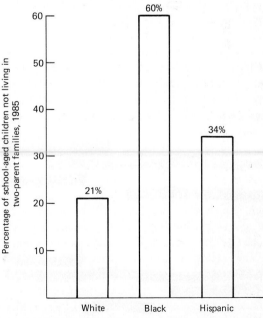

port; but an elementary-school child has fewer people to go to. When divorce takes place during adolescence, young people understandably may feel angry, sad, and hurt, but it appears that those adolescents who had few psychological problems before their parents' divorce and who are able to avoid taking sides during their parents' conflicts show few long-term adverse effects from their parents' breakup (Wallerstein and Kelley, 1974). But some research indicates that remarriage may be more difficult for adolescents than for younger children (Hetherington and Camara, 1984).

The child's sex. While children of both sexes are affected by changes in the family, there is some evidence that children are somewhat more affected by changes involving the parent of the same sex. Thus girls appear to be more affected by mothers' employment than boys, and boys more affected by fathers' absence than girls (Biller, 1981; Hoffman, 1974). Because children tend to identify with the parent of the same sex, it makes sense that girls' occupational plans would be more influenced by the mother working than would boys. A girl whose mother works is more likely to say that she wants a career outside the home than a girl whose mother does not work, but boys' work plans are not highly influenced by their mothers' employment. With respect to children's adjustment, however, several studies indicate that mothers' employment may have a positive impact on daughters but a negative impact on sons (Bronfenbrenner and Crouter, 1982).

Along similar lines, the problems that sometimes result from fathers' absence—difficulties in school, for instance—are more likely to afflict boys than girls. Boys from father-absent homes are more likely to have problems in school than other boys, but differences between girls from father-absent and father-present homes are not as great. But even boys appear to be less affected by father absence when other male role models (a stepfather, older brother, or uncle, for example) are available (Biller, 1981). When a divorced mother remarries, the impact

is more likely to be positive on sons, but negative on daughters (Peterson and Zill, 1986).

Researchers are finding also that it may be important to take the sex of the child into account when making child custody decisions after a divorce. One study of the impact of divorce on children's development, in which the children were living with their mothers following the divorce, found that problems were more likely to develop between boys and their mothers than between girls and their mothers (Hetherington, Cox, and Cox, 1978). But another study, which included children whose fathers had been granted custody after the divorce, found that in these families, problems were more likely among girls than among boys (Santrock and Warshak, 1979). Although more studies in this area are needed, it seems from these investigations that adjusting to divorce may be easier for children who live with the parent of the same sex following their parents' separation.

Short-term and long-term consequences. Changes in the family usually have more serious short-term than long-term consequences. Therefore, in studying children's reactions to events such as divorce, it is important to take into account how long it is since the event occurred. Psychologist E. Mavis Hetherington (1981), who has conducted the most extensive study of divorce to date, notes that the impact of divorce on children occurs in two phases. The first phase concerns the crisis of the divorce itself, and the short-term adjustment of the child is linked to the degree and nature of this crisis. If the divorce is extremely painful, for example, children react much more poorly to it. But if the divorce actually ends a long period of family conflict and stress, children may be better off. Sometimes, divorce provides needed stability to a family that has lived with tense relationships and uncertainty about the future for a long time. Even under the best of circumstances, however, most families go through a period of at least one year following a divorce in which they experience some distress and tension.

Problems that may result from a father's absence are more likely to affect boys than girls. Studies indicate that maintaining contact with the father after a divorce generally benefits the adolescent boy's development. Unfortunately, by two years after a divorce, most children living with their mother seldom see their father. (Rae Russel)

The second phase of the child's experience depends on the nature of his or her life in the one-parent family after divorce. Actually, the long-term adjustment of a child to his or her parents' divorce depends more on the conditions he or she experiences in the household *after* the divorce than on the divorce itself (Hetherington, 1981). Children whose families remain economically well-off, whose parents adjust well to the divorce, and who have people to turn to for support display few divorce-related problems in the long run.

The parents' response.   How parents react to a change in the family is also an important mediator of the impact of the change on the adolescent. As noted above, children whose working mothers enjoy their combination of work and family roles are themselves more likely to feel positively about mothers working and to benefit developmentally from it. Similarly, children are least likely to be harmed by divorce if conflict between their parents is minimal, if the parents maintain a friendly and cooperative relationship following the separation, if the parents themselves have sufficient emotional and economic support, and if both parents remain involved in the children's upbringing (Hetherington, 1981; Wallerstein and Kelley, 1980). In general, the degree of conflict between adolescents' parents is a better predictor of the adolescents' adjustment than is divorce in and of itself. Indeed, persistent marital conflict in intact homes may be worse for the child than divorce (Peterson and Zill, 1986). Most researchers agree that conflict, more than parental separation, contributes to maladjustment among children whose parents divorce (Hetherington and Camara, 1984).

When fathers are absent, the mother's response has a very important impact on the child. One study found, for example, that girls who experience father absence through divorce are likely to be affected differently than those who lose their fathers through death, because widows and divorcees communicate very different messages about their former spouses (Hetherington, 1972). A divorcee is far more likely to communicate bitterness and unhappiness to her daughter, which may make the girl believe that life without a man is a terrible fate. A widow, in contrast, may make her daughter feel that no man can live up to her father. Of the two groups, girls whose fathers had died felt more positively about their fathers but were most likely to be shy and withdrawn around males. The girls whose parents had been divorced felt less positively about their fathers but were most likely to seek out the company of males.

Although several studies indicate that contact with one's father after a divorce is beneficial to psychological development, the sad truth is that for most children, divorce means a genuine loss of their father. By two years after a divorce, most children living with their mother see their father rarely or not at all (Furstenberg et al., 1983). This may have especially adverse effects on adolescent boys.

Special Problems of Adolescents in Stepfamilies

Although it is difficult to make sweeping generalizations about the impact of divorce, single parenthood, or maternal employment on the development of the adolescent, several recent studies indicate that adolescents growing up in stepfamilies—especially if the remarriage has occurred during early adolescence rather than childhood—may have more problems than their peers (Zill, 1984). For example, youngsters growing up in single-parent homes are more

likely than those in intact homes to be involved in delinquent activity, but adolescents in stepfamilies are even more at risk for this sort of problem behavior than are adolescents in single-parent families (Dornbusch et al., 1985). Early adolescents in stepfamilies also are more susceptible to pressure from their peers to commit delinquent acts than are other youngsters (Steinberg, 1987d).

In general, remarriage affects adolescent girls more adversely than boys (Peterson and Zill, 1986). Most stepfamilies consist of a biological mother and a stepfather, and girls may have more problems following their mother's remarriage because the arrival of the stepfather threatens the close mother-daughter bond that may have developed when the mother was single. Among boys, in contrast, remarriage may mean that an important role model enters the household. As noted earlier, boys appear to suffer more after divorce when they do not have a male role model (Biller, 1981).

According to one study (Garbarino et al., 1984), adolescents in stepfamilies may be especially vulnerable to child abuse. You may know that child abuse is a significant national problem, but did you know that nearly half of all reported cases involve adolescents? According to a survey conducted by the National Center on Child Abuse, adolescent maltreatment accounts for 47 percent of the known cases of abuse and neglect—even though adolescents account for only 38 percent of the American population under the age of 18 (Garbarino, Sebes, and Schellenbach, 1984). If you were surprised to learn this, you are not alone; most professionals working in this area do not realize that child abuse may disproportionately involve teenagers.

Research on adolescent maltreatment is only now beginning. One study, by James Garbarino and his colleagues, points to several factors that may make a family "high-risk" for adolescent abuse: High-risk families are more likely to have stepparents and are less likely to have flexible, appropriately structured patterns of family relationships. Moreover, adolescents in families at risk for abuse and neglect are more likely to have undergone a series of stressful changes within the preceding twelve months (often, the parents' divorce), to suffer from a variety of developmental problems, and to be less socially competent.

Remarriage during the adolescent years may be extremely stressful when families are unable to accommodate the new stepparent relationship. Given what we know about family reorganization and change during adolescence, having to integrate a new type of relationship into a family system that is already undergoing a great deal of change may be more than some families can cope with. Many adolescents find it difficult to adjust to a new authority figure moving into the household, especially if that person has different ideas about rules and discipline. This appears to be especially true when the adolescent in question is already somewhat vulnerable, either because of previous psychological problems or because of a very recent divorce or other stressful event. By the same token, many stepparents find it difficult to join a family and not be accepted immediately by the children as the new parent. Stepparents may wonder why love is not forthcoming from their stepchildren. In extreme cases, relationships between adolescents and stepparents can become so strained that family violence results. Although many stepfathers and their adolescent stepchildren do establish positive relations, the lack of a biological connection between stepparent and stepchild, coupled with the stresses associated with divorce and remarriage, may make this relationship especially vulnerable to problems.

The findings of Garbarino's research underscore the need—particularly as remarriage becomes a more common part of American family life—to understand the special problems that may arise in the course of family reorganization. As our understanding of stepfamily relationships grows, it should become easier to anticipate stepfamily problems before they occur, prepare families in the process of reorganization for the

transition they are about to make, and provide special services for families who need help.

THE "GENERATION GAP"

One of the most frequently asked questions in the study of families during adolescence concerns **intergenerational conflict,** or as it is more commonly known, the "generation gap." In what sense is there a gap between adolescents and their parents, and how wide is it? In order to answer these questions, it is important to distinguish among family relationships, values and attitudes, and personal tastes. In some of these respects, there is indeed a schism between the generations. But in others, there is not.

If we consider the quality of adolescents' *relationships* with their parents, we find that there is very little gap between young people and their elders. Study after study on this issue has shown that although some adolescents and their parents have serious interpersonal problems, the overwhelming majority of adolescents feel close to their parents, respect their parents' judgment, feel that their parents love and care about them, and have a lot of respect for their parents as individuals (Kandel and Lesser, 1972; Offer, Ostrov, and Howard, 1981; Sorensen, 1973). In one study, for example, three-quarters of the adolescent respondents agreed with the statements, "I can count on my parents most of the time" and "When I grow up and have a family, it will be in at least a few ways similar to my own" (Offer, Ostrov, and Howard, 1981). If intergenerational conflict exists, it is not of the sort that seriously affects the quality or closeness of most adolescents' family relationships.

When we look at intergenerational differences in *values and attitudes,* we also find little evidence in support of a generation gap—or at least, of a schism as large as many people have been led to believe exists. Adolescents and their parents have similar beliefs about the importance of hard work, about educational and occupational ambitions, and about the personal

Contrary to myth, the overwhelming majority of young people feel close to their parents, respect their parents' judgment, and feel that their parents love and care about them. The notion that severe intergenerational conflict is common during adolescence is largely a misconception. (Erika Stone)

characteristics and attributes they feel are important and desirable (Conger, 1977a). In some areas, there exist attitudinal differences between teenagers and adults, but these differences do not appear to be any greater than those that exist within the adult or adolescent populations themselves. Indeed, when it comes to more basic values—concerning religion, work, education, and the like—diversity within the adolescent population is much more striking than are differences between the generations. Socioeconomic background, for instance, has a much stronger influence on individuals' values and attitudes than does age, and adolescents are more likely to share their parents' values than those of other teenagers who are from a different background. Wealthy adolescents growing up in affluent suburbs, for example, have educational and career plans that resemble their parents' plans for them, and their plans are very different from those of poor adolescents growing up in less prosperous areas (Conger, 1977a).

In matters of *personal taste* there is somewhat of a gap between the generations. It is most clearly seen in styles of dress, preferences in music, and patterns of leisure activity. Adolescents are more likely to be influenced by their friends than by their parents in these matters, and as a consequence, disagreements and differences in opinion between old and young often result. Indeed, it is over these matters that much of the bickering that occurs in families takes place (Montemayor, 1983). A mother and her daughter may argue about such things as the daughter's curfew, how the daughter spends her spare time, whether the daughter keeps her room clean enough, or what sorts of clothes the daughter wears. Unlike values, which develop gradually over time and are shaped from an early age, preferences and tastes are far more transitory and subject to the immediate influences of the social environment. Because adolescents spend a great deal of time with their friends (and because a good deal of that time is spent in social activities in which taste in clothes, music, etc., is especially important) teenagers' tastes are likely to be shaped to a large measure by forces outside the family.

The Myth of the Generation Gap

The notion that conflict between the generations is not characteristic of adolescence may seem surprising to you. After all, we have been hearing about the generation gap for a long time now. If the gap is not as great or as extensive as we have been led to believe—if the generation gap is a myth—to what can we attribute the perpetuation of the idea? Scholars point to three sources of confusion (Adelson, 1970; Bandura, 1964).

First, many observers have failed to make the distinction that has been made here—among relationships, values, and tastes. Because parents and adolescents may argue over matters of dress, for example, some people have taken this as an indication that family relationships are strained, distant, or conflict-ridden. But as you well know, people are perfectly capable (or at least, they ought to be) of disagreeing about things without such disagreements changing what they have in common or how they feel about each other. Moreover, because it is during adolescence that individuals develop the capacity to reason in highly sophisticated ways, it is often not until adolescence that children are willing (or able) to engage in the sorts of arguments that may be labeled problematic. As noted in an earlier chapter, individuals do not become more argumentative at adolescence—they merely become better arguers.

Second, many observers have viewed adolescents as a far more homogeneous group than they really are. A picture of young people has been presented that ignores the considerable diversity existing within this age group. It is difficult to draw simple generalizations about differences between adolescents and their parents, because it is difficult to draw generalizations about adolescents as a group. During the early 1970s, many writers, interested in demonstrating that a generation gap existed, compared the views of East and West Coast college students with those of working-class adults from Middle America. Interviewers contrasted the views of politically active Harvard and Berkeley students with those of factory workers from Pittsburgh or farmers from Nebraska. Not surprisingly, they found considerable differences in the groups' views. Had they compared adolescents and adults from similar environments—the Berkely students with affluent adults living in San Francisco or the Nebraska farmers with agriculture majors at the University of Nebraska—they would have found far less divergence (Conger, 1981).

Third, there has been a tendency in writing about the nature of adolescent-parent relationships to extrapolate findings based on studies of emotionally disturbed and delinquent adolescents to adolescents as a whole (Hill and Steinberg, 1976). Young people with psychological and social problems often have strained family relationships (Offer, Ostrov, and Howard, 1981)—which is not surprising, considering that family problems may lead to, or result from, adolescents' emotional and behavioral difficulties. Without minimizing the very real problems that some young people and their parents have, it is important to emphasize that adolescents with psychological and social problems make up a very small minority of young people and that drawing conclusions about *all* adolescents' family relationships from this highly visible, but highly unrepresentative, sample can be quite misleading. To be sure, there are times when adolescents and parents have their problems. But so are there times when younger children and their parents have problems and when adults and their parents do also. To date, no studies demonstrate that family problems are any more likely to occur during adolescence than at other times in the life span. Most systematic studies indicate that among the 25 percent of teenagers and parents who report having problems, about 80 percent had problematic relations during childhood (Rutter et al., 1976). Thus only about 5 percent of families who enjoy positive relations during childhood can expect to develop serious problems during adolescence.

CHANGES IN THE FAMILY AT ADOLESCENCE

Although it is incorrect to characterize adolescence as a time of conflict in most families, it is important to keep in mind that adolescence is a period of change and reorganization in family relationships. It is to these processes of change and reorganization in the adolescent's family that we now turn.

The Family as a System

You may remember from high school science classes that living organisms and their environments function as systems. All living systems attempt to maintain *equilibrium*, or balance.

When a change takes place that upsets this balance, the system responds by doing something to restore the equilibrium that existed previously. A change in an ecological niche, such as a forest, will provoke a series of changes among the flora and fauna living in the environment. If a new species of animal migrates into a forest, for instance, other animals' feeding habits will change, and in turn, plant life will be affected. These changes generally have the effect of maintaining the system's natural equilibrium.

The family is a system, too—a system in which relationships change in response to the changing needs and concerns of family members and in response to changes in the family's relationship with the larger society (Minuchin, 1974). And like other systems, families attempt to maintain a sense of equilibrium in their relationships. Certain implicit understandings develop within families—concerning which family members have decision-making power, how much privacy different individuals can expect to have, how much freedom and control each family member has, and the like—and these understandings form the unwritten rules according to which the system operates. Family members may not be aware of the rules under which their family works, but outsiders are usually able to see what sorts of principles and norms a family system follows.

The tendency for family systems to try to maintain their established patterns of behavior is challenged from time to time by changes to which they must adapt. When someone new moves into the household, the members of the system must find a way to reorganize and reestablish workable types of relationships and patterns of activity. (This is one of the difficulties families have following a divorce or remarriage, for example.) And when a family member changes in one way or another—psychologically or emotionally, for example—the change usually has reverberations throughout the family system.

Often, following a change in a family system, the family goes through a period of imbalance, or *disequilibrium*, before it adjusts to the change. These periods of disequilibrium can be difficult for families. They may sense that old ways of relating to one another are no longer working, but they may not realize why. Establishing new ways of dealing with one another may take some time (Steinberg, 1988). Only after a new and different equilibrium is established may the family feel comfortable again.

Relationships in families always change most dramatically during those times when individual family members are changing or when the family's circumstances are changing, since it is during these times that the family's previously established equilibrium will be upset. During these times, it is *healthy* for family relationships to change, for through such changes families restore balance to the system. Not surprisingly, one period in which family relationships usually change a great deal is adolescence.

The Life Cycle of Families

A family in its "infancy" is different from a family in its "adolescence." Like individuals, families move through a life cycle, a **family life cycle**—that is, various developmental phases in which new issues arise and different concerns predominate (Rodgers, 1973). During the first years of marriage, for example, families focus nearly all of their energy on establishing a household, finding suitable employment, and strengthening the marital relationship. During the child-bearing stage, the family's concerns shift to taking care of their young children. Families are likely to have higher medical expenses, more debts in general, and concerns about managing work and family commitments. During the "launching" stage, when children begin leaving home, families are usually less strained financially, and their concerns shift to reorganizing the household in response to their children's departure. Each stage of the family life cycle is different from those that came before and those that will follow. The life cycle of families is presented in Figure 4.4

The concerns and issues characteristic of families at adolescence arise not just because of

Adolescence is a time of changes in family relationships, as the family adjusts to the developing capabilities and changing concerns of parents and children. Although it need not be a time of difficulty, it is often a time of restructuring and altering previously established patterns of interaction. (Rae Russel)

the changing needs and concerns of the young person, but also because of changes in the adolescent's parents and because of changes in the needs and functions of the family as a unit. Consequently, in order to understand the changing nature of family relationships during the adolescent years, we must take into account not only characteristics of the developing young person, but characteristics of the adolescent's parents and of families at this stage as well.

The Adolescent's Parents at Midlife

The typical parent is between 35 and 45 years old during much of his or her first child's early adolescent years (Troll, 1975). It is important therefore to consider psychological development during this period of adulthood and ask how the concerns characteristic of this age may contribute to the changing nature of family relationships at adolescence. Only recently have those interested in human development begun to pay

attention to development during the middle adult years, but a growing body of evidence suggests that the decade between 35 and 45 is a potentially difficult time for many adults. Indeed, some theorists have gone so far as to describe it as a time of "midlife" crises (Farrell and Rosenberg, 1981; Levinson, 1978).

If we look at the nature of these midlife crises in some detail, we find that the developmental concerns of parents and adolescents are complementary (Steinberg, 1988b). First, consider the issue of biological change. At the same time that adolescents are entering into a period of rapid physical growth, sexual maturation, and ultimately, the period of the life span that society has labeled one of the most physically attractive, their parents are beginning to feel increased concern about their own bodies, about their physical attractiveness, and about their sexual appeal. In one cross-sectional study of adults of different ages, the proportion of individuals agreeing with the statement, "My greatest concern is my

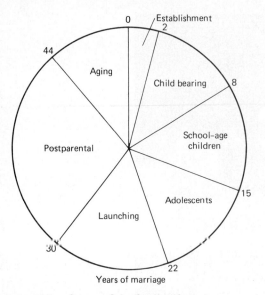

FIGURE 4.4   Stages of the family life cycle.

health," increased markedly at age 35 (Gould, 1972).

A second overlap of crises concerns perceptions of time and the future. At the same time that adolescents are beginning to develop the capability to think systematically about the future and do, in fact, begin to look ahead, their parents are beginning to feel that the possibilities for change are limited. While adolescents' ideas about the future are becoming more expansive, their parents' ideas are probably becoming more limited. Bernice Neugarten, who has studied adult personality development extensively, suggests that an important shift in time perspective takes place during midlife: before this phase in the life cycle, we tend to measure time in terms of how long we have been alive; after midlife, we are more likely to see things in terms of how much longer we have to live (Neugarten, 1975). One reason for this shift may be that midlife adults are reminded of their mortality because they see their own parents aging.

Finally, consider the issue of power, status, and entrance into the roles of adulthood. Adolescence is the time when individuals are on the threshold of gaining a great deal of status. Their careers and marriages lie ahead of them, and choices seem limitless. For their parents, in contrast, many choices have already been made—some successfully, others perhaps less so. Most adults reach their occupational plateau—the point at which they can tell how successful they are likely to be—during midlife, and many must deal with whatever gap exists between their early aspirations and their actual achievements (Gould, 1972). In sum, for adolescents, this phase in the family life cycle is a time of boundless horizons; for their parents, it is a time of coming to terms with choices made when they were younger.

This overlap of crises is likely to have an impact on family relationships. Together, the crises disrupt patterns of activity and interaction, and they often require new sorts of relationships. A father who is worried about his own physical health suddenly feels uncomfortable about playing tennis each weekend with his growing son, as they did for years when the son was younger. They may have to find new activities that they can share together. An adolescent girl with big plans for the future finds it difficult to understand why her father seems so cautious and narrow-minded when she asks him for advice. She may react by turning to her friends more often. An adolescent boy finds his mother's constant attention annoying; he doesn't see that to her, his interest in independence signifies the end of an important stage in her career as a parent. In fact, the adolescent's desire for autonomy in particular may be especially stressful for parents (Small et al., in press). While none of these situations may cause family conflict, each requires a period of adjustment on the part of parents and their children.

Although many theorists have speculated that parents' mental health at midlife is affected by the development of their adolescent children, few studies have examined this issue directly. One exception is found in the work of psychologist Susan Silverberg (Silverberg and Steinberg, 1987; Silverberg and Steinberg, in press; Steinberg and Silverberg, 1987). According to

For many adults, midlife is a time of heightened introspection and personal reevaluation. Because many parents are at this stage in the life cycle when their children are teenagers, the so-called "midlife crisis" of adulthood may coincide with the "identity crisis" of adolescence. (Ellis Herwig/Stock, Boston)

these studies, parents may be somewhat adversely affected by the transition of their child into adolescence, especially if the child is of the same sex. Mothers of daughters and fathers of sons, for example, show more psychological distress, report less satisfaction with their marriage, and experience more intense midlife identity concerns as their children begin to mature physically, get involved in dating relationships, and distance themselves from their parents emotionally. Interestingly, however, her studies indicate that parents who are deeply involved in work outside the home may be buffered against some

of these negative consequences. Having a satisfying job may help parents more successfully negotiate the family's transition into their child's adolescence.

Changes in Family Needs and Functions During Adolescence

It is not only individual family members who undergo change during the family's adolescent years. The family as a unit changes as well in its economic circumstances, its relationship to other social institutions, and its functions. One of the most important changes undergone by the family during adolescence is financial: Family finances are likely to be strained during adolescence. Children grow rapidly during puberty, and clothing for adolescents is expensive. Keeping up with the accoutrements of the peer culture—the records, cosmetics, and high-priced home video and stereo equipment—may push a family budget to the limit. Many families also begin saving money for large anticipated expenditures, such as the adolescent's college education. And in some families, parents may find themselves having to help support their own parents at a time when their children are still economically dependent. These financial demands require adjustment on the part of the family system, and they may prompt changes in patterns of consumption, activity, work, and household schedules. In some families, for instance, the mother may return to full-time work solely to earn money for her child's college expenses.

In addition to these financial pressures, the adolescent's family must cope with the increasing importance of two new contexts in which the young person spends time and invests energy: the peer group and, later in adolescence, the workplace. During the early stages of the life cycle, the child's social world is fairly narrow, and the family is the central setting. As the child grows, the school begins to take on increased significance, and relationships and concerns revolving around school must be balanced with those revolving around the family. During late childhood and early adolescence, however, the peer group becomes a setting in which close ties are formed. Families may have a tough time adjusting to the adolescent's increasing interest in forgoing family activities for peer activities. They may have arguments about the teenager's reluctance to give up time with his or her friends for family outings.

Finally, important changes in family functions also take place during adolescence. During infancy and childhood, the functions and responsibilities of the family are fairly clear: nurturance, protection, and socialization. While all of these roles are still important during adolescence, adolescents are more in need of support than nurturance, of guidance than protection, of direction than socialization. Making the transition from the family functions of childhood to the family functions of adolescence is not necessarily easy, for the shift often upsets the equilibrium established during childhood. The transition is further complicated in contemporary society, where preparation for adulthood—one of the chief tasks of adolescence that was once carried out primarily by the family—is increasingly done by other institutions, such as the school. Many families may feel at a loss to figure out just what their role during adolescence is. A 16-year-old girl once told the author that she wasn't sure whether she needed her parents any more, now that she could drive and had a job at the local fast-food restaurant.

Transformations in Family Relations at Adolescence

Together, the biological, cognitive, and social changes of adolescence, the changes experienced by adults at midlife, and the changes undergone by the family during this stage in the family life cycle set in motion a series of transformations in family relationships. Think for a moment about the relationship between parents and a 12-year-old and that between parents and an 18-year-old. In most families, there is a movement during adolescence from patterns of influence and interaction that are asymmetrical and unequal to ones in which parents and their adolescent children are on a more equal footing. And there is some evidence that early adolescence—when this shift toward more egalitarian relationships first begins—may be a time of temporary disequilibrium in the family system.

One study, by psychologist Theodore Jacob (1974), compared family interaction in the families of 11-year-old boys with interaction in the families of 16-year-old boys. He asked family groups to discuss a series of problems and reach consensus on how best to deal with them. The problems were designed to elicit a wide range of responses from adolescents and their parents. One problem, for example, asked families to decide how best to determine an adolescent's curfew. The discussions were taped, and the patterns of family interaction were examined. Jacob found that 11-year-olds were less influential than 16-year-olds (they had less influence over the family's ultimate decisions), but that the younger boys were more assertive in family discussion than the older ones (for example, they interrupted their parents more often). These findings suggest that early adolescence may be a time during which young people begin to try to play a more forceful role in the family but when parents may not yet acknowledge the adolescents' input. As a result, young adolescents may interrupt their parents more often but have little impact. By middle adolescence, however, teenagers act and are treated much more like adults. They have more influence over family decisions, but they do not need to assert their opinions through interruptions and similarly immature behavior.

Increases in the assertiveness and influence of adolescents as they get older are consistent with their changing needs and capabilities. It is adaptive for families to permit these changes to happen, because it is through such changes that adolescents learn to be more mature and independent. In fact, there is some evidence that families who resist making changes in their patterns of interaction during adolescence are more likely to experience such problems as juvenile delinquency (Alexander, 1973). This further corroborates the idea that family systems must be able to adapt when changes in family members or family circumstances make such adaptation necessary. Like the birth of a child, divorce, family crises, or other events that require adjustment, the beginning of adolescence may disrupt a delicate balance formed in the family system during childhood and challenge family members to develop new ways of interacting.

Two recent series of studies indicate that the adolescent's biological and cognitive maturation may play a role in unbalancing the family system during early adolescence. Several researchers have demonstrated that family relationships change during puberty, with conflict between adolescents and their parents increasing—especially between adolescents and their mothers—and closeness between adolescents and their parents diminishing somewhat (Hill et al., 1985a, 1985b; Papini and Sebby, 1987; Susman et al., 1987; Steinberg, 1981, 1987, 1988). Although puberty seems to distance adolescents from their parents, it is not associated with familial "storm and stress." The conflict is more likely to take the form of bickering over day-to-day issues like household chores than outright fighting. Similarly, the diminished closeness is more likely to be manifested in increased privacy on the part of the adolescent and diminished physical affection between teenagers and parents, rather than any serious loss of love or respect between parents and children (Montemayor, 1983; 1986). Research suggests that the distancing effect of puberty is temporary, though, and that relationships may become less conflicted and more intimate during late adolescence. In any event, it does appear that early adolescence may be a somewhat more strained time for the family than earlier or later. This finding is consistent with both Freudian and social-learning views of the family at adolescence, which both predict that puberty loosens emotional ties between parents and teenagers.

A different perspective on transformations in family relations emphasizes the changing cognitive capabilities of the adolescent. Psychologist Judith Smetana (1988) has looked at how the adolescent's changing social cognitive abilities (see Chapter 2) may affect parent-child relations. She finds that conflicts between teenagers and parents may result from their different approaches to defining and understanding points of contention. One common source of disagreement between teenagers and parents concerns keeping the teenager's room clean. A mother may nag her adolescent to clean up her room. But, as Smetana points out, the teenager may define the issue as a personal one ("It's my room, and I'll clean it if I want to"), while the mother may define it in broader terms ("This is a family, and we all have responsibilities around the house to keep it a nice place for all of us to live"). You can well imagine that little negotiation can take place between two people who define the same issue in such different terms, and that is indeed what happens in many families. As adolescents' social-cognitive abilities increase, however, they come to be able to see things in broader terms and find it easier to take their parent's perspective. According to Smetana, we can better understand transformations in the parent-child relationship by looking at the ways in which parents' and adolescents' reasoning change over time.

FAMILY RELATIONSHIPS AND ADOLESCENT DEVELOPMENT

Thus far we have looked at the sorts of issues and concerns faced by families during the adolescent years. We have seen that adolescence is not usually a time of dire conflict in most households, but we have also seen that families must be able to adapt to the social and psychological changes that arise at this time in the family life cycle.

In our focus on those experiences that all families share, however, we have not addressed the very important questions of how relationships differ from family to family and whether these differences have important consequences for the developing adolescent. Some parents are stricter than others. Some adolescents are given a great deal of affection, while others are treated more distantly. In some households, decisions are made through open discussion and verbal give-and-take, while in others, parents lay down the rules and children are expected to follow them. To what extent are different patterns of family relationships associated with different patterns of adolescent development? Are some styles of parenting more likely to be associated with healthy development than others?

In this section, we look at variations in parenting practices and their correlates in adoles-

cent behavior. But before we turn to this issue, an important caveat is in order.

Most of the studies of this subject are correlational; that is, they provide information about what sorts of parenting practices are *associated with* various patterns of adolescent development. But correlational studies cannot say whether certain types of parenting practices *lead to* certain adolescent behaviors. That is an entirely different matter. Although the tendency is to see child behavior as the result of parent behavior, socialization is actually a two-way, not a one-way, street (Bell, 1968). It is a known fact, for example, that parents who employ physical punishment (spanking, hitting, etc.) are more likely to have aggressive adolescents (Bandura and Walters, 1959). But we cannot be sure whether (1) physical punishment leads to adolescent aggression; (2) adolescent aggression leads to parents using physical punishment; (3) some other factor is correlated with parents using physical punishment and with adolescent aggression (a genetic predisposition to behave aggressively that adolescents inherit from their parents); or (4) some combination of these causal and correlational factors is at work. Thus when we look at the findings concerning parenting practices and adolescent development, we must keep in mind that just as parents affect their adolescents' behavior, so do adolescents affect their parents' behavior.

Variations in Parenting Styles and Their Impact on Adolescent Development

There are a variety of ways to characterize parents' behavior toward their children. One of the most useful approaches derives from the work of psychologist Diana Baumrind (in preparation). According to her work and that of others in this vein, two aspects of the parent's behavior toward the adolescent are critical: *parental responsiveness* and *parental demandingness* (Maccoby and Martin, 1983). Responsiveness refers

Working-class parents tend to place more emphasis on obedience in raising their children than do middle-class parents. One reason is that obedience is adaptive in working-class settings; a successful laborer is one who can take orders. (Leonard Speier)

to the degree to which the parent responds to the child's needs in an accepting, supportive manner. Demandingness refers to the extent to which the parent expects and demands mature, responsible behavior from the child. Parents vary on each of these dimensions. Some are warm and accepting while others are unresponsive and rejecting; some are demanding and expect a great deal of their child while others are permissive and demand very little.

Because responsiveness and demandingness are more or less independent of each other— that is, it is possible for a parent to be very demanding without being responsive and vice versa—it is possible to look at various combinations of these *two* dimensions (see Figure 4.5). Many studies of parents and children indicate that the fourfold classification scheme presented in Figure 4.5 is very important in understanding the impact of parents' behavior on the child, and psychologists have given labels to the four different prototypes presented in the table. A parent who is very responsive but not at all demanding is labeled *indulgent,* whereas one who

is equally responsive but also very demanding is labeled *authoritative.* Parents who are very demanding but not responsive are *authoritarian;* parents who are neither demanding nor responsive are labeled *indifferent.* These four general patterns are described below:

Authoritative parents are warm but firm. They set standards for the child's conduct but form expectations that are consistent with the child's developing needs and capabilities. They place a high value on the development of autonomy and self-direction but assume the ultimate responsibility for their child's behavior. Authoritative parents deal with their child in a rational, issue-oriented manner, frequently engaging in discussion and explanation with their children over matters of discipline.

Authoritarian parents place a high value on obedience and conformity. They tend to favor more punitive, absolute, and forceful disciplinary measures. Verbal give-and-take is not common in authoritarian households, because the underlying belief of authoritarian parents is that the child should accept without question the rules and stan-

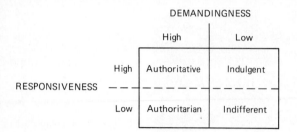

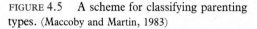

FIGURE 4.5   A scheme for classifying parenting types. (Maccoby and Martin, 1983)

dards established by the parents. They tend not to encourage independent behavior and, instead, place a good deal of importance on restricting the child's autonomy.

Indulgent parents behave in an accepting, benign, and somewhat more passive way in matters of discipline. They place relatively few demands on the child's behavior, giving the child a high degree of freedom to act as he or she wishes. Indulgent parents are more likely to believe that control is an infringement on the child's freedom that may interfere with the child's healthy development. Instead of actively shaping their child's behavior, indulgent parents are more likely to view themselves as resources which the child may or may not use.

Indifferent parents try to do whatever is necessary to minimize the time and energy that they must devote to interacting with their child. In extreme cases, indifferent parents may be neglectful. They know little about their child's activities and whereabouts, show little interest in their child's experiences at school or with friends, rarely converse with their child, and rarely consider their child's opinion when making decisions. Rather than raising their child according to a set of beliefs about what is good for the child's development (as do the other three parent types) indifferent parents are "parent-centered"—they structure their home life primarily around their own needs and interests.

The categorization proposed by Baumrind provides a useful way of summarizing and examining some of the relations between parenting practices and adolescent psychosocial development. Generally speaking, young people raised in authoritative households are more psychoso-cially competent than peers who have been raised in authoritarian, indulgent, or indifferent homes: Adolescents raised in authoritative homes are more responsible, self-assured, adaptive, creative, curious, and socially skilled. Adolescents raised in authoritarian homes, in contrast, are more dependent, more passive, less socially adept, less self-assured, and less intellectually curious. Adolescents raised in indulgent households are often less mature, more irresponsible, more conforming to their peers, and less able to assume positions of leadership. Adolescents raised in indifferent homes are often impulsive and more likely to be involved in delinquent behavior and in precocious experiments with sex, drugs, and alcohol (Pulkkinen, 1982). In general, the effects of nonresponsiveness tend to be slightly worse among girls than boys, whereas the effects of nondemandingness tend to be slightly worse among boys than girls. Although occasional exceptions to these general patterns have been noted, the evidence linking authoritative parenting and healthy adolescent development is remarkably strong, and it has been found in studies of a wide range of ethnic and socioeconomic groups (Baumrind, 1978; Bronfenbrenner, 1961; Hill, 1980; Maccoby and Martin, 1983).

The parenting a child receives is put to its most rigorous test, perhaps, when the child comes under the increased influence of agemates. Many parents are understandably concerned about the likely impact of the peer group on their adolescent's behavior. They may feel at times that the work they have done as parents will be undone when the child is exposed to peer pressure. But research has consistently shown that adolescents from authoritative households are self-directed, autonomous, and self-assured—and remain so even in the face of strong peer pressure (Devereaux, 1970). In fact, there is a good deal of evidence indicating that adolescents who have positive family relationships—the kind promoted in authoritative households—seek peer groups that reaffirm, rather than contradict, their parents' values (Hill, 1980a).

Why is authoritative parenting associated with healthy adolescent development? First, authoritative parents provide a nice balance between restrictiveness and autonomy, which on the one hand provides the young person with opportunities to develop self-reliance but on the other hand sets the sorts of standards, limits, and guidelines that developing individuals need. The authoritative family is more able than other families to adjust to new stages of the family life cycle. Because authoritative parents are flexible in their approach to parenting, they tend to shape and tailor their demands and expectations to suit the changing needs and competencies of the adolescent, a process that is likely to help the young person's continued development (Hill, 1980). Authoritative parents, for instance, are more likely to give children more independence gradually as they get older, which helps children develop self-reliance.

Second, because authoritative parents are more likely to engage their children in verbal give-and-take, they are likely to promote the sort of intellectual development that provides an important foundation for the development of psychosocial competence. Family discussions in which decisions, rules, and expectations are explained help the child to understand social systems and social relationships. This understanding plays an important part in the development of reasoning abilities, role taking, moral judgment, and empathy (Baumrind, 1978). The extensive discussion characteristic of authoritative households stimulates the adolescent's thinking.

Third, because authoritative parenting combines moderate control with a good deal of warmth, children are more likely to identify with their parents. In fact, one of the strongest predictors of identification between children and their parents is warmth in the parent-child relationship. We are more likely to identify with and imitate people who treat us with warmth and affection. A child raised warmly by parents who value self-direction will imitate his or her mother and father and display a similar preference for independence (Hill, 1980).

Finally, the child's own behavior may play a role in shaping authoritative parenting practices (Lewis, 1981a). Children who are responsible, self-directed, curious, and self-assured elicit from their parents warmth, flexible guidance, and verbal give-and-take. In contrast, children who are aggressive, dependent, or less psychosocially mature in other ways may provoke parents' behavior that is excessively harsh, passive, or distant. Parents may enjoy being around children who are responsible and independent, for example, and may treat them more warmly. In contrast, children who are continually acting up make their parents short-tempered, impatient, or distant. In other words, the relationship between adolescent competence and authoritative parenting may be the result of a reciprocal cycle in which the child's psychosocial maturity leads to authoritative parenting, which in turn leads to the further development of maturity.

Individuality and Attachment in the Adolescent's Family

Several recent studies of verbal interaction between adolescents and their parents have examined factors in the parent-child relationship that contribute to healthy adolescent development. In these studies, families are asked to discuss a problem together, and their interaction is taped and later analyzed. Psychologists Catherine Cooper and Harold Grotevant (Cooper et al., 1983; Grotevant and Cooper, 1985, 1986) have noted that families with psychologically competent teenagers interact in ways that permit family members to express their individuality yet remain attached, or connected, to other family members. In these families, verbal give-and-take is the norm, and adolescents (as well as parents) are encouraged to express their own opinions. At the same time, however, the importance of maintaining close relationships in the family is emphasized, and individuals are encouraged to consider how their actions may affect other family members.

Rather than viewing attachment and autonomy as opposites, Cooper and Grotevant's stud-

The Sexes: Are There Sex Differences in Adolescents' Family Relationships?

One question frequently asked by researchers who study adolescents and their parents is whether and in what ways there may be sex differences in patterns of family relationships. Do daughters and sons have different sorts of relationships with their mothers and fathers? Now that several studies have been completed, we have a tentative answer to this question, and it is a surprising one.

In general, differences between the family relations of sons and daughters seem quite minimal. Although there are occasional exceptions to the rule, sons and daughters report similar degrees of closeness to their parents, similar amounts of conflict, similar types of rules (and disagreements about those rules), and similar patterns of activity (Hill and Holmbeck, 1987; Montemayor and Brownlee, 1987; Youniss and Ketterlinus, 1987). Observational studies of interaction between parents and adolescents indicate that sons and daughters interact with their parents in remarkably similar ways (Cooper and Grotevant, 1987; Hauser et al., 1987).

Does this mean that sex differences in the family are absent? Not entirely. These same studies also indicate that the sex of the adolescent's *parent* may be a more important influence on family relationships than the sex of the adolescent. Many studies suggest that teenagers—males and females alike—have very different types of relationships with mothers and fathers. One of the best of these studies was conducted by psychologists James Youniss and Jacqueline Smollar (1985). They found that adolescents tend to be closer to their mother than their father and feel more comfortable talking to their mother about problems and other emotional matters. Fathers are more likely to be perceived as relatively distant authority figures who may be consulted for "objective" information (such as help with homework) but who are rarely sought for support or guidance (such as help for problems with a boyfriend or girlfriend). Interestingly, adolescents also fight more often with their mothers than their fathers, but this higher level of conflict does not appear to jeopardize the closeness of the mother-adolescent relationship. It seems safe to say that relationships between adolescents and their mothers are more emotionally intense in general, and this intensity has both positive and negative manifestations.

ies as well as those of other researchers (Campbell et al., 1984; Litovsky and Dusek, 1985) indicate that the path to healthy psychological development is likely to combine the two. In other words, adolescents appear to do best when they grow up in a family atmosphere that permits the development of individuality against a backdrop of close family ties. In Chapter 10, we will look more closely at the nature of attachment between parents and adolescents.

Other researchers have also found that healthy adolescent development is associated with particular patterns of verbal interaction. Psychiatrist Stuart Hauser and his colleagues (Hauser et al., 1984) have drawn a distinction between "enabling" and "constraining" patterns of interchange in the family. Enabling interactions include explanation, problem solving, and empathy. Constraining interactions are distracting, judgmental, or devaluing of a family member's opinion. Not surprisingly, adolescents who grow up in homes to which the family tends to interact in enabling ways score higher on measures of psychological development than those

One of the most interesting findings to emerge from these studies concerns the father-daughter relationship in particular. Most researchers have found that this relationship is especially distant. Although we are not quite sure of the reasons—some theorists have speculated that unconscious taboos against incest may make it difficult for fathers and daughters to remain close after puberty, while others have suggested that the general emotional inexpressiveness of fathers may put daughters off more than sons (Youniss and Ketterlinus, 1987)—it seems clear that this relationship is the flattest, emotionally speaking, in the family. Whether and in what ways this may affect the daughter's development is not known.

Why should mothers and fathers have such different sorts of relationships with their adolescent children? One explanation concerns difference in the socialization of men and women. We know, for example, that women in Western cultures are socialized to be more emotionally expressive than men, and this may give them talents and capabilities that permit them to form closer relationships with their children. Growing up in a household in which mothers are emotionally accessible and fathers are emotionally distant only furthers this tendency, for this provides role models for adolescents to imitate. A somewhat different explanation concerns differences in the maternal and paternal roles. The mother's role in this culture traditionally has included more of an "expressive," or emotional, component, whereas the father's role may be more "instrumental" (Parsons, 1949). Moreover, until relatively recently, patterns of work and family life were so different for mothers and fathers that it may have been difficult for fathers—whatever their socialization—to form close relationships with their children. Mothers may be closer than fathers simply because they spend more time with their children as their children develop, and time together may foster and strengthen emotional bonds.

Whatever the explanation, however, the consistency with which studies of parents and adolescents uncover different patterns of relations for mothers and fathers is striking—especially in light of changes that have taken place in sex roles in contemporary society. Although we cannot be sure of the origins of these differences, we are fairly confident that they exist, even in today's families. In discussing the parent-adolescent relationship, we clearly need to pay attention to sex differences—not necessarily differences between sons and daughters, but between mothers and fathers.

who grow up in relatively more constraining families.

Adolescents' Relationships with Siblings

Far more is known about adolescents' relations with their parents than about their relations with brothers and sisters. In general, studies suggest that sibling relationships may have characteristics that set them apart from both other family relationships, such as that between adolescents and their parents, and other relationships with peers, such as those between adolescents and their close friends (Furman and Buhrmester, 1985; Raffaelli and Larson, 1987). In one study, for example, young adolescents were asked to rate several different types of relationships (for example, with parents, siblings, friends, grandparents) along similar dimensions. As you can see in Figure 4.6, sibling relationships were rated like those with parents for companionship and importance, but they were rated more like friendships with respect to power, assistance,

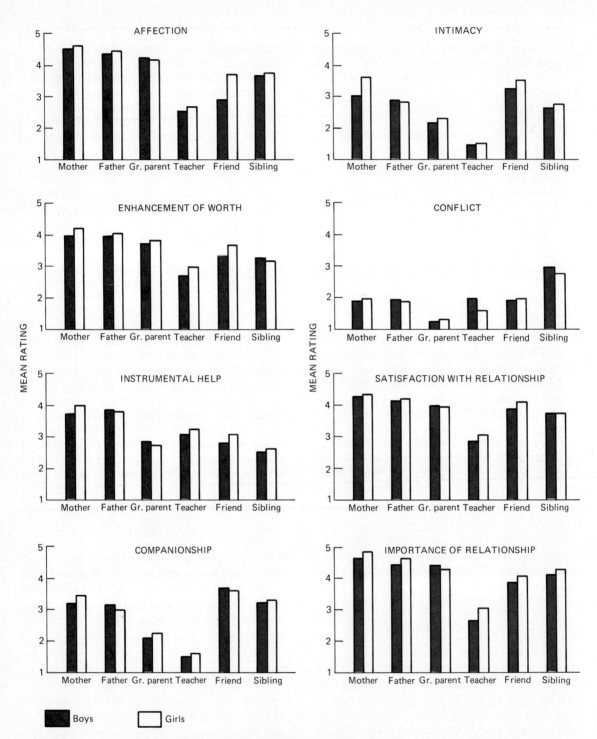

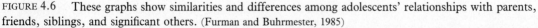

FIGURE 4.6   These graphs show similarities and differences among adolescents' relationships with parents, friends, siblings, and significant others. (Furman and Buhrmester, 1985)

and how satisfying the relationship is. One striking difference between sibling and other types of relationship involves conflict; adolescents report far higher levels of conflict with brothers and sisters than they do with anyone else. Because siblings live in close proximity to each other, they may have added opportunities for both positive and negative interaction.

One topic of interest to researchers interested in adolescents and their siblings concerns how closely siblings resemble each other in intelligence, personality, and interests. Because siblings share some genetic influences (because they have the same parents) and at least some environmental influences (because they have grown up in the same household), you might think that they would be more alike than different. But new research suggests that adolescents growing up in the same family are actually quite different from each other—far more than would be expected given their supposedly similar genetic and environmental histories. For example, siblings' scores on standard measures of personality traits are virtually uncorrelated (Plomin and Daniels, 1987). Indeed, the findings concerning differences between siblings are so consistent that one team of investigators wrote recently that "two children in the same family are as different from one another as are pairs of children selected randomly from the population" (Plomin and Daniels, 1987, p. 1).

Why might siblings be so different from each other? One explanation is offered by behavioral geneticists Robert Plomin and Denise Daniels (Plomin and Daniels, 1987; Daniels et al., 1985). They have found that siblings growing up in the same family experience their environment very differently. One brother may describe his family as very close-knit, while another may have experienced it as very distant. One girl describes her family life as plagued with argument and conflict; her sister describes it as peaceful and agreeable. In other words, even though we may assume that children growing up in the same family have shared the same environment, this may not really be the case.

Siblings may experience the same family environment differently for a variety of reasons. First, parents may treat their children differently because of their own conscious and unconscious preferences, differences in their children's temperaments, or changes in their child-rearing philosophies over time. Second, the family may itself be at different stages in its own development, and this may affect children differently. For instance, it may be different to be raised by older parents than by younger ones, and children born later in the family's history may have parents who treat them differently because of this. Finally, differences in the family's circumstances at different times may affect the way that siblings are raised. A child who is raised during a time of financial strain may have very different experiences from a sibling who grows up when the family is more comfortable.

Plomin and Daniels have found that siblings actually do describe their upbringings as very different and, moreover, that these differences in experiences are related to different patterns of development. In general, better adjusted adolescents were more likely than their siblings to report that their relationship with their mother was close, that their relations with brothers or sisters were friendly, that they were involved in family decision making, and that they were given a high level of responsibility around the house (Daniels et al., 1985).

Summary

Although discussions of adolescence and the family typically focus on how the family has been transformed in recent years, it is important to recognize that these transformations have not been accompanied by a decrease in the family's significance. Generally speaking, a combination of high warmth, moderate control, and reasoned decision making—a pattern that has come to be called *authoritative parenting*—is associated with healthy psychosocial development. Adolescents who are raised in authoritative homes are more self-directed, more socially adept, and more instrumentally competent than their peers.

Adolescence is typically portrayed as a time of strained family relationships, but this is not a very accurate picture. Adolescence, like other periods of the family life cycle, is a time of *changing* family relationships; however, these changes are not necessarily accompanied by conflict and tension. Rather, in healthy families, adolescents are encouraged to develop autonomy while remaining close and connected to their parents.

It is helpful to view the family as a system that must negotiate passages into successive stages of the family life cycle. Such transitions entail adjustment and adaptation, as families learn to accommodate to changes in individual family members and changes in the family's functions and circumstances. During early adolescence in particular, young people and their parents must cope with each other's developments. In general, parent-child relationships become more equal during adolescence, as adolescents come to play a more adult role in the family.

Less is known about adolescents' relations with their siblings than about their relations with parents. In general, sibling relations share in common elements of relationships with parents and with peers. Studies of sibling resemblance indicate that siblings are far more different from each other than one would expect. Although brothers and sisters grow up in the same family, they may have very different experiences, and these differences may contribute to different patterns of development.

Despite the temptation to make sweeping statements about the effects of the changing American family on adolescents, such generalizations tend to be of little use. The impact of various family structures on adolescent development can be understood only by examining a particular family unit and how the individuals' relationships have been affected by their circumstances. How adolescents and their parents respond to one another is more important than whether the family has one parent or two, a working mother or not. In a rapidly changing society such as that in the United States, an adolescent who has warm, concerned, and involved parents—whether they are married, divorced, or separated, and whether they are full-time workers or not—has one of the most important elements of a strong foundation that he or she will need to develop into a happy, capable, and caring adult.

Key Terms

authoritarian parenting
authoritative parenting
family life cycle

indifferent parenting
indulgent parenting
intergenerational conflict

For Further Reading

BAUMRIND, D. (1978). Parental disciplinary patterns and social competence in children. *Youth and Society, 9,* 239–276. Diana Baumrind discusses different patterns of child rearing and their effects on youngsters' development.

HETHERINGTON, E. M., and CAMARA, K. (1984).

Families in transition: The process of dissolution and reconstitution. In R. Parke (Ed.), *Review of child development research* (Vol. 7). Chicago: University of Chicago Press. A discussion of divorce and its impact on family and child development.

HILL, J. (1980). The family. In M. Johnson (Ed.), *Toward adolescence: The middle school years.* (Seventy-ninth Yearbook of the National Society for the Study of Education.) Chicago: University of Chicago Press. An extensive review of research on the family duirng adolescence.

STEINBERG, L. (ED.). (1987). Sex differences in family relations at adolescence. *Journal of Youth and Adolescence, 16* (3). Six recent studies of adolescents' family relationships.

Peer Groups

CHAPTER 5

PREVIEW

1. In contempory society, peer groups play an especially important role in the socialization of adolescents. Among the many factors that have contributed to the rise of adolescent peer groups in modern America are changes in the schools, changes in the workplace, and changes in family life.

2. One of the most hotly debated topics in the study of adolescence is whether the prominence of peer groups in contemporary society is harmful to the development of young people. Some social scientists have argued that American adolescents live in a "youth culture" that is dangerously separate from adult society. But others believe that modernization has made peer groups essential to the preparation of adolescents for adulthood.

3. The basic unit of the adolescent peer group is the clique. Cliques play an extremely important role in structuring adolescents' social activities. Generally, adolescents tend to associate with people who are from similar backgrounds and who share similar interests and attitudes.

4. The determinants of popularity during adolescence are different from the determinants of status, or leadership. Popular adolescents—like popular children and popular adults—are outgoing, friendly, and socially adept. Status in the peer group, in contrast, is much more dependent on being able to get things done that further the clique's goals.

5. Peers play a critical role in psychosocial development during adolescence. Problematic peer relationships are associated with a range of psychological and behavioral problems.

It is about 8:30 in the morning. A group of teen-agers congregate in the hallway in front of their first period classroom. They are discussing their plans for the weekend. As the first period bell sounds, they enter the classroom and take their seats. For the next 4 hours—until there is a break in their schedule for lunch—they will attend class in groups of about thirty—thirty adolescents to one adult.

At lunch, the clique meets again to talk about the weekend. They have about 45 minutes until the first afternoon period begins. After lunch, they spend another 2 hours in class—again, in groups of about thirty. The school day ends, and the clique reconvenes. They are going over to some-one's house to hang out for the rest of the day. Everyone's parents are working. They are on their own. At about 6 o'clock, they disperse and head home for dinner. A few will talk on the phone that night. Some will get together to study. They will see one another first thing the next morning.

When you stop to think about it, adoles-cents in modern society spend a remarkable amount of time with their peers. In fact, Amer-ican teenagers spend more time talking to their friends each day than in any other activity (Csikszentmihalyi, Larson, and Prescott, 1977). Virtually all adolescents spend most of each weekday with their peers while at school, and the vast majority also see or talk to their friends in the afternoon, in the evening, and over the weekend (Medrich et al., 1982). Even when ad-olescents work in part-time jobs, they are more likely to work with people their own age than with adults (Greenberger and Steinberg, 1986). And studies show that adolescents' moods are most positive when they are with their friends (Larson, 1983).

American society is very *age-segregated*. From the time youngsters enter school at the age of 5 until they graduate at age 18 or so, they are grouped with children their own age. They have little contact with people who are older or younger, outside of relatives. Because schools play such an important role in determining chil-dren's friendships, age grouping carries over into after-school, weekend, and vacation activi-ties. Little League, scouting, church groups—all are structured in a way that groups people together by age.

In contemporary society, **peer groups** have become an increasingly important context in which adolescents spend time. Modernization has led to more and more age segregation—in schools, in the workplace, and in the commu-nity. Today's teenagers spend far more time in the exclusive company of their peers than their counterparts did in the past. Indeed, the rise of peer groups in modern society gives adolescence in contemporary America some of its most dis-tinctive features. And the role of peers in shap-ing adolescent psychosocial development has be-come increasingly important.

For these reasons, understanding how ad-olescent peer groups form and what takes place within their boundaries is critical to understand-ing adolescent development in contemporary so-ciety. No discussion of adolescent identity de-velopment is complete without an examination of how and why teenagers derive part of their identity from the group they spend time with. No discussion of adolescent friendship is com-plete without an examination of teenagers' cliques and how they are formed. And no dis-cussion of adolescent sexuality is complete with-out an examination of how, and when, peer groups change from same-sex groups to mixed-sex groups.

In the previous chapter, by looking at the family *in context* and *as a context*, we were better able to understand how families affect the de-velopment of young people. Our discussion of peer groups follows a similar organization.

ADOLESCENT PEER GROUPS IN MODERN SOCIETY

Contact between adolescents and their peers is found in all cultures. But not all societies have peer groups that are as narrowly defined and age-segregated as those in modern-day America. While adolescent peer relationships are univer-sal, age-segregated peer groups are not. In ear-lier times, for example, interactions among

Even in activities outside of school, adolescents spend most of their time in age-segregated groups. (David S. Strickler)

youngsters occurred largely in the context of mixed-age groups composed of infants, children, and adolescents (Hartup, 1977). And much interaction among children occurred in the presence of their parents, because adults and children were not isolated from one another during the day. Even today, in societies that are less industrialized, young people spend a good part of the day in contact with their elders.

In contemporary America, however, age segregation is the norm. Indeed, the nature of adolescent psychosocial development in contemporary society cannot be understood without a full appreciation of just how prominent adolescents' peer groups are. Changes in the schools, changes in the workplace, and changes in the family have all led to the progressive separation of adolescents from adults and, consequently, to the rise of adolescent peer groups. Let's look at

some of these changes, which have contributed to making widespread age segregation a part of life in contemporary America.

Changes in the Schools

Educators first developed the idea of free public elementary education, with students grouped by age and achievement level, in the middle of the nineteenth century (President's Science Advisory Committee, 1974). In so doing, they established an arrangement that would eventually touch all American youngsters and encourage the development and maintenance of age-segregated peer groups. However, it was not until the second quarter of this century that most adolescents were directly affected by educational age grouping. Attending elementary school may have been common, but until 1930 or so, high school was a luxury available only to the very affluent. Thus adolescent peer groups based on friendships formed in school were not prevalent until fifty or sixty years ago.

We do not know for sure if not being in school hindered the development of adolescent peer groups. Perhaps peer groups were composed of young people living in the same neighborhood or working together. But we can be fairly certain that the forces encouraging adolescents to associate almost exclusively with people of exactly the same age were not as strong at the beginning of the century as they are today. Youngsters who were not in school were generally working and living at home, where they were likely to have a good deal of contact with adults and children (Modell, Furstenberg, and Hershberg, 1976). Even those youngsters from families wealthy enough to send their children to high school typically attended academies where children of different ages were mixed together, and it was not uncommon during the nineteenth century for "peer groups" to be composed of individuals ranging in age from 14 to 20 (President's Science Advisory Committee, 1974).

With the rise of free secondary education during the second quarter of this century, school attendance in age-grouped educational institutions became the norm for most American adolescents. Moreover, during the first part of the twentieth century, youth organizations—such as the Boy Scouts and other types of boys' clubs—became popular, which further segregated adolescents with same-aged or similarly aged peers (Kett, 1977; President's Science Advisory Committee, 1974). By 1930, then, adolescents were not only grouped with contemporaries during school hours, they were also encouraged to mix almost exclusively with peers during their spare time as well.

Today, virtually all American adolescents spend the years between ages 12 and 16 in age-grouped junior and senior high schools, and only 25 percent leave school before graduating at the age of 17 or 18 (Carnegie Commission on Policy Studies in Higher Education, 1980). The impact of this educational age grouping on adolescents' social life is dramatic. In one recent survey, in which seventh- through tenth-grade students were asked to list the people who were important to them, over two-thirds of the same-sex peers they mentioned were from the same grade in their school (Blyth, Hill, and Thiel, 1982). And participation in age-segregated organized activities—particularly among young adolescents—persists today. One recent study found that close to 80 percent of sixth-graders are involved in at least one nonschool club, extracurricular activity group, or youth organization in which they are likely to have contact only with peers of the same age (Medrich et al., 1982). Furthermore, more than half of all young people currently continue their education in colleges and universities,

Changes over the past 30 years in patterns of housing and employment have added to the separation of teenagers and adults. Many suburban neighborhoods are filled each weekday afternoon with people under the age of 18. (Paul Conklin/Monkmeyer)

many of which have fairly strong age groupings (although the groupings are not as narrowly defined as those in elementary or secondary schools). In short, as a result of changes in educational institutions over the last century, the vast majority of adolescents and youth in America now spend most of every weekday in the company of young people who, if not their exact age, are older or younger by very little.

Changes in the Workplace

A second set of factors related to the rise of adolescent peer groups during this past century concerns changes in the workplace, or more precisely, changes in the relationship between work and other aspects of daily life. With industrialization came more stringent and more carefully monitored child labor laws, which restricted ad-

olescents' participation in the world of work (Bakan, 1972). Because the implementation of tougher child labor laws coincided with the rise of secondary education, adolescents and adults (who had once shared the same daily activity—work) went their separate ways. Adolescents spent the day in school, adults at work.

In addition, the disappearance of the household as a workplace moved many adults who had been employed in family enterprises out of the home during the day and into work settings. Improvements in transportation made it possible for more and more adults to leave home each day and travel long distances to work; suburbs grew rapidly (see Figure 5.1). Thus home and work became geographically separated, and as a consequence, adolescents and adults saw less and less of each other. Between dawn and dusk each weekday, America's suburbs are filled with

FIGURE 5.1 Between 1960 and 1980, the shift of population in America has been toward suburban areas.

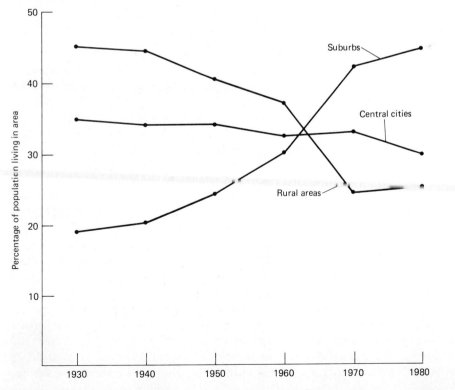

people under the age of 18. Not surprisingly, studies of adolescents' social ties show that suburban youngsters have fewer adult friends than do their urban or rural counterparts (Garbarino et al., 1978).

The segregation of adolescents from adults was also fueled by the rise in maternal employment. For example, the proportion of employed mothers of children between the ages of 6 and 17 living in two-parent households rose from 26 percent in 1948 to 68 percent in 1984. Among single mothers, whose numbers have grown rapidly during the last twenty-five years, labor-force participation rates have been even higher (U.S. Bureau of the Census, 1986). The movement of mothers out of the home and into the workplace furthered the trend, already set in motion by suburbanization, toward the development of residential neighborhoods dominated by young people during weekday mornings and afternoons. Today, between 2 and 4 million youngsters between the ages of 7 and 13—about 15 percent of all children in this age range—come home from school to houses with no adults present (Langway, Abramson, and Foote, 1981). In all likelihood, the proportion of so-called "latchkey" children among 14- to 18-year-olds is even higher, although precise figures are not available. Later in this chapter we examine how the changing nature of adolescents' after-school environment may affect their susceptibility to peer pressure.

Changes in the Family

The changes that have taken place in the structure of American family life during the last century were discussed in detail in Chapter 4. But it is worth mentioning them again briefly in the context of this discussion of adolescent peer groups because the two topics are closely related.

Perhaps the most important factor influencing the rise of adolescent peer groups was the dramatic growth of the teenage population during the 20-year period between 1955 and 1975. Following the end of World War II, many parents wanted to have children as soon as possible, creating what has come to be called the postwar "baby boom." The products of this baby boom became adolescents during the 1960s and early 1970s, creating an "adolescent boom" for about 15 years. As you can see from Figure 5.2, the size of the population aged 15 to 19 nearly doubled between 1955 and 1975 and, more important, rose from less than 7 percent of the total population to over 10 percent. During the mid-1970s, one out of every seven Americans was a teenager (United Nations, Population Division, 1976). One reason for the growth of peer groups, therefore, was the sheer increase in the number of peers that young people had. This trend, as you can see, turned downward in 1975, and the relative size of the adolescent population was projected to decrease until 1990. But during the last decade of this century—when the products of the baby boom have adolescents of their own, the size of the teenage population is expected to increase once again. In Chapter 13, we will look at one theory that links fluctuations in adolescent problems, such as crime and suicide, to changes in the size of the teenage population (Easterlin, 1980).

Adolescents also used to have much younger and older siblings than they do now. In most families today, only a few years separate most brothers and sisters. Today, the typical 15-year-old might have siblings who are 13 or 17. But 100 years ago, many infants died at birth or soon after, and as a result, children were spaced further apart. It was not uncommon for people to have siblings who were ten years younger or older than themselves (President's Science Advisory Committee, 1974). A 15-year-old might have had a 25-year-old brother or sister living at home. In other words, even within households, contact between adolescents and older individuals was more common in past eras than it is today.

Finally, the age at which young people establish a residence separate from their parents has dropped significantly over the past 100 years, from an average of about 27 to about 25 (in both cases, the age is slightly higher for

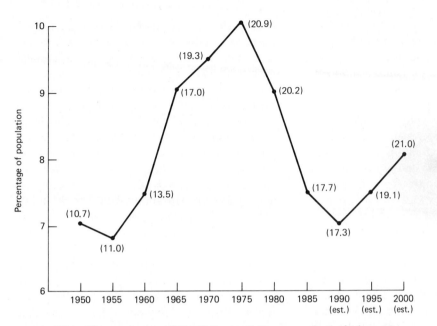

FIGURE 5.2   The percentage of the U.S. population comprised of 15- to 19-year-olds reached its highest level in 1975. It will begin to increase again by the turn of this decade. Figures in parentheses indicate the number of 15- to 19-year-olds, in millions. (From United Nations Population Division, 1976)

males, slightly lower for females [Modell, Furstenberg, and Hershberg, 1976]). Thus today's young people not only have less day-to-day contact with their parents than they did earlier in the century, they also move out of their parents' homes earlier.

THE ADOLESCENT PEER GROUP: A PROBLEM OR A NECESSITY?

There is no doubt about it: Peer groups play a more prominent role in adolescents' lives today than at any other time in history. But is the rise of peer groups in modern society a problem that needs to be remedied, or is it an inevitable—perhaps even necessary—part of life in contemporary America? This question has sparked some of the hottest arguments in the study of adolescence during the past twenty-five years.

On one side are those who say that age segregation has led to the development of a separate "youth culture," in which young people maintain attitudes and values that are different from—even contrary to—those of adults. On the other side are those who argue that industrialization and modernization have made peer groups more important, that adults alone can no longer prepare young people for the future, and that peer groups play a vital and needed role in the socialization of adolescents for adulthood. Let's look at both sides of the debate.

Is There a Separate Youth Culture?

Among the most vocal proponents of the view that age segregation has fueled the development of a separate—and troublesome—"youth culture" has been sociologist James Coleman, whose book *The Adolescent Society* (1961) presented the findings of an extensive study of the social worlds of ten American high schools. "Our adolescents are cut off, probably more than ever before, from the adult society," Coleman wrote. "They are still oriented toward fulfilling their parents' desires, but they look very much to their peers for approval as well. Consequently, our society has within its midst a set of small teenage societies, which focus teenage interests and attitudes on things far removed from adult responsibilities, and which may develop standards that lead away from those goals established by the larger society" (1961, p. 9).

What were these "teenage interests and attitudes," that Coleman was referring to, and how did they differ from the interests and attitudes of adults? Coleman felt that the most significant differences concerned the value placed on academic success. While parents felt that academic achievement should be a priority for their youngsters, adolescents lived in a social world in which academic success was frowned on, in which doing well in school did not earn the admiration of peers. Although their parents may have been pleased by straight-A report cards, the high schol students studied said that being a good student carried little weight with their friends.

"What does it take to get into the leading crowd in this school?" When Coleman asked adolescents from ten different high schools this question, he found that their answers were very consistent. For boys, overall, the most important determinants of prestige were personality and athletic success as well as having a good reputation and good looks; for girls, getting into the leading crowd depended on personality, good looks, and clothes. Good grades, particularly for girls, were near the bottom of the list. (See Figure 5.3.)

Coleman also found that social and athletic success were more likely to make adolescents feel good about themselves than academic success. All other factors being equal, students who were successful socially and athletically had significantly higher self-esteem than their peers who were successful scholastically. Getting into the most popular crowd in the school made ad-

olescents feel confident and self-assured. Doing well academically, however, did not make people more popular and did not boost adolescents' self-esteem. The less the students in a school valued academic achievement, the lower the opinion that academically successful students had about themselves. In fact, in schools in which scholastic achievement was not valued very highly, bright students were likely to be "underachievers"—that is, they were likely to perform worse in classes than would be expected on the basis of their ability. In other words, in these schools, getting good grades was a real liability, and in order to remain popular, bright students worked below their level of capability.

The Adolescent Society was written nearly thirty years ago, but many of its findings have been corroborated in more recent studies (e.g., Eitzen, 1975). It probably is fair to say that academic achievement is not valued any more by American teenagers today that it was thirty years ago. Indeed, there are some indications that, if anything, it is valued even less. As you can see in Figure 5.4, for example, academic achievement is considered less important than appearance, personality, or athletic achievement among contemporary adolescents—just as it was during the 1950s (Crockett et al., 1984).

Coleman interpreted the results of his study to mean that age segregation had so strengthened the power of the peer group that American adolescents had become alienated and unfamiliar with the values of adults. No longer were young people interested in the things their parents wanted for them. Teenagers had become separated from adult society to such an extent that they established their own society—a separate youth culture that undermined parents' efforts to encourage academic excellence and placed emphasis on sports, dating, cars, and partying. Unless steps were taken to integrate adolescents into the world of adults—such as shortening the school day and expanding opportunities for adolescents to work—society was going to have a difficult time preparing young people for adulthood. How could adolescents growing up in the "adolescent society," without sufficient contact

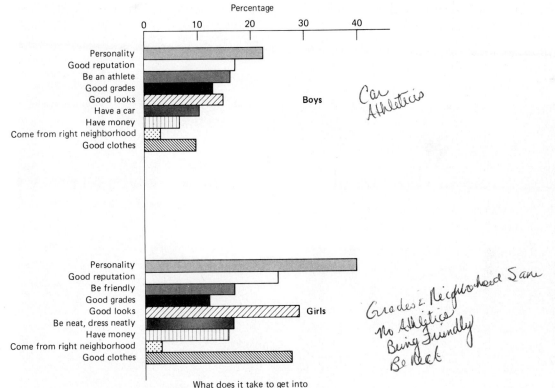

FIGURE 5.3   Boy's and girls' rankings of attributes seen as important for membership in the leading crowd in their high school during the late 1950s. (Adapted from Coleman, 1961)

with their elders, become responsible, diligent, and competent adults?

Many social scientists agreed with Coleman's observations (President's Science Advisory Committee, 1974). Growing problems—such as youth unemployment, teenage suicide, juvenile crime and delinquency, drug and alcohol use, and premarital pregnancy—were all attributed to the rise of peer groups and the isolation of adolescents from adults. Many observers of the adolescent scene noted that all of these problems increased dramatically after 1940, as peer groups became more prominent and age segregation more prevalent (Bronfenbrenner, 1974).

Debates about the increasing orientation of

American adolescents toward the peer group and away from adults are generally fueled by rhetoric rather than hard evidence. Many social commentators had suggested that peer groups had become more and more powerful during the late 1960s, but much of this was speculation. One recent study, however, looked at this issue directly, by contrasting the peer orientation of young people at three different points in time. Identical questionnaires assessing how much adolescents looked to their parents and friends for advice on a range of issues were given to groups of teenagers from the same community in 1963, 1976, and 1982 (Sebald, 1986). As might have been predicted, between 1963 and 1976 adolescents became more oriented toward their peers

Coleman found that academic success has much less impact on adolescents' self-esteem than do social and athletic success. (Polly Brown/The Picture Cube)

and less toward their parents. Between 1976 and 1982, however, this trend reversed itself somewhat, as adolescents' orientation toward their peers diminished. During this later period, boys' orientation toward their parents increased, but girls' continued to decline, although at a less dramatic rate.

Interestingly, this period of heightened peer orientation during the late 1960s coincided with a time during which several politically oriented youth movements were prominent and visible in the media (Braungart, 1979). Similarly, the decline in peer orientation during the 1970s occurred during a time of a notable decline in youth activism. One might speculate that ado-

lescents' orientation toward peers may ebb and flow with the prominence of youth movements. If this is the case, peer orientation probably is stronger in the late 1980s than during the late 1970s because political activism among youth appeared to increase earlier in the 1980s.

Has the rise of adolescent peer groups in modern society really been the cause of so many problems, however? Unfortunately, this question is very difficult to answer. While it is true that age segregation has increased over the last fifty years, society has changed in other ways during this same time—ways that may also have contributed to increases in such problems as crime and drug use. Adolescents are pressured

years. Divorce is commonplace. The economy seems to change from month to month, and competition to get a good job is fierce. The threat of nuclear war is ever-present. Is it any wonder that problems such as suicide and alcohol abuse are on the rise?

To be sure, contemporary adolescents spend more *time* in peer groups than adolescents did in past eras. But we do not know if today's young people are any more susceptible to the influence of their friends than their counterparts were previously, nor do we know if teenagers are any worse off because peer groups have come to play a more prominent role in modern society. In fact, studies of peer pressure indicate that most teenagers feel that their friends are likely to pressure them *not* to use drugs or engage in sexual activity. Adolescents do, however, report a good deal of pressure to drink alcohol, and this pressure increases during the adolescent years (Brown, Clasen, and Eicher, 1986). Adolescents exert both positive and negative influences on each other, and it is incorrect to describe the peer group as a monolithic, negative influence. Indeed, some theorists have suggested that peer groups are inevitable and *necessary* by-products of modernization. Let's now take a look at their point of view.

The Need for Peer Groups in Modern Society

In less industrialized societies, political, economic, and social institutions revolve around the family. Your occupation, your choice of a spouse, your place of residence, your treatment under society's laws, and your participation in governing the community are all tied to who your relatives are. Individuals' family ties determine whom they can trade with and how much they pay for various commodities. In short, how adults are expected to behave depends on which family they come from.

Because all adults are not expected to behave in the same way in these kinship-based societies, it is not possible to educate or socialize all young people in one large group, because

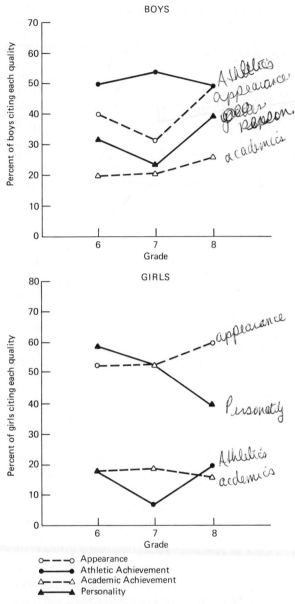

FIGURE 5.4   Percentage of boys (top) and girls (bottom) during the early 1980s who cited appearance, athletic achievement, academic achievement, and personality as qualities important for popularity.

to grow up faster today than they were fifty years ago (Elkind, 1982). In many regards, the world is a far more stressful place to grow up in now than it was in the past. Families move every few

they all have to learn somewhat different sets of norms. When norms for behavior vary from person to person they are called **particularistic norms.** Suppose, for example, that the rules for driving were particularistic—that is, that the rules of the road were different for every person. Perhaps people from families who had lived in the community for a long time would be allowed to drive at 75 miles an hour, but people from families who were new to the area would have to drive at 55. Under a particularistic system such as this, having driver education courses for high school students wouldn't make much sense, because each student would have to learn a different set of rules.

In societies in which norms are particularistic, grouping adolescents by age and sending them off to school is not an effective strategy for socializing them for adulthood, since their family ties, not their age, determine what their rights and responsibilities are. The socialization of adolescents in kinship-based socities is best accomplished in family groups, where elders can pass on the values and norms particular to the family to their younger relatives.

In contemporary societies, things are quite different. Modernization has eroded much of the family's importance as a political, social, and economic unit. Generally speaking, in modern society, all individuals are expected to learn the same set of norms, because the rules governing behavior apply equally to all members of the community. These norms are called **universalistic norms.** When you walk into a department store to buy something or when you go into a voting booth to vote, it generally makes no difference who your relatives are. Whom you are permitted to marry, what kind of work you do, where you live, and how you are treated under the law are not based on family lineage. The norms that apply to you apply to everyone.

Under these circumstances, it is not wise to limit the socialization of adolescents to the family, because doing so does not ensure that all youngsters will learn the same set of norms. In societies that require individuals to learn universalistic norms, it is more efficient to group

by age all of the individuals who are to be socialized together (Eisenstadt, 1956). Teaching is better done in schools than left up to individual families. One of the reasons we have driver education classes, for example, is that our rules for driving are universalistic—the same for everyone—and we need to make sure that individuals learn a common set of regulations, not simply the ones their parents teach them.

As the family has become a less important political and economic institution, universalistic norms have come to replace particularistic ones. And this has required a change in the way in which adolescents are prepared for adulthood. Modernization has not just created age groups—it has made them absolutely *necessary.* Without systematic age grouping in schools, it would be impossible to prepare young people for adulthood. And because age grouping in schools carries over into activities outside of school, the need for universal, school-based education has created age-segregated peer groups.

Some theorists do not see this as a bad thing. They feel that as society has become more technologically advanced, adolescents have come to play a valuable role in preparing one another for adulthood.

According to the anthropologist Margaret Mead (1978), the way in which young people are best socialized for adulthood depends on how fast their society is changing. In some cultures, cultural change is so slow that what a child needs to know to function as an adult changes very little over time. Mead called these **postfigurative cultures.** In postfigurative cultures, the socialization of young people is accomplished almost exclusively through contact between children and their elders, because the way in which older generations have lived is almost identical to the way in which subsequent generations will live. "Grandparents, holding newborn grandchildren in their arms, cannot conceive of any other future for the children than their own past lives. The past of the adults is the future of each new generation; their lives provide the ground plan" (Mead, 1978, p. 14).

Imagine, for a moment, growing up in a

In postfigurative societies cultural change is slow, and the socialization of young people is accomplished almost exclusively through contact between young people and their elders. In cofigurative societies, however, where cultural change takes place at a faster rate, much of the socialization of young people is performed by peers. (Left, George Bellrose/Stock, Boston; right, Joel Gordon)

world in which you had to know only what your grandparents knew in order to survive. In this age of computer technology, video games, robots, and space shuttles, growing up in a world in which very little changes in fifty years seems almost impossible to imagine. After all, fifty years ago television was not even on the market. Yet strange as it may seem to us now, most societies until fairly recently have been postfigurative—and they still are in much of the developing world. In other words, until fairly recently, adolescents could learn what they needed to know to be successful adults exclusively from their elders.

During the past 100 years, contemporary societies have shifted away from being postfig-urative cultures. They have become **cofigurative cultures.** In cofigurative cultures, the socialization of young people is accomplished not merely through contact between children and their elders but through contact between people of the same age. In cofigurative cultures, society changes so quickly that much of what parents are able to teach their children may be outdated by the time their children become adults. Today, we live in a cofigurative society. For adolescents in contemporary America, peers have become role models as important as parents and grandparents. As a result, adolescents increasingly need to turn to members of their own generation for advice, guidance, and information.

If you were a teenager living in a postfigurative culture, you might ask your grandfather for advice on how to hunt or farm. But if you were a teenager in today's cofigurative culture, to whom would you turn for advice on how to use a computer—your friends, who probably have grown up with computers in their homes and schools, or your grandparents, who may never even have seen a computer?

Mead believed that as society became even more rapidly changing, cofigurative cultures would be replaced by **prefigurative cultures,** in which young people would become adults' teachers. We already may be living in a prefigurative culture. Instead of parents asking, "Why can't Johnny read?" teenagers ask, "Why can't Mom and Dad program a computer?"

Do these analyses mean that the adolescents of the future will cease to profit from having close relationships with adults? Of course not. Young people will always need the support, affection, and advice of their elders. But understanding how peer groups have been made necessary by modernization casts the issue of age segregation in a new light. Despite whatever problems may have been caused by the rise of peer groups in contemporary society, there may be little we can do to make adolescent peer groups less prominent.

Current debate about the behavior and development of so-called latchkey youngsters has directed much recent attention to the costs and benefits of age segregation in contemporary society. As noted earlier, changes in patterns of employment and family life have resulted in a large number of youngsters who are not supervised by their parents after school. How big a problem is this, or is it a problem at all? Researchers disagree, and at the present time, we cannot definitely answer this question. Some researchers have argued that latchkey youngsters may have opportunities to develop responsibility and self-reliance during after-school hours because they are expected to monitor and plan their own behavior (Rodman et al., 1985). Other writers, however, have pointed out that many adolescents misbehave in the absence of adult supervision and that latchkey teenagers may be more likely to get involved in deviant or otherwise worrisome activity (Steinberg, 1986). More research on this issue is necessary before any firm conclusions can be drawn.

With no apparent end to modernization in sight, we can expect that peer groups will come to play an even greater role in the socialization of young people in the future. For this reason, it is critical that we understand how peer groups are formed, what takes place when adolescents spend time with their agemates, and how spending time in the peer group influences young people's development. It is to these questions that we now turn.

THE STRUCTURE OF ADOLESCENT PEER GROUPS

Cliques and Crowds

Adolescents' peer groups are usually organized around **cliques,** small groups of between two and twelve individuals—the average is about five or six—generally of the same sex and, of course, age (Dunphy, 1975; Hollingshead, 1949/1975). Cliques play a vital role in structuring adolescents' social activities. Usually, teenagers who are in the same clique plan their social and leisure activities together, do things together, and go places as a group. A clique of 14-year-old boys, for instance, might discuss plans for a weekend football game during lunch break, hang around together after school, and meet before going to a party so that they enter as a group.

Occasionally, several cliques—some of boys and some of girls—come together for social activities, forming a larger, more loosely organized **crowd.** Crowds are usually composed of about three or four cliques, or approximately twenty individuals. In contrast to cliques, which are smaller and more tightly knit, crowds are formed chiefly on the basis of shared activity rather than close friendship or compatibility. Many times, adolescents do things in crowds with people they aren't really very friendly with. Girls who are part of the cheerleaders' clique, for example, may not like the girls on the swimming team, but both cliques may come together occasionally when there is a big party for the athletic, or "jock," crowd.

Changes in Clique Structure During Adolescence

One reason social scientists have been interested in studying teenagers' cliques is that understanding how cliques change during adolescence helps us understand changes in adolescents' psychosocial needs and capabilities. For example, many adolescents begin to lose interest in being part of a large same-sex clique at around the time they begin dating. As their psychosocial concerns shift toward establishing intimate relationships with opposite-sex peers, the activities of the old gang start to seem dull and childish.

Studies of the structure of adolescents' peer groups often make use of a research technique called **participant observation.** In this approach, the researcher establishes rapport with a group of individuals in order to infiltrate and eventually join the group. In *Inside High School* (Cusick, 1973), for example, the author pretended to be a newcomer to the community and attended high school for a year to learn more about the adolescents' social world. As an observer who is also a participant, the researcher can observe the group's behavior under conditions that are more natural and more private than would otherwise be the case. Overhearing a ten-minute conversation in a high school locker room can be more informative than interviewing a student for three hours if the student feels uncomfortable or uneasy.

Observational studies (for example, Dunphy, 1963) of young people indicate that during early adolescence, adolescents' activities revolve around same-sex cliques. These same-sex cliques are isolated from one another, because crowds have not yet formed. Adolescents at this stage are not yet involved in parties and typically spend their leisure time with a small group of friends, playing sports, talking, or simply hanging around.

Somewhat later, as boys and girls become more interested in one another—but before dating actually begins—boys' and girls' cliques come together, marking the beginning of crowd formation. This is clearly a transitional stage. Boys and girls may go to parties together, but the time they spend there actually involves interaction with peers of the *same* sex. When youngsters are still uncomfortable about dealing with members of the opposite sex, the crowd provides a setting in which adolescents can learn more about opposite-sex peers without having to be intimate and without having to risk losing face. It is not unusual, for example, at young adolescents' first mixed-sex parties, for groups of boys and girls to position themselves at opposite sides of a room, watching each other but seldom interacting.

The crowd then enters a stage of structural transformation, generally led by the clique leaders. As youngsters become interested in dating, part of the crowd begins to divide off into mixed-sex cliques, while other individuals remain in the crowd but in same-sex groups. The shift into dating is usually led by the clique leaders, with other clique members following along. For instance, a clique of boys whose main activity is riding dirt bikes may discover that one of the guys they look up to has become more interested in going out with girls on Saturday nights than hanging out at the local racing track. Over time, they will begin to follow his lead, and their crowd at the track will become smaller and smaller.

During middle adolescence, mixed-sex cliques become more prevalent. In time, the crowd becomes composed entirely of heterosexual cliques. It is not yet time for couples to begin pairing off and leaving the crowd, however. One clique might consist of the drama students—male and female students who know each other from acting together in school plays. Another might be composed of four girls and four boys who like to drink on the weekends. The staff of the school yearbook might make up a third.

These three cliques may come together for parties and larger social activities.

What about those adolescents who are not interested in starting to date or in mixed-sex activities? What happens to them when clique activities begin to change? Many leave the crowd as its interests turn toward dating, either remaining together in a smaller same-sex clique or forming a few close friendships with same-sex peers. Others are left behind by their peers who are interested in moving on to dating. They may stop getting invitations or telephone calls about weekend activities. Not keeping up with the peer group's transition from same-sex activities into mixed-sex ones is one of the most common reasons for peer rejection during adolescence (Dunphy, 1963).

Finally, during late adolescence, the crowd begins to disintegrate. Pairs of dating adolescents begin to split off from the activities of the larger group. The crowd is replaced by loosely associated groups of couples. Couples may go out together from time to time, but the feeling of being in a crowd has disappeared. This pattern—in which the couple becomes the focus of social activity—persists into adulthood.

When viewed from a structural point of view, the peer group's role in the development of intimacy is quite clear. Over time, the structure of the peer group changes to become more in keeping with adolescents' changing needs and interests. As we shall see in Chapter 10, the adolescent's capacity for close relationships develops first through friendships with peers of the same sex. Only later does intimacy enter into opposite-sex relationships. Thus the structure of the peer group changes during adolescence in a way that parallels the adolescent's development of intimacy: As the adolescent develops increasing facility in close relationships, the peer group moves from the familiarity of same-sex activities to contact with opposite-sex peers but in the safety of the larger group. It is only after adolescent males and females have been slowly socialized into dating roles—primarily by modeling their higher-status peers—

that the safety of the crowd is no longer needed and adolescents begin coupling off.

Cliques as a Source of Adolescent Identity

As well as serving important functions in the socialization of intimacy and dating, the clique provides the adolescent with a sense of identity, by serving as a basis of comparison, or **reference group**. It is partly through comparisons with other clique members that adolescents learn about themselves and evaluate their experiences in school, at home, and in the broader peer group. Suppose, for example, that an adolescent girl feels that her parents are intolerable—that they are intrusive, overly demanding, or too strict. She discusses her situation with another girl in her clique, and in the course of their discussion, the two girls compare notes. The first adolescent discovers that life with her friend's parents would be even more difficult (at least in her eyes) than with her own. By using her friend's experience as a point of reference, she may well revise her opinion of her mother and father and perhaps even change the way she behaves toward them.

Adolescents also form judgments about their own abilities by comparing themselves to clique members. An adolescent who gets a B on a history test will feel differently about it if his clique is composed of straight-A students than if his friends all received lower grades than he did. Sometimes, adolescents leave cliques in which they have very good friends because comparing themselves to other clique members makes them feel inferior. When cliques turn to dating, for instance, adolescents who are overweight may withdraw from the group because being around their friends makes them feel fat or unattractive.

Another way in which cliques serve as reference groups is in providing their members with an identity in the eyes of *other* adolescents. Adolescents judge one another on the basis of the company they keep. Individuals become

As young people become more interested in opposite-sex relationships, the structure of adolescent peer groups changes. During early adolescence, peer activities often revolve around same-sex cliques; boys' and girls' cliques may merge to form crowds, but interaction between the sexes is limited. By late adolescence, large peer groups have begun to break down, and the crowd is replaced by loosely associated groups of couples. (Top, Alan Carey/The Image Works; bottom, Ellis Herwig/The Picture Cube)

branded on the basis of whom they hang around with. Such labels as "jocks," "brains," "socies," "druggies," and "leathers" serve as shorthand notations—accurate or inaccurate—to describe what someone is like as a person and what he or she holds as important. You might not recognize the specific labels in the aforementioned list, but in all likelihood, you will recognize the dividing lines they signify. In some schools, "jocks" are individuals who are very involved in athletics; "brains" worry about their grades; "socies' " main concern is their social life; "druggies" use drugs frequently; and "leathers" wear boots and leather jackets and work on their cars or motorcycles.

Clique identities are important not only because they are used by adolescents when talking about one another, but also because they become the basis for an adolescent's own identity. A girl who runs with the "preppies" identifies herself as a "preppy" by wearing the preppy "uniform," shopping in the preppy stores, and speaking the preppy language. After a while, "preppiness" becomes a part of her own self-concept; she wouldn't think of dressing or talking in a different way. Or consider the boys whose clique is held together because none of them likes school. By having their attitude toward school continually reinforced by one another, the boys' feelings about school become strengthened, and not liking school becomes a part of each boy's identity. Even if something very positive happens at school, it becomes difficult for someone in the clique to admit that it makes him feel good about himself. Doing well on a test or receiving a compliment from a teacher is likely to be dismissed as unimportant.

Because the adolescent's peer group plays such an important role as a reference group and a source of identity, the nature of the crowd with which an adolescent affiliates is likely to have an important influence on his or her behavior, activities, and self-conceptions. Psychologist B. Bradford Brown and his colleagues have studied how peer group membership—that is, *which* peer group the adolescent affiliates with— may affect the adolescent's development and behavior. Although most adolescents feel pressure from their friends to behave in ways that are consistent with their crowd's values and goals, the specific nature of the pressure varies from one crowd to another. Adolescents who are part of the druggie crowd report much more peer pressure to engage in misconduct, for example,

than do adolescents from the jock crowd (Clasen and Brown, 1985).

Crowd membership can also affect the way adolescents feel about themselves. Adolescents' self-esteem is higher among students who are identified with peer groups that have relatively more status in their school. In the high schools that Brown has studied, the "jocks" and "socies" are highest in status, the "druggies" and "toughs" lowest. Students who were identified with the jock or socie group had higher self-esteem than those identified with the druggie or tough group (Brown and Lohr, 1987). As the authors wrote, "Crowds are not merely fertile grounds for bolstering self-esteem through identity testing or building supportive social relationships. Crowd labels also provide one feedback on one's comparative standing among peers, which in turn may enhance or depreciate self-esteem" (1987, p. 53).

WHO CLIQUES WITH WHOM?

Steve is part of the "socie" clique. He is the president of the junior class, his family lives in the nicest neighborhood in the community, and he is extremely popular. He never misses an important party.

Julie is part of the "student" clique. She is a junior also, but she rarely runs into Steve. She is president of the honor society and assistant editor of the school newspaper. Her weekends and evenings are often spent studying.

What draws adolescents into one clique and not another? What factors influence who forms cliques with whom? Because cliques serve as a basis for adolescents' friendships and play an important role in identity development, many researchers have studied the determinants of clique composition.

Similarity as the Basis for Clique Formation

The most important influence on the composition of cliques is similarity. Adolescents' cliques typically are composed of people who are the same age, the same race, from the same socio-economic background, and at least during early and middle adolescence, of the same sex.

Age segregation. Age grouping in junior and senior high schools makes having friends who are substantially older or younger unlikely. A tenth-grader who is enrolled in tenth-grade English, tenth-grade math, tenth-grade history, and tenth-grade science simply does not have many opportunities to meet adolescents who are in different grades. Age segregation in adolescents' cliques does indeed appear to be due mostly to the structure of schools. When an adolescent's friends come from a different school, those friends are just as likely to be younger or older as they are to come from the same grade (Blyth, Hill, and Thiel, 1982).

Sex segregation. During the early and middle adolescent years, cliques also tend to be composed of adolescents of the same sex. This so-called **sex cleavage** begins in childhood and continues through most of the adolescent years, although the sex cleavage is stronger among white students than among black students (Hallinan, 1981; Sagar et al., 1983). The causes of sex segregation in adolescents' cliques are more interesting than the causes of age segregation, because schools do not separate boys and girls into different classes. Why, then, do adolescent males and females separate themselves into different cliques?

First, cliques are formed largely on the basis of shared activities and interests. Generally speaking, preadolescent and early adolescent boys and girls are interested in different things. It is not until adolescents begin dating that boys' cliques and girls' cliques mix, presumably because dating provides a basis for common activity.

A second reason for the sex cleavage in adolescent peer groups concerns young adolescents' sensitivity about sex roles. Over the course of childhood, boys and girls become in-creasingly concerned about behaving in ways that are judged to be sex-appropriate. When boys show an interest in dolls, they are often told either explicitly, by parents, friends, and teachers, or implicity, by television, books, and other mass media, "Little boys don't play with dolls. Those are for girls." And when girls start wrestling or roughhousing, they are often repri-manded and told to "act like ladies."

As a consequence of these continual re-minders that there are boys' activities and girls' activities, early adolescents—who are trying to establish a sense of identity—are very concerned about acting in sex-appropriate ways. This makes it very difficult for an adolescent girl to be part of a boys' clique, whose activities are likely to be dominated by athletics and other physical activities, and for a boy to be a part of a girls' clique, whose activities are likely to re-volve around clothing, grooming, and talking about boys (Schofield, 1981). Adolescents who go against prevailing sex-role norms by forming friendships with members of the opposite sex may be teased about being "faggots" or ostra-cized by their peers because they are "strange." Ironically, once dating becomes the norm, ado-lescents who *don't* have relationships with peers of the opposite sex become the objects of equally strong suspicion and social rejection.

Social class segregation. One of the most im-portant studies ever undertaken of adolescents' peer groups is *Elmtown's Youth* (1949/1975). In this study of adolescents in the midwestern com-munity of "Elmtown," sociologist August Holl-ingshead examined the relation between the so-cial position of adolescents' families and the composition of teenagers' cliques. He was in-terested in determining whether adolescents' cliques were segregated along class lines.

Hollingshead used such indicators as in-come, residence, and reputation in the com-munity to sort families into five different **social class** groups. In the highest class were families who were very affluent, lived in the best neigh-borhoods, and were known in the community as powerful and respected families. These "up-per-class" families had lived in the community for a long time and belonged to all the exclusive clubs and organizations. In the "lower class" were families who were poor, lived on the "wrong" side of town, and were not highly thought of in the community. In between these extremes were three groups of families: the hard-working but not very well off "working-class" families; the comfortable but not espe-cially affluent "middle-class" families; and the "upper-middle-class" families, who had money but did not quite have the reputation and pres-tige of the families in the highest class.

Hollingshead found that adolescents do in fact associate chiefly with peers from the same social class. More than 60 percent of each ado-lescent's close friendships in Elmtown High School were between teenagers from the same background. Of the remaining clique relation-ships, the vast majority were between adoles-cents of adjacent social classes (for example, "middle-class" adolescents with "upper-middle-

class" adolescents). Almost never did adoles-cents from one social class associate with stu-dents from a class that was two steps higher or lower (see Figure 5.5).

Hollingshead found similar patterns when he looked at adolescents' best friends and dating relationships: Rarely were social class lines crossed, and when they were, it was virtually always between adolescents of adjacent classes. Moreover, adolescents became even more class conscious as they got older; freshman girls and boys were nearly five times more likely than seniors to belong to cliques with adolescents of different social background.

Social class was also important in shaping the status hierarchy of the school. Hollingshead asked the adolescents to list those students who were the leaders in extracurricular and social activities and those who were shunned by most of their classmates. Over 40 percent of the lead-ers came from the two highest social classes, even though only 9 percent of the student body were from these social groups. Only 14 percent

FIGURE 5.5   The majority of teenagers are in cliques with adoles-cents from the same socioeconomic background. Virtually no cli-ques cross two class lines. (Hollingshead, 1949/1975)

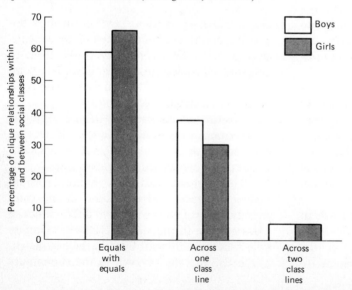

of the leaders came from the two lowest classes, even though over half the students in the school were from these social groups. And adolescents from the lower classes were far more likely to be among those who were shunned—in fact, students from the two lowest classes constituted virtually all of this group.

Several other studies conducted since the time of *Elmtown's Youth* have confirmed the importance of social class in influencing an adolescent's status in the peer group of the high school. But subsequent research has shown the pattern to be somewhat different from that suggested by Hollingshead. In *The Adolescent Society* (1961), the study on the "youth culture" of ten different high schools discussed earlier, James Coleman also looked at some of the same questions examined in *Elmtown's Youth*. Overall, as in "Elmtown," adolescents from wealthier backgrounds were proportionately more likely to occupy leadership positions in their schools. The student government leaders, the team captains, the presidents of different clubs and activities, and the students who were in the leading crowd usually came from the more affluent families. But this pattern was more characteristic of some schools than others. Specifically, Coleman found that the dominance of high school activities by middle- and upper-middle-class students is most likely to occur in communities with a high proportion of middle- and upper-middle-class families. In communities dominated by working-class families, however, middle-class adolescents have less of an advantage over the other students. In this respect, then, the social structure of the high school mirrors the social structure of the broader community in which the high school is found.

This finding has important implications for understanding how the location of an adolescent's school can have an impact on his or her social life and psychosocial development. A youngster from a poor family probably has less of a chance to become a leader in a middle-class school than in a school located in a working-class or poor neighborhood. Opportunities to develop responsibility, leadership skills, and self-confidence are more restricted for poor youngsters than they are for their affluent peers, particularly in schools dominated by middle-class families.

Race segregation. Race is not a strong determinant of clique composition during childhood, but like social class, it becomes increasingly powerful as youngsters get older. By middle and late adolescence, adolescents' peer groups typically are racially segregated. This appears to be the case, although somewhat less so, even within desegregated schools (Schofield, 1981).

There are several explanations for racial separation in adolescents' peer groups. First, because adolescents' cliques are often segregated along socioeconomic lines, peer groups that appear to be segregated because of race actually may be separated on the basis of class, since disproportionately higher numbers of minority youngsters come from economically poorer families. This explanation helps to account for the race cleavage in desegregated schools, which often bring together youngsters not only of different racial backgrounds but from varying economic backgrounds as well.

Another reason for the strong racial split in adolescents' cliques appears to be the differential levels of academic achievement of white and black adolescents (Schofield, 1981). Adolescents who are friends usually have similar attitudes toward school, similar educational aspirations, and similar school achievement levels (Berndt, 1982). Racial differences in school achievement may lead to racial separation in adolescent peer groups.

A third reason, according to one study of adolescents in a recently desegregated school, is attitudinal. In this school, the white adolescents perceived their black peers as aggressive, threatening, and hostile. The black students felt that the white students were conceited, prejudiced, and unwilling to be friends with them. These perceptions, which fed on each other, made the formation of interracial peer groups unlikely. The more the white students felt that the black students were hostile, the more the white stu-

Generally speaking, peer groups become more racially segregated as individuals get older. Adolescents' peer groups, for example, are more segregated than are those of children. (Susan Lapides/Design Conceptions)

dents acted distant and kept to themselves. But the more the white students acted this way, the more likely the black students were to feel rejected, and the more hostile they became. In many schools, adolescents' lack of familiarity with youngsters from other racial groups results in misperceptions of the others' attitudes and motives, and this misunderstanding limits interracial interaction (Schofield, 1981). In general, white students are less apt to initiate contact with black students than vice versa (Sagan et al., 1983).

One way out of this cycle of misunderstanding is to bring white and black youngsters together from an early age, before they have had time to build up prejudices and stereotypes. Interracial school busing, for example, has been far more successful in communities that began

such programs during elementary school than in districts that implemented them for the first time at the high school level. If white and black children grow up together from an early age, they are less likely to misunderstand each other and less likely to go off into separate peer groups purely on the basis of race.

An alternative approach to increasing interracial contact among adolescents involves restructuring the school environment. One study compared interaction among students in two desegregated junior high schools. One school was organized conventionally, with students grouped by grade levels and tracked into high, medium, and low ability classrooms. In the second, students were organized into "teams" composed of adolescents who varied in age and academic ability. In this unconventional school, the focus was

The Sexes: Why Are There Sex Differences in Interracial Contact?

Two findings from studies of adolescent peer groups emerge over and over again. First, a strong "sex cleavage" limits the interaction between adolescent boys and girls—at least, until dating begins. And second, adolescents have very little contact with peers from other races, even when they attend desegregated schools that have been developed to increase cross-racial interaction.

One curiosity that has been uncovered, as noted in this chapter, is that, although the "race cleavage" seems to characterize boys' as well as girls' interaction, it is much stronger among adolescent girls than boys. Specifically, although boys and girls alike are likely to interact more often with adolescents of the same race, the likelihood of white boys interacting with black boys is much greater than the likelihood of white girls interacting with black girls. Indeed, several studies suggest that cliques of young-adolescent black girls are among the most socially isolated of all adolescent groups (Damico and Sparks, 1986). This isolation seems to work both ways: White students of both sexes are less likely to talk to black girls than to any other group, and black girls are less likely than any other group to initiate contact with whites.

No one is quite sure why black females face this predicament, but at least three hypotheses may be offered. One researcher has suggested that a special tension exists between white and black girls that does not exist between white and black boys (Schofield, 1982). She suggests that as sex and romance become more important during early adolescence, students become increasingly competitive for the attention of opposite-sex students. Although both boys and girls seek this attention, it may be more important for girls, who may rely more on the prestige derived from dating popular boys as an index of their social status in school. Boys, in contrast, may look to athletics more for status and may be slightly less concerned about getting the attention of girls in their classes. The heightened concern for male attention introduces a greater level of competition into adolescent girls' social relations, and this competition may underlie white and black girls' reluctance to interact.

An alternative explanation concerns the special role that white girls may play in the communication network of the school. One team of researchers (Damico and Sparks, 1986) has suggested that from an early age white girls try to develop personalized relationships with their teachers. By junior high school, these girls may have become an important source of "inside information" for students in the school about teachers and classes. Thus white girls may find themselves more centrally located within the school's social network than black girls. Black girls may receive fewer social overtures from other students because they are perceived as less tied into the school's network.

Finally, sex differences in the degree to which peer interaction is racially segregated may be based in differences between the activity patterns of girls and boys in general. As you will read in Chapter 10, adolescent boys are more likely than girls to spend time in large group activities, such as sports, and girls are more likely to spend time talking in pairs or in small groups. The large group activities of boys may simply provide greater opportunities for cross-racial interaction to take place—as when white and black students are on the same team, for example. In contrast, the focus of adolescent girls on more intimate peer relations may make them less likely to interact with individuals whom they perceive—correctly or not—to have different values and norms for behavior. In other words, sex differences in the structure of adolescent peer activities may make cross-racial contact easier for boys than girls.

on student participation in class activities and on group assignments in which team members had to work together (Damico and Sparks, 1986). Although students in both schools most often interacted with students of the same sex and race, students in the unconventional school were more likely to interact with students of the other race; the formal requirements for teamwork apparently carried over into more informal contact. Team members who had been working together in class, for example, would wander together to the cafeteria or into another activity after class had ended. The unconventional school structure increased cross-racial interaction among both white and black students alike, but it did not seem to be as powerful for females as for males. Like other studies (Schofield, 1982), this study found that black females are more often excluded from cross-racial interaction than are black males, even when structures are put into place to encourage interracial contact. (See the accompanying box on p. 173.)

Shared Interests as a Basis for Clique Formation

Thus far we have seen that adolescents' cliques are usually composed of adolescents who are the same age, in the same grade in school, from the same social class, and of the same race. But what about factors beyond these? Do adolescents who associate with one another also share certain interests and activities? Generally speaking, they do. Two factors appear to be especially important in determining adolescent clique membership and friendship patterns: orientation toward school and orientation toward the teen culture.

Orientation toward school. Adolescents and their friends tend to be similar in their attitudes toward school, in their school achievement, and in their educational plans (Berndt, 1982; Epstein, 1983b). Adolescents who earn high grades, study a great deal, and plan to go on to college usually have friends who share these activities and aspirations. One reason for this is

that how much time a student devotes to schoolwork affects his or her involvement in other activities. Someone who is always studying will not have many friends who are out late at night partying, because the two activities conflict. By the same token, someone who wants to spend afternoons and evenings out having fun will find it difficult to remain friends with someone who prefers to stay home and study. Students also may influence each other's academic performance. Given two students with similar records of past achievement, the student whose friends do better in school is likely to achieve more than the student whose friends do worse (Epstein, 1983).

Orientation toward the teen culture. Adolescents and their friends generally listen to the same type of music, dress similarly, spend their leisure time in similar types of activities, and have similar patterns of drug use (Berndt, 1982). It would be very unlikely, for example, for a "jock" and a "druggie" to be part of the same clique, because their interests and attitudes are so different. In most high schools, it is fairly easy to see the split between cliques—in how people dress, where they eat lunch, how much they participate in the school's activities, and how they spend their time outside of school.

Earlier in this chapter, we considered the question of whether age segregation in contemporary society has created a separate "youth culture." However, on the basis of what we know about adolescents' cliques, it would appear that high schools are dominated not by a single monolithic youth culture but by a series of distinct youth *cultures*. People have a tendency to see adolescents as constituting a far more homogeneous group than they actually do. To be sure, there may be some very real differences between adolescents' tastes and those of adults. But the differences *within* the adolescent population— between "jocks" and "druggies," or between "socies" and "leathers"—are substantial and important.

Because leisure activities seem to be such a

Leisure activities, tastes in music and dress, and patterns of drug and alcohol use are strong determinants of clique composition during adolescence. Teenagers tend to have friends who share their tastes, attitudes, and interests. (Joel Gordon)

strong determinant of clique composition, many adults have expressed concern over the influence of peers in the socialization of delinquent activity and drug and alcohol use. Parents often feel that if their youngster runs with the wrong crowd, he or she will acquire undesirable interests and attitudes. They express concern, for instance, when their child starts spending time with peers who seem to be less interested in school or more involved with drugs. But which comes first, joining a clique or being interested in a clique's activities? Do adolescents develop interests and attitudes because of who their friends are, or is it more the case that people with similar interests and tastes are likely to become friends?

This question has been examined by social psychologist Denise Kandel (1978) in a longitudinal statewide study of New York high school students. Students completed a battery of questionnaires once during the beginning weeks of a school year and again toward the end of the year.

They answered questions concerning a range of activities and interests, including delinquency, drug use, and educational aspirations. In addition, through the use of an intricate coding system that kept information anonymous and confidential, respondents provided the identities of their close friends. By examining patterns of attitudinal and behavioral change over the course of the school year and comparing these shifts with patterns of friendship formation and change, Kandel was able to determine whether adolescents were attracted to one another because of their initial similarity or whether they became similar as a result of the friendship.

Kandel found that both *selection*—choosing a friend on the basis of similarity—and *socialization*—becoming more similar as a result of the friendship—are at work. Moreover, on almost every dimension studied—including delinquency, drug use, and attitudes toward school—selection and socialization operated with about equal weight. In other words, similarity among adolescent friends is about equally due to their selecting one another as friends to begin with as it is to the influence that friends have on one another.

Popularity, Rejection, and Status in the Peer Group

Thus far, our discussion has focused on how and why peer groups and cliques serve as the basis for adolescents' social activities. But what about the *internal* structure of cliques? Within a crowd or a clique, what determines which adolescents are the leaders and which the followers?

To answer this question we must first draw a distinction between popularity and status. **Popularity** refers to how well-liked someone is. The chief determinant of a youngster's popularity during adolescence is his or her social skill. Popular adolescents act appropriately in the eyes of their peers, are skilled at perceiving and meeting the needs of others, and are confident without being conceited. Additionally, popular adolescents are friendly, cheerful, good-natured, humorous, and, you may be surprised to learn, intelligent (Hartup, 1983; Hollingshead, 1949/ 1975). (Contrary to myth, popular adolescents are more intelligent than unpopular ones. This is because intelligent individuals are better at figuring out how to behave in ways that will get them liked. Remember also that being intelligent is not the same as being a "brain.") Interestingly, the determinants of popularity in adolescent peer groups are the same for boys and girls and are the same for older and younger individuals. People of all ages like to be around others who make them feel good, who know how to have a good time, and who are able to communicate well.

An interesting ethnographic study of early adolescent girls provides insight into the dynamics of popularity. An **ethnography** is an observational study in which the researcher spends time in a natural setting, like a school cafeteria, and records detailed field notes describing individuals' behavior and interactions. Ethnographic techniques are widely used by anthro-pologists who study other cultures, and they are increasingly used by researchers interested in studying adolescent peer relations.

Ethnographer Donna Eder (1985) spent two years observing interactions between early adolescent girls in various extracurricular and informal settings in their middle school (the cafeteria, the hallway, at school dances). In this school, the cheerleaders were considered the elite crowd, and girls who made the cheerleading squad were immediately accorded social status. Other girls then attempted to befriend the cheerleaders as a means of increasing their own status. This, in turn, increased the cheerleaders' popularity within school, since they became the most sought-after friends. The girls who were successful in cultivating friendships with the cheerleaders then became a part of this high-status group and themselves became more popular.

This popularity had a price, however, as one eighth-grader explained to the researcher:

> A lot of times, people don't talk to the popular kids because they're kind of scared of them and they don't know their real personality. So that's kind of a bummer when you're considered to be popular because you don't usually meet a lot of other people because they just go, "Oh." (Eder, 1985, p. 162)

Paradoxically, popularity in many cases led to these girls being disliked. As Eder explains, "There are limits to the number of friendships that any one person can maintain. Because popular girls get a high number of affiliative offers, they have to reject more offers of friendship than other girls. Also, to maintain their higher status, girls who form the elite group must avoid associations with lower-status girls. . . . These girls are likely to ignore the affiliative attempts of many girls, leading to the impression that they are stuck-up. . . . Shortly after these girls reach their peak of popularity, they become increasingly disliked" (Eder, 1985, p. 163).

In general, the determinants of social rejection and isolation during adolescence are the opposite of those associated with popularity—in other words, unpopular adolescents are less socially adept than their peers. They may be timid, tactless, or conceited. They interfere with the group's having fun, either by being unenthusiastic or by constantly drawing attention to themselves.

Generally, social scientists believe that it is important to distinguish between adolescents who are actively rejected by their friends and those who are simply ignored or neglected. Rejected adolescents are more likely to behave in ways that are negative and that bother others—they may be tactless, conceited, aggressive, or egotistical. Neglected adolescents suffer more from problems of omission than commission. They may be overly timid, shy, or lacking in enthusiasm, or may find it difficult to socialize with their peers in appropriate ways (Coie and Dodge, 1983). Rejected adolescents are lonelier than neglected adolescents and more likely to develop psychological and emotional problems (Asher and Wheeler, 1985).

Many psychologists believe that rejected and neglected youngsters lack the social skills and social understanding necessary to be popular with peers. In recent years, therefore, several teams of psychologists have developed programs designed to improve the social skills of unpopular youngsters. Two types of intervention appear to have promise, especially when they are combined. Interventions designed to teach conversational skills—self-expression, questioning others about themselves, and leadership—have been shown to improve adolescents' abilities to get along with peers. Interventions designed to make adolescents more acceptable to their peers—in which unpopular adolescents participate in group activities with popular adolescents under the supervision of the psychologists—have been shown to improve adolescents' self-conceptions and their acceptance by others (Bierman and Furman, 1984). When combined, these types of programs can remedy the deficiencies of both rejected and neglected adolescents.

The most popular adolescents are not always the leaders of their cliques. In contrast to popularity, an adolescent's **status**—that is, whether he or she is perceived as a leader—is associated with the ability to accomplish the things that the group wants done. For example, a girl may not be the most well-liked member of her clique, but she may be the group's leader because she is good at organizing parties and other social activities. A boy who is a good all-around athlete may be looked up to by his friends but may not be as popular as someone who is funnier and more good-natured.

Status in the peer group is highly related to the group's activities. Consequently, as adolescents' interests change, so do their cliques' status hierarchies—the arrangement of a group's members from highest status to lowest status. We all know people who were leaders during elementary school but somehow lost their prestige during high school. The reason is that unlike the determinants of popularity—which do not change much during childhood and adolescence—the determinants of status shift as peer activities change. For example, during early adolescence, boys who are physically mature and athletically talented may command a great deal of status, because sports are important activities at this age (Savin-Williams, 1976). As athletics become less important, however, athletic prowess is less likely to be related to status, because being a talented athlete is less likely to help achieve the group's goals. During middle adolescence, when same-sex cliques give way to mixed-sex crowds, competence in dating becomes a more important influence on the status hierarchies of adolescents (Dunphy, 1963).

Status hierarchies are established very quickly when adolescents who do not know one another are brought together—in a summer camp, for instance. Within the first week of a clique's formation, the leaders have emerged (Sherif and Sherif, 1969; Savin-Williams, 1979). Status hierarchies in adolescents' peer groups are established through a process called **anchoring** (Sherif and Sherif, 1969). When a clique begins to form, status positions are not yet clear; no one has emerged as the definite leader of the

Within the peer group, members generally play well-defined roles that differ in terms of status and popularity. The sociocenter is extroverted and a specialist in humor; he or she is well-liked but not necessarily highest in status. (Jim Anderson/Woodfin Camp & Associates)

group. After a couple of days, it becomes clear who the high status *and* low status members of the clique will be. The obvious leaders and the obvious followers emerge first. But status differentiation is still fuzzy between the two extremes of the continuum. It is not apparent, for instance, who the second or third most powerful members will be. With more time, the individuals of moderate status begin to fall into their place in the hierarchy.

The high-status members of cliques often have tremendous power over the other clique members and over the group's internal structure. One study of boys' groups at a summer camp provided several illustrations of the role that high-status individuals play in establishing and maintaining a group's hierarchy (Savin-Williams, 1976). The researcher, Ritch Savin-Williams, worked as a camp counselor and carefully recorded his campers' behavior in order to determine how status hierarchies are formed. Here he describes a change at the low end of his cabin's heirarchy. (The boys are referred to as A, B, C, D, and E, on the basis of their position in the hierarchy, with A being the highest-status member of the group):

> On Day 11 the cabin group went hiking, and A and B, as was usual, ran ahead of the group. E (at that time D) attempted to tag along, much to the consternation of the other two. Angrily, A nicknamed E the "shadow." During lunch the next day, A decided to give E a hard time clearing and cleaning the table, demanding seconds and "accidentally" squirting catsup on the table. B and others readily joined in the fun. While E enjoyed the attention, he was not so fond of the verbal and physical ridicule that was his fate for the next week and a half. . . . E received an inordinate barrage of agonistic behavior. During the second 9 days of camp, A and B quadrupled the number of times they dominated him over that of the first 9 days. Not to be outdone, the two boys below E in the hierarchy quintupled their domination over him during the same period. The net effect was to lower E and raise D one notch. . . . The important facet of the illustration above . . . is the demonstration of A's power and influence on the behavior of the other group members. (Savin-Williams, 1976)

THE PEER GROUP AND PSYCHOSOCIAL DEVELOPMENT

Regardless of the structure or norms of a particular peer group, peers play an extremely important role in the psychological development of adolescents. Problematic peer relationships are associated with a range of serious psychological and behavior problems during adolescence and adulthood. Individuals who are unpopular or who have poor peer relationships during childhood and adolescence are more likely than their socially accepted peers to be low achievers in school, to drop out of high school, to have a range of learning disabilities, to show higher rates of delinquent behavior, and to suffer from an array of emotional and mental health problems as adults (Hartup, 1983). Although it is likely that poorly adjusted individuals have difficulty making friends, there is now good evidence that psychological problems result from as well as cause problems with peers (Hartup, 1983).

Peers also play a crucial role in promoting (or hindering) normal psychosocial development. In later chapters we examine in detail the importance of peers in the development of identity, autonomy, intimacy, sexuality, and achievement, but it is worthwhile to comment briefly on these subjects here. In the realm of *identity,* peers provide the sorts of models and feedback that adolescents cannot get from adults. In the context of the peer group, young people can try on different roles and personalities and experiment with different identities with greater ease than at home. Because peers are often experiencing the same sorts of identity-related dilemmas, adolescents can discuss their concerns with friends who are facing similar questions and struggles (Erikson, 1968). During early adolescence, in particular, the peer group may serve as a way station in the development of identity; as adolescents begin to develop a separate sense of self that is differentiated from the family (Brown et al., 1986a). And as we have seen, experience in the peer group can be an important influence on adolescents' self-image. Being rejected or unpopular during adolescence can have a devastating impact on a young person's self-esteem.

Experience in the peer group also is vital for the development and expression of *autonomy.* The process of developing more mature and more independent relationships with parents is accompanied by the establishment of more mature relationships with peers. In addition, the peer group provides a context for adolescents to test out decision-making skills, in an arena where there are fewer adults present to monitor and control their choices (Hill and Holmbeck, 1986). And many theorists have suggested that it is only through experience with peers that adolescents evolve independent values and guidelines for moral behavior, since it is only in the absence of powerful authority figures that young people learn to make moral decisions on the basis of their own principles, rather than based on those that have been handed down by parents, teachers, or other adults (Piaget, 1932).

Intimacy and *sexuality,* of course, are much more common between peers than between adolescents and adults, for a variety of reasons. Perhaps most critical is that both intimacy and sexuality require interaction between two individuals who are relative equals. Moreover, sexual relationships and close intimacy within the family context would be likely to disrupt important functions of family relationships (Hartup, 1977). It is therefore the adolescent's peer group that generally plays the central role in socializing youngsters in appropriate sexual behavior and in developing the capacity for intimate friendship. Without peers, development in each of these domains would be severely limited. Indeed, some writers have even suggested that establishing healthy intimate relationships during adolescence can help an adolescent who has undergone a moderate degree of psychological "damage" during childhood (Sullivan, 1953a).

Finally, peers are an important influence on *achievement*-related behavior. Although they may play a less influential role than parents or teachers, peers undoubtedly influence adolescents' educational and occupational plans (Epstein, 1983b). We noted earlier, for example, that adolescents' attitudes toward school are shaped by their friends. In addition, because of the important role played by agemates in the establishment and maintenance of sex roles, the peer group helps to maintain sex differentials in achievement situations. For instance, during the middle high school years, girls who perform well academically may be totally cut off from social activities with their peers (Coleman, 1961). The threat of peer rejection may force some young women into performing less well in school than they otherwise might.

Several studies of adolescents' activities indicate that the time adolescents spend with peers is one of the most enjoyable parts of the day (Csikszentmihalyi and Larson, 1984). One reason is that activities with friends are typically organized around having a good time, in contrast to activities with parents, which are more likely to be organized around household chores and the enforcement of parental rules (Larson, 1983; Montemayor, 1982). Contrary to stereo-types, the family and the peer group are not in competition with each other; adolescents who have disagreeable relations with their mothers, for example, are likely to spend more time with their fathers, not with their friends. Rather than being competing institutions, the family and peer group seem to provide contrasting opportunities for adolescent activities and behaviors. The family is organized around work and other tasks, and may be important in the socialization of responsibility and achievement. The peer group provides more frequent opportunity for interaction and leisure, which contributes to the development of intimacy and enhances the adolescent's mood and psychological well-being.

Summary

The fact that peers play an important role in influencing adolescent development is incontrovertible. And as contemporary society continues its trend toward modernization, peer groups will come to play an increasingly prominent role in the lives of adolescents. For this reason, it is important to understand how adolescents' peer groups are structured and how peers can affect young people's psychosocial development.

Most research on adolescents' peer groups has been descriptive. We now have a good understanding of why peer groups have risen in prominence during the past half century, of how peer groups are organized into cliques, and of the determinants of clique composition. We also understand how the structure of the peer group changes over the course of adolescence. We know less about the processes through which peer groups influence adolescent development, however.

It is tempting but misleading to draw generalizations about the nature of the peer group during adolescence and to ask whether the influence of *the* peer group—as if all peer groups were the same—is a good or a bad thing. We certainly would not want to make sweeping statements about the impact of the family, the school, or the workplace without taking into account the particular nature of a household, a classroom, or a job setting. By the same token, it is not wise to draw general conclusions about the impact of the peer group without knowing more about the specific peer group in question. The influence of the peer group varies, from one adolescent to another, from one peer group to another, and of course, across different societies and cultures. Studies of contemporary adolescents indicate that the time they spend with peers is generally very positive and enjoyable.

In the previous chapter, we saw that a good deal of research has been devoted to understanding how families differ and to assessing the effects of these differences. Yet comparable research on adolescents' peer groups is lacking. How do peer groups differ from one another, and are these differences important? How is the development of autonomy affected by being in a clique with an autocratic leader? How is the development of intimacy affected by the shift from same-sex to mixed-sex peer groups, and why are some adolescents better able to make this shift than others? How are adolescents affected by having friends who are from different backgrounds? These are all important questions that have yet to be answered. As we have noted, peers can and do play an important and necessary role in fostering healthy development—indeed, healthy development is unlikely to take place in the absence of peers. But undoubtedly, peers can also play a role in hindering healthy development and in promoting undesirable behavior. How a particular adolescent is influenced by his or her peers—for better and for worse—and how peer groups differ in their impact on their members are questions that social scientists are now beginning to address.

Key Terms

anchoring
cliques
cofigurative cultures
crowds
ethnography
participant observation
particularistic norms
peer groups

popularity
postfigurative cultures
prefigurative cultures
reference group
sex cleavage
social class
status
universalistic norms

For Further Reading

COLEMAN, J. (1961). *The adolescent society*. Glencoe, Ill.: Free Press. The classic study of ten midwestern high schools which provided evidence that adolescents had formed a separate "youth culture."

CSIKSZENTMIHALYI, M., AND LARSON, R. (1984). *Being adolescent*. New York: Basic Books. A study of how adolescents spend their time, and how they feel in a variety of activities and settings.

EPSTEIN, J., AND KARWEIT, N. (1983). *Friends in school*. New York: Academic Press. A collection of articles on peer influence and interaction during high school.

HOLLINGSHEAD, A. (1949/1975). *Elmtown's youth and Elmtown revisited*. New York: Wiley. Hollingshead's study of social class and social life among high school students in "Elmtown."

MEAD, M. (1978). *Culture and commitment*. Garden City, N.Y.: Anchor. A fascinating analysis of the important role played by peers in rapidly changing societies.

Schools

CHAPTER 6

PREVIEW

1. High school attendance was not made compulsory for adolescents until well into the twentieth century. Since that time, high schools, colleges, and universities have come to play an increasingly prominent role in the lives of young people.

2. Educators have long debated the goals of secondary education and the approaches schools should take to meet them. The focus of the debate has shifted several times over the years. Today, critics of the schools are calling for more stringent standards and more challenging course work.

3. Researchers have devoted a great deal of attention to examining factors that distinguish successful schools from unsuccessful ones. Social scientists have looked at variations in school curricula, at different types of school organization and structure, and at factors that make the atmosphere of the high school classroom conducive to learning. Good schools are characterized by shared values that emphasize learning, a governance structure in which teachers have a good deal of freedom, and strong links to the surrounding community.

4. Many observers believe that schools are not especially well suited to the needs and capabilities of all adolescents. Students' experiences in school depend a lot on the place they occupy in the school's structure.

The study of schools is important to social scientists and policymakers who are interested in influencing adolescent development, because it is through educational institutions that the greatest number of young people can most easily be reached. When, for example, politicians felt that the United States had lost its scientific edge over the Soviet Union—as they did in the 1950s—schools were called upon to see to it that students took more courses in math and science (Conant, 1959). When policymakers felt that society ought to do something to close the economic gap between the races—as they did in the 1960s—schools were called upon to implement desegregation programs so that all individuals would have equal schooling and equal economic opportunity (Coleman et al., 1966). When social scientists felt that adolescents were growing up unfamiliar with the world of work—as they did in the 1970s—schools were asked to provide opportunities for work-study and classes in career education (President's Science Advisory Committee, 1974). And when economists felt that America was losing its competitive edge in the world economy—as they did in the 1980s—schools were called upon to return to the "basics" and become more academically demanding (National Committee on Excellence in Education, 1983).

Because of the important role it has come to play in modern society, the educational system has been the target of a remarkable amount of criticism, scrutiny, and social science research. Parents, teachers, educational administrators, and researchers debate what schools should teach, how schools should be organized, and how schools might best teach their students. They debate such issues as whether high schools should stick to instructing students in the basics—reading, writing, and arithmetic—or offer a more diverse range of classes designed to prepare young people for adulthood socially and emotionally as well as intellectually; whether students learn more in small schools and small classes or whether it is more efficient to consolidate resources into larger schools that can offer more varied courses and activities. They ask such questions as these:

How should school districts be organized?

Should early adolescents be schooled in separate junior high schools? With younger students? With older students?

Should students be grouped by ability ("tracked"), or should students with different interests and abilities take classes together?

What sort of atmosphere should teachers establish in the classroom?

How important is classroom discipline?

These questions have proven difficult to answer. Nevertheless, they remain extremely important. Virtually all American adolescents under the age of 16 and the vast majority of 16- and 17-year-olds are enrolled in school. More than half of all youth now continue their education beyond high school graduation—in technical schools, colleges, and universities. During most of the year, the typical student spends more than one-third of his or her waking hours each week in school or in school-related activities. Not only are schools the chief educational arena for adolescents in America, they also play an extremely important role in defining the young person's social world and in shaping the adolescent's developing sense of identity and autonomy. It is therefore crucial that we understand how best to plan them.

SECONDARY EDUCATION IN AMERICA

Consider the data presented in Figure 6.1. Today, virtually all young people between the ages of 14 and 17 are enrolled in school. Fifty years ago, only about half of this age group were students, and at the turn of the century, only one in ten (D. Tanner, 1972).

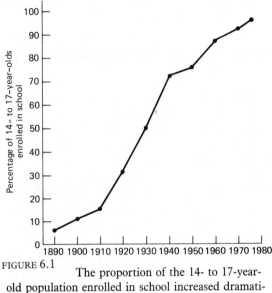

FIGURE 6.1   The proportion of the 14- to 17-year-old population enrolled in school increased dramatically between 1910 and 1940. (D. Tanner, 1972)

Not only are there considerably more youngsters enrolled in school today than there were 50 years ago; today's students also spend more days per year in school. In 1920, for example, the average school term was 162 days, and the average student attended only 121 days, or 75 percent of the term. By 1968, however, the school term had been lengthened to nearly 180 days, and the average student was attending over 160 days of school each year—about 90 percent of the days that school was open (President's Science Advisory Committee, 1974). In many European countries, the school year is even longer. In England, for example, high school students spend 220 days in school each year (National Commission on Excellence in Education, 1983). Although some critics of American schools have called for lengthening our school year (National Commission on Excellence in Education, 1983), others have pointed out that simply expanding the school year, without changing what takes place in school, may be misguided (Boyer, 1983).

Adolescents also remain in school longer

now than they did in past eras. In 1924, fewer than one-third of all youngsters entering the fifth grade eventually graduated from high school; today, about 75 percent of all fifth graders will eventually graduate on time, and a substantial number of those who do not graduate on schedule eventually get their diploma through equivalency programs or continuation schools. More than 50 percent of high school graduates will go on to college (Wetzel, 1987). Over the course of the twentieth century, then, schools have become increasingly prominent settings in the life of the average American adolescent.

The Origins of Compulsory Education

In the introductory chapter of this book, a controversial question was raised: Should high school attendance be compulsory, or should adolescents be permitted to leave school when they turn 14 years old? Although today it is difficult to imagine teenagers *not* spending their days in school, it has been only within the past fifty years that schools have come to play such a prominent role in defining the nature of adolescence in America. When considering education in contemporary society, therefore, one might well begin by asking why mandatory high school attendance developed in the first place.

The rise of secondary education in America was the result of several historical and social trends at the turn of the century. Most important were industrialization, urbanization, and immigration. Following widespread industrialization during the late nineteenth century, the role of children and young adolescents in the workplace changed dramatically. With the economy expanding, many families who at one time had needed their children in the labor force for financial reasons were able to make ends meet without the labor of their young. Furthermore, as the nature of the workplace changed, employers recognized that they needed workers who were more skilled and more reliable than youngsters. Many of the unskilled jobs of the nineteenth century were replaced by jobs that

During the second quarter of this century, high schools began to play an increasingly important role in the lives of American adolescents. (Culver Pictures)

sory elementary education had been introduced during the nineteenth century. Now social reformers began calling for free public education beyond childhood. Eager to improve living conditions for the urban masses, they envisioned education as a means of improving the life circumstances of the poor and working classes. And eager to ensure that the problems of cities did not get out of hand, many saw compulsory secondary education as a means of social control. High schools would take thousands of idle young people off the streets, it was argued, and keep them in a social institution in which they could be supervised and kept out of trouble. Eager, too, to see that foreign-born immigrants were well socialized into the American way of life, reformers presented universal secondary education as a necessary part of the process of "Americanization": It was a way of homogenizing a population characterized by increasing—and to many, increasingly uncomfortable—ethnic and cultural diversity (Church, 1976; D. Tanner, 1972). By 1915, the idea of universal compulsory education for adolescents had gained widespread acceptance.

required more specialized talents—operating complicated manufacturing equipment, for example. The few unskilled jobs that remained required strength beyond the capacity of many youth (Church, 1976). Social reformers also expressed concern over the dangers of children working in factories, and organized labor—an increasingly powerful force during the early 1900s—sought to protect not only the welfare of children but the security of their own employment. Child labor laws narrowed and limited the employment of minors (Bakan, 1972). Together, these changes in the workplace kept many youngsters out of the labor force.

During this same period, the nature of life in American cities was also changing markedly. Industrialization brought with it urbanization and, along with the rising rate of immigration during the early twentieth century, new problems for urban centers. The effects of a rapidly expanding economy were seen in the tenements and slums of America's cities: poor housing, overcrowded neighborhoods, crime. Compul-

The Rise of the Comprehensive High School

Prior to the early twentieth century, before secondary education became compulsory, high schools were designed for the elite. In curriculum, staff, and student composition, they were similar to the colleges of the day (Church, 1976), the emphasis being for the most part on classical liberal-arts instruction (D. Tanner, 1972).

By 1920, however, educators saw a need for curricular reform. Compulsory secondary education had changed the social composition of the schools; many educators argued for a corresponding diversification in the secondary school curriculum. Now that secondary education was aimed at the masses, schooling was seen not merely as a means of intellectual training but as a way of preparing youth for life in modern society. It was argued that education, especially for the majority, should include preparation for work and citizenship roles. Training in Latin and Greek was dropped in many high schools, and the concept of electives was proposed. Vocational education was introduced for the non-college-bound. Many courses in "general" education (in contrast to the more limited college preparatory curriculum) were added—such as home economics and shop (Church, 1976; D. Tanner, 1972).

The 1920s marked the birth of what came to be known as the **comprehensive high school,** an educational institution that would meet the needs of a diverse and growing population of young people. Classes in general education, college preparation, and vocational education were all housed under one roof. As can be seen in Figure 6.1, the proportion of high school-aged individuals enrolled in school jumped dramatically in the years between World War I and World War II—from 32 percent in 1920 to over 73 percent in 1940. This was also a time of tremendous change in the high school curriculum. During these years, new courses were added in music, art, family life, health, physical education, and other subjects designed to prepare adolescents for family and leisure as well as work roles.

The high school had come a long way from its exclusive focus on the intellectual development of the economic elite at the turn of the century. By the 1950s, its concern had broadened to include the social and intellectual development of all young people. And today, despite all the questioning and criticism that have been aimed at it over the years, the comprehensive high school remains the cornerstone of the American system of secondary education.

CURRICULUM: RIGOR OR RELEVANCE?

One of the most difficult issues that society has faced since the birth of the comprehensive high school concerns its curriculum. Suppose you were asked to make a list of the things you think

young people need to know in order to function as competent, responsible, and satisfied adults. Which items on your list should be the responsibility of high schools? Should high school curricula be limited to the traditional academic subjects, or should schools play a broader role in preparing young people for adulthood, by providing instruction more directly relevant to work, family, leisure, and citizenship? Should students receive instruction only in English, mathematics, science, and social studies, or should they take courses as well in "general education"—in subjects such as art, home economics, health, sex education, driver education, and personal finance? Which courses should be required, and which should be left as electives? As you can see, these are extremely hard questions to answer. Furthermore, if you were to discuss these questions with your classmates, you would probably find little consensus.

In recent years, politicians and parents have sounded the cry for schools to scale down their general education offerings and place greater emphasis on the traditional academic subjects: English, mathematics, science, social studies, and a new "basic"—computer science (National Commission on Excellence in Education, 1983). Several social commentators have argued that educators—in high schools and colleges alike—have lost sight of the common core of knowledge and values that serves as the intellectual foundation of our society (Bloom, 1987). To observers who are unfamiliar with the history of America's high schools, this plea for limiting the high school curriculum to the "essentials" sounds like a fresh and timely idea. But while returning to the basics may indeed be seen as a welcome change, this is by no means the first time that educational critics have called for a more rigorous and more focused curriculum. When the question of high school curriculum is approached historically, we find that the pendulum has swung back and forth several times between calls for academic rigor and calls for real-world relevance.

During the early years of the comprehensive high school, for example, the pendulum swung away from a purely academic curriculum and toward more varied course offerings in vocational and general education. In response to the beginning of the Cold War and the launching of the first space satellite, Sputnik, by the Soviet Union, however, educators called for a return to more rigorous academic preparation. At the time, many politicians and educators were concerned that America was losing ground to the Soviet Union because high schools were not spending enough time on math and science. They believed that the "watered-down" curriculum offered by comprehensive high school had left American youth unprepared to face the challenge of communism (D. Tanner, 1972).

During the late 1960s, though, as the Cold War died down, the educational pendulum swung back toward relevance. Educational reformers claimed that schools were not preparing young people for the roles they would encounter as adults (Church, 1976). They felt that adolescents should spend less time in school and more time in community and work settings. Programs such as career education and experiential education were implemented in many school districts so that young people could receive "hands-on" experience in the "real world" (President's Science Advisory Committee, 1974). During this time period, students also became more vocal and demanded more courses in relevant and practical subject areas. Schools began to offer an increasingly wide range of electives for students to choose among. By the late 1970s, over 40 percent of all high school students were taking a general, rather than college preparatory or vocational, course of study, and 25 percent of their educational credits came from work experience outside of school, remedial coursework, and courses aimed at personal growth and development (National Commission on Excellence in Education, 1983).

During the 1980s, the pendulum swung back again toward the "basics." Several proposals called for more demanding curricula (Adler, 1982; National Commission on Excellence in Education, 1983). One set of writers bemoaned what they called the "shopping-mall high

school," where students were given too much freedom in choosing courses and schools were more concerned with keeping students happy than with seeing that genuine and important learning took place (Powell et al., 1985). The achievement test scores of American high school students had fallen steadily, and by 1981 they were lower than they had been when Sputnik was launched. This time, however, the prodding for academic rigor came not from a Soviet threat but to meet the threat of economic competition from Japan and Western Europe. Noting that America was losing its competitive edge in the world market, educational reformers called for more academic rigor in the schools as a means of preparing young people for the workplace of the future. One group, for example, called for schools to implement more demanding academic requirements, tougher standards for graduation, and longer school days (National Commission on Excellence in Education, 1983). Thus the current fascination with "back to basics" is a product of the times in which we live.

You may well wonder why our ideas about the content of the high school curriculum have changed so often. Are we not able to make up our minds about the purpose and responsibilities of educational institutions? Why aren't we able to develop a high school curriculum that works and stick with it? One reason is that high schools, like other social institutions, are embedded in the broader society. As society changes, so does the sort of preparation young people need to develop into capable and competent adults. Another reason lies in the tension—perhaps an unresolvable tension—between the desire to offer a common education to all students and the obligation to recognize that students present schools with an amazingly diverse array of talents and interests. In all likelihood, the "back to basics" movement of the 1980s will eventually give way to another return to "relevance" (perhaps under a different label), as social change once again makes educational reform necessary. The "fresh" educational proposals of the 1980s will seem as outmoded in the future as yesterday's do today.

"Relevance" became an important issue in secondary education during the 1970s. Here a group of high school students learn how to produce their own television show. (David S. Strickler/The Picture Cube)

SCHOOL STRUCTURE AND ORGANIZATION

In addition to debating the issue of curriculum, social scientists have also discussed the ways in which secondary schools should be organized. In this section we examine the research on four aspects of school structure and organization: (1) school and classroom size; (2) different approaches to age grouping, in particular, whether young adolescents should be grouped with younger students, with older students, or separately; (3) tracking, the grouping of students in classes according to their academic abilities; and (4) school desegregation.

School and Class Size

When it comes to schools, is bigger better? The most extensive data on the effects of *school size* on adolescents come from a series of studies conducted by ecological psychologist Roger Barker and his colleagues (Barker and Gump, 1964). These researchers were interested in how the size of a school influences the variety of classes and extracurricular activities available to

students and the students' participation in them. About half of all American high school students attend small schools, with a student body of 600 or fewer (Boyer, 1983).

Large schools offer more varied instruction than do small schools. But as can be seen from Figure 6.2, the variety of courses offered in a school increases substantially only when the size of the school increases dramatically. For example, a 100 percent increase in school size yields only a 17 percent increase in the variety of instruction. In other words, while a school with 2,000 students might offer 50 different classes, a school with 4,000 students would offer only 58.

Perhaps the most interesting findings, however, concern participation in nonacademic activities. One might expect that in addition to providing a more varied curriculum, large schools would be able to offer a more diverse selection of extracurricular activities to their students, and indeed they do. Large schools can afford to have more athletic teams, after-school clubs, and student organizations. In fact, Barker found that nearly four times the number of nonacademic activities were available to students

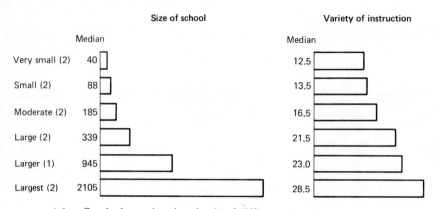

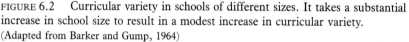

FIGURE 6.2   Curricular variety in schools of different sizes. It takes a substantial increase in school size to result in a modest increase in curricular variety. (Adapted from Barker and Gump, 1964)

attending very large high schools as were available to students in small schools.

But because the large schools also contained so many more students, actual participation in different activities was only half as high in the large schools as in the smaller schools. In Barker's terminology, the large schools were **overmanned**—they had many more students per activity than necessary. As a result, students tended more often to be observers than participants in school activities. For instance, during the fall, a small school and a large school might each field teams in football, soccer, and cross-country running, together requiring a total of 100 students. An individual's chances of being one of those 100 students are greater in a school that has only 500 students than in a school with an enrollment of 4,000.

Because students in small schools are more likely than students in large schools to be active in a wider range of activities, they are more likely to report doing things that help them develop their skills and abilities, allow them to work closely with others, and make them feel needed and important. In a small school, chances are that, sooner or later, most students will find themselves on a team, in the student government, or in an extracurricular organization. Students in small schools also are more

likely to be placed in positions of leadership and responsibility, and they more often report having done things that made them feel confident and diligent. School size especially affects the participation of students whose grades are not very good. In large schools, academically marginal students often feel like outsiders; they rarely get involved in school activities. In small schools, however, these students feel a sense of involvement and obligation equal to that of more academically successful students.

Several recent studies of American high schools have echoed this sentiment (Boyer, 1983; Goodlad, 1984). Although large schools may be able to offer a more diverse curriculum or provide greater material resources to their students, the toll that school size may take on student learning and engagement appears to exceed the benefits of size. One writer has suggested that instead of dismantling schools with 1,500 or 2,000 students, these schools be reorganized into smaller units, each composed of several hundred students—"schools within schools," as these units are sometimes called (Boyer, 1983). In this way, students could take advantage of the large school's resources but would not suffer the feelings of anonymity found so often in a large, impersonal institution.

It is important to keep in mind, of course,

Generally speaking, research has shown that adolescents in large classes learn just as much as adolescents in small ones. An important exception, however, is remedial education: here, adolescents benefit from smaller classes and one-on-one instruction. (Meri Houtchens-Kitchens/The Picture Cube)

that not all large schools are impersonal, overmanned institutions. Many large high schools are able to create a strong sense of involvement among their students and provide ample opportunities for all interested students to participate in school activities (Lightfoot, 1983). What takes place *within* a school is likely to be a far more important determinant of how students behave than simply how large the institution is (Hill, 1980b).

Between 1980 and 1985, numerous reports on American high schools appeared, all of them filled with suggestions for school reform (Boyer, 1983; Goodlad, 1984; Lightfoot, 1983; Powell et al., 1985; Sizer, 1984). In each case, the researchers had spent hours observing what takes place in various high schools—large and small; rural, suburban, and inner-city; public and private—and attempted to articulate just what it

was in the school environment and program that distinguished good schools from bad schools. Although the reports were not always consistent, several themes emerged that point to five general conclusions about good schools.

First and foremost, good schools emphasize intellectual activities. They create this atmosphere in different ways, depending on the nature and size of the student body, but in these good schools, a common purpose—quality education—is valued and shared by students, teachers, administrators, and parents. Learning is more important to students than school athletics or social activities, and seeing that students learn is more important to teachers and administrators than seeing that they graduate.

Second, good schools have teachers who are committed to their students and who are given a good deal of freedom and autonomy by the school administration in the way that this commitment is expressed in the classroom. In all schools, of course, teachers have curricular requirements that they must fulfill. But in good schools, teachers are given relatively more authority to decide how their lessons are planned and how their classes are conducted. When teachers are given this sort of say in school governance, they may find it easier to make a commitment to the shared values of the institution.

Third, good schools constantly monitor themselves in order to become even better. Rather than viewing questions and concerns about school policies and practices as threatening, principals and other administrators welcome opportunities for dialogue and discussion. As one writer pointed out (Lightfoot, 1983), one of the ironies of the good schools she visited was that they understood their own imperfection. When school personnel encourage flexibility, openness to change, and the exchange of ideas, they set a tone for the entire school that may even trickle down into the classroom and result in more stimulating student-teacher interaction.

Fourth, good schools are well integrated into the communities they serve. Active attempts are made to involve parents in their youngsters' education. Links are forged between the high school and local colleges and universities, so that advanced students may take more challenging and stimulating courses for high school credit. Bridges are built between the high school and local employers, so that students begin to see the relevance of their high school education to their occupational futures.

Finally, and perhaps obviously, good schools are composed of good classrooms. In good classrooms, students are active participants in the process of education, not passive recipients of lecture material. Innovative projects replace rote memorization as a way of encouraging learning. Students are challenged to think critically and debate important issues, rather than asked simply to regurgitate yesterday's lessons.

There is no evidence that these goals can only be achieved in small classes, as one might think. In contrast to studies of school size, studies of *class size* indicate that variations within the typical range of classroom sizes—twenty to forty students—do not generally affect students' scholastic achievement (Rutter, 1983). Students in classes with forty students learn just as much as students in classes with twenty students. However, in situations that call for highly individualized instruction or tutoring, smaller classes appear to be more effective. For example, in remedial education classes, where teachers must give a great deal of individual attention to each student, small classes are valuable. As Michael Rutter (1983) points out, one important implication of these findings is that it may be profitable for schools that maintain regular class sizes of twenty-five or thirty students to increase the sizes of these classes by a student or two in order to free instructors and trim the sizes of classes for students who need specialized, small-group instruction.

Approaches to Age Grouping

A second issue that social scientists have examined in the study of school structure and organization concerns the way in which schools group students of different ages. Early in this century, most school districts separated youngsters into an elementary school (which had either six or eight grades) and a secondary school (which had either four or six grades). However, many educators felt that the two-school system was unable to meet the special needs of young adolescents. During the early years of compulsory secondary education, the establishment of separate schools for young adolescents began, and the **junior high school** was born.

According to Joan Lipsitz, whose book, *Growing Up Forgotten* (1977), focuses on early adolescents, a special concern of proponents of separate schools for young adolescents was the "leakage" of many young people from the educational system during the seventh, eighth, and ninth grades. Many students dropped out of school during the early adolescent years. Moreover, some educators felt that early adolescents needed to be separated from younger and older students because of their "peculiarities of disposition." One writer, for instance, called on the school system to check the "physical, mental and moral evils that accompany and grow out of adolescence," warning about "perverted sex habits" such as "self-abuse," "looseness," the reading of "trashy" novels, and the "frequenting [of] moving picture houses" (Bennett, 1919).

In response to these concerns, a few school districts created two-year junior high schools (for seventh and eighth graders). But by far the most popular organization to emerge was the 6-3-3 system, in which the seventh, eighth, and ninth graders were regrouped into a separate school. In more recent years, the **middle school**—a three- or four-year school housing the seventh and eighth grades with one or more younger grades—has gained a certain popularity, replacing the junior high school in some districts. Proponents of middle schools point to the earlier maturation of young people today and the greater similarity of fifth- and sixth-graders to their older peers than to their younger ones.

What is known about the differential effects of these various arrangements? From the point of view of the developing adolescent, are some organizational schemes superior to others? As

Lipsitz notes (1977), there is not a great deal of systematic information available on the impact of different age-grouping arrangements on young people's development and behavior. According to her, we have yet to figure out how to meet the special needs of young adolescents. What little research exists indicates that there are very few differences between going to a middle school and going to a junior high school (Hill, 1978). Perhaps more interesting, though, a recent series of studies indicates that housing young adolescents in eight-year elementary schools—paradoxically, the model popular at the turn of the century—may be preferable to placing them in separate schools.

The most comprehensive study of the impact of different school organizations on the developing adolescent was conducted by sociologists Roberta Simmons and Dale Blyth (1987). These researchers studied youngsters in the Milwaukee public schools for a five-year period.

Some of these students were in school districts organized around the 6-3-3 arrangement, while others were in schools using an 8-4 plan. The researchers were interested in the impact of having to change schools at different ages. They compared shifts in adolescents' self-esteem, grade-point averages, participation in extracurricular activities, and feelings of anonymity as the students moved through each of the two arrangements. In the 8-4 arrangement, students change schools only once, whereas in the 6-3-3 arrangement, they must make two transitions.

As shown in Figure 6.3, adolescent boys' and girls' self-esteem is affected quite differently by the different school arrangements. For boys, self-esteem rises throughout the years between sixth and tenth grades, with the exception of the year between ninth and tenth grades for those in a 6-3-3 arrangement, during which self-esteem remains essentially unchanged. For girls, self-esteem rises throughout the five years in the

FIGURE **6.3**   For boys and girls, self-esteem is affected differently by different school arrangements.

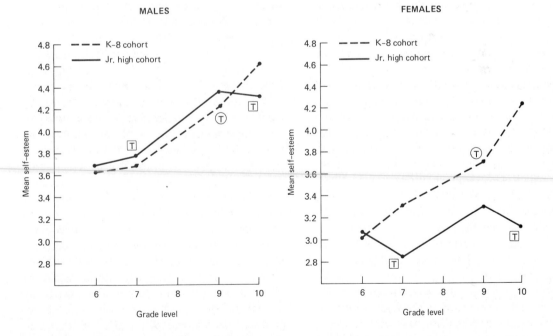

The symbol ☐T☐ indicates a year of transition for the junior high cohort;
Ⓣ indicates a year of transition for the K–8 cohort

8-4 arrangement—as with the boys in this arrangement. But the girls in the 6-3-3 arrangement show two dramatic drops in self-esteem, during each of the transitions into a new school (that is, between the sixth and seventh grades and between the ninth and tenth grades).

The data on youngsters' participation in extracurricular activities again favored the 8-4 arrangement, this time for both boys and girls. Over the five-year period, extracurricular participation decreased slightly for boys in the 6-3-3 plan, whereas it increased slightly for boys in the 8-4 plan. For girls, the differences were more striking. Although sixth graders in both types of schools participated in the same number of extracurricular activities, in the eighth grade, girls who were in the 8-4 arrangement participated in about twice as many activities as did girls in the 6-3-3 organization, and in the tenth grade, they participated in nearly three times as many. The findings concerning students' grade-point averages and feelings of anonymity paint a somewhat different picture. Students' grades declined *whenever* they had to change schools, regardless of the timing of the transition. Similarly, whenever students changed schools, their feelings of anonymity increased for a time.

The researchers concluded that, while all school transitions may have a temporary negative impact on adolescents' psychological well-being and social participation, changing schools may be harder—and consequently may have a more deleterious impact—the earlier it occurs during adolescence. This view is consistent with the authors' "developmental readiness" hypothesis, which we examined in Chapter 1. There we saw evidence that puberty, too, may be more disruptive if it occurs early. Simmons and Blyth also contend that the impact of several simultaneous changes is worse than the impact of any one change alone. Thus the early school transition is particularly hard for girls, because changing schools following the sixth grade often coincides with the onset of puberty and with their initiation into dating (Simmons et al., 1987). Although the effects for boys do not seem as severe, there is evidence that for them, too, the

8-4 arrangement may be preferable to the 6-3-3 plan.

Another study evaluated a school district's changeover from an organization in which ninth-graders were grouped with seventh- and eighth-graders (a 6-3-3 arrangement) to one in which ninth- and tenth-graders were housed in a school separate from older and younger students (a 6-2-2-2 arrangement; [Blyth, Hill, and Smyth, 1981]). These researchers were interested in whether the presence of older students affected the feelings and behavior of younger students. Many parents in the school district had expressed concern that the ninth-graders exerted a negative influence on the younger adolescents, and they favored separating grades seven through twelve into three two-year schools. Parents felt, for example, that young adolescents were more likely to be exposed to drugs and alcohol when they attended school with older youngsters.

The researchers examined the impact of the different grade-level arrangements on self-esteem, extracurricular participation, drug and alcohol use, dating and sexual behavior, perceptions of the school environment, and victimization. They found that the presence of older students negatively affected younger students at all grade levels. Interestingly, the ninth-graders were more adversely affected by being placed with tenth-graders than were either seventh- or eighth-graders by being placed with ninth-graders. For example, the ninth-grade boys who were moved to schools with tenth-graders were less likely to participate in extracurricular activities, less likely to assume leadership positions, more likely to use marijuana and alcohol, more sexually active, more likely to feel anonymous, and more likely to be picked on. Ninth-grade girls in schools with tenth-graders also were less likely to participate in school activities, less likely to assume leadership positions, more likely to use drugs and alcohol, and more likely to feel anonymous. For seventh- and eighth-graders, the removal of the ninth-graders had positive effects: The transfer of older students to a different school increased the participation

Recent studies indicate that changing schools often or early during adolescence may affect school achievement and self-esteem negatively. In general, a two-school arrangement, in which junior high school is eliminated, may be preferable to the more widely used three-school arrangement. Young adolescents are more likely to flourish in school when they attend an elementary school through the eighth grade and then graduate to a high school. (Frederik D. Bodin/Stock, Boston)

of younger students in school activities, decreased substance use, decreased feelings of anonymity, and decreased the likelihood of victimization.

These findings pose a dilemma for those hoping for simple solutions to problems in school organization. Removing ninth-graders from junior high schools and placing them with tenth-graders appears to benefit the younger students who remain in the junior high school. But doing so may place the ninth-graders at a disadvantage. As the authors suggest, different methods of school organization have different effects on students of different ages, and what may help some may harm others. Nevertheless, these studies indicate that early adolescents may benefit from changing schools less often and remaining somewhat separate from older peers.

Although some aspects of the transition into secondary school may be difficult for students to negotiate, not all students experience the same degree of stress during the transition. The Simmons and Blyth studies indicate that students experiencing the transition earlier in ado-

lescence have more difficulty with it than those experiencing it later. Other studies indicate that adolescents who have close friends before and during the transition into secondary school adapt more successfully to the new school environment (Berndt, 1987). Consistent with this, students who have more academic and psychosocial problems before the transition into middle or junior high school—that is, during elementary school—cope less successfully with the transition (Safer, 1986). Evidently, the transition into secondary school is not the sort of stressor that has uniform effects on all students. More vulnerable adolescents and adolescents with fewer sources of social support may be more susceptible to the adverse consequences of this stressor than their hardier or more socially protected peers.

Tracking

In some schools, students with different academic abilities and interests do not attend classes together. Some classes are designated as more challenging and rigorous and are reserved for students identified as especially capable. Other classes in the same subject area are designated as average classes and are taken by most students. Still others are designated as remedial classes and are reserved for students having academic difficulties. The process of separating students into different levels of classes within the same school is called **tracking.** Not all high schools use tracking systems. In some schools, students with different abilities take all of their classes together.

Educators have debated the pros and cons of tracking for years (Rutter, 1983). Its proponents argue that tracking allows teachers to design class lessons that are more finely tuned to students' abilities. Tracking may be especially useful at the high school level, where students must master certain basic skills before they can learn such specialized subjects as science, math, or foreign languages. It is extremely difficult for a teacher to teach algebra, for example, in a classroom in which some students are already familiar with the subject but others have difficulty with simple multiplication and division. If too much time is spent on the basics, little time will be spent on algebra, and the more advanced students may become bored. But if the lessons are aimed solely at the advanced students, those who have not yet mastered the basics will be confused and frustrated. If students are tracked, proponents say, these problems can be avoided.

Unfortunately, however, tracking creates problems of its own. Students who are placed in the remedial track are likely to be labeled by their peers as slow or stupid. Their self-esteem may suffer, and they may eventually come to see themselves as failures (Rutter, 1983). What is more, because schools play such an important role in influencing adolescents' friendships, when students are tracked they tend to socialize only with peers from the same academic group (Rosenbaum, 1976). Tracking can contribute to the polarization of the student body into different subcultures that feel hostile toward each other. The students in the advanced track may feel superior and look down on other students,

and the students in the remedial track may feel angry and resentful. Finally, some critics of tracking point out that decisions about track placements often discriminate against poor and minority students and may hinder rather than enhance their academic progress (Rosenbaum, 1976). Some school counselors assume, for example, that black or poor youngsters are not capable of handling the work in advanced classes and may assign them to average or remedial classes, where less material is covered and the work is less challenging. According to one study, a very good student from a disadvantaged background has only a 50 percent chance of being assigned to the academic, or college prep, track (Vanfossen et al., 1987). Other studies, however, indicate that student ability is a stronger influence on track placement than student background (Alexander and Cook, 1982).

Research on tracking indicates that students' academic achievement is not greatly affected—positively or negatively—by the use of such systems. There is evidence, however, that students' course selection and plans for the future are negatively affected by placement in a lower track (Vanfossen et al., 1987). In light of the adverse psychological impact that tracking has on students in the nonacademic tracks, many researchers now feel that the costs of tracking outweigh the benefits. Mixed-ability classes may have some psychological advantages for less able students without impeding the academic progress of their more able peers (Rutter, 1983).

School Desegregation

Since the landmark Supreme Court ruling in *Brown* v. *Board of Education* (1954), many of the nation's school districts have enacted changes aimed at desegregating their schools. Underlying the Court's ruling was the belief that segregation in schools impedes the academic and economic progress of students from racial minorities and, in addition, fosters hostility and misunderstanding between individuals of different backgrounds. Even if racially segregated

The Sexes: Ability Grouping and Sex Differences in Mathematics Achievement

According to a recent review, differences in the mathematics achievement of boys and girls, which favor boys, are well documented (Fennema and Peterson, 1985). Although in elementary school girls generally outscore boys on tests of math achievement, during junior and senior high school, boys are more likely to take math classes and are more likely to outperform girls. These sex differences are important, because students emerging from high school with little preparation in mathematics are unlikely to be able to enter college programs (such as engineering) and occupations (such as scientist) that require training in math. Decisions that young women make early in their educational careers therefore may have important long-term implications for their occupational and educational futures.

Many psychological explanations have been offered for the flipflop in math achievement during early adolescence, including (1) that girls come to see math achievement as part of the masculine role and develop negative attitudes toward math as a consequence, (2) that girls have fewer role models of successful mathematicians or scientists and, consequently, are less likely to aspire to enter these fields; and (3) that girls receive pressure from their male peers not to excel in math class (Hallinan and Sorensen, 1987). We examine some of these explanations in Chapter 12 as part of our discussion of adolescent achievement. As Hallinan and Sorensen point out, however, psychological explanations of sex differences in math achievement ignore organizational aspects of schools that may have important effects. In particular, they suggest that tracking biases in the math curriculum operate against the assignment of girls to high-ability math classes.

These researchers examined mathematics ability-group assignments in a large sample of fourth- through seventh-graders. They were interested in whether assignment to the high-ability group was influenced by the student's math ability, his or her sex, or a combination of both. They found, not surprisingly, that a student's ability weighed heavily in the assignment process, with more able students more likely to be assigned to the high-ability group. But they also found that the benefits of being high in math ability were greater for boys than girls. In other words, high-ability girls were less likely to be assigned to the high-ability group than were boys of comparable talent (Hallinan and Sorensen, 1987).

The authors then asked whether this assignment process differentially hurt the math achievement of girls. Specifically, if girls who should have been assigned to the high-ability group were not, perhaps these girls had less opportunity to learn than they would otherwise have had. Surprisingly, though, analyses suggested that the high-ability girls' actual math achievement was not diminished by the biased ability grouping process. High-ability girls in the high-ability group achieved just as much during the year as high-ability girls in the average group. As the authors point out, however, this is no cause for complacency. For one thing, it still may be too early in these girls' careers to see the cumulative effect of not being exposed to the most challenging math instruction. For another, the biased assortment of youngsters into math tracks may have long-term implications for future course selection. Even if the immediate effect on math achievement is small, an adolescent girl who is not assigned to a high-ability math class—despite her talent—may come to develop more negative attitudes toward math than she might have otherwise.

schools appear equivalent on various indices of quality (for example, the amount of money spent on educational materials and programs), segregated schools are inherently unequal, the Court argued, because "to separate [black youngsters] from others solely because of their race generates a feeling of inferiority as to their status in the community that may affect their hearts and minds in a way unlikely ever to be undone" (*Brown* v. *Topeka Board of Education*, 1954). Since the Court's ruling, many school districts have adopted measures designed to create voluntary desegregation (for example, permitting families to choose among different schools within a large catchment area rather than assigning students to specific schools on the basis of their residence). Others have enacted policies aimed at mandatory desegregation (assigning students of different racial background to specific schools in order to create predetermined racial balances) (Bradley and Bradley, 1977).

Few subjects have generated as much controversy in recent years—not only among the general public but in social science circles as well—as has the desegregation of public schools. Researchers have examined the impact of desegregation on a wide range of outcomes, including adolescents' academic achievement, racial attitudes, educational and occupational ambitions, social behavior, friendship formation, and psychosocial development. Literally hundreds of studies have been conducted (Campbell, 1977).

Despite the considerable legal basis for desegregation, research on the effects of desegregation programs on high school students has not been overwhelmingly encouraging. Several sets of studies point to this disappointing conclusion. First, research indicates that desegregation has surprisingly little impact on the achievement levels of either black or white youngsters (St. John, 1975). Second, there is some evidence that black youngsters' self-esteem is higher when they attend schools in which they are in the majority—a phenomenon true not only for black youth, but for all youth (Rosenberg, 1975). Third, as we saw in the previous chapter, interracial contact, even in desegregated schools, is

rare, largely because of the reluctance on the part of white students to form cross-racial friendships (Hallinan and Teixeira, 1987). Fourth, studies indicate that immediately following the imposition of a desegregation program, white enrollment in a school declines as white families move or withdraw their child from the public school, although the high rate of "white flight" appears to be most pronounced during the first year of a desegregation program and slows shortly thereafter (Wilson, 1985).

As sociologist Jomills Braddock (1985) points out, however, focusing on the short-term impact of desegregation may provide only a very narrow means of assessing its costs and benefits. He notes that black youngsters who have attended desegregated high schools—especially boys—are more likely to graduate and to continue their education in desegregated institutions. Because blacks graduating from predominantly white colleges earn more when they enter the labor force than blacks who attend predominantly black colleges, it seems that youngsters who attend desegregated high schools may reap advantages in the labor force later on, as young adults. Moreover, black graduates of predominantly white schools are more likely to work in integrated environments and live in integrated neighborhoods during adulthood. Taken together, these studies suggest that desegregated high school programs indeed benefit black youth, but that these benefits may not be apparent until adulthood. Furthermore, these studies suggest that desegregation during high school does appear to help break down racial barriers in society at large.

It also may not be advisable to make sweeping generalizations about the impact of school desegregation without looking further at the processes inside the school and how they are affected (or not affected) by its racial composition. Segregation may be maintained in "desegregated" schools through tracking, seating assignments, and class scheduling. One would need information on how school policies and procedures were changed and on how students, teachers, and administrators responded to the

School desegregation and busing continue to be controversial, and still there are no solid conclusions about the costs and benefits of desegregation to adolescent development. (Peter Southwick/Stock, Boston)

changes. All desegregated schools are not the same (Campbell, 1977). Consider, for example, the differences between two desegregated schools. Each has achieved a 50-50 racial balance. But in one school, the black and white students are taught in different classes; in the other, the classes themselves are all integrated. Obviously, it makes little sense to view these schools as having similar environments merely because they are both classified as "desegregated."

Finally, not all children and families respond in the same way to changes in the racial composition of their school. Some parents and students are enthusiastic about such changes, whereas others are apprehensive. Thus in any comprehensive study of the effects of school de-

segregation, it would be important to know how children of different ages are affected, how children from different racial and socioeconomic backgrounds are affected, how parents' attitudes toward desegregation affect the child's reaction, and so forth. These and other factors are likely to mediate the impact of desegregation on the adolescent (St. John, 1975).

THE IMPORTANCE OF SCHOOL CLIMATE

Most social scientists and educators now agree that the school-related factors most important in influencing learning and psychosocial development during adolescence concern the more immediate environment of the school and classroom. As noted earlier, in good schools, the classroom environments encourage dialogue between teachers and students and among students, and learning is emphasized over memorization. According to Michael Rutter (1983), various aspects of the school and classroom *climate* have important effects on youngsters' learning and achievement. Specifically, the way teachers interact with students, the way classroom time is used, and the sorts of standards and expectations teachers hold for their students are all more important than the size of the school, the way that age groups are combined, or the racial composition of the school.

Using a questionnaire called the Classroom Environment Scale, Edison Trickett and Rudolph Moos have studied the ways in which classroom environments differ and the extent to which these differences are associated with students' behavior and performance (Moos, 1978; Moos and Trickett, 1974; Trickett, 1978; Trickett and Moos, 1973). The questionnaire is completed by students and measures nine classroom dimensions: involvement, affiliation, teacher support, task orientation, competition, order and organization, rule clarity, teacher control, and innovation.

One of Trickett's recent studies, for instance, compared samples of classrooms from five different categories of schools: urban, rural, suburban, vocational, and alternative (Trickett, 1978). As shown in Figure 6.4, classroom environments differ considerably on these nine dimensions, indicating that differences in global characteristics among schools are sometimes reflected in differences in the more immediate environments to which their students are exposed. For example, the differences between alternative and vocational schools are particularly striking: whereas the classrooms in alternative schools typically emphasize interpersonal factors, the classrooms in vocational schools are more likely to be oriented around rules and regulations.

What sort of climate brings out the best in students? Considered together, the results of several studies indicate that the same factors which promote psychosocial development in the home—warmth, high standards, and moderate control—also promote positive behavior in the classroom. Students and teachers are more satisfied in innovative than control-oriented classes and in classes that combine a moderate degree of structure with high student involvement and high teacher support. In these classes, teachers encourage their students' participation but do not let the class get out of control. Classes that are too task-oriented, particularly when they also emphasize teacher control, tend to make students feel anxious, uninterested, and unhappy (Moos, 1978). The pattern of classroom variables associated with positive student behavior and attitudes, then, is reminiscent of the *authoritative* family environment. Similarly, an overemphasis on control in the classroom in the absence of support is reminiscent of the *authoritarian* family, while a lack of clarity and organization is reminiscent of the *indulgent* or the *indifferent* family—and these styles may affect adolescents detrimentally. Students do best when their teachers spend a high proportion of time on lessons (rather than on setting up equipment or dealing with discipline problems), begin and end their lessons on time, provide clear feedback to students on what is expected of them and on their performance, and give ample praise to students when they perform well (Rutter, 1983). A good high school teacher, in other words, bears a striking resemblance to a good parent.

This general pattern of findings has been replicated in several other studies. In an extensive program of research on young adolescents in London schools, for example, Michael Rutter and his colleagues (Rutter et al., 1979) found that after controlling for differences in students' backgrounds and abilities before entering secondary school, school climate was significantly associated with student performance, attendance, and delinquency. Generally speaking, schools in which teachers were supportive but firm and maintained high, well-defined standards for behavior and academic work had fewer problems, higher rates of attendance, lower rates

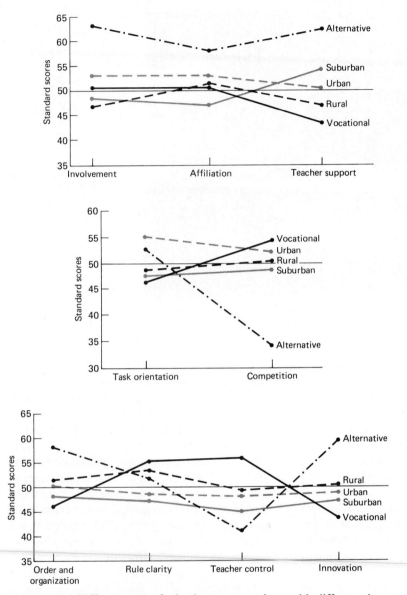

FIGURE 6.4   Different sorts of schools present students with different class-room environment. (Adapted from Trickett, 1978)

of delinquency, and higher scores on tests of achievement. This pattern is remarkably similar to that uncovered in studies comparing public and private high schools (Coleman, Hoffer, and Kilgore, 1982). In these studies, too, students' achievement was higher in schools that were somewhat more structured and demanding—no matter whether the school was public or private.

As Rutter (1983) explains, being an effective teacher entails two distinct processes: gaining and maintaining students' attention and instructing students in the subject matter. A

Students perform better when their teachers maintain well-defined, high standards for behavior and academic work and behave in a supportive but firm manner. (Elizabeth Crews/Stock, Boston)

teacher who is a good lecturer will not be an effective teacher if he or she lacks classroom management skills. Managing a classroom effectively entails more than merely knowing how to discipline students once they become unruly, however. In fact, teachers who spend too much time on disciplining the few students who misbehave run the risk of losing the interest of the rest of the class. Especially in junior high school classrooms, where young adolescents may not yet have developed a high level of self-control in the absence of guidelines from adults, maintaining students' attention depends on having well-organized lesson plans, teaching in a way that involves and engages the whole class, and using creative and innovative approaches to instruction. As most experienced teachers know, disorganized lesson plans and frequent interruptions for discipline can quickly lead to chaos in the classroom. The National Commission on Excellence in Education (1983), for example, recommended that schools adopt and enforce firm disciplinary codes and that continually disrup-

tive students be removed from classrooms in order to permit teachers to spend more time on teaching and less on discipline.

It is important to keep in mind that not all students are affected the same way by a given school or classroom climate. Although the "authoritative" school climate (high supportiveness, moderate structure, clear expectations, and firm discipline) appears in general to be preferable to other types of atmosphere, students vary in the extent to which they flourish under different degrees of support, structure, and control. It may be more helpful to think of the authoritative school climate as a general category within which good teachers vary their methods from time to time to suit the needs of particular students. For example, teachers who are demanding, challenging, and somewhat critical of inferior work are more successful with high-ability students, while teachers who are relatively more supportive, warmer, and more encouraging are more successful with students of lower academic ability (Brophy, 1979).

Several studies also point to the importance of teachers' expectations of students. When teachers expect more of their students, they actually learn more; when teachers expect less, they learn less. This phenomenon is known as the **self-fulfilling prophecy** (Rosenthal and Jacobson, 1968). Unfortunately, research suggests that teachers are likely to base their expectations in part on students' ethnic and socioeconomic background. In much the same way that these factors may influence tracking decisions, as we saw earlier, they may consciously and unconsciously shape teachers' expectations, which, in turn, affect students' learning. Thus, for example, teachers may call on poor or minority students less often than on their affluent or white peers—conveying a not-so-subtle message about whose responses the teacher believes are more worthy of class attention (Good and Brophy, 1984). It is not difficult to see how years of exposure to this sort of treatment can adversely affect a student's self-concept and interest in school. Indeed, teacher biases against lower-class children may make it difficult for students from lower socioeconomic groups to attain a level of academic accomplishment that would permit upward mobility.

Teachers and school personnel, of course, are not the only influences on adolescents' behavior in school. Several writers have noted that the peer group's values and norms also exert an important influence. In *The Adolescent Society* (1961), for example, James Coleman found that high schools vary a great deal in the extent to which the prevailing peer culture emphasizes academic success as a route toward status and popularity. In schools in which academic success is not valued by the student body, students are less likely to achieve grades that are consonant with their tested ability. In other words, a bright student who attends a school in which getting good grades is frowned upon by other students will actually get lower grades than he or she would in a school in which scholastic success is generally admired.

As we noted in the previous chapter on peer groups, however, cliques and crowds differ enormously in the extent to which they encourage or discourage academic success (Clasen and Brown, 1985). It therefore is misleading to generalize about the impact of peer groups on adolescents' engagement in school without knowing more about the specific peer group in question. Some peer groups (e.g., the "brains") may place a great deal of pressure on their members to succeed in school and may engage in behaviors (e.g., studying together) that promote school success. Other groups, in contrast, may actively discourage school success. An especially telling example of this is seen in a recent ethnographic study of black male peer groups in an inner-city school (Fordham and Ogbu, 1987). In the peer groups studied, pressure was put on the group members *not* to achieve, because succeeding in school was seen as "acting white" and breaking from the group's ethnic identity. Thus those students with high aspirations found themselves having to choose between succeeding in school and keeping their friends, a position that few adolescents of any race would want to find themselves in.

EDUCATING ACADEMICALLY HANDICAPPED AND GIFTED ADOLESCENTS

The large, comprehensive high school is often geared to the needs of the average student. Adolescents who deviate from this norm are therefore less likely to be schooled in a way that is suitably matched to their capabilities and interests. This state of affairs is particularly problematic for young people whose level of academic achievement is extremely low or extremely high, relative to their peers. It is estimated that close to 10 percent of the children and youth in America need special education of some kind because of a behavioral, emotional, or intellectual handicap (Lipsitz, 1977). Estimates of the number of gifted adolescents—who also would benefit from special educational treatment—are harder to make, because criteria for defining "giftedness" vary considerably from state to state and from school to school (Gallagher, 1979). Actually, in both areas there has been a trend away from the use of global labels to categorize students and toward greater specificity in describing and defining each individual student's strengths and weaknesses.

Although special programs do sometimes exist for mentally retarded, learning disabled, and gifted adolescents, funding for these programs is generally meager. The programs that do exist are usually implemented at the elementary rather than secondary or postsecondary level. In the case of special education, for example, more funding goes to programs serving preschool and elementary school students, and relatively little goes to programs serving adolescents (Lipsitz, 1977). In the case of adolescents who are classified as gifted in one way or another, funding agencies and the public often have extremely ambivalent feelings about spending money on students perceived as having an intellectual advantage when there remain adolescents in need of remedial or compensatory education (Gallagher, 1979). Yet most experts feel that any student who deviates significantly from peers in talent or ability—on either side of the continuum—benefits from educational programs tailored to meet his or her specific needs.

During the past twenty-five years, the dominant issue in the education of adolescents with special educational needs has revolved around the extent to which these youngsters should be integrated into classrooms with more typical students. In special education circles, the issue revolves around the concept of **mainstreaming,** the integration of adolescents with educational handicaps into regular classrooms (Turnbull and Schultz, 1979). (Mainstreaming, whenever possible, is required by federal law.) In discussions of the treatment of academically gifted adolescents, it revolves around the choice between acceleration and enrichment. **Acceleration** involves having a student move through a regular academic program at a faster than average rate;

enrichment entails the provision of additional, broadening educational experiences (Keating, 1979).

Before 1950, few special programs for educationally handicapped or academically gifted students existed. All students were generally taught in regular classrooms, and some were either held back or placed ahead as their school performance seemed to warrant. During the late 1950s and early 1960s, special programs were initiated for gifted students in many schools; but these efforts were short-lived, and few programs survived the 1960s. By the mid-1970s, however, specialized education for the gifted began to receive attention once more, and new programs were implemented (Tannenbaum, 1979). Separate programs for the educationally handicapped increased considerably during the late 1960s and early 1970s, until legislation requiring mainstreaming, enacted during the mid-1970s, shifted practices back toward the integration of these students into regular classrooms (Turnbull and Schultz, 1979). Mainstreaming remains widely used today.

It is clear that there are costs and benefits associated with both the integration and the segregation strategies. They are analogous to the issues involved in the pros and cons of tracking. On the one hand, it is possible that in specially designed classes, with instructors who are specially trained to work with exceptional students, youngsters may be taught in ways that are more appropriately geared to their needs and capabilities.

On the other hand, separating adolescents merely on the basis of their intellectual abilities may have undesirable effects on their psychosocial development. Youngsters who are segregated in special classes may be stigmatized by their peers and their opportunities for social interaction with a wide range of peers curtailed. And adolescents who are in regular classes may themselves suffer, by being denied the opportunity to interact with individuals whose interests and abilities are different from those of the average adolescent.

POSTSECONDARY EDUCATION IN AMERICA

The Accessibility and Diversity of Higher Education

The early part of the twentieth century was an important time in the development not only of secondary schools but also of postsecondary educational institutions in the United States. Although colleges and, to a lesser extent, universities had existed for some time previously, not until the latter part of the nineteenth century did diversity in institutions of higher education begin to develop. Early postsecondary institutions were typically small, private liberal arts colleges, often with a strong theological emphasis. But during a relatively brief period bridging the nineteenth and twentieth centuries, these colleges were joined by a host of other types of institutions, including large private universities, technical colleges, professional schools, publicly financed state universities, land-grant colleges, urban universities, and two-year community colleges (Brubacher and Rudy, 1976).

Although postsecondary educational institutions multiplied and became more varied during the early part of this century, enrollment in college was still a privilege enjoyed by very few young people. In 1900, only 4 percent of the 18- to 21-year-old population was enrolled in college; and by 1930, the proportion had grown to some 12 percent. Even as recently as 1950, fewer than one in five young people were enrolled in college (Church, 1976). During the first half of the twentieth century, then, colleges and universities were not prominent in the lives of most American youth.

How different the state of affairs is today. Paralleling the rise of secondary education between 1920 and 1940, postsecondary education grew dramatically between 1950 and 1970 (see Figure 6.5). By 1960, one-third of all young people were entering college directly after high school graduation. College enrollments, which numbered about 1 million in 1930, had risen to

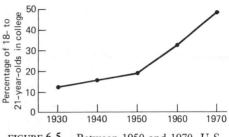

FIGURE 6.5 Between 1950 and 1970, U.S. college enrollments expanded markedly.

more than 3 million by 1960 and to nearly 8.5 million by 1970. Today, nearly half of the 18- to 19-year-old population is enrolled in college. Although there were large increases in the enrollment of minority youth during the 1970s, the proportion of minority youth enrolled in higher education fell during the early 1980s (Wetzel, 1987).

If there are two dominant characteristics that distinguish the development of postsecondary education in contemporary America from that in other parts of the world, they are diversity and accessibility (Brubacher and Rudy, 1976). In countries other than the United States, postsecondary education is likely to be monopolized by monolithic public universities, and relatively few adolescents continue their formal education beyond high school (President's Science Advisory Committee, 1974). Individuals are often separated into college- and non-college-bound tracks early in adolescence, typically on the basis of standardized national examinations. In fact, rather than housing all high school students in comprehensive high schools such as those found in the United States, many European nations separate students during early adolescence into schools for college-bound youngsters and schools designed to provide vocational and technical education.

Although the accessibility and diversity of its postsecondary educational institutions have been commended by many, the American system of higher education has not been without its critics (Brubacher and Rudy, 1976). Some observers have suggested that educational diversity has been gained at the expense of quality. With so many different options and electives for young people to choose among, it has been hard for colleges to ensure that all students receive a high-quality education. Others have pointed out that it is difficult for many young people to obtain adequate information about the range of alternatives open to them and that students are often poorly matched with the colleges they enter (President's Science Advisory Committee, 1974). The large enrollments of high schools make it difficult for school counselors to give each student individualized advice.

Most significant, although many more young people enroll in college today than in previous years, a very large number do not graduate. Perhaps as a consequence of increasing accessibility, poor matching, and a lack of "consumer" knowledge among college applicants, rates of college attrition are high: Only four of every ten students who enter college in the United States graduate from the same college four years later. Of the 60 percent of students who leave the school they entered, about half eventually finish college, either returning to that particular college or transferring to another. Half, however, never obtain a college degree. Of the students who drop out of college, about half do so during their first year (Pantages and Creedon, 1978). In other words, while a great deal has been done to make college *entrance* more likely, rates of college *graduation* lag far behind.

The Community Colleges

More than one-third of all college students are enrolled in two-year community colleges, a disproportionate number of them minority and lower-income students (Dougherty, 1987; Pincus, 1980). For many adolescents, entering the local community college after graduating from high school has become a near-automatic transition (President's Science Advisory Committee, 1974). Community colleges typically provide three types of offerings: (1) two-year terminal programs, generally geared for entry into a spe-

cific occupation; (2) two-year college-preparation programs, intended for students who wish eventually to enter four-year institutions; and (3) courses for individuals who wish to attend school but may not be interested in completing a formal academic or vocational program.

Community colleges played a major role in absorbing the new entrants to higher education in the 1960s and 1970s. It was hoped that these two-year schools would fill a special educational need for students whose career choices do not require a four-year college degree and for students who want to continue in school beyond high school graduation but need time or additional preparation before entering a four-year school. Although these schools have undoubtedly served these purposes for many students, two-year colleges have increasingly faced problems similar to those experienced by the comprehensive high school—and have been the target of much criticism as a result (Pincus, 1980).

Like the comprehensive high school, community colleges have struggled with many problems inherent in trying to serve a wide range of students with diverse needs and capabilities. In many respects, they have been more successful for students who eventually transfer into four-year colleges than for students who enter two-year terminal programs (President's Science Advisory Committee, 1974). Indeed, several studies have indicated that community colleges do not have a good record in placing students with specific vocational interests in jobs that are consistent with the training they have received (Pincus, 1980). One extensive study, for example, found that private technical schools are far more effective in placing their graduates in appropriate jobs than are public community colleges. One reason for this is that community colleges are slower than private technical schools in adapting to the needs of a changing labor market (Wilms, 1975). Community colleges, caught in a bureaucratic morass, have difficulty implementing curricular changes promptly, and they sometimes continue to offer courses in technical areas long after the demand for workers in those fields has waned. They may turn out hundreds

Community colleges attempt to serve a wide range of students with diverse needs. Several studies indicate that community colleges have failed to prepare students adequately for careers because they are slow to adapt to the changing needs of the labor market. (Alan Carey/The Image Works)

of computer technicians, for example, into a community that has an oversupply of people looking for these sorts of jobs. Private, profit-making schools, in contrast, are able to change their course offerings frequently and fine-tune their curricula to the changing demands of the job market.

The record of community colleges for students whose ultimate goal is a four-year college degree is not encouraging either, according to one recent review (Dougherty, 1987). This author concluded that students who aspire to a four-year college degree attain less educationally and economically if they begin their education at a two-year community college than if they start at a four-year college. This is not necessarily the case for students who enter community

colleges intending only to complete two years of college, however. Nonetheless, the evidence indicates that although two-year colleges have become an important means of access to higher education for low-income and minority youth, the limitations of the institution may contribute to continued class and race stratification.

SCHOOLS AS A CONTEXT FOR ADOLESCENT DEVELOPMENT

It is difficult to generalize about the effects of schools on students. Many critics view high schools as either modified prisons or junior country clubs, depending on whether they serve poor youngsters or wealthy ones (Friedenberg,

1967). True, some schools *are* little more than holding vats for adolescents, in which concerns over discipline and safety overshadow teaching and learning, and others are little more than social gathering places, where what goes on outside the classroom is far more important than what takes place within.

But there are many, many excellent high schools in the United States that are exciting and stimulating places, where adolescents grow intellectually and psychologically and where they learn a great deal about themselves and the world they live in. Perhaps you were fortunate enough to have attended such a school—to have had interested and interesting teachers, challenging classes, and opportunities to participate in a range of satisfying extracurricular activities. If so, then you know that high schools can play a very important role in young people's development.

Nevertheless, many observers feel that the majority of secondary schools do not promote adolescent learning and development as much as they might. One pessimistic review concluded, for example, that while high schools are moderately successful in promoting learning among the best and brightest students, they are alarmingly unsuccessful in reaching the individuals who need them the most. Students who enter high school deficient in basic reading, writing, and arithmetic skills gain virtually nothing intellectually from their years of high school attendance. Their performance on tests of achievement does not improve between ninth and twelfth grades (Stipek, 1981).

Other studies, however, suggest that, whatever the shortcomings of schools may be, staying in school is preferable to dropping out, as far as cognitive development is concerned. (We look more closely at the causes and consequences of dropping out in a subsequent chapter on achievement.) One study contrasted the performance of dropouts and graduates on a battery of standardized tests of achievement administered during late adolescence (Alexander et al., 1985). The study took into account differences in achievement levels that existed before the dropouts had left school (two years before the assessment was conducted), because dropouts are more likely than graduates to show achievement problems early in their educational careers. Adolescents who stayed in school gained far more intellectually over the two-year interval than did the dropouts in a variety of content areas. More important, the results showed that the adverse effects of dropping out were most intense among socioeconomically disadvantaged students. Paradoxically, then, those students who are most likely to leave school prior to graduation may be most harmed by doing so.

One other way of assessing the contribution of schools to adolescents' intellectual development is by comparing early adolescents' intellectual gains during the school year with their gains during the summer. An ingenious study by Heyns (1982) did just this. Using information on the academic progress of students measured at three points in time—the beginning of the school year, the end of the school year, and the beginning of the next year—she was able to see how the academic progress of students during the summer compared with their academic progress during the school session. Her results were surprising and point once again to the importance of school for minority and disadvantaged youth. Among white students, rates of academic progress during the school year and during the summer were comparable. Among black students, however, the pattern was different. Although rates of progress during the school year were more or less equal to those of white students, during the summer months, black students' scores actually declined. In other words, if it were not for the effects of school on cognitive development, the discrepancy between white and black youngsters' achievement scores would be much greater than it currently is.

Far less is known about the impact of schools on the psychosocial development of adolescents. Some observers have noted that most schools are not structured to promote psychosocial development, with their excessive focus on conformity and obedience and their lack of encouragement for creativity, independence, and self-reliance (Friedenberg, 1967; Hill, 1980b). But there are very many good schools, in which students not only learn the academic material taught in classes, but learn about themselves, their relationships with others, and their society as well. Schools differ from each other, and it may be difficult to generalize about the impact of schools on adolescent development without knowing more about the particular school in question.

Studies also show that students' experiences within a school can vary widely according to the track they are in, the peer group they belong to, and the extracurricular activities in which they participate. It seems safe to say that academically talented and economically advantaged students have a more positive experience in school than their less capable or less affluent counterparts—positive not only with respect to what they learn in class, but with respect to the impact of school on their feelings about themselves as individuals. Their teachers pay more attention to them, they are more likely to hold positions of leadership in extracurricular organizations, and they are more likely to experience classes that are engaging and challenging. In other words, the structure of a school—its size, its tracking policy, its curriculum—provides different intellectual and psychosocial opportunities for students who occupy different places within that structure. The best answer to the question, "How do schools affect adolescent development?" is another question: "Which schools and which adolescents?"

In the introduction, we noted that policymakers are now beginning to question the wisdom of requiring that all young people remain in school through most of adolescence. How can we demand that all adolescents attend school, they ask, if we cannot demonstrate that they all benefit from such attendance? It is a hard question to ponder. But maybe the answer lies not in changing the age at which people are permitted to leave school, but in changing the nature of schools and in making schools more responsive to all students.

Summary

In contemporary society, schools have come to play an increasingly prominent role in the lives of young people. Researchers have examined a wide range of factors thought to distinguish successful from unsuccessful schools. They have discovered that the most important factors are related not to the overall structure or organization of the school but, rather, to what goes on inside the classroom. Successful schools are schools that have effective teachers, and effective teachers are teachers who—like effective parents—are warm, firm, supportive, and talented.

Ever since the inception of compulsory secondary education, policymakers, educators, and social scientists have debated about the goals of secondary schools and the means schools should adopt to meet them. Today, the focus is on making high schools more rigorous. Twenty years ago, the debate centered on making education more relevant. Ten years into the future, the issue will have shifted once again. No clear consensus has emerged on the purpose of secondary education in contemporary society, and it is unlikely that one ever will. In a diverse and heterogeneous society, schools must meet the needs of a wide range of adolescents with varied capabilities and interests. And in a rapidly changing world, we must be able and willing to transform schools as the nature of adolescence, and the demands and needs of society, change.

More research is needed on adolescents and schools that will bridge our understanding of educational processes and our knowledge about adolescent development. As we understand more about the stresses associated with puberty, for example, we will be better able to plan youngsters' school transitions so that they do not coincide with periods of psychological vulnerability. As we understand more about the nature of cognitive development during adolescence, we will be better able to devise teaching strategies that stimulate intellectual growth rather than simply communicate facts and figures. And as we learn more about the problems young people face in becoming capable and responsible adults, we will be better able to judge what role schools should—and should not—play in easing the transition into adulthood. In short, as we come to understand more about adolescent development, we will be better able to design schools with adolescents' needs in mind.

Key Terms

acceleration
comprehensive high school
enrichment
junior high school
mainstreaming

middle school
overmanning
self-fulfilling prophecy
tracking

For Further Reading

BROPHY, J., AND EVERTSON, C. (1976). *Learning from teaching: A developmental perspective.* Boston: Allyn & Bacon. A discussion of factors related to effective classroom teaching.

CHURCH, R. (1976). *Education in the United States.* New York: Free Press. A comprehensive history of the development of schools in America.

LIGHTFOOT, S. (1983). *The good high school.* New York: Basic Books. Profiles of several good high schools and a discussion of their similarities and differences.

POWELL, A., FARRAR, E., AND COHEN, D. (1985). *The shopping mall high school.* Boston: Houghton Mifflin. An extensive critique of the nature and structure of contemporary high schools.

RUTTER, M. (1983). School effects on pupil progress: Research findings and policy implications. *Child Development, 54,* 1–29. A review of research on how students' achievement is affected by the schools they attend.

The Adolescent Workplace

CHAPTER 7

PREVIEW

1. Many American adolescents work while attending school. The student-worker, however, is a relatively new phenomenon. In previous eras, the worlds of school and work were separate. Today, the typical high school student works more than fifteen hours each week.

2. Adolescents generally take on formal part-time jobs when they reach age 15 or 16. However, many young people work before this age informally in their neighborhood or around the house on assigned chores.

3. Only recently have researchers begun to study the work environments of young people. These studies challenge widely held assumptions about the value of early work experience. Far from being conducive to learning and psychological development, many adolescents' jobs are monotonous, unchallenging, and stressful.

4. The impact of work on adolescents' development depends on the nature of the work setting. Given the types of jobs most adolescents hold, it is not surprising to learn that working during high school has costs as well as benefits. Research indicates that extensive involvement in a part-time job during the school year may lead to problems at school and increased drug and alcohol use.

We typically do not think of the world of work as a place that figures significantly in the lives of most young people. Most discussions of the contexts of adolescence are limited to the family, the peer group, and the school. Yet in primitive and modern societies; in urban, suburban, and rural areas; in past eras as well as in the present, adolescents have provided labor for the adults around them. And in contemporary society, the workplace is increasingly becoming a context where young people spend a considerable amount of time.

Most youngsters who were enrolled in high school during the 1980s held part-time jobs at one time or another during the school year. More than 80 percent of today's high school students will have worked before graduating. But although working while attending high school may currently be the norm, only recently has part-time employment become prevalent among American adolescents. In fact, the widespread employment of students represents an important break from past eras, in which going to school and working were mutually exclusive activities.

Whenever a social change of this magnitude occurs, social scientists want to know the reasons behind it. Large-scale changes in the social context in which adolescents live usually have important implications for adolescent development. Is the growth of teenage employment due to economic inflation, increased job opportunities for young people, or changing values among American youth? Is teenage work a passing fad, or is it a phenomenon that is here to stay? How has employment changed the daily lives of American teenagers? Has it affected their mental health, their relationships with friends and family members, their attitudes toward education? Has the adolescent workplace had an impact on what goes on in adolescents' families, at school, or in the peer group?

The role of work during adolescence has been an issue of considerable debate among educators and policymakers. As noted in the previous chapter, many social scientists and social critics have recommended that adolescents be given greater opportunity to gain work experience during their high school years (President's Science Advisory Committee, 1974; National Panel on High School and Adolescent Education, 1976; National Commission on Youth, 1980; Carnegie Commission on Policy Studies in Higher Education, 1980). These educators and policymakers have argued that working helps adolescents develop a sense of independence, brings young people and adults closer together, and teaches young people important skills that they will need as adults. In short, adolescent work experience has been presented as a means of easing the transition into adult roles. But does working actually live up to these expectations?

These are some of the questions we will examine in this chapter, as we look at the world of adolescent work—at the jobs adolescents hold, at what goes on inside the adolescent workplace, and at the impact of employment on adolescents' development. Compared with research on the family, the peer group, and the school, research on adolescents in the workplace is far less extensive, and we shall find that many important questions remain unanswered. Nevertheless, the adolescent workplace has been the focus of several recent studies, and the results of this research may surprise you. Contrary to the widely held belief that early work experience helps to build character, some studies show that the impact of working on adolescents' psychological and social development can be harmful as well as beneficial.

ADOLESCENTS AND WORK IN AMERICA

The Separation of Youth from the Workplace

The segregation of young people from the work of adults has not always characterized adolescence in American society. Before 1925—when continuing on in high school was the exception, not the rule—most teenagers entered the work

In previous eras, adolescents played an important role in farming. Early work experience of this sort readied young people for the work they would perform during adulthood. (The Bettmann Archive)

force by the time they turned 15 years old. Teenagers from all but the most affluent families left school between the ages of 12 and 15 and entered the labor force as full-time workers (Modell, Furstenberg, and Hershberg, 1976). Adolescents were either students or workers, but not both.

During the second quarter of this century, however, the school began to replace the workplace as the setting in which most adolescents spent their weekdays. As secondary education grew and became more widespread among different social and economic segments of American society, more youngsters remained in school well into middle and late adolescence, and fewer elected to work. Compulsory education laws were passed in most states that required youngsters to remain in school until at least the age of 16, and part-time jobs were not plentiful. Furthermore, a variety of child labor laws were enacted to restrict youngsters' employment (Kett, 1977).

As a result of these social and legislative changes, the employment of American teenagers in the formal labor force declined steadily during the first four decades of this century. As labor force expert Beatrice Reubens points out,

It is true that a tradition has long existed in the United States that it was respectable, even praiseworthy to work one's way through school, but [before 1940] the numbers [of students who worked] were not large. Prior to World War II, attending school and holding a . . . job were almost exclusive activities. (Reubens, Harrison, and Rupp, 1981, p. 296)

An incredible reversal had taken place in a period of about twenty-five years. Early in the century, most adolescents were workers, not students. By the middle of the century, most adolescents had become students, not workers. In 1940, only 5 percent of 16- and 17-year-old male high school students worked during the school year. Less than 2 percent of female students of this age were employed (U.S. Department of Commerce, 1940).

The Emergence of the Student-Worker

The situation began to change again between 1940 and 1950. The rise of a separate workplace, composed almost exclusively of adolescents, was under way. Examining this phenomenon in detail provides a nice example of how changes in society can transform the nature of adolescence.

Following the end of World War II, sectors of the American economy that needed large numbers of part-time employees expanded rapidly (Ginzberg, 1977). In particular, the postwar period was a time of tremendous growth in retail stores and restaurants. Between 1950 and 1976, the retail trade sector of the economy (which includes all jobs in which people sell finished products to consumers) expanded by 96 percent, and the service sector (which includes all jobs in which people provide services to others), by 172 percent. As economist Eli Ginzberg observed in 1977, "More than three out of every five new jobs created [since 1950] have been in retail trade or services, where many jobs are part-time and wages are traditionally low" (1977, p. 47). Employers, particularly in businesses such as fast-food restaurants, needed workers who were willing to work part-time for relatively low wages and for short work shifts. Many employers looked to teenagers to fill these jobs. Consequently, over the past twenty-five years or so, one out of every three new entrants

into the labor force has been a young person (Ginzberg, 1977, p. 45).

Another reason for the phenomenal rise of the adolescent workplace is the dramatic increase during the last twenty years in the cost of living for the typical American teenager. Although inflation took its toll on people of all ages, it hit teenagers especially hard (see the accompanying box). For example, the cost of being a teenager rose more than 20 percent between 1975 and 1979, and more than 15 percent in 1979 alone. In both periods, the rate of inflation on typical teen items, such as records and movie tickets, rose considerably faster than the rate of inflation overall. But unlike many adults who receive cost-of-living salary increases commensurate with the rate of inflation, many adolescents rely on a weekly allowance from their parents, which usually does not rise as economic indicators change. As prices rose and allowances held steady, adolescents looking for spending money were drawn into the world of work (Rotbart, 1981).

As shown in Figure 7.1, the proportion of high school students holding part-time jobs rose dramatically from 1940 on. By 1980, according to a nationwide survey conducted for the National Center for Education Statistics (Lewin-Epstein, 1981), about two-thirds of all high school seniors and about half of all high school sophomores held part-time jobs during the week prior to the survey. More recent estimates indicate that the proportion of working high school students has not changed appreciably since this time (Bachman et al., 1986). By current estimates, at any one time during the school year, well over 6 million American high school students are working.

In less than half a century, adolescence had undergone a remarkable change. In 1940, it was virtually unheard of for a high school student to hold a regular part-time job during the school year. Today, it is almost unheard of for a high school student not to work.

In the past it was young people from less affluent families who were more likely to work; today the opposite is true. Working during high

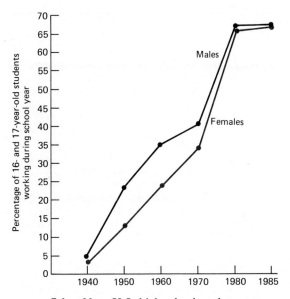

FIGURE 7.1   More U.S. high school students are working during the school year now than at any other time in recent history.

The Transition to Adult Work Roles in Contemporary Society

As we saw in Chapter 3, social scientists interested in adolescence have long been concerned with the extent to which transitions into adult roles are gradual (continuous) or abrupt (discontinuous). In many traditional societies the transition of adolescents into adult work roles is gradual and continuous. In most contemporary societies, in contrast, the transition into the world of adult work is often discontinuous. Adolescents generally grow up unfamiliar with the work adults perform and typically do not acquire hands-on experience in adult work activities until they themselves have reached adulthood.

The transition most American adolescents experience has both continuous and discontinuous aspects. On the one hand, American adolescents are more likely than adolescents in comparably industrialized countries to have part-time work experience before reaching adulthood. On the other hand, this work experience is seldom in the sorts of jobs they will be likely to occupy as adults.

There are several reasons for the lack of continuity in work roles found in contemporary society. As the workplace has changed, with fewer and fewer jobs requiring unskilled labor, so have the skills and knowledge necessary to participate successfully in the world of work. It therefore has become increasingly unlikely that an adolescent growing up in modern society will be well equipped before graduating from high school to handle the sorts of work performed by most adults. Most jobs in offices and stores now require that workers be college-educated.

Because the family has come to play a less central part in society's economic activities (unlike the case in many traditional societies, in which the family is the primary economic and work unit), children and adolescents have become increasingly divorced from the work of their parents. Virtually all children spend most of the day in school. Few spend even part of their day in settings in which they are able to

school is more common among middle- and upper-middle-class teenagers, presumably because these youngsters have an easier time finding employment. Jobs in the adolescent workplace are more likely to be located in suburban areas, where the more affluent families reside. The national survey cited above revealed, for example, that the teenagers most likely to work came from families earning between $20,000 and $25,000 annually. Least likely to be employed were teenagers from families with annual incomes below $7,000 (Lewin-Epstein, 1981).

Not only are more high school students working today than ever before, but those who do work are working for considerably more hours than adolescents have in the past (Greenberger and Steinberg, 1986). The average high school sophomore put in close to 15 hours per week at a job, and the average senior, about 20 hours per week (Bachman et al., 1986; Lewin-Epstein, 1981). Considering that the average school day runs for about 6 hours, today's typical working adolescent is busy with school or work commitments for close to 50 hours a week.

Coping with Kidflation

One explanation for the dramatic increase in teenage employment during recent years is the remarkable increase during this same time in the cost of being an American teenager. The following article provides some insight into the phenomenon called "kidflation."

"It's hard to be a kid today because you've got a lot to worry about, including money, which is one of the biggest problems," explains Miss [Lauren] Krzywkowski, a seventh grader in Cleveland. She says the $1-a-week allowance she usually gets is insufficient to buy the snacks and other things she enjoys. "I wish I was back in the good old days when you could go to the store with 10 cents and have a field day," she says. . . .

Although the government doesn't keep such statistics, and private research is very limited, there are indications that the buying power of children has shrunk significantly over the past five years. Because even dime and quarter increases in the cost of children's items often mean huge leaps in terms of percentages (and weekly allowances), "kidflation" in some cases has outpaced the adult variety.

[On the basis of] conversations with over 50 children, this newspaper compiled a "market basket" of 15 items frequently purchased by children, then determined from manufacturers approximately what has happened to the retail prices of those items. While the resulting "Kiddie Consumer Price Index" isn't scientific, and prices may vary from city to city, it offers some insight into what the younger generation is up against.

The kiddie market basket includes among other items, gum, ice cream, candy, records, toys, fast food, and a ticket to a major league baseball game. The total would have cost $14.29 on December 31, 1975. By that same day in 1979, the price for the basket had risen 21 percent to $17.27, and by the end of 1980 it was up a further 17 percent to $20.13. The Consumer Price Index, meanwhile, rose 14 percent from 1975 to 1979, and then an additional 12 percent from 1979 to 1980.

While the numbers indicate that until 1979, kids had fared pretty well compared with adults, a look at children's incomes in the period suggests otherwise. Unfortunately for kids, income from allowances, paper routes, babysitting, and mowing lawns isn't tied to the Kiddie Consumer Price Index. . . .

Many parents tend to set their allowance payments by age, rather than need. At the Callahan house in Cleveland for example, 11-year-old Ricky receives the same $5 weekly that his older brother, Michael, got before he turned 12. At that point, Michael's income was doubled to $10 a week. "My mom gives me the same amount as she gave him," Ricky says, "But he could get more things with it when he was 11."

. . . Being astute consumers is only one tack kids have taken to keep themselves afloat financially. Educators say that an increasing number of children have begun to look for outside jobs at an earlier age. "It just floors me that even in the fourth grade, kids are earning money," says Helen Rindsberg, coordinating teacher for consumer economic education in the Cincinnati public school system. Mrs. Rindsberg says a survey of ninth-grade students in some Cincinnati economics classes found about 50 percent have outside jobs.

Source: D. Rotbart, "Allowances Stay Flat, Candy Rises—and Kids Lose Their Innocence," *Wall Street Journal*, March 2, 1981, pp. 1 ff.

see adults on the job. And even fewer, of course, actually accompany their parents to work. As a result, many adolescents grow up without much exposure to the adult workplace, and many do not gain this exposure until they are ready to enter the job market.

Although youngsters in contemporary America do not enter the formal labor force until the age of 15 or 16, many individuals have worked on an informal basis during childhood. We can identify four phases in the transition of young people into adult work roles:

Today, adolescents usually work in jobs that are unrelated to the careers they will pursue as adults. (Jill Cannefax/EKM-Nepenthe)

1. *Household work:* During childhood, most boys and girls are assigned chores around the house (White and Brinkerhoff, 1981). Typically, they help in the kitchen, help care for younger siblings, and help in such tasks as yardwork and cleaning. Families who own and operate a business such as a store or a farm may require children to work in the family enterprise. However, family businesses, once popular in America, are relatively rare today.

2. *Informal part-time employment:* By late childhood and during early adolescence, many youngsters begin to take on employment outside the home on an informal basis for other family members or neighbors. Babysitting is a common source of income for many young adolescents, as are gardening, house cleaning, and newspaper delivery (Greenberger and Steinberg, 1983).

3. *Formal part-time employment:* As adolescents reach the age required for formal employment in their home state, they generally enter the formal labor force as part-time employees in the adolescent workplace. Typically, this occurs between the ages of 14 and 16. Students take on jobs after school, in the evenings, and on weekends, with many working fifteen hours or more weekly on a regular schedule. Although most jobs open to teenagers pay only the minimum wage, they pay more than the informal jobs held by younger adolescents (Greenberger and Steinberg, 1983).

4. *Full-time employment:* Full-time employment in the adult workplace usually begins shortly after an individual has completed his or her schooling.

Teenage Employment in America and in Other Nations

The extent and nature of teenage employment vary considerably from country to country. In most traditional societies, work life and family life are not as distinct as they are in contemporary America, and youngsters are typically integrated into the world of work before they reach adolescence (Whiting and Whiting, 1975). If the society subsists on farming, children are taught how to farm at an early age. If the society subsists on hunting, children are taught how to hunt. Although young people who are still acquiring work skills may be given tasks that are more elementary than those performed by their elders, adolescents and adults work side by side, and a distinct adolescent workplace—such as that in the United States—is not usually found. Whereas we draw a distinction between schooling and work in contemporary society, in many traditional societies, the two activities are essentially the same.

In developing nations, where industrialization is still in a relatively early stage and a large percentage of the population is poor, adolescents generally leave school early—at least by American standards. In these countries, most adolescents enter into full-time employment by the time they are 15 or 16, in jobs similar to those they will hold as adults. Very often, adolescents work for their families. The pattern in these countries closely resembles America at an earlier stage in its own industrialization: school for adolescents of the extremely affluent; work for the majority of teenagers.

The contrast with other comparably industrialized countries is the most interesting, for it reveals that the high school student-worker is a distinctively American phenomenon. In most highly industrialized countries other than the United States, adolescents are more likely to defer employment until their education is completed. As shown in Figure 7.2, for example, during 1979, over two-thirds of all American 16- and 17-year-old adolescents were working while attending school; but in Canada, only about 37 percent of this group was employed, in Sweden, only about 20 percent, and in Japan, less than 2 percent (Reubens, Harrison, and Rupp, 1981). In these countries and others in Western Europe, young people generally move from school directly into full-time employment without an intervening period of formal part-time work. In the United States today, it is more common for youngsters to move from full-time school with no formal employment (during early adolescence), to a combination of school and part-time work (during middle and late adolescence), to full-time work (sometime during late adolescence or early adulthood).

How can we account for these differences between the United States and other industrialized countries? First, part-time employment opportunities are not as readily available elsewhere as they are in America. Fast-food restaurants, although increasingly popular in other countries, are not seen on every major street. Second,

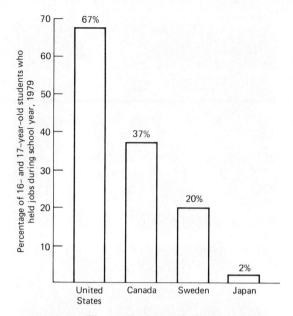

FIGURE 7.2   The employment of high school students is far more common in the United States than in other industrialized countries. (Reubens, Harrison, and Rupp, 1981)

the scheduling of part-time jobs in other countries is not well suited to the daily routines of students. In Europe, for example, the school day lasts well into the late afternoon, and relatively few shops are open in the evenings. In the United States, many adolescents leave school early in the afternoon and go straight to their part-time jobs, where they work until nine or ten o'clock in the evening. Third, in most other industrialized countries, the employment of children is associated with being poor, and there is a strong stigma attached to having one's children work. Many middle-class parents do not feel that it is appropriate for their children to have jobs while attending school. Finally, schools demand much more out-of-school time in countries other than the United States; it is not uncommon for a European high school student, for example, to be assigned four or five hours of homework nightly. The average American high school student rarely spends this amount of time *weekly* on homework (Reubens, Harrison, and Rupp, 1981; Greenberger and

Steinberg, 1986). However, the employment rate among students in some other industrialized nations is on the rise, particularly in Great Britain, Sweden, and Canada. As the service and retail industries in these countries grow, the rate of student employment may come to resemble that in the United States.

THE ADOLESCENT WORKPLACE TODAY

Common Adolescent Jobs

The range of jobs open to adolescents who wish to work in the formal labor force is rather limited. Most surveys indicate that the proportion of adolescents who hold challenging or interesting jobs is very, very small. A substantial proportion of working high school students are employed in restaurants—staffing fast-food counters, preparing food, waiting on customers, clearing tables, seating guests, or washing dishes. About 17 percent of all working high school students work in these sorts of jobs. The remainder tend to work in other types of retail establishments—as cashiers or sales clerks (jobs that fall into these categories, outside of food service work, account for about 20 percent of *happen* working teenagers); in offices, as clerical assistants (10 percent); or as unskilled laborers (also about 10 percent). Unlike in previous eras, very few teenagers today are employed on farms or in factories (Lewin-Epstein, 1981).

The Adolescent Work Environment

In one series of studies of adolescents who work, the researchers examined teenagers' work environments. They were especially interested in collecting information about the degree to which adolescents had contact with adults on their jobs and about the sorts of tasks teenagers were given (Greenberger and Steinberg, 1981; Greenberger, Steinberg, and Ruggiero, 1982). If working is going to be a positive influence on youngsters'

The part-time employment of teenagers reached an all-time high in the early 1980s. Studies of the impact of employment on adolescent development, however, suggest that there may be costs associated with working more than fifteen or twenty hours per week during the school year. (Rick Mansfield/The Image Works)

development, they reasoned, it is likely to be so only if the work environment provides opportunities for learning and self-reliance. Most of the workers studied were employed in one of six types of work: food service (for example, fast-food counter worker); clerical (file clerk in an office); retail (cashier in a store); manual labor (gardener); and skilled labor (assistant automobile mechanic). Using an elaborate coding system to record on-the-job activities, the researchers observed what went on in the work settings. They recorded the tasks adolescents performed (for example, cleans table), the things they said ("May I help you?"), and the people with whom they interacted (an adult customer). They also interviewed the adolescent workers and had them complete a series of questionnaires about their experiences at work.

The results were surprising. Unlike adolescents in traditional societies, whose work typi-

The Sexes: Sex Differences in the Adolescent Workplace

One of the topics that social scientists interested in work have studied extensively concerns sex differences in the labor force. It is well documented that men and women typically work in different types of jobs and that men generally are paid higher wages—even when they do the same work as women. This disparity has been an important concern to many people who feel that such sex differences in patterns of work are unfair and serve to maintain economic inequities between the sexes. Are the same sorts of disparities found in teenagers' jobs? The answer seems to be yes (Lewin-Epstein, 1981; Greenberger and Steinberg, 1983).

Generally, boys are more likely to work as manual laborers, skilled laborers, gardeners, busboys, janitors, and newspaper deliverers. Girls are more likely to be employed as food servers, house cleaners, and babysitters. Moreover, boys almost never work as secretaries, receptionists, babysitters, nurse's aides, or house cleaners; and girls almost never as "busgirls," dishwashers, gardeners, manual laborers, janitors, or newspaper deliverers (see accompanying figure). A study of over 3,000 adolescents in southern California revealed that boys work longer hours than girls, and that "boys'" jobs pay better than "girls'" jobs. In fact, the average hourly wage for boys is about 15 percent higher than it is for girls (Greenberger and Steinberg, 1983).

These findings are important because they indicate that youngsters are exposed to the sorts of sex differences characteristic of the adult workplace long before they reach adulthood. However, one question that cannot be answered is whether sex differences in adolescents' work experience are due to the different preferences of boys and girls (that is, whether boys and girls *choose* to work in different kinds of jobs) or to discrimination in the labor force (that is, whether employers choose boys for some jobs and girls for others). Could it be that sex differences in job preferences are established even *before* adolescence? In order to answer this question, one needs to look at patterns of work during childhood.

Were you given household chores when you were growing up? If you had a sibling of the opposite sex, were your chores the same, or were they different? Recent research suggests that in most families, the separation of "boys' " work and "girls' " work begins early in childhood, and that chores become even more sex-typed as children get older. Among young children, for example, boys and girls are equally likely to be given the chore of washing dishes. By the time children are a little older, however, this has become a "girls' " job. The opposite is true for various sorts of manual labor around the house, such as yardwork, which becomes more and more a "boys' " job as children get older (White and Brinkerhoff, 1981).

On the basis of these studies, it seems that young people learn lessons about the sex-

cally brings them into extensive contact with adults, the young people observed in the studies spent as much time on the job interacting with other adolescents as they did with their elders. In the typical fast-food restaurant, for example, nearly all of the workers were teenagers, the work supervisor was usually not much older, and the customers were often young people, too. Few of the teenage workers surveyed reported having formed close relationships with adults at work. They were unlikely to see their adult supervisors or coworkers outside of work, felt reluctant to go to the adults they knew at work with personal problems, and generally reported feeling less close to adults at work than to other people in their lives (Greenberger and Steinberg, 1981).

The studies also indicated that most teen-

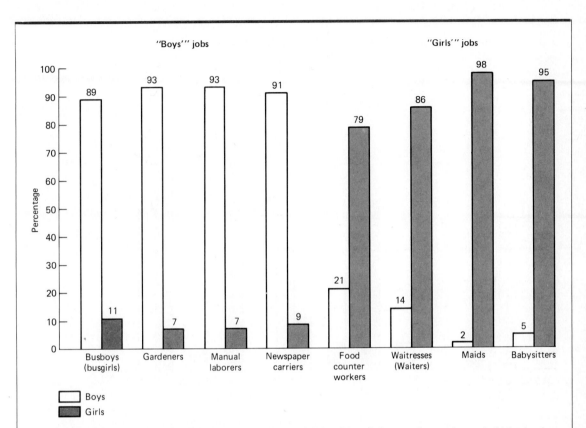

"Boys'" jobs   "Girls'" jobs

Percentage of boys versus girls in common adolescents' jobs. Some jobs are almost always held by boys, whereas others are almost always held by girls.

appropriateness of various work roles at an early age. And these lessons have important implications for the subsequent occupational development of males and females. Adolescent males and females aspire to different jobs and expect to enter different occupations. Early work experience, it appears, reinforces and readies adolescent boys and girls for the sex roles they will be likely to encounter in the workplace as adults.

Mastery Orientation not stimulated.

agers' jobs are pretty dreary. Few jobs permit adolescents to behave independently or make decisions, they receive little instruction from their supervisors, and they are rarely required to use the skills they have been taught in school (Greenberger and Steinberg, 1986). As an illustration of this point, consider the following contrast: The average adolescent worker spends less than 6 percent of time on the job in such activities as reading, writing, or arithmetic; but he or she spends more than 25 percent of the time cleaning or carrying things.

With occasional exceptions, most teenagers' jobs are repetitive, monotonous, and unlikely to be intellectually stimulating. Some are even highly stressful, requiring that youngsters work under intense time pressure without much letup (Greenberger and Steinberg, 1986).

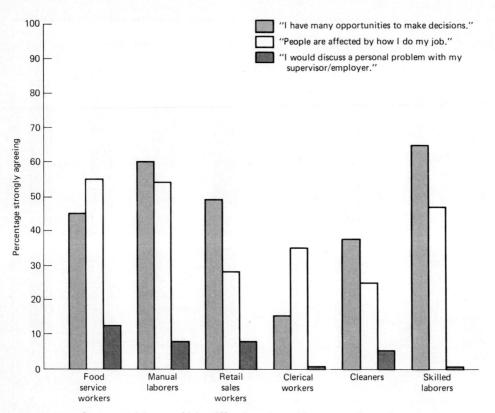

FIGURE 7.3   Common adolescents' jobs differ along several important dimensions. (Greenberger and Steinberg, 1986)

Differences among adolescents' jobs. Of course, not all jobs provide adolescents with identical work environments; some jobs are better than others.

As shown in Figure 7.3, differences among the six most common types of jobs are most pronounced in the opportunities they provide for adolescents to take initiative. Food service positions, retail jobs, and jobs in skilled labor provide the greatest opportunity to exercise initiative; cleaning jobs, the least. Opportunities for social interaction also vary across the job types. Food service and retail work involve the highest levels of social interaction; cleaning jobs, the lowest. However, the nature of social interaction in fast-food restaurants differs from that in retail stores: In food service work, adolescents

interact chiefly with other adolescents; in retail work, their interaction is often with adults. Adolescents' jobs vary least along the dimensions measuring opportunities for learning. Overall, the results of the study favor retail jobs, at least with respect to the opportunities these jobs provide adolescents for learning, initiative, and social contact (Greenberger and Steinberg, 1986).

Work through School-Sponsored and Volunteer Programs

Although the majority of teenagers who work are in the labor force as paid part-time workers, many young people work through work-experience and volunteer programs designed to teach them valuable skills and information. Psychol-

The Burger Blues

The fast-food industry employs more American teenagers than does any other specific segment of the labor market. Given the results of the observational study described in the text, it is not surprising to learn that many adolescents who work in fast-food restaurants are unhappy with their jobs.

> Low pay, distasteful working conditions, and autocratic bosses are hardly a new story to the millions of teenagers that the fast-food industry depends upon to peddle the billions of hamburgers, fries, and shakes it sells every year. But . . . few youngsters realize when they apply for a fast-food job that they will be doing better than average if they don't get disgusted and quit within four months. . . .
>
> "I quit because I didn't like the way the managers treated us," says a 17-year-old who was a cashier at an Atlanta McDonald's last summer. "The managers," she says, "are real snotty. They yell at the workers in front of customers and call you stupid. At the end of August, fifteen of us quit because of one manager. Otherwise, most of us would have kept working after school." . . .
>
> Low pay is a constant irritant. A 16-year-old who quit an Atlanta Wendy's last fall says he was "doing more work than I was getting paid for" at $2.65 an hour. "Sometimes I'd have to work twelve hours a day. Other times there weren't enough of us for lunch-time crowds. One month we went through five assistant managers. When I get another job it won't be in fast foods."
>
> To be sure . . . a number of fast-food employees . . . [feel] well-treated. "I like working here," says an Alabama fast-food worker. "It gives me a chance to meet new people." Another teen-ager, who makes $2.65 an hour as a Burger King food handler, says, "It's a lot of fun. The managers are nice to work for. I work pretty much the time I want to." And a young man working the counter in a Florida store says, "All the hard work is rewarding in the long run because the manager is a friend, parent, counselor, adviser, teacher, and boss."
>
> More numerous, however, [are] comments such as [this] one from a counter employee in Texas who complained: "Management puts tremendous mental strain on the employees. We have all learned how to successfully steal enough money . . . to make working here with all the bull and pressure worthwhile."

Source: J. Montgomery, "Low Pay, Bossy Bosses Kill Kids' Enthusiasm for Food-Service Jobs," *Wall Street Journal*, March 15, 1979, pp. 1 ff.

ogist Stephen Hamilton (1981) has suggested that a well-designed work-experience program can be an important supplement to adolescents' formal schooling. Rather than working in the sorts of routinized and unstimulating jobs typically found in the adolescent workplace, adolescents who choose to participate in experiential learning programs may serve as apprentices to skilled craftsmen; give their services to the elderly, the handicapped, or the disadvantaged; tutor younger students who are having difficulty in school; or help to clean up or refurbish their neighborhood. These sorts of work experiences may not provide the income that paid employment does; but in the view of some young people, the personal satisfaction gained may be more important than the income earned working in the adolescent workplace.

WORKING AND ADOLESCENT DEVELOPMENT

The Development of Responsibility

Most people believe that working builds character, teaches adolescents about the "real" world, and helps young people prepare for adulthood. Like many of the widely held views of adolescence that have gone unquestioned over

Many young people work as volunteers in hospitals, schools, and community centers. According to some psychologists, these sorts of service activities may enhance psychosocial development. (Alan Carey/The Image Works)

the years, these assumptions are not entirely supported by hard facts. Indeed, recent studies indicate that working during adolescence may even have some costs to young people's development.

One study examined the impact of employment on young people growing up during the Great Depression. The researchers found that boys who took on part-time jobs outside the home became more adultlike as a result: "Boys . . . who were employed showed a much greater interest in adults and spent more time with them . . . than other children. . . . Economic hardship and jobs increased their desire to associate with adults, to 'grow up' and become adult. This adult orientation is congruent with other behavioral correlates of roles in the household economy, including the responsible use of money . . . energetic or industrious behavior . . . and social independence" (Elder, 1974, pp. 81–82). Because very few girls worked outside the home during the Depression (most remained home and performed household labor so that their mothers could enter the labor force), the impact

of employment on the development of responsibility among girls was not studied.

Studies of more contemporary youth also support the view that holding a job may help adolescents become more personally responsible (Steinberg, Greenberger, Garduque, Ruggiero, and Vaux, 1982). For example, in studies of southern California youngsters, standardized measures of responsibility were used to study adolescents before they entered their first part-time job and one year later. The study used a comparison group of nonworking teenagers, who were also studied at two times. The findings indicated that teenagers who work, compared with their peers who do not, are more likely to grow in self-reliance (the ability to manage themselves) and develop a more mature "work orientation" (the ability to complete work tasks and take pride in doing so). There is no evidence, however, that working enhances adolescents' self-esteem (Bachman et al., 1986).

These findings support the idea that working can have a positive impact on youngsters' development. But other findings, especially

Mastery Orientation

It is widely believed that working helps teenagers develop a greater sense of responsibility and healthier attitudes toward work. Recent research on the costs and benefits of adolescent employment, however, call this belief into question. (Carolyn Hine/The Picture Cube)

those pertaining to the issue of adolescents' sense of responsibility to others, are not as favorable. Generally, working does not enhance adolescents' feelings of social obligation, social tolerance, or social belongingness (Greenberger and Steinberg, 1986). It does not make adolescents feel more concern for the well-being of others. If anything, working seems to make youngsters more individualistic. Moreover, adolescents who have jobs are more likely to express cynical attitudes toward work and to endorse unethical business practices. For example, it has been found that workers are more likely to agree with such statements as, "Anyone who works harder than he or she has to is a little bit crazy" (an item from a scale designed to measure cynicism) and, "In my opinion, it's all right for workers who are paid a low salary to take little things from their jobs to make up for it" (an item from the scale measuring acceptance of unethical business practices; see Table 7.1

[Steinberg, Greenberger, Garduque, Ruggiero, and Vaux, 1982]).

What can we make of these findings? Why would working make youngsters more self-reliant but at the same time more cynical about work and less concerned about the welfare of others? Perhaps the answer has something to do with the nature of the work most adolescents perform. Think for a moment about the job environment of most teenagers. Their work is dull, monotonous, and often stressful. Even if you have never worked in such a job, you can certainly imagine that working under these conditions could make people feel cynical and protective of their own interests above all else.

Money and Its Management

One specific aspect of responsibility that working is believed to affect is money management. Because the average working teenager earns be-

TABLE 7.1   SCALES USED TO MEASURE "CYNICISM TOWARD WORK" AND "TOLERANCE OF UNETHICAL BUSINESS PRACTICES"

SAMPLE ITEMS FROM THE "CYNICISM TOWARD WORK" SCALE	SAMPLE ITEMS FROM THE "TOLERANCE OF UNACCEPTABLE BUSINESS PRACTICES" SCALE
People who work harder at their jobs than they have to are a little crazy.	People who break a few laws to make a profit aren't doing anything I wouldn't do in their position.
Most people today are stuck in dead-end, go-nowhere jobs.	Workers are entitled to "call in sick" when they don't feel like working.
Hard work really doesn't get you much of anything in this world.	It doesn't matter if a businessman bends the law a little to make a profit.
There's no such thing as a company that cares about its employees.	In my opinion, it's all right for workers who are paid a low salary to take little things.
If I had the chance, I'd go through life without ever working.	It's acceptable to me if a teenage worker cheats a little on the amount of income tax he or she pays the government.
People who take their work home with them probably don't have a very interesting home life.	

Source: Steinberg et al., 1982.

tween $200 and $250 each month, holding a job may provide many opportunities for learning how to budget, save, and use money responsibly. Research indicates, however, that few teenagers exercise a great deal of responsibility when it comes to managing their earnings. One national survey, for example, showed that the majority of working teenagers spent most of their earnings on their own needs and activities (Johnston et al., 1982). Few adolescents who work save a large percentage of their income for their education, and fewer still use their earnings to help their families with household expenses (see Table 7.2). Instead, the picture of the contemporary working teenager that emerges from these studies is one of self-indulgent materialism. Wages are spent on designer clothing, expensive stereo equipment, movies, and eating out. A fair proportion of the earnings are spent on drugs and alcohol (Greenberger and Steinberg, 1986).

According to one social scientist, today's working teenagers may suffer from **premature affluence** (Bachman, 1983). As he put it, in an article entitled "Do High School Students Earn Too Much?":

A fairly popular assumption these days is that students should have a great deal of freedom in spending their part-time earnings, so that in making their own choices and occasionally their own mistakes they will get some reality experiences and "learn the value of a dollar." . . . The problem is that the "reality" faced by the typical high school student with substantial part-time earnings is just not very realistic. In the absence of payment for rent, utilities, groceries, and the many other necessities routinely provided by parents, the typical student is likely to find that most or all of his/her earnings are available for discretionary spending. . . . It seems likely that some will experience what I've come to call "premature affluence"—affluence because $200 or more per month represents a lot of "spending money" for a high school student, and premature because many of these individuals will not be able to sustain that level of discretionary spending once they take on the burden

TABLE 7.2   HIGH SCHOOL SENIORS IN 1982: WHERE THEIR EARNINGS WENT (Entries Are Percentages)

	MALES[1]	FEMALES[1]		MALES[1]	FEMALES[1]
Please think about all the money you earned during the past year, including last summer. About how much of your past year's earnings have gone into:			*as clothing, stereo, TV, records, other possessions, movies, eating out, other recreation, hobbies, gifts for others, and other personal expenses?*		
A. *Savings for your future education?*			None	4	5
None	48	50	A little	21	17
A little	23	21	Some[2]	38	34
Some[2]	19	19	Most[3]	36	44
Most[3]	11	10			
B. *Savings or payments for a car or car expenses?*			E. *Helping to pay family living expenses (groceries, housing, etc.)?*		
None	35	58	None	56	55
A little	19	16	A little	26	25
Some[2]	29	18	Some[2]	13	14
Most[3]	17	9	Most[3]	5	6
C. *Other savings for long-range purposes?*					
None	48	48			
A little	26	25			
Some[2]	18	20			
Most[3]	8	8			
D. *Spending on your own needs and activities—things such*					

[1] Number of cases are approximately 1500 for males and 1520 for females.
[2] Combines two categories: "Some" and "About half."
[3] Combines three categories: "Most," "About all," and "All."
Source: Bachman, 1983.

of paying for their own necessities. (1983, p. 65)

What might be some of the effects of premature affluence? According to one team of researchers, some of the consequences may be increased cynicism about the value of hard work and a lack of interest in working harder than is absolutely necessary, increased interest in buying drugs and alcohol, and the tendency to develop more materialistic attitudes (Greenberger and Steinberg, 1986). The very experience that many adults believe builds "character" may actually teach adolescents undesirable lessons about work and the meaning of money.

Occupational Deviance in the Adolescent Workplace

It comes as no surprise to learn that some adolescents, like some adults, behave at work in ways that would certainly upset their employers—if their employers knew. Do adolescents who suffer from the "burger blues" actually do things at work to retaliate for their unpleasant working conditions? There is not a great deal of research on this question, but one study that has examined deviant behavior in the adolescent workplace revealed relatively high rates of misconduct among adolescent workers, even in the early months of their first jobs (Ruggiero,

Greenberger, and Steinberg, 1982). Adolescent workers completed a questionnaire that examined several categories of **occupational deviance.** The workers, who were assured that their responses would remain confidential and anonymous, were asked to check whether and how often they had committed each of nine acts (see Figure 7.4). After nine months on the job, more than 60 percent had committed at least one "deviant" act. About 38 percent of working teenagers in the sample were "nonoffenders," about 38 percent "occasional offenders," and about 24 percent "relatively frequent offenders."

Because comparisons between adolescent and adult workers were not made, it would be erroneous to conclude that adolescents necessarily make bad or untrustworthy workers. Fur-

thermore, it is not clear from the study whether adolescents learned these deviant behaviors in the workplace or merely used the work setting as a context in which to display behaviors learned elsewhere. Nevertheless, the findings challenge the idea that the workplace is invariably a positive influence on the socialization of young people.

Some studies have also examined the time-honored belief that having a job deters youngsters from delinquent and criminal activity. Studies that have focused on youngsters known to be more likely to get involved in delinquent behavior—inner-city youth, for example—do not show that working deters delinquency. In general, workers are no less likely to engage in delinquent behavior than nonworkers (Gottfred-

FIGURE 7.4   Some first-time workers do things on the job that their employers would not be pleased about. (Ruggiero, Greenberger, and Steinberg, 1982)

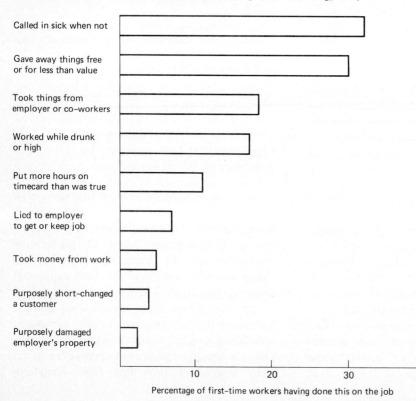

Percentage of first-time workers having done this on the job

son, 1985). Studies of more representative samples of youngsters, however, suggest that employment during high school may be associated with *increased* delinquent behavior. In particular, workers—especially those who work long hours—are more likely than nonworkers to get into fights, commit vandalism and theft, and buy and sell drugs (Bachman et al., 1986; Greenberger and Steinberg, 1986). It is not clear from these studies, however, whether working actually leads to higher levels of delinquency or whether adolescents who are already involved in delinquent activities are more likely to choose to work long hours.

Adolescent Work Experience: The Effect on Later Employment

In addition to the claim that working promotes the development of responsibility, some proponents of work experience for adolescents have argued that young people can learn a great deal about the world of work from holding a part-time job. It is often pointed out, for example, that schools do not teach students how to find employment, fill out a job application, behave during a job interview, or perform responsibly on the job—all skills that adults in modern society need. Early work experience, it is claimed, is the best way to help young people make the transition into adult work roles (President's Science Advisory Committee, 1974).

Several studies have shown that work experience does in fact help young people learn important information about the world of work that is not typically taught in the high school. Adolescents who work—whether in school-sponsored career education programs, in government-sponsored youth employment programs, or in the part-time labor force—score higher on a variety of tests designed to measure career-planning skills, career maturity, and occupational knowledge (Owens, 1982; Steinberg, 1982). It has been found, for example, that adolescents who have held paying jobs have more knowledge about consumer and financial matters; they are more likely to know how credit

cards work, how store owners set prices on their items, and how to decide which of two items is the better bargain (Steinberg, Greenberger, Garduque, and McAuliffe, 1982). Studies of adolescents enrolled in school-sponsored career education programs also indicate that work experience may teach young people about money and personal finances. Participants in such programs score higher on measures of "survival skills," such as balancing a checkbook or planning a personal budget, than do students without work experience (Owens, 1982). These sorts of skills are extremely important for successful adulthood in modern societies, and it is encouraging to see that these capabilities can be acquired through working.

Learning about the world of work is one thing. But does this knowledge increase the adolescent's chances of landing a full-time job later? This question has been the focus of a great deal of research, but as yet there are few clear answers. It seems that individuals who work during high school have a small advantage later on over their peers who did not work as students (Stevenson, 1978). However, although students who work during high school have a small advantage in landing a future job, the advantage is short-lived. Full-time employment is more likely and earnings are higher immediately after graduation for students who have had work experience; but within a few years, those who did not work during high school are just as likely to be employed and are likely to earn just as much money (Freeman and Wise, 1982).

The Effects of Long Work Hours

Several studies indicate that working more than fifteen or twenty hours a week may jeopardize adolescents' schooling and psychological well-being. Youngsters who work long hours are absent from school more often, are less likely to participate in extracurricular activities, report enjoying school less, spend less time on their homework, and earn lower grades (Damico, 1984; Steinberg, Greenberger, Garduque, and McAuliffe, 1982; Wirtz et al., 1987). Students

Studies show that teenagers who work more than fifteen or twenty hours a week during the school year are forced to cut back their participation in extracurricular activities. (Jaye R. Phillips/The Picture Cube)

who work long hours may miss out on family activities, such as eating dinner together or spending time together on weekends (Greenberger et al., 1980). Young people who spend more time at work report growing more distant from their parents and friends (Steinberg, Greenberger, Garduque, Ruggiero, and Vaux, 1982). And working long hours is associated with higher rates of alcohol, marijuana, cocaine, and cigarette use (Bachman et al., 1986; Greenberger, Steinberg, and Vaux, 1981).

The adverse impact of working long hours on schooling is especially troublesome in light of studies pointing to achievement problems of American youngsters (see Chapter 12). Not only does working seem to lead to increased absenteeism and decreased time spent on homework and school activities, intensive involvement in a part-time job early in a student's education—

during sophomore year in high school, for example—may actually increase the likelihood of dropping out of school (Damico, 1984). Moreover, students who work a good deal have less ambitious plans for further education while in high school and complete fewer years of college (Mortimer and Finch, 1986).

Several studies also indicate that extensive employment among high school students may take its toll on the educational process in other ways. When students work a great deal, they must develop strategies for protecting their grade point averages. These strategies include taking easier courses, cutting corners on their homework assignments, copying homework from friends, and cheating (Greenberger and Steinberg, 1986; McNeil, 1984). Teachers respond by assigning less homework and by using class time for students to complete assignments that otherwise would be done outside of school (McNeil, 1984).

Youth Unemployment

Although the employment of teenagers has become commonplace in contemporary America, a sizable minority of young people who wish to work are nevertheless unable to find jobs. Much attention has been given to the problem of **youth unemployment** over the past two decades, but there remains a good deal of controversy over the nature of the problem and possible solutions to it.

In discussing the problem of unemployment among the young, several points need to be understood. First, most young people in this country do not have great difficulty finding full-time employment after they graduate from high school or college. For example, one team of researchers, using data collected by the U.S. Department of Labor, found that more than 90 percent of all teenage boys were either in school, working, or both. Only 5 percent were out of school, unemployed, and looking for full-time work (Feldstein and Ellwood, 1982). Much of the unemployment of young people is attributable to their involvement in other productive activities, such as school, rather than to deficiencies in job skills or constraints in the labor force (Mare et al., 1984).

Second, most young people who are out of school and out of work are unemployed for only short periods of time. Nearly half of the unemployed youth in the survey mentioned above had been out of work for one month or less; only 10 percent had been unemployed for as long as six months. An important conclusion to keep in mind, therefore, is that long-term unemployment is a problem that afflicts a very small minority of young people.

A third point is that the majority of unemployed youth are high school dropouts. Black youth are more likely to experience unemployment than white youth, and unemployment is more common among teenagers who come from low-income families and live in areas that have high overall unemployment rates and where competition for available employment is severe (Freeman and Wise, 1982). Their unemployment problems may have more to do with poverty and related factors than with youth or inexperience. Most studies show that unemployment during adolescence and young adulthood results primarily from a combination of economic and social factors, rather than from a lack of motivation on the part of unemployed individuals.

Finally, the consequences of unemployment during adolescence and young adulthood appear to be worse in the short term than in the long run. Unemployment is not a condition that stays with a person throughout his or her life. Researchers have found that most people who have been unemployed as teenagers are eventually able to secure stable full-time employment. Youth unemployment is a problem mostly because it is associated with higher rates of crime, drug abuse, and violence (Freeman and Wise, 1982).

Nevertheless, for the minority of youngsters who experience long-term difficulty in finding and holding a full-time job, chronic unemployment is an onerous condition filled with hopelessness. Because of the serious effects of chronic unemployment during young adulthood on individuals' later lives, many different approaches have been taken over the years in trying to solve the youth unemployment problem. Most social scientists now feel that strengthening the economy in general, in order to create a greater demand for workers, and encouraging young people to complete high school are the two most promising approaches. Programs that create temporary jobs for teenagers, such as CETA, may have a short-term financial payoff for the individuals who obtain these jobs, but they do little to ease the unemployment problem in the long run. Some of these programs have even encouraged youngsters to drop out of high school, which further hurts their chances of landing a good job later on. Researchers have also found that training programs designed to prepare young people for work, such as vocational education, are not very successful in actually placing individuals in permanent jobs. Finishing high school and receiving a solid education still appear to be the best means of preparing for full-time work (Freeman and Wise, 1982).

One proposal for dealing with the problem of youth unemployment that has the support of many policymakers is the expansion of service opportunities for young people who are out of school but not yet ready for work (Committee for the Study of National Service, 1980). Service activities, in which young people are paid for their time, could be used to provide preemployment training for young people and involve them in helping to solve many of society's pressing and important problems. At present, very few service activities for young people are sponsored at a national level in the United States. The largest, of course, is military service, but this is attractive to only a minority of young people. Such programs as VISTA and the Peace Corps generally involve older youth. Many people have called for the creation of a network of **nonmilitary service** opportunities, through which young people could work on a variety of social and environmental projects, such as staffing day-care centers for children, helping to restore historic buildings, providing assistance to the elderly, or cleaning up the environment.

Some proponents of youth service would like to see a system in which all young people—not only those with employment problems—would be encouraged to spend at least one year after leaving or graduating from high school in a service activity of their choosing.

Summary

Although we often overlook its significance in the daily life of most young people, the workplace is an important context for the developing adolescent. In recent years, increasing numbers of high school students have entered the labor force as part-time workers in the retail and service industries. Whereas in 1940 virtually no students worked during the school year, today about two-thirds of all high school seniors hold part-time jobs while they are in school. The situation is different from that in other countries, where the employment of high school students is still relatively uncommon. In less industrialized countries, most adolescents do not continue in school past the age of 12 or 13, and those who stay in high school do not work while they are students. In countries that are comparable to the United States in industrialization, adolescents generally defer their entry into the work force until they have completed their education.

Contrary to widely held assumptions about the positive, character-building properties of early work experience, research on the impact of working on adolescent development indicates that working may have more costs than benefits. On the positive side, adolescents who work show gains in self-reliance and in their knowledge of practical information about the world of work. On the negative side, however, adolescents who work a great deal develop cynical attitudes about working; do less well in school; become less involved in family and peer activities; increase their use of drugs and alcohol; and may be more likely to become involved in delinquent activity.

One explanation for the mixed impact that working appears to have on teenagers is the nature of the jobs and work environments open to them in contemporary society. In general, adolescents' jobs are monotonous, unchallenging, and stressful.

There are important lessons to be learned from the material in this chapter that extend beyond the study of adolescents at work. Many of the assumptions we have about adolescence—including the assumption that working builds character—do not hold up when we examine them scientifically. In order to understand how adolescents develop in contemporary society, we need to collect detailed information on the nature of their activity and on the context in which it occurs. This applies to the study of schools, families, and peer groups, as well as to the study of work environments. As we begin to learn more about the contexts in which young people live, we will better understand how the course of adolescent development is shaped by the social and physical environment.

Key Terms

nonmilitary service
occupational deviance

premature affluence
youth unemployment

For Further Reading

BORMAN, K., AND REISMAN, J. (EDS.). (1986). *Becoming a worker*. Norwood, NJ: Ablex. A collection of articles on the preparation of individuals for work.

CARNEGIE COMMISSION ON POLICY STUDIES IN HIGHER EDUCATION. (1980). *Giving Youth a Better Chance*. San Francisco: Jossey-Bass, A panel of experts explains why work opportunities for young people should be expanded.

FREEMAN, R., AND WISE, D. (EDS.). (1982). *The youth labor market problem: Its nature, causes, and consequences*. Chicago: University of Chicago Press. A collection of articles by economists that examines the causes and correlates of youth unemployment.

GREENBERGER, E., AND STEINBERG, L. (1986). *When teenagers work: The psychological and social costs of adolescent employment*. New York: Basic Books. A summary of research on adolescent employment in contemporary society.

STEINBERG, L., GREENBERGER, E., GARDUQUE, L., RUGGIERO, M., AND VAUX, A. (1982). Effects of working on adolescent development. *Developmental Psychology. 18*, 385–395. A longitudinal study of the effects of part-time employment on teenagers' psychological and social development.

PART THREE

Psychosocial Development During Adolescence

Identity

CHAPTER 8

PREVIEW

1. Identity development involves changes in the way people think and feel about themselves. Adolescence is an especially important time for changes in identity because of the physical, intellectual, and social transformations characteristic of the period.

2. Researchers and theorists have taken three approaches to the study of identity during adolescence. One emphasizes changes in the way individuals conceive of themselves, a second focuses on changes in the way individuals feel about themselves, and the third emphasizes changes in the degree to which individuals feel secure about who they are and where they are headed.

3. An especially important perspective on adolescent identity development comes from the work of Erik Erikson, who believes that adolescents in contemporary society go through a series of "identity crises," during which they struggle to establish a coherent sense of self-definition. Recent research, while not yet conclusive, appears to support Erikson's view.

4. Sex differences in identity development have received considerable attention from researchers. During adolescence, pressure to conform to prevailing sex-role stereotypes may intensify, and differences in the behavior of males and females may widen. As sex roles change, however, many current ideas about differences between the sexes in the realm of identity development may have to be reconsidered.

A voice sobs within me. "There you are, that's what's become of you: you're uncharitable, you look supercilious and peevish, people dislike you and all because you won't listen to the advice given you by your own better half." Oh, I would like to listen, but it doesn't work; if I'm quiet and serious, everyone thinks it's a new comedy and then I have to get out of it by turning it into a joke, not to mention my own family, who are sure to think I'm ill, make me swallow pills for headaches and nerves, feel my neck and head to see whether I'm running a temperature, ask if I'm constipated and criticize me for being in a bad mood. I can't keep that up: if I'm watched to that extent, I start by getting snappy, then unhappy, and finally I twist my heart round again, so that the bad is on the outside and the good is on the inside and keep on trying to find a way of becoming what I would so like to be, if . . . there weren't any other people living in the world.

Thus wrote Anne Frank in *The Diary of a Young Girl.*

Some, but not all, adolescents share Anne's feelings of self-consciousness and confusion. For these young people, adolescence is a time of "identity crisis." For other adolescents, this period is one of more gradual and subtle change. As you may recall from your own adolescence, there are few experiences that can be as trying— or as exhilarating—as questioning who you really are and, more important, who you would like to be.

Because changes—whether gradual or abrupt—take place during adolescence in the way people view and feel about themselves, the study of identity development has been a major focus of research and theory on adolescents. In this chapter, we examine whether adolescence is indeed a time of major changes in identity and how the course of adolescent identity development is shaped by the nature of life in contemporary society.

IDENTITY AS AN ADOLESCENT ISSUE

Changes in the way in which we see and feel about ourselves occur throughout the life cycle.

You have probably heard and read about the so-called "midlife crisis," for example, an identity crisis thought to occur during middle age. Many adults in their forties feel unsure about the marital and occupational decisions they have made and wonder whether they should change their lifestyle or their job before it becomes too late or too difficult to break away from past decisions and commitments (Neugarten and Datan, 1974). And certainly, there are important changes in self-conceptions and in self-image throughout childhood. When a group of 4-year-olds and a group of 10-year-olds are asked to describe themselves, the older children display a far more complex view of themselves. While young children restrict their descriptions to lists of what they own or what they like to do, older children are more likely to tell you also about their personality.

If in fact changes in identity occur throughout the life cycle, why have researchers interested in identity development paid so much attention to adolescence? One reason is that the changes in identity which take place during adolescence involve the first substantial reorganization and restructuring of the individual's sense of self at a time when he or she has the intellectual capability to appreciate fully just how significant the changes are. Although important changes in identity certainly occur during childhood, the adolescent is far more self-conscious about these changes and feels them much more acutely. If you have read Anne Frank's diary or other accounts of the adolescent identity crisis in such works as *Hamlet, A Separate Peace, Manchild in the Promised Land, The Catcher in the Rye,* or *The Member of the Wedding,* you know that young people can be all too painfully aware of their changing sense of self.

Another reason for the attention that researchers and theorists have given the study of identity development during adolescence concerns the fundamental biological, cognitive, and social changes characteristic of the period. Puberty, as we saw in Chapter 1, brings with it dramatic changes in physical appearance and alters the adolescent's self-conceptions and relationships with others. It is not hard to see why puberty plays an important role in provoking identity development during adolescence. When you change the way you look—when you have your hair cut in a different way, lose a great deal of weight, or get a new pair of glasses—you sometimes feel as if your personality has changed, too. During puberty, when adolescents are changing so dramatically on the outside, they understandably have questions about changes that are taking place on the inside. For the adolescent, undergoing the physical changes of puberty may prompt fluctuations in the self-image and a reevaluation of who he or she really is.

The broadening of intellectual capabilities during early adolescence, just as it provides new ways of thinking about problems, values, and interpersonal relationships, also permits adolescents to think about themselves in new ways. We saw in Chapter 2 that it is not until adolescence that the young person is able to think in systematic ways about hypothetical and future events. For this reason, it is not until adolescence that individuals typically begin to wonder, "Who will I become?" "What possible identities are open to me?" or "What am I really like?" Because the preadolescent child's thinking is concrete, it is impossible for him or her to think seriously about being a different person. But the changes in thinking that take place during adolescence open up a whole new world of alternatives.

Finally, we saw in Chapter 3 that the changes in social roles that occur at adolescence open up a new array of choices and decisions for the young person that were not concerns previously. In contemporary society, adolescence is a time of important decisions about work, marriage, and the future. Facing these decisions about your place in society not only provokes questions about who you are and where you are headed—it necessitates them. At this point in the life cycle, young people must make important choices about their careers and their commitments to other people, and thinking about these questions prompts them to ask more questions about themselves: "What do I really want out of life?" "What things are important to me?" "What kind of person would I

In contemporary society, adolescence is a time when different career possibilities are considered and explored. Here, a young girl works as a hospital volunteer to discover whether she is suited to a career in health services. (Michael Hayman/Stock, Boston)

really like to be?" Questions about the future, which inevitably arise as the adolescent prepares for adulthood, raise questions about identity.

Identity development is complex and multifaceted. Actually, it is better understood as a series of interrelated developments—rather than one single development—that all involve changes in the way individuals view themselves in relation to others and in relation to the broader society in which they live. As you can imagine, studying identity development is an extremely challenging task, because the concept of identity is very elusive and difficult to measure. There is little agreement among social scientists on how best to measure an individual's identity. Generally speaking, researchers and theorists have taken three different approaches to the question of how the individual's sense of identity changes over the course of adolescence. Each approach focuses on a different aspect of identity development.

The first approach emphasizes changes in self-conceptions—the ideas that individuals have of themselves as regards various traits and attributes. An entirely different approach focuses on adolescents' self-esteem—how positively or negatively individuals feel about themselves. Finally, a third approach emphasizes changes in the sense of identity—the sense of who one is, where one has come from, and where one is going.

CHANGES IN SELF-CONCEPTIONS

During adolescence, important shifts occur in the way individuals think about and characterize themselves—that is, in their **self-conceptions**. As individuals mature intellectually and undergo the sorts of cognitive changes described in Chapter 2, they come to conceive of themselves in more sophisticated and differentiated ways. As we saw in that chapter, adolescents are much more capable than children of thinking about abstract concepts. This intellectual advantage affects the way in which individuals characterize themselves. Compared with children, who tend to describe themselves in relatively simple, concrete terms, adolescents are more likely to employ complex, abstract, and psychological self-characterizations (Rosenberg, 1986). For example, compare these two self-descriptions—one by a 9-year-old boy, the other by a girl just three years older:

"My name is Bruce C. I have brown eyes. I have brown hair. I have brown eyebrows. I'm nine years old. I love! sports. I have seven people in my family. I have great! eye sight. I have lots! of friends. I live on 1923 Pinecrest Drive. I'm going on ten in September. I'm a boy. I have an uncle that is almost seven feet tall. My school is Pinecrest. My teacher is Mrs. V. I play hockey! I'm almost the smartest boy in the class. I love food! I love fresh air. I love school." (9-year-old boy)

"My name is A. I'm a human being. I'm a girl. I'm a truthful person. I'm not pretty. I do so-so

in my studies. I'm a very good cellist. I'm a very good pianist. I'm a bit tall for my age. I like several boys. I like several girls. I'm old fashioned. I play tennis. I am a very good musician. I try to be helpful. I'm always ready to be friends with anybody. Mostly I'm good, but I lose my temper. I'm not well-liked by some girls and boys. I don't know if boys like me or not." (12-year-old girl) (Montemayor and Eisen, 1977)

Although there are several concrete elements in the older child's description (she mentions her musical interests and abilities, for example), we also see the emergence of more psychological and interpersonal descriptors (her reference to her moodiness and friendliness, for instance, and her concern over whether boys like her). This trend toward responding with more abstract characterizations continues throughout adolescence, as the youngster becomes more intellectually, psychologically, and socially sophisticated.

Self-conceptions change in structure as well as content at adolescence. Structurally, self-conceptions become more *differentiated* and better *organized* (Hill and Palmquist, 1978; Livesley and Bromley, 1973; Montemayor and Eisen, 1977). Consider first the movement toward greater differentiation. In answer to the question, "Who am I?" adolescents are more likely than children to link traits and attributes describing themselves to specific situations, rather than using them as global characterizations. While a preadolescent child might say "I am nice" or "I am friendly" and not specify when or under what conditions, an adolescent is more likely to say "I am nice *if* I am in a good mood," or "I am friendly *when* I am with people I have met before." The realization that one's personality is expressed in different ways in different situations is one example of the increased differentiation that characterizes the self-conceptions of youngsters as they mature toward adulthood.

There is another way in which self-conceptions become more highly differentiated at adolescence. As opposed to characterizations provided by children, adolescents' self-descriptions

Self-conceptions become more differentiated during adolescence. Young people are able to see, for example, that they may be perceived differently by their parents and their siblings. (Joel Gordon)

take into account *who* is doing the describing (Livesley and Bromley, 1973). Teenagers differentiate between their own opinions of themselves and the views of others. Suppose you asked a group of youngsters to describe how they behaved when they were with other people. Instead of saying, "I am shy" or "I am outgoing," an adolescent would be more likely to say, "People think I'm not at all shy, but most of the time, I'm real nervous about meeting other kids for the first time." Adolescents also recognize that they may come across differently to different people, another type of differentiation in self-conceptions that does not appear until this

point in time: "My parents think I'm quiet, but my friends know I really like to party a lot."

With this shift toward increased differentiation in self-conceptions comes better organization and integration (Harter, 1983). When children are asked to describe themselves, the traits and attributes they list remain somewhat disparate, like items haphazardly placed on a grocery list. Adolescents, however, are likely to organize and integrate different aspects of their self-image into a more logical, coherent whole. Whereas a younger child may list a sequence of several traits that appear to be contradictory ("I am friendly. I am shy."), an adolescent will attempt to organize apparently discrepant bits of information into more highly organized statements ("I am shy when I first meet people, but after I get to know them, I'm usually pretty friendly.")

Understanding how self-conceptions change during adolescence helps to explain why issues of identity begin to take on so much importance at this time in the life span. As individuals' self-conceptions become more abstract and as they become more able to see themselves in psychological terms, they become more interested in understanding their own personalities and why they behave the way they do. You may recall having wondered as a teenager about your personality development, about the influences that shaped your character, about how your personality had changed over time. "Am I more like my father or like my mother? Why do my sister and I seem so different? Will I always be so shy?" Although these sorts of questions may seem commonplace to you now, in all likelihood, you did not think about these things until adolescence, when your own self-conceptions became more abstract and sophisticated.

CHANGES IN THE SELF-IMAGE

As noted in the introduction to this book, ever since G. Stanley Hall initially suggested that adolescence was a time of "storm and stress," researchers and theorists have asked whether adolescence is a more difficult time for the developing person than earlier or later periods in the life span. For many years, in fact, the idea that adolescence is inherently stressful for the individual was accepted without question. The noted psychoanalytic theorist Anna Freud, for example, once wrote that adolescence was a "developmental disturbance" (1969). Even today, most portrayals of young people in fiction, in film, or on television present the stereotypic teenager as moody, self-conscious, and in a general state of psychological distress. One of the manifestations assumed to result from the stress of adolescence involves problems in the adolescent's **self-esteem**—how the individual feels about himself or herself.

Despite what we see in the movies, however, research has not supported the view that adolescence is a time of tumultuous upheaval in self-image. Nor is adolescence the time of "rebirth" Rousseau once cast it as. As one team of researchers put it, in discussing their study of changes in adolescents' perceptions of themselves between ages 11 and 18, "The person who enters adolescence is basically the same as that who exits it" (Dusek and Flaherty, 1981, p. 39). Although adolescents' feelings about themselves may fluctuate somewhat, particularly during the very early adolescent years (late elementary school and junior high school), from about eighth grade on, self-esteem remains stable; individuals with high self-esteem as children are likely to have high self-esteem as adolescents. There is no apparent loss of self-esteem during adolescence. If anything, over the course of middle and late adolescence, self-esteem *increases* (O'Malley and Bachman, 1983; Nottelmann, 1987; Rosenberg, 1986; Savin-Williams and Demo, 1984). Just as the "storm and stress" view of adolescence is not supported in studies of family relations, neither does it appear to apply to adolescent self-esteem.

There is some evidence, however, that for a brief and temporary period during early adolescence, minor problems in self-image may arise. Roberta Simmons and her colleagues have completed a series of studies that shed light on when and why these problems in self-image are likely to occur. Simmons and her associates (Simmons, Rosenberg, and Rosenberg, 1973) employed an extensive questionnaire to assess three aspects of adolescents' self-image: their self-esteem (how positively or negatively they feel about themselves), their **self-consciousness** (how much they worry about their self-image), and the **stability of their self-image** (how much they feel that their self-image changes from day to day). They hypothesized that young adolescents would show the lowest levels of self-esteem, the highest levels of self-consciousness, and the shakiest self-image.

Consistent with their expectations, these researchers found that fluctuations in the self-image are most likely to occur between the ages of 12 and 14. Compared with older adolescents (15 years and older) and with preadolescents (8 to 11 years old), early adolescents have lower self-esteem, are more self-conscious, and have a more unstable self-image than other youngsters (see Figure 8.1). Generally speaking, the small but reliable differences between the preadolescents and the early adolescents are greater than those between the younger and older adolescents, which indicates that the most marked fluctuations occur during the transition into adolescence, rather than over the course of adolescence itself (Simmons, Rosenberg, and Rosenberg, 1973).

According to sociologist Morris Rosenberg (1986), it is important to differentiate between two aspects of self-perceptions in looking at studies of fluctuations in self-esteem. The **barometric** aspect of our **self-esteem** refers to the extent to which our feelings about ourselves shift and fluctuate rapidly, moment to moment. Perhaps you can remember times as a teenager—or even as an adult—when you entered a room full of people feeling confident and suddenly felt nervous and insecure, only to engage in a pleasant interaction with someone an hour later and feel confident once again. You were experiencing fluctuations in your barometric self-esteem.

Your **baseline self-esteem,** in contrast, is less transitory and less likely to fluctuate mo-

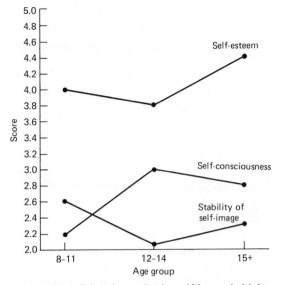

FIGURE 8.1   Disturbance in the self-image is highest during early adolescence. (Derived from Simmons, Rosenberg, and Rosenberg, 1973)

ment to moment. This aspect of self-image is relatively stable over time and unlikely to be easily shifted by immediate experiences. Even if you feel momentarily insecure when entering a room full of new people, your integral, or baseline, self-esteem has not shifted. Indeed, individuals with high baseline self-esteem would readily dismiss transient feelings of insecurity as having more to do with the situation than with themselves.

Studies that report very high stability in self-esteem over adolescence are likely tapping the individual's baseline self-esteem, which is unlikely to change dramatically over time. This may be because the determinants of baseline self-esteem are themselves relatively stable factors such as social class (middle-class adolescents have higher self-esteem than their peers), sex (boys have higher self-esteem than girls), birth order (oldest or only children have higher self-esteem), and academic ability (more able adolescents have higher self-esteem [Bachman and O'Malley, 1986; Savin-Williams and Demo, 1983]). In contrast, studies that show fluctuation

and volatility in self-image during early adolescence are probably focusing on the barometric self-image, which, by definition, is more likely to fluctuate. It seems safe to say, therefore, that although individuals' baseline self-image does not change markedly over adolescence, early adolescence is a time of increased volatility in the barometric self-image (Rosenberg, 1986). In other words, young adolescents are more likely than children or older adolescents to experience moment-to-moment shifts in self-esteem. Interestingly, the extent to which an individual's barometric self-esteem is volatile is itself a fairly stable trait—that is, young adolescents whose self-image fluctuates a lot moment to moment are likely to develop into older adolescents who experience the same thing (Savin-Williams and Demo, 1983).

Although an individual's baseline self-image is probably a better overall indicator of how a person feels about him- or herself, fluctuations in barometric self-image can be distressing and uncomfortable—as most of us know well (Rosenberg, 1986). Consistent with this, studies indicate that young adolescents report higher levels of depression than preadolescents or older teenagers (Simmons, Rosenberg, and Rosenberg, 1973). Moreover, young adolescents with the most volatile self-image report the highest levels of anxiety, tension, psychosomatic symptoms, and irritability (Rosenberg, 1986).

Volatility in the barometric self-image during early adolescence probably is due to several interrelated factors. First, the sort of egocentrism common to young adolescents, discussed in Chapter 2, may make the young adolescent painfully aware of others' reactions to his or her behavior. Second, as individuals become more socially active, they begin to learn that people play games when they interact and, consequently, they learn that it is not always possible to tell what people are thinking on the basis of how they act or what they say. This ambiguity may leave the young adolescent, relatively unskilled at this sort of "impression management," puzzled and uncomfortable about how he or she is *really* viewed by others. Finally, because of the increased importance of peers in early adolescence, young adolescents are especially interested in their peers' opinions of themselves. For the first time, they may have to come to terms with contradictory messages that they get from their parents ("I think that hairstyle makes you even more beautiful") versus their peers ("You'd better wear a hat until your hair grows back!"). Hearing contradictory messages probably generates a certain degree of uncertainty about oneself (Rosenberg, 1986).

Variations in Self-Esteem

Not all adolescents undergo the same degree of fluctuation in self-esteem, nor are all adolescents' levels of self-esteem comparable. Several studies have shown that early adolescent girls are more vulnerable to disturbances in the self-image than any other group of youngsters. Specifically, their self-esteem is lower, their degree of self-consciousness higher, and their self-image shakier than is the case for boys (Rosenberg and Simmons, 1972; Simmons, Brown, Bush, and Blyth, 1978; Simmons and Rosenberg, 1975). They are more likely to say negative things about themselves, feel insecure about their abilities, and worry about whether other people like being with them.

Why would girls have greater difficulty during early adolescence than boys? At this point, the answer is not entirely clear, but it appears to be related to the ambivalent attitudes that young girls have toward their sex roles as well as to their higher degree of concern about peer relationships—opposite-sex relationships in particular. Compared with other youngsters, young girls seem to worry a great deal about dating and being popular in school. Yet they are also worried about doing well academically. Other adolescents care about these things, of course, but they have a more casual, less worried atti-

Several recent studies have shown that white adolescent females may be more vulnerable to self-image problems than other teenagers. Many young women feel caught in a bind between pressures to be academically successful and pressures to be popular with peers. (J.D. Sloan/The Picture Cube)

tude. Adolescent girls may feel caught in a bind between pressures to do well academically and pressures to do well socially. As we saw in Chapter 5, getting good grades in school is at the bottom of the list of attributes adolescent girls feel are important for being accepted into the leading crowd (Coleman, 1961). Several studies have shown that adolescents who worry a lot about being popular are most likely to feel self-conscious and are most likely to have unstable views of themselves (Simmons and Rosenberg, 1975). Because young girls appear to be more concerned than boys about dating and peer acceptance, they may experience a greater number of self-image problems.

It is important to interpret these findings in light of the fact that early adolescence typically coincides with the transition into secondary school. Social expectations change when youngsters change schools. Students in junior high schools place greater emphasis on looks, popularity, dating, and opposite-sex relationships than do students in elementary schools, and girls who have begun to mature physically may be especially susceptible to the pressures of the new value system they encounter when they change schools. Suddenly, girls with little dating experience may be asked out by older boys and feel pressured to fit into a new social system, in which popularity depends on being a desirable date. These new pressures may lead to increased concerns over physical appearance and popularity and, as a consequence, to disturbances in the self-image.

Studies also indicate that an adolescent's **social class**—as indexed by his or her parents' occupations, education, or income—is an important determinant of self-esteem, especially as the individual moves into middle and later adolescence. In general, middle-class youngsters have higher self-esteem than their peers, and this discrepancy grows greater over the course of adolescence. One explanation for this is that middle-class youngsters do better in school than their peers, and this success leads to enhanced self-esteem (Demo and Savin-Williams, 1983). Although it once was believed that enhanced

self-esteem leads to school success (rather than vice vera), this has not been found to be true (Bachman and O'Malley, 1986; Bohrnstedt and Felson, 1983).

The context in which adolescents develop has a substantial impact on changes in the self-image, however. Some research indicates, for example, that high school–aged youngsters who live in a social environment or go to a school in which their ethnic or socioeconomic group is in the minority are more likely to have self-image problems than those who are in the majority (Rosenberg, 1975). This seems to be true with regard to religion, socioeconomic status, race, and family structure (single-parent or two-parent home). Black teenagers, for example, have a higher opinion of themselves when they go to schools in which black students are a majority than when they attend predominantly white schools, where they may feel out of place and pressured to play down their cultural heritage. By the same token, Jewish adolescents have higher self-esteem in schools in which there are many other Jewish students than in schools in which Jews comprise a small minority of the student body.

Research on changes in self-image during adolescence has helped paint a new picture of adolescence as a developmental period. In contrast to views that were popular even as recently as twenty-five years ago, adolescence is now viewed as a time of gradual rather than tumultuous change in the individual's self-image. Through studies of young adolescents, psychologists have learned more about vulnerable adolescent populations and about the sorts of stresses that make early adolescence an especially difficult time. Instead of adhering to the view that adolescence is an inevitably difficult time for *all* young people, researchers are coming to understand that certain factors seem to worsen stress during adolescence and that some youngsters are more susceptible to its adverse effects. In the future, we will be better prepared to design preventive mental health programs for young teenagers and head off adolescent psychological difficulties before they begin.

Youngsters who attend schools in which they are in the racial minority may suffer greater self-esteem problems than their peers who attend schools in which they are in the majority. Although desegregation may have a positive impact on minority youngsters' academic achievement, this benefit may be counterbalanced by the apparently negative impact of desegregation on minority youngsters' self-image. (Owen Franken/Stock, Boston)

THE ADOLESCENT IDENTITY CRISIS

In the view of some theorists, the study of adolescent identity development entails more than merely examining the expansion of self-conceptions or temporary fluctuations in self-image. If you were asked to talk about your own identity development, what sorts of things would you mention? Perhaps you would talk about the development of a sense of purpose, or the clarification of your long-term plans and values, or the growing feeling of knowing who you really are and where you are headed. If these are the sorts of things that come to mind when you think about identity development, you are thinking about an aspect of development that psychologists refer to as the **sense of identity.** The dominant view in the study of adolescent identity development emphasizes precisely these aspects of psychosocial development, and the theorist whose work has been most influential in this area is Erik Erikson.

Erikson's Theoretical Framework

Few theorists have influenced the study of adolescence as much as Erik Erikson, a neo-Freudian psychoanalyst who has written extensively on psychosocial development throughout the life cycle, but who has paid special attention to the development of identity during adolescence (1959, 1963, 1968). Erikson's theory of the human life cycle developed out of his clinical and cross-cultural observations of young people at various stages of development. He views the developing person as moving through a series of eight psychosocial crises over the course of the life span. Each crisis, although present in one form or another at all ages, takes on special significance at a given period of the life cycle because biological and social forces interact to bring the crisis into prominence. Erikson believes that the establishment of a coherent sense of identity is the chief psychosocial crisis of adolescence.

In Erikson's model, each psychosocial crisis defines an "age" or "stage" of the life span (see Figure 8.2). Each crisis is a sort of challenge that the individual must resolve. The crises are *normative,* in the sense that they are an inevitable part of being alive and growing older. Erikson describes each of the eight crises as a continuum with positive and negative poles. The crisis of infancy, for example, is labeled "trust versus mistrust." By this Erikson means that during infancy, the child must be able to establish a feeling of trust, or security, with its caregivers. Infants must come to feel that they can depend on their caregivers for love, attention, and nurturance. Resolving each crisis, though, does not entail coming through the crisis either entirely positively or entirely negatively, nor does it mean resolving the issue once and for all. "It is instead a matter of tipping the balance more in one direction (i.e., toward one end of the continuum) than in another" (Gallatin, 1975, p. 175). In other words, it is important that the infant come through the first stage of development feeling more secure than insecure.

In Erikson's view, each crisis builds on the previous ones. Specifically, the successful resolution of each challenge depends on the healthy resolution of the challenges that have preceded it. An infant who has not successfully resolved the crisis of trust versus mistrust, for example, will have a difficult time with the crises he encounters through the rest of the life cycle. He may be always somewhat hesitant about becoming close with other people because, deep down inside, he fears that others will let him down. With respect to adolescent identity develop-

FIGURE 8.2   The eight stages of development and their corresponding psychosocial crises, according to Erikson (1959).

I Infancy	Trust vs. mistrust						
II Early childhood		Autonomy vs. shame, doubt					
III Play age			Initiative vs. guilt				
IV School age				Industry vs. inferiority			
V Adolescence					Identity vs. identity diffusion		
VI Young adult						Intimacy vs. isolation	
VII Adulthood							Generativity vs. Self- absorption	
VIII Mature age								Integrity vs. disgust, despair

ment, then, Erikson believes that the successful resolution of the crisis of **identity versus identity diffusion** depends on how the individual has resolved the previous crises of childhood. Without a healthy sense of trust, autonomy, initiative, and industry, it is difficult to establish a coherent sense of identity. Moreover, the way in which the adolescent resolves the crisis of identity will have an impact on his or her struggle with the crises of adulthood. Far from seeing adolescence as a separate period of the life cycle, Erikson believes that what takes place during adolescence is much intertwined with what has come before and what will follow.

Identity and identification. Some of the most important influences on the child's developing personality are the identifications the youngster has formed over the years with parents, siblings, teachers, and other significant models. Children are motivated, consciously and unconsciously, to identify with other people for several reasons. First, these models generally possess certain qualities the child sees as desirable—power, privileges, and the like—and the child believes that by becoming like the admired figures, he or she will share, vicariously as well as actually, some of their envied qualities. Second, in the child's mind, similarity with an admired figure is a route to nurturance and affection, both from that figure (who, presumably, will look favorably on being imitated) and from people who are affectionate toward that figure (who, presumably, will treat the child similarly to the way they treat the target of the child's identification). Finally, the child identifies with other people because he or she is directly rewarded and reinforced for doing so; certain models are presented as desirable, and the child is praised when he or she acts like them (Kagan, 1958).

As a consequence of the child's conscious attempts to imitate certain models and unconscious strivings to be like them, the youngster's personality and behavior come to resemble, in part, the personalities and actions of these other individuals. As the child develops, many of these attributes become incorporated into his or

The adolescent's sense of identity is shaped partly through interactions with peers. (Peter Southwick/ Stock, Boston)

her personality. A child, for example, may sometimes display her father's timidity and at other times her mother's assertiveness. Another may speak with inflections that bear an uncanny resemblance to his older brother's. A third may have facial expressions very like his father's. This process of incorporation is called **identification.** In ways that we are not necessarily aware of, we have many personality traits and mannerisms that resemble those of our parents and others with whom we have identified.

The identifications we form as children are not complete, unchanging internalizations of other people's personalities. Rather, identifications are partial and incomplete, often transitory, and often contradictory. Think, for example, how quickly young children identify with various television heroes and how quickly these identifications are shed: When the new television season begins, the child, like the television network, retains some heroes and drops others. By the time a youngster has reached adolescence, his or her sense of self is still undergoing a tremendous amount of revision. The bits and pieces—part identifications, as Erikson calls them—have not been integrated into a coherent, balanced whole.

Identity versus Identity Diffusion

Before adolescence, the child's identity is like patches of fabric that have not yet been sewn together. But by the end of adolescence, these patches will be woven into a patchwork quilt that is unique to the individual. This process of integration is at the center of the fifth psychosocial crisis described by Erikson: the crisis of identity versus identity diffusion. As Erikson describes it, "From among all possible and imaginable relations, [the young person] must make a series of ever-narrowing selections of personal, occupational, sexual, and ideological commitments" (1968, p. 245). The maturational and social forces that converge at adolescence force young people to reflect on their place in society, on the ways that others view them, and on their options for the future.

Coming to terms with who you are as well as with who you might become is a challenge that requires pulling together your past, your present, and your future. The influence of the past is represented by the young person's previous identifications, many of which are retained in one form or another and incorporated into the emerging sense of self. The influence of the present is also felt, for it is in the present context that the adolescent consciously and unconsciously repudiates some aspects of his or her past and holds on to others. And finally, the importance of the future is found in the adolescent's anticipation of who he or she might become, an anticipation that guides many of the choices and decisions that are made in the course of the struggle for self-definition. Achieving a balanced and coherent sense of identity is an intellectually and emotionally taxing process.

According to Erikson, it is not until adolescence that one even has the mental or psychological capacity to tackle this task.

The key to resolving the crisis of identity versus identity diffusion, argues Erikson, lies in the adolescent's interactions with others. Through responding to the reactions of people who matter, the adolescent selects and chooses from among the many elements that could conceivably become a part of his or her final identity. The other people with whom the young person interacts serve as a mirror that reflects back to the adolescent information about who he or she is and who he or she ought to be. As such, the responses of these important others shape and influence the adolescent's developing sense of identity. Through others' reactions, we learn whether we are competent or clumsy, attractive or ugly, socially adept or tactless. Perhaps more important, especially during periods when our sense of identity is still forming, we learn from others what it is we do that we ought to keep doing, and what it is we do that we ought not to do.

Forging an identity, therefore, is a social as well as mental process. Erikson places a great deal of weight on the role of the young person's society (and, especially, on those individuals who have influence over the adolescent) in shaping the adolescent's sense of self. The adolescent's final identity is the result of a mutual recognition between the young person and society: The adolescent forges an identity, but at the same time, society identifies the adolescent.

The Social Context of Identity Development

The social context in which the adolescent attempts to establish a sense of identity exerts a tremendous impact on the nature and outcome of the process. Clearly, if adolescents' identities are forged out of a recognition on the part of society, society will play an important role in determining which sorts of identities are possible alternatives; and of those that are genuine options, which are desirable and which are not.

Consider, for example, the impact on an adolescent's identity development of deciding whether to go on to college after high school. In some communities, young people are expected to continue their education after graduating. Those going on to college are not admired for doing so—they are expected to do so. They may even be judged on the basis of *which* college they plan to attend. Those who choose not to attend college or who for one reason or another are not able to are viewed disparagingly.

In other communities, however, going on to college is the exception rather than the rule. Acceptance at a college is viewed as an important accomplishment, worthy of special commendation. The students who go on to college may be especially admired and congratulated for doing so. But their peers who do not attend college are not looked down on—after all, they are following the norms for members of their community. Obviously, attending or not attending college in these two kinds of communities has very different meanings. And as a consequence, the same decision will have a different impact on the adolescent's identity in one community than it would in the other.

Because the adolescent's attempt to establish a sense of identity is so clearly linked to the roles his or her society designates as acceptable pathways into adulthood, the course of identity development will vary in different cultures, among different subcultures within the same society, and over different historical eras. For example, the career options open to women in contemporary society have changed dramatically in the past twenty-five years, and, consequently, so has the nature of adolescent girls' identity development. In the past, most young women assumed that their adult identity would be exclusively tied to marriage and family life. But today, far more alternative identities are open to women. As a result, the process of choosing among different alternatives has become more complicated than it once was.

The social context in which an adolescent develops also determines to a large extent whether the youngster's search for self-defini-

tion will take the form of a full-blown crisis or whether it will be a more manageable challenge. Generally speaking, the more alternatives available to the young person and the more arenas in which decisions must be made, the more difficult establishing a sense of identity will be. Growing up in contemporary America, where adolescents have a range of careers to decide among, for example, is far more likely to provoke an occupational identity crisis than is growing up in a small agrarian community in which each young person continues farming the family's land. The rapid rate of social change has raised new and more complicated sets of questions for young people to consider—questions not only about occupational plans but about values, lifestyles, and commitments to other people. No longer are all young people expected to follow the same narrow path into adulthood: marriage and children for all, work for men, and homemaking for women. Today, male and female adolescents alike must ask themselves *if* they want to remain single, live with someone, or marry; *if* and *when* they want to have children; and *how* they plan to incorporate these choices into their career plans. Consequently, the likelihood of going through a prolonged and difficult identity crisis is probably greater today than it has ever been.

The psychosocial moratorium.   The complications inherent in identity development in modern society have created the need, Erikson argues, for a **psychosocial moratorium**—a time-out during adolescence from the sorts of excessive responsibilities and obligations that might restrict the young person's pursuit of self-discovery. Adolescents in contemporary America are given a moratorium of sorts by being encouraged to remain in school for a long time, where they can think seriously about their plans for the future without making irrevocable decisions.

During the psychosocial moratorium, the adolescent can experiment with different roles and identities, in a context that permits and encourages this sort of exploration. The exper-

Suspension of action

imentation involves trying on different postures, personalities, and ways of behaving—sometimes to the consternation of the adolescent's parents, who may wonder why their child's personality seems so changeable. One week, an adolescent girl will spend hours putting on make-up; the next week she will insist to her parents that she is tired of caring so much about the way she looks. An adolescent boy will come home one day wearing boots and a leather jacket and acting tough, and a few weeks later, he will discard the tough-guy image for that of serious student. Sometimes, parents describe their teenage children as going through "phases." Much of this behavior is actually experimentation with roles and personalities.

Having the time to experiment with roles is an important prelude to establishing a coherent sense of identity. But role experimentation can take place only in an environment that allows and encourages it (Gallatin, 1975). Without a period of moratorium, a full and thorough exploration of the options and alternatives available to the young person cannot occur, and identity development will be somewhat impeded. In other words, according to Erikson, adolescents must grow into adulthood—they should not be forced into it prematurely.

It is clear, however, that the sort of moratorium Erikson describes is an ideal; indeed, some might even consider it to be a luxury of the affluent. Many young people—perhaps even most—do not have the economic freedom to enjoy a long delay before taking on the responsibilities of adult life. For many youngsters, alternatives are not open in any realistic sense, and introspection only interferes with the more pressing task of survival. Does the 17-year-old who must drop out of school to work a full-time factory job go through life without a sense of identity? Do youngsters who cannot afford a psychosocial moratorium fail to resolve the crisis of "identity versus identity diffusion"?

Certainly not. But from an Eriksonian point of view, the absence of a psychosocial moratorium in some adolescents' lives—owing either to restrictions they place on themselves or to restrictions placed on them by others or by their life circumstances—is truly lamentable. The price these youngsters pay is not in failing to develop a sense of identity but in lost potential. You may know people whose parents have forced them into prematurely choosing a certain career or who have had to drop out of college and take a job they really did not want because of financial pressures. According to Erikson, without a chance to explore, to experiment, and to choose among options for the future, these young people may not realize all that they are capable of becoming. In theory, these individuals should encounter difficulties in resolving the subsequent crises of intimacy, generativity, and integrity.

Resolving the Identity Crisis

Is establishing a sense of identity a consciously felt achievement? According to Erikson, it is. It is experienced as a sense of well-being, a feeling of "being at home in one's body," a sense of knowing where one is going, and an inner assuredness of recognition from those who count. It is a sense of sameness through time—a feeling of continuity between the past and the future.

Establishing a coherent sense of identity is a lengthy process. Most writers on adolescence and youth believe that identity exploration continues well into young adulthood. But rather than thinking of the adolescent as going through *an* identity crisis, it probably makes more sense to view the phenomenon as a series of crises that may concern different aspects of the young person's identity and that may surface—and resurface—at different points in time throughout the adolescent and young adult years. As Erikson writes, "A sense of identity is never gained nor maintained once and for all . . . it is constantly lost and regained, although more lasting and more economical methods of maintenance and restoration are evolved and fortified in late adolescence" (1959, p. 118). During adolescence, the feeling of well-being associated with establishing a sense of identity is somewhat fleeting. Ultimately, however, the identity crisis of ado-

Role experimentation during adolescence often involves trying on different looks, images, and patterns of behavior. According to theorists such as Erik Erikson, having time to experiment with roles is an important prelude to establishing a coherent sense of identity. (Hazel Hankin)

lescence, when successfully resolved, culminates in a series of basic life commitments: occupational, ideological, social, religious, ethical, and sexual (Bourne, 1978a).

PROBLEMS IN IDENTITY DEVELOPMENT

Given the wide variations in developmental histories that individuals bring to adolescence and the wide variations in the environments in which adolescence is experienced, it is not surprising to find differences in the ways in which individuals approach and resolve the crisis of identity versus identity diffusion. Problems in identity development can result when an individual has not successfully resolved earlier crises or when the adolescent is in an environment that does not provide the necessary period of moratorium. Three sorts of problems have received special attention from Erikson. They are labeled identity diffusion, identity foreclosure, and negative identity, respectively.

Identity Diffusion

Identity diffusion (sometimes called identity confusion) is characterized by an incoherent, disjointed, incomplete sense of self. Identity diffusion can vary in degree from a mild state of not quite knowing who you are while in the midst of an identity crisis to a more severe, psychopathological condition that persists beyond a normal period of exploration. It is marked by disruptions in the individual's sense of time (some things seem to happen much faster than they really do, while others seem to take forever); excessive self-consciousness, to the point that it is difficult to make decisions; problems in work and achievement-related activities; difficulties in forming intimate relationships

From Carson McCullers's The Member of the Wedding

One of the most wonderful and memorable stories of an adolescent's struggle to establish a sense of identity is told in Carson Mc-Cullers's novel *The Member of the Wedding*. Set in the South during the mid-1940s, the story revolves around the identity development of Frankie Addams, a 12-year-old girl who has her first encounter that summer with the sort of self-examination and introspection we have come to associate with the adolescent years. At one point during the summer, she changes her name to F. Jasmine Addams.

"Why is it against the law to change your name?"

Berenice sat in a chair against the pale white light of the window. She held the newspaper open before her, and her head was twisted down and to one side as she strained to see what was printed there. When F. Jasmine spoke, she folded the paper and put it away on the table.

"You can figure that out," she said. "Just because. Think of the confusion."

"I don't see why," F. Jasmine said.

"What is that on your neck?" said Berenice. "I thought it was a head you carried on that neck. Just think. Suppose I would suddenly up and call myself Mrs. Eleanor Roosevelt. And you would begin naming yourself Joe Louis. And John Henry would try to pass off as Henry Ford. Now what kind of confusion do you think that would cause?"

"Don't talk childish," F. Jasmine said. "That is not the kind of changing I mean. I mean from a name that doesn't suit you to a name you prefer. Like I changed from Frankie to F. Jasmine."

"But it would still be a confusion," Berenice insisted. "Suppose we all suddenly changed to entirely different names. Nobody would ever know who anybody was talking about. The whole world would go crazy." . . .

"Listen," F. Jasmine said. "What I've been trying to say is this. Doesn't it strike you as strange that I am I, and you are you? I am F. Jasmine Addams. And you are Berenice Sadie Brown. And we can look at each other, and touch each other, and stay together year in and year out in the same room. Yet always I am I, and you are you. And I can't ever be anything else but me, and you can't ever be anything else but you. Have you ever thought of that? And doesn't it seem to you strange?"

Source: Carson McCullers, *The Member of the Wedding* (New York: Bantam, 1974; orig. pub. 1946), pp. 107–109.

with others; and concerns over sexuality. Identity confusion is reflected not just in problems of identity; it manifests itself in the areas of autonomy, intimacy, sexuality, and achievement as well.

A classic example of an adolescent in the throes of identity diffusion is Holden Caulfield in the novel *The Catcher in the Rye*. He has flunked out of several prep schools, has severed most of his friendships, and has no sense of where he is headed. At one point in the book, for example, walking up Fifth Avenue in New York City, Holden says, "Every time I came to the end of a block and stepped off the goddam curb, I had this feeling that I'd never get to the other side of the street. I thought I'd just go down, down, down, and nobody'd ever see me again. Boy, did it scare me" (Salinger, 1964, pp. 197–198).

Identity Foreclosure

Some young people bypass—either willingly or unwillingly—the period of exploration and experimentation that precedes the establishment of a healthy sense of identity. Instead of considering a range of alternatives, these adolescents prematurely commit themselves to a role, or series of roles, and settle upon a certain identification as a final identity. In essence, these individuals are not given—or do not take advantage of—a psychosocial moratorium. For example, a college freshman who made up his mind about becoming a doctor at the age of 13 may enroll in a rigid pre-med curriculum without considering other career possibilities. The circumvention of the identity crisis is called **identity foreclosure**.

Typically, the roles adopted in the process of identity foreclosure revolve around the goals set for the young person by parents or other authority figures. The adolescent may be led into these roles directly or forced into them indirectly by being denied a true period of psychosocial moratorium. Perhaps the parents of the would-be doctor have arranged their child's school schedule and summer vacations so that all of his or her spare time is spent taking extra science courses. No time is left for role experimentation or introspection. Individuals who have bypassed the identity crisis have made commitments, but they have not gone through a period of experimentation before making them. Identity foreclosure can be viewed, then, as a kind of interruption of the identity development process, an interruption that interferes with the individual's discovery of his or her full range of potentials.

Negative Identity

Occasionally, adolescents appear to select identities that are obviously undesirable to their parents and their community. The examples are familiar: The daughter of the local police chief who repeatedly gets into trouble with the law; the son of prestigious and successful parents who refuses to go to college; the child of a devoutly religious family who insists that he or she is a confirmed atheist. Because the establishment of a healthy sense of identity is so intimately tied to the recognition of the adolescent by those who count in his or her life, the adoption of a so-called **negative identity** is a sign that problems in identity development have arisen. The adolescent who adopts a negative identity is indeed recognized by those around him or her but not in a way that fosters healthy development.

Usually, selecting a negative identity is an attempt to forge *some* sense of self-definition in an environment that has made it difficult for the young person to establish an acceptable identity. This appears to be especially likely when, after repeatedly trying and failing to receive positive recognition from those who are important in their lives, adolescents turn to a different, perhaps more successful, route to being noticed—adopting a negative identity. Consider this example: The son of successful parents is a good student but not quite good enough to please his excessively demanding parents. He feels he is a nobody in his parents' eyes. So the boy drops out of school to play guitar in a band—something his parents vehemently oppose. To paraphrase Erikson, this adolescent, like most youngsters, would rather be somebody "bad" than nobody at all.

RESEARCH ON ERIKSON'S THEORY

Determining an Adolescent's Identity Status

Erikson's theory has had a far-reaching impact on current views of identity development during adolescence. Although the theory has a great deal of intuitive appeal, many of the concepts are vague and difficult to measure. How would you determine whether someone was in a state of identity diffusion? Where would you draw the line between someone who has genuinely established a coherent sense of identity and one who, in Erikson's terms, has "foreclosed" the process? One of the challenges faced by researchers in this area has been to find valid and reliable ways of measuring Erikson's very interesting ideas.

The most extensive attempt to do this is an interview measure of identity development constructed by psychologist James Marcia and his

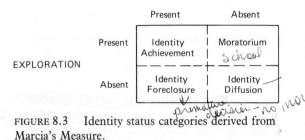

COMMITMENT

	Present	Absent
Present	Identity Achievement	Moratorium *school*
Absent	Identity Foreclosure	Identity Diffusion

EXPLORATION

premature decision – no moratorium

FIGURE 8.3 Identity status categories derived from Marcia's Measure.

colleagues, called the Identity Status Interview (Marcia, 1966, 1976). The focus of this interview, which covers identity exploration in three areas—occupation, ideology, and interpersonal relations—is on the individual's personal commitments and the efforts he or she has undertaken to forge them. Based on the interview responses, individuals are rated on two dimensions: (1) the degree to which they have made commitments and (2) the degree to which they engaged in a sustained search in the process (see Figure 8.3). On the basis of these ratings, the judges assign young people to one of four categories: *identity achievement* (the individual has established a coherent sense of identity, that is, has made commitments after a period of crisis and experimentation); *moratorium* (the individual is in the midst of a period of crisis and experimentation); *foreclosure* (the individual has made commitments but without a period of crisis or experimentation); and *identity diffusion* (the individual does not have firm commitments and is not currently trying to make them). Several other researchers also have begun using a questionnaire to measure identity status (Grotevant and Adams, 1984).

Generally speaking, research employing the Identity Status Interview and its paper-and-pencil derivatives has supported Erikson's theory. For example, identity achievers are psychologically healthier than other individuals on a variety of measures: They score highest on measures of achievement motivation, moral reasoning, intimacy with peers, and reflectiveness. Individuals

Parents who encourage their children to make early occupational choices may deny them a period of psychosocial moratorium during which they can experiment with different roles and discover their full range of potential. (Lew Merrim/Monkmeyer)

in the moratorium category score highest on measures of anxiety, show the highest levels of conflict over issues of authority, and are themselves the least rigid and authoritarian. Individuals classified as being in the foreclosure group have been shown to be the most authoritarian and to have the highest need for social approval, the lowest level of autonomy, and the greatest closeness to their parents. Individuals in a state of identity diffusion display the highest level of psychological and interpersonal problems: They are the most socially withdrawn and show the lowest level of intimacy with peers (Bourne, 1978b).

What sorts of parenting practices are associated with these different identity statuses? Research has only begun to examine this issue, but generally speaking, individuals whose identity development is healthy are more likely to come from homes characterized by warm, not excessively constraining relations (Grotevant and Cooper, 1986). As we saw in Chapter 4, individuals who grow up in these environments are encouraged to assert their individuality but to remain connected to their families at the same time. Typically, the absence of parental warmth is associated with problems in making commitments—the most extreme case being identity diffusion—whereas the absence of parental encouragement of individuality is associated with problems in engaging in extensive exploration (Campbell, Adams, and Dobson, 1985).

In order to examine the development of a sense of identity, researchers using the Identity Status Interview have done both cross-sectional studies (comparing individuals of different ages) and longitudinal studies (following the same individuals over a period of time). Perhaps the most significant finding to emerge from this line of research is that establishing a coherent sense of identity generally does not occur much before age 18 (Marcia, 1980). In general, when comparisons are made among groups of youngsters of different ages over the span from ages 12 to 24, differences in identity status are most frequently observed between groups in the 18- to 21-year-old range. Few consistent differences emerge in comparisons of teenagers in the middle adolescent years, suggesting that, although self-examination may take place throughout adolescence, the consolidation of a coherent sense of identity does not begin until very late in the period (Adams and Jones, 1983; Archer, 1982). The late teens and early twenties appear to be the critical times for the crystallization of a sense of identity. As Alan Waterman has noted, "The

results of numerous studies confirm that, in general, (college) senior men and women have a stronger sense of personal identity than do their freshman counterparts and that the identity commitments held as seniors are more likely to have been arrived at through the successful resolution of identity crisis" (Waterman, 1982, p. 346). Thus, it appears that the establishment of a sense of identity is a developmental issue that extends will into late adolescence and perhaps even into early adulthood.

The movement toward identity achievement that occurs between ages 18 and 21 among college students appears to be primarily in the area of occupational commitments. Alan Waterman and his associates (Waterman and Waterman, 1971; Waterman, Geary, and Waterman, 1974; Waterman and Goldman, 1976), who followed samples of college students for several years, found that during the college years, vocational plans solidify, but religious and political commitments are not as clearly established. More specifically, individuals emerge from college with more clearly defined occupational plans but no firm religious or political commitments (Waterman, 1982). In fact, college seems to undermine students' "traditional" religious beliefs—the beliefs that they acquired from their parents—without replacing them with others. Students who enter college as devout Catholics, for example, may graduate having lost some of their commitment to Catholicism but without having developed any new religious commitments instead.

A recent study by Raymond Montemayor and his colleagues supports the idea that the freshman year of college may be an important time in the process of identity development. A group of students were assessed before entering college and again toward the end of their freshman year. Before entering college, half of the adolescents were judged to be in a state of identity diffusion and 40 percent in a state of moratorium—consistent with the notion that the identity crisis is unlikely to be resolved during high school. Eight percent were in the identity achievement status, and the rest were judged to

During the college years, many individuals begin to develop clearer vocational identities. Many colleges sponsor career days and offer job counseling services. (Stu Rosner/Stock, Boston)

be foreclosed. What happened to these individuals as college freshmen? Over the first year of college, the most common pathway was either remaining diffused or in a state of moratorium or moving from one of the "committed" statuses (identity achievement or identity foreclosure) to one of the "noncommitted" statuses (diffusion or moratorium). In other words, while freshman year may "shake up some students and cause them to reexamine previously held commitments, students who are uncertain to begin with . . . remain so. . . . The freshman year appears to produce uncertainty in many students but does not help to resolve it" (Montemayor, Brown, and Adams, 1985, p. 7).

Although these studies bring us closer to a direct test of Erikson's model, their reliance on college students does not tell us whether movement toward a more clearly defined sense of self

is a general characteristic of development between the ages of 18 and 21 or whether it is more specifically attributable to the experience of going to college.

Do young people need to go to college in order to develop a clear sense of identity? Unfortunately, because there are so few developmental studies among noncollege youth, we have little way of answering this question. But the results of one study comparing identity development in college and noncollege youth are quite interesting. Gordon Munro and Gerald Adams (1977) compared a sample of college students with a same-aged (18–21) sample of noncollege working youths. The working youths were actually *more* likely to have established a sense of identity—more in the area of ideological commitments than in vocational commitments. This finding suggests that for many young peo-

Does College "Cause" Identity Development? Why Correlation Is Not Causation

One problem often faced by researchers who study adolescent development is to determine whether two factors that are associated with each other, or *correlated*, have any *causal* connection to each other. For example, we might find that smart people eat a great deal of fish (that intelligence and eating fish are correlated), but it wouldn't necessarily be correct to conclude on the basis of this finding that eating fish *causes* people to become smarter. It might be the case, instead, that smart people are more aware of the nutritional benefits of eating seafood and choose to eat seafood more often—in which case we might be correct in saying that being smart "causes" people to eat more fish. Or it might be the case that some other factor—living near the ocean, for example—is associated both with being smart and eating fish, making it only appear that intelligence and the consumption of seafood are independently related. It is much more difficult to demonstrate that one thing causes another than to demonstrate that the two are merely correlated. As the social science maxim goes, "Correlation is not causation."

Even social scientists forget this occasionally. The author of an article on identity development, in discussing his studies of college students, wrote that "College clearly facilitates identity development in the area of vocational plans" (Waterman, 1982, p. 347). He cited evidence from several longitudinal studies of young people, which showed that as students moved from the freshman to senior years, the clarity of their occupational identity increased. But did *college* really facilitate (help or cause) their identity development?

Actually, without a sample of noncollege youth to serve as a comparison group, we have no way of telling. It might be the case that *all* young adults undergo significant identity development between the ages of 18 and 21, regardless of whether they go to college—in which case, both college attendance and identity development would be correlated with a third factor, going from 18 to 21 years of age. Or it might be that youngsters who have a developing sense of identity are more likely to enroll in and stay in school than their peers who have a less clear sense of who they are—in which case it would be more accurate to say that identity development facilitated college attendance. Both of these explanations are entirely plausible, and both would account for the greater clarity of seniors' plans than those of freshmen. But in neither case would we be correct in concluding that college "facilitates" identity development.

Drawing causal interpretations from correlational data is not an uncommon practice. But it is one that you should be wary of whenever you read research. If an author suggests or implies that something caused something else, ask yourself whether other plausible explanations were adequately ruled out. College may indeed facilitate the development of occupational identity. But we can't be sure yet.

ple, college may prolong the psychosocial moratorium, especially in matters of political and religious belief. It would be interesting to know whether this extended moratorium has any long-term benefits or costs to later identity development. A study addressing this question would require that the samples of college and noncollege individuals be reassessed sometime during adulthood. Thus far, such a study has not been undertaken.

Shifts in Identity Status

As you will recall, Erikson theorizes that the sense of identity developed during adolescence is constantly lost and regained, that the challenge is not resolved once and for all at one point in time. If, according to Erikson's model, identity crises surface and resurface throughout the life cycle, we ought to find that individuals move from one identity status to another, particularly during the adolescent and young adult years.

This appears to be precisely the case. In one study that followed students over a one-year period (Adams and Fitch, 1982), nearly 60 percent of the students classified as experiencing identity diffusion at the beginning of the study were no longer in this category one year later. Changes in status also occurred for half of the students initially placed in the moratorium category. In two other longitudinal studies, each spanning a four-year period (Waterman, Geary, and Waterman, 1974; Waterman and Goldman, 1976), the degree of shifting was 50 percent in one study and 33 percent in the other for students classified as experiencing identity diffusion, and 91 percent and 100 percent for students initially classified as being in the midst of a moratorium.

These sorts of shifts are not surprising, of course, since both the diffusion and moratorium categories are, theoretically, unstable ones. But in these same longitudinal studies, about one-third of each of the identity achievement and foreclosure groups *also* shifted status over the course of one year; and, over the course of four years, more than half of the students initially classified as foreclosures and one-third of those initially classified as identity achievers moved into a different group. In other words, some individuals who at one point had apparently resolved the identity crisis (had been classified as identity achievers) actually had not resolved it— at least, in any final sense. The weight of the evidence collected to date, therefore, suggests that identity status classifications made during adolescence and young adulthood probably represent short-term, temporary states, rather than long-term, enduring traits. As Erikson has suggested, revising and maintaining one's sense of self-definition is a challenge that continues beyond adolescence.

Development of Ethnic Identity

In recent years, researchers have begun to study more intensively American adolescents from minority groups—blacks, Hispanics, Asians, and American Indians. This research has tended to focus more on problematic aspects of development, however, such as unemployment, teenage pregnancy, or delinquency, rather than on more normative aspects of adolescence, such as the development of identity or intimacy. Studies of problem behavior among minority adolescents are important when they shed light on the dimensions, causes, and consequences of these problems and provide information with which to compare the behavior of white adolescents. Nonetheless, it is misleading and disparaging to limit our research on minority adolescents to the study of problem behavior, because there is reason to believe that most minority youngsters— like most white youngsters—progress through adolescence without major difficulty. We do not know, however, whether the progression through the developmental challenges of adolescence follows the pattern described in most theories and research, because virtually all of our knowledge about *normative* aspects of adolescent development derives from studies of white youth—white, middle-class youth, to be precise. Consequently, we must be cautious about generalizing these results to nonwhite populations. Furthermore, as studies of normative aspects of development among minority youth begin to appear, we must be cautious about generalizing the findings from one minority group to another: Black, Hispanic, Asian, and American Indian adolescents may share the fact that they are members of ethnic minorities, but their similarities may end there. Even within these broad ethnic categories there are substantial differences in adolescents' experiences between Mex-

The Sexes: Are There Sex Differences in the Route to a Sense of Identity?

Many writers have argued that male and female adolescents approach the crisis of identity from different perspectives and resolve it through different means. Some theorists have gone so far as to say that although Erikson's framework, which places the crisis of identity developmentally earlier than the crisis of intimacy, is a reasonable model of psychosocial development for males, it does not adequately account for development among girls (Gallatin, 1975). They argue that girls are much more interpersonally oriented than boys and that as a consequence, girls are likely to face the challenge of intimacy before they deal with the crisis of identity—or at the very least, that girls pursue their sense of identity *through* their relationships with others. Girls learn about themselves, it is argued, in the context of friendships and close relationships, whereas boys forge a sense of identity by being autonomous and independent (Douvan and Adelson, 1966).

There is undoubtedly some truth to the idea that males and females approach and resolve the psychosocial issues of adolescence differently; how could they help but do so, given the strong pressures on them to adhere to two different sets of behavioral standards?

But linking male identity development to autonomy and independence and female identity development to intimacy and other interpersonal pursuits is no longer as useful as it once was. Although one classic study of adolescents conducted during the early 1960s (Douvan and Adelson, 1966) concluded that "there is not one adolescent crisis, but two major and clearly distinctive ones—the masculine and the feminine" (p. 350), research carried out during the 1980s has pointed to similarities rather than differences in the ways in which males and females struggle with the task of self-definition (Adams and Fitch, 1982; Grotevant and Thorbecke, 1982). Were the early descriptions of sex differences in identity development erroneous, or are these recent studies off the mark?

In answering this question, we must bear in mind that sex differences—or for that matter similarities—in identity development can be understood only against the backdrop of the social context in which development takes place. Assessing the studies in a historical context sheds some light on the controversy. For many adolescent girls, particularly twenty or thirty years ago, the roles of adulthood open to them *were* primarily interper-

ican-American and Puerto Rican adolescents, for instance, or between Japanese-American and Chinese-American adolescents.

For all individuals, but especially for those who are not part of the white majority, integrating a sense of **ethnic identity** into their overall sense of personal identity is likely to be an important task of late adolescence, perhaps as important as establishing a coherent occupational, ideological, or interpersonal identity (Phinney and Alipuria, 1987). According to several writers (Cross, 1978; Kim, 1981, cited in Phinney and Alipuria, 1987), the process of ethnic-identity development follows in some re-

spects the process of identity development in general, with an unquestioning view of oneself being displaced or upset by a crisis. Following the crisis, the individual may become immersed in his or her own ethnic group and turn against the white majority culture. Eventually, as the value and importance of having a strong ethnic identity become clear, the individual establishes a more coherent sense of personal identity that includes this ethnic identity and, with growing confidence, attempts to help others deal with their own struggles with ethnic identity.

Do members of ethnic minorities have more difficulty than white adolescents in resolving the

sonal in nature, so it comes as no surprise that the crisis of identity manifested itself for these young women through their relationships with others. After all, in Erikson's model, identity is pursued with one eye toward the future. But today, as new generations of adolescent girls face a society that presents them with greater and more diverse options for the future, especially in terms of occupation, their identity explorations are likely to extend further into the realms of autonomy and independence than they have in the past.

In this regard, it is interesting to note that some studies show that adolescent males move through the process of identity development faster than females (Marcia, 1980). If young women appear to take more time resolving the crisis of identity than young men do, perhaps it is because the options and alternatives open to women in contemporary society are more confusing, more complicated, and more rapidly changing than they are for men. As noted earlier, the length of a moratorium needed to experiment with enough roles is linked to the complexity of the choices the young person faces.

This is not to say that the outcomes of the identity development process are the same for males and females, however, or that the similarities that may characterize identity

development during adolescence persist into adulthood. Society has still not fully come to terms with women's interest in careers, and, consequently, the task of integrating occupational and interpersonal commitments into a coherent and satisfying sense of self is likely to be more difficult for women than men. Whereas men are apt to follow the predictable sequence of normative crises outlined by Erikson—a pattern largely determined by their occupational development (Levinson, 1978)—women's lives diverge more from one another and in some senses are more complicated by the commitments of marriage and parenthood (Baruch, Barnett, and Rivers, 1983). Accordingly, even though boys and girls may go through similar struggles in establishing a sense of identity in adolescence, the consequences of resolving the crisis may have clearer and more immediate advantages for men than women. Thus, for example, achieving a coherent sense of identity during adolescence is a strong predictor of life satisfaction and of becoming married as an adult for men, but for women, it predicts neither (Kahn et al., 1985). Whatever similarities exist between boys and girls in their search for identity as adolescents, the structure of adult experience introduces important differences into the process—and, consequently, the outcome.

identity crisis, however? Researchers are just now beginning to examine this question, and the answer is still not known. The little research that has been done suggests more similarities than differences in the *process* through which identity development occurs. One difference, though, appears to be quite important, if perhaps not very surprising: Having a strong ethnic identity is associated with higher self-esteem among minority youngsters, especially among black and Hispanic youth, but this is not the case among white youth (Phinney and Alipuria, 1987). It would seem, therefore, that establishing a sense of ethnic identity is more important

to individuals who are part of an ethnic minority than for those who are part of a majority.

SEX-ROLE STEREOTYPES AND IDENTITY DEVELOPMENT

Gender is a critical component of one's identity. From birth, boys and girls are socialized to behave in "sex-appropriate" ways—that is, to conform to society's standards for acceptable masculine and acceptable feminine behavior. In American society, strong sex-role stereotypes prevail among children, adolescents, and adults.

Traits such as logical, independent, ambitious, and aggressive are considered masculine; and traits such as gentle, sociable, empathic, and tender are considered feminine (Broverman et al., 1972).

Individuals very in their degrees of masculinity and femininity. Some are decidedly more masculine than feminine, and others are decidedly more feminine than masculine. But some people have a high degree of both masculinity and femininity. For instance, some people are highly ambitious (a trait usually considered masculine) and highly sensitive (a trait usually considered feminine). Individuals who are both highly masculine and highly feminine are said to be **androgynous** (Bem, 1975).

Researchers have begun to take an interest in the relation between sex-role stereotypes and adolescent identity development. Are teenagers, for example, pressured more than children to behave in stereotypically masculine or feminine ways? If so, to what extent does a person's compliance with prevailing sex-role stereotypes affect his or her self-image?

Sex-Role Socialization During Adolescence

There is some thought that pressures to behave in "sex-appropriate" ways intensify during adolescence, especially for girls. This idea, called the **gender intensification hypothesis** (Hill and Lynch, 1983), is that many of the sex differences observed between adolescent boys and girls are due not to biological differences but to an acceleration in their socialization to act in stereotypically masculine and feminine ways.

Psychologists John Hill and Mary Ellen Lynch (1983) have summarized some of the research that bears on this issue. They note that at adolescence, girls become more self-conscious and experience more disruptions in self-image than boys; that achievement behavior becomes more sex-stereotyped, with girls beginning to excel in verbal skills and boys in spatial skills; and that girls become more invested in and more competent at forming intimate friendships. As

we saw in the chapter on cognitive development, it is impossible to rule out totally the biological explanations for some of these sex differences, because patterns of hormonal change at puberty differ markedly for boys and girls. Nonetheless, according to Hill and Lynch, it seems reasonable to conclude that at least in some areas, sex-role socialization does intensify during adolescence. As teenagers begin to date, for example, it may become more important for them to act in ways that are consistent with sex-role expectations and that meet with approval in the peer group. Boys who do not act masculine enough and girls who do not act feminine enough may be less popular and may be less accepted by their same- and opposite-sex peers.

In many respects, sex-role identity, already an important part of the self-concept during childhood, may become an even more important aspect of identity during adolescence. As we shall see in the chapters on intimacy, sexuality, and achievement, the intensification of sex-role socialization during adolescence has important implications for understanding sex differences in a range of different issues. For example, girls' achievement in high school may be lower than boys' because doing well in school is not perceived as appropriately feminine, and girls who earn high grades may pay a price in popularity.

Masculinity, Femininity, and the Adolescent's Self-Image

If sex-role socialization becomes more intense during adolescence, we would expect to find that conformity to sex-role expectations is an important influence on the adolescent's self-image. Do more feminine girls and more masculine boys feel better about themselves than do their peers, or are boys and girls both better off being somewhat androgynous—as some psychologists suggest (Bem, 1975; Spence and Helmreich, 1978)?

Recent research on sex-role identity during adolescence suggests that the answer to this question may differ for males and females. The benefits of androgyny to youngsters' self-image are greater for girls than for boys. For example,

Androgynous girls—girls who have a mix of masculine and feminine traits—have a more positive self-image and are more accepted by their peers than are extremely feminine or extremely masculine girls. (Barbara Alper)

one study examined the relation between adolescents' self-image, their acceptance by peers, and their scores on standardized measures of masculinity, femininity, and androgyny. Although androgynous girls felt better about themselves than either very masculine or very feminine girls, it was the masculine boys (not the androgynous boys) who showed the highest levels of self-acceptance. This may have been due to the fact that peer acceptance during adolescence was also highest for androgynous girls and masculine boys (Massad, 1981). These findings suggest that it is easier for girls to behave sometimes in masculine ways during adolescence than it is for boys to act occasionally in feminine ways. Consistent with research on younger children (Lynn, 1966), during adolescence—at least in contemporary American society—males who do not conform to traditionally masculine sex-role norms are judged more deviant than females whose behavior departs from exclusively feminine roles.

At first glance, this finding may seem to contradict something we noted earlier—that during adolescence, pressures to conform with sex-role norms increase more for girls than for boys. If this is so, why is it that boys suffer greater self-image problems when they deviate from what is viewed as appropriate for their gender?

The answer is that although girls may be pressured to adopt (or maintain) certain feminine traits during adolescence, they are not necessarily pressured to relinquish all elements of masculinity. In contrast, boys are socialized from a very early age not to adopt feminine traits and are judged deviant if they show signs of femininity. In other words, girls can be highly pressured during adolescence to behave in feminine ways without necessarily being punished or labeled deviant for exhibiting some masculine traits at the same time; thus for girls, androgyny is a viable alternative to exclusive femininity. Girls may feel increasingly pressured to dress nicely and wear make-up when they reach adolescence; but they are not pressured to give up athletics or other typically masculine interests. But boys, from childhood on, are pressured not to behave in feminine ways—even if the femininity is in the context of androgyny. Their gen- der-role socialization does not intensify during adolescence as much as it does for girls because it is so intense to begin with.

Summary

Identity emerges as a concern during adolescence because of the biological, cognitive, and social changes characteristic of development during this period of the life cycle. Together, these changes provoke changes in the adolescent's self-concept, fluctuations in self-image, and a struggle to establish a coherent sense of identity. Much of the work on adolescent identity development has followed from the theories of Erik Erikson, who characterizes adolescence as a time of identity crisis. According to this view, the adolescent forges a sense of identity by experimenting with different roles and personalities. This process culminates, in late adolescence or early adulthood, in the making of occupational and interpersonal commitments to be carried out in adulthood. Many researchers and theorists have commented on the notable sex differences that are apparent at adolescence. Despite pressures on males and females to behave in different ways, however, the fundamental task of self-definition remains the same for adolescent girls and boys: to establish a sense of self that links one's unique past with one's present, with an eye toward one's hopes for the future.

During the past two decades, we have made many advances in our ability to describe the progressions that adolescents move through as their self-conceptions, self-image, and sense of identity develop. It can now be stated with some confidence how self-conceptions expand and become more sophisticated, when problems in self-image are likely to arise during early adolescence, and how older adolescents progress toward a more coherent sense of self-definition. Now that much of this work is completed, researchers can turn their attention to more challenging questions: Why does identity development follow the pattern that it does? How are the various aspects of identity development related? And how does the broader context of adolescence shape and influence the young person's developing sense of self?

Key Terms

androgynous *highly masculine + feminine*

barometric self-esteem *fluctuation of*

baseline self-esteem *stable*

ethnic identity

gender intensification hypothesis *during adolescence*

identification

identity achievement

identity diffusion

identity foreclosure

identity versus identity diffusion

negative identity

part identifications

psychosocial moratorium

self-conceptions *as see self*

self-consciousness *too regularly in self concept*

self-esteem *what one feels about self*

self-image stability *how one feels about change from day to day in self image*

sense of identity *how feel secure about self identity*

social class *social position of family or person according to power, money, reputation + achievement*

For Further Reading

ERIKSON, E. (1968). *Identity: Youth and Crisis*. New York: Norton. In this book, Erikson presents his theory of identity development during adolescence.

MONTEMAYOR, R., AND EISEN, M. (1977). The development of self-conceptions from childhood to adolescence. *Developmental Psychology, 13,* 314–319. This is a study of age differences in children's self-conceptions.

ROSENBERG, M. (1986). Self-concept from middle childhood through adolescence. In J. Suls and A. Greenwald (Eds.), *Psychological perspectives on the self*. (Vol. 3). Hillsdale, NJ: Erlbaum. A review of research on self-concept and self-esteem during adolescence.

WATERMAN, A. (1982). Identity development from adolescence to adulthood: An extension of theory and a review of research. *Developmental Psychology, 18,* 341–358. An extensive review of research on Erikson's ideas about identity development during adolescence.

Autonomy

CHAPTER 9

1. The development of a healthy sense of autonomy is a fundamental concern during adolescence. Because adolescents in contemporary society spend so much time away from the direct supervision of adults, understanding the processes through which young people become responsible and self-reliant is extremely important.

2. Research on the growth of autonomy during adolescence has focused on three aspects of the adolescent's developing sense of independence: emotional autonomy, which concerns the adolescent's changing relationships with parents; behavioral autonomy, which concerns changes in decision-making abilities, susceptibility to pressures from other people, and feelings of self-reliance; and value autonomy, which concerns changes in the adolescent's beliefs, morals, and values.

3. Studies of influences on the development of autonomy show that the most autonomous adolescents have warm, not distant, relationships with their parents and come from authoritative families, in which independence was granted progressively throughout childhood and adolescence.

4. Although early writings on the development of autonomy linked adolescent independence with rebellion and family conflict, more recent research indicates that this view is incorrect. Responsible autonomy is more likely to be achieved through a gradual and surprisingly undramatic process. Establishing a healthy sense of independence need not be a struggle for adolescents, and rebellion and family conflict are likely to be indicators of problems, not progress.

You are about to leave the house:
"Where are you going?"
"Out."
"Out where?"
"Just out."
"Who are you going with?"
"A friend."
"Which friend?"
"Mom, just a friend, okay? Do you have to know everything?"
"I don't have to know everything. I just want to know who you're going out with."
"Debby, okay?"
"Do I know Debby?"
"She's just a friend, okay?"
"Well, where are going?"
"Out."

—Delia Ephron, *Teenage Romance*

For most adolescents, establishing a sense of **autonomy** is as important a part of becoming an adult as is establishing a sense of identity. Becoming an autonomous person—a self-governing person—is one of the fundamental developmental tasks of the adolescent years.

Although we often use the words *autonomy* and *independence* interchangeably, in the study of adolescence, *autonomy* means something slightly different from *independence*. Independence generally refers to individuals' capacity to behave on their own. The growth of independence is surely a part of becoming autonomous during adolescence, but, as you will see in this chapter, autonomy has emotional and cognitive as well as behavioral components.

During adolescence, there is a movement away from the dependency typical of childhood toward the autonomy typical of adulthood. But the growth of autonomy during adolescence is often misunderstood. Autonomy is often confused with rebellion, and becoming an independent person is often equated with breaking away from the family. This perspective on autonomy goes hand in hand with the idea that adolescence is inevitably a time of stress and turmoil. But as we saw in the last chapter, the view that adolescence is a period of "storm and stress" has been questioned repeatedly by recent research. The same sort of rethinking has taken place with regard to the development of autonomy. Rather than viewing adolescence as a time of spectacular and active rebellion, researchers are coming to see the growth of autonomy during adolescence as gradual, progressive, and although important, relatively undramatic.

The development of autonomy during adolescence is vital in contemporary society, where increasingly adolescents are faced with difficult decisions about lifestyles, values, and behavior. "Should I do what I think is right, or should I go along with my friends in order to stay popular?" "Is it all right to live with someone before getting married?" "How much say should my parents have over where I go to college or what I do with my life?" In earlier eras, these sorts of questions did not come up as frequently as they do today because the range of choices open to young people was not as great. Living together before getting married was virtually unheard of, for example; the question of whether it was acceptable seldom arose. Norms and standards were clearer and more universal, and as a result, making decisions was easier.

Because today's adolescents spend so much time away from the direct supervision of adults, either by themselves or with their peers, learning how to govern their own behavior in a responsible fashion is a crucial task for contemporary youth. As we saw in earlier chapters, with increasing numbers of single-parent and two-career households, more young people are expected to supervise themselves for a good part of the day (Steinberg, 1986). Many young people feel pressured—by parents, by friends, and by the media—to grow up quickly and to act like adults at an early age (Elkind, 1982). One 13-year-old must make plane reservations to fly back and forth between his separated parents' homes. Another is pregnant and, afraid to tell her parents, must seek counseling on her own. A third is expected to take care of his younger siblings each afternoon because both of his parents work. In many regards, the demands on young people to behave independently are greater today than ever before.

There is a curious paradox to all of this, however. At the same time that adolescents have been asked to become more autonomous psychologically and socially, they have become less autonomous economically. Because of the extension of schooling well into the young adult years for most individuals, financial independence may not come until long after psychological independence has been established. Many young people who are emotionally independent find it frustrating to discover that they have to abide by their parents' rules as long as they are being supported economically. They may feel that the ability to make their own decisions has nothing to do with financial dependence. A 16-year-old who drives, has a part-time job, and has a serious relationship with his girlfriend, for example, may be independent in these respects, but he is nonetheless still dependent on his parents for food and shelter. His parents may feel that as long as their son lives in their home, they should decide how late he can stay out at night. The adolescent may feel that his parents have no right to tell him when he can come and go. This sort of difference of opinion can be a real source of problems and confusion for teenagers and their parents, particularly when they have difficulty agreeing on a level of independence for the adolescent. Disagreements over autonomy-related concerns are at the top of the list of quarrel-provokers between adolescents and parents (Montemayor, 1986).

AUTONOMY AS AN ADOLESCENT ISSUE

Like identity, autonomy is a psychosocial concern that surfaces and resurfaces during the entire life cycle. The development of independent behavior begins long before puberty. Erik Erikson (1963), whose theory of psychosocial development we examined in the previous chapter,

believes that autonomy is the central issue of toddlerhood, in the same sense that identity is the central issue of adolescence. Young children, he observes, try to establish an initial sense of autonomy when they begin to explore their surroundings on their own and assert their desire to do as they please. If you have spent any time with 3-year-olds, you know that one of their favorite expressions is "No!" In some regards, the early adolescent's behavior captured in the excerpt that began this chapter is quite similar. The toddler who insists on saying "no" and the young adolescent who insists on keeping her whereabouts secret are both demonstrating their growing sense of independence and autonomy.

Although childhood and adolescence are important periods for the development of autonomy, it is a mistake to suggest that issues of autonomy are resolved once and for all by young adulthood. Questions about our ability to function independently arise whenever we find ourselves in positions that demand a new degree of self-reliance. Following a divorce, for example, someone who has depended on a spouse over the years for economic support, guidance, or nurturance must find a way to function more autonomously and independently. During late adulthood, autonomy may become a significant concern of the individual who suddenly finds it necessary to depend on others for assistance and support.

If establishing and maintaining a healthy sense of autonomy is a lifelong concern, why has it attracted so much attention among scholars interested in adolescence? When we look at the development of autonomy in relation to the biological, cognitive, and social changes of adolescence, it is easy to see why. Consider first the impact of puberty. Some theorists (for example, A. Freud, 1958) have suggested that the physical changes of early adolescence trigger changes in the young person's emotional relationships at home. Adolescents' interest in turning away from parents and toward peers for emotional support—a development that is part of establishing adult independence—may be sparked by

The development of autonomy becomes an especially salient issue during adolescence as young people find themselves moving into positions that demand independent and responsible behavior. (Sybil Shackman/Monkmeyer)

their emerging interest in sexual relationships and their concern over such things as dating and intimate friendships. In some senses, puberty drives the adolescent away from exclusive emotional dependence on the family. Furthermore, the changes in stature and physical appearance occurring at puberty may provoke changes in how much autonomy the young person is granted by parents and teachers. Youngsters who simply *look* more mature may be given more responsibility by adults around them. A father may look at his son—who now stands several inches taller than he—and say, "You're older now. It's time you began taking more responsibility around the house."

The cognitive changes of adolescence also play an important role in the development of autonomy. Part of being autonomous involves being able to make our own decisions. When we turn to others for advice, we often receive conflicting opinions. If you are deciding between staying home to study for an exam and going out to a party, your professor and the person throwing the party would probably give you different advice. As an adult, you are able to see that each individual's perspective influences his or her advice. The ability to see this, however, calls for a level of intellectual abstraction not available until adolescence. Being able to take other people's perspectives into account, reason in more sophisticated ways, and foresee the future consequences of alternative courses of action all help the young person to weigh more effectively the opinions and suggestions of others and reach his or her own independent decisions. The cognitive changes of adolescence also provide the logical foundation for changes in the young person's thinking about social, moral, and ethical problems. These changes in thinking are important prerequisites to the development of a system of values that is based on the individual's own sense of right and wrong and not merely on rules and regulations handed down by parents or other authority figures.

Finally, changes in social roles and activities during adolescence are bound to raise concerns related to independence, as the adolescent moves into new positions that demand increasing degrees of responsibility and self-reliance. Being able to work, to marry, to drive, to drink, and to vote, to name just a few activities that are first permitted during adolescence, all require a certain degree of autonomy—the ability to manage oneself responsibly in the absence of monitoring by parents or teachers. Becoming involved in new roles and taking on new responsibilities place the adolescent in situations that require and stimulate the development of independent decision-making abilities and the clarification of personal values. A teenager might not really think much about the responsibilities associated with taking a job, for example, until he or she actually ends up in one. Choosing whether to drink does not become an important question until the adolescent begins to approach the legal drinking age. And deciding what one's political leanings are becomes a more pressing concern when the young person realizes that he or she has the right to vote.

THREE TYPES OF AUTONOMY

We have talked a great deal thus far about the need to develop a sense of autonomy during adolescence. But what does it really mean to be an autonomous or independent person? If you give the question some thought, you will realize that its answer is rather complicated. One way to approach the question is to begin by thinking of people whom you would describe as independent. Why did you pick them? Is it because they seem to be able to rely on themselves rather than depending excessively on others for support or guidance? Is it because they can make their own decisions and follow them through, withstanding pressures to go against what they really know is right? Or it is perhaps because they are independent thinkers—people who have strong principles and values that they won't compromise?

Each of these characterizations is a reasonable enough description of what it means to be independent, yet each describes a different sort of independence. The first involves what psychologists call **emotional autonomy**—that aspect of independence related to changes in the individual's close relationships. The second characterization corresponds to what is sometimes called **behavioral autonomy**—the capacity to make independent decisions and follow through with them. The third characterization involves an aspect of independence referred to as **value autonomy**—which is more than simply being able to resist pressures to go along with the demands of others; it means having a set of principles about right and wrong, about what is important and what is not. We will examine each of these three aspects of autonomy in turn.

THE DEVELOPMENT OF EMOTIONAL AUTONOMY

The relationship between children and their parents changes repeatedly over the course of the life cycle. Changes in the expression of affection, the distribution of power, and patterns of verbal interaction, to give a few examples, are likely to occur whenever important transformations take place in the child's or the parents' competencies, concerns, and social roles. During infancy, for example, the child is extremely, often exclusively, dependent on his or her parents for affection and for survival. But this emotional bond gradually gives way to a more complicated arrangement of interpersonal ties that usually includes agemates and adults outside the family (for example, teachers). Such transformations are related to the child's entrance into the world of day care or school, where important relationships with others are formed; to the child's growing capacity to function independently; and to changes in parents' own emotional needs.

Changes in social roles and personal capabilities transform relationships in the adolescent's family, too as we saw in Chapter 4. By the end of adolescence, individuals are far less emotionally dependent on their parents than they were as children. One can see this in several ways. First, older adolescents do not generally rush to their parents whenever they are upset, worried, or in need of assistance. Second, they do not see their parents as all-knowing or all-powerful. Third, adolescents often have a great deal of emotional energy wrapped up in relationships outside the family; in fact, they may feel more attached to a boyfriend or a girlfriend than to their parents. And finally, older adolescents are able to see and interact with their parents as people—not just as their parents. Many parents find, for example, that they can confide in their adolescent children, something that was not possible when their children were younger, or that their adolescent children can easily sympathize with them when they have had a hard day at work. These sorts of changes in the adolescent-parent relationship all reflect the development of emotional autonomy.

Emotional Autonomy and Detachment

Early writings on emotional autonomy were influenced by psychoanalytic thinkers such as Anna Freud (1958), who argued that the physical changes of puberty cause substantial disruption and conflict inside the family system. The reason, Freud believed, is that intrapsychic conflicts that have been repressed since early childhood are reawakened at early adolescence by the resurgence of sexual impulses. (These conflicts revolved around the young child's unconscious attraction toward the parent of the opposite sex and ambivalent feelings toward the parent of the same sex.) The reawakened conflicts, Freud believed, are not dealt with consciously and explicitly by the adolescent and his or her parents but are expressed as increased tension among family members, occasional arguments, and a certain degree of discomfort around the house. Adolescents and their parents may get on each other's nerves for no apparent reason. As a consequence of this tension, early adolescents are driven to separate themselves, at least emotionally, from their parents and turn their emotional energies to relationships with peers—in particular, peers of the opposite sex. Psychoanalytic theorists call this process of separation **detachment**, because it appeared as if the early adolescent were attempting to sever the attachments that had been formed during infancy and strengthened throughout childhood.

Detachment, and the accompanying storm and stress inside the family, were viewed by Freud and her followers as normal, healthy, and inevitable aspects of emotional development during adolescence. According to Freud, tension and conflict are an inherent part of family life for most adolescents. In fact, Freud believed that the absence of conflict between an adolescent and his or her parents signified that the young person was having problems growing up. This view was compatible with the idea that adolescence was an inherently tumultuous time,

a perspective that, as you know, dominated ideas about adolescence for many, many years.

Studies of adolescents' family relationships have not supported Freud's idea, however. In contrast to predictions that high levels of adolescent-parent tension are the norm, that adolescents detach themselves from relationships with their parents, and that adolescents are driven out of the household by unbearable levels of family conflict, every major study done to date of teenagers' relations with their parents has shown that most families get along quite well during the adolescent years (Offer, 1969; Offer, Ostrov, and Howard, 1981; Douvan and Adelson, 1966; Kandel and Lesser, 1972). Although parents and adolescents may bicker more often than they did during earlier periods of development, there is no evidence that this bickering significantly diminishes closeness between parents and teenagers (Hill and Holmbeck, 1986). One team of researchers, for example, who asked adolescents and children of different ages to rate how close they were to their parents, found that 19-year-old college students reported being just as close as fourth graders (Hunter and Youniss, 1982).

The psychic and interpersonal tension believed to arise at puberty does not show up in markedly strained family relationships. Although adolescents and their parents undoubtedly modify their relationships during adolescence, their emotional bonds are by no means severed. This is an important distinction, for it means that emotional autonomy during adolescence involves a *transformation*, not a breaking off of family relationships. Adolescents can become emotionally autonomous from their parents *without* becoming detached from them (Hill and Holmbeck, 1986).

Why did the early psychoanalytic theories of adolescence depict the period as a time of inevitable family tension? One reason is that Freud and her colleagues conducted most of their work with adolescents who were having psychological problems. Their observations may apply to the family relationships of psychologically troubled teenagers, but they appear not to

Every major study conducted to date of teenagers' family relations has shown that young people and their parents feel quite close to one another. Contrary to stereotypes, there is no evidence that family relations are any more strained during adolescence than during other periods of life. (Richard Kalvar/Magnum)

be accurate descriptions of the families of psychologically normal adolescents. Today, in contrast to Freud's view, many researchers believe that high levels of family tension during adolescence are a sign of family problems, not an indication that development is proceeding in a healthy direction.

Emotional Autonomy and Individuation

As an alternative to the classic psychoanalytic perspective on adolescent detachment, some theorists have suggested that the development of emotional autonomy be looked at in terms of the adolescent's developing sense of **individuation.** One such theorist is the noted psychoanalyst Peter Blos. "Individuation," writes Blos, "implies that the growing person takes increasing responsibility for what he does and what he is, rather than depositing this responsibility on the shoulders of those under whose influence

and tutelage he has grown up" (1967, p. 168). The process of individuation, which begins during infancy and continues well into late adolescence, involves a gradual, progressive sharpening of one's sense of self as autonomous, as competent, and as separate from one's parents. Individuation, therefore, has a great deal to do with the development of a sense of identity, in that it involves changes in how we come to see and feel about ourselves. The process does not involve stress and turmoil. Rather, individuation entails relinquishing childish dependencies on parents in favor of more mature, more responsible, and less dependent relationships. Adolescents who have been successful in establishing a sense of individuation can accept responsibility for their choices and actions instead of looking to their parents to do it for them (Josselson, 1980). For example, rather than rebelling against her parents' midnight curfew by deliberately staying out later, a girl who has a healthy sense of individuation might take her parents aside before going out and say, "This party to-night may last longer than midnight. If it does, I'd like to stay a bit longer. Suppose I call you at eleven o'clock and let you know when I'll be home. That way, you won't worry as much if I come home a little later."

Several studies of the growth of emotional autonomy have appeared in recent years. These studies indicate that the development of emotional autonomy is a long process, beginning early in adolescence and continuing well into young adulthood. In one (Steinberg and Silverberg, 1986), a questionnaire measuring four aspects of emotional autonomy was administered to a sample of 10- to 15-year-olds. The four components were (1) the extent to which adolescents' *de-idealized* their parents ("My parents sometimes make mistakes"); (2) the extent to which adolescents were able to see their *parents as people* ("My parents act differently with their own friends than they do with me"); (3) *nondependency,* or the degree to which adolescents depended on themselves, rather than their parents, for assistance ("When I've done something wrong, I don't always depend on my parents to straighten things out"); and (4) the degree to which the adolescent felt *individuated* within the relationship with his or her parents ("There are some things about me that my parents do not know"). As you can see in Figure 9.1, scores on three of the four scales—all except "perceives parents as people"—increased over the age period studied.

In another study, in which adolescents were interviewed about their family relationships, similar findings emerged. The researchers also found that older adolescents were more likely to de-idealize their parents. For example, one adolescent said about his father, "I used to listen to everything. I thought he was always right. Now I have my own opinions. They may be wrong, but they're mine and I like to say them" (Smollar and Youniss, 1985, p. 8).

De-idealization may be one of the first aspects of emotional autonomy to develop, because adolescents may shed their childish images of their parents before replacing them with more

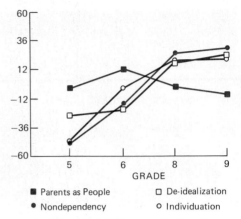

FIGURE 9.1   Age differences in four aspects of emotional autonomy. (Steinberg and Silverberg, 1986)

mature ones. Although middle adolescents are less likely than young adolescents to hold on to idealized pictures of their parents, when it comes to seeing their parents as individuals, 15-year-olds are no more emotionally autonomous than 10-year-olds. Even during the high school years, adolescents appear to have some difficulty in seeing their parents as individuals beyond their roles as parents. This aspect of emotional autonomy may not develop until much later—perhaps not until young adulthood (Smollar and Youniss, 1985; White, Speisman, and Costos, 1983). This aspect of emotional autonomy appears to develop later in adolescents' relations with their fathers than with their mothers, because fathers seem to interact less often with their adolescents in ways that permit them to be seen as individuals (Youniss and Smollar, 1985).

Most theorists now believe that healthy individuation is fostered by close, not distant, family relationships (Grotevant and Cooper, 1986). The evidence is very strong that tense family relationships during adolescence indicate problems, not positive development. Researchers have found, for example, that adolescents who feel the most autonomous—that is, those who are most likely to feel that they have been granted "enough" freedom by their parents—are not the ones who have severed relationships at home. In fact, just the opposite is the case:

Autonomous adolescents report being quite close to their parents, enjoy doing things with their families, have few conflicts with their mothers and fathers, feel free to turn to their parents for advice, and say they would like to be like their parents (Kandel and Lesser, 1972). Rebellion, negativism, and excessive involvement in the peer group are more common among psychologically immature than mature adolescents (Josselson, Greenberger, and McConochie, 1977a, 1977b). Even during the college years, students who live away from home (which is in its own way a type of autonomy), as opposed to remaining in their parents' home and commuting to school, report more affection for their parents, better communication, and higher levels of satisfaction in the relationship (Sullivan and Sullivan, 1980). Strained family relationships appear to be associated with a lack of autonomy during adolescence, rather than with its presence. Emotional autonomy develops best under conditions that encourage both individuation and emotional closeness.

Emotional Autonomy and Parenting Style

As we saw in Chapter 4, adolescents' development is affected differently by different styles of parenting. In particular, independence, responsibility, and self-esteem are all fostered by parents who are authoritative (friendly, fair, and firm), rather than authoritarian (excessively harsh), indulgent (excessively lenient), or neglectful (excessively aloof). Let us now look more closely at these findings in light of what we know about the development of emotional autonomy.

In authoritative families, guidelines are established for the adolescent's behavior and standards are upheld; but they are flexible and open to discussion. Moreover, these standards and guidelines are explained and implemented in an atmosphere of closeness, concern, and fairness. Although parents may have the final say when it comes to their child's behavior, the decision that is reached usually comes after consultation and discussion—with the child included. In discussing an adolescent's curfew, for example, authoritative parents would sit down with their child and explain how they arrived at their decision and why they picked the hour they did. They would also ask the adolescent for his or her suggestions and consider them carefully in making a final decision.

It is not difficult to see why the sort of give and take found in authoritative families is well suited to the child's transition into adolescence. Because standards and guidelines are flexible and adequately explained, it is not hard for the family to adjust and modify them as the child matures emotionally and intellectually. At some point, for example, a teenager may ask his or her parents to consider establishing a later curfew, and authoritative parents would think about the request seriously and discuss it openly. Gradual changes in family relations that permit the young person more independence and encourage more responsibility but that do not threaten the emotional bond between parent and child—in other words, changes that promote increasing emotional autonomy—are relatively easy to make for a family that has been flexible and has been making these sorts of modifications in family relationships all along (Baumrind, 1978).

In authoritarian households, where rules are rigidly enforced and seldom explained to the child, adjusting to adolescence is more difficult for the family. Authoritarian parents may see the child's increasing emotional independence as rebellious or disrespectful, and they may resist their adolescent's growing need for independence, rather than react to it openly. Authoritarian parents, on seeing that their daughter is becoming interested in boys, may implement a rigid curfew in order to restrict her social life. Instead of encouraging autonomy, authoritarian parents may inadvertently maintain the dependencies of childhood, by failing to give their child sufficient practice in making decisions and taking responsibility for his or her actions. In essence, authoritarian parenting may interfere with adolescent individuation.

When closeness is absent as well, the problems are compounded. In families in which excessive parental control is accompanied by extreme coldness and punitiveness, the adolescent may rebel against parents' standards explicitly, in an attempt to assert his or her independence in a visible and demonstrable fashion (Hill and Holmbeck, 1986). Adolescents whose parents refuse to grant reasonable curfews are the ones who typically stay out the latest. Such rebellion is not indicative of genuine emotional autonomy, though; it is more likely to be a demonstration of the adolescent's frustration with his or her parents' rigidity and lack of understanding.

In indulgent and neglectful families, a different sort of problem arises. These parents do not provide sufficient guidance for their children, and as a result, youngsters who are raised permissively do not acquire adequate standards for behavior. Someone who has never had to abide by his parents' rules as a child faces tremendous difficulty learning how to comply with rules as an adult. Unfortunately, the policeman who issues a speeding ticket or a boss who issues a dismissal slip is less sympathetic toward rule breaking than were the permissive parents— who seldom asked their child to do anything he or she did not want to do. At adolescence, youngsters who have been raised permissively find themselves faced with a myriad of decisions and few guidelines on which to base them. We often forget that although young adolescents are more intellectually and emotionally mature than children, they are still not ready to be entirely on their own. In the absence of parents' guidance and rules, permissively reared teenagers often turn to their peers for advice and emotional support—a practice that can be problematic when the peers are themselves still relatively young and inexperienced. Not surprisingly, adolescents whose parents have failed to provide sufficient guidance are likely to become psychologically dependent on their friends—emotionally detached from their parents, perhaps, but not genuinely autonomous. The problems of parental permissiveness are also exacerbated by a lack of closeness, as is the case in neglectful families.

Some parents who have raised their children permissively until adolescence are caught by surprise by the consequences of not having been stricter earlier on. The greater orientation toward the peer group of permissively raised adolescents may involve the young person in behavior that his or her parents disapprove of. As a consequence, some parents who have been permissive throughout childhood shift gears at adolescence and become autocratic, as a means of controlling a youngster over whom they feel they have lost control. For instance, parents who have never placed any restrictions on their child's afternoon activities during elementary school suddenly begin monitoring their teenager's social life once she enters junior high school. Shifts like these are extremely hard on adolescents—just at the time when they are seeking greater autonomy, their parents become more restrictive. Having become accustomed to relative leniency, adolescents whose parents change the rules in the middle of the game may find it difficult to accept standards that are being strictly enforced for the first time.

THE DEVELOPMENT OF BEHAVIORAL AUTONOMY

Some years ago, a remarkable news story came out of Milpitas, California, a small town in the northern part of the state. The story was later popularized in the film *River's Edge*. A group of high school students had discovered the corpse of one of their classmates in a ravine near the school. Although they knew that their discovery should be reported immediately, several days passed before any of the students told the police, school officials, or even their parents. Many of the students were worried that one of their friends had been involved in the girl's death, and the peer pressure to cover up the incident— at least temporarily—was enormous. Eventually word got out, and an official investigation was

Parents who have been extremely lenient before adolescence may face the consequences of not having been stricter when they discover that their children are involved in behavior of which they disapprove. (Joseph Koudelka/Magnum)

conducted. Several of the youngsters came forward and revealed what they knew. Still, many adults wondered why the students had not done something immediately (Kaye, 1982).

Granted, this is an extreme and unlikely situation. Very few adolescents ever find themselves pressured into covering up something as serious as the death of another person. But the Milpitas incident provides a useful introduction to our discussion of behavioral autonomy. Would most adolescents have acted like the Milpitas students? Is peer pressure as coercive a force as this incident would lead us to believe it is? Why can some youngsters withstand pressure from their friends to act contrary to what they know is right, whereas others are unable to resist conforming to the peer group's wishes?

We noted at the beginning of this chapter that being able to make decisions independently as a teenager is critical in contemporary society. Changes in the family, in the workplace, and in the peer group have further distanced young people from their elders. As adolescents increasingly find themselves in situations where adults are not present and where they must make decisions and take responsibility for their actions, the extent to which they are capable of independent choices and autonomous behavior takes on a special importance. Deciding how to deal with pressures from peers, parents, and other sources of influence—when to conform to them and when to stand up to them, when to follow others' advice and when to reject it—is a difficult challenge for young people.

One of the most popular misconceptions about adolescent development is that adolescents demonstrate autonomy by rebelling against the wishes of their parents. But were the Milpitas adolescents acting autonomously by not reporting the incident to their parents? Of course not. In our discussion of emotional autonomy, we saw that rebellion is associated with psychological immaturity, not maturity. We should note that in many instances, rebelling

Emotional Autonomy in Two Cultures

Emotional autonomy is most easily established by adolescents whose families adjust their relationships to the growing competencies and concerns of the child. Therefore, we would expect to find fewer autonomy-related difficulties, such as parent-adolescent conflict, in families where parents are relatively strict during childhood, in order to help their children learn guidelines and standards for appropriate behavior, but become less controlling as their children approach adolescence and learn to govern themselves. In contrast, we would expect to find more problems with the reverse pattern—permissiveness during childhood and greater restrictions during adolescence.

In a comparative study of adolescents in Denmark and the United States, psychologists Denise Kandel and Gerald Lesser examined the development of emotional autonomy among Danish and American adolescents in relation to the parenting practices they had grown up with. In both countries, autonomy was highest among adolescents whose parents set fewer specific rules for them and whose family relationships were positive.

But that was where the similarity between the two countries ended. Considerably higher levels of adolescent autonomy and lower levels of parental authoritarianism were reported by the Danish adolescents. For example, in Denmark, 76 percent of the 15-year-old boys and 73 percent of the 15-year-old girls surveyed felt that their parents gave them enough freedom, compared with only 55 percent and 62 percent of American boys and girls of the same age. In Denmark, only

15 percent of the adolescents reported having an authoritarian relationship with their mothers, and only 31 percent with their fathers, as opposed to 43 percent and 53 percent in the United States samples. Moreover, Danish parents imposed fewer specific rules (about homework, television viewing, and dating, for example) on their adolescent children than did American parents—explaining, perhaps, why the Danish adolescents were more likely to feel autonomous.

Why were levels of autonomy so much higher, and authoritarianism so much lower, in Denmark? Kandel and Lesser speculate as follows:

> In the United States parents treat their adolescents as children longer than in Denmark. Danish adolescents are expected to be self-governing; American adolescents are not. . . . Having delayed the adulthood training—that is, teaching the children self-discipline—the parents are faced in the United States with adolescents who are in fact more dependent on them psychologically. . . . We would suggest that children in the United States are subject to a delayed socialization pattern, both in terms of autonomy from parental control as an adolescent and perhaps controls and limits as an earlier child. We would speculate that, as young children, Danes are subject to stronger discipline than the Americans. If this were indeed true, the discipline exercised at an early age would create a child who as an adolescent is far more disciplined and one to whom, as a consequence, the parent can afford to give freedom (p. 89).

Source: D. Kandel and G. Lesser, *Youth in Two Worlds* (San Francisco: Jossey-Bass, 1972).

against one's parents or other authorities is done not out of independence but in the service of conforming to one's peers. One recent study indicated, in fact, that during early adolescence individuals become more emotionally autonomous from their parents but *less* autonomous from their friends (Stemberg and Silverberg, 1986). Merely substituting one source of influence (the peer group) for another (the family), though, is hardly evidence of growth toward independence. Excessive adherence to the pressures of one's friends is not more autonomous than is excessive adherence to the pressures of one's parents. Just what is meant, then, by behavioral autonomy?

All individuals—at any age—are susceptible to the pressures of those around them. The opinions and advice of others, especially people whose knowledge and judgment we respect, are, and should be, important influences on our choices and decisions. Surely, then, we would not want to say that the behaviorally autonomous adolescent is entirely free from the influence of others. Rather, an individual who is behaviorally autonomous is able to turn to others for advice when it is appropriate, weigh alternative courses of action based on his or her own judgment and the suggestions of others, and reach an independent conclusion about how to behave (Hill and Holmbeck, 1986). Let's look more closely at why and how changes in behavioral autonomy occur during adolescence. Researchers have looked at this in three domains: changes in decision-making abilities, changes in susceptibility to the influence of others, and changes in feelings of self-reliance.

Changes in Decision-Making Abilities

The more sophisticated reasoning processes employed by the adolescent permit him or her to hold multiple viewpoints in mind simultaneously, allowing comparisons among them to be drawn—an ability that is crucial for weighing the opinions and advice of others. In addition, because adolescents are better able to think in hypothetical terms, they are more likely to consider the possible long-term consequences of choosing one course of action over another. And the enhanced role-taking capabilities of adolescence permit the teenager to consider another person's opinion while taking into account that person's perspective. This is important in determining whether someone who gives advice has special areas of expertise, particular biases, or vested interests that one should keep in mind. Taken together, these cognitive changes result

in improved decision-making skills and, consequently, in the individual's greater ability to behave independently.

A study by Catherine Lewis (1981b) sheds a good deal of light on these issues. She presented over 100 adolescents ranging in age from 12 to 18 with a series of "problems" that they were to help another teenager solve. The adolescents listened to a tape recording of an agemate, who described a difficult decision that he or she was facing. They were then asked to try and "help [the agemate] with what to think about." They were told to "try to 'get into it' by thinking of friends with similar problems or by imagining that [they] were in that situation" (p. 540). The problems concerned becoming involved in different sorts of risky situations, revising an opinion of someone who had previously been respected, or reconciling different pieces of advice from two "experts." One of the problems, for example, focused on a teenager's indecision about whether to have cosmetic surgery:

> I've been thinking about having this operation. It won't make me healthier or anything, but I'd like to have it because it would make me look better since I've always had this ugly thing like a bump on my cheek. I could have an operation to remove it. I'm trying to decide whether to have the operation, and I can't decide. Do you think I should have the operation? (Lewis, 1981b, p. 540)

Lewis looked at adolescents' responses along five dimensions: whether they were aware of risks; whether they were aware of likely future consequences; whether parents, peers, or outside specialists were recommended as consultants; whether attitudes were revised in light of new information; and whether the adolescent recognized and cautioned against the vested interests of people giving advice. The adolescents were grouped by grade level, with seventh and eighth graders forming one group, tenth graders a second group, and twelfth graders a third group. The results of the study are shown in Figure 9.2.

Along four of the five dimensions studied,

By the time young people reach late adolescence, they have developed fairly sophisticated decision-making abilities. Compared with younger teenagers, for example, high school seniors are better able to anticipate the long-term consequences of their decisions and more likely to understand the personal biases that advice givers sometimes have. (Ann McQueen/Stock, Boston)

the age groups differed, with older adolescents demonstrating more sophisticated decision-making abilities. The older adolescents were more likely to be aware of risks; more likely to consider future consequences; more likely to turn to an independent specialist as a consultant; and more likely to realize when vested interests existed and to raise cautions about accepting advice from people who might be biased. For example, in response to the dilemma about cosmetic surgery, a twelfth grader who was considering the consequences of such a decision noted, " 'Well, you have to look into the different things . . . that might be more important later on in your life. You should think about, will it have any effect on your future and with, maybe, the people you meet. . . .' " In response to the same dilemma, an eighth grader advised: " 'The

different things I would think about in getting the operation is like if the girls turn you down on a date, or the money, or the kids teasing you at school' " (pp. 541–542). The younger child did not look at the decision's long-term implications.

Decision-making abilities improve over the course of the adolescent years, with gains continuing well into the later years of high school. These developments provide the cognitive tools for behavioral autonomy: being able to look ahead and assess risks and likely outcomes of alternative choices, being able to recognize the value of turning to an independent "expert," and being able to see that someone's advice may be tainted by his or her own interests. Whether these changes in decision-making abilities translate into changes in actual behavior, however, is

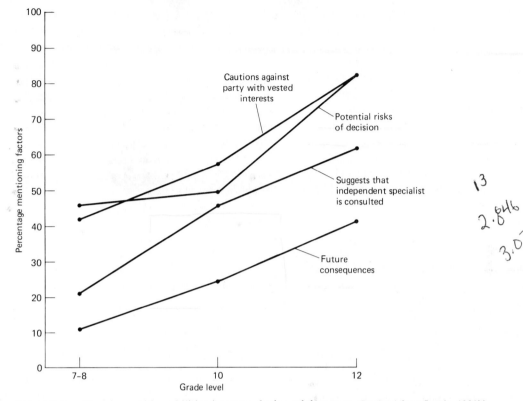

FIGURE 9.2   Decision-making abilities improve during adolescence. (Derived from Lewis, 1981b)

a different matter. Older adolescents may be more *intellectually* skilled when it comes to decision making, but are they actually more able to resist pressures to conform? It is to this question that we now turn.

Changes in Conformity and Susceptibility to Influence

As the adolescent comes to spend more time outside the family, the opinions and advice of others—not only peers but adults as well—become more important. At a certain point, for example, adolescents seek their friends' advice, rather than their parents', on how to dress. They may turn to a teacher or guidance counselor for advice on what courses to take in school, instead

of bringing such questions home. Understandably, a variety of situations arise in which adolescents may feel that their parents' advice may be less valid than the opinions of others.

And there are issues that might be talked over with more than one party. For example, a teenager trying to decide whether to take on a part-time job after school might discuss the problem with her parents; but she might also turn to friends and ask their advice on the same question. When friends and parents disagree, adolescents must reconcile the differences of opinion and reach their own, independent conclusions.

In situations in which parents and peers give conflicting advice, do teenagers tend to follow one group more often than the other? Adolescents are often portrayed as being extremely susceptible to the influence of peer pressure— more so than children or young adults—and as stubbornly resistant to the influence of their parents. But is peer pressure really more potent during adolescence than during other times in the life cycle? Would the Milpitas students have acted differently had they been older or younger?

Researchers have studied conformity and peer pressure during adolescence by putting adolescents in situations in which they must choose between the pressures of their parents and the pressures of their peers or between their own wishes and those of others—typically, parents or friends. For example, an adolescent might be told to imagine that he and his friends discover something on the way home from school that looks suspicious. His friends tell him that they should keep it a secret. But the adolescent tells his mother about it, and she advises him to report it to the police. He then would be asked by the researcher to say what he would do.

In general, studies that contrast parents' and peers' influences indicate that in some situations, peers' opinions are more influential, while in others, parents' are more influential. Specifically, adolescents are more likely to conform to their peers' opinions when it comes to short-term, day-to-day, and social matters— styles of dress, tastes in music, choices among leisure activities, and so on. This is particularly true during junior high school and the early years of high school. When it comes to long-term questions concerning educational or occupational plans, however, or questions of values, religious beliefs, or ethics, teenagers are primarily influenced by their parents (Brittain, 1963; Young and Ferguson, 1979). Some studies have also looked at adolescents' willingness to seek advice from adults outside their family. These studies indicate that in situations calling for objective information (the facts about getting admitted to a particular college) rather than opinion (whether the college is supposed to be a friendly place), teenagers are likely to turn to outside experts such as their teachers (Young and Ferguson, 1979).

Similar findings emerge from studies of the consultants adolescents turn to when they have problems (Wintre, Hicks, McVee and Fox, in press). In general, when the adolescent's problem centers around a relationship with a friend, he or she chooses to turn to a peer, and this preference becomes stronger with age. But adolescents' willingness to turn to an adult for advice with problems—especially problems that involve adolescents and their parents—remains very strong and increases as individuals move toward late adolescence. This suggests that older adolescents are quite willing to turn to adult experts whose advice they consider valuable.

Considered together, the findings derived from these studies are consistent with some of the findings we looked at earlier on changes in adolescents' decision-making abilities. With age,

Adolescents are more likely to conform to their peers' opinion when it comes to short-term, day-to-day, and social matters such as styles of dress. But when it comes to long-term questions or issues concerning basic values, parents remain more influential than peers. (Shirley Zeiberg)

adolescents become increasingly likely to turn to "experts" for advice. On social matters, the "experts" are friends; on issues requiring specific objective information, teachers and other adults likely to have the necessary knowledge are the authorities; and on questions of values, ethics, and plans, parents remain the advisers of choice. More important, the results of these studies indicate that peer pressure—or, for that matter, parental pressure—is likely to be ineffective in some situations and powerful in others.

Studies that contrast the influence of peers and adults do not really get to the heart of peer pressure, however, because most peer pressure operates when adults are absent from the scene—at a party, on the way home from school, on a date. In order to get closer to this issue, researchers have studied how adolescents respond when placed between the pressure of their friends and their own opinions of what to do. For example, an adolescent might be asked whether he would go along with his friends' pressure to vandalize some property even though he did not want to do so (Berndt, 1979).

In general, most studies using this approach show that conformity to peers is higher during early and middle adolescence than during preadolescence or later adolescence (Berndt, 1979; Brown, Clasen, and Eicher, 1986; Krosnick and Judd, 1982; Steinberg and Silverberg, 1986). This is especially true when the behavior in question is antisocial, such as cheating, stealing, or trespassing, and especially true for boys. These findings are in line with studies of delinquency—which, as we shall see later in this chapter, is often committed by young people in groups and is more common during middle adolescence (Berndt, 1979). Moreover, several studies indicate that adolescents who are more susceptible to peer pressure to engage in delinquent activity actually are more likely to misbehave than their more autonomous friends (Brown, Clasen, and Eicher, 1986).

Although we know that conformity to peer pressure is greater during early adolescence than before or after, it is not exactly clear just why

this is so. One interpretation is that adolescents are more susceptible to peer influence during this time because of their heightened orientation toward the peer group. Because they care more about what their friends think of them, they are more likely to go along with the crowd to avoid being rejected (Brown, Clasen, and Eicher, 1986). It is also possible that this heightened conformity to peer pressure during early adolescence is a sign of a sort of emotional way station between becoming emotionally autonomous from parents and becoming a genuinely autonomous person (Steinberg and Silverberg, 1986). In other words, the adolescent may become emotionally autonomous from parents before he or she is emotionally ready for this degree of independence and may turn to peers to fill this void. Each of these accounts suggests that *susceptibility to peer pressure* increases as youngsters move into early adolescence, peaks at around age 14, and declines thereafter. Each of these explanations has been supported by research (Brown, Clasen, and Eicher, 1986; Steinberg and Silverberg, 1986).

A different version of the same story focuses on the *strength of peer pressure*. It may be, for instance, that individuals' susceptibility to peer pressure remains constant over adolescence but that the peer pressure itself increases and then decreases over the period. Early adolescent peer groups may exert more pressure on their members to conform than groups of younger or older individuals, and the pressure may be strong enough to make even the most autonomous teenagers comply. Although this is an appealing alternative explanation—particularly to adolescents who appeal to their parents by saying, "No one will talk to me if I don't do it!"— studies have not borne it out. In fact, it appears that peer pressure to misbehave increases steadily throughout adolescence, beyond the age at which it would be expected to diminish (Brown, Clasen, and Eicher, 1986).

When we put the findings on peer pressure, peer conformity, and parental conformity together, then, the following picture emerges. During childhood, boys and girls are highly oriented toward their parents and far less so toward their peers. Peer pressure is not especially strong. As they approach adolescence, children become somewhat less oriented toward their parents and more oriented toward their peers, and peer pressure begins to escalate. As a result, during preadolescence, there is little net gain in behavioral autonomy—overall levels of conformity do not change, but the source of influence shifts. During early adolescence, conformity to parents continues to decline and both conformity to peers and peer pressure continue to rise—again, little change in overall behavioral autonomy. It is not until middle and late adolescence, therefore, that genuine increases in behavioral autonomy occur, for it is during this time period (between the ninth and twelfth grades) that conformity both to parents *and* to peers declines even though peer pressure continues to increase (see Figure 9.3).

FIGURE 9.3   During adolescence, susceptibility to peer pressure increases and then falls, while susceptibility to parental pressure decreases. Perceptions of the strength of peer pressure increase throughout the period.

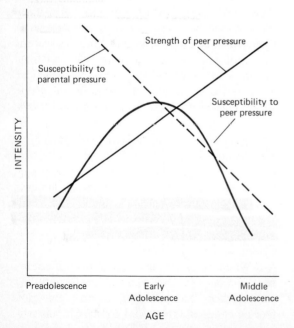

Within a group of teenagers of the same age, there are some who are highly autonomous, others who are easily influenced by their peers, others who are oriented toward their parents, and still others who are swayed by both peers and parents, depending on the situation. In order to differentiate better among youngsters who differ in their level of behavioral autonomy, a group of researchers led by Edward Devereux and Urie Bronfenbrenner devised an ingenious strategy (Devereux, 1970).

Like other researchers studying behavioral autonomy, Devereux and Bronfenbrenner presented groups of adolescents with a series of dilemmas and asked how they would resolve them. But a new dimension to the procedure was added: The questionnaires were administered under three different conditions. In one condition, before receiving the questionnaires, the adolescents were told that their answers would not be seen by anyone other than the researchers, who would keep their responses confidential and anonymous (the researchers called this the *baseline* condition). In another condition, the youngsters were told that their answers would be circulated around the classroom, so that their classmates could see how each person responded (the *peer* condition). In the third condition, youngsters were told that their responses would be made available to their parents and teachers (the *adult* condition).

By comparing each youngster's responses in the baseline condition with those given in the peer and adult conditions, the researchers were able to determine how much each youngster shifted his or her answers in response to the different audiences. They then classified each adolescent into one of four groups: *autonomous* youngsters (those who shifted answers minimally from their baseline responses); *peer-oriented* youngsters (those who shifted answers in the peer condition); *adult-oriented* youngsters (those who shifted answers in the adult condition); and *chameleons* (those who shifted answers in all conditions).

The researchers then looked at the family experiences of youngsters in each of the four groups. In general, autonomous youngsters and adult-oriented youngsters were likely to have come from homes in which their parents were warm and moderately controlling—the typical authoritative household. "Chameleons" tended to come from warm but permissive homes. Peer-oriented children were likely to have parents who were less nurturant and either extremely controlling or extremely permissive. Although the early studies were conducted in the United States, similar research was subsequently completed in other countries, and the same connections between parenting styles and adolescent autonomy were observed (Devereux, 1970). Like emotional autonomy, then, behavioral autonomy appears to be associated with authoritative, rather than with permissive or autocratic, parenting.

Although it is tempting to conclude from these and other studies that authoritative parenting *fosters* the development of autonomy, we must be careful about drawing this conclusion, since the direction of effects could work just as plausibly the other way around. Perhaps responsible, independent children elicit warm and democratic behavior from their parents, whereas less autonomous youngsters invoke harsher discipline or parental nonchalance. In all likelihood, both processes are at work—children are affected by their parents, and parents are affected by their children. Authoritative parenting probably leads to adolescent autonomy, which in turn leads to more authoritative parenting.

Studies of peer pressure across cultures. Although only a small number of researchers have looked at cross-cultural differences in behavioral autonomy, common sense and casual observation both suggest that the power of the peer group varies from one culture to another as does the degree to which parents and peers operate as opposing forces. American youngsters, for example, tend to be more peer-oriented than their counterparts in the Soviet Union but less peer-oriented than British teenagers (Devereux, 1970). Furthermore, when adolescents are asked to choose between an ethical and an unethical choice in an experiment, American youngsters are swayed by adults toward the ethical choice and by their peers toward the unethical choice, but Soviet youngsters are influenced by adults and peers in the same direction (Bronfenbrenner, 1967). Opposing pressures from parents and peers, then, are apparently more prevalent in some cultures than in others and perhaps more so in the United States and England than in other countries.

Much has been made about the negative influence of the peer culture on American adolescents' development. But whether the conflicting pulls experienced by American teenagers are necessarily problematic is a difficult question to answer. Some theorists, such as Jean Piaget, have argued that conflict between different sets of values is necessary for moral development. As Devereux explains:

> Growing up in an atmosphere of adult-peer cross pressure is apparently part of the standard experience for the American child. In contrast . . . Soviet children . . . apparently perceive their peer group as carrying the same norms as those of their parents and teachers. At face value, it appears that Soviet society has rather successfully harnessed the powerful sanctioning force of the peer collective to work for, rather than against, the development and maintenance of morally approved behavior in children. Our observations generally confirm the impression that, in fact, Soviet children are better behaved, as judged by conventional standards. However, in light of our theorizing about the roots of autonomy, we must also wonder whether the moral character of the Soviet adult—unchallenged and untested by dissonance and cross pressure—is as secure and self-regulating as that of the American adult who has successfully survived the trials and tests of childhood and youth in our society. (Devereux, 1970, pp. 126–127)

Changes in Feelings of Self-Reliance

A third approach to the study of behavioral autonomy focuses on adolescents' own judgments of how autonomous they are. When adolescents of different ages are asked to complete standard-

Conformity to peers—especially in situations involving antisocial or delinquent behavior—is higher during early and middle adolescence than during other points in the lifespan. According to some theorists, some forms of "social delinquency" may result from youngsters' heightened susceptibility to the influence of their friends. (Joel Gordon)

ized tests of self-reliance, for example, the results show that subjective feelings of autonomy increase steadily over the adolescent years and, contrary to stereotypes, that adolescent girls report feeling more self-reliant than adolescent boys (Greenberger, 1982; Steinberg and Silverberg, 1986). This is especially interesting in light of the findings concerning susceptibility to peer pressure, discussed earlier, since it indicates that adolescents may describe themselves as gaining in self-reliance during a period when their susceptibility to peer pressure may be increasing (see Figure 9.4). Although adults may view giving in to peer pressure as a sign of diminished autonomy, adolescents may not see their own behavior in this light. Boys especially see going along with the crowd as something that says very

little about their own sense of independence (Steinberg and Silverberg, 1986).

THE DEVELOPMENT OF VALUE AUTONOMY

The development of value autonomy entails changes in the adolescent's conceptions of moral, political, ideological, and religious issues. Three aspects of the development of value autonomy during adolescence are especially interesting. First, adolescents become increasingly abstract in the way they think about things. Take the example of an 18-year-old who is deciding whether to participate in a disruptive demonstration at his state capital against policies

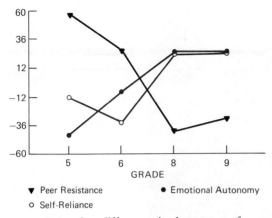

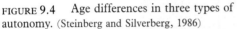

FIGURE 9.4   Age differences in three types of autonomy. (Steinberg and Silverberg, 1986)

that indirectly support apartheid. Instead of looking at the situation only in terms of the specifics of apartheid, he might think about the implications of knowingly violating the law in general. Second, during adolescence, beliefs become increasingly rooted in general principles that have some ideological basis. So an 18-year-old might say that demonstrating against apartheid is acceptable because promoting racial equality is more important than living in accord with the law, and breaking a law is legitimate when the status quo maintains racial discrimination. Finally, beliefs become increasingly founded in the young person's own values and not merely in a system of values passed on by parents or other authority figures. Thus an 18-year-old may look at the issue of apartheid in terms of what he himself believes, rather than in terms of what his parents have told him to do.

Much of the growth in value autonomy can be traced to the cognitive changes characteristic of the period. With the adolescent's enhanced reasoning capabilities and the further development of hypothetical thinking comes a heightened interest in ideological and philosophical matters and a more sophisticated way of looking at them. The ability to consider alternative possibilities and to engage in thinking about thinking allows for the exploration of differing value

systems, political ideologies, personal ethics, and religious beliefs.

But the growth of value autonomy is encouraged by the development of emotional and behavioral independence as well. As we shall see in a moment, there is some evidence that the development of value autonomy occurs later (between ages 18 and 20) than does the development of emotional or behavioral autonomy, which takes place during early and middle adolescence. As young people gain increasing distance from the emotional dependencies of childhood, they rely less on their parents' beliefs and values. The establishment of emotional autonomy provides the adolescent with the ability to look at his or her parents' views more objectively. When young people no longer see their parents as omnipotent and infallible authorities, they may seriously reevaluate the ideas and values that they accepted without question as children.

And as adolescents begin to test the waters of independence behaviorally, they may experience a variety of cognitive conflicts caused by having to compare the advice of parents and friends and having to deal with competing pressures to behave in given ways. These conflicts may prompt the young person to consider, in more serious and thoughtful terms, what it is that he or she really believes. This struggle to clarify values, provoked in part by the exercise of behavioral autonomy, is a large part of the process of developing a sense of value autonomy.

Moral Development During Adolescence

Moral development has been the most widely studied aspect of value autonomy during adolescence. The dominant theoretical viewpoint for some time now has been a perspective that is grounded in Piaget's theory of cognitive development. As you will recall from the discussion in Chapter 2 of changes in thinking processes during adolescence, the emphasis within the Piagetian, or **cognitive-developmental,** perspective is on changes in the structure and or-

The growth of value autonomy during adolescence is often reflected in adolescents' increased interests in political and ideological matters. Research indicates that the development of value autonomy can be traced to the cognitive changes characteristic of the period. (Sybil Shelton/Peter Arnold)

ganization of thought rather than on changes in its content. Theories of morality that stem from the cognitive-developmental viewpoint similarly emphasize shifts in the type of reasoning that individuals use in making moral decisions and not changes in the content of the decisions they reach or the action they take as a result.

Theorists who have taken a Piagetian standpoint argue that the way in which individuals think about moral problems undergoes structural, qualitative change over the course of childhood and adolescence. Moral development proceeds through a series of stages, with each stage entailing a more advanced type of reasoning. Although the initial formulation of the cognitive-developmental perspective on morality was presented by Piaget himself, the theory was subsequently expanded by Lawrence Kohlberg, and it is Kohlberg's work that is more relevant to the study of value autonomy during adolescence.

Kohlberg's theory.   Consider the following dilemma:

In Europe, a woman was near death from a very bad disease, a special kind of cancer. There was one drug that the doctors thought might save her. It was a form of radium that a druggist in the same town had recently discovered. The drug was expensive to make, but the druggist was charging ten times what the drug cost him to make. He paid $200 for the radium and charged $2,000 for a small dose of the drug. The sick woman's husband, Heinz, went to everyone he knew to borrow the money, but he could only get together about $1,000, which was half of what it cost. He told the druggist that his wife was dying, and asked him to sell it cheaper or let him pay later. But the druggist said, "No, I discovered the drug and I'm going to make money from it." Heinz got desperate and broke into the man's store to steal the drug for his wife.

Should the husband have done that? Was it right or wrong? (Kohlberg and Gilligan, 1972)

According to Kohlberg, whether you think that Heinz should steal the drug is less important than the reasoning behind your answer. Kohlberg suggested that there are three levels of moral reasoning—the **preconventional** level, which is dominant during most of childhood; the **conventional** level, which is usually dominant during late childhood and early adolescence; and the **principled** (or postconventional) level, which emerges sometime during the adolescent or young adult years. He further divided these three levels into six stages, with each level composed of two stages. As shown in Table 9.1, preconventional thinking is characterized by reference to external and physical events. Preconventional moral decisions are not based on society's standards, rules, or conventions (hence the label, *pre*conventional). Children at this stage approach moral dilemmas in ways that focus on the rewards and punishments associated with different courses of action. One preconventional child might say that Heinz should not have stolen the drug because he could have gotten caught and sent to jail. Another might say that Heinz was right to steal the drug because people would have been angry with him if he had let his wife die.

Conventional thinking about moral issues focuses not so much on tangible rewards and punishments but on how an individual will be judged by others for behaving in a certain way. In conventional moral reasoning, special importance is given to the roles people are expected to play and to society's rules, social institutions, and conventions. One behaves properly because, in so doing, one receives the approval of others and helps to maintain the social order. The correctness of society's rules is not questioned, however—one "does one's duty" by upholding and respecting the social order. A conventional thinker might say that Heinz should not have stolen the drug because stealing is against the law. But another might counter that Heinz was right to steal the drug because it is what a good husband is expected to do. According to most studies of moral reasoning, the majority of adolescents and adults think primarily in conventional terms.

Principled thinking is relatively rare. At this level of reasoning, society's rules and conventions are seen as relative and subjective rather than as authoritative. One may have a moral duty to abide by society's standards for behavior—but only insofar as those standards support and serve human ends. Thus occasions arise in which conventions ought to be questioned and when more important principles—such as justice, fairness, or the sanctity of human life—take precedence over established social norms. For instance, a principled response might be that Heinz should not have stolen the drug because in doing so he violated an implicit agreement among members of society—an agreement that gives each person the freedom to pursue his or her livelihood. However, another principled thinker might respond that Heinz was right to steal the drug because someone's life was at stake, and preserving human life is more important than preserving individual freedoms. Whereas conventional thinking is oriented toward society's rules, principled thinking is founded on more broadly based moral principles and is oriented toward the individual's personal conscience. For this reason, it is the development of principled reasoning that is especially relevant to the discussion of value autonomy.

Like Piaget, Kohlberg believed that moral development proceeds in an orderly fashion; individuals develop through the stages in a fixed, irreversible sequence, in an order that is presumed to be universal. Thinking at each of the stages, according to Kohlberg, is qualitatively different from thinking at other stages; and the higher stages are more advanced and more mature than the lower ones. Moral development is stimulated by having to struggle with moral conflicts and, in particular, from being exposed to levels of thinking that are more advanced.

Researchers assess individuals' levels of moral thinking by examining their responses to a series of moral dilemmas, such as the story

LEVEL ONE: PRECONVENTIONAL	CHILD'S RESPONSE TO THEFT OF DRUG
Stage 1 *Obedience-and-punishment orientation:* The child obeys rules to avoid punishment. There is as yet no internalization of moral standards.	*Pro:* Theft is justified because the drug did not cost much to produce.
	Con: Theft is condemned because Heinz will be caught and go to jail.
Stage 2 *Naive hedonistic and instrumental orientation.* The child's behavior is motivated by a selfish desire to obtain rewards and benefits. Although reciprocity occurs, it is self-serving, manipulative, and based on a marketplace outlook: "You can play with my blocks if you let me play with your cars."	*Pro:* Theft is justified because his wife needs the drug and Heinz needs his wife's companionship and help in life.
	Con: Theft is condemned because his wife will probably die before Heinz gets out of jail, so it will not do him much good.

LEVEL TWO: CONVENTIONAL	CHILD'S RESPONSE TO THEFT OF DRUG
Stage 3 *"Good boy"—"nice girl" morality.* The child is concerned with winning the approval of others and avoiding their disapproval. In judging the goodness or badness of behavior, consideration is given to a person's intentions. The child has a conception of a morally good person as one who possesses a set of virtues, hence the child places much emphasis upon being "nice."	*Pro:* Theft is justified because Heinz is unselfish in looking after the needs of his wife.
	Con: Theft is condemned because Heinz will feel bad thinking of how he brought dishonor on his family: his family will be ashamed of his act.
Stage 4 *"Law-and-order" orientation.* The individual blindly accepts social conventions and rules. Emphasis is on "doing one's duty," showing respect for authority, and maintaining a given social order for its own sake.	*Pro:* Theft is justified because Heinz would otherwise have been responsible for his wife's death.
	Con: Theft is condemned because Heinz is a lawbreaker.

[handwritten marginal note: To gain approval]

LEVEL THREE: PRINCIPLED	CHILD'S RESPONSE TO THEFT OF DRUGS
Stage 5 *Social-contract orientation.* The individual believes that the purpose of the law is to preserve human rights and that unjust laws should be changed. Morality is seen as based upon an agreement among individuals to conform to laws that are necessary for the community welfare. But since it is a social contract, it can be modified so long as basic rights like *life* and *liberty* are not impaired.	*Pro:* Theft is justified because the law was not fashioned for situations in which an individual would forfeit life by obeying the rules.
	Con: Theft is condemned because others may also have great need.
Stage 6 *Universal ethical principle orientation.* Conduct is controlled by an internalized set of ideas, which, if violated, results in self-condemnation and guilt. The individual follows self-chosen ethical principles based upon abstract concepts (e.g., the equality of human rights, the Golden Rule, respect for the dignity of each human being) rather than concrete rules (e.g., the Ten Commandments). Unjust laws may be broken because they conflict with broad moral principles.	*Pro:* Theft is justified because Heinz would not have lived up to the standards of his conscience if he had allowed his wife to die.
	Con: Theft is condemned because Heinz did not live up to the standards of his conscience when he engaged in stealing.

about Heinz and the drug. These dilemmas are presented either in an interview, in which case the adolescents' responses are recorded, transcribed, and coded (Kohlberg and Gilligan, 1972), or in a questionnaire, in which adolescents respond to the dilemmas in a sort of multiple-choice format (Rest, Davison, and Robbins, 1978). The responses of individuals are classified as falling into one of the six stages described above. Here, for example, are two answers given in response to the dilemma about Heinz and the drug. One response is classified as conventional, the other as principled (from Rest, cited in Kohlberg, 1969, pp. 379–380):

(Conventional): He should steal the drug. He was only doing something that was natural for a good husband to do. You cannot blame him for doing something out of love for his wife; you would blame him if he did not love his wife enough to save her.

(Principled): This is a situation which forces him to choose between stealing and letting his wife die. In a situation where the choice must be made, it is morally right to steal. He has to act in terms of the principle of preserving and respecting life.

The first response is considered conventional because the respondent has evaluated the situation in terms of whether Heinz is adhering to established conventions. The respondent has emphasized what a "good" husband should do—rather than discussing Heinz's choice in terms of a more abstract moral principle. The second response is considered principled because the respondent has evaluated the situation in terms of a general ethical principle—in this case, the principle of "preserving and respecting life."

Research on Kohlberg's theory. Kohlberg's theory and its derivatives (for example, Gilligan, 1982) have generated a wealth of research and have for the past twenty-five years dominated the study of moral development during adolescence. An important alternative to Kohlberg's

model was proposed in the late 1970s by psychologist Carol Gilligan (1977, 1982), who argued that Kohlberg's view of morality placed too much emphasis on a type of moral orientation characteristically employed by men. Gilligan's perspective is discussed in the box on pages 294–295.

Studies have confirmed Kohlberg's suggestion that moral reasoning becomes more principled over the course of childhood and adolescence (Hoffman, 1980). Moreover, development appears to proceed through the sequence described in Kohlberg's theory (Colby et al., 1983). Preconventional reasoning (stages 1 and 2) dominates the responses of children; stage 3 responses begin to appear during preadolescence; stage 4 responses emerge during middle adolescence; and principled reasoning (stages 5 and 6) does not appear until late adolescence. Consistent with the view that moral development is stimulated by a modest degree of cognitive conflict, researchers have found also that advanced levels of moral reasoning are more common among children raised in families in which parents encourage their children to participate in family discussions and in which the level of conflict in family discussions is neither extremely low nor extremely high (Holstein, 1972; Haan, Smith, and Block, 1968).

Kohlberg's suggestion that moral development proceeds in *stages*, however, has not been confirmed. Do you recall the discussion in Chapter 2 of research on Piaget's theory of cognitive development? At that time it was pointed out that strong evidence does not exist for his view that cognitive development occurs in stages. The same conclusion seems to apply to Kohlberg's theory of moral development (Hoffman, 1980). In order to demonstrate that moral judgment develops in stages, we would need to show that individuals whose reasoning is at a given stage almost always use this level of reasoning and rarely employ a higher or lower level of reasoning. Yet in several recent studies, it has been found that individuals do not always reason in a consistent way; about one-third of the people

The Sexes: Do a Man and a Woman Speak About Moral Problems "In a Different Voice"?

Few theories have generated as much controversy among psychologists as Lawrence Kohlberg's theory of the development of moral reasoning. In addition to criticizing it as culturally biased, critics have argued that his view of what constitutes "more advanced" moral reasoning is oriented to how men typically view moral problems and underrepresents an equally valid approach to morality that women happen to use more often. The most compelling argument in this spirit was made by psychologist Carol Gilligan in her book, *In a Different Voice* (1982).

Essentially, Gilligan argues that Kohlberg's scheme places great weight on what she calls an orientation to *justice*. This is an orientation toward problems of inequality or oppression that holds out as its ideal a morality of reciprocity and equal respect. From this perspective—or "voice," as Gilligan would call it—the most important consideration in making a moral decision would be whether the individuals involved were treated "fairly" by the ultimate decision.

An equally valid alternative to the justice orientation, says Gilligan, emphasizes *caring*. From this perspective, the focus is on problems of abandonment and detachment, and the ideal is a morality of attention to others and responsiveness to human need. As opposed to the justice orientation, which is rooted in the premise that moral decisions are best made from a detached position of "objectivity" ("rules are rules," "fair is fair"), the caring orientation is rooted in the belief that our moral decisions should be shaped by our attachments and our responsiveness to others.

An example may help to clarify the distinction. In responding to the Heinz dilemma, discussed on page xxx, individuals with a justice orientation cast the problem as a conflict between Heinz's desire to save his wife and the druggist's right to engage in his business—a conflict between the abstract values of life and property. Individuals with a caring orientation, in contrast, see the dilemma in entirely different terms: as a dilemma of responsiveness. The question is not whether the druggist has a right to property that outweighs other rights but rather why the druggist is not being responsive to the needs of another person. Rather than seeing society as functioning with a system of rules or abstract principles, individuals with a caring orientation view society as functioning

studied used two different levels of reasoning at the same time, and close to 10 percent used three different levels (Colby et al., 1983; Walker, de Vries, and Trevethan, 1987). Individuals developed advanced levels of reasoning (stages 4 and 5) very gradually and not at all in a stagelike fashion. Indeed, stage 4 reasoning did not emerge suddenly during middle adolescence but developed slowly and steadily over a period of ten or fifteen years (Fischer, 1983).

Thus while Kohlberg provided a generally useful description of the changes in moral thinking that occur during adolescence, it seems that moral development—particularly after childhood—is more quantitative in nature than stagelike. Elements of new and more advanced forms of reasoning do appear with age, but aspects of earlier forms of reasoning are present at all ages, and different levels of reasoning are called into use at different times and in different situations. While a young child's responses to moral dilemmas would in all likelihood be clearly and consistently preconventional, an adolescent's responses would probably be a mixture of preconventional and conventional, and a young adult's a mixture of preconventional, conven-

through the interconnection of human relationships.

Theories of morality and of human development in general, argues Gilligan, have emphasized the sort of intellectual, individualistic, and detached reasoning characteristic of the justice orientation as the index of mental health and have given short shrift to emotional, interpersonal, and attachment concerns. The pinnacle of psychological health in most theories is the individual who can function independently, argues Gilligan, rather than the person who can function *interdependently*. We see this not only in abstract theories of development, but in the way in which our children are socialized to emphasize competition over cooperation, and assertiveness over concern for others. In Kohlberg's theory, this bias toward detached individualism is reflected in the elevation to the highest level of morality of a view that places abstract principles of individual rights over all other considerations. In her book, Gilligan presented evidence that women are likely to approach moral problems from a caring orientation, rather than from the justice orientation idealized in Kohlberg's theory.

In more recent studies, Gilligan and others have found that both men and women are capable of approaching moral problems from the perspectives of justice and caring but that women may be more likely to give caring-oriented responses before justice-oriented ones, whereas men are more likely to follow the opposite pattern (Ford and Lowery, 1986; Gilligan, 1986; Walker, de Vries, and Trevethan, 1987). When individuals are prompted to hear a moral problem in a different voice, they appear to be able to do so—regardless of their sex. In other words, men are capable of viewing a moral problem from a caring orientation and women are capable of viewing a problem from a justice orientation.

Gilligan's work suggests that there are two distinct voices to be heard in moral debates and that society—especially a society governed primarily by men—may be more inclined to listen to one voice than another. The fact that most of the major theories of human development have been constructed by men—Freud, Piaget, Erikson—also has biased our views of what mental health is. But while Gilligan's studies suggest that there may be sex differences in our tendencies to *prefer* one orientation, her work also indicates that men and women can adopt both perspectives. By helping children to hear and speak with *both* voices, we may encourage the development of more complete—and more moral—people.

tional, and principled answers. It does not make much sense, then, to try to classify adolescents into "stages" of moral development.

Nevertheless, the idea that individuals become more principled in their thinking during adolescence is relevant to our discussion of value autonomy. Although individuals may not enter a stage of principled thinking during adolescence, they do begin to place greater emphasis on abstract values and moral principles during the adolescent years. Studies by James Rest and his colleagues (Rest, Davison, and Robbins, 1978) have shown this to be true. These researchers worked within Kohlberg's framework but employed the questionnaires about moral reasoning rather than interview. Instead of classifying individuals as being in one stage or another, Rest and his associates focused on the relative proportions of principled and nonprincipled arguments appealing to individuals at different ages.

Overall, their studies indicate that the appeal of principled moral reasoning increases over the course of adolescence, while the appeals of preconventional and of conventional reasoning both decline. During the high school years, the proportion of principled responses given by individuals increases from about 25 percent to about 33 percent. Over the course of late adolescence and early adulthood, the proportion increases further, to about 45 percent. (The appeal of principled thinking appears to increase both with age and with schooling, with most adults reaching a plateau after completing their formal education.) Thus Rest's studies provide support for the idea that value autonomy grows during adolescence, particularly during the late adolescent years.

Moral reasoning and moral behavior.   It is one thing to reason about moral problems in an advanced way, but it is another thing to *behave* consistently with one's reasoning. Some critics have argued that although Kohlberg's theory may provide a window on how people think about abstract and hypothetical dilemmas of life and death, it does not tell us very much about the ways people reason about day-to-day problems or the ways people behave when they find themselves in situations that might evoke moral considerations. As for the first of these concerns, research indicates that people reason about life-and-death dilemmas in ways parallel to their reasoning about moral dilemmas that they actually encounter in their everyday life (Walker, de Vries, and Trevethan, 1987). As for the second of these concerns, many studies indicate that individuals' behavior is related to the way in which they reason about hypothetical moral dilemmas. For example, individuals who are capable of reasoning at higher stages of moral thought are less likely to commit antisocial acts, less likely to cheat, less likely to conform to the pressures of others, more likely to engage in political protests, and more likely to assist others in need of help (Rest, 1983).

Of course, moral behavior and moral reasoning do not always go hand in hand. Most of us have found ourselves in situations where we have behaved less morally than we would have liked to act. According to one writer, however, we would not expect that moral behavior would follow exactly from moral reasoning, because

other factors enter into moral decision making that complicate matters (Rest, 1983). In tests measuring moral reasoning, assessments are made in a social vacuum, but such vacuums rarely exist in the real world. For example, you may realize in the abstract that complying with highway speed limits is important because such limits prevent accidents, and you may obey these limits most of the time when you drive. But you may have found yourself in a situation in which you weighed your need to get somewhere in a hurry (perhaps you were late for an important job interview) against your moral belief in the importance of obeying speeding laws and decided that in this instance you would behave in a way inconsistent with your belief. Situational factors influence moral choices, and they also influence moral reasoning. When individuals perceive that they will be severely hurt by behaving in a morally advanced way (for example, if standing up for someone will lead to severe punishment), they are less likely to reason at a higher moral level (Sobesky, 1983). Moral reasoning is an important influence on moral behavior, but neither can be considered out of context.

Political and Religious Thinking During Adolescence

Less is known about the development of political or religious thinking during adolescence than about moral development, but research in these areas is generally consistent with the view that beliefs become more principled, more abstract, and more independent during the adolescent years. Let us look first at changes in youngsters' political beliefs.

Political thinking during adolescence.   Between the sixth and twelfth grades, political thinking becomes more conceptual and principled and less simplistic and pragmatic (Gallatin, 1980). One researcher who has studied the development of political ideology during adolescence extensively is Joseph Adelson (1972). He suggests that political thinking changes during

Value Autonomy Across Cultures

We noted earlier that the growth of emotional and behavioral autonomy is affected by the broader context in which adolescents develop. Is the same true for value autonomy? Is principled thinking promoted to different degrees in different cultural contexts?

One study of the moral judgments of young people in more than a dozen countries points to at least one cultural variable that may make a difference: Value autonomy is more likely to develop in environments characterized by more *cultural pluralism* (Garbarino and Bronfenbrenner, 1976). Pluralistic environments—in which different subgroups are free to espouse different values and norms—expose young people to a variety of standards, thereby generating the sort of cognitive conflict that is thought to stimulate more advanced levels of moral reasoning. In contrast, in *monolithic* settings, the adolescent is presented with a more pervasive and universal set of standards, and the likelihood of moral conflicts arising due to competing pulls is much smaller. We would expect, therefore, that young people growing up in monolithic environments would be more oriented to the values of authority figures and less autonomous in their judgments.

Researchers James Garbarino and Urie Bronfenbrenner compared adolescents' responses to moral dilemmas across countries with various levels of cultural pluralism. Ratings of pluralism in thirteen countries were based on some twenty factors, such as the presence of effective constitutional limitations on the government's power, a competitive electoral system, freedom for opposing groups, and freedom of speech. Countries ranked highest in pluralism were the United States, West Germany, Switzerland, the Netherlands, and Sweden. Countries ranked lowest in pluralism were Poland, Hungary, Czechoslovakia, and the Soviet Union.

The adolescents' responses to a series of moral dilemmas were scored in the degree to which they were oriented toward the pressures of authority. Consistent with theoretical predictions, adolescents from highly pluralistic countries were least authority oriented. The most authority-oriented youngsters were those from Hungary and the Soviet Union; the least, from Sweden and the Netherlands. A culturally pluralistic cultural environment—in some regards, a large-scale version of the authoritative household, which we have seen is associated with adolescent autonomy—may provide the levels of cognitive conflict necessary to promote the development of more independent moral judgments.

adolescence in several important ways. First, it becomes more abstract. In response to the question, "What is the purpose of laws?" for example, 12- and 13-year-olds are likely to reply with concrete answers—"So people don't kill or steal," "So people don't get hurt," and so on. Older adolescents, in contrast, are likely to respond with more abstract and more general statements—"To ensure safety and enforce the government," and "They are basically guidelines for people. I mean, like this is wrong and this is right and to help them understand" (Adelson, 1972, p. 108).

Second, political thinking during adolescence becomes increasingly less authoritarian and rigid. Young adolescents are inclined toward obedience, toward authority, and toward an uncritical, trusting, and acquiescent stance toward government. For example, when asked what might be done in response to a law that is not working out as planned, the young adolescent will "propose that it be enforced more rigorously." An older teenager may suggest, instead, that the law needs reexamination and perhaps amendment. In contrast to older adolescents, younger adolescents are "more likely to favor

Whereas younger adolescents express belief in autocratic rule and support existing laws, older adolescents are more likely to challenge authority and argue that laws should be reexamined. Here, adolescents speak out against a local school board on the subject of budget cuts. (Susan Lapides/Design Conceptions)

one-man rule as [opposed to] representative democracy; . . . [show] little sensitivity to individual or minority rights; [and are] indifferent to the claims of personal freedom" (Adelson, 1972, p. 108). Although we often complain about the political leaders we elect to office, we can be thankful that we don't have to live under the autocratic thumbs of young adolescents!

Of special significance is the development during middle and late adolescence of a roughly coherent and consistent set of attitudes—a sort of ideology—which does not appear before this point. This ideology is, in Adelson's words, "more or less organized in reference to a more encompassing . . . set of political principles" (1972, p. 121).

Shifts in all three of these directions—increasing abstraction, decreasing authoritarianism, and increasing use of principles—are similar to those observed in studies of moral development, and they support the idea that value autonomy begins to emerge during the late

adolescent years. The movement away from authoritarianism, obedience, and unquestioning acceptance of the rulings of authority is especially interesting because it suggests, further, that an important psychosocial concern for adolescents revolves around questioning the values and beliefs emanating from parents and other authority figures and trying to establish their own priorities.

Religious beliefs during adolescence. Religious beliefs, like political beliefs, also become more abstract and principled during the adolescent years. Specifically, adolescents' beliefs become more oriented toward spiritual and ideological matters and less oriented toward rituals, practices, and the strict observance of religious customs (Wuthnow and Glock, 1973). For example, while 87 percent of all adolescents pray, and 95 percent believe in God, 60 percent of all young people feel that organized religion does not play a very important role in their lives

(Farel, 1982). Compared with children, adolescents place more emphasis on the internal aspects of religious commitment (such as what an individual believes) and less on the external manifestations (such as whether an individual goes to church [Elkind, 1978]).

Generally speaking, the stated importance of religion—and especially of participation in an organized religion—declines somewhat during the adolescent years. More high school students than older adolescents attend church regularly, and not surprisingly, more of the younger adolescents state that religion is important to them (Yankelovich, 1974). Interestingly, several studies have indicated that the decline in the importance of religion during late adolescence appears to be more noteworthy among college than noncollege youth (Yankelovich, 1974), suggesting that college attendance may play some part in shaping (or, as the case may be, unshaping) young people's religious beliefs. As we saw in Chapter 8, studies of identity development during the college years have indicated that over the course of college, students' traditional religious commitments are shaken but are not replaced with alternative beliefs (Waterman, 1982). Late adolescence appears to be a time when individuals reexamine and reevaluate many of the beliefs and values they have grown up with. Consistent with other developments in the area of value autonomy, young people's religious beliefs are likely to become more personalized and less bound to the traditional religious practices they may have been exposed to when they were younger.

Although religious cults and dramatic religious conversion have attracted a great deal of attention in the popular media, they remain rare phenomena among American adolescents and often reflect nonreligious concerns. Membership in a religious cult is often associated with a preceding period of psychological stress, identity diffusion, rootlessness, and with dissatisfaction with mainstream societal values (Conger, 1977a; Wuthnow and Glock, 1973). Contrary to sensationalized stereotypes, most adolescents who maintain an interest in organized religion remain affiliated with the religion they have been exposed to as children and continue with this affiliation as they move into adulthood. The most popular single religious group among U.S. adolescents who belong to one is evangelical Christianity—just as it is among U.S. adults (Religion in America, 1984). And contrary to the fears of many parents—fueled by media reports—most interest in religious cults occurs during young adulthood, not adolescence (Neilsen, 1987).

Summary

In this chapter we have looked at the development of autonomy during the adolescent years. Specifically, we have examined the growth of independence in three distinct but highly interrelated areas—emotional autonomy, behavioral autonomy, and value autonomy. Generally, emotional and behavioral autonomy are likely to surface as psychosocial concerns somewhat earlier during adolescence than value autonomy, which usually does not become a prominent concern until middle or late adolescence.

In contrast to popular stereotypes, the development of autonomy during adolescence does not typically involve rebellion, nor is it usually accompanied by strained or tense family relationships. Especially in households characterized by authoritative patterns of decision making, warmth, and flexibility, family relationships during adolescence move toward increasing maturity gradually and smoothly. Moreover, adolescents raised in authoritative households show the greatest gains in emotional, behavioral, and value autonomy.

Relinquishing the longstanding—and unsupported—notion that psychological health during adolescence is reflected in parent-child conflict and in adolescent rebellion has paved the way for new and better research into the causes and correlates of autonomy. We are now beginning to understand how healthy families are able to adjust their relationships in response to the growing and changing capabilities of the adolescent. Researchers no longer see parental and peer influences as opposing forces and, instead, have turned their attention to the study of factors that enable the young person to make responsible decisions and function with a healthy degree of independence. In addition, they now understand how moral, political, and religious thinking parallel each other during late adolescence and how the development of value autonomy is related to the young person's growing sense of identity.

As a whole, research on the development of autonomy during adolescence indicates that becoming an emotionally, behaviorally, and intellectually independent person need not be a struggle. If establishing a sense of independence is difficult, the source of difficulty lies in the context in which a young person grows up, not in the nature of adolescence itself. Indeed, problems in the development of a healthy sense of autonomy appear more often than not to be either an understandable reaction against excessively controlling circumstances or the foreseeable outcome of growing up in the absence of any clear standards at all.

Key Terms

autonomy - self governing
behavioral autonomy - make own decision + follow through
cognitive-developmental perspective
conventional moral reasoning
detachment

emotional autonomy
individuation
preconventional moral reasoning
principled moral reasoning
value autonomy

For Further Reading

BERNDT, T. (1979). Developmental changes in conformity to peers and parents. *Developmental Psychology, 15,* 608–616. A study of age differences in youngsters' susceptibility to the influence of parents and peers.

DOUVAN, E., AND ADELSON, J. (1966). *The adolescent experience.* New York: Wiley. Although nearly twenty-five years old, this remains a classic study of autonomy and family relations.

HILL, J., AND HOLMBECK, G. (1986). Attachment and autonomy in adolescence. In G. Whitehurst (Ed.), *Annals of child development* (Vol 3.). Greenwich, Conn.: JAI Press. A review of the literature on autonomy in adolescence.

KOHLBERG, L., AND GILLIGAN, C. (1972). The adolescent as philosopher: The discovery of the self in a postconventional world. In J. Kagan and R. Coles (Eds.), *Twelve to sixteen: Early adolescence.* New York: Norton. A discussion of moral development during the adolescent years, from a cognitive-developmental perspective.

STEINBERG, L., AND SILVERBERG, S. (1986). The vicissitudes of autonomy in early adolescence. *Child Development, 57,* 841–851. A study of age and sex differences in emotional and behavioral autonomy.

Intimacy

CHAPTER 10

PREVIEW

1. During adolescence, remarkable changes take place in the capacity of individuals to form close relationships with other people and, consequently, in the types of relationships they form. The growth of intimacy is a fundamental feature of adolescent psychosocial development.

2. Intimacy first emerges in friendships with same-sex peers, usually during preadolescence. It is not until late adolescence that opposite-sex relationships become intimate. The development of intimacy in adolescence occurs prior to and independent of the development of sexuality.

3. In many ways, adolescent girls demonstrate more interest in, and a greater capacity for, intimacy than do adolescent boys. Girls develop close relationships earlier, are more interpersonally sensitive, and place greater emphasis on intimacy in their early sexual relationships.

4. Dating during early and middle adolescence does not appear to contribute very much to the development of intimacy. In fact, some theorists believe that dating may do more to encourage shallowness and superficiality than genuine intimacy.

One of the most remarkable things about adolescence is the way in which close relationships change during these years. Think about the friendships you had as a child and compare them with those you had as a teenager. Think about the boyfriends or girlfriends that children have and the boyfriends or girlfriends of adolescents. And think about relationships between parents and their children, and how these relationships change during adolescence. In all three cases, adolescents' relationships are closer, more personal, more involved, and more emotionally charged. During adolescence, in short, relationships become more intimate.

At the outset, it is necessary to draw a distinction between *intimacy* and *sexuality*. The word *intimacy*—at least as it is used in the study of adolescence—does not have a sexual or physical connotation. Rather, an intimate relationship is an emotional attachment between two people characterized by concern for each other's well-being; a willingness to disclose private, and occasionally sensitive, topics; and a sharing of common interests and activities. Two individuals can therefore have an intimate relationship without having a sexual one. And by the same token, two people can have a sexual relationship without being especially intimate.

The development of intimacy during adolescence involves changes in the adolescent's *need* for intimacy, changes in the *capacity* to have intimate relationships, and changes in the extent to which and the way in which this capacity to be intimate is *expressed*. Although the development of intimacy during adolescence is almost always studied in relation to friendships with peers, adolescents' intimate relationships are by no means limited to other teenagers. Parents often have intimate relationships with their adolescents, especially when their children have reached a sufficient level of maturity. Siblings, even with many years between them, are often close confidants. Sometimes young people even form intimate relationships with adults who are not in their immediate family. Unfortunately, though, we know very little about adolescent intimacy in relationships other than with peers,

because research on close friendships during adolescence has nearly always dealt with young people and their agemates. As you read this chapter, you should therefore bear in mind that most of what is known about the development of intimacy over the course of adolescence is derived from studies of adolescents' relationships with peers and that the study of intimacy with other people is virtually uncharted territory. It would be fascinating to know more about the types of friendships adolescents form with people who are older or younger.

Obviously, one of the central issues in the study of intimacy during adolescence is the onset of dating. Although the young person's initiation into opposite-sex relationships is undoubtedly important, it is not the only noteworthy change that occurs in close relationships during adolescence. Adolescence is also an important time for changes in what we look for in friends, in our capacity to be intimate with people of *both* sexes, and in the way we express our closeness with friends.

INTIMACY AS AN ADOLESCENT ISSUE

Intimacy is an important concern throughout most of the life span. Friends and confidants provide support when we are feeling emotionally vulnerable, assistance when we need it, and companionship in a variety of activities and contexts (Weiss, 1974). During childhood, not having friends is associated with a range of psychological and social problems (Hartup, 1983). And in adulthood, having at least one intimate friendship is beneficial to your health: People who have others to turn to for emotional support are less likely to suffer from psychological and physical disorders (Myers, Lindentthal, and Pepper, 1975). Without question, close relationships are extremely important to people of all ages. Why, then, is the development of intimacy especially important during adolescence?

One reason is that it is not until adolescence that truly intimate relationships—relationships

Children's friendships center around shared activities. Not until adolescence are friendships based on the sorts of bonds that are formed between individuals who care about, know, and understand each other in a special way. (Alan Carey/The Image Works)

characterized by openness, honesty, self-disclosure, and trust—first emerge. Although children certainly have important friendships, their relationships are different from those formed during adolescence. Children's friendships are activity-oriented, for example, built around games and shared pastimes. To a child, a friend is someone who likes to do the same things he or she does. But teenagers' close friendships are more likely to have a strong emotional foundation; they are built on the sorts of bonds that form between people who care about and know and understand each other in a special way.

Another reason for the importance of intimacy during adolescence concerns the changing nature of the adolescent's social world: during early adolescence, the increasing importance of peers and, during late adolescence, the increasing importance of opposite-sex peers. In the previous chapter, we looked at the young person's growing orientation toward peers as part of the development of emotional autonomy. In this chapter, we look at changes in adolescent peer relations again but in a different light—as part of the development of intimacy.

Why do such important changes take place in close relationships during adolescence? Several theorists have answered this question by pointing to significant links between the development of intimacy during adolescence and the biological, cognitive, and social changes of the period (Berndt, 1982). Puberty and its attendant changes in sexual impulses often raise new issues and concerns requiring serious, intimate discussion. Some young people feel hesitant to discuss sex and dating with their parents and turn instead to relationships outside the family. As Elizabeth Douvan and Joseph Adelson noted in *The Adolescent Experience* (1966), "[The adolescent] is discovering, and trying to interpret and control, a changed body, and with it new and frightening impulses, and so requires the example and communion of peers" (pp. 178–179). Sexual maturation may also provoke intimacy between adolescents and their parents, when young people turn to their mothers or fathers for advice, information, and guidance (Kandel and Lesser, 1972).

Advances in thinking—especially in the realm of *social cognition*—are also related to the development of intimacy during adolescence (Hill and Palmquist, 1978). The growth of social cognition during adolescence, as we saw in Chapter 2, is reflected in the young person's more sophisticated conceptions of social relationships and in improvements in interpersonal understanding and communication. These changes permit adolescents to establish and maintain far more mature relationships, characterized by higher levels of empathy, self-disclosure, and responsiveness to each other's thoughts and feelings. Robert Selman, who has studied the development of role-taking abilities during childhood and adolescence, points out that the limitations in preadolescents' ability to look at things from another person's point of view may make intimate interpersonal relationships a cognitive impossibility (1980). It is hard to be an intimate friend to someone when you are unable to empathize with that person. Consistent with this, researchers have found that children and adolescents who are better at understanding and empathizing with their peers are more likely to have close friends and are more likely to be socially accepted (Kurdek and Krile, 1982; McGuire and Weisz, 1982). Improvements in social competence and gains in intimacy during adolescence, therefore, are partly attributable to improvements in social cognition (Ford, 1982).

We can also point to changes in the adolescent's social roles as potentially affecting the development of intimacy. Perhaps most simply, the behavioral independence that often accompanies the transition from childhood into adolescence provides greater opportunities for adolescents to be alone with their friends, engaged in intimate discussion. Adolescents spend more time talking to their friends than in any other

activity (Csikszentmihalyi and Larson, 1984). Moreover, the recognition of adolescents as "near adults" may prompt their parents and other adults to confide in them and turn to them for support. Shared experiences, such as working, as well as the development of emotional autonomy, may help give young people and their parents more of a basis for friendship and communication (Youniss and Smollar, 1985). Finally, changes in the structure of schools during early adolescence, often giving younger teenagers more contact with older ones, may promote new types of peer relationships (Blyth, Hill, and Smyth, 1981).

During the course of preadolescence and adolescence, relationships are gradually transformed—from the friendly but activity-oriented friendships of childhood to the more self-conscious, more analytical, and more intimate relationships of adulthood. In the next section, we examine why and how this transformation occurs.

THEORETICAL PERSPECTIVES

The most important theoretical perspectives on the development of intimacy during adolescence are those of Harry Stack Sullivan (1953a) and Erik Erikson (1968). Like Erikson, whose theory of adolescent identity development was discussed at length in Chapter 8, Sullivan took a far less biological view of development than had other psychoanalytic theorists, such as Anna Freud. Instead, Sullivan emphasized the social aspects of growth, suggesting that psychological development can best be understood when looked at in interpersonal terms.

By shifting the emphasis from biological to interpersonal aspects of development, Sullivan changed the view of adolescence in a very important way. Like Freud, Sullivan viewed adolescence as a time of struggle and potential difficulty. But in contrast to the more traditional psychoanalytic view of adolescence, Sullivan argued that the struggles of the period are interpersonal, not intrapsychic. They involve trans-

inter personal – relations between people
intra personal – with in ones self

formations in the adolescent's relationships with others. In particular, the challenges of adolescence (and, indeed, according to Sullivan, of the entire life cycle) revolve around trying to satisfy our changing interpersonal needs.

Sullivan's Theory of Interpersonal Development

According to Sullivan, development is characterized by two general tendencies: the **pursuit of satisfaction**, which is a biological drive; and the **pursuit of security**, which is a psychosocial drive. The pursuit of satisfaction is what makes us eat when we are hungry or drink when we are thirsty. The pursuit of security makes us seek relationships with others who will make us feel happy and safe. Both of these pursuits, Sullivan believed, intensify when they are not satisfied. Sullivan claimed, for example, that when our needs for security are thwarted, we feel anxious and we become even more driven to seek out others.

As the child develops, different interpersonal needs surface that lead either to feelings of security (when the needs are satisfied) or to feelings of anxiety (when the needs are frustrated). Sullivan charted a developmental progression of needs, beginning in infancy and continuing through adolescence (see Table 10.1): the **needs for contact and for tenderness** (infancy), the **need for adult participation** (early childhood), the **need for peers and for peer acceptance** (middle childhood), the **need for intimacy** (preadolescence), the **needs for sexual contact and for intimacy with a peer of the opposite sex** (early adolescence), and the **need for integration into adult society** (late adolescence [Sullivan, 1953b]). These changing interpersonal needs define the course of interpersonal development through different phases of the life span. During middle childhood, for example, youngsters need to be accepted into peer groups, or else they feel rejected and ostracized.

In Sullivan's view, the security derived from having satisfying relationships with others is the "glue" that holds together a sense of self.

TABLE 10.1   INTERPERSONAL NEEDS ASSOCIATED WITH DIFFERENT DEVELOPMENTAL ERAS: SULLIVAN'S THEORY

DEVELOPMENTAL EPOCHS	INTERPERSONAL NEEDS
Infancy (0 to 2–3 yrs.)	Need for contact with people
	Need for tenderness from the mothering one
Childhood (2–3 to 6–7 yrs.)	Need for adult participation in the child's play
Juvenile era (6–7 to 12–14 yrs.)	Need for peer playmates
	Need for acceptance into peer society groups
Preadolescence (8–10 to 12–14 yrs.)	Need for intimacy and consensual validation in same-sex chumships
Early adolescence (12–14 to 17–18 yrs.)	Need for sexual contact
	Need for intimacy with an opposite-sex peer
Late adolescence (17–18 yrs. to adult)	Need for integration into adult society

Source: Sullivan, 1953b.

Identity and self-esteem are gradually built up through interpersonal relationships. Like Erikson, Sullivan viewed psychosocial development as cumulative: The frustrations and satisfactions we experience during earlier periods affect our later relationships and developing sense of identity. The child who as an infant has his or her need for contact or tenderness frustrated will approach interpersonal relationships in subsequent eras with greater anxiety, a more intense need for security, and a shakier sense of self.

When important interpersonal transitions arise (for example, during childhood, when the social world is broadened to include significant relationships with peers), having a solid foundation of security in past relationships will aid in the successful negotiation of the transition.

An individual who is very anxious about forming relationships with others is likely to have trouble forming new types of relationships, because they threaten an already shaky sense of security. A child who does not have a strong sense of security may have many friends in elementary school but may be too afraid to form intimate friendships when she reaches preadolescence. She may try to continue having the sorts of friendships she had as a child—friendships that focus on playing games, for example, rather than talking—long after her friends have outgrown getting together to "play." As a result, she may be rejected by her peers and feel lonely and isolated.

Sullivan's view of interpersonal development during adolescence.   With this brief introduction to Sullivan's theory in mind, we can now look more closely at his views of development during adolescence. Looking back at the progression of interpersonal needs that Sullivan mapped out, we see that he distinguished between intimacy and sexuality and, perhaps more important, that he suggested that the need for intimacy—which surfaces during preadolescence—precedes the development of heterosexual relationships—which do not emerge until adolescence. In other words, Sullivan believed that the capacity for intimacy first develops before adolescence and in the context of same-sex, not opposite-sex, relationships. One of the main challenges of adolescence, according to Sullivan, is making the transition from the nonsexual, intimate, same-sex friendships of preadolescence to the sexual, intimate, opposite-sex friendships of late adolescence.

Sullivan divided the years between childhood and adulthood into three periods: *preadolescence, early adolescence,* and *late adolescence.* During preadolescence, children begin to focus their attention on relationships with a few close friends, generally of the same sex. It is through these friendships—"chum relationships," as Sullivan called them—that the need for intimacy is first satisfied. With chums, the young person learns to disclose and receive intimate, private

information and to build a close, mutual friendship that is based on honesty, loyalty, and trust. Sullivan believed that these relationships could even have a corrective influence, helping to repair interpersonal problems that might have developed during childhood. A good preadolescent friend, for example, can help overcome feelings of insecurity that have developed as a result of poor family relationships.

Not all youngsters feel secure enough as preadolescents to forge these more mature, intimate friendships, however. The feelings of insecurity are so strong for some that anxiety holds them back. As a result, some youngsters never fully develop the capacity to be intimate with others, a limitation that takes its toll on relationships throughout adolescence and adulthood. In other words, Sullivan felt that forming intimate friendships during preadolescence is a prerequisite to forming close relationships as an adolescent or young adult.

According to Sullivan, the preadolescent era comes to an end with the onset of puberty. Early adolescence is marked by the emergence of sexuality, in the form of a biologically based, powerful sex drive. As a consequence of this development, a change in the preferred "target" of the adolescent's need for intimacy takes place. He or she must begin to make a shift from intimate relationships with members of the same sex to intimate relationships with members of the opposite sex.

Like all interpersonal transitions, the movement from same-sex into opposite-sex relationships can be fraught with anxiety. For adolescents who do not have a healthy sense of security, it can be scary to leave the safety of nonsexual same-sex friendships and venture into the world of opposite-sex relationships, dating, and sexuality. Some adolescents' fears of dating have been overcome through counseling programs that allow them to practice dating skills in a safe and secure setting. For instance, one program had male adolescents who had fears of dating try out newly learned interpersonal skills with females who were working for the counselors (McGovern, Arkowitz, and Gilmore,

During middle adolescence individuals often begin to make the transition from same-sex into opposite-sex friendships. For some teenagers, the transition can be an awkward one. (Bohdan Hrynewych/Southern Light)

1975). The program successfully reduced the adolescents' inhibitions.

The chief challenge of adolescence, according to Sullivan, is to integrate the individual's established need for intimacy with the emerging need for sexual contact in a way that does not engender an excessive degree of anxiety. Just as Erikson views adolescence as a time of experimentation with different identities, Sullivan saw adolescence as a time of experimentation with different types of interpersonal relationships. Some adolescents choose to date many different people to try to find out what they are looking for in a relationship with someone else. Others get involved very deeply with a boyfriend or girlfriend in a relationship that lasts throughout their entire adolescence. Others may have a series of serious relationships. And still others keep intimacy and sexuality separate. They may develop close platonic relationships with opposite-sex peers, for example, or they may have

sexual relationships without getting very intimate with the people they have sex with. And just as Erikson views role experimentation as a healthy part of the adolescent's search for identity, Sullivan viewed the adolescent's experimentation with different types of relationships as a normal way of handling new feelings, new fears, and new interpersonal needs. For many young people, experimentation with sex and intimacy continues well into late adolescence.

If the interpersonal tasks of adolescence have been negotiated successfully, the young person enters late adolescence able to be intimate, able to enjoy sex, and most critical, able to experience intimacy and sexuality in the same relationship. This accomplished, the adolescent turns to the interpersonal needs of late adolescence: carving his or her niche in adult society. This latter task, in some senses, is reminiscent of the adolescent identity crisis described by Erikson.

Erikson's View of Intimacy

Erik Erikson believes that development during the adolescent and young adult years revolves around two psychosocial crisis: the crisis of identity versus identity diffusion, prominent during adolescence, and the crisis of **intimacy versus isolation,** prominent during early adulthood (1968). Erikson's ideas on the subject of intimacy are far less developed than his ideas on the issue of identity. Nonetheless, his view of the relationship *between* intimacy and identity is important to understand and provides somewhat of a contrast to Sullivan's perspective.

Erikson feels that in a truly intimate relationship, two individuals' identities become fused in such a way that neither person's identity is lost. Together, two people who are in love form a couple that has its own life, its own future, and its own identity. Yet the partners do not lose their own sense of individuality. When two people marry, for example, becoming a part of a couple becomes an important part of each person's identity, but it doesn't erase the sense of self that each person had before the marriage.

It follows, Erikson reasons, that adolescents must establish a sense of identity before they are capable of real intimacy. Without a secure sense of identity, people are afraid and unwilling to make serious commitments to others: They fear that they will lose their identity in the relationship. A young woman who is struggling to establish an occupational identity, for example, may feel that getting seriously involved with someone may impede her progress toward discovering who *she* really is as an individual.

Relationships between individuals who have not yet established a sense of identity may look intimate, but generally they are not. Adolescents who throw themselves into going steady often display a sort of "pseudointimacy." On the surface, their relationship may seem to be close, but a more careful examination usually reveals a sort of shallow, superficial intimacy. The couple may proclaim their faith in each other, for instance, but deep down they may be mistrustful or afraid to voice their fears. They may say that

they are open with each other, but they may not disclose what they are really feeling, for fear of losing the relationship. They may say that they will stay together forever, but they have trouble making any concrete plans for the future that include each other. According to Erikson, this type of pseudointimacy is to be expected during adolescence. After all, it is difficult to commit yourself to someone else before you yourself know who you are.

Erikson and Sullivan each sees the development of intimacy and the development of identity as going hand in hand throughout adolescence, with changes in one realm of psychosocial development affecting changes in the other. Whereas Sullivan's concern was primarily with the adolescent's need and capacity for intimacy (hence, his focus on early adolescence), Erikson's has been with the expression of intimacy (hence, his focus on late adolescence). Close relationships are used as a safe context in which adolescents confront difficult questions of identity; yet at the same time, the development of an increasingly coherent and secure sense of self provides the foundation upon which adolescents build and strengthen intimate relationships with others. Although we may speak of them as though they are independent processes, the development of intimacy and identity—along with the development of autonomy, sexuality, and achievement—are highly interrelated.

A Theory of Relationship Maturity

Recently, Kathleen White and her colleagues (White, Speisman, Costos, and Smith, 1987) have proposed a model of **relationship maturity,** in which individuals are described as moving through a series of qualitative stages in their close relationships with others. According to White, relationship maturity refers to the level of maturity the adolescent or young adult brings to his or her relationships with parents, lovers, or close friends. Three stages of relationship maturity have been described by the researchers:

Level 1: Self-Focused. At this stage, individuals are still wrapped up in their own needs and their own perspectives. Their view of the other person is simplistic, and their emotional responses in the relationship are extreme—love or hate. As a consequence of this simplistic view of things, the self-focused individual responds to the other's actions in simplistic ways—either by trying to hold on to the relationship or by trying to flee from it. As a prototype of this sort of individual, the researchers offer Alexis Colby, the power-hungry ex-wife in the popular television series *Dynasty*.

Level 2: Role-Focused. Role-focused individuals behave in ways that are dominated by conformity and conventionality. In their close relationships, they attempt to keep things nice, avoid controversy, and control their emotions. Although their close relationships are important to them, role-focused individuals generally are more concerned with conforming with the appropriate roles and norms in a relationship (what the "good" boyfriend does; what the perfect daughter is "supposed" to do) than with the partner as an individual. They do not cast their relationships or their partners in extreme terms, as do self-focused individuals, but differences between individuals or complications in the relationship are disregarded or minimized. As an example of a role-focused individual, the authors give the character Edith Bunker, from the once popular television show *All in the Family*.

Level 3: Individuated-Connected. Individuals functioning at this level of relationship maturity are both highly individuated themselves and able to form close, intimate relationships with others that acknowledge the complexity and contradictions in close relationships. Differences in outlook are not only tolerated but are encouraged, because individuated-connected individuals value these differences as part of what makes each partner unique and the relationship vital. Within

the context of a strong relationship, individuals are encouraged to assert and express their individuality. Cliff Huxtable, the father on the *Bill Cosby Show*, is presented as an example of the individuated-connected person.

These stages of relationship maturity are reminiscent of those proposed by other theorists working from a cognitive-developmental perspective (for example, Selman, Kohlberg, and Turiel). As in these other theories, the individual is thought to progress from a level of functioning that is narrow and concrete (here, self-focused), into one that is tied to social conventions and rules (here, role-focused), and perhaps into one based on more abstract principles (here, the individuated-connected stage). According to White and her colleagues, individuals progress through these three stages between childhood and young adulthood, with children most often functioning at the self-focused level, and adolescents most often at the role-focused level. Not all individuals are believed to move into the individuated-connected level, and if they do, it is typically not expected to happen until early adulthood. Research on this theory is now underway, and it is difficult to say at this time whether studies of young people will support the model.

RESEARCH ON THE DEVELOPMENTAL COURSE OF INTIMACY

Several interesting hypotheses about the development of intimacy during adolescence can be derived from these theories of interpersonal development during adolescence. First, we would expect that intimate relationships with peers seldom appear much before preadolescence. Second, we would hypothesize that these intimate relationships are distinct from sexual relationships, which do not emerge until later in adolescence. Third, Sullivan's theory suggests that intimate relationships first appear primarily in

Identity and Intimacy: Two Tests of Erikson's Model

As we have seen, Erikson believes that the establishment of a coherent sense of identity is a prerequisite to the successful resolution of the young adulthood crisis of intimacy versus isolation. In order to test this hypothesis, a team of researchers studied the development of identity and intimacy in a group of male college undergraduates (Orlofsky, Marcia, and Lesser, 1973). Separate measures of identity development and intimacy development were administered to fifty-three male students, and the relation between each student's levels of identity and intimacy achievement was examined. The measure of identity development was the Identity Status Interview discussed in Chapter 8. The measure of intimacy was a similarly structured interview that focused on the individual's current and past relationships.

Students were interviewed twice, once to determine their identity status and once to determine their intimacy status. The four identity classifications were *identity achievement* (the student has established a coherent sense of identity); *moratorium* (the student is still in the midst of identity exploration); *foreclosure* (the student has circumvented the crisis of identity by prematurely foreclosing the exploration process); and *identity diffusion* (the student is extremely confused or cynical about making commitments).

The four intimacy classifications were *intimate* (the student has and continues to develop close mutual relationships with others and has an intimate relationship with a woman); *preintimate* (the student has the qualities that predispose him toward intimacy but has not yet had an intimate relationship with a woman); *pseudointimate* or *stereotyped* (the student has immature and superficial relationships with others; he may appear to be involved in an intimate relationship but in reality is only "going through the motions"); and *isolate* (the student shows no signs of any enduring close relationships). Identity and intimacy classifications were made independent of each other so that the raters would not be biased.

If the developmental sequence described by Erikson is correct, the researchers argued, one would expect all students who demonstrate a mature capacity for intimacy also to have achieved a coherent sense of identity. However, one would not expect all students who have established a sense of identity necessarily to demonstrate mature intimacy. One

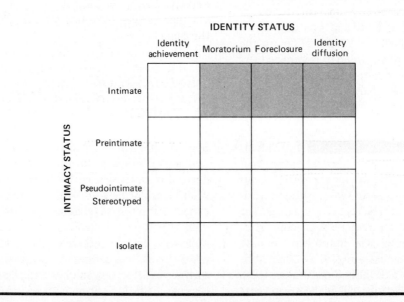

would expect some of them to be still in the midst of the "intimacy crisis."

Consistent with Erikson's theory, most of the individuals classified as intimate were also classified as having achieved a sense of identity, and all of the individuals classified as isolates were classified as being either in the foreclosure group or in the identity diffusion category. Preintimate individuals were most likely to be classified as being in the moratorium group, and pseudointimate individuals were most likely to be classified as either identity diffused or foreclosed.

However, contrary to the most conservative interpretations of Erikson's model— which would predict that *none* of the individuals who had not resolved the identity crisis would be classified as intimate—some of the intimate individuals were still in the midst of the identity moratorium, and a handful of them were classified as having experienced identity foreclosure. Thus while having resolved the identity crisis successfully appears to increase the likelihood of successfully resolving the crisis of intimacy, it does not appear to be essential in all cases. Although the findings therefore lend some support for the idea that the development of identity is a prerequisite to the development of intimacy, they indicate that for some individuals, identity and intimacy may develop at the same time.

A similar study was carried out with young women, but it focused on the relation between intimacy and individuation rather than identity (Levitz-Jones and Orlofsky, 1985). A group of college women were given a **projective test** designed to measure their level of individuation, and their scores on this measure were examined in relation to their scores derived from the intimacy interview described earlier. (A projective test is a test in which the subject responds to an abstract or vague picture, like an inkblot, and is assumed to "project" his or her inner feelings in the answer.) In this study, the researchers introduced a new intimacy status category, *merger*, to indicate individuals who had become involved in an excessively dependent relationship at the expense of their own autonomy.

As hypothesized, women who scored higher on the measure of intimacy were more likely to have scored higher on the measure of individuation, leading the authors to conclude that "the capacity for intimacy . . . in young womanhood is associated with and perhaps dependent on the capacity to feel secure and confident as a separate individual" (p. 167). In contrast, women in the low-intimacy and merger groups appeared, on the basis of their scores on the projective measure, to have had difficulty in individuating from their parents. These two groups differed in the way in which this problem was manifested, however. Whereas the women in the merger category appeared to act out their conflicts over dependency through their relationships with others, women in the low-intimacy groups appeared to shun closeness altogether. As was the case among males, however, a small number of women who evidenced problems of individuation nevertheless scored high on the intimacy measure— suggesting once again that resolving issues of identity may not be a prerequisite to entering into intimate relationships for all individuals.

In both of the studies, incidentally, only a small percentage of the men or women demonstrated a mature capacity for intimacy. Although one might be tempted to attribute this to widespread difficulty on the part of contemporary adolescents in establishing a healthy sense of identity (which, consequently, would impair their ability to enter into intimate relationships), it may be that the level of intimacy assessed via the interview measure employed is achieved only later in young adulthood, as Erikson had initially suggested. The development of intimacy may be a long, gradual process that begins in preadolescence but that does not culminate until well beyond the adolescent decade.

Sources: J. Orlofsky, J. Marcia, and I. Lesser. (1973). "Ego Identity Status and the Intimacy Versus Isolation Crisis of Young Adulthood," *Journal of Personality and Social Psychology, 27,* 211–219; E. Levitz-Jones and J. Orlofsky. (1985). "Separation–Individuation and Intimacy Capacity in College Women," *Journal of Personality and Social Psychology, 49,* 156–169.

same-sex friendships during preadolescence and early adolescence and that intimacy gradually extends, during the middle and late adolescent years, to opposite-sex relationships that have a decidedly sexual air about them. Let's examine the research on each of these hypotheses, as we look at changes during adolescence in the nature of friendship, the display of intimate behavior, and the targets of intimacy.

Changes in the Nature of Friendship

"How do you know that someone is your best friend?" When this question is posed to children and adolescents of different ages, younger and older respondents give different sorts of answers. Consider, for example, the following two responses—the first from a kindergarten child, the second from a sixth grader (from Berndt, 1981, p. 180):

"I sleep over at his house sometimes. When he's playing ball with his friends, he'll let me play. When I slept over, he let me get in front of him in four-squares [a playground game]. He likes me."

"If you can tell each other things that you don't like about each other. If you get into a fight with someone else, they'd stick up for you. If you can tell them your phone number and they don't give you crank calls. If they don't act mean to you when other kids are around."

These two examples illustrate the most important trend in the development of children's conceptions of friendship: it is not until early adolescence that such features as self-disclosure and loyalty are mentioned as important dimensions of friendship. Thomas Berndt (1981), for example, compared the responses of kindergarten children, third-graders, and sixth-graders to questions about their conceptions of close friendship. The children's responses were classified into one of eight categories, including *play or association* ("He calls me all the time"), *prosocial behavior* ("She helps me do things"), *intimacy or trust* ("I can tell her secrets"), and *loyal*

support ("He'll stick up for me when I'm in a fight"). In general, responses mentioning prosocial behavior and association were equally frequent across all age groups—in fact, they were among the most frequent types of responses at all ages. But answers mentioning intimacy and loyalty, which were virtually absent among the kindergarten students, increased dramatically between the third and sixth grades.

A similar study revealed comparable results (Bigelow and LaGaipa, 1975). The researchers looked at the typical age at which different sorts of friendship conceptions first emerge. Not until seventh grade did individuals mention intimacy, and not until this time did children mention "common interests" or "similar attitudes and values" (see Figure 10.1). As in Berndt's study, the researchers found that responses mentioning prosocial behavior and common activities were high in all age levels. One team of writers suggest that it may be important to differentiate between companionship, which appears much before adolescence, and intimacy, which may not emerge until considerably later (Buhrmester and Furman, 1987).

That conceptions of friendship come to place greater weight on such dimensions as intimacy, loyalty, and shared values and attitudes during early adolescence is consistent with Sullivan's theory. As adolescents' needs for intimacy increase, so might the emphasis that they place on intimacy as an important component of friendship. The findings are also consistent with what we know about other cognitive changes characteristic of early adolescence. As you will recall from Chapter 2, adolescents have greater facility than children in thinking about abstract concepts, such as intimacy and loyalty. And adolescents' judgments of others are more sophisticated, more psychological, and less tied to concrete attributes than are those of children.

Several studies indicate that the importance of intimacy continues to increase throughout early and middle adolescence. But an interesting pattern of change occurs around age 14. During middle adolescence (between ages 13 and 15), particularly for girls, concerns about loyalty and

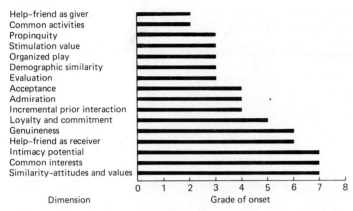

Dimension

FIGURE 10.1   Children and adolescents have different conceptions of "friendship." Some sorts of conceptions do not appear until the fifth or sixth grade. (Derived from Bigelow and LaGaipa, 1975)

anxieties over rejection become more pronounced and may temporarily overshadow concerns about intimate self-disclosure (Douvan and Adelson, 1966; Coleman, 1974). As Elizabeth Douvan and Joseph Adelson explain:

> The girls in this age group [14–16] are unique in some respects, that is, different from both older and younger girls. What stands out in their interviews is the stress placed on security in friendships. They want the friend to be loyal, trustworthy, and a reliable source of support in any emotional crisis. She should not be the sort of person who will abandon you or who gossips about you behind your back. . . . With so much invested in the friendship, it is no wonder that the girl is so dependent on it. . . . The girl is likely to feel like the [patient] in that famous *New Yorker* cartoon, who, getting up from the couch, takes a pistol from her purse, and says [to her psychoanalyst]: "You've done me a world of good, Doctor, but you know too much." (1966, pp. 188–189)

How might Sullivan have explained this pattern? Why might loyalty become such a pressing concern for girls during the middle adolescent years? One possible answer is that at this age, girls may feel more anxious about their relationships because they are beginning to make the transition into opposite-sex relationships. These transitions, as Sullivan noted, can sometimes make us feel insecure. Perhaps it is anxiety over dating and heightened feelings of insecurity that cause adolescent girls temporarily to place a great deal of emphasis on the trust and loyalty of their close friends.

Changes in the Display of Intimacy

In addition to placing greater emphasis on intimacy and loyalty in defining friendship than children do, teenagers are also more likely actually to display intimacy in their relationships. According to Sullivan, we should be able to see this in patterns of self-disclosure. Compared with children, adolescents should be more likely to share intimate feelings and thoughts with their friends. To investigate this issue, one team of researchers examined age differences in the degree to which youngsters had intimate knowledge about their best friends (Diaz and Berndt, 1982). Although fourth- and eighth-graders had comparable degrees of knowledge about *nonintimate* characteristics of their best friends (such as the friend's telephone number or birth date), eighth graders knew significantly more things about their friends that could be classified as

The development of intimacy generally surfaces first in same-sex friendships. Research suggests that intimate friendships develop earlier among girls than boys.
(Rae Russel)

intimate (such as what their friends worry about or what they are proud of). Along similar lines, another study showed that, between the fifth and eleventh grades, increasingly more adolescents agree with such statements as, "I know how [my friend] feels about things without his [or her] telling me," and "I feel free to talk to [my friend] about almost everything" (Sharabany, Gershoni, and Hofman, 1981). Consistent with Sullivan's viewpoint, then, during preadolescence and early adolescence, youngsters' friendships become more personal. One recent study, however, suggests that individuals' desire for speaking intimately—sharing close secrets, for example—does not increase between childhood and early adolescence, as might be expected to occur (Buhrmester and Furman, 1987). Unfortunately, this study only included youngsters between the second and eighth grades, so it is difficult to know whether the desire for this sort of closeness does not increase during adolescence at all or whether the increase simply occurs after junior high school.

Individuals also become more responsive toward close friends during adolescence (Berndt, 1982). This can be interpreted as another indicator of their increased capacity for intimacy. Before preadolescence, for example, children are actually *less* likely to help and share with their friends than with other classmates (perhaps because children are more competitive with their friends than with other youngsters and do not want to feel inferior). By about fourth grade, children treat their friends and other classmates similarly when it comes to sharing and cooperation. But by the time they have reached eighth grade, one team of researchers found, friends are "more generous and more helpful toward each other than toward other classmates" (Berndt, 1982, p. 1452).

In addition, during the course of adolescence, individuals become more interpersonally sensitive—they show greater levels of empathy and social understanding—in situations in which they are helping or comforting others. Compared with children, adolescents are more likely to understand and acknowledge how their friends feel when those friends are having problems. For instance, one researcher asked children and adolescents how they would help a younger friend who had been scared by a horror movie on television. The children were more likely to deny their friend's feelings ("You're getting to be a big kid now. . . . There's no reason to be upset. Don't make it so big"); but the adolescents were more likely to respond sensitively and supportively ("The movie *was* scary, and I know 'cause it scared me too. . . . Just remember the picture isn't true—it's all camera angles and stuff") (Burleson, 1982).

Changes in the "Targets" of Intimacy

According to Sullivan, adolescence is a time of noteworthy changes in the "targets" of intimate behavior. During preadolescence and early adolescence, intimacy with peers is hypothesized to replace intimacy with parents, and during late adolescence, intimacy with peers of the opposite sex is thought to take the place of intimacy with same-sex friends. Actually, this view appears to be only somewhat accurate. As we shall see, new "targets" of intimacy do not *replace* old ones. Rather, new targets are *added to* old ones.

Parents and peers as targets of intimacy. The increasing intimacy between teenagers and their friends during the course of adolescence is generally not accompanied by a decrease in intimacy toward parents. Declines in intimacy between adolescents and their parents, which appear to occur during early adolescence, are temporary. By the end of adolescence, young people and their parents are quite close. One study, for example, compared levels of intimacy between adolescents and their best friends, their moth-

Although intimate, opposite-sex relationships begin to develop during middle adolescence, they do not replace friendships with same-sex peers. Rather, new types of relationships appear to be added to old ones. (Joe Gordon)

ers, and their fathers (Hunter and Youniss, 1982). Thirty adolescents in each of four different age groups—9, 12, 15, and 19—were asked to rate the three relationships along four measures of intimacy: (1) their willingness to discuss problems with the other person, (2) their ability to talk through disagreements, (3) feelings of companionship, and (4) the degree of intimate knowledge possessed by the other person. Ratings across these measures were summed to form overall intimacy scores for each of the three relationships (see Figure 10.2).

As expected, intimacy between adolescents and their best friends increased across the four groups. And from age 12 on, adolescents described their relationships with their best friends as more intimate than those with their mothers or fathers. But this difference between parent and peer intimacy was due to increases in intimacy with peers, not to decreases in intimacy with parents. Intimacy between adolescents and their mothers was equal across the four groups, and intimacy between adolescents and their fathers appeared to increase slightly between ages 9 and 12, to decrease slightly between ages 12 and 15 (returning to the level at 9 years of age), and to remain steady between ages 15 and 19. In this study and in several others, adolescents of both sexes described their relationships with their mothers as more intimate than those with their fathers (Kandel and Lesser, 1972; Youniss and Smollar, 1985).

Findings consistent with these were obtained when nearly 2,500 students in a large midwestern school district were asked to list the important people in their lives—people they cared about, went to for advice, or did things with (Blyth, Hill, and Thiel, 1982). The number of peers listed increased over the course of the age range studied (from grades seven through ten). But no changes were found across this same age range in the percentage of adolescents listing their mothers or fathers—in each grade, for both boys and girls, about 93 percent of the adolescents sampled listed their parents. Similarly, studies of adolescents' preferences for social support show that the likelihood of turning

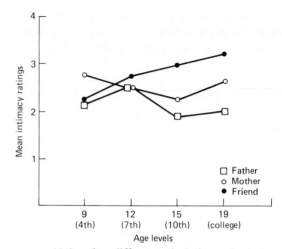

FIGURE 10.2   Age differences in intimacy in three relationships. (Adapted from Hunter and Youniss, 1982)

to a peer during a time of trouble increases during adolescence but that the likelihood of turning to a parent remains constant (Kneisel, 1987). In other words, even though adolescents begin to see their friends as increasingly important sources of emotional support, they do not cease needing or using their parents for the same purpose.

An important transition appears to take place sometime between the fifth and eighth grades, however. During this period, peers become the most important source of companionship and intimate self-disclosure, surpassing parents and, interestingly, other family members, such as siblings, as well (Buhrmester and Furman, 1987). Peers may become increasingly important as targets of intimacy not simply because of their similar age, but because they do not share the same family with the adolescent. As adolescents begin the process of individuation, they may need to seek intimacy outside the family as a means of establishing an identity beyond their family role.

Adolescents also have very different sorts of intimate relationships with parents and peers, and these differences point to different ways in which mothers, fathers, and friends may contribute to the social development of the young person. Even in close families, parent-adolescent relations are characterized by an imbalance of power, with parents as nurturers, advice givers, and explainers whom adolescents turn to because of their experience and expertise. Adolescents' interactions with their friends, in contrast, are more mutual and balanced and are more likely to provide adolescents with opportunities to express alternative views and engage in an equal exchange of feelings and beliefs (Hunter, 1984). Rather than viewing one type of relationship as more or less intimate than the other, it seems wiser to say that both types of intimacy are important, for each influences a different aspect of the adolescent's developing character in important ways. Intimacy with parents provides opportunities to learn from someone older and wiser; intimacy with friends provides opportunities to share experiences with someone who has a similar perspective and degree of expertise.

In general, these findings on age changes in intimacy with parents and peers are similar to the findings discussed in the chapter on autonomy: Although the importance of peer relationships undoubtedly increases during adolescence, the significance of family relationships does not decline. Contrary to widely held stereotypes about adolescents' social relationships, then, parents do not cease to be important sources of influence or, as we see here, targets of intimacy. Throughout adolescence, parents and adolescents remain close; parents—especially mothers—remain important confidants; and both mothers and fathers continue to be significant influences on the young person's behavior and decisions. Indeed, even in adolescence being close to one's parents has a more positive impact on psychological health than being close to one's friends (Greenberg, Siegel, and Leitch, 1983), and studies show that the quality of the relationship adolescents have with their parents may have an influence on the quality of the relationship they have with close friends (Gold and Yanof, 1985). Increasingly, psychologists are coming to see family relationships and peer relationships as influencing each other, rather than

competing with each other. Although studies certainly support this view of the adolescent's social world, it seems clear that peers take on an increasingly important role in the individual's social life over the course of adolescence. Although peers do not *replace* parents, they clearly contribute to the adolescent's social development in a unique and beneficial way.

Other family members as targets of intimacy. Comparatively little is known about adolescents' relationships with siblings and with members of their extended family. In the midwestern survey discussed above, only about 10 percent of the adolescents who had a brother or a sister failed to list a sibling as an important person in their life. Furthermore, more than two-thirds of the adolescents with brothers or sisters listed all of their siblings as significant (Blyth, Hill, and Thiel, 1982). Adolescents typically rate their relationship with their "favorite" brother or sister as having about the same level of intimacy as their relationship with their best friend (Greenberger et al., 1980). When researchers do not specify that the sibling be a "favorite" brother or sister, however, the relationship is usually described as less intimate than the adolescent's relationship with parents *or* friends (Buhrmester and Furman, 1987). It would be interesting to know whether siblings serve similar functions during adolescence to close friends outside the family; unfortunately, this is an area of research that has not been carried out in any detail.

Approximately 80 percent of adolescents list at least one member of their extended family (grandparents, aunts, uncles, and cousins) as significant in their lives, with extended family members constituting about one-fifth of all people listed as important (Blyth, Hill, and Thiel, 1982). Contact with extended family is infrequent, however, either through actual visits or via the telephone. (More than half the extended family members mentioned lived outside the adolescent's area.) One might suspect, therefore, that although adolescents consider grandparents, aunts, uncles, and cousins to be important, these relatives rarely serve as targets of intimacy.

There appears to be an especially steep drop-off in intimacy with grandparents between childhood and adolescence (Buhrmester and Furman, 1987).

Adults outside the family as targets of intimacy. As noted in an earlier chapter, many observers of the changing nature of adolescence in contemporary society have lamented the increasing segregation of young people from nonfamily adults, especially in the suburbs, where intergenerational contact is rare (Bronfenbrenner, 1974). How much contact do adolescents have with adults other than family members, and how close are these relationships?

Few studies have looked at this question directly, and it is difficult to answer it with any precision. Generally speaking, however, it appears that adolescents have only a modest number of adults outside the family who are important to them, and these relationships appear to be significantly less close than those between adolescents and their parents or between adolescents and their friends. In the study of midwestern students discussed previously, for example, at least one nonfamily adult appeared on 60 percent of adolescent boys' lists and on 75 percent of girls' lists (Blyth, Hill, and Thiel, 1982). But the *number* of nonfamily adults on the average adolescent's list paled in comparison to the number of nonfamily peers: Three times as many peers as nonfamily adults were listed by adolescents as important people in their lives.

There is also the issue of the *frequency* of adolescents' contact with these adult friends and the degree of intimacy that they share. In one study comparing adolescents living in urban, suburban, and rural environments, the average urban youngster named only two nonfamily adults who were seen at least once a month, and the average suburban youngster, only one (Garbarino et al., 1978). Another study, of working suburban high school students, assessed the degree to which adolescents formed close relationships with adults on the job (Greenberger et al., 1980; Greenberger and Steinberg, 1981). Only 39 percent of the teenagers surveyed felt even "moderately close" to an adult they knew from work; less than 10 percent reported that they would "definitely" discuss personal problems with an adult from work; only 3 percent reported having contact with an adult work supervisor outside the job; and with one exception, teenagers felt less close to adults from work than to any other important people they were asked about—the only individuals who ranked lower than work supervisors were teachers (see also Buhrmester and Furman, 1987). Overall, then, it appears that close relationships between adolescents and adults other than their parents are relatively rare. At least with regard to intimacy outside the family, age segregation is a common feature of many adolescents' social life.

Same-Sex versus Opposite-Sex Friendships

It is not until middle or even late adolescence that intimate relationships with opposite-sex peers begin to be important. Consistent with Sullivan's theory, studies of preadolescents and young teenagers point to a very strong sex cleavage in adolescents' friendships, with boys rarely reporting friendships with girls, and girls rarely reporting friendships with boys (Hallinan, 1981). Indeed, gender is the single most important determinant of friendship during preadolescence, playing a considerably more powerful role than, for example, race or socioeconomic background (Schofield, 1981). (Age is also an important determinant of preadolescents' friendships, but it is difficult to study, since the structure of most elementary schools—at least in America—makes it hard for children to develop friendships with older or younger peers.)

The schism between boys and girls during early adolescence is due to a variety of factors. First, despite whatever changes may have taken place in American society with regard to sex-role socialization during the past twenty years, it is still the case that preadolescent and early adolescent boys and girls have different interests, engage in different sorts of peer activities, and perceive themselves to be different from

Despite supposed changes in sex-role socialization, early adolescents tend to have exclusively same-sex friendships because—quite simply—boys and girls have different, sex-stereotyped interests. (Frank Sitemen/The Picture Cube)

each other (Schofield, 1981). In one recent study, for example, an interviewer asked a young adolescent boy why boys and girls sit separately in the school lunchroom. "So they can talk," the boy replied. "The boys talk about football and sports and the girls talk about whatever they talk about" (Schofield, 1981, p. 68).

But perhaps a more interesting reason for the low frequency of cross-sex friendships during early adolescence is the concern of some adolescents that contact with members of the opposite sex will be interpreted as a sign of romantic involvement (Schofield, 1981). As one girl put it, "If you talk with boys they [other girls] say that you're almost going with him." Another girl from the same class remarked that boys and girls rarely work together on class projects, "because people like to work with their friends. . . . When you're working on a project . . . your friend has to call and come over to your house. If it's a boy, it can be complicated" (Schofield, 1981, p. 69).

The discomfort that younger adolescents feel about cross-sex relationships is vividly illustrated in the following observation of three preadolescent boys in an amusement park:

The boys seem very interested in the girls they see, and there is considerable whispering and teasing about them. Tom had received a small coin bank as a prize which he decides that he no longer wishes to keep. At this time we are standing in line for a roller coaster directly behind three girls—apparently a year or two older than these twelve-year-olds—one of whom is wearing a hooded jacket. Frank tells Tom to take the bank and "stuff it in her hood," which Tom does to the annoyance of his victim. When she turns around, Tom and Hardy tell her that Frank did it, and of course Frank denies this, blaming Tom. The girls tell the boys to shut up and leave them alone. As things work out, Hardy has to sit with one of these girls on the ride and he clearly appears embarrassed, while Tom and Frank are vastly amused. After the ride Tom and Frank claim that they saw Hardy holding her. Frank said that he saw them holding hands, and Tom said: "He was trying to go up her shirt." Hardy vehemently denies these claims. A short while later we meet these girls again, and Frank turns to Hardy, saying "Here's your honey." The girl retorts as she walks away, "Oh, stifle it." (Fine, 1981, p. 43)

Friendly interactions between early adolescent boys and girls, when they do occur, typically involve "overacting attraction or romantic interest in such a pronounced or playful way that the indication of interest can be written off as teasing or fooling around" (Schofield, 1981, p. 71).

The transitional period—between same-sex nonsexual relationships and opposite-sex sexual ones—appears to be a somewhat trying time for adolescents. This period usually coincides with the peer group's shift from same-sex cliques to mixed-sex crowds, which we examined in Chapter 5. The interpersonal strains and anxieties inherent in the transition show up in the high levels of teasing, joking around, and overt discomfort young adolescents so often display in situations that are a little too close to being romantic or sexual. As one researcher put it, intimacy between boys and girls before middle adolescence appears to be "impeded at least partly because . . . children are aware that they are approaching the age when they may begin to become deeply involved with each other in a romantic or sexual way" (Schofield, 1981, pp. 69–71).

These observations support Sullivan's claim that intimacy between adolescent boys and girls is relatively slow to develop and generally tinged with an air of sexuality. Contrary to his notion that cross-sex intimacy comes to *replace* intimacy with peers of the same sex, however, researchers have found that intimate relationships between adolescents of the same sex continue to develop throughout adolescence. They clearly are not displaced by the eventual emergence of intimacy between adolescent males and females (Shara-

bany, Gershoni, and Hofman, 1981). Although researchers find that the likelihood of opposite-sex peers appearing on adolescents' lists of people who are important to them increases between the seventh and tenth grades, the number of same-sex peers listed remains constant, at around five (Blyth, Hill, and Thiel, 1982).

Actually, intimacy between the sexes increases during early adolescence (Buhrmester and Furman, 1987), but many adolescents in grades seven through ten—half of all males and about one quarter of all females—do not list a single opposite-sex peer as a significant person in their lives (see Figure 10.3). When females do include opposite-sex peers, the boys they list are often older and often from another school, suggesting that opposite-sex intimacy occurs primarily in the context of dating—again, consistent with predictions derived from Sullivan's theory. Similarly, when boys list girls as important friends, they generally are of the same age or younger (Blyth, Hill, and Thiel, 1982). Interestingly, having an intimate relationship with an opposite-sex peer is more strongly related to boys' general level of interpersonal intimacy than it is to girls' (Buhrmester and Furman, 1987). This suggests that opposite-sex relationships may play a more important role in the development of intimacy among adolescent boys than girls.

INTIMACY AND PSYCHOSOCIAL DEVELOPMENT

Intimate friendships during adolescence play an important role in the young person's overall psychological development, particularly in the realms of identity and sexuality. Both Sullivan and Erikson have stressed the role of friendship in helping the adolescent establish a coherent sense of identity. Close friends serve as a sounding board for adolescents' fantasies and questions about the future. Adolescents often talk to their friends about the careers they hope to follow, the people they hope to get involved with, and the life they expect to lead after they leave

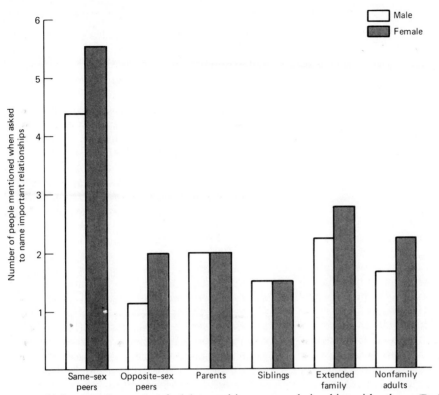

Male
Female

FIGURE 10.3   The frequency of adolescents' important relationships with others. (Derived from Blyth, Hill, and Thiel, 1982)

home. Friends provide advice on a range of identity-related matters—from how to act in different situations to what sorts of occupational and educational paths to pursue. Not surprisingly, adolescents who report having at least one close friendship report higher levels of self-esteem than their peers who do not. However, it is not clear whether intimacy leads to self-esteem or whether adolescents with already high self-esteem are more likely to develop close friendships (Berndt, 1982).

Peers also play an extremely important part in socializing adolescents into the roles of adulthood. This is especially the case when it comes to sex roles. The pressure that adolescents exert on each other to behave in what they deem as sex-appropriate ways is often remarkably strong (Fine, 1981; Schofield, 1981).

As we shall see in the next chapter, friends are also important agents of sexual socialization during adolescence: Teenagers are far more likely to discuss sex with their friends than with their parents. Through close friendships, adolescents learn a great deal about sex and about ways of dealing with members of the opposite sex—lessons that are less likely to be learned from parents or other adults.

Adolescent Loneliness

According to several surveys of high school and college students, late adolescence is one of the loneliest times in the life span. Although we often think of the elderly as being lonely, most studies show that the highest levels of loneliness are reported not by older adults but by adoles-

The Sexes: Are There Sex Differences in Intimacy?

It is often noted that intimacy develops earlier in girls than in boys, that intimate relationships are more common among girls throughout adolescence, and that girls experience more intimacy in their relationships than boys do. In most respects, as we shall see, these observations are absolutely true.

When asked to name the people who are most important to them, adolescent girls—particularly in the middle adolescent years—list more friends than boys do, and girls are more likely to mention intimacy as a defining aspect of close friendship. In interviews, adolescent girls express greater interest in their close friendships, talk more frequently about their intimate conversations with friends, and express greater concern about their friends' faithfulness and greater anxiety over rejection. Girls are more likely than boys to make distinctions in the way they treat intimate and nonintimate friends, and girls appear to prefer to keep their friendships more exclusive, being less willing to include other classmates in their cliques' activities. Intimacy with same-sex friends increases markedly between childhood and early adolescence among girls but does not show a similar increase among boys. Indeed, when self-disclosure is taken as the measure of intimacy, it is clear that boys' friendships with other boys do not approach girls' friendships with other girls until late in adolescence, if at all (Buhrmester and Furman, 1987). Girls also appear to develop intimate relationships with boys earlier than boys do with girls (see figure). And girls appear to be more sensitive than boys and more empathic when comforting friends who are distressed (Berndt, 1981, 1982; Blyth, Hill, and Thiel, 1982; Burleson, 1982; Coleman, 1980; Douvan and Adelson, 1966; Sharabany, Gershoni, and Hofman, 1981). In these very numerous—and very important—respects,

the expression of intimacy therefore appears to be more advanced among adolescent girls than boys.

Yet on some measures, adolescent boys and girls show similar degrees of intimacy in their interpersonal relationships. Although girls are more likely to mention self-disclosure when asked to define close friendship, boys and girls report similar levels of actual self-disclosure in their same-sex friendships and have equivalent degrees of intimate knowledge about their best friends (Diaz and Berndt, 1982; Sharabany, Gershoni, and Hofman, 1981). In group situations, boys and girls are equally likely to help their friends (Zeldin, Small, and Savin-Williams, 1982). Boys and girls report comparable levels of intimacy with their mothers, with the majority of adolescents feeling closer to their mothers than to their fathers, but boys report greater intimacy with fathers than girls do (Blyth and Foster-Clark, in press; Kandel and Lesser, 1972; Youniss and Smollar, 1985). As we noted in Chapter 4, the father-daughter relationship is generally more distant than other parent-child relationships in adolescence.

On the face of it, it appears that intimacy is a more *conscious* concern for adolescent girls than for boys. But this does not mean that intimacy is absent from boys' relationships. "Boys may spend less time in conversations about their emotions and ideas than girls, but they may [nevertheless] acquire a deep understanding of each other by spending time together" (Berndt, 1982, p. 1450). It is important to recognize, therefore, that boys and girls have different *types* of friendships. Consequently, they express intimacy in somewhat different ways. Observations of youngsters on a camping trip, for example, showed that although boys and girls are

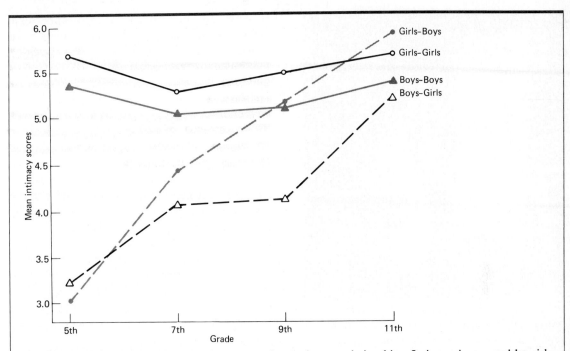

Age differences in reported intimacy in same- and opposite-sex relationships. Intimacy is reported by girls before boys. (Adapted from Sharabany, Gershoni, and Hofman, 1981)

equally helpful when their friends are in need, boys were more likely to help *physically* (perhaps by helping someone set up a tent), but girls were more likely to help *verbally* (by explaining to someone how to put up a tent [Zeldin, Small, and Savin-Williams, 1982]). In general, boys' friendships are more oriented toward shared activities than toward the explicit satisfaction of emotional needs—as is often the case for girls; and the development of intimacy between adolescent males may be a quieter, more subtle phenomenon.

Many theorists have suggested that these sex differences in intimacy are the result of different patterns of socialization (see Blyth and Foster-Clark, in press), with females more strongly encouraged to develop and express intimacy—especially verbal intimacy—than males. Other factors could be at work,

however, that lead to the greater expression of certain types of intimacy in females' than in males' relationships. One set of writers, for example, notes that social pressures on males and females *during adolescence* are quite different and may lead to differences in expressions of intimacy in certain types of relationships (Blyth and Foster-Clark, in press). For instance, theorists have noted that **homophobia**—the fear of homosexuality—is stronger among adolescent males than adolescent females and leads to suppressed intimacy in relationships between adolescent boys (Kite, 1984). One reason adolescent boys may not be as intimate in their friendships as adolescent girls may be that adolescent boys are nervous that expressions of intimacy—even without sexual contact—will be taken as a sign of their sexual orientation.

Studies indicate that lonely adolescents have lower self-esteem than their peers who have at least one intimate friendship. It is not known, however, whether loneliness leads to self-esteem problems or whether adolescents with low self-esteem are less likely to make friends. (Rick Smolan/Stock, Boston)

cents and youth (Cutrona, 1982). Because adolescents may have developed strong needs for intimacy but may not yet have forged the social relationships necessary to satisfy these needs, they may be especially prone to feelings of social isolation. Being with other people who have active social lives can also be hard. Feelings of loneliness are intensified when we feel that the people around us are happier and more socially active than we are. The college student who remains back in his room while the rest of his suitemates are out on a weekend evening is likely to feel lonelier than the student who is in his room but knows that the student next door is having an equally miserable night.

According to an extensive study of loneliness among students at UCLA (Cutrona, 1982), nearly half of all students experience great loneliness during the first months of college. Leaving behind the familiarity of one's family, high school friends, and a hometown boyfriend

or girlfriend, and entering a large, impersonal institution can be a very difficult transition. In an earlier chapter, we noted that half of all students who drop out of college do so during their first year. Loneliness is a contributing factor in many cases. Researchers find that loneliness is equally likely to be experienced by male and female students, by students from different ethnic groups, and by students living in dormitories and in off-campus housing (Cutrona, 1982).

Although many students experience severe loneliness during their first year in college, these feelings subside somewhat for most people by the end of the year. However, a signficant number of students never overcome their initial feelings of social isolation and continue to feel lonely throughout college. This has led researchers to ask what enables some students to adjust to the transition into college and eventually form friendships whereas other students remain lonely.

The results of the UCLA study indicate that the likelihood of overcoming loneliness is strongly related to students' attitudes. Students who remain lonely do many of the same things as students who eventually overcome their loneliness. Both groups are equally likely to go to parties, join clubs, and strike up conversations with strangers in class. Although the groups' behavior does not differ, their attitudes do. Students who eventually form friendships are more likely to have high initial expectations for their social life and to maintain them even though they may be lonely when they first arrive on campus. In contrast, students who remain lonely are likely to adjust their expectations and lower their initial goals. They are more likely to tell themselves that they do not need friends or that their schoolwork is far more important than their social lives. By rationalizing their loneliness, they may increase their chances of staying lonely.

College counselors can help lonely students overcome their feelings not only by teaching them how to be more socially assertive but also by helping them change their beliefs and expectations about social relationships. It may not be sufficient, for example, simply to encourage lonely students to join campus organizations or participate in activities that are likely to bring them into contact with potential friends. Even though they may get out and meet people, the pessimistic attitudes that many lonely students have in social situations may impede their social adjustment.

ADOLESCENT INTIMACY IN OPPOSITE-SEX RELATIONSHIPS

Dating

Opposite-sex relationships during middle and late adolescence may play an important role in furthering the development of intimacy, although there are surprisingly few studies of how adolescents are affected by their boyfriends or girlfriends. Sullivan believed that establishing intimate relationships with peers of the opposite sex was the chief developmental task of middle and late adolescence. The capacity for intimacy, which initially develops out of same-sex friendships, eventually is brought into cross-sex relationships. In some senses, then, Sullivan viewed relationships between boyfriends and girlfriends as a context in which intimacy is *expressed* rather than learned.

Some theorists have speculated that this view may be more accurate for females than for males. In American society, boys are not encouraged to develop the capacity to be emotionally expressive, particularly in their relationships with other males. During middle adolescence, as we have seen, girls may be better than boys at certain types of intimacy—self-disclosure and interpersonal understanding, for example. Girls, therefore, are more likely than boys to enter into relationships capable of being intimate and eager for emotional closeness. Some studies of early sexual relationships confirm this idea: For adolescent girls, early sexual relationships are far more likely to involve love, emotional involvement, and intimacy. For this reason, some writers have suggested that girls play an important role in teaching boys how to be more open, more sensitive, and more caring (Simon and Gagnon, 1969). In other words, whereas for girls cross-sex relationships may provide a context for further *expression* of intimacy, for boys they may provide a context for the further *development* of intimacy. This notion is consistent with the finding, discussed earlier, that opposite-sex relationships may play a more important role in the development of intimacy among boys than among girls, who may develop and experience intimacy earlier with same-sex friends (Buhrmester and Furman, 1987).

There is a big difference between the sort of learning that takes place in a long-term, intimate relationship between two people and the lessons that are learned through casual dating. Dating is a well-established social institution in American adolescent life. Most adolescent girls begin dating around age 13 or 14, and most boys between ages 14 and 15. Although early maturers begin dating somewhat earlier than late maturers (Simmons and Blyth, 1987), age norms within the adolescents' school are more important in determining the age at which dating begins than is the adolescent's level of physical development. In other words, a physically immature 14-year-old who goes to school where it is expected that 14-year-olds date is more likely to date than a physically mature 14-year-old who lives in a community where dating is typically delayed until 16 (Dornbusch et al., 1981). Sexual behavior, however, as we shall see in the next chapter, is more strongly influenced by biological development (Udry et al., 1985). By the age of 16, more than 90 percent of adolescents of both sexes have had at least one date, and during the later years of high school, more than half of all students average one or more dates weekly. Only 15 percent of high school students date less than once a month. About 75 percent of high school students have become steadily involved with someone else by the end of high school (Dickenson, 1975).

Given the prevalence of dating among contemporary adolescents, it is almost embarrassing to say that we know virtually nothing about the

The role of dating in the development of intimacy is not entirely clear. Recent studies indicate that boys may learn more about being intimate from girls than vice versa. (Hazel Hankin)

impact or significance of dating relationships for adolescent development. In particular, the role of *dating* in the development of intimacy is not at all clear. Some young people—especially boys—may learn how to be more intimate through dating. But for the majority of young people, dating appears more likely to foster superficiality, rather than self-disclosure; shallow sociability, rather than genuineness; and the avoidance of real closeness (Douvan and Adelson, 1966). All in all, "pseudointimacy" is as likely an outcome of dating as is intimacy. Why is this so?

At least in American society, dating is highly ritualized, and a premium is placed on physical attractiveness rather than on other, perhaps more important, attributes (Walster et al., 1966). On dates, young people are apt to follow fairly rigid "scripts," adhering closely to conventional and stereotyped social roles, particularly during early and middle adolescence. It is not until adolescence that dating relationships begin to be characterized by a level of emotional depth and maturity that can be described as intimate (Douvan and Adelson, 1966). But even among college juniors and seniors, intimate dating relationships may be fairly rare. Less than one quarter of the male or female students interviewed in studies of psychosocial development were judged as having relationships that were truly intimate. More than half either had relationships that were stereotyped and shallow, excessively (and unhealthily) dependent, or they had no close relationships at all (Levitz-Jones and Orlofsky, 1985; Orlofsky, Marcia, and Lesser, 1973).

"Dating" during adolescence can mean a variety of different things, of course, from group activities that bring males and females together (without much actual contact between the sexes); to group dates, in which a group of boys and girls go out jointly (and spend part of the time in couples and part of the time in large groups); to casual dating in couples; to serious involvement with a steady boyfriend or girlfriend. More adolescents have experience in mixed-sex group activities like parties or dances than dating, and more have experience in dating than in having a serious boyfriend or girlfriend (Tobin-Richards, 1985).

One reason that we may not know very much about the impact of dating on adolescent development is that researchers have not paid enough attention to differences among various types of dating activities. There is some evidence, for example, that especially for girls, it may be important to differentiate between group versus couple activities in examining the impact of dating on psychological development. Evidently, participating in mixed-sex activity in group situations—going to parties or dances, for example—may have a positive impact on the psychological well-being of young adolescent girls, while serious dating in couples may have a more negative effect (Tobin-Richards, 1985).

The reasons for this are not entirely clear, but researchers believe that pressures on girls to engage in sexual activity when they are out alone on dates or involved with a steady boyfriend may have a negative impact on their mental health (Simmons and Blyth, 1987). Although boys may feel peer pressure to become sexually active, this may be a very different sort of pressure—with very different consequences—from what girls feel. Because boys generally begin dating at a later age than girls—and date people who are younger rather than older—beginning to date in couples may be less anxiety-provoking for the adolescent boy, who has the advantage of a few additional years of "maturity," than for the adolescent girl.

Given the generally high level of superfi-

How to Go on a Date

Intimacy between adolescent males and females is slow to develop, and early dating experiences can be tortuous for tongue-tied teenagers, as Delia Ephron illustrates:

GIRL: Look around the restaurant at the other couples. Wonder if people are looking at the two of you as a couple. Hope that they are.

BOY: Out of sight, under the table, wipe finger on pants. Did anything come off? Look down, then look up quickly to see if your date had any idea what you were doing. Smile at her.

GIRL: Stop meeting his eye. Look down at your paper placemat and fold the edge of it over and over.

BOY: Bang the bowl of a spoon with your fork to try to flip it into the air. Notice what you are doing and stop. Put down fork and try desperately to think of something to say.

GIRL: Run your finger along the edge of the placemat, tracing its rim. Appear to be fascinated by the rim. Appear to study its every curve and turn while you worry—I can't think of anything to say. I knew this would happen. I knew it, I knew it, I knew it!

BOY: You know you heard a joke last week in school—now what was it? Who told it to you? Oh yeah, him. What was it? Put fork down. Try to remember. Pick it up, you can't remember, put it down, put hands in lap, put hands back on table, pick up knife and twirl it. What was it?

GIRL: Stop studying the placemat and instead look curiously and intently around the restaurant. Scrutinize the people at the next table. Scrutinize the pictures on the walls. Pray: Please God, let me think of something to say. Please, I'll do anything, just let me think of something. Oh, this is unreal! I knew that this would happen. I knew it and I was right! Oh God, please!!! I'll never ask for anything else, just let me have this, please. This is awful. This is the worst! Suppose the entire rest of the date goes by and I can't think of anything. Suppose I have to sit here in silence. I'll die, I'll absolutely die. Oh God, please!!!!!!

Source: Delia Ephron, *Teenage Romance* (New York: Viking, 1981), pp. 79–81.

ciality operating in most adolescents' dating relationships, it comes as no surprise that early and intensive dating—for example, becoming "seriously involved" before age 15—has a somewhat stunting effect on interpersonal development. This is probably true for both sexes, but researchers have focused primarily on girls, because boys are less likely to begin serious dating quite so early. Compared with their peers, girls who begin serious dating early are more socially immature, more superficial, and less imaginative (Douvan and Adelson, 1966).

This is not to say that dating is not a valuable source of interpersonal experience for the adolescent. Adolescent girls who do not date at all show signs of retarded social development, excessive dependency on their parents, and feelings of insecurity (Douvan and Adelson, 1966), and adolescent boys who date and go to parties regularly have a stronger self-image and report greater acceptance by their friends (Tobin-Richards, 1985). It is not clear, of course, whether a moderate degree of dating *leads to* higher levels of social development or whether more socially advanced adolescents are simply more likely to date and go to parties. Nonetheless, it does seem that for girls in particular, *early* and *intensive* involvement with a boyfriend may do more harm than good. All in all, a moderate degree of dating, with serious involvement delayed until late adolescence, appears to be the most potentially valuable pattern. Perhaps adolescents need more time to develop the capacity to be intimate through same-sex friendships and less pressured group activities before they enter intensively into the highly ritualized and not very intimate relationships encouraged through dating.

During late adolescence, many partners move in with each other without being married. The prevalence and social acceptability of living together outside of marriage—once considered scandalous in most circles—increased dramatically during the 1960s and 1970s and by the early 1980s was a familiar, if perhaps even commonplace, part of the American social landscape (Bureau of the Census, 1985). Indeed, in many segments of the young adult population, moving in with a boyfriend or girlfriend is now seen as yet another stage in the development of a relationship—somewhere between going steady and marriage.

Despite their valiant efforts, researchers have failed to uncover anything distinctive, much less remarkable, about couples who live together without being married (Macklin, 1978). Interactions between nonmarried partners living together look very much like interactions between married partners, with the main exception being that married partners are more likely to pool their financial resources (Schwartz and Blumstein, 1983). Answering the big question— Does living together before marriage make for a better or worse marriage?—has proven to be elusive. In general, studies show that living together has virtually no impact on long-term marital adjustment or marital stability (Macklin, 1978). One study did show, however, that during the *first year* of marriage, individuals who had *not* lived together previously reported getting along better than their counterparts who married after living together (Watson, 1983). The reason: Couples who had lived together previously probably enjoyed their psychological honeymoon before getting married.

Breakups Before Marriage

"For all the concern with the high incidence of divorce in contemporary America," wrote psychologists Charles Hill, Zick Rubin, and Letitia Peplau, "marital separation accounts for only a small proportion of the breakups of intimate male-female relationships among American couples. For every recorded instance of the ending of a marriage, there are many instances, typically unrecorded, of the ending of a relationship among partners who were dating or 'going together'" (1979, p. 64). Surprisingly, very few studies of breaking up have been conducted, despite its obvious significance to the parties involved. One exception is an extensive study of over 100 breakups of college couples.

Hill, Rubin, and Peplau followed 231 cou-

Between 1960 and 1970, the increase in the number of unmarried couples living together was phenomenal. And the trend toward unmarried cohabitation continued at an even more dramatic rate during the 1970s. (Ellis Herwig/Stock, Boston)

ples in the Boston area over a period of two years. Questionnaires covering a wide range of psychological and social topics were completed by both members of each couple several times over the course of the study. By the end of the two-year period, 103 couples (45 percent of the original group) had broken up, the average amount of time that these relationships had lasted was 16 months.

On the basis of the questionnaires completed at the beginning of the study, could the breakups have been predicted in advance? According to the results of this study, a variety of factors considered together could significantly predict which relationships would eventually break up and which ones would remain intact. Couples who remained together reported higher levels of intimacy and love to begin with, were equally committed to each other (rather than

one person being significantly more involved than the other), and were highly similar on such characteristics as age, educational plans, SAT scores, and physical attractiveness. Similarity of attitudes, religion, and social class (as assessed by parents' education levels) were *not* good predictors of staying together.

Breakups were most likely to occur at three times of the year, reflecting the sensitivity of students' social relationships to the school calendar: May–June, September, and December–January. Evidently, having to make vacation plans, changes in living arrangements, and changes in school plans prompt many couples to reevaluate the status of their relationship.

As the authors point out, there are two sides to every breakup. Although, in the majority of cases, it was possible to identify a "breaker-upper" and a "broken-up-with"—in the sense of who was primarily responsible for ending things—couples did not always agree on who *wanted* to end the relationship: Respondents were biased toward saying that "they themselves, rather than their partners, were the ones who wanted to break up." Moreover, members of a couple often had different perceptions of why the relationship ended. The factors typically mentioned were boredom, differences in interests, and the woman's desire to be independent. Less often mentioned was one of the partners having a romantic interest in someone else.

Contrary to beliefs about women being more romantic than men, this and previous studies provide some evidence that men fall in love more readily than women and that women fall out of love more easily than men. For example, it was more often the woman who ended the relationship, frequently because she had become the less involved partner. And rejected men took breaking up harder than did rejected women—they often could not reconcile themselves to the fact that they were no longer loved and that the relationship had ended. Men also found it more difficult than women to stay friends after the relationship ended.

Why the sex differences? The authors give two interpretations, one economic, the other interpersonal. First, women may take a more practical stance toward relationships, because, "in most marriages, the wife's status, income, and life chances are far more dependent on her husband's than vice versa. . . . For this reason . . . the woman cannot allow herself to fall in love too quickly, nor can she allow herself to stay in love too long with the wrong person. Men, on the other hand, can afford the luxury of being romantic." Second, "the emphasis upon social-emotional matters in women's socialization may lead women to be more sensitive than men to the quality of their interpersonal relationships, both in the present and projecting into the future. . . . Because of greater interpersonal sensitivity and discrimination, it may also be more important for women than for men that the quality of a relationship remain high."

Incidentally, although the song says that "breaking up is hard to do," it is harder on the person being broken up with: "Breaker-uppers" feel considerably less depressed, less lonely, and happier—albeit guiltier—even one year after the breakup.

Adolescent Marriage and Divorce

Most Americans marry for the first time in their middle twenties, with men, on the average, marrying at a somewhat later age than women. In 1986, the median age at first marriage was 25.7 for men, and in 1985 it was 23.3 for women. Generally, from the late 1950s on and particularly during the past fifteen years, the average age at which American men and women first marry has risen steadily, no doubt due to the increasing labor force involvement of young women, the increasing acceptance of cohabitation, higher rates of college enrollment among

FIGURE 10.4   First marriage occurs at a much later age today than it did thirty years ago.

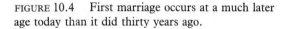

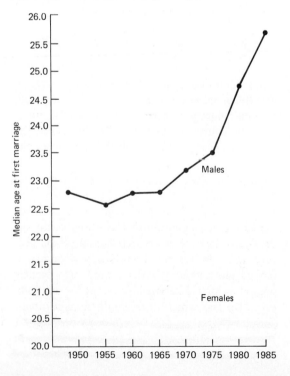

women, and the increasing availability of contraception (see Figure 10.4). As a consequence, the percentage of married teenagers has diminished substantially in recent decades. In 1960 and 1970, one in ten teenage women was married. In 1986, this had declined to one in twenty (Wetzel, 1987).

The trend toward delayed marriage is probably for the better. The younger people are when they marry, the greater their chances of experiencing marital problems and divorce. Indeed, the divorce rate among men who marry in their teens is three times that of men who marry in their late twenties, and the divorce rate of women who marry before turning 18 is four times that of women who marry in their late twenties (Lewis and Spanier, 1979). There are considerable ethnic differences in teenage divorce rates, however. Proportionately more black 18- and 19-year-olds are divorced or separated than Hispanic youths of this age, and more Hispanic youths are divorced or separated than white youths (U.S. Bureau of the Census, 1982).

Why are teenage marriages so susceptible to divorce? The higher rate of marital instability among the young is not surprising, given the array of other factors often characteristic of early marriage. Teenagers are more likely than adults to marry because of premarital pregnancy (the most common reason for marriage during adolescence), they are more likely to be under economic stress, and they are more likely to have low levels of education and, therefore, poor job prospects. On several counts, teenagers who marry are likely to begin married life with problems that require a tremendous degree of coping and that, consequently, do not bode well for marital success. Premarital pregnancy, economic stress, and low levels of education are associated with higher divorce rates at *all* ages. In other words, teenagers' marriages are more likely to end in divorce because teenagers who marry are more likely to have the problems that lead to divorce among couples of all ages.

Not all adolescents who marry get divorced, of course. Adequate financial resources, a long-standing relationship before marriage, having completed high school, and delaying pregnancy until at least one year into married life are among the factors most predictive of marital success (Burchinal, 1965). Not surprisingly, these same factors—education, income, long engagement, and delayed childbearing—are also highly predictive of marital success among adults.

Summary

The onset of puberty, the growth of more advanced forms of social cognition, and the movement of young people into new settings and roles all provoke the development of more intimate relationships during adolescence. Over the course of the adolescent years, individuals become more capable of emotional closeness, and they become more interested in seeking it in their relationships with other people. In addition, the adolescent's social world broadens considerably: Close relationships with peers come to supplement (but not replace) close relationships in the family; and close relationships with opposite-sex peers come to supplement (but not replace) close relationships with friends of the same sex.

The developmental course of intimacy follows a pattern described initially by Sullivan. Usually, adolescents develop the capacity for intimacy through preadolescent and early adolescent relationships with same-sex peers. Intimate, cross-sex relationships develop relatively late during adolescence. Generally, girls' friendships evidence more verbal intimacy than boys' friendships, and opposite-sex relationships may play a special role in the development of intimacy among adolescent males. Although many teenagers begin dating between the ages of 13 and 15, these relationships are not usually very intimate. Rather, early dating relationships typically follow highly ritualized "scripts," in which teenagers are more likely to play stereotypic roles than really be themselves. Although little is known about the impact of dating on development, several studies indicate that early and intensive involvement in dating may, for a variety of reasons, do more harm than good—especially among adolescent girls.

Most of what is known about intimacy during adolescence comes from studies of teenagers' friendships. While the understanding of adolescents' relationships with peers has broadened considerably within the past decade, there remain substantial gaps in what is known about changes in interpersonal closeness during adolescence. In many regards, research on intimacy during adolescence has lagged behind research on identity, autonomy, and sexuality. Why, for example, are there such consistent sex differences in the development of intimacy? How do intimate relationships with parents and siblings change during adolescence? What do teenagers learn about intimacy from boyfriends or girlfriends? And how are changes in intimate relationships linked to changes in the adolescent's evolving sense of self and emerging sense of independence? As research on intimacy continues to expand, it will become possible to provide at least preliminary answers to these questions.

Key Terms

homophobia
intimacy versus isolation
need for adult participation
need for integration into adult society
need for intimacy
need for peers and for peer acceptance
needs for contact and for tenderness

needs for sexual contact and for a loving relationship with a peer of the other sex
projective test
pursuit of satisfaction
pursuit of security
relationship maturity

For Further Reading

ASHER, S., AND GOTTMAN, J. (EDS.). (1981). *The development of children's friendships.* Cambridge: Cambridge University Press. A collection of articles on friendship during childhood and adolescence.

BUHRMESTER, D., AND FURMAN, W. (1987). The development of companionship and intimacy. *Child Development, 58,* 1101–1113. A study of relationships among children and young adolescents.

SULLIVAN, H. S. (1953). *The interpersonal theory of psychiatry.* New York: Norton. Sullivan's most extensive statement of his theory of interpersonal development.

YOUNISS, J. (1980). *Parents and peers in social development: A Sullivan-Piaget perspective.* Chicago: University of Chicago Press. A theoretical examination of the different roles played by parents and peers in the process of socialization.

Sexuality

CHAPTER 11

PREVIEW

1. Sexuality is an important concern during adolescence, not only because of the physical changes of puberty but because of the new social meaning given to sex during this time in the life cycle.

2. Contrary to stereotypes that American society is too permissive when it comes to matters of sex, American society in comparison with many other cultures appears to be relatively restrictive. And, contrary to many adults' fears, most contemporary adolescents are not promiscuous.

3. Premarital sex has become a part of the average teenager's social life. No longer can early sexual activity be dismissed as something limited to an unusual minority of adolescents. As a consequence, society is now faced with a pressing need for earlier and more effective sex education. Fortunately, evaluations of new approaches to sex education are encouraging.

4. Although patterns of sexual activity are similar for males and females, there are important sex differences in the sexual socialization of young people. Early sexual experience is imbued with very different meanings for young men and women. Unfortunately, we know more about initial reactions to sexual experience than we do about the place of sex in the lives of adolescents.

How have teenagers' attitudes toward sex changed in recent decades? Should society be worried about sexual activity among young adolescents, or is teenage sex no more troublesome than many of the other new and adultlike activities that young people engage in? Does sex education prevent unwanted pregnancies, or does it encourage young people to begin sexual activity earlier? Should adolescents have access to contraceptives, and if so, should their parents be told? To what extent is interest in sex at adolescence driven by the hormonal changes of puberty and to what extent is it culturally conditioned?

Perhaps because these issues continue to be so controversial, discussions of adolescent sexuality are often filled with empty rhetoric, rather than solid information. Only recently have systematic and scientific data on the sexual behavior of young people begun to be gathered. Consequently, only in the past few decades has it become possible to separate myths about adolescent sexuality from reality.

In this chapter, we examine adolescent sexuality in contemporary society with an eye toward dedramatizing and demystifying an aspect of adolescent behavior that has received a great deal more media attention than systematic research investigation. In order to present a more accurate picture of adolescent sexuality, we will need to step back and look at sexual behavior and development during adolescence in context—in the context of society and how it has changed and in the context of adolescence as a period in the life cycle and how it has changed.

SEXUALITY AS AN ADOLESCENT ISSUE

Like other aspects of psychosocial development, sexuality is not an entirely new issue that surfaces for the first time during adolescence. Children, of course, are known to be curious about their sex organs and at a very early age derive pleasure (if not what adults would label orgasm) from genital stimulation—as the famous sex researcher Alfred Kinsey pointed out many years ago (Kinsey, Pomeroy, and Martin, 1948). Psychoanalytic theorists have long believed that even infants experience a form of sexual arousal and that sexuality, rather than emerging for the first time at adolescence, surfaces in different forms at different points during childhood. Overt sex play prior to adolescence is common in many societies. Indeed, in some cultures, the sexual stimulation of young children is encouraged and seen as a vital prelude to adult sexual adjustment (Ford and Beach, 1951).

And of course, sexual activity and sexual development continue after adolescence. Although there is little transformation in the form that sexual behavior takes during adulthood, there are nevertheless important changes throughout the adult years in the frequency of sexual activity and in the meaning and importance of sex. Particularly during middle and late adulthood, when concerns over changes in physical appearance and physical attractiveness may be heightened, individuals may readjust how they conceive of and feel about themselves as sexual beings (Neugarten and Datan, 1974). Middle-aged adults, for example, may go through a difficult period in which they wonder whether they are still sexually appealing. Thus while sexual development may be more dramatic and, for this reason, more obvious before adulthood, it by no means ceases at the end of adolescence.

Nonetheless, most of us would agree that adolescence is a fundamentally important time—if not the most important time in the life cycle—for the development of sexuality. There are several reasons for this. Perhaps most obvious is the link between adolescent sexuality and puberty. There is an increase in the sex drive in early adolescence as a result of hormonal changes (Udry, 1987). Although children may be capable of experiencing sexual arousal and pleasurable sexual feelings, they are not as aware as adolescents of sexual impulses or of their own sexual desires. Moreover, it is not until puberty that individuals become capable of sexual reproduction. Before puberty, children are certainly

Although sexuality is undoubtedly an important psychosocial issue during adolescence, sexual concerns do not surface for the first time at this stage in the life span. It is normal for children to be curious about sex and about their sex organs at an early age. (Fredrik D. Bodin/Stock, Boston)

capable of kissing, petting, masturbating, or even having sexual intercourse. But it is not until puberty that males can ejaculate semen or females begin to ovulate, and the fact that pregnancy is a possible outcome of sexual activity changes the nature and meaning of sexual behavior markedly—for the adolescent and for others. What had previously been innocuous sex play becomes serious business when pregnancy is a genuine possibility. Finally, as we saw in Chapter 1, not until puberty do individuals develop the secondary sex characteristics that serve as a basis for sexual attraction and as dramatic

indicators that the young person is no longer physically a child.

But the increased importance of sexuality at adolescence is not due solely to puberty. The cognitive changes of adolescence play a part in the changed nature of sexuality as well. One of the obvious differences between the sexual play of children and the sexual activity of adolescents is that children are not especially introspective or reflective about sexual behavior. Sex during adolescence is the subject of sometimes painful conjecture ("Will she or won't she?"), decision making ("Should I or shouldn't I?"), hypothetical thinking ("What if he wants to do it tonight?"), and self-conscious concern ("Am I good-looking enough?"). As we saw in the previous chapter, one of the chief tasks of adolescence is to figure out how to deal with sexual desires and how to incorporate sex successfully and appropriately into social relationships (Sullivan, 1953a). Much of this task is cognitive in nature, and much of it is made possible by the expansion of intellectual abilities that takes place during the period.

In addition to the influence of the physical changes of puberty and the growth of sophisticated thinking capabilities on sexuality in adolescence, the new social meaning given to sexual and dating behavior at this time in the life cycle makes sexuality an especially important psychosocial concern. Much of this new meaning has to do with the young person's social transition into adulthood. You may have played "doctor" with your friends when you were a little child, but—as you well know—the game meant something quite different then from what it would if you were to play it now. Although younger children may engage in sex play, and although even infants may experience sexual arousal, it is not until adolescence that sexual activity begins to take on the social meaning it will continue to have throughout adulthood. With all due respect to Freud and Kinsey, one must place the sex play of children in proper perspective. Sullivan, for example, despite his psychoanalytic orientation, believed that sex play before adolescence had more to do with simple curiosity than with true sexuality (1953a). Adolescence is a turning point in the development of sexuality because it marks the onset of deliberate sexually motivated behavior that is recognized, both by oneself and by others, as primarily and explicitly sexual in nature.

HOW SEXUALLY PERMISSIVE IS AMERICA?

It is impossible to understand sexuality as a psychosocial phenomenon without taking into account the social milieu in which adolescents learn about and first experience sexual activity. Although we tend to think of sex as something that adolescents are inevitably anxious or concerned about, it is no more true to suggest that sexuality is always riddled with problems during adolescence than it is to say that all adolescents have problems in establishing a sense of identity or in developing a sense of autonomy. Like any other aspect of psychosocial growth, the development of sexuality is determined largely by its context. Of particular importance is the way in which adolescents and children are exposed to and educated about sexuality—a process called **sexual socialization.** Many aspects of sexual socialization are important. Later in this chapter, for example, we will look at the different sexual roles that males and females are socialized to play. For the moment, however, let's raise a different set of questions about the socialization of young people—whether male or female—for adult sexuality.

When did you first learn about sex? How much were you exposed to as a child? Was it something that was treated casually around your house or something that had an air of mystery to it? Was your transition into adult sexual activity gradual or abrupt?

As you know from previous chapters, the passage of adolescents into adulthood is believed to be easier and less stressful when transitions between the two eras are gradual, or continuous (Benedict, 1934). One aspect of the adolescent passage that anthropologists have examined ex-

tensively from this perspective is the transition of young people into adult sexual roles. In *Patterns of Culture* (1934), Ruth Benedict observed that anxiety over sex—thought to be common among teenagers in contemporary society—was absent in many traditional cultures. Margaret Mead's observations of young people in Samoa and New Guinea (1939) provided evidence that sexual development at adolescence was placid, not tumultuous—calm, not stressful—in societies where sexual experimentation was treated openly and casually during childhood and where special attention was not drawn to the adolescent's changed sexual status.

Think about some of the things you learned gradually and casually as a child—learning your way around the kitchen, for example—and imagine how different things would have been had this learning been handled the way most families handle sexual socialization. Suppose from an early age your parents had treated cooking food as if the activity had special, mysterious significance. Suppose you had never been permitted to see anyone actually cooking food, that you had been prohibited from seeing movies in which people cooked food, and that you had been excluded from any discussions of cooking. Nevertheless, imagine that you knew that *something* went on in the kitchen and that there was some special activity that adults did there which you would be permitted, and expected, to do when you grew up. Perhaps you even overheard other kids at school talking about cooking, but you still weren't sure just what the activity was or what one was supposed to do (or not do). Imagine how confused and ambivalent and anxious you would feel.

In many respects, this is how families in contemporary society handle sexual socialization. By being so secretive about sex when children are young and so worried about it when they are adolescents, Mead and Benedict argued, contemporary societies have turned sexuality into a problem for young people. Adolescents today are understandably confused and concerned about sex because their sexual socialization is so discontinuous.

Mead's and Benedict's observations of sexual socialization in traditional societies also indicated that cultures vary considerably in the ways in which they handle the sexual development of children and adolescents. Their observations were further borne out in *Patterns of Sexual Behavior* (1951), perhaps the most extensive study to date of sexual behavior in different cultural contexts. In this enormous undertaking, Clellan Ford and Frank Beach catalogued the sexual socialization and activity of children and adolescents in over 200 societies. The diversity in attitudes and behaviors uncovered by Ford and Beach is quite remarkable. Moreover, it helps to place debates over the sexual "permissiveness" of contemporary America in a somewhat sobering perspective. Drawing on hundreds of studies undertaken by cultural anthropologists over the years, Ford and Beach categorized societies into three groups: restrictive societies, semirestrictive societies, and permissive societies. As we shall see, present-day America is anything but permissive.

Sexual Socialization in Restrictive Societies

In **restrictive societies,** the adolescent's transition into adult sexual activity is highly discontinuous. Pressure is exerted on youngsters to refrain from sexual activity until they either have undergone a formal rite of passage or have married. In many restrictive societies, adolescents are forced to pursue sex in secrecy. Within the broad category of restrictive societies, of course, there are wide variations in the degree of restrictiveness and in the methods used to discourage sexual activity before marriage. For example, in some societies, such as the Cheyenne of Colorado and Montana, the sexual activity of young people is controlled by separating the sexes throughout childhood and adolescence. Boys and girls are not permitted to play together and never associate with each other before marriage in the absence of chaperones. In other societies, such as the Ashanti of the Guinea coast in Africa, sexual activity before the attainment of

adult status is restricted through the physical punishment and public shaming of sexually active youngsters. Other restrictive societies are less severe in their approach and attempt to deter young people from sexual activity primarily by preventing them from accidentally observing it. Among the Kwoma (New Guinea), before having sex parents make sure that their children are asleep (Ford and Beach, 1951).

Sexual Socialization in Semirestrictive Societies

In **semirestrictive societies,** "adult attitudes toward . . . premarital affairs in adolescents are characterized by formal prohibitions that are . . . not very serious and in fact are not enforced" (Ford and Beach, 1951, p. 187). The transition into adult sexual activity is somewhat, but not entirely, discontinuous. For example, among the Alorese of Indonesia, sexual activity among youngsters is formally prohibited; but children playing together often imitate the sexual behavior of their elders, and unless this play is brought explicitly to the attention of adults, little is done about it. Similarly, among the Andamanese (Southeast Asia), "premarital promiscuity is common, and the parents do not object as long as the love affairs are kept secret" (Ford and Beach, 1951, p. 187). In many semirestrictive societies, it is premarital pregnancy, rather than premarital sex, that is objectionable, and unmarried adolescents whose sexual activity has resulted in pregnancy are often forced to marry.

Generally speaking, the sexual socialization of children and adolescents in America has followed either a restrictive or a semirestrictive pattern, depending on the particular historical period and social group in question. At the time of the publication of *Patterns of Sexual Behavior* almost forty years ago, Ford and Beach classified America as restrictive. And some would argue that this classification is still valid today. For the most part, for example, American children are likely to be discouraged from (or even punished for) masturbation; sexual exploration is frowned upon, and sex play is discouraged. Adults rarely mention sexual matters in the presence of children; there even are laws prohibiting children from being exposed to sexual activity on television or in the movies. During adolescence, sexual activity—and in particular, sexual intercourse—between unmarried youth is discouraged. Adults openly try to discourage young people—especially young women—from becoming sexually active by lecturing them on the virtues of virginity, by not openly discussing matters of sex and pregnancy, and by making it difficult for young people to obtain contraception.

At the same time, however, some aspects of sexual socialization appear to place contemporary America more in the semirestrictive category. Adolescent boys and girls are not typically segregated; boys and girls often date without chaperones present; and premarital sex is not generally punished with public humiliation. Adolescents are encouraged to date, although adults know that dating provides a context for sexual activity. And it does seem at times as if we attempt only halfheartedly to enforce prohibitions against premarital sexual activity. Many parents are well aware that young people are sexually active, and they prefer to look the other way rather than restrict children's activities.

Sexual Socialization in Permissive Societies

In **permissive societies,** the transition of young people into adult sexual activity is highly continuous and usually begins in childhood. Whether contemporary America is restrictive or semirestrictive may be subject to debate, but by no stretch of the imagination is it a permissive society—at least in comparison with many of the cultures described by Ford and Beach. Consider, for example, these descriptions of sexual socialization in some of the societies they categorized as permissive:

Among the Pukapukans of Polynesia, where parents simply ignore the sexual activities of young children, boys and girls masturbate freely and openly in public. Among the Nama Hottentot [Southwest Africa] no secret is made of autogenital stimulation in early childhood. Young Trobriand [Melanesia] children engage in a variety of sexual activities. In the absence of adult control, typical forms of amusement for Trobriand girls and boys include manual and oral stimulation of the genitals and simulated coitus. Young Seniang [New Hebrides] children publicly simulate adult copulation without being reproved. . . . Lesu [New Ireland] children playing on the beach give imitations of adult sexual intercourse, and adults in this society regard this to be a natural and normal game. . . .

Most of the societies that permit children free sex play . . . also allow them opportunity to observe adult sexual behavior and to participate in discussions of sexual matters. . . . On Ponape [Caroline Islands] children are given careful instruction in sexual intercourse from the fourth or fifth year. Trukese [Caroline Islands] children receive no formal tutelage, but they learn a great deal by watching adults at night and by asking their elders about sexual matters. . . .

The Lepcha of India believe that girls will not mature without benefit of sexual intercourse. Early sex play among boys and girls characteristically involves many forms of mutual masturbation and usually ends in attempted copulation. By the time they are eleven or twelve years old, most girls regularly engage in full intercourse. . . . Sexual life begins in earnest among the Trobrianders at six to eight years for girls, ten to twelve for boys. Both sexes receive explicit instruction from older companions whom they imitate in sex activities. . . . At any time a couple may retire to the bush, the bachelor's hut, an isolated yam house, or any other convenient place and there engage in prolonged sexual play with full approval of their parents. (Ford and Beach, 1951, pp. 188–191)

ADOLESCENTS' SEXUAL VALUES AND BEHAVIOR

Attitudes Toward Sex

Most social scientists agree that adolescents' attitudes toward sex—and toward premarital sex in particular—became more liberal during the

Although adolescents became more sexually permissive during the 1970s, they did not become promiscuous. Most sexually active teenagers today are likely to be monogamous. (Barbara Alper/Stock, Boston)

late 1960s and 1970s and have become only slightly more conservative since then (Chilman, 1986). But the meaning of this change in attitudes is often misunderstood. Three points must be kept in mind. First, while it is certainly true that teenagers became more tolerant of sexual relations before marriage, it is also true that adults themselves became more permissive of premarital sex during this same time period (Clayton and Bokemeier, 1980). In other words, society as a whole, not simply young people, changed its views toward sex. Second, the changes in attitudes toward premarital sex among adolescents during the late 1960s and early 1970s and the trend toward greater conservatism during the early 1980s cannot be understood apart from many other attitudinal changes that took place during this historical era. Although attitudes toward premarital sex changed, many other attitudes shifted in the same direction (for example, attitudes toward racial equality and women's rights). Thus trends in sexual attitudes are best understood as a part

of a larger attitudinal shift. Finally, although adolescents became more permissive of premarital intercourse, they did not become proponents of promiscuity, "free love," or casual sex. What happened was that being emotionally involved, rather than being legally married, became the important criterion for judging the acceptability of sexual involvement. The vast majority of young people today subscribe to a view that is best characterized as "permissiveness with affection" (Reiss, 1960). Most endorse the view that "It's all right for young people to have sex before getting married if they are in love with each other" (Sorensen, 1973).

Although young people have become more permissive over the past three decades, adolescents clearly do not favor sexual promiscuity or sexual exploitation. Surveys indicate that the majority of adolescents believe that openness, honesty, and fidelity are important elements of a sexual relationship. Many enter into monogamous relationships, in which each partner is expected to remain sexually loyal (Sorensen,

1973). Although an adolescent may have a series of sexual partners over a period of time, he or she is likely to be monogamous within each relationship, a pattern known as **serial monogamy.** And most young people oppose "exploitation, pressure, or force in sex; sex solely for the sake of physical enjoyment without a personal relationship; and sex between people too young to understand what they are getting into" (Conger, 1977a, p. 283).

Another important trend in young people's changing attitudes toward sex has been the decline in popularity of the double standard. In past eras, many people believed that premarital sex was permissible for men but not for women. But most adolescents today believe that males and females should follow the same standards for premarital sexual behavior (Ferrell, Tolone, and Walsh, 1977; King, Balswick, and Robinson, 1977). This shift toward a single standard of sexual conduct, which began during the late 1960s and accelerated during the early 1970s, was related, no doubt, to other large-scale attitudinal shifts in matters related to women's rights and sexual equality.

During the 1970s, a new value system emerged that emphasized individuality and personal independence (Yankelovich, 1982). Over 85 percent of all adolescents believe that "It's right that people should make their own moral code, deciding for themselves what's moral and immoral." Choosing not to be permissive is just as acceptable as behaving permissively: Although most young people do not believe that marriage is a necessary prerequisite for sexual intercourse, very few adolescents believe that individuals who wait until marriage before having sex are foolish (Sorensen, 1973). It appears, then, that what has taken place—not only in sexual values and attitudes but across a range of topics—has been a shift away from conformity to institutionalized norms and toward a perspective that places greater emphasis on the individual's personal judgment and values (Conger, 1975). To put it most succinctly, "Doing your own thing" became the watchword of the 1970s and 1980s. Today, despite stereotypes and par-

ents' concerns to the contrary, most adolescents are neither preoccupied with sex nor anxious about it. Indeed, as we shall see, being sexually active during adolescence—and being comfortable about it—has become part of the normal adolescent experience.

Sexual Behavior

Because of the controversies surrounding premarital intercourse, most of the research conducted on the sexual behavior of adolescents has focused on this single activity. While this is undoubtedly an important topic of concern, it is also wise to remember that a good deal of the sexual activity of adolescents—even sexually experienced adolescents—involves activities other than sexual intercourse, such as necking and petting. Moreover, because most individuals do not begin their sexual careers with intercourse but progress toward it through stages of gradually increasing intimacy, it is important to view intercourse as one activity in a long progression, rather than as an isolated behavior.

The stages of sexual activity. When do individuals first begin expermenting with sex, and is there a fairly common order of activities in which adolescents proceed toward intercourse? One study examined this question by asking older adolescents (ranging in age from 18 to 23) if they had ever engaged in any of nine sexual behaviors, and, if so, to recall the age at which they first experienced each (DeLamater and MacCorquodale, 1979). Figure 11.1 (page 348) presents the average age of experience and the prevalence of each of the behaviors surveyed. Note that these are prevalence rates and not indicators of current activity, since the researchers asked whether an individual had *ever* engaged in the behaviors in question.

Figure 11.1 indicates that the developmental sequence in which males and females engage in various sexual activities is remarkably similar. Necking and petting are more common activities and occur earlier than genital contact or intercourse, which in turn occur earlier than oral sex. The "first base, second base, third base, all the way" sequence of adolescent sexual behavior appears to be the norm for most contemporary American youth. Furthermore, if you compare the figures for boys and girls, you will see that, although boys engage in these activities at a somewhat earlier age than girls, the similarities in age of first experience and in prevalance are far more striking than the differences. Researchers who have asked young adolescents about current sexual activity directly (rather than asking older ones to recall their past experiences), have found a very similar developmental pattern (Vener and Stewart, 1974).

The one exception to this general similarity between males and females in the progression of sexual activity is masturbation. The prevalence of masturbation among adolescent boys is extremely high—nearly universal by the age of 19—but it is only half as prevalent for girls by this age. Moreover, boys typically begin masturbating before age 14, but the age of first masturbation is extremely variable for girls—some begin during early adolescence, but many girls do not begin masturbating until after they have become sexually active with boys (Gagnon, 1972). Thus if we were to place masturbation on a list of activities that includes those activities graphed in Figure 11.1, it would fall at or near the top of the list for males but near the bottom for females.

There is some evidence that the progression of sexual activity shown in Figure 11.1 is more common among white adolescents than among blacks (Smith and Udry, 1985). White adolescents are likely to follow a more predictable pattern that includes more petting and takes longer to move toward intercourse. Blacks, in contrast, are more likely to move toward intercourse at an earlier age and without as many intervening steps. As the authors of one recent study note, "Put simply, a young white virgin who had experienced necking on a date is not likely to immediately proceed to intercourse at the next date; for black adolescents, however, necking may be one of the few heterosexual behaviors engaged in before intercourse (Smith and Udry, 1985, p. 1202). This difference has an important implication for our understanding of adolescent pregnancy. Virtually all adolescents who are virgins find themselves unprepared for contraception when they begin necking, but the more gradual progression of sexual activity among whites is less likely to be affected by this lack of preparation than is the case among blacks. This may place young black adolescents at greater risk for pregnancy.

Adolescent premarital intercourse.

The prevalence of premarital intercourse among contemporary American youth.   Estimates of the prevalence of premarital intercourse among American adolescents vary considerably from study to study, depending on the nature of the sample surveyed and the year and region in which the study was undertaken. Only a few studies have examined premarital intercourse among adolescents younger than age 15. These indicate that, overall, about 17 percent of boys and 5 percent of girls have intercourse by age 15 but that there are vast regional and ethnic differences in the prevalence of sexual activity during the junior high school years (Dreyer, 1982; Miller and Simon, 1980). Thus, while only 12 percent of white males are sexually active by this age, 19 percent of Hispanic males and 42 percent of black males are (Hayes, 1987). The comparable figures for girls are 5 percent, 4 percent, and 10 percent, respectively. As noted earlier, the prevalance of early sexual activity is extremely culturally variable, and such variability is apparent even within American society.

Data from the 1983 National Longitudinal Survey of Youth provide perhaps the best estimate of the prevalance of sexual activity among American adolescents today. The data on the age of first intercourse are displayed in Figure 11.2 (page 348) to show the *cumulative* percentage of sexually experienced adolescents at each age. As you can see, at all ages, boys are more likely to have had sexual intercourse than girls, and about one-half of all adolescents have had

The Sexes: The Influences of Hormones and Friends on Adolescent Sexual Behavior

We noted earlier that increased interest in sex at adolescence is likely to have both biological and social causes. Specifically, adolescents are thought to become interested in sex in part because of increases in sex hormones at puberty and in part because sexual activity becomes accepted—even encouraged—in their peer group. But is one set of factors more important than the other? One recent series of studies, by J. Richard Udry and his colleagues (Smith, Udry, and Morris, 1985; Udry, 1987; Udry, Talbert, and Morris, 1986) suggests that a fuller understanding of adolescent sexual behavior comes from looking at biological and social influences *in interaction* rather than at either set of influences alone. However, the way in which hormones and friends influence sexual behavior at adolescence appears to be different for males than females.

According to Udry's studies, boys' and girls' initial interest in sex is influenced primarily by the surge in certain hormones—**testosterone,** to be specific—at puberty. Adolescents with higher levels of androgens (testosterone is an androgen) are more likely than their peers to report masturbating, thinking about sex, and planning to have sexual intercourse within the next year. This hormonal change therefore appears to increase adolescents' interest in sex and in their arousal when exposed to sexual stimuli.

Motivation to have sex is one thing; becoming sexually active is another. How important is the rise in testosterone levels at puberty in determining the onset of sexual intercourse? The answer appears to differ in boys and girls. Among boys, but not girls, the increased level of androgens is directly related to the likelihood of their being sexually active. Younger boys who were more mature biologically were more likely to be sexually active than older boys whose hormone levels were lower. Boys' sexual behavior is not *entirely* dependent on their hormone levels, however. The studies also found that boys who are more popular with girls in their school are more likely to initiate sex early than are boys who are less popular with girls. Although there is also some evidence that boys whose friends are sexually active are themselves more likely to be involved in sex, this seems more to do with hormones' influences than with friends' influence. Boys tend to have friends who are at a similar level of pubertal development and therefore may be more likely to have high testosterone levels and be sexually active. All in all, the evidence

intercourse by their eighteenth birthday—about the time of high school graduation. The figure also shows that the sex difference in the age of beginning sexual activity is more pronounced among young than older adolescents.

As you can see from Figure 11.3 (page 349), however, there are substantial ethnic differences in age of sexual initiation. We noted above that black adolescents are more likely to begin sexual activity earlier than other adolescents and to progress toward intercourse more quickly. This

is readily apparent from Figure 11.3, which shows the cumulative percentage of sexually active adolescents at each age, separately for white, black, and Hispanic youth. These data indicate that black adolescents are much more likely to have had sexual intercourse at each age and that ethnic differences in the ages at which sex begins are most dramatic early in adolescence. Studies also indicate that rates of sexual activity are higher among economically disadvantaged youth, in all ethnic groups.

provided in these studies indicates a very strong biological influence on the sexual behavior of adolescent boys.

As you know from the earlier chapter on biological development during adolescence, androgens, including testosterone, contribute to increases in boys' sex drive as well as to the development of secondary sex characteristics like facial hair. Because of this, it is difficult to determine whether increases in androgens lead to increased sexual activity because of the increased sex drive (which may make boys with higher testosterone levels *want* to have sex more) or because of changes in their physical appearance (which may make them more attractive to girls). In girls, however, although androgens are responsible for increases in the sex drive, a different set of hormones—estrogens—are primarily responsible for changes in appearance, including breast development. Because of this, it is possible to study whether increased interest in sex among adolescent girls is more influenced by increases in sex drive or by changes in physical appearance (and, presumably, their sexual attractiveness to boys). Thus far, the answer appears to be both, although the effects of high androgen levels in girls seem to be stronger than the effects of changes in physical appearance.

Despite the effects of hormones on girls' sex drive, though, Udry's studies show that social factors are far more important in influencing girls' involvement in sexual inter-course than boys'. Although increases in androgens lead to increased interest in sex among girls, whether this interest is translated into behavior depends on their social environment. Among girls with high levels of androgens, those who have sexually permissive attitudes and friends who are sexually active are likely to engage in intercourse. But girls whose social environment is less encouraging of sex—even girls with high levels of androgens—are unlikely to be sexually active. In other words, whereas hormones seem to have a direct and powerful effect on the sexual behavior of boys, the impact of hormones on the sexual behavior of girls seems to depend on the social context in which they live.

To what can we attribute this sex difference? Udry hypothesizes that boys develop in an environment that is more uniformly tolerant and encouraging of sexual behavior than girls do. In this environment, all boys need is the jolt that the increase in androgens provides in order to become sexually active. For girls, however, the environment is more varied. Some girls develop within a context that permits or even encourages sexual activity; other do not. Although the increase in androgens also provides a jolt to the sexual motivation of the adolescent girl, if she develops within a context that places social controls on sexual activity, this hormonal awakening will not be translated into sexual experience.

There is a large difference, of course, between having intercourse once and being sexually active on a regular basis—a distinction that seems to get lost in discussions of sexual activity among youth. How frequently do teenagers have intercourse? The average sexually experienced high school girl has sexual intercourse between two and three times each month. However, about 15 percent of the high school–aged girls who report having had sexual intercourse have done so only once (Zelnick, Kantner and Ford, 1981). Interestingly, although black youngsters generally begin sexual activity at an earlier age than their peers, sexually active black teenagers have intercourse less frequently than other sexually active adolescents (Hayes, 1987). Among sexually experienced college students, only half have intercourse regularly (DeLamater and MacCorquodale, 1979). There also is little evidence that young people are sexually promiscuous: According to the national study discussed earlier, the majority of teenage respondents who

Nine Sexual Behaviors	Male				Female			
	Student n = 509		Nonstudent n = 262		Student n = 476		Nonstudent n = 401	
	Percent of respondents aged 18 to 23 who have done this	Age at first experience	Percent of respondents aged 18 to 23 who have done this	Age at first experience	Percent of respondents aged 18 to 23 who have done this	Age at first experience	Percent of respondents aged 18 to 23 who have done this	Age at first experience
Necking	97	14.2	98	13.9	99	14.8	99	14.9
French kissing	93	15.3	95	15.1	95	15.8	95	16.0
Breast fondling	92	15.8	92	15.5	93	16.6	93	16.6
Male/female genitals	86	16.6	87	16.3	82	17.2	86	17.5
Female/male genitals	82	16.8	84	16.7	78	17.4	81	17.8
Genital apposition	77	17.1	81	16.8	72	17.6	78	17.9
Intercourse	75	17.5	79	17.2	60	17.9	72	18.3
Male oral/female genitals	60	18.2	68	17.7	59	18.1	67	18.6
Female oral/male genitals	61	18.1	70	17.8	54	18.1	63	18.8

FIGURE 11.1   The age of first experience and prevalence rates for various sexual behaviors are very similar for males and females and for students and nonstudents. (Derived from DeLamater and MacCorquodale, 1981)

had engaged in premarital intercourse had had only one sexual partner, and fewer than 10 percent had had more than three (Zelnick, Kantner, and Ford, 1981). Consistent with their attitudes toward premarital sex, teenagers' sexual behavior is not promiscuous.

FIGURE 11.2   About half of all adolescents today have had sexual intercourse by age 18. Boys generally become sexually active at an earlier age than girls. (Hayes, 1987)

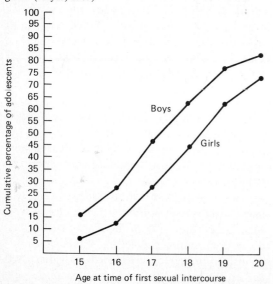

Cumulative percentage of adolescents

Age at time of first sexual intercourse

Changes in patterns of adolescent premarital intercourse.   We noted earlier that attitudes toward premarital intercourse during adolescence have become increasingly liberal since the mid-1960s and became especially so during the early 1970s. Not surprisingly, accompanying this shift in attitudes has been an equally noteworthy shift in the actual prevalance of adolescent premarital sex. The major changes have not been in behaviors such as necking and petting, but in the incidence and prevalence of intercourse among teenagers (Vener and Stewart, 1974). Presumably, teenagers have long distinguished between intercourse and other sexual activities in their values and actions, and what has shifted during the past three decades has been their stance specifically toward intercourse.

Three trends are of special interest. First, the overall percentage of American adolescents—of all ages—who have engaged in premarital sex accelerated markedly during the early 1970s but declined somewhat during the early 1980s, especially among black youth (Hayes, 1987; Ventura, 1984). For example, the proportion of high school youth who have had premarital intercourse rose from about 20 percent before the mid-1960s, to about 35 percent during the early 1970s, to approximately 50 percent in the late 1970s, and is about 40 per-

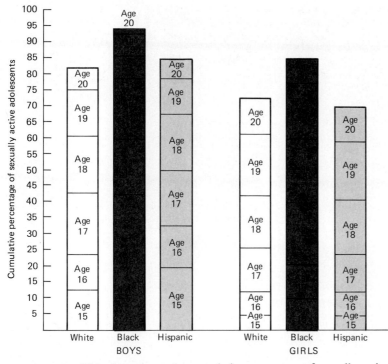

FIGURE 11.3   This chart shows the cumulative percentage of sexually active adolescents at various ages, by sex and ethnicity. (Hayes, 1987)

cent today (Hayes, 1987). Among college students, the increase has been equally notable, but it occurred primarily during the period 1966–1973, when the prevalence rate rose from about 40 percent to about 75 percent; changes in the prevalence of premarital sex among college students since then have been less dramatic (Dreyer, 1982).

Second, the median age at which adolescents first engage in intercourse declined during this same time period. For example, in 1971, the average age at first intercourse was 16.4 years. By 1976, this had declined to 16.1 years. As we shall see in a later section, these figures are important to consider in discussions of sex education, because they indicate that programs which do not begin until the later years of high school may be too late for a substantial number of young people. Indeed, as of 1982, one-third of adolescent girls living in metropolitan areas

had had sexual intercourse before turning 16 (Zelnick, Kantner, and Ford, 1981).

Finally, the greatest recent increases in prevalence of premarital intercourse have been among white females. Before 1966, there were substantial gaps between boys and girls and between black females and white females. As Figure 11.4 shows, since about 1965 the proportion of sexually experienced high school males has doubled, but the proportion of sexually experienced high school females has *more than quadrupled*. Among college students, the proportion of boys who have had premarital intercourse has increased by 36 percent since 1965; for girls, the increase has been a remarkable 300 percent (Dreyer, 1982). As noted earlier, sex differences in rates of premarital intercourse today are minimal.

A similar, though less dramatic, picture of change emerges when we look at the prevalence

About 50 percent of American young people have had sexual intercourse by the time of high school graduation. By the end of college, about 80 percent are sexually experienced. (Joel Gordon)

of premarital intercourse among black and white teenage women. Between 1971 and 1976, the prevalence of premarital intercourse among black 15- to 19-year-old females increased by 19 percent. But during this same time period, there was a *41 percent increase* in the proportion of sexually experienced white girls of the same age (Zelnick, Kantner, and Ford, 1981). Between 1976 and 1982, however, the percentage of black 15- to 19-year-olds who are sexually experienced declined, while the comparable percentage among white teenagers continued to increase. Thus rates of premarital intercourse in different subgroups of American adolescents have converged with the passing of time.

Adolescent sexual behavior in perspective. What are we to make of these trends? First, it is essential to note that most social scientists agree that the increase in sexual activity among young people is genuine and not merely due to an increase in people's willingness to report that they have been sexually active. Changes in pat-

terns of self-disclosure probably have taken place, and these may have affected the results of surveys taken at different times; but sufficient evidence has been amassed to date to warrant the conclusion that in behavior, and not just in reports, more young people are sexually active, and more are sexually active at earlier ages than at any other time in the country's recent history. Whether adults approve or not, sexual activity has become a part of the *normal* American teenager's life.

Nevertheless, it is important to understand these trends for what they really are. Although many parents, educators, and other adults are alarmed and concerned about sexual activity among the young, it is clear that for most adolescents, sexual involvement is accompanied by affection, emotional involvement, and commitment to a relationship and that by no stretch of the imagination can the majority of today's young people be described as promiscuous or morally lax in matters of sex.

Although it is interesting to speculate on

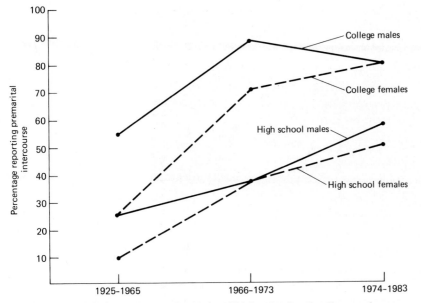

FIGURE 11.4   Changes in the percentage of high school and college males and females who have experienced sexual intercourse in three historical eras. (Derived from Dreyer, 1982, and Hayes, 1987)

the causes of these changes in adolescents' sexual behavior—the increased availability of the birth control pill, the overall liberalization of social attitudes, and the earlier age of puberty have all been suggested—the more pressing issue is how society ought to react to the changed nature of sex during adolescence. Premarital sex is not limited to males, to minority youngsters, or to adolescents with emotional problems. It is a part of life for the average teenager. The longer we ignore this—by failing to provide adequate sex education, by limiting the accessibility of effective contraception, and by not dealing with the issue squarely—the more difficulties society, and young people in particular, will face.

Psychological and Social Characteristics of Sexually Active Adolescents

For many years, researchers studied the psychological and social characteristics of adolescents who engaged in premarital sex. During an era when such activity was relatively rare, it made sense to try to find out which teenagers were more likely to be sexually active. These early studies, as psychologist Philip Dreyer notes, suggested that

for boys sexual activity is often part of a larger pattern of adolescent rebellion, rejection of parental controls, aggressive acting out, alienation from school, and association with older peers who flaunt their sexual experience as a badge of masculinity. For young adolescent girls, on the other hand, sexual activity is part of a larger pattern of low self-esteem, feeling rejected and not loved at home, passive dependent longing for nurturance, disinterest in school, and association with an older boyfriend who provides the assurance and affection which the girl lacks (1982, p. 575).

However, a very different picture emerges today:

As sexual activity becomes increasingly popular among teenagers, these large group images of the

The percentage of American adolescents having premarital sex increased dramatically during the early 1970s. Today, adolescents become sexually active at a much earlier age than was the case previously. (Joel Gordon)

rebellious, aggressive boy and the passive, insecure girl, both of which perpetuate the old notion that sex is not part of the well-adjusted, happy teenager's life, are increasingly inaccurate and misleading. To a greater and greater extent, as the percentages of sexually active youth indicate, sexual activity is becoming part of the teenage experience and is being experienced by all types of young people, not just those who use sex as a way to express personal frustrations or to meet dependency and security needs (Dreyer, 1982, p. 575).

Several recent studies support the contention that sexual activity during adolescence is decidedly *not* associated with low self-esteem, fatalistic attitudes, or psychological disturbance. One study, for example, showed that adolescents who became sexually active earlier than their peers had levels of self-esteem and life satisfaction similar to that of other adolescents (Jessor et al., 1983). Another study indicated that unmarried girls who became pregnant were more likely to have high self-esteem and strong feelings of efficacy than the reverse (Robbins, Kaplan, and Martin, 1985). It does seem to be the

case, however, that early sexual activity is associated with a more general attitude and behavioral profile that includes involvement with drugs and alcohol, a low level of religious involvement, tolerance of deviant behavior, a lower value on academic achievement, and a higher orientation toward independence (Jessor et al., 1983).

Researchers also have asked whether adolescents who become sexually active earlier than their peers have different family histories than other adolescents. In general, studies have not supported the widely held view that monitoring by parents and communication between parents and children have a strong impact on adolescent sexual behavior (Moore et al., 1986; Newcomer and Udry, 1984). That is, in general, adolescents whose parents keep close tabs on them or who discuss sex with them are neither more nor less likely to be sexually active. Instead, it appears that, for reasons yet unknown, the adolescent's family structure is important. In general, adolescents whose parents are in the process of divorcing as well as girls who live in single-parent households—regardless of when (or if) a divorce took place—are more likely to be sexually active than their peers (Newcomer and Udry, 1987). One hypothesis, consistent with what we saw in the earlier chapter on the adolescent's family, is that parental divorce temporarily disrupts the adolescent's behavior, leading him or her into early involvement with sex, drugs, alcohol, and minor delinquency.

Why should growing up in a single-parent home affect girls' sexual behavior more than that of boys, however? At least two possibilities exist. One possibility, which we encountered earlier in this chapter, is that social influences on girls' sexual behavior are in general more varied than those of boys. Boys' parents may not attempt to exert great control over their sexual activity regardless of whether the household has one parent or two. Consequently, boys from one- and two-parent homes may be equally likely to be sexually active. Girls' sexual behavior, in contrast, may be more subject to parents' controls. Single-parent homes are typically more permissive than two-parent homes (Dornbusch et al., 1985), and this difference in control may be enough to make a difference in girls' sexual activity. Because monitoring appears to have little impact on adolescent sexual activity, however, this explanation is not sufficient. An alternative possibility is that single-parent mothers are more likely to be dating than married mothers and in so doing, may inadvertently be role models of sexual activity to their adolescents. To the extent that this modeling effect is stronger between parents and children of the same sex, we would expect to find a more powerful effect of growing up in a single-parent home on the sexual behavior of daughters than sons.

Adolescents' Use of Contraceptives

One of the reasons for the great concern of adults over the sexual activity of adolescents is the failure of many sexually active young people to use birth control measures regularly. According to data collected in 1982, only half of all young women reported having used some method of birth control the first time they had intercourse, and nearly one-sixth of all 15- to 19-year-old sexually active women reported never having used any contraception. About 40 percent of sexually active teenagers use birth control sporadically. While these figures are still worrisome, they show a clear improvement in adolescent contraceptive behavior during the last decade. In 1976, for example, nearly two-thirds of sexually active young women reported that they had not used contraception during their first intercourse, and more than 35 percent reported never using birth control. In general, older adolescents are more likely to use contraception than younger ones, and adolescents are more likely to use contraception when they plan in advance to have sex than when intercourse is unplanned (Hayes, 1987).

Among adolescents who do use contraception, the most popular method is by far the birth control pill, which is used by approximately 60 percent of sexually active teenage girls. About 20 percent of girls report that their partner uses condoms, and an additional 5 percent report using a diaphragm. Withdrawal, a highly ineffective method of preventing pregnancy, unfortunately is still used by a large number of teenagers, as is the rhythm method—a method of birth control that requires more regular menstrual cycling than many teenagers have and more careful monitoring of menstrual cycling than most teenagers are capable of. Other methods, such as the intrauterine device (IUD), are not widely used by teenagers (Hayes, 1987).

Why do so few adolescents use contraception regularly? Social scientists point to several factors. First, for a sizeable minority of adolescents, contraceptives are not readily available—or if they are, young people may not know where to get them. Approximately 15 percent of adolescent girls and 25 percent of adolescent boys reported that they did not use contraceptives when they had sex for the first time because they could not get them (Hayes, 1987). This is likely to be an especially important barrier among younger adolescents, who may feel uncomfortable discussing their sexual activity with parents or other adults whose help or consent may be necessary in order to obtain birth control. Having ready access to a free, confidential family planning service that does not require parents' consent is a strong predictor of whether adolescents will use contraceptives at all or use them consistently (Chilman, 1980).

Second, many young people are insufficiently educated about sex, contraception, and pregnancy. For example, according to one national survey, nearly one-third of all adolescents believe that "If a girl truly doesn't want to have a baby, she won't get pregnant even though she may have sex without taking any birth control precautions" (Sorensen, 1973). Many young people also do not fully understand that the likelihood of pregnancy varies over the course of a woman's menstrual cycle, and more than half mistakenly believe that it is during menstruation that the risk of pregnancy is greatest (Zelnick and Kantner, 1973). At the time of first intercourse, about one-third of all teenagers who do not use contraception fail to do so because they don't know about contraception or didn't think about using contraceptives (Hayes, 1987). Among sexually active teenagers, 20 percent of all girls and more than 40 percent of all boys usually "just trust to luck" that pregnancy will not result from intercourse (Sorensen, 1973). Unfortunately, not very many sexually active adolescents who fail to use contraception remain lucky for very long.

Psychological factors also play a role in adolescents' failure to use contraception. Although it certainly is a misconception that many young women unconsciously want to become pregnant, many young people nevertheless do not recognize the seriousness of pregnancy and take the possiblity lightly (Hayes, 1987). More than 25 percent of non-users report that they or their partners simply did not want to use birth control. From a cognitive perspective, the limited ability of young adolescents to engage in long-term, hypothetical thinking, and their occasionally egocentric tendency to believe that they are immune from the forces that affect others may impede their consideration of pregnancy as a likely outcome of sexual activity. Perhaps most important, many adolescents fail to use birth control because doing so would be tantamount to admitting that they are planfully and willingly sexually active (Cvetkovich et al., 1975). Going on the pill or purchasing a condom requires an adolescent to acknowledge that he or she is having sexual relations. For many young people, this is an extremely difficult admission to make. This may be especially true for young women who feel ambivalent and guilty about sleeping with someone for the first time.

One recent study of "sex guilt" documented the role that emotional factors play in influencing contraceptive use. In this study, college students' sexual behavior, contraceptive use, and feelings of sex guilt were charted between 1973 and 1983. Individuals who feel very guilty about having sex are less inclined to be sexually active, but when they are, they are also less inclined to use effective contraception—perhaps because their guilt inhibits their ability to plan for sex (Gerrard, 1987). When sexual standards become more permissive, as they did during the 1970s, many individuals who would otherwise feel guilty about having sex are drawn into sexual relationships. Unfortunately, their feelings of guilt are not changed by the aura of permissiveness and as a consequence, they have sex without using effective contraception. As attitudes became more conservative, during the early 1980s, the study showed that fewer individuals were sexually active, but those who were used contraception more effectively. Presumably, during more conservative times individuals who feel guilty about sex have enough support to abstain from sexual activity. One lesson from these studies is that inducing feelings of guilt about sex may have different consequences for sexual behavior depending on the prevailing social norms. During conservative periods, the guilt may inhibit sexual activity; during times of liberal attitudes, however, sex guilt may actually increase careless sex.

Taken together, this evidence suggests that there is a great deal that adults can do to improve the contraceptive behavior of adolescents. First, adults can see that contraceptives are made accessible to the young people who feel they need them. Second, adults can provide sex education at an early enough age to instruct young people in the fundamentals of pregnancy and birth control before, rather than after, the adolescents have become sexually active. And finally, parents and teachers can make adolescents feel more free to talk about their sexual interests and concerns, so that young people will be more apt to look at their own behavior seriously and thoughtfully.

Given the statistics regarding contraceptive use by young people, it comes as no surprise to learn that one in every ten American female adolescents, and nearly 30 percent of all American girls who are not virgins, become pregnant before marriage at least once (Zelnick, Kantner, and Ford, 1981). Although contraceptive use has increased somewhat over the past ten years, so has sexual activity among young teenagers, whose contraceptive use is extremely rare. In a later chapter, we look closely at the extent, causes, and consequences of teenage pregnancy.

Homosexual Activity During Adolescence

Few subjects generate as much concern—not only among adolescents but among adults as well—as homosexualitiy. Much of this concern stems from confusion and misinformation about the nature and antecedents of homosexuality. In attempting to separate fact from myth, we need to keep in mind several important distinctions.

First, there is an important distinction between engaging in homosexual activity or having homosexual feelings, on the one hand, and having an exclusive and enduring preference for sexual activity with people of the same sex, on the other. It is not uncommon, for example, for young adolescents to engage in sex play with members of the same sex or to have questions about the nature of their feelings for same-sex peers. Indeed, one study indicated that by age 16, over 20 percent of adolescent boys had engaged in homosexual activity to the point of orgasm (Kinsey, Pomeroy, and Martin, 1984).

But even though many adolescents have such homosexual experiences, nearly all young people—92 percent, in fact—develop an exclusive preference for heterosexual relationships by the end of adolescence. And contrary to myths bout the increasing prevalence of homosexuality in contemporary American society, the proportion has remained at or near this level since the mid-1940s, when researchers began studying the phenomenon (Hunt, 1974).

A second distinction is that between homosexuality as an exclusive preference and homosexuality as an interest that may exist simultaneously with strong heterosexual interests. Many people mistakenly view sexual preference as an "either-or" attribute, with individuals being either exclusively heterosexual or exclusively homosexual. In fact, of the 8 percent of Americans who do not develop an exclusive preference for heterosexual relationships, only one-third are exclusively homosexual in their orientation. Nearly twice as many describe themselves as having *both* heterosexual and homosexual interests (Conger, 1977a).

Finally, a great deal of confusion about homosexuality results because people tend to confuse sexual preference (the extent to which someone prefers heterosexual activity, homosexual activity, or both), sex-role behavior (the extent to which an individual behaves in traditionally "masculine" or "feminine" ways), and gender identity (which gender an individual believes he or she is psychologically). There is no simple connection between an adolescent's sexual preference and his or her sex-role behavior. Thus individuals with strong or even exclusive preferences for homosexual relationships exhibit the same range of masculine and feminine behaviors characteristic of individuals with strong or exclusive heterosexual interests. In other words, exclusively homosexual men (like exclusively heterosexual men) may act in very masculine, very feminine, or both masculine and feminine ways; and the same holds true for exclusively homosexual and exclusively heterosexual women. Along similar lines, individuals with homosexual interests are generally not confused about their gender identity—at least, no more confused than are individuals with heterosexual interests.

Studies of the antecedents of homosexuality generally have focused on two sets of factors: biological influences, such as hormones, and social influences, including the parent-child relationship and early patterns of play. More is known about the development of homosexuality among men than women—the prevalence of homosexuality is much greater among men than women—but the weight of the evidence thus far suggests that an adolescent's sexual preference is likely to be shaped by a complex interaction of social and biological influences (Green, 1980, 1987). Although simple comparisons of hormonal functioning among homosexual and heterosexual adults have not pointed to clear or consistent differences, it appears that *early* biological predispositions may channel some youngsters into patterns of play and social relationships that can lead to the development of homosexuality. Studies suggest that sex hormones may influence preferences for aggressive activities, which, consequently, may be related to preferences for stereotypically masculine or feminine behavior. Thus, for example, boys who are biologically predisposed toward timidity may avoid rough play as young children and gradually come to prefer activities that are more typical of young girls.

These early behavioral preferences may come to affect the parent-child relationship in ways that increase the likelihood of an individual developing a homosexual orientation. Several studies suggest that a higher proportion of homosexuals than heterosexuals report having had problems in their early family relationships and, specifically, in their relationships with their father. The stereotype of the homosexual's father as cold and distant once was rejected as an artifact of poor research designs, which focused exclusively on unhappy or psychologically distressed homosexuals (who, given their psychological distress, might be expected to report disrupted family relationships). But more carefully designed studies have offered at least par-

tial confirmation of this notion. Both male and female homosexuals are more likely than heterosexuals to describe their fathers as distant and rejecting. Whereas male homosexuals are more likely than heterosexuals to report having had close and generally positive relationships with their mothers, female homosexuals are more likely than heterosexuals to describe their mothers as cold and unpleasant (Bell et al., 1981).

It is difficult to conclude that these disruptions in the parent-child relationship are the primary cause of homosexuality, however. Researchers now believe that, at least for many male homosexuals, early, biologically-influenced preferences for feminine behavior may alienate these boys from their fathers and from other boys, and these youngsters may grow up seeking the affection from males that they did not receive as children. One recent study, for example, showed that the majority of young boys who behave like girls—so-called "sissy boys"—grow up to be homosexual adults (Green, 1987). Several other studies also suggest that nonconformity with gender roles during early childhood is an important predictor of adult homosexuality (Bell et al., 1981).

Although these studies point to certain factors that appear more often than not in the early histories of homosexuals, the research evidence does not indicate that *all* individuals who show patterns of gender nonconformity or who have distant relations with their fathers inevitably become homosexual. Nor does research show that all homosexuals have identical developmental histories. For example, while it is true that homosexuals are more likely than heterosexuals to describe their parents in negative terms, not all homosexuals feel this way. Indeed, only about half do, suggesting that a large number of homosexuals had quite positive family relationships growing up. And, of course, many heterosexuals describe their parents in exceedingly negative terms. Similarly, although the majority of boys with persistently feminine behavior preferences may grow up to be homosexual, a substantial number of boys with this preference do not.

Approximately 8 percent of the young adult population is either partially or exclusively gay. Contrary to public opinion, homosexuality is not considered by mental health experts to be a form of psychopathology, an indicator of psychological disturbance, or a condition warranting psychological treatment. (Joel Gordon)

It is important to bear in mind that homosexuality is not considered by mental health experts to be a form of psychopathology, an indicator of an underlying psychological disturbance, or a condition warranting psychological treatment. Perhaps as we begin to understand more about the interplay among biological and social factors that contribute to the development of a homosexual orientation, our attitudes toward homosexuality will change for the better. Indeed, as one expert noted, "Society tends to treat . . . homosexuals as if they had a choice about their sexual orientation, when in fact they have no more choice about how they develop than heterosexuals do" (Marmor, quoted in Brody, 1986, p. 17).

SEX EDUCATION

One part of the sexual socialization of young people is sex education. Adolescents receive information about sex, pregnancy, and contraception in a variety of settings and through a variety of informal and formal means. It is important to distinguish, therefore, between formal and informal education (Spanier, 1976). In many traditional societies, where preparation for adult sexuality is highly continuous, most sex education is done informally by the adolescents' elders. In contemporary society, adults may play a role in the formal sex education of adolescents, but the informal sex education of young people is generally left up to their peers. Indeed, during

Many young people receive some sort of formal sex education through school-based programs. But some experts believe that these classes have been only partially effective because of their emphasis on the biological aspects of sex rather than the psychosocial issues surrounding sexuality. (Alan Carey/The Image Works)

the adolescent years, it is peers—not parents or teachers—who are the leading source of information on sex. In fact, by the time individuals reach adolescence, they are likely to report that they cannot talk freely to their parents about sex (Sorensen, 1973).

Many adolescents receive some sort of classroom instruction on sexual matters—whether through high school health classes, biology classes, classes designated exclusively for the purpose of sex education, or educational programs administered through youth or religious organizations. Such classes and programs, if they are available, are likely to be targeted toward adolescents rather than toward children and preadolescents (Kirkendall, 1981).

Given the important role played by informal sex education in traditional societies, it is unfortunate that so little is known about the processes and consequences of informal sex education among contemporary youth. We do know, however, that the lessons learned from peers and dating partners have considerably

greater impact on the sexual activities of young people than do formal sex education programs.

Until recently, most evaluations of formal sex education programs administered through schools rated them remarkably disappointing (Spanier, 1976). The consensus among experts was that most sex education programs failed because they emphasized the biological over the emotional aspects of sex (and thus did not prepare adolescents for making decisions about sexual involvement), because they came too late in high school (and thus did not reach adolescents before they became sexually active), and because they focused primarily on changing students' knowledge rather than their behavior (and thus did not directly affect patterns of sexual activity or contraceptive use).

A new wave of sex education programs has been developed, and initial evaluations of these programs have been more encouraging. According to a recent review of these programs by a panel of the National Academy of Sciences, sex education courses that focus on increasing youngsters' knowledge about sex, contraception, and pregnancy should begin early and should be combined with courses designed to teach decision-making skills and interpersonal assertiveness. They should teach adolescents the skills they need to resist peer pressure to become sexually active. In addition, the panel recommended that the media take a more socially responsible position and portray sexual relationships and the responsibilities of parenthood more accurately on television and in movies (Hayes, 1987).

The panel also recommended that contraceptive services be expanded for teenagers. Noting that adolescents are often reluctant to seek contraceptives from their physicians and more inclined to use the services of clinics, the experts recommended that sex education programs include clear information on how to use and obtain contraceptives and that communities consider developing school-based clinics in which adolescents can receive information about contraception and obtain contraceptives. Research suggests that the combination of sex education and school-based clinics is more effective in deterring adolescent pregnancy than sex education programs alone (Zabin et al., 1986). Indeed, studies show that increasing adolescents' knowledge about sex has little impact—positive or negative—on their sexual behavior (Hanson et al., 1987).

Sexually Transmitted Diseases

Helping youngsters understand sex, pregnancy, and contraception is an important goal of sex education programs for adolescents. Helping them avoid the risks of **sexually transmitted diseases,** or STDs, is another. STDs—once called "venereal diseases"—are caused by viruses, bacteria, or parasites that are transmitted through sexual contact (Mahoney, 1983). The most common STDs among adolescents are **gonorrhea** (caused by a bacterium), **chlamydia** (caused by a parasite), and **herpes** (caused by a virus). In the cases of gonorrhea and chlamydia, the main symptoms are painful urination and a

discharge from the penis, vagina, or urethra. If untreated, either disease can lead to disorders of the reproductive system and sterility. Antibiotic treatment of gonorrhea and chlamydia is relatively simple, but, unfortunately, many individuals who have these diseases do not have the symptoms, which makes it less likely that they will seek treatment.

The symptoms of herpes are tiny, itching blisters that turn into open sores on the penis, vulva, or cervix. These symptoms are sometimes accompanied by headaches, fever, and pelvic pain. The signs of herpes may appear and then disappear, only to reappear again. Herpes is transmitted through direct contact with open sores and can therefore be transmitted only when symptoms are present. Although there are medications that can be used to relieve the symptoms of herpes, to date there is no cure. The main risks of herpes are increased likelihood of cervical cancer in women, and, during pregnancy, the increased likelihood of miscarrige or damage to the newborn's central nervous system.

During the 1980s, a new and far more serious STD commanded the world's attention: **AIDS** or **Acquired Immune Deficiency Syndrome.** AIDS is transmitted through bodily fluids, especially semen, during sexual intercourse, or blood when drug users share needles. Before information was available about the transmission of AIDS, some individuals were infected through blood transfusions in hospitals. Now hospitals routinely screen blood for the AIDS virus, and this means of transmission is extremely rare today.

AIDS itself has no symptoms, but the AIDS virus attacks the body's immune system, interfering with the body's ability to defend itself against life-threatening diseases like pneumonia or cancer. About 25 percent of all individuals who are infected with the virus develop complications within five years; about half of all people in the United States known to have AIDS have died as a result.

Thus far, the incidence of AIDS in the United States has been concentrated primarily within two groups, homosexual men and drug users who use needles. This does not mean, however, that other individuals are not susceptible to the AIDS virus or that they are somehow protected from its transmission. (In Africa, it is the heterosexual population that is dying from AIDS.) For this reason, many sex education programs around the country have begun to incorporate information on AIDS, and adolescents are being taught how to protect themselves from the virus.

There is still no cure for AIDS, although medical researchers around the world are working furiously on the problem. Most experts note that the best way for sexually active teenagers to protect themselves is by using condoms, the only known protection (other than abstinence) against the AIDS virus. Unfortunately, however, a survey of adolescents in the San Francisco area, a city with a high incidence of AIDS, indicated that while most adolescents knew that AIDS was transmitted through intercourse, only 60 percent were aware that using a condom lowers the risk of getting the disease (DiClemente et al., 1986).

Does Sex Education Encourage Sexual Activity?

Although some adults fear that making sex education more explicit and contraceptives more easily available to adolescents will encourage more sexual activity, studies indicate that this is not the case (Furstenberg et al., 1985; Hanson et al., 1987). In most European countries, where sex is discussed with adolescents more openly and where contraceptives are easier for teenagers to obtain, adolescent pregnancy is much rarer than it is in the United States. Although encouraging youngsters toward celibacy may be morally appealing to some, comparisons of the United States with other industrialized countries indicates that whereas rates of *pregnancy* among American teenagers are far higher than they are among foreign youth, rates of *sexual activity* are no higher (Jones et al., 1985). Thus the problem in contemporary America is not sexual activity

among the young; it is careless, unprotected sexual activity.

THE MEANING OF SEX FOR ADOLESCENTS

It is one thing to describe the extent of sexual activity among adolescents; it is quite another to understand its meaning (Miller and Simon, 1980). Indeed, a great deal more is known about teenagers' attitudes toward sex and about how early and how often adolescents engage in sex than is known about the meaning of sex to young people or how sexual experience affects young people's psychosocial development. It is easy to lose sight of the more human aspects of sex amidst the mountains of statistics on premarital intercourse.

Any discussion of the psychosocial significance of sexual experience during adolescence must be sensitive to the very substantial sex differences in the way in which early sexual activity is experienced. Despite the convergence of males' and females' *rates* of sexual activity, the early sexual experiences of adolescent boys and girls are usually very different in nature and, as a consequence, are imbued with very different *meanings*. In other words, the sexual behavior of males and females may be similar, but the sexual socialization of males and females is quite different.

As noted earlier, the typical adolescent boy's first sexual experience is in early adolescence, through masturbation (Gagnon, 1972). At the outset, then, the sexual socialization of the adolescent boy typically places sex outside of an interpersonal context. To use a distinction offered by John Gagnon (1972), the adolescent male is experienced in matters of sexuality before he moves into the realm of **sociosexuality**— the merging of sexuality into social relationships. Before adolescent boys begin dating, they have generally already experienced orgasm and know how to arouse themselves sexually. For males, the development of sexuality during adolescence revolves around efforts to integrate the

There are substantial gender differences in the way in which early sexual activity is experienced psychologically. For adolescent boys, early sexual relationships are often brief, impersonal, and associated with a sense of achievement. (Rick Smolan/Stock, Boston)

capacity to form close relationships into an already existing sense of sexual capability.

Yet at the time of first intercourse, boys are likely to keep matters of sex and intimacy separate. Boys often have as their first partner someone they describe as a "casual date" or "pickup" (Carns, 1973). Indeed, in one-third of the cases, boys never sleep with their first sexual partner again, and fewer than 25 percent of adolescent boys sleep with their first partner more than five times after their first time together (Simon, Berger, and Gagnon, 1972). Generally, it is the male member of a couple who is likely to initiate sex, and interestingly, the typical male reports more love for a woman who lost her virginity with him than for a woman who lost her virginity with a previous partner. His own loss of virginity, however, has no impact on his feelings of affection in a relationship (Peplau, Rubin, and Hill, 1977). These findings suggest that the early sexual experiences of males are often interpreted not in terms of intimacy and emotional involvement but in terms of achievement, or "scoring." And males typically report that the people to whom they describe their first sexual liaison—generally, male peers—are overwhelmingly approving (Carns, 1973; Miller and Simon, 1980). It is little surprise, when looked at in light of these findings, that the most common immediate reactions among adolescent males to having intercourse for the first time are "excitement" (46 percent), "satisfaction" (43 percent), exhilaration (43 percent), or "happiness" (43 percent) (Sorensen, 1973).

The typical girl's first experience is likely to be very different and likely to leave her feeling very differently as well. Although the majority of adolescent girls masturbate, masturbation is a far less prevalent activity among girls than among boys; it often occurs later in adolescence, sometime after the girl has already experienced sex with a boy; and it is far less regularly practiced. Thus the typical adolescent girl, in contrast to the typical boy, is more likely to experience sex for the first time in an interpersonal relationship. Unlike her male counterpart, then, the adolescent girl begins her sexual career not alone but with someone else. For her, the development of sexuality involves the integration of sexual activity into an existing capacity for intimacy and emotional involvement. The girl's sexual script is one that, from the outset, tinges sex with romance, love, and intimacy.

In addition to this gender difference in the relation between sexuality and sociosexuality, boys and girls encounter a set of social attitudes that differ in a very important way: Despite the gradual erosion of the double standard, society is much more discouraging of sexual activity outside the context of emotional involvement among adolescent girls than boys (Carns, 1973). Because of the possibility of pregnancy, the po-

From J. D. Salinger's The Catcher in the Rye

The sexual socialization of adolescent males often revolves around themes of achievement and "scoring." Yet despite the sexual bravado typically demonstrated by adolescent boys, many of them feel as uncomfortable and anxious about losing their virginity as girls do. Holden Caulfield, the protagonist of J. D. Salinger's classic novel *The Catcher in the Rye,* explains why.

> If you want to know the truth, I'm a virgin. I really am. I've had quite a few opportunities to lose my virginity and all, but I've never got around to it yet. Something always happens. . . . The thing is, most of the time when you're coming pretty close to doing it with a girl—a girl that isn't a prostitute or anything, I mean—

she keeps telling you to stop. The trouble with me is, I stop. . . . I can't help it. You never know whether they really *want* you to stop, or whether they're just scared to hell, or whether they're just telling you to stop so that if you *do* go through with it, the blame'll be on you, not them. . . . The trouble is, I get to feeling sorry for them. I mean most girls are so dumb and all. After you neck with them for a while, you can really *watch* them losing their brains. You take a girl when she really gets passionate, she just hasn't any brains. I don't know. They tell me to stop, so I stop. I always wish I *hadn't,* after I take them home, but I keep doing it anyway.

Source: J. D. Salinger, *The Catcher in the Rye* (New York: Bantam, 1981; orig. pub. 1951), p. 92.

---

tential adverse consequences of premarital sexual activity are far more serious for girls than for boys. For this reason, society monitors the sexual activity of girls more carefully, and girls are more likely to be encouraged to take a cautious approach in matters of sex. Although the "permissiveness with affection" standard is increasingly being applied to both genders, the "affection" criterion is likely to be more stringent for adolescent girls than boys. Even as recently as 1980, more college students believed that it was immoral for a woman to sleep with many men than believed it was immoral for a man to sleep with many women (Robinson and Jedlicka, 1982).

Not surprisingly, then, at the time of first intercourse, the adolescent girl's first sexual partner is likely to be a person she describes as someone she was "planning to marry" or was "in love with" at the time (Carns, 1973; Kallen and Stephenson, 1982). In contrast with men, nearly two-thirds of all young women have sex with their first partner many times thereafter (Simon, Berger, and Gagnon, 1972). There is a social meaning to losing one's virginity that is still today very different for young women and for young men, and women typically report feel-

ing more love for a man if he was their first sexual partner (Peplau, Rubin, and Hill, 1977). After having intercourse for the first time, the typical adolescent girl is more likely to encounter disapproval or mixed feelings on the part of others in whom she confides (generally speaking, peers) than is the typical boy (Carns, 1973). And she is more likely to report feeling "afraid" (63 percent), "guilty" (36 percent), "worried" (35 percent), and "embarrassed" (31 percent) than happy, excited, or exhilarated (Sorensen, 1973). Thus for the adolescent girl, early sexual experience is nearly always tied to emotional involvement and an enduring relationship and, more often than not, complicated by fears of becoming pregnant and ambivalence over the social and moral significance of losing her virginity. Although young women are more likely today than they were fifteen years ago to admit to their friends that they have lost their virginity soon after the event has occurred, boys still are more likely than women to tell their friends soon after having intercourse for the first time because it is easier to do so when the act has not been accompanied by emotional involvement (Kallen and Stephenson, 1982).

According to Sullivan (1953a), one of the

chief psychosocial tasks of adolescence is to integrate sexual activity into a satisfying close relationship. But it is clear that boys and girls approach this task from quite different vantage points. For the boy, the pursuit of sexual experience is tinged with achievement; for the girl, it is tinged with romantic love and intimacy.

Summary

Sexuality is an important concern during adolescence, not only because of the biological changes of puberty but because sexual activity takes on new social meaning during this time in the life cycle. One of the most important developmental tasks of the adolescent years is to incorporate sexuality successfully into close, intimate relationships. This task may be made more difficult in contemporary society by the highly discontinuous nature of sexual socialization.

Concerns about sex education, teenage pregnancy, and adolescent contraceptive behavior have generated emotional arguments about the sexual values and sexual activity of adolescents that are often based on fiction rather than fact. For example, although premarital sex has become more common during the past twenty-five years, young people have not in any way become more promiscuous.

Researchers interested in adolescent sexual behavior have focused primarily on young people's attitudes toward premarital sex and on the prevalence of various sexual activities among young people of different ages. Studies of this sort have made it clear that sexual activity, and specifically sexual intercourse, is now part of the average teenager's life. Accordingly, there is a pressing need for better and more effective sex education for young people. Surveys of adolescents make it clear that premarital sex can no longer be treated as something that only an unusual minority of teenagers engage in. Yet while this research has provided needed factual information on the sexual attitudes and behavior of adolescents, it unfortunately has not led to a greater understanding of the meaning of sex for young people or of the role of sexual activity in adolescent psychosocial development.

Although we have a partial picture of the way in which adolescents respond to their initial sexual experiences, we know surprisingly little about the ways in which being sexually active affects the adolescent's psychological functioning and well-being. Perhaps in our concern over studying whether certain psychological or social characteristics increase the likelihood of an adolescent becoming sexually active we have lost sight of the fact that for most young people, sex is a natural part of the growing capacity for mature intimacy. As a consequence of this neglect, we understand very little about the ways in which sexuality is integrated into the adolescent's whole realm of experience. How are adolescents affected by having a serious sexual relationship with a boyfriend or girlfriend? Does being sexually active affect the teenager's self-esteem? How, if at all, are patterns of achievement in school influenced by sexual experience? These are important questions that experts have yet to address.

Key Terms

Acquired Immune Deficiency Syndrome (AIDS)
chlamydia

gonorrhea
herpes
permissive societies

restrictive societies
semirestrictive societies
serial monogamy
sexual socialization

sexually transmitted disease (STD)
sociosexuality
testosterone

For Further Reading

DREYER, P. (1982). Sexuality during adolescence. In B. Wolman (Ed.), *Handbook of developmental psychology.* Englewood Cliffs, N.J.: Prentice-Hall. A review of research on teenagers' sexual attitudes and behavior.

FORD, C., AND BEACH, F. (1951). *Patterns of sexual behavior.* New York: Harper & Row. The classic study of sexual behavior in cross-cultural perspective.

HAYES, C. (ED.). (1987). *Risking the future: Adolescent sexuality, pregnancy, and childbearing.* Washington: National Academy Press. The comprehensive report of the National Academy of Sciences on sexuality and pregnancy among American youth.

MILLER, P., AND SIMON, W. (1980). The development of sexuality in adolescence. In J. Adelson (Ed.), *Handbook of adolescent psychology.* New York: Wiley. An extensive discussion of the psychological aspects of sexual development during adolescence.

UDRY, J. R. (1987). Hormonal and social determinants of adolescent sexual *initiation.* In J. Bancroft (Ed.), *Adolescence and puberty.* New York.: Oxford University Press. A study of how biological and social influences interact to influence the development of sexuality.

Achievement

CHAPTER 12

PREVIEW

1. Adolescence is an important time for the development of achievement because during this period of the life cycle individuals make major decisions about their educational and occupational futures.

2. A variety of theories have been offered to explain why some youngsters achieve more in school than others. Many theorists have focused on differences in youngsters' motivation to succeed. Others have examined the beliefs adolescents hold about the causes of their successes and failures. Still others have pointed to differences in adolescents' opportunities for success and to the roles of significant adults and peers.

3. Educational and occupational achievement are highly interconnected. Doing well in school generally leads to higher levels of educational attainment, which in turn leads to more prestigious and better-paying employment. In general, there are strong socioeconomic differences in educational and occupational attainment.

4. Occupational plans do not begin to crystallize until middle adolescence. Even then, the process of choosing a career is a long one for most individuals. It may last well through the final years of college. Occupational plans are influenced by a complex array of individual and environmental factors.

Because adolescence typically is a time of preparation for the roles of adulthood, considerable attention has been paid to the development and expression of achievement during these years. Broadly defined, achievement concerns the development of motives, capabilities, interests, and behavior that have to do with performance in evaluative situations. More specifically, the study of achievement during adolescence has focused on young people's performance in educational settings and on their hopes and plans for future scholastic and occupational careers. Since most young people form their first realistic educational and vocational plans during adolescence, researchers have long been interested in the factors that appear to play the greatest role in influencing individuals' futures.

Achievement is a particularly important consideration in the study of adolescence in contemporary society. American society places an extraordinary emphasis on achievement, competition, and success—more so than on cooperation, for example, or the development of satisfying interpersonal relationships (McClelland, 1961). During childhood and adolescence, youngsters are continually tested to determine how they stand scholastically in relation to their peers. In most industrialized societies, the amount of education a person has completed and the job he or she holds—two of the most important indicators of achievement—provide a basis for individuals' self-conceptions, their image in the eyes of others, and the life style they follow (Featherman, 1980). Not surprisingly, one of the first things we ask about other people when first introduced is what sort of work they do.

A second reason for the importance of achievement in the study of adolescence in contemporary society concerns the range and rapidly changing nature of the choices faced by today's young people. Unlike youth in most traditional cultures, adolescents in modern societies are confronted with a phenomenally wide array of difficult occupational and educational decisions before they turn 25. Beyond such fundamental questions as what type of career to follow and whether to continue with schooling after high school, there are other difficult issues to ponder: what specific sorts of jobs should be pursued within a particular career path, what kind of educational preparation would be most appropriate, and how entry into the labor force is best negotiated. For the college student contemplating a career in business, for instance, is it better to major in business administration or is it better to follow a liberal arts course of study? How early is it necessary to decide which aspects of business to specialize in? Is it necessary to go to graduate school, or do employers prefer applicants with work experience in place of an advanced degree? These are all difficult questions to answer. And they are made more difficult because the nature of education and work changes so rapidly in contemporary society. Many young people lack adequate sources of information upon which to base decisions about their occupational and educational futures.

Finally, achievement is a particularly important issue in the study of adolescence in contemporary society because of wide variation in levels of educational and occupational success. By the end of high school, many adolescents demonstrate a high enough level of academic achievement to enter selective colleges and universities; yet a sizable number of their peers enter adulthood unable even to read a newspaper or understand a bus schedule. Although the majority of adolescents today complete high school and go on to college, a substantial number leave high school before graduating. Similar disparities exist in the occupational achievements of young people: Most youth make the transition from school to work without a great deal of difficulty, but a significant number experience long bouts of unemployment. Even within the population of young people who enter the labor force, there is considerable variation in earnings and in occupational status. Many important questions in the study of adolescent achievement, therefore, concern factors that distinguish between young people who are successful—however success is defined—and those who are not.

ACHIEVEMENT AS AN ADOLESCENT ISSUE

As noted above, in contemporary society, achievement is a lifelong concern. Educational institutions—even for young children—stress performance, competition, and success on tests of knowledge and ability. Children are acutely aware of their relative standing in matters of academic achievement. They are sensitive to differences in the ways that successful and unsuccessful youngsters are treated by their teachers; they understand that youngsters are assigned to learning groups on the basis of past performance; and they are probably more aware than their teachers think of how well or poorly other students in their class are performing. Many elementary students turn to their peers after their teacher returns a graded assignment and immediately ask, "How did you do?" There is ample evidence that much of the socialization of achievement-related motives takes place relatively early in childhood. By preadolescence, the importance individuals place on achievement, the extent to which they are afraid of failure, and the degree to which they feel nervous or anxious when they take tests are well established (Feld, 1967).

Concerns over achievement continue throughout adulthood as well. Many adults change jobs or careers at one time or another because their interests or aspirations change. And like their younger counterparts, adults for the most part place a premium on success. American society is highly stratified. Certain jobs are designated as high in status and others as less prestigious. Work and occupational attainment therefore play an important role in shaping the adult's values, self-concept, and self-esteem (Featherman, 1980). Changes in an individual's work situation—because of job re-

definition or job loss, for example—can exert a powerful impact on an individual's sense of competence, purpose, and identity. A successful adult who is laid off from a job may feel a dramatic loss of self-worth and dignity. But receiving a major promotion or raise—even after many years of employment—is still a significant source of satisfaction for most adults. It is clear, then, that development in the realm of achievement neither begins nor ends during adolescence.

Achievement during the adolescent years, though, merits special attention for several reasons. First, the fact that adolescence is a time of preparation for adult work roles raises questions about the nature of the preparation that young people receive and the processes through which they sort themselves (or are sorted) into the occupational roles that may influence the remainder of their lives. Few would debate that a good deal of vocational development takes place after adolescence. But many of the factors that narrow an individual's educational options and vocational alternatives are prominent during the high school and college years, and it is important to ask how such options are defined and how early educational and occupational decisions are made.

Second, although differences in school performance and achievement are apparent as early as the first grade, not until adolescence do individuals begin to appreciate fully the implications of these differences for immediate and future success. During childhood, for example, children's occupational plans are made to a large extent on the basis of fantasy and passing interests, without any realistic assessment of their practicality or feasibility. Not until adolescence do individuals begin to evaluate their occupational choices in light of their talents, abilities, and opportunities.

Third, it is clear that the educational and occupational decisions made during adolescence are more numerous, and the consequences more serious, than those characteristic of childhood. For example, in most elementary schools, al-

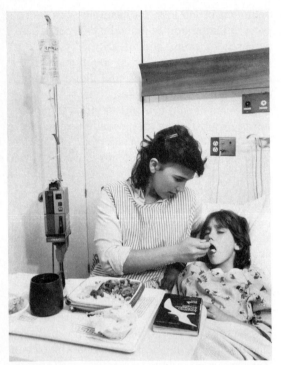

Achievement-related issues take on increased prominence during adolescence because it is during this time that individuals must begin to make important decisions about their educational and occupational futures. Volunteer experiences can help adolescents clarify their future plans. (Billy E. Barnes/Stock, Boston)

though children may be grouped by ability—groupings that have implications for subsequent achievement—they generally are all exposed to fairly similar curricula and have few opportunities to veer from the educational program established by their school system. In high school, however, students can select how much science and math they want to take, whether they wish to study a foreign language, whether they want to pursue an academic or vocational track—even whether they want to remain in school once they have reached the legal school-leaving age. Moreover, it is during adolescence that most individuals decide whether they want to pursue post-secondary education or enter a full-time job

directly from high school. All of these decisions have important implications for the sort of choices and plans the adolescent will make in the future, which in turn will influence his or her earnings, lifestyle, identity, and subsequent psychosocial development.

It is neither surprising nor coincidental that many achievement-related issues surface for the first time during adolescence rather than during early or later periods of development. One reason concerns the social definition of adolescence. In virtually all societies, adolescence is the period when important educational and occupational decisions are made, and society has structured its educational and work institutions accordingly. In America, for example, it is not until adolescence that individuals attain the status necessary to decide whether they will continue or end their formal education. And it is not until adolescence that people are allowed to enter the labor force in an official capacity, since child labor regulations typically prohibit the employment of youngsters under the age of 14 or so. The transition from school to work—one of the central issues in the study of achievement during adolescence—is in part a *socially* defined transition and one that is determined by society as a passage to be negotiated during adolescence.

Not until adolescence are individuals cognitively capable of seeing the long-term consequences of educational and occupational choices or of realistically considering the range of scholastic and work possibilities open to them. Thus a second reason for the prominence of achievement-related issues at adolescence concerns the advent of more sophisticated forms of thinking. The ability to think in hypothetical terms, for example, raises new achievement concerns for the individual (Should I go to college after I graduate or work for a while?) and at the same time permits the young person to think through these concerns in a logical and systematic fashion (If I decide to go on to college, then . . .).

Finally, the emergence of many achievement concerns at adolescence is tied to the biological changes of puberty. As noted in Chapter

2, not until early adolescence do sex differences in achievement test performance begin to emerge, with boys scoring higher on tests of mathematics and girls outscoring boys on tests of verbal skills. As we shall see, sex differences in achievement-related motives and beliefs appear around puberty as well. These sex differences are related primarily to the differential responses that boys and girls receive from others following changes in their appearance at puberty and to differences in the ways that adolescent boys and girls view themselves. Boys may be encouraged to pursue course work (and, by implication, careers) in math and science, girls in the arts and humanities. This differential treatment may have important implications for sex differences in educational and occupational attainment.

In this chapter, we look at the nature of achievement during the adolescent years. As you will see, the extent to which an adolescent is successful in school and in preparing for work is influenced by a complex array of personal and environmental factors. In addition, we shall find that development in the realm of achievement is cumulative, in that youngsters who are successful early are likely to reap the benefits of the educational system, continue to succeed in school, and to complete more years of education than their peers. This success, in turn, gives them an advantage in the labor market, since the prestige and status of individuals' entry-level jobs are largely dependent on their educational background.

If there is a theme to this chapter, it is that at least with respect to achievement during adolescence, the rich get richer and the poor get poorer. More often than not, personal and environmental influences on achievement complement rather than correct each other, in the sense that individuals who bring personal advantages to the world of achievement—talent, a motive to succeed, high aspirations for the future—are also likely to grow up in an environment that supports and maintains achievement success. We begin with a look at one set of factors that

may differentiate the "rich" from the "poor" early in their schooling—long before adolescence, in fact: their motives to succeed and their beliefs about the causes of their successes and failures.

ACHIEVEMENT MOTIVES AND ACHIEVEMENT BELIEFS

The Development of Achievement-Related Motives

Need for achievement. One of the longest-standing notions in the study of achievement is that individuals differ in the extent to which they strive for success and that this differential striving—which can be measured independently of sheer ability—helps to account for different degrees of actual achievement. Two students may both score 100 on an intelligence test, but if one student tries much harder than the other to do well in school, their actual grades may differ. The extent to which an individual strives for success is referred to as his or her **need for achievement** (McClelland et al., 1953). Need for achievement is an intrinsically motivated desire to perform well that operates even in the absence of external rewards for success. A student who tries very hard on an assignment that is not going to be graded probably has a very strong need for achievement.

Several researchers have examined the childhood antecedents of need for achievement. Generally, researchers have found that adolescents who have a strong need for achievement come from families where parents have set high performance standards, have rewarded achievement success during childhood, and have encouraged autonomy and independence (Winterbottom, 1958; Rosen and D'Andrade, 1959). Equally important, however, this training for achievement and independence generally takes place in the context of warm parent-child relationships in which the child forms close identifications with his or her parents (Shaw and White, 1965). Put most succinctly, *authoritative* parenting, coupled with parents' encouragement of success, is likely to lead to the development of a strong need for achievement.

Fear of failure.   One psychological factor that interacts with need for achievement in influencing adolescents' performance is a related, and in some ways complementary, motive—**fear of failure**. Fear of failure, which is often manifested in feelings of anxiety in test-taking or other evaluative situations, sometimes can interfere with successful performance. In some situations—generally, when the situation involves an easy task, and feeling somewhat anxious helps to focus attention—a modest amount of anxiety appears to improve performance. If, for instance, you were asked to do something repetitive—such as count the number of times the letter *t* appears in this paragraph—you would do a better job if you were told that your performance would be taken into account in determining your grade in the class. The moderate anxiety that this contingency would generate would stop

your mind from wandering and help you concentrate on an otherwise boring task (Spielberger, 1966).

Usually, though, anxiety interferes with successful performance. This is especially true when the task involves learning something new or solving a complex problem (Spielberger, 1966). In most of the achievement situations faced by adolescents in school, therefore, anxiety hinders rather than facilitates success. Throughout elementary and junior high school, test anxiety becomes an increasingly strong predictor of poor performance on achievement tests (Hill and Sarason, 1966). Students who feel very nervous during tests do worse, all other factors being equal, than students who feel relaxed.

Fear of failure and need for achievement work together. In classical psychological terms, the two motives together form what is called an **approach-avoidance conflict** (Atkinson and Feather, 1969). Need for achievement drives us to approach success, and fear of failure influences us to avoid failure. How much effort an adolescent exerts in a particular achievement situation depends on the relative intensity of the

Because it usually produces anxiety, fear of failure can interfere with successful performance in test situations. (Rae Russel)

two motives. For example, two adolescents who have equal athletic abilities and equally strong needs for achievement may not learn how to swim at the same rate if one has a much stronger fear of failure than the other and feels pessimistic about his ability to learn. This latter adolescent's motive to avoid failure may outweigh his motive to approach success, and he may give up more quickly than his peer. By measuring both need for achievement and fear of failure, psychologists are able to make more accurate predictions about how individuals will behave when challenged than they can by simply measuring need for achievement.

Fear of success. In addition to the influence of need for achievement and fear of failure, individuals' orientation toward achievement may be influenced by their **fear of success** (Horner,

1970). Some individuals may actually be afraid of succeeding if they believe that the social costs of doing well—being rejected by their friends, for example—are greater than the benefits. Initially, psychologists believed that adolescent girls were more likely to fear success than adolescent boys because the consequences of succeeding were more mixed for girls than boys. Subsequent research has not supported this notion uniformly, suggesting rather that sex differences in fear of success may be apparent only during early adolescence (Ishiyama and Chabassol, 1985). In other words, before adolescence and during the high school years and after, boys are just as likely as girls to fear success. During the junior high school years, however, girls are more likely to fear success than boys.

Sex differences in fear of success during early adolescence may have a good deal to do with sex-role orientation, which, as we discussed

In Horner's studies women tended to project negative themes onto the image of a career woman, leading Horner to suggest that "fear of success" may undermine many women's need for achievement. More recent studies indicate that sex differences in fear of success may be limited to early adolescence. (Peter Southwick/Stock, Boston)

The Sexes: Patterns of Math and Science Achievement in Adolescent Boys and Girls

We noted in an earlier chapter on cognitive development that sex differences in cognitive skills during adolescence are trivial. On standardized tests of intellectual abilities, girls and boys perform at about the same level, and when sex differences are observed, they are small—too small, indeed, to make a meaningful difference in adolescents' school performance. Despite this absence of sex differences in ability, girls in general are less likely than boys to pursue advanced courses in math and science, and those girls who do are more likely to drop out before finishing (Kavrell and Petersen, 1984). Studies of college students show that women are exceedingly underrepresented among graduates whose degrees are in math, engineering, and the physical science but overrepresented among graduates whose degrees are in the humanities and education (Eccles, Adler, and Meece, 1984). Because high school preparation undoubtedly influences college course choices, which in turn affect career choices, educators have been interested in understanding why sex differences in math achievement emerge in adolescence. In essence, if adolescent girls and adolescent boys have equal math ability, why do they show different patterns of math and science achievement during high school?

Psychologists have offered several explanations. The first concerns sex differences in the social consequences of succeeding in school and in math classes in particular. We noted earlier that fear of success may be more prevalent among women than men during early and middle adolescence than during childhood or adulthood (Butler and Nissan, 1975; Hoffman, 1977; Ishiyama and Chabas-

sol, 1985). This finding and other research on achievement-related conflicts among adolescent girls (Rosen and Aneshensel, 1975) suggest that the social world of adolescent peer groups may make it difficult for adolescent girls to integrate positive feelings toward achievement—especially toward achievement in stereotypically masculine subject areas—into their sense of identity (Douvan and Adelson, 1966). Of special importance for girls is the relation between academic achievement, the development of a feminine identity, and social relations with boys.

In Horner's original research on fear of success, many of the negative themes that surfaced in young women's stories had to do with social rejection by men as a result of academic or occupational success. Their stories portrayed unsuccessful women as unattractive and lonely. Children, however, do not associate such negative consequences with achievement. As psychologists Judith Bardwick and Elizabeth Douvan (1971) explain: "Until adolescence the idea of equal capacity, opportunity, and life style [for men and women] is held out to [girls]. But sometime in adolescence the message becomes clear that one had better not do too well, that competition is aggressive and unfeminine, that deviation threatens the heterosexual relationship" (p. 152).

In other words, adolescent girls may not fear "success" per se, but they may be wary of other consequences—not necessarily negative consequences, but often merely complicated consequences—that may befall them as a result of their achievement. Girls are more likely to have been socialized to believe that their achievement is out of their control, and

in an earlier chapter, refers to the degree to which an individual exhibits stereotypically masculine or feminine behaviors. Several studies have indicated that fear of success is lower in

individuals who score high on measures of masculinity—both masculine and androgynous individuals (Cano, Solomon, and Holmes, 1984). These studies suggest that it is not sex but sex-

they are consequently more likely to feel helpless in response to failure (Dweck and Light, 1980). During adolescence, when concerns over dating and socializing may be paramount, and when the sense of self is shaky and the view of the future cloudy, achievement may carry a different connotation for girls than it does for boys. Actually, one study indicated that *both* men and women had negative feelings about women's occupational success, suggesting that women's fear of success may be just as much due to a cultural bias against women succeeding as to an achievement-related motive prevalent among females (Monahan, Kuhn, and Shaver, 1974).

A second account focuses on sex differences in attitudes toward mathematics. Although girls and boys are equally likely to report liking math, girls are less likely than boys to believe that taking math classes will be useful to their future careers (Kavrell and Petersen, 1984). As a result, girls may place less value on achievement in math classes and may be less inclined to continue a math curriculum and more inclined to drop out of advanced math classes (Eccles et al., 1984). Thus, it appears that sex differences in career expectations may influence early attitudes toward math classes, which in turn influence math attainment. As we shall see later in this chapter, sex differences in adolescents' occupational ambitions are still quite marked. Unfortunately, to the extent that young adolescent girls opt out of advanced math classes, they limit their chances of moving into occupations that require preparation in math and only perpetuate occupational sex stereotypes.

Psychologist Jacqueline Eccles and her colleagues have argued that these sex differences in course selection may be related to sex differences in achievement attributions and beliefs. Parents, in particular, may pass on different expectations to sons and daughters, regardless of similarities in sons' and daughters' actual achievement. Parents of sons are more likely to believe that their child's success in math is due to his intrinsic math ability, whereas parents of daughters are more likely to attribute their child's math success to hard work. Parents of sons are also more likely than parents of daughters to think that taking advanced math courses is important (Parsons, Adler, and Kaczala, 1982). To make matters worse, studies also indicate that school counselors and teachers also endorse views that support math achievement among boys but discourage it among girls (Kavrell and Petersen, 1984).

Studies show that grades in school decline during early adolescence, for both boys and girls. This decline has been attributed to harder grading practices by teachers (Kavrell and Petersen, 1984) and to the declining importance of achievement to adolescents as they approach high school (Elmen and Steinberg, 1988). But the decline in grades in math and science may evoke very different responses in boys and girls. Boys, who have been told that they are good at math and that math is important, may simply try harder to do better. Girls, who receive less support for achievement in math from both adults (who may inadvertently socialize them to believe that math is difficult and not very useful) and peers (who may convey the message that success in math is not attractive), may respond by avoiding math entirely. This response is easy to understand: By the time an adolescent girl has reached the point in her high school career that she is able to choose among electives, she has been socialized to believe that math is difficult, that math classes are not especially worthwhile, and that success in math is inconsistent with being popular and attractive.

role socialization that may influence youngsters' beliefs about the perils of succeeding. Because early adolescent girls are often expected to hide or play down aspects of their personality that are traditionally masculine, sex differences in fear of success may be especially pronounced during early adolescence. Later, when pressures to conform to traditional sex roles may lessen, sex differences in fear of success may diminish (Hill and Lynch, 1983).

The Importance of Attributions

Researchers have questioned the usefulness of asserting the existence of global achievement-related motives that are expressed equally in a variety of situations. The relation between an individual's internal needs and fears, on the one hand, and his or her actual effort and performance, on the other, varies in different situations. Someone who has a strong need for achievement might express this need to different degrees in academic and in social situations—or even in different sorts of academic and different sorts of social situations—depending on her past experiences and her perception of the specific situation. Because of this, individuals' actual performance in achievement situations may not be strongly related to their general achievement motives.

Adolescents make judgments about their likelihood of succeeding or failing and exert different degrees of effort accordingly. Consider, for instance, the different ways that two individuals might approach a card game. Someone who believes that the outcome of the game is based on luck rather than skill will not try as hard as someone who feels that how he or she plays the game makes a difference.

For this reason, psychologists have increasingly turned their attention to studying how individuals' perceptions of achievement situations influence their behavior in them (Stipek and Weisz, 1981). Researchers interested in **achievement attributions** (Dweck and Wortman, 1980) have studied how the attributions individuals make for their success or failure influence their performance. According to these theorists, individuals attribute their performance to a combination of four factors: ability, effort, task difficulty, and luck. When individuals succeed and attribute their success to "internal" causes, such as their ability or effort, they are more likely to approach future tasks confidently and with self-assurance. If, however, individuals attribute

their success to "external" factors outside their own control, such as luck or having an easy task, they are more likely to remain unsure of their abilities. Not surprisingly, individuals high in achievement motivation are likely to attribute their successes to internal causes (Powers and Wagner, 1984).

How youngsters interpret their failures is also important in influencing their subsequent behavior. Some youngsters try harder in the face of failure, whereas others withdraw and exert less effort. According to psychologist Carol Dweck (Dweck and Light, 1980), when individuals attribute their failures to a lack of effort, they are more likely to try harder on future tasks. Individuals who attribute their failure to factors that they feel cannot be changed (bad luck, lack of intelligence, task difficulty) are more likely to feel helpless and exert less effort in subsequent situations.

Suppose, for instance, a student takes the SAT examination and receives a score of 500. He then is told by his guidance counselor that the SAT is a measure of intelligence and that his score reflects how smart he is. The counselor tells the student that he can retake the test if he wants to but that he should not expect to score much higher than 500. Now imagine a different student, who also scored 500 on the test. She is told by her guidance counselor that effort has a great deal to do with scores on the SAT and that she can raise her score by trying harder. In all likelihood, the first student would not try as hard the next time he takes the test as the second student would, because the first student is more likely to feel helpless.

Students who are led to believe that their efforts do not make a difference—by being told, for example, that they are stupid or that the work is too difficult for them—develop **learned helplessness**: the belief that their failure is inevitable (Dweck and Light, 1980). As a result, these students try less hard than their peers and do not do as well. Research on adolescents' attributions for success and failure suggests that instead of dismissing low-achieving students as having "low needs for achievement" or "low intelligence," teachers and other school personnel can help students achieve more by helping them learn to attribute their performance to factors that are under their own control (Wilson and Linville, 1985).

ENVIRONMENTAL INFLUENCES ON ACHIEVEMENT

Ability and effort may play a large role in influencing individual performance, but opportunity and situational factors also have a great deal to do with achievement (Featherman, 1980). Many of the differences in academic or occupational achievement observed among adolescents are due not to differences in adolescents' abilities, motives, or beliefs, but to differences in the environments in which these abilities and motives are expressed.

School environments differ markedly—in physical facilities, in opportunities for pursuing academically enriched programs, and in classroom atmosphere, for example. Many school districts, plagued with shrinking tax bases, are characterized by decaying school buildings, outdated equipment, and textbook shortages. In some schools, problems of crime and discipline have grown so overwhelming that attention to these matters has taken precedence over learning and instruction. Many young people who genuinely want to succeed are impeded not by a lack of talent or motivation but by a school environment that makes academic success virtually impossible.

The school, of course, is not the only environment that makes a difference in adolescent achievement, and few would argue that schools should accept full responsibility for adolescents who do not succeed at a level consonant with their ability. If anything, the evidence suggests that important aspects of the *home* environment are better predictors of adolescents' academic achievement than important aspects of the school environment (Coleman et al., 1966).

Researchers have focused on three ways in which the adolescent's home may influence his or her level of achievement. First, studies have shown that authoritative parenting is linked to school success during adolescence. In one recent study, sociologist Sanford Dornbusch and his colleagues (Dornbusch et al., 1987) demonstrated that adolescents whose parents were authoritative consistently performed better in school than their peers whose parents were permissive or autocratic. Interestingly, the poorest school performance was observed among adolescents whose parents were inconsistent in their child rearing. That is, even though adolescents whose parents were autocratic received lower grades than students whose parents were authoritative, adolescents whose parents used a mixture of autocratic and permissive techniques performed even worse. In general, these findings are in line with a good deal of research suggesting that consistent, authoritative parenting is associated with a wide array of benefits to the adolescent, including higher achievement motivation, greater self-esteem, and enhanced competence (Maccoby and Martin, 1983).

A second way in which the family influences adolescent achievement is through parents' encouragement. Studies have shown that adolescents' achievement is directly related to the level of achievement their parents expect them to attain. Adolescents whose parents expect them to go on to college are more likely to do so than adolescents of equal ability whose parents expect less of them (Featherman, 1980).

Finally, studies have also shown that the quality of an adolescent's home environment—as measured simply in terms of the presence of such items as a television set, dictionary, encyclopedia, newspaper, vacuum cleaner, and other indicators of family income—is more strongly correlated with youngsters' levels of academic achievement than is the quality of the physical facility of the school they attend, the background and training of their teachers, or the level of teacher salaries paid by the school district (Armor, 1972).

With this in mind, it is important to point out that a disheartening number of young people in this country—a disproportionate number of

Many American young people grow up in environments that present tremendous obstacles to their educational and occupational success. (Mary Ellen Mark/Archive Pictures)

them from minority groups—live in overcrowded, inadequate housing and come from families that are under severe economic and social stress. Their neighborhoods may be dangerous centers of crime and violence. And their diets may be sorely deficient in protein and other nutrients necessary for intellectual development. These obstacles to success disproportionately afflict youngsters from minority backgrounds. Put succinctly, many American youngsters do not grow up in an atmosphere that is conducive to academic achievement.

There is also evidence that friends influence adolescent achievement as well. But contrary to the notion that the influence of the peer group on adolescent achievement is always negative, recent studies suggest that the impact of friends on adolescents' school performance depends on the academic orientation of the peer group. Having friends who earn high grades and aspire to further education appears to enhance adolescent achievement, whereas having friends who earn

low grades or disparage school success may interfere with it. For example, according to one extensive study of friends in school (Epstein, 1983a), students' grades changed over time in relation to the grades of their friends. Students with best friends who achieved high grades in school were more likely to show improvements in their own grades than students who began at similar levels of achievement but had friends who were not high achievers. Peers also exerted a small but significant influence on each other's college plans. Among low-achieving adolescents, for example, those with high-achieving friends were more likely to plan to continue their education than those with low-achieving friends.

The potential negative impact of friends on achievement is vividly seen in a recent study of black male peer groups in an inner-city school (Fordham and Ogbu, 1986). These researchers found that bright black students in this school had to live down the "burden of acting white" and face criticism from their peers, who referred to them as "brainiacs." When a small group of these students were placed in an environment in which all their peers were high achievers, the derision and negative labeling did not occur, however.

Situational factors affect occupational as well as educational attainment. In the opinion of many social critics, strong institutional barriers impede the occupational attainment of women and members of ethnic minorities (Ogbu, 1978). These barriers may be especially strong during adolescence, when young people are steered away from some educational and occupational pursuits and toward others—not on the basis of ability or interest but because of gender, socioeconomic background, or race. Anthropologist John Ogbu (1974) has argued that many minority youth do not believe that the labor market will be open to them and, consequently, do not believe that there is sufficient payoff for investing a great deal of time in schoolwork. Studies by sociologist James Rosenbaum (1976, 1978) indicate that the ways in which schools determine which students are exposed to which curricula restrict the opportunites of those students who are placed in the slower tracks and perpetuate these students' academic disadvantages. The courses they encounter are likely to be less stimulating and less intellectually enriching than those taken by their peers. And students placed in the slower tracks tend to come disproportionately from minority groups and the economically disadvantaged— partly because their academic test scores warrant remedial placement, but partly as a consequence of their social background (Featherman, 1980).

Even after adolescence, a variety of social obstacles may lead to differences in occupational attainment among various ethnic groups and between men and women. Sociologist Margaret Marini (1980) finds, for example, that although men and women enter the labor force at similar levels of occupational status, men have much greater occupational mobility—primarily because their movement is not constrained, as is women's, by marital and childbearing commitments. The single most powerful influence on sex differences in the years of schooling completed, for example, is not that men and women have different abilities and motives, but that women marry younger (Marini, 1978). Because women tend to marry younger than men, they tend to leave school earlier.

Thus although psychological factors play an important role in determining occupational and scholastic success, it is impossible to examine achievement during adolescence thoroughly without taking into account the broader environment in which individuals pursue their educational and occupational careers. Moreover, distinguishing between motivational and environmental factors is hard: They typically go hand in hand. Living in an environment that offers few opportunities for success induces feelings of learned helplessness, which in turn leads individuals to feel that exerting any effort to succeed is futile. Attending school in an environment where achievement is not encouraged engenders attitudes and beliefs inconsistent with striving for achievement. Rather than viewing achievement during adolescence as determined by one single factor, such as ability, it is more accurate to say that patterns of achievement are the result of a cumulative process that includes a long history of experience and socialization in school, in the family, at work, and in the peer group.

EDUCATIONAL ACHIEVEMENT

Educational achievement is usually defined in one of three ways: the grades students earn in school, their performance on standardized tests of **academic achievement,** or the number of years of schooling completed—a measure of achievement referred to as **educational attainment.** These different measures of educational achievement are, not surprisingly, interrelated, but they are less tied to each other than one would expect.

The Importance of Socioeconomic Status

No one factor adequately accounts for differences in adolescents' levels of educational achievement. Generally speaking, mental ability—as assessed by IQ tests—is highly correlated with performance on achievement tests (not surprisingly, since IQ tests and achievement tests are designed to tap similar abilities), moderately correlated with school grades, and only mildly correlated with educational attainment (Featherman, 1980).

Grades in school—and to an even greater extent, educational attainment—are influenced by a wider range of factors than simply an adolescent's intellectual abilities. Grades, for example, are influenced by teachers' judgments of students' mastery of the material, and these judgments may be influenced by teachers' evaluations of students' effort and behavior in the classroom. How many years of school an adolescent completes is likely to be influenced by his or her family background as well as by school performance. Two adolescents may have similar grade-point averages, but if one comes from a poor family and cannot afford to go to college, the two will have different levels of educational attainment. In the words of sociologist David Featherman, "High intelligence begets good grades, and both assist one in acquiring above-average education, but . . . it is obvious that some persons fail to achieve their educational potentials while others ultimately obtain degrees and certification in spite of more modest accomplishments in school or average mental ability" (1980, p. 696).

Socioeconomic status and educational achievement.

One of the most powerful influences on educational achievement is the socioeconomic status of the adolescent's family. Middle-class adolescents score higher on basic tests of academic skills, earn higher grades in school, and complete more years of schooling than their working-class and lower-class peers (Garbarino and Asp, 1981). Although some of the socioeconomic gaps in school achievement appear to be closing, many disparities between the social classes remain strong, and the importance of socioeconomic status in determining educational achievement remains substantial (Featherman, 1980).

Adolescents who come from lower socioeconomic levels are more likely to score lower than their peers on standardized tests of achievement, and youngsters who come from more advantaged households are more likely to score higher. Similarly, youngsters whose parents have gone to college are more likely to attend college themselves than are those whose parents did not. And those youngsters whose parents completed high school are more likely to attend college than are those whose parents did not (Johnson, 1975). Socioeconomic status, therefore, influences both achievement and attainment and, as a consequence, influences occupational achievement as well. However, you should bear in mind that variations *within* socioeconomic categories are often as substantial as differences *between* categories. Not all youngsters from affluent backgrounds have higher levels of educational achievement than adolescents from poorer families, and many youngsters from economically disadvantaged households go on to receive college and postcollege degrees.

Socioeconomic differences in ability, motivation, and school performance.

One reason that family background is related to educational achievement is that children from lower socioeconomic levels are more likely to enter elementary school scoring low on tests of basic academic competence. These initial differences are due both to genetic and to environmental factors. Middle-class adults generally have higher IQs than lower-class adults, and this advantage is passed on to middle-class children—both through inheritance and through the benefit that middle-class youngsters receive from growing up under more favorable environmental conditions (Featherman, 1980). Affluent youngsters receive better health care and better nutrition, for example, both of which contribute to their higher performance on intelligence tests. The disadvantages of poorer youngsters in achievement test scores persist—and may even increase—throughout elementary and secondary school (Coleman et al., 1966). Because progress in high school depends so heavily on having a solid foundation of basic academic competence, adolescents who enter secondary school without having mastered basic academic skills quickly fall behind. Many then leave high school before graduating.

Studies also suggest that parents from higher social classes are more likely to be involved in their adolescent's education, through formal parent-teacher organizations, like the PTO, and through conferences with their child's teachers (Stevenson and Baker, 1987). They are also more likely to have information about their child's school and to be responsive to their child's school problems and to help select more rigorous courses for their child to take (Baker and Stevenson, 1986). Because adolescents whose parents are involved in their schooling perform better than adolescents whose parents are not, youngsters from higher social classes may achieve more in school than their less advantaged peers (Stevenson and Baker, 1987).

With regard to motivation, several studies indicate that working-class and lower-class parents are less likely than middle-class parents, on average, to rear their chidren in ways that encourage the development of achievement motivation (by encouraging autonomy and independence in the context of affection and high achievement expectations [Rosen, 1956]). Moreover, working-class and lower-class parents are less likely to look upon education as valuable in its own right and are more likely to view schooling primarily as a path to vocational success (Conger, 1977a). Thus they are less likely than middle-class parents to encourage academic achievement in the absence of any hard evidence that such achievement pays off in the job market. Finally, growing up under stressful and frustrating conditions may lead to the development of learned helplessness (Dweck and Light, 1980).

Socioeconomic differences in opportunity. Many of the reasons for socioeconomic differences in school achievement are environmental, however, and cannot be attributed solely to ability or motivational differences on the part of students or parents. Adolescents from economically disadvantaged backgrounds, for example, are more likely to face financial problems, which limit their opportunities for further education, thus limiting their educational ambitions and attainment. Economically disadvantaged adolescents are less likely to grow up in a community with large numbers of role models of scholastically successful individuals and are less likely than middle-class youngsters to be rewarded by their peers for academic achievement. And as we noted earlier, youngsters from lower socioeconomic levels, particularly those from nonwhite backgrounds, are more likely to be denied access to academic enrichment—through tracking, discrimination, and the sheer unavailability of these programs in the schools they attend (Conger, 1977a).

Socioeconomic differences in school achievement—however measured—obviously reflect the cumulative and combined effects of a variety of influences, and it is simplistic to explain group differences in achievement without considering these factors simultaneously. What is perhaps more interesting—and more worthy of scientific study—is to ask what it is about the many youngsters from economically disadvantaged backgrounds who are successful that accounts for their overcoming the tremendous odds against them. Although more research on this subject is sorely needed, several findings suggest that what might be most important is the presence of warm and encouraging parents who raise their children authoritatively, take an interest in their children's academic progress, and hold high aspirations for their children's educational attainment (Bachman, 1970; Simp-

Youngsters from socioeconomically advantaged backgrounds typically outscore their less affluent peers on measures of achievement. But are social class differences in achievement due to differences in ability, differences in motivation, or differences in opportunity? (Abigail Heyman/Archive Pictures)

son, 1962). In other words, positive family relations and parents' encouragement can in some circumstances overcome the negative influence of socioeconomic disadvantage.

Changes in Educational Achievement over Time

As noted in Chapter 6, more students are going on to postsecondary education today than ever before. In other words, levels of educational attainment in America have risen substantially over the past half century. For example, whereas in 1937 only 15 percent of the students enrolled in the fifth grade eventually entered college, by 1982, this figure had risen to well over 50 percent. In 1985, 58 percent of recent high school graduates enrolled in postsecondary programs (Wetzel, 1987).

These overall trends are encouraging, but several variations from this pattern have drawn the concern of educators in recent years. Notably, although high school graduation rates have increased in years among minority youth, college enrollment rates in these groups have

actually declined (see Figure 12.1). Thus, for example, whereas one-third of black high school graduates enrolled in college in 1976, only one-fourth did so in 1985. Similarly, the proportion of Hispanic high school graduates enrolling in college dropped from 36 percent in 1976 to 27 percent in 1985 (Fiske, 1987). Most experts attribute the decline to cutbacks in financial aid. The decline in minority student college enrollment is all the more troubling in light of other data, discussed later in this chapter, indicating that levels of academic achievement among minority youth, as indexed by standardized tests, have risen more steeply in recent years than scores among nonminority students (Congressional Budget Office, 1986).

Trends in academic achievement have not paralleled trends in educational attainment in many respects. For example, as Figures 12.2 and 12.3 indicate, between 1970 and 1980, average scores on the Scholastic Aptitude Test (SAT) declined by about fifty points but rose by about fifteen points between 1980 and 1984 (Congressional Budget Office, 1986). Scores on other tests of achievement, such as the Iowa

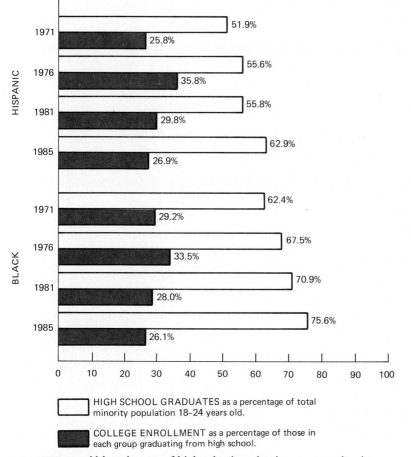

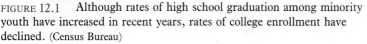

FIGURE 12.1   Although rates of high school graduation among minority youth have increased in recent years, rates of college enrollment have declined. (Census Bureau)

Tests of Basic Skills, a widely used standardized test, showed a similar pattern of decline during the late 1960s and 1970s and an increase during the early 1980s (see Figure 12.2 [Congressional Budget office, 1986]). Although scores have been improving, there is clearly cause for concern. According to recent estimates, nearly 40 percent of all 17-year-olds cannot draw inferences from written material presented to them. Only 33 percent can solve mathematical problems that require several steps, and only 20 percent can write a persuasive essay. In a recent comparison with adolescents from other industrialized countries, American youngsters scored last on more than one-third of the nineteen tests given and never came in first or second. In some economically distressed urban areas, close to half of all adolescents are functionally illiterate (National Commission on Excellence in Education, 1983).

The general picture that has emerged from studies of achievement trends over time is one of substantial decline followed by modest increases in recent years. There are noteworthy

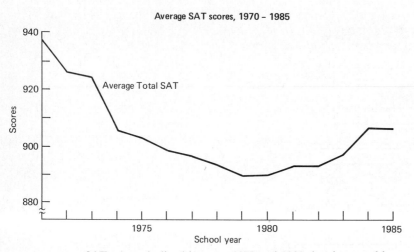

FIGURE 12.2   SAT scores declined between 1970 and 1980, but increased between 1980 and 1984. (Congressional Budget Office, 1986)

differences in trends within the adolescent population, however. Overall, the greatest gains in recent years have been among minority students, particularly blacks, and among urban youth (Congressional Budget Office, 1986).

Recent analyses suggest that the pattern of decline and recent upturn is attributable mainly to the cohort of individuals born between the years 1955 and 1962—the main years of the postwar baby boom (Congressional Budget Office, 1987). For reasons not yet entirely understood, these youngsters as a group scored lower on most standardized tests of achievement than those who were born earlier or later. Many fac-

FIGURE 12.3   Adolescents' scores on most standardized tests of achievement, such as the Iowa Tests of Basic Skills, were lower during the 1970s than before or after. (Congressional Budget Office, 1986)

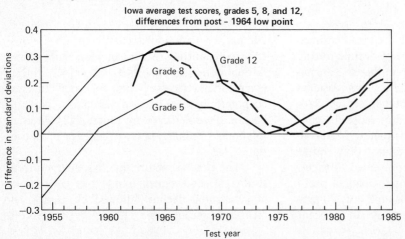

tors have been suggested to account for this phenomenon, but no one explanation appears to suffice. The most likely causes, according to a recent comprehensive study, were changes in school practices such as homework assignments and course content (which resulted in less demanding schooling among the baby boomers), variations in patterns of drug and alcohol use (these substances, which may depress achievement levels, were used by a larger proportion of baby boom adolescents), and changes in family size (baby boom families were larger, and youngsters from larger families typically score lower on achievement tests than youngsters from smaller families). Interestingly, three factors that are often blamed for the decline in achievement scores apparently have been falsely accused: There is no evidence that changes in television viewing habits, increases in mothers' employment, or increases in the divorce rate contributed to the decline in achievement seen during the 1970s (Congressional Budget Office, 1987).

Dropping Out of High School

There was a time when leaving high school before graduating did not have the dire consequences that it does today. With changes in the labor force, however, have come changes in the educational requirements for entry into the world of work. Today educational attainment is a powerful predictor of adult occupational success and earnings. Not surprisingly, high school dropouts are far more likely than graduates to live at or near the poverty level, experience unemployment, depend on government-subsidized income maintenance programs, and be involved in delinquent and criminal activity.

Although dropping out of high school is less prevalent now than it was twenty-five years ago, a substantial number of today's adolescents leave high school before graduating. The national dropout rate declined from 40 percent in 1960 to 25 percent in 1965, but it has not changed substantially since then. However, many youngsters who do not graduate on time

eventually complete their high school education by returning to school or through a General Education Development (GED) program. The proportion of individuals who have not completed a high school degree by age 29 is only 14 percent ("Youth and America's Future," 1988).

When dropout rates are examined for different racial groups, we find that black youngsters drop out of high school at a slightly higher rate than white youngsters (both are near the national average) but that Hispanic youngsters drop out at about twice the rate of other youth. One reason for this is the large proportion of Hispanic youth who are not English-speaking; a lack of proficiency in English is a major determinant of dropping out (Steinberg et al., 1984).

Given the findings on school achievement discussed earlier, the research evidence on the other correlates of dropping out comes as no surprise. In addition to the prevalence of dropping out among Hispanic youngsters and among youngsters who are not fluent in English, adolescents who leave high school before graduating are more likely to come from lower socioeconomic levels, poor communities, large families, single-parent families, and households where little reading material is available. In short, adolescents who drop out of school are more likely to come from socially and economically disadvantaged backgrounds (Bachman, Green, and Wirtanen, 1972; Rumberger, 1983).

Coupled with this socioeconomic disadvantage, adolescents who drop out of high school also are more likely to have had a history of poor school performance, low school involvement, poor performance on standardized tests of achievement and intelligence, and negative school experiences. Many high school dropouts have had to repeat one or more grades in elementary school. By the time youngsters have reached the ninth grade, for example, it is possible to predict—with over 90 percent accuracy—which adolescents will complete high school simply by knowing each individual's age (which indicates whether he or she has been held back in school), IQ, socioeconomic background, and achievement test scores (Walters and Kranzler, 1970). More remarkably, one researcher was able to identify youngsters who would become high school dropouts with 75 percent accuracy at the time the individuals were in the *third* grade, solely on the basis of family background variables, achievement test scores, elementary school grades, and IQ scores (Lloyd, 1978).

The picture that emerges, then, is that dropping out of high school is not so much a decision that is made during the adolescent years but, like other aspects of adolescent achievement, the culmination of a long process. For the dropout, this process is characterized by a history of repeated academic failure and increasing alienation from school.

OCCUPATIONAL ACHIEVEMENT

During early and middle adolescence, school is the setting in which achievement is most often expressed. During late adolescence, the focus shifts to the world of careers and work. Although we often think of school and work as separate domains, achievement is one aspect of psychosocial development during adolescence that links them together. Rather than thinking of educational achievement and occupational achievement as separate, it is more useful to think of them as different manifestations of the same basic psychosocial phenomena.

Occupational and educational achievement are linked primarily through educational attainment. The number of years of schooling an individual completes is the single best indicator of his or her eventual occupational success. It is not simply that adolescents benefit in the labor force by having a high school diploma or a college degree. Although these credentials matter, research shows that each year of education—even without graduating—adds significantly to occupational success. In other words, individuals who have completed three years of college earn more money, on average, than individuals who have completed only one year, even though neither group has a college degree in hand. You may be surprised to learn, however, that *grades* in high school and college are virtually unrelated to occupational success. A few years after graduation, "A" students and "C" students hold similarly prestigious jobs and earn comparable amounts of money (Garbarino and Asp, 1981).

Researchers interested in occupational achievement during adolescence have examined several issues, including the ways in which young people make decisions about their careers and the influences on their occupational aspirations and expectations. We begin with a look at the development of adolescents' occupational plans.

The Development of Occupational Plans

The development of occupational plans during adolescence can be viewed in many respects as paralleling, or even as a part of, the identity development process. As with developing a coherent sense of identity, the development of occupational plans follows a sequence that involves an examination of one's traits, abilities, and interests; a period of experimentation with different work roles; and an integration of influences from one's past (primarily, identification with familial role models) with one's hopes for the future. And as is also the case with identity development, occupational role development is profoundly influenced by the social environment in which it takes place.

Today, the dominant theoretical viewpoint in the study of the development of occupational plans is that of Donald Super (1967). Super suggests that occupational plans develop in stages, with adolescence as an important time for the crystallization of plans that are more realistic, less based on fantasy, and more grounded in the adolescent's assessment of his or her talents. Prior to adolescence, individuals express occupational interests, but these are much like fantasies and have little to do with the plans they will eventually make. When children are asked what they want to be when they grow up, they are likely to respond with occupations that are exciting, glamorous, or famil-

Educational attainment is an extremely strong determinant of occupational achievement, especially among Black and Hispanic adolescents. Young people who graduate from college are more successful in the world of work than individuals who do not continue their schooling after high school. (Janice Fullman/The Picture Cube)

iar—a teacher, a policeman, a baseball player, a movie star.

With the advent of more sophisticated thinking capabilities during early adolescence, however, and as the economic and practical realities of adulthood become imminent, young people begin to consider career alternatives in a more systematic fashion. They plan educational and work activities to suit their career interests, and they evaluate career decisions in terms of long- as well as short-term consequences. Instead of merely being attracted to glamorous or exciting jobs, adolescents think about such mundane realities as the need to earn a living.

According to Super, between ages 14 and 18 individuals first begin to crystallize a vocational preference. During this period of **crystallization,** individuals begin to formulate ideas about appropriate work and begin to develop occupational self-conceptions that will guide subsequent educational decisions. Although adolescents may not settle on a particular career at this point, they do begin to narrow their choices according to their interests, values, and abilities. One adolescent may decide that she wants a career in which she works with people. Another may decide that she wants a career in which she can earn a great deal of money. A third may think about a career in science. During this period, the adolescent begins to seek out information on his or her tentative choice and make plans for the future (Osipow, 1973). The process is reminiscent of the sort of role experimentation described by Erik Erikson (1968) in his theory of adolescent identity development. In both cases, during middle adolescence, alternative identities are considered and evaluated on the basis of exploration, experimentation, and self-examination.

Following the period of crystallization is a

period of **specification,** occurring roughly between the ages of 18 and 21. During this period, the young person recognizes the need to specify his or her vocational interests and begins to seek appropriate information to accomplish this. In many regards, a similar process is followed during the stage of specification as during the stage of crystallization: alternatives are considered, information is sought, decisions are made, and preferences are consolidated. The chief difference, however, is that during the period of specification, more narrowly defined career pursuits within a general career category are considered (rather than general career categories themselves). For example, during the period of crystallization, a young person may decide that he wants to pursue a career in the field of mental health, without being able to specify a vocational preference within this general category. During the specification stage, he might begin to consider and compare a variety of careers within the mental health profession—social work, educational counseling, clinical psychology, psychiatry, and so on—and make choices among them.

According to Super's theory, three stages characterize the process of vocational development during adulthood. In the **implementation** stage—roughly between the ages of 21 and 24—the individual completes the relevant training for his or her career, executes whatever plans are necessary to qualify for career entry, and obtains an entry-level job. Between the ages of 25 and 35, during the stage of **stabilization,** the individual settles down within a field of work. Hereafter, he or she may change positions but is unlikely to change vocation. Finally, in the stage of **consolidation**—during the thirties and mid-forties—the individual's focus is on establishing skills, seniority, and status in order to gain a comfortable career position during the later years of work (Osipow, 1973).

Although the chronological ages given in Super's theory must be taken as only rough guidelines, his perspective is an influential one, and it has shaped the way in which career counselors advise young people. Perhaps most im-

portant, Super's perspective reminds us that vocational development comes relatively late during adolescence and that a good deal of growth in this arena takes place during the young adult years. This has become increasingly true in contemporary society, as more and more young people have chosen to continue their education in college and postpone their entrance into a career until their mid-twenties. Changes in the broader environment in which adolescents develop—in this case, changes in the accessibility of higher education—can exert a powerful influence on the developmental course of vocational planning.

Influences on Occupational Choices

What makes one individual choose to become an attorney and another, a teacher? Why do some students pursue careers in business while others major in engineering? Researchers have long been interested in the reasons that individuals end up in certain careers. While Super's developmental theory has helped us understand the general stages of career planning, it does not shed light on why certain careers appeal to some individuals but not to others. In other words, Super's theory focuses on *how* and *when* individuals make career choices, rather than on *why* they make the career choices they do.

The influence of personality traits and interests on occupational plans. Many theorists interested in why people enter different occupational fields have examined the role of personality factors—traits, interests, and values—in the process of career selection. They believe that individuals select careers that match, in one way or another, certain elements of their personality. Perhaps the most widely cited perspective of this sort is that of John Holland (1973).

After years of extensive analysis of jobs and the people who select them, Holland determined that career choices can be viewed as a reflection of basic personality styles. Certain occupational environments are well suited to individuals with certain personalities, and others are not. Suc-

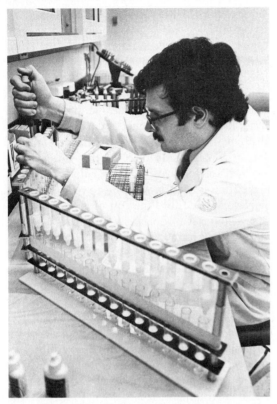

According to John Holland's model of career choice, individuals who are "investigative" are well-suited for jobs that permit the use of conceptual and theoretical skills. Scientists, for example, often have investigative personalities. (Joel Gordon)

cessful career choice, in Holland's model, entails the matching of a particular personality type—a given set of interests and personality characteristics—with a vocation that allows the expression of these traits. By answering questions on a standardized personality inventory, an individual can determine which of six basic personality dimensions are characteristic of himself or herself and can then examine directories in which occupations have been classified according to the same typology. (More than one dimension may emerge as important to someone's personality; indeed, the overall *pattern* of personality factors, rather than one dominant factor, is what is considered important.)

The basic personality factors, according to Holland, are

1. *Realistic:* Individuals who are realistic prefer practical jobs—often requiring physical labor and motor coordination rather than interpersonal skills. A construction worker probably has realistic interests.

2. *Investigative:* Individuals who are investigative are oriented toward thinking rather than acting. They are often interested in work in which they can use conceptual and theoretical skills. Scientists are often investigative.

3. *Social:* Individuals who are social enjoy being involved in interpersonal situations and social interaction. They are often interested in work in which they can help other people. Counseling is a good example of a job that permits the expression of social interests.

4. *Conventional:* Individuals who are conventional like structured job environments and prefer to subordinate their own personal needs to the needs of others. They often seek to work under the direction of supervisors. Office clerks are typically conventional.

5. *Enterprising:* Individuals who are enterprising are often verbally skilled and interested in supervising and directing other people. They often seek work situations in which they can attain power and status. A sales manager for a large corporation is likely to be enterprising.

6. *Artistic:* Individuals who are artistic show strong needs for artistic self-expression and prefer tasks that are unstructured and that emphasize physical skills or interpersonal interaction. Artists, musicians, and actors have artistic interests.

After completing Holland's personality inventory—called the **Self-Directed Search**—an individual better understands his or her vocational profile—which of the six orientations are dominant and which are less important. Because different occupations typically offer different degrees of opportunity to express each of the six orientations, a good career choice, in Holland's view, is one that provides the best fit between a person's pattern of orientations and a vocation's characteristics. Someone whose dominant orientation is artistic, social, and enterprising, for example, would be better suited to a career in acting than in accounting.

Other theoretical frameworks focusing on the fit between individual personality characteristics and work environments are popular as well, and batteries of inventories are available to help individuals learn more about their vocational interests. Two of the best-known measures are the **Strong Vocational Interest Blank** and the **Kuder Preference Record**. These inventories can play an important role in helping to clarify individuals' vocational preferences and in suggesting career possibilities that may warrant further investigation.

There are important limitations to theories of career choice that are based solely on personality traits, however. First, as Jeylan Mortimer and her colleagues have demonstrated (Mortimer and Lorence, 1979), it is clear that interests and abilities are not fixed during adolescence and young adulthood. They continue to develop and change during the adult years. Indeed, one of the most important influences on personality development during adulthood is work itself! Thus through working in a job that emphasizes certain personality characteristics, requires certain abilities, or reinforces certain values, individuals begin to change in these directions. Consequently, a job that may seem like a bad match during early adulthood may, over time, become a good match, as the adult employee grows and changes in response to the work environment. For example, an individual may not have especially social interests but may, because of a tight job market, end up in a teaching position after graduating from college. Over time, the more he interacts with his students, the more he may come to like the interpersonal aspects of his job. Eventually, he may come to feel that having opportunities for social interaction on the job is very important.

A second problem with theories of career choice that emphasize personality dimensions is that they may underestimate the importance of other factors that influence and shape vocational decisions. It is all well and good, for example, for an adolescent to discover that he or she is well suited for a career in medicine; but the realization is of little value if the young person's family cannot afford the cost of college or medical school. An adolescent girl may discover, through taking a vocational preference inventory, that she is well suited for work in the area of construction or building, but she may find that her parents, peers, teachers, and potential employers all discourage her from following this avenue of employment. Put most simply, career choices are not made solely on the basis of individual preference; they are the result of an interaction among individual preference, social influence, and important forces in the broader social environment. It is to these influences and forces that we now turn.

Social and environmental influences on occupational plans.

The influence of parents and peers. Parents and peers influence adolescents' occupational plans in a variety of ways. One commonly noted finding is that adolescents' occupational ambitions and achievements are highly correlated with the ambitions and achievements of those around them (Duncan, Featherman, and Duncan, 1972). Youngsters from middle-class families are more likely than their less advantaged peers to aspire to and enter middle-class occupations. In addition, apart from their own socioeconomic status, youngsters who have many friends from middle-class backgrounds are more likely than those who have many friends from lower socioeconomic levels to aspire to high-status occupations (Simpson, 1962).

A variety of explanations have been offered for the fit between adolescents' ambitions and the socioeconomic status of those around them. First and perhaps most important, occupational attainment—the prestige or status an individual achieves in the world of work—depends strongly on educational attainment (Alexander and Eckland, 1975). As we saw earlier, educational attainment is greatly influenced by socioeconomic status. Thus because middle-class adolescents are likely to complete more years of schooling than their lower-class peers, economically advantaged adolescents are more likely to seek and enter higher-status occupations.

Second, middle-class parents, as we noted earlier, are more likely to raise their children in ways that foster the development of strong needs for achievement (Rosen, 1956) and interest in career exploration (Grotevant and Cooper, 1988). The development of achievement motivation, which has an impact on school performance, also has an impact on youngsters' occupational ambitions—both directly (in that individuals with strong needs for achievement will express these needs by aspiring to occupations that provide opportunities to achieve status or wealth) and indirectly, through the effects of achievement motivation on academic achievement (in that youngsters who are successful in school are likely to be encouraged to seek higher-status occupations and engage in identity exploration).

Third, the same opportunities that favor economically advantaged youngsters in school situations better facilities, more opportunities for enrichment, greater accessibility of higher education—also favor middle-class youngsters in the world of occupations. Because their parents, for example, are more likely to work in positions of power and leadership, middle-class youngsters often have important family connections and sources of information about the world of work that are less available to youngsters from poorer families. In addition, coming from a family that is economically well-off may provide an adolescent with more time to explore career options and wait for an especially desirable position

rather than having to take the first job that becomes available, out of economic necessity.

Fourth, parents, siblings, and other important sources of influence serve as models for adolescents' occupational choices (Grotevant and Cooper, 1988). Although it is true that some young people establish career choices through the explicit rejection of their parents' careers, the weight of the evidence suggests that adolescents' and parents' vocations are more similar than different, particularly when the adolescent's family relationships have been warm and close and when strong identifications have formed. As we saw in our discussion of mothers' employment in Chapter 4, adolescents are especially influenced by the work roles of the parent of the same sex. This finding has become increasingly important as growing numbers of women enter the labor force and hold high-status occupations. Daughters of women who are happily employed outside the home are far more likely themselves to seek careers in addition to marriage and family responsibilities than are adolescent girls whose mothers are not employed (Leslie, 1986). Moreover, young women whose mothers occupy high-status occupations are more likely to do so themselves when they enter the labor force (Hoffman, 1974).

Finally, parents—and to a lesser extent peers—influence adolescents' occupational plans by establishing a value context in which certain occupational choices are encouraged and others are discouraged. According to sociologist Melvin Kohn (1977), middle-class families and middle-class schools encourage children to value autonomy, self-direction, and independence—three features that are more likely to be found in middle-class than in working-class jobs. They are told, implicitly and explicitly, how important it is to have freedom, power, and status. Adolescents who have been raised to value attributes that are characteristic of middle-class jobs will, not surprisingly, seek those attributes when they plan their careers. They will look for jobs that offer independence and power. In working-class families, in contrast, children are more likely to be raised to value obedience and conformity—

Although some young people establish career choices by rejecting their parents' occupations, the majority of adolescents select careers that are similar to, rather than different from, those of their parents. Parent-child similiarity in occupational choices is greatest in families with warm, close relationships. (Eric Roth/The Picture Cube)

two characteristics that are highly valued in most working-class jobs. For youngsters from this socioeconomic background, jobs that appeal to these values will be relatively more attractive. They will have been raised to value such things as job security and not having to worry too much about making high-pressured decisions. Indeed, to many working-class youngsters, the high-stress world of the business executive is not at all an attractive career possibility.

The broader context of occupational choice. Adolescents' occupational choices are made, of course, in a broader context that profoundly influences the nature of their plans. At different times, different employment opportunities arise, and young people—particularly by the time they

reach the end of their formal schooling—are often very aware of the prospects for employment in different fields. Understandably, they often tailor their plans in response to what they perceive as the needs and future demands of the labor market.

One problem faced by young people in making career plans is obtaining accurate information about the labor market needs of the future and the appropriate means of pursuing positions in various fields. Psychologist Harold Grotevant, who has studied adolescents' occupational plans extensively (Grotevant and Durrett, 1980), notes that the majority of young people do not have educational plans that are consistent with the educational requirements of the jobs they hope to enter. Even among high school seniors who perceived themselves as having "considerable" knowledge of the fields they planned to enter, approximately one-fifth were planning on too little education and nearly one-third, too much education, given the requirements of the careers to which they aspired. One goal of career educators is to help adolescents make more informed choices about their careers.

Summary

Achievement is an important arena of psychosocial development during adolescence because this period of the life cycle typically is a time of preparation for the occupational roles of adulthood. The development of achievement-related motives, beliefs, and behaviors has received special attention because of the tremendous emphasis placed in most industrialized countries on status, success, and attainment. Researchers have focused primarily on adolescents' achievement in the educational and occupational domains, examining the nature, antecedents, and consequences of academic achievement, educational attainment, and occupational plans.

Differences in adolescents' levels of achievement are due not only to differences in their abilities and motives but also to differences in the opportunities they have to express and develop their potential. An extensive literature documents the importance of social class as an influence on both educational and occupational achievement.

Although it is possible to distinguish among various indicators of achievement, they are all highly interconnected. Early success in school leads to later success in school; later success in school leads to higher levels of educational attainment; and higher levels of educational attainment lead to higher-status jobs and greater earning power. Thus in order to understand the course of achievement during adolescence, it is essential to understand its cumulative nature.

The process of choosing a career is a lengthy one in contemporary society. Because career options have expanded and changed so dramatically, and because more and more individuals choose to enter college after high school, many adolescents do not decide on a career until well into early adulthood. In much the same way that the adolescent identity crisis has been prolonged by modernization, so has the process of occupational choice.

Perhaps the most significant problem facing social scientists interested in achievement during adolescence concerns disparities in the educational and occupational achievements of youngsters from different social backgrounds. Beginning in early childhood, through no doing of their own, many individuals find themselves on an educational and occupational course that directs them toward low levels of academic achievement, curtailed schooling, and limited occupational mobility. They emerge from adolescence with little hope for and few dreams for the future. Understanding how this course is set in motion—and understanding what can be done to reverse it—continues to be a pressing social issue.

Key Terms

academic achievement

achievement attributions

approach-avoidance conflict

consolidation

crystallization

educational attainment

fear of failure

fear of success

implementation
Kuder Preference Record
learned helplessness
need for achievement

Self-Directed Search
specification
stabilization
Strong Vocational Interest Blank

For Further Reading

DWECK, C., AND ELLIOT, E. (1983). Achievement motivation. In E. M. Hetherington (Ed.), *Handbook of child psychology* (Vol. 4). (4th ed.). New York: Wiley. A comprehensive review of research and theory concerning achievement motives and beliefs.

FEATHERMAN, D. (1980). Schooling and occupational careers: Constancy and change in worldly success. In O. Brim, Jr., and J. Kagan (Eds.), *Constancy and change in human development*. Cambridge: Harvard University Press. An extensive review of the cumulative process of achievement during childhood, adolescence, and adulthood.

OGBU, J. (1974). *The next generation: An ethnography of education in an urban neighborhood*. New York: Academic Press. An insightful examination of the problems faced by youngsters in inner-city schools.

OSIPOW, S. (1973). *Theories of career development* (2nd ed.). New York: Appleton-Century-Crofts. A review of the major theories of career choice.

Psychosocial Problems in Adolescence

CHAPTER 13

PREVIEW

1. Although the vast majority of young people move through the adolescent years without experiencing major difficulty, some encounter serious psychological and behavioral problems such as substance abuse, depression and suicide, unplanned pregnancy, and conduct disorders (including crime and delinquency).

2. In general, women who bear children early are likely to suffer disruptions in their educational and occupational careers that can have dire long-term consequences. However, teenage mothers differ considerably in the routes that their adult lives take.

3. Studies of drug and alcohol use indicate that most adolescents have experimented with alcohol and marijuana, that many have used one or both of these drugs regularly, that alcohol is clearly the drug of choice among teenagers, and that most teenagers have not experimented with other drugs.

4. Although most adolescents violate the law at one time or another, a relatively small number of adolescents account for a relatively high proportion of serious criminal activity. These delinquents typically come from disorganized families who have mistreated their children and failed to instill in them proper standards of behavior or the psychological foundations of self-control.

5. Depression is probably the most common psychological disturbance among adolescents. It is more likely to be the result of interacting sets of environmental conditions and individual predispositions than the result of either set of factors alone.

6. A variety of explanations have been suggested for the observation that different types of problem behavior often occur together during adolescence. These explanations have focused on the relative size of the adolescent population, birth-order effects, underlying personality dispositions, and the impact that one form of problem behavior may have on involvement in another.

Although the vast majority of young people move through the adolescent years without experiencing major difficulty, some encounter serious psychological and behavioral problems that disrupt not only their lives but the lives of those around them. Problems such as substance abuse, depression and suicide, unplanned pregnancy, and disorders of conduct (including crime and delinquency), while certainly not the norm during adolescence, do affect a worrisome number of teenagers. Moreover, these problems indirectly touch the lives of all of us, either through the personal contact we may have with a troubled young person or indirectly, through increased taxes for community services or heightened anxiety about the safety of our neighborhoods. The young person who drops out of school before graduation, for example, not only jeopardizes his or her own occupational career—reason enough to discourage dropping out of school—but also runs the risk of falling into the welfare system and becoming dependent on public assistance.

In the previous chapters, which examined normative aspects of adolescent psychosocial development, the more problematic aspects of adolescent behavior and development were deliberately de-emphasized, in order to dispel the erroneous stereotype of adolescence as an inherently troubled time. As you now know from reading these chapters, research shows that most individuals emerge from adolescence with positive feelings about themselves and their parents; the ability to form, maintain, and enjoy close relationships with same- and opposite-sex peers; and the basic capabilities needed to take advantage of a range of educational and occupational opportunities. Most settle into adulthood relatively smoothly and begin establishing their work and family careers with little serious difficulty. Although the transition into adulthood may appear forbidding to the young adolescent approaching many weighty decisions about the future, statistics tell us that for a remarkably high proportion of youth, the transition is relatively peaceful. One in ten adolescent girls gets pregnant before she is twenty, but nine in ten do not. Twenty percent of students do not complete high school by the societally expected age, but 80 percent do, and a substantial number of young people who leave school prematurely later receive a high school diploma.

This is not to gloss over the fact that many healthy adolescents at one time or another experience bouts of self-doubt, periods of family squabbling, academic or vocational setbacks, or broken hearts. But it is important to keep in mind as we look at psychosocial problems in adolescence that there is an important distinction between the *normative*, and usually transitory, difficulties that are encountered by many, many young people—and many adults, for that matter—and the serious psychosocial problems that are experienced by a relatively small minority of youth.

SOME GENERAL PRINCIPLES

The mass media like nothing more than to paint extreme pictures of the world in which we live. One way in which this exaggerated view of the world is most obvious is in the presentation (both in entertainment and in news shows) of teenage problem behavior. Rarely are portrayals of sex, psychological difficulty, drug use, or delinquency accurate: On television, one experiment with marijuana inevitably leads to drug addiction and school failure. A breakup with a boyfriend is followed by a suicide attempt. An after-school prank develops into a life of crime. A couple's passionate necking session on the beach fades into a commercial, and when the program returns, the adolescent girl is on her way to a life of single parenthood and welfare dependency. Those of you for whom adolescence was not that long ago know that these "facts" about adolescent problem behavior are rarely true, but we are so often bombarded with images of young people in trouble that it is easy for all of us to get fooled into believing that adolescence equals problems.

One of the purposes of this chapter—in addition to describing and discussing some of the more prevalent psychosocial problems among young people today—is to put these problems in perspective. It is therefore helpful, before we look at several problems in detail, to lay out some general principles about adolescent problem behavior that apply to a range of problems. First, we need to distinguish between *occasional experimentation* and *enduring patterns of dangerous or troublesome behavior.* Research shows that rates of occasional, usually harmless, experimentation far exceed rates of enduring problems. For example, the majority of adolescents experiment with alcohol sometime before high school graduation, and the majority will have been drunk at least once, but, as we shall see, relatively few teenagers will develop drinking problems or permit alcohol to adversely affect their school or personal relationships.

Second, we need to distinguish between problems that have their origins and onset in adolescence and those that have their roots in earlier periods of development. It is true, for example, that some teenagers fall into patterns of criminal or delinquent behavior during adolescence, and for this reason we tend to associate delinquency with the adolescent years. But studies suggest that most teenagers who have recurrent problems with the law had problems at home and at school from an early age; in some samples of delinquents, the problems were evident as early as preschool (Loeber and Stouthamer-Loeber, 1987). In other words, simply because a problem may be displayed *during* adolescence does not mean that it is a problem *of* adolescence.

Third, it is important to remember that some, although not all, of the problems experienced by adolescents are relatively transitory in nature and are resolved by the beginning of adulthood, with few long-term repercussions in most cases. Substance abuse, delinquency, and unemployment are three good examples of problems that tend to follow this pattern: rates of drug and alcohol use, unemployment, and delinquency are all higher within the adolescent and youth population than in the adult population, but most individuals who have abused

drugs and alcohol, been unemployed, or committed delinquent acts as teenagers grow up to be sober, employed, law-abiding adults. Individuals for whom problem behavior persists into adulthood are likely to have had a problematic childhood as well as a problematic adolescence. The fact that some of the problems of adolescence seem to disappear on their own with time does not make their prevalence during adolescence any less significant, but it should be kept in mind when rhetoric is hurled back and forth about the "inevitable" decline of civilization at the hands of contemporary youth.

Fourth, as should be evident, problem behavior during adolescence is virtually never a direct consequence of going through the normative changes of adolescence itself. Popular theories about "raging hormones" causing oppositional or deviant behavior have no scientific support whatsoever, for example, nor do the widely held beliefs that problem behaviors are manifestations of an inherent need to rebel against authority, or that bizarre behavior results from having an "identity crisis." As you learned in previous chapters, the hormonal changes of puberty have only a modest direct effect on adolescent behavior; rebellion during adolescence is atypical, not normal; and few adolescents experience a tumultuous identity crisis. When a young person exhibits a serious psychosocial problem, such as depression, the worst possible interpretation is that it is a normal part of growing up. It is more likely to be a sign that something is wrong.

Finally, there is growing consensus among scientists interested in adolescence that a relatively small proportion of the adolescent population accounts for a relatively high proportion of the serious problems seen in this age group. Studies suggest that there is considerable overlap among the problems of substance abuse, school failure, unplanned pregnancy, unemployment, and delinquency. Many of the youngsters who have drug and alcohol problems are the same youngsters who leave school before graduation, get involved in criminal behavior, bear children out of wedlock, and have difficulty

In discussions of adolescent problem behavior, it is important to distinguish between occasional experimentation and enduring patterns of dangerous or troublesome behavior. Although the majority of adolescents experiment with alcohol sometime before high school graduation, and the majority will have been drunk at least once, relatively few teenagers will develop drinking problems or permit alcohol to adversely affect their school or interpersonal relationships. (Harriet Gans/The Image Works)

finding work. This troubled subgroup is disproportionately composed of poor, inner-city, non-white youngsters—which suggests that many of the problems we associate with adolescence may have more to do with class, region, and race than with adolescence itself. Later in this chapter, we shall examine current thinking about the so-called **problem behavior syndrome** (Jessor and Jessor, 1977).

In this chapter, we examine the nature, prevalence, consequences, and relief of four sets of problems typically associated with adolescence: *teenage pregnancy and childbearing, drug and alcohol use, conduct disorders and delinquency,* and *depression and suicide.* In each case, we ask three central questions: How many, and which, young people have problems in this area? What do we know about factors that contribute to problems in this area? And, finally, what approaches to prevention and intervention have the most promise? We begin our survey with one of the more controversial contemporary concerns: teenage pregnancy and childbearing.

TEENAGE PREGNANCY AND CHILDBEARING

Prevalence

Given the high rate of sexual activity and poor record of contraceptive use among contemporary adolescents (see Chapter 11), it comes as little surprise to learn that many young women become pregnant before the end of adolescence. Recent statistics indicate that nearly one-fourth of American young women experience pregnancy before the age of 18 and about 45 percent before their twenty-first birthday. Among black youth, over 40 percent experience pregnancy by age 18 and nearly two-thirds by age 21. These rates are actually slightly lower than they were in the 1970s, not because rates of sexual activity have declined, but primarily because of more effective contraceptive use among sexually active teenagers (Hayes, 1987).

It is important to keep in mind that not all adolescent pregnancies result in childbirth. About 40 percent of all teenage pregnancies are aborted, and slightly more than 10 percent end in miscarriage. Among women who carry their pregnancy full term, the vast majority—over 90 percent—keep and raise the infant, while one in ten chooses to have the child adopted. Thus, of the approximately 1 million pregnancies recorded among teenage women in 1984, approximately half ended in abortion or miscarriage, about 45 percent resulted in the birth of an infant who would be raised by his or her mother (with or without the help of a spouse or other family members), and about 5 percent resulted in the birth of an infant put up for adoption (Hayes, 1987).

Nature of the Problem

It is important to distinguish between pregnancies and actual births—a distinction that seems often to get lost in debates over the consequences of teenage pregnancy. Because of the many pregnant adolescents choosing abortion, the *birth rate* among teenage women is far lower than it would otherwise be, and it may surprise you to learn that the birth rate among adolescent women today is considerably lower than it was in previous eras. Contrary to the popular idea that teenage childbearing has reached epidemic proportions in this country is the truth of the matter: relatively more women gave birth to an infant before reaching adulthood in previous decades than is the case today—by a large margin. For example, in 1955 the rate of childbearing among women between the ages of 15 and 19 was ninety births per 1,000 women. In 1984, by contrast, it was about fifty births per 1,000 women (Furstenberg et al., 1987).

If teenage childbearing is less prevalent today than in earlier eras, why does the issue receive so much attention in the popular press?

FIGURE 13.1   In 1985, approximately one-fourth of all sexually active young women became pregnant, and approximately half of these women became parents. (Children's Defense Fund, 1988)

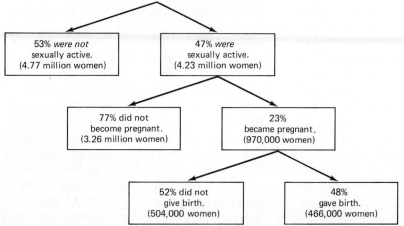

First, while the rate of childbearing may be lower today than before, the proportion of teenage childbearing that occurs *out of wedlock* is much higher. In earlier eras, adolescents who became pregnant were much more likely to marry before the child was born. Their pregnancy and childbearing did not cause as much concern, because they were "legitimated" by marriage. One source estimates that about half of all adolescent women who married during the late 1950s were pregnant at the time of marriage (Furstenberg et al., 1987). As recently as 1955, out-of-wedlock births accounted for only about 14 percent of all births to young women. But by 1984, this had skyrocketed to more than 55 percent (Furstenberg et al., 1987). Clearly, society is more tolerant of single parenthood and of nonmarital pregnancy (social scientists prefer the term *nonmarital* to the more commonly used *premarital*, because the former does not imply that marriage will necessarily take place at a later date), and many more women choose this option today than did so in the past. Nonetheless, one reason for the special concern about teenage childbearing in the popular press is that such a high proportion of it occurs outside of marriage. Whether this *should* be a concern, however— questions of morals aside for the moment—is still hotly debated, as we shall see in a moment. Indeed, there is some evidence that the fates of a large group of adolescent mothers are *worsened*, not bettered, by marrying the father of their child.

A second reason for widespread concern is that rates of teenage childbearing vary markedly across ethnic and socioeconomic groups. White and middle-class women are more likely to abort their pregnancies than are non-white and poor women, and, as a consequence, the problem of teenage childbearing is densely concentrated among economically disadvantaged, black, and Hispanic youth. Among white young women, 41 percent of all births occur outside of marriage; among black women of the same age, the figure is nearly 90 percent (Furstenberg et al., 1987). The rate for Hispanic women falls somewhere in between; interestingly, young Mexican women are more likely to bear their first child within marriage (the pattern similar to whites'), whereas young Puerto Rican women are more likely to bear children out of wedlock (the pattern similar to blacks') (Darabi et al., 1987). Because minority youth are likely to experience other problems as well, such as school failure or substance abuse, early childbearing is likely to take place in the context of limited social and economic resources. One problem that researchers have in studying adolescent childbearing is to disentangle the effects of childbearing itself from those of factors like economic stress.

Contributing Factors

Many myths permeate discussions of the causes of adolescent pregnancy and complicate what is actually a fairly simple matter. About the only reliable difference between young women who do and do not become pregnant during adolescence is effective contraceptive use. We have seen in previous chapters that sexual activity among American young people is high and contraceptive use sporadic and inadequate. Studies of adolescent contraceptive use, as we have seen, suggest that misinformation about sex and pregnancy, a lack of access to contraceptives, and adherence to the "personal fable" that unprotected intercourse is not going to result in conception all contribute to teenage pregnancy. No scientific evidence exists indicating that most— or even many—teenagers who become pregnant consciously or unconsciously want to have a baby. Studies comparing pregnant teenagers who do and do not terminate their pregnancies show that teenagers can make well-reasoned decisions about abortion and are not psychologically harmed if they choose abortion (Hayes, 1987). Moreover, studies suggest that an important factor accounting for the racial and socioeconomic differences in adolescent childbearing is that white and middle-class adolescent women perceive themselves as having more to lose— economically and careerwise—by having a child so early in life than do their minority and poor counterparts. By expanding educational and oc-

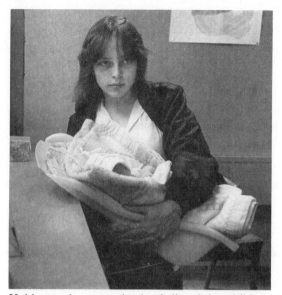

Unitl recently, most scientists believed that children born to teenage mothers were at great risk for a range of health and behavioral problems. New and more sophisticated studies, however, indicate that many of the problems that plague children born to adolescent mothers are due primarily to poverty and to the absence of a father figure for the child rather than to the mother's age. (Polly Brown/Archive Pictures)

cupational opportunities for poor and minority women, a greater number may realize that delaying childbearing may be preferable (Hayes, 1987).

The Role of the Father

Until recently, little was known about the male partners of pregnant adolescents. Now, however, research by Arthur Elster and Michael Lamb indicates that this group of males may share a number of distinguishing characteristics that differentiate them from their peers who do not impregnate adolescent women. Most important has been the discovery that the sexual partners of adolescent girls are less likely to be adolescents themselves than to be young adults and more likely than their peers to have had problems with school, with work, with drugs and alcohol, and with the law (Elster et al., 1987).

The discovery that higher rates of problem behavior characterize this population of men helps to explain why in some cases marriage may not be the best response to teenage pregnancy for the woman.

Consequences

As noted above, because teenage childbearing tends to go hand in hand with a variety of other problems—the most critical of which is poverty—it is extremely difficult to know whether any problems of teenage mothers or their children are due to the mother's young age or to other, correlated factors. Separating the effects of early childbearing from poverty is a matter of more than theoretical importance: If early childbearing is in fact a problem in and of itself, it would be important to direct preventive programs at deterring adolescent pregnancy (either by discouraging sexual activity or by encouraging effective contraceptive use) and childbearing (by encouraging adoption and abortion). But if *poverty*, not the mother's age, is the key, an entirely different set of strategies would be called for, aimed not at youngsters' sexual behavior but at all individuals' economic circumstances. It is extremely important, therefore, to ask whether and in what ways a mother's age at the time she gives birth affects her and her child's well-being.

The prevailing wisdom until recently was that children born to teenage mothers were at great risk for a range of health and behavioral problems in the short and long term, including low birth weight, conduct problems, hyperactivity, and achievement difficulties. New and more sophisticated studies, however, temper this conclusion. These new studies indicate that many of the problems believed to plague children born to adolescent mothers are due primarily to the environment of poverty and single parenthood these children grow up in, rather than to the mother's age. In general, children born to middle-class adolescents differ little from their counterparts born to older mothers, and children born to poor adolescents are similar to children born to equally poor adults. One important exception to this general similarity between the children of adolescent and adult mothers is that adolescent mothers—even of similar socioeconomic origin—interact with their infants less often in ways that are known to be beneficial to the child's cognitive and social development (Brooks-Gunn and Furstenberg, 1986). To what extent this actually jeopardizes the child's development, however, is not known with any certainty. Although studies suggest that children born to adolescent mothers are more likely to have school problems, more likely to be involved in misbehavior and delinquent activity, and more likely themselves to be sexually active at an early age (Furstenberg et al., 1987), it is difficult to link these behaviors to mothers' practices. We know from other studies that many of the problem behaviors seen among children of adolescent mothers are prevalent among poor children growing up in single-parent homes. Because adolescent mothers are more likely than adult mothers to be both unmarried and poor, their children are at greater risk of developing a variety of psychological and social problems. In other words, the greater incidence of problems among offspring of adolescent mothers may be due to the overall environment in which their children grow up, rather than to the ways in which they are raised by their mothers. Indeed, an extensive long-term follow-up study by Frank Furstenberg and his colleagues (1987) suggests that problems among children born to adolescent mothers are more likely to occur when the mothers themselves have economic and marital problems and when the adolescent mother has continued to have children.

Furstenberg's study of the long-term consequences of adolescent parenthood indicates that serious problems associated with it directly involve the teenage mother, however. His research indicates that discussions about the adverse consequences of teenage childbearing should focus more on its impact on the childbearer than the child. In general, women who bear children early are likely to suffer disruptions in their educational and occupational careers, and these disruptions can have dire long-term consequences. Not only are adolescent mothers more likely to come from a poor background, but they are also more likely to remain poor than their equally disadvantaged peers who delay childbearing until after their schooling is completed. Adolescent childbearing, then, can contribute to a vicious cycle of welfare dependency: individuals who grow up in families dependent on welfare are more likely to have children early in life, which generally means that their economic opportunities will be limited by having to change educational and occupational plans. The result often is continued dependence on public assistance by the adolescent mother and, therefore, her child—who, like his or her mother, grows up with welfare as a part of life. Although we can in theory separate the effects of poverty on children from the effects of adolescent childbearing, in reality the two usually go together, and the end result is that children born to adolescent mothers are more likely than other children to suffer the effects of malnutrition—in the womb as well as in the world—and environmental deprivation.

Yet the news is not always bad, and having a child early in life does not cast in concrete a life of poverty and misery for the mother and her youngster. Studies show that there is considerable diversity among teenage mothers in the routes that their adult lives take. As Furstenberg and his colleagues point out (1987), women who remained in high school and delayed subsequent childbearing fared a great deal better over the long run—as did their children—than their counterparts who dropped out of school or had more children relatively early on. Marriage tends to be a "high-risk" strategy (Furstenberg et al., 1987). In some cases, when a stable relationship is formed and economic resources are available, marriage improves the mother's and the child's chances for life success; this seems to be especially true for women who marry somewhat later. In other cases, however, a hasty decision to marry in the absence of a stable relationship and economic security actually worsens many other problems.

Treatment and Prevention

Although there are stories of young women whose lives are not devastated by early childbearing, in general, studies like Furstenberg's suggest that there are not many such successes. In general, the successes are women who have avoided dire poverty, rather than women who have achieved great economic success. Although the picture of adolescent parenthood appears less uniform or dire than typically painted in the popular press, there is still consensus among experts that it is important to try to prevent teenage pregnancy and childbearing. Unfortunately, this task is more easily said than done. To date, few strategies have proven effective on a large scale. One approach that we can be cautiously optimistic about involves a combination of school-based sex education and school-based health clinics through which adolescents can receive information about sex and pregnancy as well as contraception. Evaluations indicate that this combination of sex education and clinic actually diminishes the rate of teen pregnancy, even within inner-city communities characterized by high rates of adolescent pregnancy and childbearing (Zabin et al., 1986). Unfortunately, as you might suspect, many parents have objected to such programs in their community, fearing that they will stimulate teenage sexual activity. However, most studies indicate that these fears—however intuitively reasonable—are unwarranted (Furstenberg et al., 1987).

Research on the consequences of adolescent childbearing also suggests that many of the negative effects of having children early could be prevented or at least minimized by lessening the disruptive economic impact of teenage parenthood on young women's lives. What do we know about the factors that work toward this end? First, it is clear that marrying the father of the child may place the adolescent mother at greater risk if the father is not capable of supporting himself economically, much less his family. Studies show, in contrast, that if the father is able to find a good job and remain employed, he can be an important source of psychological and economic support and a healthy influence on the mother and child. Given the problems characteristic of male partners of adolescent mothers discussed earlier, however, it is all too likely that marriage may diminish, rather than enhance, an adolescent mother's economic circumstances. In addition, marriage places the adolescent mother at greater risk of having another child relatively soon, which further jeopardizes her already precarious economic situation. One of the factors most likely to worsen the problems of teenage mothers is having yet another child (Furstenberg et al., 1987). Moreover, teenage marriage, as you know, is very likely to end in divorce (see Chapter 10), which itself is an additional stressor on the mother and child.

Adolescent mothers therefore cannot always look to the father of the child to help break the cycle of poverty that afflicts young parents. However, they can, in many cases, look to their own parents for support, and this seems to be an effective strategy. Teenage mothers who move in with their own family for a short time are more likely to enjoy educational and occupational success than their counterparts who live on their own, studies show. The family's help allows the young mother to return to school or find employment. Without this help, many young mothers must drop out of school and find and pay for child care, which often is more costly than the income their low-paying jobs generate. Without a high school diploma, these women have little chance of improving their economic situation and, consequently, improving the opportunities for their child.

Because it is so important for young mothers to have adequate incomes and the chance for adequate employment, many policymakers have called for changes in the ways that schools treat pregnant students and for changes in the provision of day care. Among the most important are adaptations in school schedules and the development of school-based child-care centers, so that pregnant students can remain in school after the birth of their child; the expansion of subsidized child care for young mothers who are out of school, so that the economic benefits of having a job are not outweighed by the costs of suitable child care during the workday; and the expansion of family planning services to adolescent mothers so that they can prevent yet another pregnancy.

ADOLESCENT DRUG AND ALCOHOL USE

Our society sends young people mixed messages about drugs and alcohol. Television programs aimed at preadolescents urge viewers to "Just Say NO!" but the televised football games and adult situation comedies that many of these same viewers watch tell them, no less subtly, that having a good time with friends is virtually impossible without something alcoholic to drink. Many celebrities idolized by teenagers speak out against cocaine and marijuana, but many equally famous stars admit to using these same drugs. For each dollar spent by the Lung Association or American Cancer Society aimed at deterring cigarette smoking, many, many more are spent by cigarette manufacturers, aimed at convincing us that cigarettes make us sexy, powerful, and chic.

The mixed signals sent to young people about drugs and alcohol reflect, no doubt, the inconsistent way that we view these substances as a society: Some drugs (like alcohol or Valium) are fine, as long as they are not abused, but others (like cocaine or LSD) are not; some drinking (enough to relax at a party) is socially appropriate, but too much (enough to impair an automobile driver) is not; some people (those over 21) are old enough to handle drugs, but others (those under 21) are not. It is easy to see why teenagers do not follow the dictates of their elders when it comes to alcohol and drugs. How then, should we view drug and alcohol use among teenagers, when our backdrop is a society that much of the time tolerates, if not actively encourages, adults to use these same substances?

As with most of the problem behaviors that are common during adolescence, discussions of teenage drug and alcohol use are often filled more with rhetoric than with reality. The popular stereotype of contemporary young people is that they use and abuse a wide range of drugs more than their counterparts did previously, that the main reason adolescents use drugs and alcohol is peer pressure, and that the "epidemic" level of drug and alcohol use among American teenagers is behind many of the other problems associated with this age group—including academic underachievement, early pregnancy, suicide, and crime. The simplicity of these assertions is certainly tempting—after all, what could be more reassuring than to identify the "real" culprit (drugs) and the "real" causes (peers) of all of the maladies of young people? And what could be even more comforting than the belief that if we simply teach young people to "say no" to their peers, these problems will all disappear?

Unfortunately, what we would like to believe about adolescent drug and alcohol use is not necessarily identical to what the facts are. As we shall see in this section, although there are grains of truth to many of the popular claims about the causes, nature, and consequences of teenage alcohol and drug use, there are many widely held misconceptions about this subject, too.

Prevalence of Drug and Alcohol Use

Each year since 1975, a group of researchers from the University of Michigan has surveyed a nationally representative sample of over 16,000 American high school seniors on several aspects of their lifestyle and values, including their use and abuse of a variety of drugs. Because of the size and representativeness of the sample of respondents, this survey, called *Monitoring the Future* (Johnston, O'Malley, and Bachman, 1986), is the best source of information about patterns of adolescent drug and alcohol use. The most recent statistics available from these researchers are from the graduating class of 1985, and these are summarized in Figure 13.2, which indicates the prevalence and recency of use of eleven types of drugs, and Figure 13.3, which indicates the

Is there any doubt that our society sends young people mixed messages about drugs and alcohol? On this billboard, an advertisement against driving while intoxicated (DWI) was placed next to one promoting beer consumption. (AP/Wide World Photos)

percentage of high school seniors who are daily, or near-daily users.

These figures describe several interesting patterns. As you can see in Figure 13.2, the two major "legal" drugs—alcohol and cigarettes—are by far the most commonly used substances, both in terms of prevalence (the percentage of teenagers who have *ever* used the drug) and in terms of recency of use (the percentage of teenagers who have used the drug *within the last month*). Nearly all teenagers have tried alcohol, and more than two-thirds have tried cigarettes. About half of all seniors have tried marijuana, and about one-fourth have smoked marijuana at least once within the last month. After marijuana, however, the percentage of young people who have tried various other drugs drops precipitously, and the percentage of seniors who have used any of the other drugs within the last month is very small (Johnston et al., 1986).

Prevalence statistics, especially those that tap whether an individual has *ever* tried the substance in question, tell us little about the nature and extent of drug use from the standpoint of adolescents' health and well-being. It is one

thing to have tried alcohol or marijuana, but it is something else to use either of these substances so often that one's life and behavior are markedly affected. One of the best ways of examining this issue is to look at the percentage of young people who report using any of these substances daily or near daily (at least 20 times in the last 30 days) basis. These data are found in Figure 13.3. Here we see that cigarettes are the only drugs used by a substantial number of high school seniors daily (about 20 percent smoke daily) and that of the remaining drugs, only alcohol and marijuana are used daily by even a modest percentage (5 percent) of teenagers. Many adults welcome these statistics and find them reassuring—and in some senses they are. More disquieting, however, is an important statistic *not* in this table: Over one-third of all seniors report having abused alcohol (had more than five drinks in a row) at least once in the past two weeks (Johnston et al., 1986).

Taken together, the findings from these surveys cast doubt on some of the most fervently held stereotypes about adolescent drug use. It is true that many adolescents smoke cigarettes,

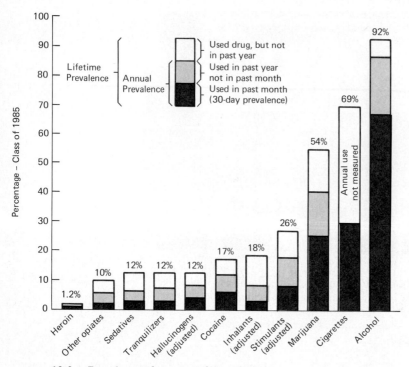

FIGURE 13.2   Prevalence of recency of use of eleven types of drugs among seniors in the class of 1985. (Johnston et al., 1986)

which is certainly cause for concern, and that many adolescents who drink do so in excess from time to time. But the data also indicate that only a very small proportion of young people have serious drug dependency problems (which would lead to daily use) or use hard drugs at all. Moreover, it is very unlikely that drug and alcohol use lurk behind the wide assortment of adolescent problems for which they are so frequently blamed. Rather, the pattern suggests that most adolescents have experimented with alcohol and marijuana, that many have used one or both of these drugs regularly, that alcohol is clearly the drug of choice among teenagers (some of whom drink to excess), and that most teenagers have not experimented with other drugs. From a health and safety standpoint, therefore, education about alcohol and cigarette use and abuse is more urgently needed and may potentially affect a larger percentage of

young people than education about any other drug type.

Because the *Monitoring the Future* study has tracked patterns of drug and alcohol use over time, we can use these data to examine changes in adolescents' use of various substances. Changes over time in the percentages of seniors reporting daily or near-daily use of marijuana or alcohol are graphed in Figure 13.4. You can see from these figures that the proportion of seniors reporting daily use of marijuana peaked in the late 1970s, declined steadily during the early 1980s, and leveled out during the mid-1980s. The pattern for alcohol is similar, if less striking: Daily alcohol use increased during the mid-1970s, peaked during the late 1970s, declined somewhat during the early 1980s, and has remained essentially unchanged since that time. For the most part, other drugs have followed a similar pattern of either decline or no change in

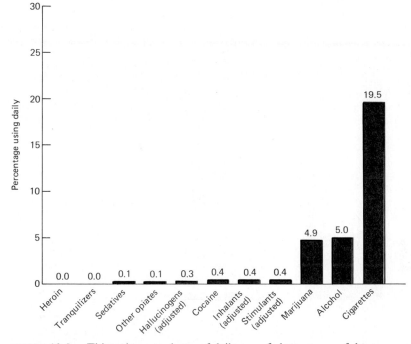

FIGURE 13.3   Thirty-day prevalence of daily use of eleven types of drugs among seniors in the class of 1985. (Johnston et al., 1986)

prevalence of use since the early 1980s. One notable exception is cocaine, however, which was used more frequently and more widely by high school seniors during the mid-1980s than previously (Johnston et al., 1986).

These figures treat different drugs as if their use is independent; many adolescents who use drugs have used more than one, and several researchers have studied the sequence through which adolescents experiment with different drugs. In general, most studies indicate that young people experiment with beer and wine before cigarettes or hard liquor, which precede marijuana use, which in turn precedes the use of other illicit drugs (cocaine, stimulants, LSD [Kandel, 1980]). But although experimentation may follow this sequence, this does not mean that alcohol use invariably *leads to* marijuana use or that marijuana use necessarily *leads to* experimentation with harder drugs. In fact, there is little evidence to support the idea that marijuana

is an inevitable "stepping stone" to hard drug use. The fact that such a sequence does exist, however, suggests that virtually all users of hard drugs have also tried alcohol, cigarettes, and marijuana and, moreover, that one way to prevent adolescents from experimenting with more serious drugs is to stop them from experimenting with alcohol and marijuana. In fact, studies show that adolescents who have not experimented with alcohol or marijuana by the time they are 21 are unlikely *ever* to use these or other drugs (Kandel and Logan, 1984). For this reason, alcohol and marijuana are considered "gateway" drugs, in the sense that they form a "gate" through which individuals pass before using harder drugs. Whether an individual passes through the gate, however, is influenced by many other factors beyond his or her previous patterns of drug use.

What to make of this mass of numbers, figures, and trends is not entirely clear. As you

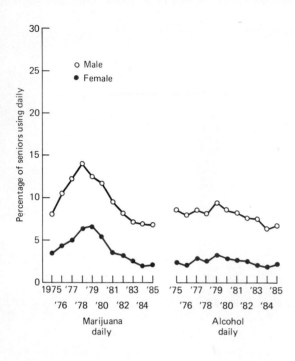

FIGURE 13.4   Trends in thirty-day prevalence of daily use of marijuana, alcohol, and cigarettes, by sex. Note: Daily use for alcohol and marijuana is defined as use on 20 or more occasions in the past thirty days. (Johnston et al., 1986)

can probably imagine, the picture is sufficiently complicated that the statistics can be used to argue for virtually any position. Perhaps the most reasonable reading is that the overall pattern of adolescent drug and alcohol use is not as bad as politicians and the popular media would have us believe but that there nevertheless is little reason to feel complacent. True, drug and alcohol use is lower now than it has been in previous years, but the decline in use that began in the early 1980s has stopped, and cigarette, alcohol, and marijuana use are all still too high, in an absolute sense. Moreover, there is some evidence that experimentation with drugs begins at an earlier age now than previously, so that the problem may not concern the prevalence of drug use among high school seniors but, instead, early experimentation with drugs among their younger counterparts. For example, more adolescents begin smoking cigarettes, drinking alcohol, and using marijuana *before* high school than during high school itself (Johnston et al., 1986). Many psychologists believe that early experimentation with drugs is more harmful than experimentation at a later age. Younger adoles-

cents may lack the psychological maturity or judgment necessary to use drugs in moderation or under safe circumstances, and younger adolescents may face unique developmental challenges that drug use interferes with (Baumrind and Moselle, 1985).

Causes and Consequences of Adolescent Drug and Alcohol Use

Adolescent drug and alcohol use is determined by a number of interrelated factors, and attempts to find the *sole* cause of this set of behaviors have not been fruitful. In looking at the causes of drug and alcohol use, it is especially important to keep in mind the distinction between occasional experimentation and regular, problematic use. Because the majority of adolescents have experimented with alcohol and marijuana, one can speculate that occasional alcohol and marijuana use has become normative among American high school students and, consequently, that there are plenty of normal, healthy young people who have used these drugs at least once.

The proportion of seniors reporting daily use of marijuana peaked in the late 1970s, declined steadily during the early 1980s, and leveled off during the mid-1980s. Although most adolescents have experimented with alcohol and marijuana, only a very small proportion of young people have serious drug-dependency problems or use hard drugs at all. (Arlene Collins/Monkmeyer Press)

Excessive alcohol or drug use, or, more precisely, alcohol or drug *abuse,* is a different matter. Young people who abuse drugs and alcohol are more likely to experience problems at school, to experience psychological distress and depression, to engage in "unprotected" sexual activity, and to become involved in dangerous or deviant activities, including crime, delinquency, and truancy (Irwin, 1986; Jessor and Jessor, 1977). Alcohol and drugs are typically implicated in adolescent automobile crashes, the leading cause of death and disability among American teenagers (Douglass, 1982), and in other fatal and nonfatal accidents, such as drownings, falls, and burns (Irwin, 1986). Adolescent substance abusers also expose themselves to the long-term health risks of excessive drug use that stem from addiction or dependency; in the case of cigarettes, alcohol, and marijuana, these risks are substantial and well-documented—among them,

cancer, heart disease, and kidney and liver damage.

Because of the clear and harmful consequences of drug and alcohol abuse during adolescence, much time and money has been spent studying its antecedents. Generally, four main sets of "risk factors" have emerged from this research, and the more risk factors that are present for an individual, the more likely he or she is to use and abuse drugs (Newcomb, Maddahian, and Bentler, 1986). First, individuals with certain personality characteristics—present before adolescence—are more likely to develop drug and alcohol problems than their peers. These characteristics include *anger, impulsivity, depression, and achievement problems* (Brook et al., 1986).

Second, individuals with *distant or hostile family relationships* are more likely to develop substance abuse problems than are their peers who grow up in close, nurturing families (Barnes, 1984). Drug-abusing youngsters are more likely than their peers to have parents who are excessively permissive (perhaps to the point of neglect), uninvolved, or rejecting. They are also more likely to come from homes in which one or both parents uses drugs or is tolerant of drug use (Brook, Whiteman, and Gordon, 1983; Brook, Whiteman, Gordon, and Brook, 1984; Newcombe, Huba, and Bentler, 1983).

Third, individuals with drug and alcohol problems are more likely to have *friends who also use and tolerate the use of drugs,* both because they are influenced by these friends and because they are drawn to them. As you read in Chapter 5, whether and how often adolescents use drugs is an important defining characteristic of peer groups—abstainers tend to have other abstainers as friends, users tend to have other users. Recent studies suggest that drug-using adolescents seek drug-using peers and that drug-using peers encourage even more drug use among their friends (Kandel, 1978).

Finally, adolescents who begin to use drugs a good deal are generally at a point in their own psychological development when they are especially susceptible to the influences around them that may lead them to make the transition into drug use and other deviant behavior (Jessor and Jessor, 1977). Periods of so-called **transition-proneness** are characterized by a high level of tolerance of the problem behavior in question, alienation from school and from family relationships, minimal involvement in religious activity, and general apathy. During transition-prone periods, adolescents are likely to experiment with many different problem behaviors, including drugs, alcohol, and delinquency.

In summary, research on the causes of adolescent drug and alcohol use suggests that a youngster's involvement is the consequence of a set of converging risk factors. Generally, the more of these risk factors an individual has, the more likely he or she is to develop a drug or alcohol problem, in part because their effect is cumulative, but in part because the presence of one of the four risk factors often predisposes the adolescent toward another. For example, adolescents with distant family relationships are more likely to choose drug-using friends than are adolescents with close family relations (Foster-Clark and Blyth, 1987). At the same time, however, the absence of one of the four risk factors can buffer an adolescent against the ill effects of the others. Positive achievement experiences in adolescence or close family relationships can buffer a teenager against the potential negative impact of having an impulsive or aggressive personality (Brook et al., 1986).

Prevention of Drug and Alcohol Problems

Considered together, these studies of adolescent drug and alcohol use suggest that merely encouraging adolescents to say "No!" to drugs—however simplistically appealing this strategy—is unlikely to substantially diminish substance abuse. Rather, findings from scientific studies of the antecedents of adolescent substance abuse problems point to several potentially more fruitful recommendations about the prevention of abuse. First, the studies of personality risk factors suggest that it is possible to identify before adolescence individuals who may be predisposed toward developing problems. Parents might monitor these youngsters more carefully, for example. Second, studies of family risk factors indicate that many adolescent problem behaviors actually have their roots in childhood family relationships, which suggests the need for early intervention in families experiencing difficulty. Third, studies of peer risk factors suggest that an adolescent's friends have an important influence on the adolescent's behavior and that parents and other involved adults have reason to be concerned if their child begins to run with a drug-using crowd. Finally, studies of transition-proneness suggest that there may be periods of heightened vulnerability in an adolescent's development when he or she may need more attention and protection by adults.

JUVENILE DELINQUENCY AND DISORDERS OF CONDUCT

Although social scientists continue to disagree about the causes and treatment of delinquent behavior during adolescence, there is one point on which there is tremendous agreement—violations of the law are far more common among adolescents and young adults than among any other age segment of the population. Part of this pattern stems from the fact that certain violations, called **status offenses**, are by definition limited to minors. Status offenses, such as truancy, running away from home, or using alcohol, are behaviors that are not against the law for adults but that nevertheless violate established codes of conduct for juveniles. Even if we discount status offenses, however, research shows that both *violent crimes*, such as assault, rape, and murder, and *property crimes*, such as robbery, theft, and arson, increase in frequency between the preadolescent and adolescent years, peak during the high school years, and decline somewhat during young adulthood (Federal Bureau of Investigation, 1983). Individuals under the age of 18, who comprise about one-quarter of the population, account for about half of all property crimes, and individuals between the ages of 18 and 24, who comprise a little more than one-tenth of the population, account for well over one-third of all violent crimes (U.S. Bureau of the Census, 1985).

Rates of crime among American youth have followed a pattern over time that is strikingly similar to that seen when rates of drug use are examined over time. Between 1950 and 1980, roughly speaking, there were steady increases in juvenile arrests for virtually all classes of misbehavior. In the early 1980s, the rate of youthful criminal activity leveled off, and it has dropped slightly since then (Farrington, 1986). Because the curves for substance abuse and delinquent activity parallel each other and are similar to several other trends in adolescent problem behavior—such as suicide and academic underachievement—some social scientists have proposed more general explanations for the inverted U-shaped pattern found across a relatively wide class of problems (Easterlin, 1980). In the box on page 418, we take a look at one of these explanations.

Most of the data we have on adolescent misbehavior comes from official arrest records. Consequently, it is important to keep in mind that the "official" figures on adolescent crime may both *underreport* and *selectively report* rates of misbehavior. Underreporting results from the fact that many adolescents commit offenses that are undetected by authorities or that are handled outside official reporting procedures—for example, when an adolescent caught shoplifting is reprimanded by the storekeeper instead of being referred to the police. (Only about one-third of crimes are ever reported to the police [Krisberg et al., 1986].) Selective reporting results from the fact that lower-class and minority youngsters are more likely to be arrested and to be treated more harshly than are other youngsters who commit similar offenses, so official statistics may artificially inflate the proportion of crimes committed by poor, minority youth.

An alternative to relying on official records is to go to adolescents directly and ask them about their involvement in various criminal or status offenses. Several researchers have done this, promising the respondents anonymity and confidentiality. The results of these surveys have been surprising, to say the least. They do not necessarily provide a more accurate picture of juvenile crime, but they certainly provide a *different* one. Three conclusions are especially interesting. First, the surveys indicate that a very large proportion of adolescents—between 60 and 80 percent, depending on the survey sample—have engaged in delinquent behavior at one time or another (Gold and Petronio, 1980; Huizinga and Elliot, 1985). Most of these behaviors were not serious crimes, but they nevertheless were genuine status or criminal offenses.

Second, in contrast to official records, which indicate a disproportionate involvement of minority youth in delinquent activities, the surveys indicate that once social class is taken into account, there are relatively few ethnic or racial differences in the prevalence of delinquent activity—in either minor or serious misbehavior. According to data from the 1980 National Youth Survey, for example, nearly equal proportions of white, black, and Hispanic youth admitted to having committed some type of delinquent activity (65 percent among whites, 72 percent among blacks, and 59 percent among Hispanics), and equal proportions admitted having committed a serious crime—about 13 percent in each group. Moreover, there are no racial differences in the prevalence of chronic, or repeat, offenders (Krisberg et al., 1986). There are *social class* differences in serious criminal activity, however, which are often attributed to race or ethnicity.

Finally, the surveys indicate that even though minority youth do not commit more delinquent behavior than white youth—and do not commit more *serious* delinquent behavior than white youth, either—minority youth are far more likely to be arrested and far more likely to be treated harshly by the juvenile justice system. Black adolescents are seven times more likely to be arrested than white adolescents for minor offenses and twice as likely to be arrested for serious crimes (Krisberg et al., 1986). Minority youth in general are more likely to be sent to correctional facilities than are white youth who commit similar offenses (Krisberg et al., 1986). Thus the reason for the stereotype of the nonwhite juvenile offender is the higher proportion of arrests in this group, not the higher proportion of delinquent and criminal activity. In addition, the disproportionate number of nonwhite youth living in poverty contributes to racial differences in criminal activity.

Although studies indicate that most adolescents—regardless of their social backgrounds—do *something* that violates the law at one time or another, the vast majority of teenagers who violate the law do so only once. Thus, while most adolescents have violated the law, a relatively small number of adolescents account for a relatively high proportion of serious criminal activity. One estimate is that about 15 percent of the teenage population accounts for more than half of all adolescent delinquent activity and that an even smaller proportion accounts for virtually *all* serious activity (Gold and Petronio, 1980). It is important, therefore, in thinking about the causes of delinquent behavior, to distinguish between delinquent behavior that is serious and chronic and delinquent behavior that is less worrisome. As you will see momentarily, these two sets of delinquent behavior have very different antecedents.

Causes of Delinquent Behavior

In general, the earlier an adolescent's "criminal career" begins, the more likely he or she is to become a chronic offender, commit serious and violent crimes, and continue committing crimes as an adult. The older an adolescent is when the delinquent activity first appears, the less worrisome his or her behavior is likely to become. For purposes of discussion, therefore, it is helpful to distinguish between youngsters who begin misbehaving before adolescence and those whose delinquent activity first appears during adolescence. The causes and the consequences of delinquency that begins during preadolescence are quite different from those of delinquency that begins during adolescence.

Unsocialized delinquents. In general, youngsters whose problems with the law begin before adolescence are very psychologically troubled. Most of these delinquents are male, many are poor, and a disproportionate number come from homes in which divorce has occurred. More important, however, chronic delinquents typically come from disorganized families with hostile, neglectful parents who have mistreated their children and failed to instill in them proper standards of behavior or the psychological foundations of self-control. The idea that family factors may underlie this type of delinquency—because of either genetic or environmental influences—is supported by observations that preadolescent delinquency tends to run in families. Many ad-

Surveys indicate that a very large proportion of adolescents—between 60 and 80 percent, depending on the survey sample—have engaged in delinquent behavior at one time or another. Most of these behaviors were not serious crimes, but nevertheless they were chargeable offenses. (Joel Gordon)

olescents who have been in trouble with the law from an early age have siblings who have had similar problems (Loeber and Stouthamer-Loeber, 1987).

Some social scientists have referred to these youngsters as **unsocialized delinquents** (Gleuck and Gleuck, 1950), because they have not adequately acquired the norms and standards of society. A healthy conscience develops out of close and supportive family relationships early in life, and it is likely that among many unsocialized delinquents this process was disrupted. Indeed, several studies indicate that many of these individuals had psychological and social problems, such as excessive aggression, that were observable very early—in some cases, as early as preschool. Contrary to popular belief, there is no evidence that these individuals have low self-esteem, or that raising their self-esteem does anything to diminish their propensity to-

ward misbehavior. As you will read, the prognosis for change in this group of adolescents is very grim.

Socialized delinquents. In contrast to youngsters who begin their delinquent careers before adolescence, those who begin after adolescence do not always show signs of psychological abnormality or severe family pathology. Typically, the offenses committed by these youngsters do not develop into serious criminality, and typically these individuals do not violate the law after adolescence. Usually, their misbehavior is limited to a small number of offenses, and if they are caught and dealt with swiftly, they are unlikely to continue misbehaving. Because these individuals have apparently learned the norms and standards of society and are reasonably healthy psychologically, social scientists refer to them as **socialized delinquents** (Miller, 1958).

Current research indicates that some family factors may be associated with socialized delinquency. In particular, there is some evidence that these youngsters are less carefully monitored by their parents (Dornbusch et al., 1985; Patterson and Stouthamer-Loeber, 1985). But there also is evidence that the role of the peer group may be very important (Brown, Clasen, and Eicher, 1986). Specifically, studies show that much of this kind of delinquent activity occurs in group situations in which adolescents are pressured by their friends to go along with the group. In Chapter 9, you read about studies of age differences in susceptibility to peer pressure, which show that susceptibility increases between preadolescence and middle adolescence and then declines. It comes as no surprise, therefore, to discover that much socialized delinquency follows the same pattern: Rates are low during preadolescence, peak during middle adolescence, and drop off as adolescence ends (Berndt, 1979). The difference between adolescents who do and who do not engage in socialized delinquency may be related to two factors: the extent to which their parents monitor them and their susceptibility to peer pressure.

Treatment and Prevention of Juvenile Delinquency

Given the important differences between the causes of unsocialized and socialized delinquency, one would expect that these two groups would be best served by different sorts of preventive and after-the-fact interventions. In order to lower the rate of unsocialized delinquency, we would need to either prevent disruption in family relationships from occurring in the first place or try to repair the psychological damage that these youngsters have suffered because of their upbringing. These strategies are easier proposed than done, however. Our society is hesitant to intervene to prevent family disruption, because we typically wait until we see a sign of trouble in a family before acting. Unfortunately, waiting until after family disruption has occurred before intervening may have little bene-

fit, for research shows that the outlook for delinquents who have begun their criminal careers early is not very good. Various attempts at therapy and other sorts of tretment have not, by and large, proven successful. Some studies show that placing these youngsters in group homes—essentially, in the care of surrogate parents—may be successful occasionally. But the sorry truth is that most chronic delinquents, despite our attempts to treat them, go on to commit serious and violent crimes and continue their criminal behavior into adulthood.

The prognosis for the socialized delinquent

In general, youngsters whose problems with the law begin before adolescence are psychologically troubled youth. Most of these delinquents are male, many are poor, and a disproportionate number come from homes in which divorce has occurred. These delinquents typically come from disorganized families with hostile, neglectful parents who have mistreated their children and failed to instill in them proper standards of behavior or the psychological foundations of self-control. (Susan Lapides/Design Conceptions)

is, as you would guess, much better. Because they have internalized a basic foundation of norms and moral standards, it is easier to help them control their own behavior and stop misbehaving. Three types of strategies have a good chance of succeeding. First, by helping these youngsters learn to resist peer pressure, we can give them the necessary psychological tools to avoid being drawn into misbehavior simply to go along with the crowd (Kaplan, 1983). Second, by training parents to monitor their children more effectively, we can minimize the number of opportunities adolescents have to engage in peer-oriented misbehavior (Loeber and Stouthamer-Loeber, 1987). Finally, by treating delinquency seriously when it occurs—making sure an adolescent knows that his or her misbehavior has definite consequences—we can deter an adolescent from doing the same thing again in the future.

ADOLESCENT DEPRESSION AND SUICIDE

As you know, adolescence is a time of many demands: Teenagers must adapt to changes in their physical apperance, to the new expectations of others, and to new social roles. These demands may prompt extensive self-examination and introspection in an attempt to establish a coherent sense of identity, a healthy sense of autonomy, and an accurate accounting of one's strengths and weaknesses. Most individuals emerge from adolescence confident, with a healthy sense of who they are and where they are headed. But in some instances, the changes and demands of adolescence may leave a teenager feeling helpless, confused, and pessimistic about the future. Although minor fluctuations in self-esteem during early adolescence are commonplace—as you read in Chapter 8—it is not normal for adolescents (or adults, for that matter) to feel a prolonged or intense sense of hopelessness or frustration. Such young people are likely to be psychologically depressed and in need of professional help.

In its mild form, **depression** is probably the most common psychological disturbance among adolescents (Weiner, 1980), but problems in measuring and defining depression make it difficult to say exactly how prevalent the disorder is. It is helpful to distinguish between depressive symptoms anad depression as a disorder. Many more individuals have occasional depressive symptoms than suffer from the clinical disorder that is recognized as depression by professionals. According to some large-scale surveys, about 25 percent of adolescents have depressive feelings, but less than 3 percent of adolescents would be characterized as severely depressed according to standard diagnostic criteria (Chartier and Ranieri, 1984). There is a dramatic increase in the prevalence of depressive feelings around the time of puberty; depression is half as common during childhood as it is during adolescence. Interestingly, whereas depressive feelings are more common among boys than girls prior to adolescence, depression is much more common among females than males after puberty. This sex difference in the prevalence of depression (see the box on page 421) persists throughout most of adulthood (Rutter and Garmezy, 1983).

The Nature of Adolescent Depression

Although we typically associate depression with feelings of sadness, there are other symptoms that are important signs of the disturbance, and sadness alone, without any other symptoms, may not indicate depression in the clinical sense of the term. One way of thinking about depression is to consider its four sets of symptoms (Chartier and Ranieri, 1984). Depression has *emotional* manifestations, including dejection, decreased enjoyment of pleasurable activities, and low self-esteem. It has *cognitive* manifestations, such as pessimism and hopelessness. Depressed individuals also have *motivational* symptoms, including apathy and boredom. Finally depression usually has *vegetative*, or physical features, such as a loss of appetite, difficulties sleeping, and loss of energy.

more people in age group → more problems

Is "Cohort-Crowding" a Common Cause of Adolescent Disturbance?

If you were to graph the rates of the four sets of problems discussed in this chapter between 1955 and 1985, you would be startled by the similarity in the curves. Between 1960 and 1980, rates of out-of-wedlock births, adolescent drug and alcohol use, juvenile crime, and teenage suicide skyrocketed. Sometime around 1980, each of the four curves began to level off, and following that time, most showed a slight decline. Although rates of these four problems are still too high today, the remarkable increase in their prevalence that characterized the 1960s and 1970s has clearly abated. Even if we look at something less dramatic—high school seniors' scores on the Scholastic Aptitude Test (SAT), for instance—we find a parallel trend: Scores worsened between 1960 and 1980, and then the decline leveled off. Since that time, scores have improved slightly.

Some social scientists believe that the similarities in these indicators of adolescent troubles are more than coincidental. Specifically, they have argued that rates of adolescent problems—from the fatal to the mundane—are related to the size of the adolescent population. The more "crowded" a cohort of adolescents is (a cohort, as you read in Chapter 3, is a group of individuals born during the same era), the more prevalent problems will be in that generation. The smaller the cohort, the lower the rate of problems. Predictions made from this **birth-cohort theory** (Easterlin, 1980) about changes in rates of problem behavior over time have been astonishingly accurate.

If you turn back for a moment to page 157, you will see a graph that depicts the percentage of the American population comprised of 15- to 19-year-olds. If you were to add younger adolescents into the figure, the curve would shift slightly to the right, and the peak in the graph would occur around 1980. This increase reflects the movement into adolescence of the baby boom cohort, the large group of individuals born dur-

ing the twenty years after World War II. The picture parallels exactly the pattern found when adolescent problems are graphed: A moderate increase from 1955 until 1960, a dramatic increase between 1960 and 1980, and a decline thereafter. In other words, as the adolescent cohort became more populous, problems increased, but when the growth of this cohort leveled off, so did its rate of problem behavior.

Because rates of adolescent problem behavior are always adjusted for the size of the adolescent population (for example, the juvenile crime rate is reported in terms of crimes per 1,000 adolescents), fluctuations over time in *rates* of out-of-wedlock births, drug and alcohol use, crime, or suicide do not happen simply because there are more adolescents around to get into trouble. Rather, there appears to be something about being a member of a crowded generation that increases the risk of an individual getting into trouble.

Why should crowdedness increase problem behavior? One explanation is that when a cohort is crowded, its members must compete more fiercely for economic and social resources—for college admissions, for jobs, for marriage partners, for housing—and that this competition intensifies pressure on individuals. While most individuals are able to manage this pressure, some react by turning to drugs, crime, or other self- or socially destructive behavior. The competition for resources may be enough to push a slightly vulnerable youngster over the edge from health to deviance.

An alternative explanation of the birth-cohort phenomenon focuses on family size (Zajonc, 1976). In relatively more crowded cohorts there is greater percentage of youngsters from large families. These individuals, the theory goes, have received proportionately less attention from their parents and other caregivers and therefore have had less opportunity to profit from the sorts of parent-child interactions that promote healthy social

①more competition
②less attention in large families
③no strong bonds with society

and cognitive development. In other words, in a large birth cohort there may be relatively more children who have not had the most favorable family relationships and who, consequently, may be more vulnerable to developing psychological and behavioral problems.

An additional explanation for the observation that trends in adolescent problem behaviors often parallel one another is that different problem behaviors, such as precocious sexual activity, drug and alcohol use, and delinquency, often go hand in hand. Three theories about why this is so have been offered. First, because individuals who are involved in one type of problem behavior are more likely than their peers to be involved in a second type of problem behavior (for instance, adolescents who use drugs are more likely than nondrug users to be involved in delinquent activity), some researchers, most prominent among them psychologist Richard Jessor, have described a **problem behavior syndrome** (Jessor and Jessor, 1977). Jessor and his colleagues believe that there is an underlying cause or basis for a wide array of adolescent problems. According to this theory, the underlying cause is *unconventionality* in both the adolescent's personality and social environment (Donovan and Jessor, 1985). Unconventional individuals are tolerant of deviance in general, not highly connected to school or to religious institutions, and very liberal in their social views. They are more likely to engage in a wide variety of **risk-taking behavior**, including experimentation with illegal drugs, sex without contraception, and delinquent activity. Unconventional environments are those in which a large number of individuals share these same attitudes. If such a problem behavior syndrome does indeed exist, we would expect to find that increases in the rate of one type of problem (for example, drug use) would be accompanied by increases in the rate of another type of problem (for example, delinquency), because each increase actually reflects increases in the same underlying cause (unconventionality).

A somewhat different view has been proposed by sociologist Denise Kandel. Kandel and her associates have shown that involvement in a given problem behavior may itself lead to involvement in a second one. For example, the use of illicit drugs other than marijuana (for example, cocaine, heroin) increases the chances that an adolescent will become premaritally pregnant (Yamaguchi and Kandel, 1987). Thus, problem behaviors may cluster together not only because of an underlying trait such as unconventionality, but because some activities—drug use in particular—may place the young person at risk for involvement in others.

According to a third view, **social control theory** (Hirschi, 1969), individuals who do not have strong bonds to society's institutions—such as the family, the school, or the workplace—will be likely to deviate and behave unconventionally in a variety of ways. This view suggests that the apparent clustering of different problem behaviors in a segment of the youth population may stem from an underlying weakness in the attachment of these youngsters to society. This underlying problem leads to the development of an unconventional attitude, to membership in an unconventional peer group, or to involvement in one or several problem behaviors that may set a chain of problem activities in motion.

The birth-cohort theory is especially intriguing because it permits us to make predictions about the future—something social scientists are generally reluctant to do. Although we obviously do not know for sure how the next generations of adolescents will fare, an examination of actual and projected population trends gives us some idea of what we may have in store. As you can see from the graph on page 157, the decline in the size of the adolescent population will soon halt. This is because the baby boom cohort began having children of their own during the 1970s, and these children—who will, by virtue of the sheer size of their parents' cohort, be members of a crowded cohort—will begin to enter adolescence during the late 1980s and early 1990s. By the year 2000, the size of the adolescent population will be even greater than it was in 1980. These trends suggest that the rate of adolescent problem behavior will begin to rise again during the 1990s and continue to increase as we move toward the end of this century.

Obviously, the size of the adolescent cohort is not the only factor affecting the rate of problem behavior among young people. You can probably think of other explanations for large-scale fluctuations in adolescent problems, including changes in teenagers' access to drugs, changes in the rate of divorce, or widespread changes in attitudes and values that affect adolescents as well as adults. But the birth-cohort theory helps us understand, once again, that it is difficult to make sense out of adolescent behavior without considering the context in which young people grow up. Part of that context includes the number of individuals who are adolescents at the same time.

Depression during adolescence is often accompanied by other psychosocial or behavioral problems, which occasionally lead to difficulties in diagnosis or treatment. This appears to be a special problem for professionals working with very young adolescents. Because their sense of self-esteem may be especially fragile, young adolescents may find it difficult to admit self-critical thoughts and feelings of helplessness to themselves or to others. Some depressed adolescents, particularly those under 16, indicate their problems through excessive fatigue, hypochondria (excessive worry about health problems), or difficulties in concentration. Others may ward off their depression through restless, unproductive activity—in an "effort to keep one step ahead of having time to think" (Weiner, 1980, p. 456). And others may make appeals for help by running away, behaving rebelliously, or becoming involved in delinquent or antisocial activity. Although these behaviors often indicate problems other than depression, behavior problems are sometimes signs of underlying depression when they appear suddenly and follow a loss of one sort or another. Take the example of a teenager who has an excellent academic record and has never been in trouble with the law. If his grades fall dramatically following his parents' divorce and he becomes involved in delinquent activity, he may be suffering from depression.

Diagnosing and studying depression among adolescents has been a tricky business for two very different reasons. On the one hand, professionals have been tempted to attribute nearly *all* observable difficulties to unseen depression. In instances of "masked depression," behaviors such as school phobia, running away from home, or anorexia nervosa were thought to hide, or mask, the "real" problem—depression. Now, however, it is widely recognized that not all adolescents with behavior problems are necessarily depressed but that depression and other problems can coexist in some cases (Chartier and Ranieri, 1984). In cases in which the main problem seems not to be depression, a careful clinician would certainly want to probe to see if depressive symptoms were present but would not necessarily jump to the conclusion that depression and behavior problems always go hand in hand.

On the other hand, the popular stereotype of adolescents as "normally disturbed" leads many parents and teachers to fail to recognize genuine psychological problems when they appear. You can probably imagine a parent's description of an adolescent daughter who is critical of herself (which can be an emotional manifestation of depression), unduly negative (a possible cognitive manifestation), bored with everything (a possible motivational manifestation), and not very interested in eating (a possible vegetative manifestation). It would be easy for this parent to overlook a potentially very real problem and dismiss her daughter's mood and behavior as normal. Obviously, not all instances of self-criticism or apathy reflect psychological

The Sexes: Why Are There Sex Differences in Rates of Teenage Depression?

Before adolescence, boys are somewhat more likely to exhibit depressive symptoms than girls, but after puberty the sex difference in the prevalence of depression reverses significantly. From early adolescence until very late in adulthood, women report far more depression than men. Why might adolescence mark a turning point in this pattern?

Psychologists do not have a clear answer at this time. Although the fact that the emergence of a strong sex differential coincides with puberty suggests a biological explanation, there actually is little evidence that the sex difference in depression is directly attributable to sex differences in hormonal changes (Rutter and Garmezy, 1983). More likely, changes in social relationships around the time of puberty may leave girls more vulnerable than boys to some forms of psychological distress, and depression may be a stereotypically feminine way of manifesting it. To better understand this process, it helps to look at what we know about sex differences in depression among adults.

Although women are more likely than men to experience depression in adulthood, the sex differential among adults is limited to married individuals (Gove, 1972). Comparisons of single, divorced, and widowed individuals show no higher rates of depression among women than men and, in some cases, higher rates among men than women. These findings argue against straightforward biological explanations and suggest instead that there is something about the institution of marriage that contributes to women's higher rate of depression (Bernard, 1973). One explanation is that the role of wife in our society is relatively powerless and not especially gratifying.

Knowing this and knowing that intimate relationships between the sexes often begin at puberty, we can speculate that the emergence of sex differences has something to do with the social role that the adolescent girl may find herself in as she enters the world of boy-girl relationships. As you read in previous chapters, this role may bring conflict over achievement, due to fears that success will be perceived as unattractive; heightened self-consciousness over physical appearance; and increased concern over popularity with peers. Since many of these feelings may provoke helplessness, hopelessness, and anxiety, adolescent girls may be more susceptible to depressive feelings. To make matters worse, pressures on young women to behave in sex-stereotyped ways, which intensify during adolescence (Hill and Lynch, 1983), may lead girls to adopt some behaviors and dispositions—passivity, dependency, and fragility, for example—that they have been socialized to believe are part of the feminine role.

This is not to say, of course, that boys do not have their share of mental health problems during adolescence as well. In fact, boys are far more likely than girls to develop drug and alcohol problems and to commit criminal and delinquent acts. One way to cast the difference is that adolescent girls are more likely to manifest psychological distress through processes that turn the distress inward (such as depression), whereas boys are more likely to show distress through processes that turn the distress outward (such as aggression). There may be sex differences in the expression of depression, but neither sex has cornered the market on problems.

While minor fluctuations in self-esteem during early adolescence are commonplace, it is not normal for adolescents to feel a prolonged or intense sense of hopelessness or frustration. Such young people are likely to be psychologically depressed and in need of professional help. In its mild form, depression is probably the most common psychological disturbance among adolescents. (Patt Blue/Archive)

disturbance. But a good rule of thumb is that an individual who displays three or more of the signs of depression for two weeks should probably consult a professional.

Adolescent Suicide

Each year, approximately one out of every 1,000 American adolescents attempts suicide. Fortunately, the vast majority of these attempts—over 98 percent—are not successful. Contrary to myth, adolescents' suicide attempts are rarely impulsive reactions to immediate distress, such as breaking up with someone. Rather, adolescents who attempt to kill themselves usually have made appeals for help and have tried but have not found emotional support from family or friends. As psychologist Irving Weiner has observed, "Communication is a key aspect of adolescent suicidal behavior, probably more so

than it is in adults—a larger percentage of whose suicidal behavior reflects a wish to die rather than to bring about changes in how others are treating them" (1980, p. 459). Research also shows that suicidal youth are more likely than nonsuicidal youth to have come from disrupted or conflict-ridden homes and to feel rejected by one or both of their parents (Weiner, 1980). In many cases, alcohol or drug problems are present.

Only a very small proportion of the adolescent population attempts suicide. You may have read that suicide is a leading cause of death among young people, but this is primarily because very few young people die from other causes, such as disease. Although the rate of suicide rises rapidly during the middle adolescent years, it continues to rise throughout adulthood, and suicide is a much more common cause of death among adults than it is among young people (Rutter and Garmezy, 1983; Weiner, 1980). Completed suicide is more common among older adults than adolescents and more common among men than women. Attempted suicide, however, is more common during adolescence than during adulthood and far more common among adolescent girls than boys (Rutter and Garmezy, 1983).

The adolescent suicide rate increased alarmingly between 1950 and 1980—the suicide rate among 15- to 19-year-olds, for example, quadrupled between 1955 and the end of the 1970s (National Center for Health Statistics, 1982). A variety of explanations have been given for the increase in suicide among American youth, including pressures to grow up earlier, increasing rates of divorce, less contact with adults, high rates of residential mobility, and having to face an unpredictable job market (Bronfenbrenner, 1974; Rutter, 1979). These theories, while intuitively reasonable, however, have not been systematically tested. Moreover, around 1980, the adolescent suicide rate leveled off and has not increased since (Wetzel, 1987). Any theory of the causes of adolescent suicide would have to account for the leveling off of the rate after 1980 as well as for the pre-1980 increase (see box on pages 418–421.)

Recently, several researchers have noted that adolescent suicides sometimes occur in clusters—as if there is some sort of contagion effect. A youngster may attempt suicide, and shortly thereafter, a rash of attempts will be reported in the same school district or in nearby communities. This pattern of multiple suicides has raised concerns about the advisability of publicizing adolescent suicides and suicide attempts. It was initially thought that publicity surrounding suicide would help increase community awareness of the problem and that such news coverage ultimately would lower the suicide rate. Because a number of studies now demonstrate that publicity increases the likelihood of further suicide attempts, however, this strategy is being reconsidered (Gould and Shaffer, 1986; Phillips and Carstensen, 1986). Instead, efforts are more likely to be aimed at diminishing the pressures,

Contrary to myth, adolescents' suicide attempts are rarely impulsive reactions to immediate distress, such as breaking up with someone. Rather, adolescents who attempt to kill themselves usually have made appeals for help and have tried to seek—but have not found—emotional support from family or friends. (Nancy Hays/Monkmeyer)

drug problems, and family difficulties believed to lead adolescents to consider taking their life.

Causes and Treatment of Adolescent Depression

A variety of theories have been proposed to account for the onset of depression during adolescence, and current consensus is that depression is likely to be the result of interacting environmental conditions and individual predispositions rather than either set of factors alone. Depression may result when individuals who are predisposed toward it are exposed to chronic or acute circumstances that precipitate a depressive reaction. Individuals who are not predisposed toward depression are able to withstand a great deal of stress, for instance, without developing any psychological problems. Other individuals, who have strong predispositions toward the disorder, may become depressed in the face of circumstances that most of us would consider to be quite normal.

Research has focused both on individual predispositions toward depression and on the environmental circumstances likely to precipitate the disorder. Because depression has been found to have a strong genetic component, it is believed that at least some of the predisposition toward depression is biological and may be related to problematic patterns of *neuroendocrine functioning* (*neuroendocrine* refers to hormonal activity in the brain and nervous system). Other researchers have focused more on the *cognitive set* of depressed individuals, suggesting that people with tendencies toward hopelessness, pessimism, and self-blame are more likely to interpret events in their lives in ways that lead to the development of depression. Some theorists (Seligman and Peterson, 1986) believe that these sorts of cognitive sets develop during childhood and play a role in the onset of depression during adolescence.

Researchers who have been more concerned with the environmental determinants of depression have focused on three different sets of conditions. According to one viewpoint, depression is due to some sort of loss—the loss of an important relationship (for example, as a result of parents' divorce or death), the loss of something safe and familiar (moving to a new neighborhood), or the loss of self-esteem (failing at something important) (Weiner, 1980). Other scientists have contrasted the immediate environments of depressed and nondepressed individuals and have found that depressed individuals receive less reinforcement from their activities and relationships (e.g., Lewinsohn, 1975). Finally, chronic or acute stress can trigger psychological distress, of which depression is a likely manifestation (Newcomb et al., 1981). Al-

though these various environmental perspectives on depression are derived from different theories about the causes of psychological distress, they are certainly consistent with each other: An important loss (failing to gain admission to a sought-after college) can be described as a "stressor," for example, or as something that leads to a "reduction in reinforcement." They share the notion that negative conditions in the environment, broadly defined, may trigger depressive reactions in individuals predisposed in that direction.

You read earlier that the prevalence of depression increases during adolescence. Can these various theories about the causes of depression account for this? For the most part, they can. Biological theorists can point to the hormonal changes of puberty, which are likely to have implications for neuroendocrine activity. Cognitive theorists can point to the onset of hypothetical thinking at adolescence, which may result in new (and perhaps potentially more depressing) ways of viewing the world. Theorists who emphasize environmental factors draw attention to the new environmental demands of adolescence, such as changing schools or beginning to date, all of which may lead to feelings of loss, heightened stress, or diminished reinforcement. Thus there are many good reasons to expect that the prevalence of depression would increase as individuals pass from childhood into adolescence.

The treatment of depression during adolescence is very similar to its treatment at other points in the life span. Clinicians use a wide range of approaches, including biological therapies employing antidepressant medication (these address the neuroendocrine problem, if one exists); psychotherapies designed to help depressed adolescents understand the roots of their depression, increase the degree to which they experience reinforcement in their daily activities, or change the nature of their cognitive set; and family therapies, which focus on changing patterns of family relations that may be contributing to the adolescent's symptoms (Chartier and Ranieri, 1984).

Summary

Although the vast majority of young people move through the adolescent years without experiencing major difficulty, some encounter serious psychological and behavioral problems that disrupt not only their lives but the lives of those around them. Problems such as substance abuse, depression and suicide, unplanned pregnancy, and disorders of conduct (including crime and delinquency), while certainly not the norm during adolescence, affect a worrisome number of teenagers. Interestingly, there is considerable overlap among the problems of substance abuse, unplanned pregnancy, unemployment, and delinquency: a relatively small proportion of the adolescent population accounts for a relatively high proportion of the serious problems seen in this age group. This troubled subgroup is disproportionately composed of poor, inner-city, nonwhite youngsters.

In general, women who bear children early are likely to suffer disruptions in their educational and occupational careers, and these disruptions can have dire long-term consequences for the adolescent. Although studies indicate that children of adolescent mothers fare less well than other youngsters, many of their problems are due primarily to growing up in an environment of poverty and single parenthood rather than to having a young mother. It is important to keep in mind, however, that there is considerable diversity among teenage mothers in the routes that their adult lives take.

Findings from studies of drug and alcohol use cast doubt on some of the most fervently held stereotypes about adolescent involvement with these substances. The overall pattern suggests that most adolescents have experimented with alcohol and marijuana, that many have used one or both of these drugs regularly, that alcohol is clearly the drug of choice among teenagers (some of whom drink to excess), and that most teenagers have not experimented with other drugs. Young people who abuse drugs and alcohol are more likely to experience problems at school, to experience psychological distress and depression, to engage in unprotected sexual activity, and to become involved in dangerous or deviant activities, including crime, delinquency, automobile accidents, and truancy. Research on the causes of adolescent drug and alcohol use suggests that a youngster's involvement with drugs and alcohol is the consequence of four sets of converging risk factors: personality traits such as anger and impulsivity; distant family relationships; peers who use drugs and alcohol; and tolerance for deviant behavior.

Although most adolescents violate the law at one time or another, a relatively small number of adolescents account for a relatively high proportion of serious criminal activity. In general, the earlier an adolescent's "criminal career" begins, the more likely he or she is to become a chronic offender, commit serious and violent crimes, and continue committing crimes as an adult. These delinquents typically come from disorganized families with hostile, neglectful parents who have mistreated their children and failed to instill in them proper standards of behavior or the psychological foundations of self-control. In general, the prognosis for these chronic delinquents is not good, and many continue their criminal activities into adulthood. In contrast to youngsters who begin their delinquent careers prior to adolescence, those who begin after adolescence do not always show signs of psychological abnormality or severe family pathology.

In its mild form, depression is probably the most common psychological disturbance among adolescents. Depression during adolescence is often accompanied by other psychosocial or behavioral problems, which occasionally leads to difficulties in diagnosis or treatment. The prevalence of depressive feelings dramatically increase around the time of puberty; depression is half as common during childhood as it is during adolescence. Whereas depressive feelings are more common among boys than girls prior to adolescence, depression is much more common among females than males after puberty. Current consensus is that depression is more likely to be the result of an interacting set of environmental conditions and individual predispositions than the result of either set of factors alone. The treatment of depression during adolescence is very similar to the treatment of this disorder at other times in the life span. Clinicians use a wide range of approaches, including biological therapies, psychotherapies, and family therapies.

Only a very small proportion of the adolescent population attempts suicide. Although the rate of suicide rises rapidly during the middle adolescent years, it continues to rise throughout adulthood, and suicide is a much more common cause of death among adults than it is among young people.

A variety of explanations have been suggested for the observation that different types of problem behavior often occur together during adolescence. These explanations have focused on the relative size of the adolescent population, birth-order effects, underlying personality dispositions that may increase the likelihood of risk-taking behavior, and the impact that involvement in one form of problem behavior may have on involvement in another. As researchers begin to better understand how and why problem behaviors are interrelated, we will gain a clearer understanding of how to best identify and help young people who are most at risk for psychological and social pathology.

Key Terms

birth-cohort theory
depression
problem behavior syndrome
risk-taking behavior
social control theory

socialized delinquency
status offenses
transition-proneness
unsocialized delinquency

For Further Reading

CHARTIER, G., AND RANIERI, D. (1984). Adolescent depression: Concepts, treatments, prevention. In P. Karoly and J. Steffen (Eds.), *Adolescent behavior disorders: Foundations and contemporary concerns.* Lexington, Mass.: Lexington. A review of research and theory on the nature of adolescent depression.

DONOVAN, J., AND JESSOR, R. (1985). Structure of problem behavior in adolescence and young adulthood. *Journal of Consulting Clinical Psychology, 53,* 890–904. A study of several components of the "problem behavior syndrome."

EASTERLIN, R. (1980). *Birth and fortune.* New York: Basic Books. The most comprehensive presentation of the evidence for the impact of "cohort crowding."

FURSTENBERG, F., JR., BROOKS-GUNN, J., AND MORGAN, S. (1987). *Adolescent mothers in later life.* New York: Cambridge University Press. A longitudinal follow-up of the lives of 300 women who were adolescent parents.

LOEBER, R., AND STOUTHAMER-LOEBER, M. (1986). Family factors as correlates and predictors of juvenile conduct problems and delinquency. In M. Tonry and N. Morris (Eds.), *Crime and justice* (Vol. 7). Chicago: University of Chicago Press. A review of research on the familial antecedents and correlates of delinquency.

Glossary

academic achievement Achievement that is measured by standardized tests of scholastic ability or knowledge

acceleration The movement of academically gifted adolescents through a regular school program at a faster than average rate

achievement The psychosocial domain concerning behaviors and feelings in evaluative situations

achievement attributions The beliefs one holds about the causes of one's successes and failures

adolescent growth spurt The dramatic increase in height and weight that occurs during puberty

adrenal androgens A group of hormones, secreted by the adrenal gland, which affect growth and behavior at puberty

adrenal cortex A part of the adrenal gland which secretes many of the hormones that stimulate bodily change at puberty

adrenocorticotropic hormone (ACTH) A substance secreted by the pituitary gland that stimulates the release of hormones by the adrenal cortex

age of majority The designated age at which an individual is recognized as an adult member of the community

AIDS (autoimmune deficiency syndrome) A sexually transmitted disease that devastates the body's immune system

anchoring The process through which status hierarchies are formed in peer groups

androgen One of the sex hormones secreted by the gonads, found in both sexes, but in higher levels among males than among females following puberty

androgynous Possessing both highly masculine and highly feminine traits

anorexia nervosa An eating disorder found chiefly among young women, characterized by dramatic and severe self-induced weight loss

approach-avoidance A conflict in which the individual is both pulled toward and pushed away from a given stimulus

asynchronicity of growth The fact that different parts of the body grow at different rates at puberty, which sometimes results in the appearance of gawkiness or awkwardness during early adolescence

authoritarian parenting A style of parenting characterized by punitive, absolute, and forceful discipline, in which a premium is placed on obedience and conformity

authoritative parenting A style of parenting characterized by warmth, firm control, and rational, issue-oriented discipline, in which emphasis is placed on the development of self-direction

autonomy The psychosocial domain concerning the development and expression of independence

barometric self-esteem The aspect of self-esteem that fluctuates across situations

basal metabolism rate The minimum amount of energy used by the body during a resting state

baseline self-esteem The aspect of self-esteem that is relatively stable across situations and over time

behavioral autonomy The capacity to make independent decisions and follow through with them

birth-cohort theory A theory that links an individual's behavior to his or her membership in a particular cohort

brother-sister avoidance The avoidance of any contact or interaction between brothers and sisters from the onset of puberty until one or both persons is married—part of the process of social redefinition at adolescence in many societies

bulimia An eating disorder found chiefly among young women, characterized primarily by a pattern of binge eating and self-induced vomiting

chlorosis An eating disorder of adolescent women prevalent at the turn of the century;

also referred to as the "green sickness" because of the greenish tinge it produced in the complexion

chlamydia A sexually transmitted disease caused by a parasite

cliques Small, tightly knit groups of between two and twelve friends, generally of the same sex and age

cofigurative cultures Cultures in which the socialization of young people is accomplished not only through contact with elders but also through contact between people of the same age

cognitive conflict The state of cognitive disequilibrium believed to stimulate the growth of new and more sophisticated abilities

cognitive-developmental (Piagetian) A perspective on development, based on the work of Piaget, that takes a qualitative, stage-theory approach

comprehensive high school An educational institution that evolved during the first half of this century, offering a varied curriculum and designed to meet the needs of a diverse population of adolescents

concrete operations The third stage of cognitive development, according to Piaget, spanning the period roughly between age 6 and early adolescence

continuous transition A passage into adulthood in which adult roles and statuses are entered into gradually

consolidation According to Super, the stage during which individuals, typically during their thirties and forties, focus on attaining seniority and status in their occupations in order to attain a comfortable career position during their later years of work

conventional moral reasoning The second level of moral development, according to Kohlberg, which develops during late childhood and early adolescence; characterized by reasoning that is based on the rules and conventions of society

cross-pressure study A research strategy employed in the study of behavioral autonomy, in which adolescents are asked to choose between conforming to the wishes of peers and the wishes of adults

cross-sectional design A research strategy in which two or more groups of individuals of different ages or stages are compared along some dimension of interest

crowds Large, loosely organized groups of young people, composed of several cliques and typically organized around a common shared activity

crystallization According to Super, the stage during which individuals, typically between the ages of 14 and 18, first begin to formulate their ideas about appropriate occupations

depression A psychological disturbance characterized by low self-esteem, decreased motivation, sadness, and difficulty finding pleasure in formerly enjoyable activities

detachment In psychoanalytic theory, the process through which adolescents sever emotional attachments to their parents or other authority figures

developmental readiness The idea that adolescents may be more psychologically ready for certain experiences at one point in development than at another

didactic teaching The socialization of young people through lecturing or similar means of teaching; typical of socialization in industrialized societies

discontinuous transition A passage into adulthood in which adult roles and statuses are entered into abruptly

early adolescence The period spanning roughly ages 11 through 14, corresponding approximately to the junior or middle high school years

educational attainment The number of years of schooling completed by an individual

emotional autonomy The establishment of more adultlike and less childish close relationships with family members and peers

endocrine system The system of the body that produces, circulates, and regulates hormones

enrichment The provision of special programs

for students to whom the regular curriculum may not be sufficiently stimulating

epiphysis The closing of the ends of the long bones in the body, which terminates growth in height; one of the markers of the end of puberty

estrogen One of the sex hormones secreted by the gonads, found in both sexes, but in higher levels among females than among males following puberty

ethnic identity The aspect of one's sense of identity concerning ancestry or racial group membership

ethnography A type of research in which individuals are observed in their natural settings

extrusion The practice of separating children from their parents and requiring them to sleep in other households—part of the process of social redefinition at adolescence in many societies

family life cycle The sequence of phases through which families develop as their needs and concerns change

fear of failure The extent to which an individual fears failing in an evaluative situation

fear of success The extent to which an individual fears succeeding in an evaluative situation

feedback loop A cycle through which two or more bodily functions respond to and regulate each other, such as that formed by the hypothalamus, the pituitary gland, and the gonads

follicle-stimulating hormone (FSH) One of the major gonadotropins secreted by the pituitary gland

formal operations The fourth stage of cognitive development, according to Piaget, spanning the period from early adolescence through adulthood

Gender Intensification Hypothesis The idea that pressures to behave in sex-appropriate ways intensify during adolescence

genetic epistemology The study of how knowledge develops

gonadotropins Substances that stimulate the gonads to release sex hormones

gonorrhea A sexually transmitted disease caused by a bacterium

growth hormone (GH) One of the chief hormones stimulating bodily growth at puberty

herpes A sexually transmitted disease caused by a virus

homophobia The unwarranted fear of homosexuals or homosexuality

hypothalamus A part of the lower brain stem that controls the functioning of the pituitary gland

identification The unconscious process through which children incorporate aspects of their parents' (or other models') personalities into their own

identity The psychosocial domain concerning feelings and thoughts about the self

identity achievement The positive outcome of the crisis of identity, characterized by a healthy, coherent, and secure sense of self

identity diffusion (identity confusion) The incoherent, disjointed, incomplete sense of self characteristic of not having resolved the crisis of identity successfully

identity foreclosure The premature establishment of a sense of identity, before sufficient role experimentation has occurred

identity versus identity diffusion According to Erikson, the normative crisis characteristic of the fifth stage of psychosocial development, predominant during adolescence

imaginary audience The belief, often brought on by the heightened self-consciousness of early adolescence, that everyone is watching and evaluating one's behavior

implementation According to Super, the stage during which individuals, typically between the ages of 21 and 24, complete the training relevant for their careers

impression formation The aspect of thinking that concerns the ways in which individuals' judgments of other people are formed and organized

indifferent parenting A style of parenting characterized by low warmth and low demandingness

indulgent parenting A style of parenting characterized by high warmth but low demandingness

individuation The progressive sharpening of one's sense of being an autonomous, independent person

information processing A perspective on cognition that derives from the study of artificial intelligence and attempts to explain cognitive development in terms of the growth of specific components of the thinking process (for example, memory)

initiation The ceremonial induction of the young person into adulthood

intergenerational conflict Tensions often thought to be inherent in relations between the adolescent and adult generations; thought by most scholars to have been overestimated

intimacy The psychosocial domain concerning the formation, maintenance, and termination of close relationships

intimacy versus isolation According to Erikson, the normative crisis characteristic of the sixth psychosocial stage of development, predominant during young adulthood

junior high school An educational institution designed during the early era of public secondary education, in which young adolescents are schooled separately from older adolescents

Kuder Preference Record A widely used test designed to help individuals clarify vocational plans

late adolescence (youth) The period spanning roughly ages 18 through 21, corresponding approximately to the college years

learned helplessness The acquired belief that one is not able to influence events through one's own efforts or actions

longitudinal design A research strategy in which one group of individuals is studied over a period of time as they move through different ages or stages

luteinizing hormone (LH) One of the major gonadotropins secreted by the pituitary gland

luteinizing hormone-releasing factor (LH-RF) The substance secreted by the hypothalamus that stimulates the pituitary gland to release luteinizing hormone

mainstreaming The integration of adolescents with educational handicaps into regular classrooms

menarche The time of first menstruation, one of the important changes to occur among females during puberty

middle adolescence The period spanning roughly ages 15 through 18, corresponding approximately to the high school years

middle school An educational institution housing seventh- and eighth-grade students with adolescents who are one or two years younger

need for achievement A need that influences the extent to which an individual strives for success in evaluative situations

need for adult participation According to Sullivan, the chief interpersonal need of early childhood

need for integration into adult society According to Sullivan, the chief interpersonal need of late adolescence

need for intimacy According to Sullivan, the chief interpersonal need of preadolescence

need for peers and for peer acceptance According to Sullivan, the chief interpersonal need of middle childhood

needs for contact and for tenderness According to Sullivan, the chief interpersonal needs of infancy

needs for sexual contact and for a loving relationship with a peer of the other sex According to Sullivan, the chief interpersonal needs of early adolescence

negative identity The selection of an identity that is obviously undesirable in the eyes of significant others and the broader community

nonmilitary service The involvement of young people in activities that serve some social or economic need of society

obesity The condition of being more than twenty percent overweight

observational learning The socialization of young people through exposing them to adult models; typical of socialization in nonindustrialized societies

occupational deviance The commission of acts at work that are illegal or unethical

ovaries The female gonads

overmanning The presence of too many individuals relative to the number of opportunities available for participation in the activities of a setting

participant observation A research technique in which the researcher "infiltrates" a group of individuals in order to study their behavior and relationships

particularistic norms Guidelines for behavior that vary from one individual to another; more commonly found in less industrialized societies

part identifications The bits and pieces of past identifications formed during childhood that the young person brings to the stage of identity versus identity diffusion

peak height velocity The point at which the adolescent is growing most rapidly

peer groups Groups of individuals of approximately the same age

permissive societies Societies in which sexual activity during childhood and adolescence is not greatly restrained

personal fable An adolescent's belief that he or she is unique and therefore not subject to the rules that govern other people's behavior

personal responsibility The ability to take responsibility for oneself and manage one's own affairs

pituitary gland One of the chief glands responsible for regulating levels of hormones in the body

popularity The degree to which an individual is liked by his or her peers

postfigurative cultures Cultures in which the socialization of young people is accomplished almost exclusively through contact between children and their elders

preconventional moral reasoning The first level of moral development, according to Kohlberg, typical of children and characterized by reasoning that is based on the rewards and punishments associated with different courses of action

prefigurative cultures Cultures in which young people socialize their elders, rather than vice versa

premature affluence Having more income than one can manage maturely

preoperational period The second stage of cognitive development, according to Piaget, spanning roughly ages 2 through 5

principled reasoning The third level of moral development, according to Kohlberg, which may develop during late adolescence; characterized by reasoning that is based on abstract moral principles

problem behavior syndrome A social and psychological constellation that may put individuals at risk for a wide variety of problem behaviors, including delinquency, drug and alcohol use, and precocious sexual activity

projective test A psychological test in which the individual is asked to respond to a vague or ambiguous stimulus as a means of assessing his or her attitudes, interests, traits, or motives

propositional logic An abstract system of logic that forms the basis for formal operational thinking

pseudostupidity The overcomplication of relatively simple cognitive problems, which may result from the growth of cognitive abilities at adolescence

psychometric A perspective on cognitive development concerned primarily with the measurement of quantitative changes in intelligence through the use of standardized tests

psychosocial Referring to aspects of development that are both psychological and social in nature, such as developing a sense of identity or sexuality

psychosocial moratorium A period of time during which individuals are free from excessive obligations and responsibilities and can therefore experiment with different roles and personalities

puberty The biological changes of adolescence

pursuit of satisfaction According to Sullivan, the basic biological tendency that pushes individuals toward pleasurable, satisfying, or life-sustaining experiences

pursuit of security According to Sullivan, the basic psychological tendency that pushes individuals toward the safety of secure interpersonal relationships

recursive thinking Thinking about what someone else is thinking that you are thinking (and so on)

reference group A group against which an individual compares himself or herself

relationship maturity The level of sophistication and intimacy of one's closest relationships

restrictive societies Societies in which adolescents are pressured to refrain from sexual activity until they have married or undergone a formal rite of passage into adulthood

risk-taking behavior Behavior that is pursued simply because it is risky. Risk taking is thought to be linked to adolescent problem behavior

rite of passage A ceremony or ritual marking an individual's transition from one social status to another, and especially, marking the young person's transition into adulthood

role taking The aspect of thinking concerning the assessment of others' thoughts and feelings

secondary sex characteristics The manifestations of sexual maturation at puberty, including the development of breasts, the growth of facial and body hair, and changes in the voice

second-order thinking Thinking about the process of thinking

secular trend The tendency, over the past two centuries, for individuals to be larger in stature and to reach puberty earlier, due primarily to improvements in health and nutrition

self-conceptions The collection of traits and attributes individuals use to describe or characterize themselves

self-consciousness The degree to which an individual is preoccupied with his or her self-image

Self-Directed Search A personality inventory developed by Holland used to help individuals better understand their vocational interests

self-esteem The degree to which individuals feel positively or negatively about themselves

self-fulfilling prophecy The idea that individuals' behavior is influenced by what we expect of them

self-image stability The degree to which an individual feels that his or her self-image changes from day to day

semirestrictive societies Societies in which pressures against adolescent sexual activity exist but are not vigilantly enforced

sense of identity The extent to which individuals feel secure about who they are and who they are becoming

sensorimotor The first stage of cognitive development, according to Piaget, spanning the period roughly between birth and age 2

serial monogamy Having a series of sexual relationships over time in which one is monogamous within each relationship

set point A physiological level or setting (of a specific hormone, for example) that the body attempts to maintain through a self-regulating system

sex cleavage The separation of girls and boys into different cliques, common during late childhood and early adolescence

sexuality The psychosocial domain concerning the development and expression of sexual feelings

sexual socialization The process through which adolescents are exposed to and educated about sexuality

Sexually Transmitted Disease (STD) Any of

a group of diseases, including gonorrhea, herpes, chlamydia, and AIDS, passed on through sexual contact

social class The social position of an individual or family in society as determined by wealth, power, reputation, or achievement

social cognition The aspect of cognition that concerns thinking about other people, interpersonal relationships, and social institutions

social control theory A theory of delinquency that links deviance with the absence of bonds to society's main institutions

social conventions The norms that govern everyday behavior in social situations

social redefinition The process through which an individual's position or status is redefined by society

social responsibility The ability to cooperate with and take responsibility for others

socialized delinquency Delinquent activity that is primarily the result of conforming to one's peer group

sociocenter The highly popular member of a peer group who is generally the best at keeping interpersonal relationships in the group smooth

sociosexuality The aspect of sexuality that is merged with social relationships

specification According to Super, the stage during which individuals, typically between the ages of 18 and 21, first begin to consider narrowly defined occupational pursuits

stabilization According to Super, the stage during which individuals, typically between the ages of 25 and 35, settle down within a field of work

status The degree to which an individual is perceived as a leader by his or her peers

status offenses Violation of the law that pertain to minors but not to adults

Strong Vocational Interest Blank A widely used test designed to help individuals clarify vocational plans

task leader The high-status member of a peer group who is generally the best at planning and implementing the group's activities

testes The male gonads

testosterone One of the sex hormones secreted by the gonads, found in both sexes but in higher levels among males than females

thyroid One of the many glands secreting the hormones that stimulate bodily growth at puberty

thyroid-stimulating hormone (TSH) A substance secreted by the pituitary gland that stimulates the release of hormones by the thyroid gland

tracking The grouping of students, according to ability, into different levels of classes within the same school grade

transition-proneness A social and psychological period of heightened readiness to try new behaviors, especially problem behaviors

universalistic norms Guidelines for behavior that apply to all members of a community; more common in industrialized societies

unsocialized delinquency Delinquent activity that is primarily the result of inadequate socialization

value autonomy The establishment of an independent set of values and beliefs

youth unemployment The unemployment of young people, especially 16- to 24-year-olds who are not enrolled in school

References

Adams, G., and Fitch, S. (1982). Ego stage and identity status development: A cross-sequential analysis. *Journal of Personality and Social Psychology, 43*, 574–583.

Adams, G., and Jones, R. (1983). Female adolescents' identity development: Age comparisons and perceived child-rearing experience. *Developmental Psychology, 19*, 249–256.

Adelson, J. (1970). What generation gap? *New York Times Magazine*, January 18, pp. 10–45.

Adelson, J. (1972). The political imagination of the young adolescent. In J. Kagan and R. Coles (Eds.), *Twelve to sixteen: Early adolescence*. New York: Norton.

Adelson, J. (1979). The generalization gap. *Psychology Today*, 33–37.

Adler, I., and Kandel, D. (1982). A cross-cultural comparison of sociopsychological factors in alcohol use among adolescents in Israel, France, and the United States. *Journal of Youth and Adolescence, 11*, 89–113.

Adler, M. (1982). *The Paideia proposal: An educational manifesto*. New York: Macmillan.

Alexander, J. (1973). Defensive and supportive communications in normal and deviant families. *Journal of Consulting and Clinical Psychology, 40*, 223–231.

Alexander, K., and Cook, M. (1982). Curricula and coursework: A surprise ending to a familiar story. *American Sociological Review, 47*, 626–640.

Alexander, K., and Eckland, B. (1975). School experience and status attainment. In S. Dragastin and G. Elder, Jr. (Eds.), *Adolescence in the life cycle*. Washington, D.C.: Hemisphere.

Alexander, K., Natriello, G., and Pallas, A. (1985). For whom the cognitive bell tolls: The impact of dropping out on cognitive performance. *American Sociological Review, 50*, 409–420.

Archer, S. (1982). The lower age boundaries of identity development. *Child Development, 53*, 1551–1556.

Armor, D. (1972). School and family effects on black and white achievement: A reexamination of the USOE data. In F. Mosteller and D. Moynihan (Eds.), *On Equality of Educational Opportunity*. New York: Random House.

Aro, H., and Taipale, V. (1987). The impact of timing of puberty on psychosomatic symptoms among fourteen- to sixteen-year-old Finnish girls. *Child Development, 58*, 261–268.

Asher, S., and Wheeler, V. (1985). Children's loneliness: A comparison of rejected and neglected peer status. *Journal of Consulting and Clinical Psychology, 53*, 500–505.

Atkinson, J., and Feather, N. (1969). *A theory of achievement motivation*. New York: Wiley.

Bachman, J. (1970). *Youth in transition*. Vol. 2: *The impact of family background and intelligence on tenth-grade boys*. Ann Arbor: Institute for Social Research, University of Michigan.

Bachman, J. (1983). Premature affluence: Do high school students earn too much? *Economic Outlook USA, Summer*, 64–67.

Bachman, J., Bare, D., and Frankie, E. (1986). Correlates of employment among high school seniors. Paper available from the Institute for Social Research, University of Michigan, Ann Arbor.

Bachman, J., Green, S., and Wirtanen, I. (1972). *Youth in transition*. Vol. 3: *Dropping out—problem or symptom?*. Ann Arbor: Institute for Social Research, University of Michigan.

Bachman, J., and O'Malley, P. (1986). Self-concepts, self-esteem, and educational experiences: the frog pond revisited (again). *Journal of Personality and Social Psychology, 50*, 35–46.

Bakan, D. (1972). Adolescence in America: From idea to social fact. In J. Kagan and R. Coles (Eds.), *Twelve to sixteen: Early adolescence*. New York: Norton.

Baker, D., and Stevenson, D. (1986). Mothers' strategies for school achievement: Managing the transition to high school. *Sociology of Education, 59*, 156–167.

Bandura, A. (1964). The stormy decade: Fact or fiction? *Psychology in the School, 1*, 224–231.

Bandura, A., and Walters, R. (1959). *Adolescent aggression*. New York: Ronald Press.

Bardwick, J. (1971). *Psychology of women*. New York: Harper & Row.

Bardwick, J., and Douvan, E. (1971). Ambivalence: The socialization of women. In V. Gernick and B. Moran (Eds.), *Women in sexist society: Studies in power and powerlessness*. New York: Basic Books.

Barenboim, C. (1981). The development of person perception in childhood and adolescence: From behavioral comparisons to psychological constructs to psychological comparisons. *Child Development, 52*, 129–144.

Barker, R., and Gump, P. (1964). *Big school, small school: High school size and student behavior*. Stanford, Calif.: Stanford University Press.

Barnes, G. (1984). Adolescent alcohol abuse and other problem behaviors: Their relationship and common parental influences. *Journal of Youth and Adolescence, 13*, 329–348.

Baruch, G., Barnett, R., and Rivers. C. (1983). *Lifeprints*. New York: McGraw-Hill.

Baumrind, D. (1978). Parental disciplinary patterns and social competence in children. *Youth and Society, 9*, 239–276.

Baumrind, D. (In progress). *Family socialization and developmental competence in middle childhood*. Unpublished manuscript.

Baumrind, D., and Moselle, K. (1985). A developmental perspective on adolescent drug abuse. *Advances in Alcohol and Substance Abuse, 4*, 41–67.

Bayley, N. (1949). Consistency and variability in the growth of intelligence from birth to eighteen years. *Journal of Genetic Psychology, 75*, 165–196.

Bell, R. (1968). A reinterpretation of the direction of effects in studies of socialization. *Psychological Review*, 75, 81–95.

Bell, A., Weinberg, M., and Hammersmith, S. (1981). *Sexual preference: Its development in men and women*. Bloomington, IN: Indiana University Press.

Bem, S. (1975). Sex-role adaptability: One consequence of psychological androgyny. *Journal of Personality and Social Psychology*, 31, 634–643.

Benedict, R. (1934). *Patterns of culture*. Boston: Houghton Mifflin.

Bennett, G. (1919). *The junior high school*. Baltimore: Warwick and York.

Berkowitz, M. (1985). The role of discussion in moral education. In M. Berkowitz and F. Oser (Eds.), *Moral Education: Theory and Application* (pp. 197–218). Hillsdale, NJ: Erlbaum.

Bernard, J. (1973). *The future of marriage*. New York: Bantam.

Berndt, T. (1979). Developmental changes in conformity to peers and parents. *Developmental Psychology*, 15, 608–616.

Berndt, T. (1981). Relations between social cognition, nonsocial cognition, and social behavior: The case of friendship. In J. Flavell and L. Ross (Eds.), *Social cognitive development: Frontiers and possible futures*. Cambridge: Cambridge University Press.

Berndt, T. (1982). The features and effects of friendship in early adolescence. *Child Development*, 53, 1447–1460.

Berndt, T. (1987). Changes in friendship and school adjustment after the transition to junior high school. Paper presented at the biennial meetings of the Society for Research in Child Development, Baltimore.

Bierman, K., and Furman, W. (1984). The effects of social skills training and peer involvement on the social adjustment of preadolescents. *Child Development*, 55, 151–162.

Bigelow, B., and LaGaipa, J. (1975). Children's written descriptions of friendship. *Developmental Psychology*, 11, 857–858.

Biller, H. (1981). Father absence, divorce, and personality development. In M. Lamb (Eds.), *The role of the father in child development* (2nd ed.). New York: Wiley.

Bloom, A. (1987). *The closing of the American mind*. New York: Simon and Schuster.

Blos, P. (1967). The second individuation process of adolescence. In R. S. Eissler et al. (Eds.), *Psychoanalytic study of the child* (Vol. 15). New York: International Universities Press.

Blyth, D., and Foster-Clark, F. (In press). Gender differences in perceived intimacy with different members of adolescents' social networks. *Sex Roles*.

Blyth, D., Hill, J., and Smyth, C. (1981). The influence of older adolescents on younger adolescents: Do grade-level arrangements make a difference in behaviors, attitudes, and experiences? *Journal of Early Adolescence*, 1, 85–110.

Blyth, D., Hill, J., and Thiel, K. (1982). Early adolescents' significant others: Grade and gender differences in perceived relationships with familial and non-familial adults and young people. *Journal of Youth and Adolescence*, 11, 425–450.

Blyth, D., Simmons, R., Bulcroft, R., Felt, D., Van Cleave, E., and Bush, D. (1980). The effects of physical development on self-image and satisfaction with body image for early adolescent males. In F. G. Simmons (Ed.), *Handbook of community and mental health* (Vol. 2). Greenwich, Conn.: JAI Press.

Blyth, D., Simmons, R., and Zakin, D. (1985). Satisfaction with body image for early adolescent females: The impact of pubertal timing within different school environments. *Journal of Youth and Adolescence*, 14, 227–236.

Bohrnstedt, G., and Felson, R. (1983). Explaining the relations among children's actual and perceived performances and self-esteem: A comparison of several causal models. *Journal of Personality and Social Psychology*, 45, 43–56.

Bourne, E. (1978a). The state of research on ego identity: A review and appraisal. Part I. *Journal of Youth and Adolescence*, 7, 223–251.

Bourne, E. (1978b). The state of research on ego identity: A review and appraisal. Part II. *Journal of Youth and Adolescence*, 7, 371–392.

Boyer, E. (1983). *High school*. New York: Harper & Row.

Braddock, J. (1985). School desegregation and black assimilation. *Journal of Social Issues*, 41, 9–22.

Bradley, L., and Bradley, G. (1977). The academic achievement of black students in desegregated schools: A critical review. *Review of Educational Research*, 47, 399–449.

Braungart, R. (1979). Reference groups, social judgments, and student politics. *Adolescence*, 14, 135–157.

Brittain, C. (1963). Adolescent choices and parent/peer cross-pressures. *American Sociological Review*, 28, 385–391.

Brody, J. (December 16, 1986). Effeminacy and homosexuality. *The New York Times*, p. 17.

Bronfenbrenner, U. (1961). Some familial antecedents of responsibility and leadership in adolescents. In L. Petrullo and B. Bass (Eds.), *Leadership and interpersonal behavior*. New York: Holt, Rinehart and Winston.

Bronfenbrenner, U. (1967). Response to pressure from peers versus adults among Soviet and American school children. *International Journal of Psychology*, 2, 199–207.

Bronfenbrenner, U. (1974). The origins of alienation. *Scientific American*, 231, 53–61.

Bronfenbrenner, U. (1975). Reality and research in the ecology of human development. *Proceedings of the American Philosophical Society*, 119, 439–469.

Bronfenbrenner, U. (1979). *The ecology of human development*. Cambridge, Mass.: Harvard University Press.

Bronfenbrenner, U., and Crouter, A. (1982). Work and family through time and space. In S. Kamerman and C. Hayes (Eds.), *Families that work: Children in a changing world*. Washington: National Academy Press.

Brook, J., Whiteman, M., and Gordon, A. (1983). Stages

of drug use in adolescence: Personality, peer, and family correlates. *Developmental Psychology, 19,* 269–277.

Brook, J., Whiteman, M., Gordon, A., and Brook, D. (1984). Paternal determinants of female adolescent's marijuana use. *Developmental Psychology, 20,* 1032–1043.

Brook, J., Whiteman, M., Gordon, A., and Cohen, P. (1986). Dynamics of childhood and adolescent personality traits and adolescent drug use. *Developmental Psychology, 22,* 403–414.

Brooks-Gunn, J., and Furstenberg, F., Jr. (1986). The children of adolescent mothers: Physical, academic, and cognitive outcomes. *Developmental Review, 6,* 224–251.

Brooks-Gunn, J., and Ruble, D. (1979). The social and psychological meaning of menarche. Paper presented at the biennial meeting of the Society for Research in Child Development, San Francisco.

Brooks-Gunn, J., and Ruble, D. (1982). The development of menstrual-related beliefs and behaviors during early adolescence. *Child Development, 53,* 1567–1577.

Brooks-Gunn, J., and Warren, M. (1985). The effects of delayed menarche in different contexts: Dance and nondance students. *Journal of Youth and Adolescence, 14,* 285–300.

Brooks-Gunn, J., and Warren, M. (1987). Biological contributions to affective expression in young adolescent girls. Paper presented at the biennial meetings of the Society for Research in Child Development, Baltimore.

Brophy, J. (1979). Teacher behavior and its effects. *Journal of Educational Psychology, 71,* 733–750.

Broverman, I., Vogel, S., Broverman, D., Clarkson, F., and Rosenkrantz, P. (1972). Sex-role stereotypes: A current appraisal. *Journal of Social Issues, 28,* 59–78.

Brown, A. (1975). The development of memory: Knowing, knowing about knowing, and knowing how to know. In H. Reese (Ed.), *Advances in child development and behavior* (Vol. 10). New York: Academic Press.

Brown, B., Clasen, D., and Eicher, S. (1986). Perceptions of peer pressure, peer conformity dispositions, and self-reported behavior among adolescents. *Developmental Psychology, 22,* 521–530.

Brown, B., Eicher, S., and Petrie, S. (1986). The importance of peer group ("crowd") affiliation in adolescence. *Journal of Adolescence, 9,* 73–96.

Brown, B., and Lohr, M., (1987). Peer-group affiliation and adolescent self-esteem: An integration of ego-identity and symbolic-interaction theories. *Journal of Personality and Social Psychology, 52,* 47–55.

Brown, B., Lohr, M., and McClenahan, E. (1986). Early adolescents' perceptions of peer pressure. *Journal of Early Adolescence, 6,* 139–154.

Brubacher, J., and Rudy, W. (1976). *Higher education in transition* (3rd ed.). New York: Harper & Row.

Bruch, H. (1973). *Eating disorders.* New York: Basic Books.

Brumberg, J. (1982). Chlorotic girls, 1870–1920: A historical perspective on female adolescence. *Child Development, 53,* 1468–1477.

Buhrmester, D., and Furman, W. (1987). The development of companionship and intimacy. *Child Development, 58,* 1101–1113.

Bullough, V., (1981). Age at menarche: A misunderstanding. *Science, 213,* 365–366.

Burchinal, L. (1965). Trends and prospects for young marriages in the U.S. *Journal of Marriage and the Family, 27,* 243–254.

Burleson, B. (1982). The development of comforting communication skills in childhood and adolescence. *Child Development, 53,* 1578–1588.

Butler, R., and Nissan, M. (1975). Who is afraid of success? And why? *Journal of Youth and Adolescence, 4,* 259–270.

Campbell, B. (1977). The impact of school desegregation: An investigation of three mediating factors. *Youth and Society, 9,* 79–111.

Campbell, E., Adams, G., and Dobson, W. (1984). Familial correlates of identity formation in late adolescence: A study of the predictive utility of connectedness and individuality in family relations. *Journal of Youth and Adolescence, 13,* 509–526.

Cano, L., Solomon, S., and Holmes, D. (1984). Fear of success: The influence of sex, sex-role identity, and components of masculinity. *Sex Roles, 10,* 341–346.

Carnegie Commission on Policy Studies in Higher Education. (1980). *Giving Youth a Better Chance.* San Francisco: Jossey-Bass.

Carns, D. (1973). Talking about sex: Notes on first coitus and the double sexual standard. *Journal of Marriage and the Family, 35,* 677–688.

Chartier, G., and Ranieri, D. (1984). Adolescent depression: Concepts, treatments, prevention. In P. Karoly and J. Steffen (Eds.), *Adolescent behavior disorders: Foundations and contemporary concerns.* Lexington, MA: Lexington.

Chilman, C. (1980). Social and psychological research concerning adolescent childbearing: 1970–1980. *Journal of Marriage and the Family,* November, pp. 793–805.

Chilman, C. (1986). Some psychosocial aspects of adolescent sexual and contraceptive behaviors in a changing American society. In J. Lancaster and B. Hamburg (Eds.), *School-age pregnancy and parenthood: Biosocial dimensions.* New York: Aldine de Gruyter.

Clark, R., and Delia, J. (1976). The development of functional persuasive skills in childhood and early adolescence. *Child Development, 47,* 1008–1014.

Clasen, D., and Brown, B. (1985). The multidimensionality of peer pressure in adolescence. *Journal of Youth and Adolescence, 14,* 451–468.

Church, R. (1976). *Education in the United States.* New York: Free Press, 1976.

Clausen, J. (1975). The social meaning of differential physical and sexual maturation. In S. E. Dragastin and G. H. Elder, Jr. (Eds.), *Adolescence in the life cycle.* New York: Halsted Press.

Clayton, R., and Bokemeier, J. (1980). Premarital sex in the seventies. *Journal of Marriage and the Family*, November, pp. 759–775.

Cohen, Y. (1964). *The transition from childhood to adolescence.* Chicago: Aldine.

Coie, J., and Dodge, K. (1983). Continuities and changes in children's social status: A five-year longitudinal study. *Merrill-Palmer Quarterly, 29,* 261–281.

Colby, A., Kohlberg, L., Gibbs, J., and Lieberman, M. (1983). A longitudinal study of moral judgment. *Monographs of the Society for Research in Child Development, 48* (Serial No. 200).

Coleman, J. (1961). *The adolescent society.* Glencoe, Ill.: Free Press.

Coleman, J. (1974). *Relationships in adolescence.* Boston: Routledge & Kegan Paul.

Coleman, J. (1980). Friendship and the peer group in adolescence. In J. Adelson (Ed.), *Handbook of adolescent psychology.* New York: Wiley.

Coleman, J., Campbell, E., Hobson, C., McPartland, J., Mood, A., Weinfeld, F., and York, R. (1966). *Equality of educational opportunity.* Washington, D.C.: U.S. Government Printing Office.

Coleman, J., Hoffer, T., and Kilgore, S. (1982). *High school achievement: Public, Catholic and other private schools compared.* New York: Basic Books.

Committee for the Study of National Service. (1979). *Youth and the needs of the nation.* Washington, D.C.: Potomac Institute.

Committee for the Study of National Service. (1980). *National youth service: What's at stake?* Washington, D.C.: Potomac Institute.

Comstock, G., Chaffee, S., Katzman, N., McCombs, M., and Roberts, D. (1978). *Television and human behavior.* New York: Columbia University Press.

Conant, J. (1959). *The American high school today.* New York: McGraw-Hill.

Conger, J. (1975). Current issues in adolescent development. *Master Lectures on Developmental Psychology.* Washington, D.C.: American Psychological Association.

Conger, J. (1977). *Adolescence and youth* (2nd ed.). New York: Harper & Row.

Conger, J. (1981). Freedom and commitment: Families, youth, and social change. *American Psychologist, 36,* 1475–1484.

Congressional Budget Office (1986). *Trends in educational achievement.* Washington: U.S. Congress.

Congressional Budget Office (1987). *Educational achievement: Explanations and implications of recent trends.* Washington: U.S. Congress.

Cooper, C., and Grotevant, H. (1987). Gender issues in the interface of family experience and adolescents' friendship and dating identity. *Journal of Youth and Adolescence, 16,* 247–264.

Cooper, C., Grotevant, H., and Condon, S. (1983). Individuality and connectedness in the family as a context for adolescent identity formation and role taking skill. In H.

Grotevant and C. Cooper (Eds.), *Adolescent development in the family.* San Francisco: Jossey-Bass.

Crockett, L., and Dorn, L. (1987). Young adolescents' pubertal status and reported heterosocial interaction. Paper presented at the biennial meetings of the Society for Research in Child Development, Baltimore.

Crockett, L., Losoff, M., and Petersen, A. (1984). Perceptions of the peer group and friendship in early adolescence. *Journal of Early Adolescence, 4,* 155–181.

Cross, W. (1978). The Thomas and Cook models of psychological nigrescence: A literature review. *Journal of Black Psychology, 4,* 13–31.

Csikszentmihalyi, M., and Larson, R. (1984). *Being adolescent.* New York: Basic Books.

Csikszentmihalyi, M., Larson, R., and Prescott, S. (1977). The ecology of adolescent activity and experience. *Journal of Youth and Adolescence, 6,* 281–294.

Cusick, P. (1973). *Inside high school.* New York: Holt, Rinehart & Winston.

Cutrona, C. (1982). Transition to college: Loneliness and the process of social adjustment. In L. Peplau and D. Perlman (Eds.), *Loneliness: A sourcebook of current theory, research, and therapy.* New York: Wiley.

Cvetkovich, G., Grote, B., Bjorseth, A., and Sarkissian, J. (1975). On the psychology of adolescents' use of contraceptives. *Journal of Sex Research, 11,* 256–270.

Damico, R. (1984). Does working in high school impair academic progress? *Sociology of Education, 57,* 157–164.

Damico, S., and Sparks, C. (1986). Cross-group contact opportunities: Impact on interpersonal relationships in desegregated middle schools. *Sociology of Education, 59,* 113–123.

Daniels, D., Dunn, J., Furstenberg, F., Jr., and Plomin, R. (1985). Environmental differences within the family and adjustment differences within pairs of adolescent siblings. *Child Development, 56,* 764–774.

Danner, F., and Day, M. (1977). Eliciting formal operations. *Child Development, 48,* 1600–1606.

Darabi, K., and Ortiz, V. (1987). Childbearing among young Latino women in the United States. *American Journal of Public Health, 77, 25–28.*

DeLamater, J., and MacCorquodale, P. (1979). *Premarital sexuality: Attitudes, relationships, behavior.* Madison: University of Wisconsin Press.

Demo, D., and Savin-Williams, R. (1983). Early adolescent self-esteem as a function of social class: Rosenberg and Pearlin revisited. *American Journal of Sociology, 88,* 763–774.

Devereux, E. (1970). The role of peer group experience in moral development. In J. Hill (Ed.), *Minnesota Symposium on Child Psychology* (Vol. 4). Minneapolis: University of Minnesota Press.

Diaz, R., and Berndt, T. (1982). Children's knowledge of a best friend: Fact or fancy? *Developmental Psychology, 18,* 787–794.

DiClemente, Zorn, J., and Temoshok, L. (1986). Adolescents and AIDS: A survey of knowledge, attitudes and beliefs about AIDS in San Francisco. *American Journal of Public Health*, 76, 1443–1445.

Dickenson, G. (1975). Dating behavior of black and white adolescents before and after desegregation. *Journal of Marriage and the Family*, 37, 602–608.

Donovan, J., and Jessor, R. (1985). Structure of problem behavior in adolescence and young adulthood. *Journal of Consulting and Clinical Psychology*, 53, 890–904.

Dornbusch, S., Carlsmith, J., Gross, R., Martin, J., Jennings, D., Rosenberg, A., and Duke, P. (1981). Sexual development, age, and dating: A comparison of biological and social influences upon one set of behaviors. *Child Development*, 52, 179–185.

Dornbusch, S., Carlsmith, J., Bushwall, S., Ritter, P., Leiderman, P., Hastorf, A., and Gross, R. (1985). Single parents, extended households, and the control of adolescents. *Child Development*, 56, 326–341.

Dornbusch, S., Ritter, P., Liederman, P., Roberts, D., and Fraleigh, M. (1987). The relation of parenting style to adolescent school performance. *Child Development*, 58, 1244–1257.

Dougherty, K. (1987). The effects of community colleges: Aid or hindrance to socioeconomic attainment? *Sociology of Education*, 60, 86–103.

Douglass, R. (1982). Youth, alcohol, and traffic accidents. In *Alcohol and health: Monograph No. 4*. Washington: National Clearinghouse for Alcohol Information.

Douvan, E., and Adelson, J. (1966). *The adolescent experience*. New York: Wiley.

Dreyer, P. (1982). Sexuality during adolescence. In B. Wolman (Ed.), *Handbook of developmental psychology*. Englewood Cliffs, N.J.: Prentice-Hall.

Duncan, O., Featherman, D., and Duncan, B. (1972). *Socioeconomic background and achievement*. New York: Seminar Press.

Duncan, P., Ritter, P., Dornbusch, S., Gross, R., and Carlsmith, J. (1985). The effects of pubertal timing on body image, school behavior, and deviance. *Journal of Youth and Adolescence*, 14, 227–236.

Dunphy, D. (1975). The social structure of urban adolescent peer groups. *Sociometry*, 1963, 26, 230–246. Reprinted in R. Grinder (Ed.), *Studies in adolescence* (3rd ed.). New York: Macmillan.

Dusek, J., and Flaherty, J. (1981). The development of the self-concept during the adolescent years. *Monographs of the Society for Research in Child Development*, 46 (Serial No. 191).

Dweck, C., and Light, B. (1980). Learned helplessness and intellectual achievement. In J. Garber and M. Seligman (Eds.), *Human helplessness*. New York: Academic Press.

Dweck, C., and Wortman, C. (1980). Achievement, test anxiety, and learned helplessness: Adaptive and maladaptive cognitions. In H. Krohne and L. Laux (Eds.), *Achievement, stress, and anxiety*. Washington, D.C.: Hemisphere.

Easterlin, R. (1980). *Birth and fortune*. New York: Basic Books.

Eccles, J., Adler, T., and Meece, J. (1984). Sex differences in achievement: A test of alternate theories. *Journal of Personality and Social Psychology*, 46, 26–43.

Eder, D. (1985). The cycle of popularity: interpersonal relations among female adolescents. *Sociology of Education*, 58, 154–165.

Eisenstadt, S. N. (1956). *From generation to generation*. Glencoe, Ill.: Free Press.

Eitzen, D. (1975). Athletics in the status system of male adolescents: A replication of Coleman's *The Adolescent Society*. *Adolescence*, 10, 267–276.

Elder, G., Jr. (1974). *Children of the Great Depression*. Chicago: University of Chicago Press.

Elder, G., Jr. (1980). Adolescence in historical perspective. In J. Adelson (Ed.), *Handbook of adolescent psychology*. New York: Wiley.

Elkind, D. (1967). Egocentrism in adolescence. *Child Development*, 38, 1025–1034.

Elkind, D. (1978). Understanding the young adolescent. *Adolescence*, 13, 127–134.

Elkind, D. (1982). *The hurried child*. New York: Addison-Wesley, 1982.

Elkind, D. (1985). Egocentrism redux. *Developmental Review*, 5, 218–226.

Elkind, D., Barocas, R., and Rosenthal, R. (1968). Combinatorial thinking in adolescents from graded and ungraded classrooms. *Perceptual and Motor Skills*, 27, 1015–1018.

Elmen, J., and Steinberg, L. (1988). Achievement orientation in early adolescence: Social correlates and developmental patterns. Paper presented at the biennial meeting of the Society for Research on Adolescence, Alexandria, VA.

Elster, A., Lamb, M., Peters, L., Kahn, J., and Tavare, J. (1987). Judicial involvement and conduct problems of fathers of infants born to adolescent mothers. *Pediatrics*, 79, 230–234.

Epstein, J. (1983a). Selecting friends in contrasting secondary school environments. In J. Epstein and N. Karweit (Eds.), *Friends in school*. New York: Academic Press.

Epstein, J. (1983b). The influence of friends on achievement and affective outcomes. In J. Epstein and N. Karweit (Eds.), *Friends in school*. New York: Academic Press.

Erikson, E. (1959). Identity and the life cycle. *Psychological Issues*, 1, 1–171.

Erikson, E. (1963). *Childhood and society*. New York: Norton.

Erikson, E. (1968). *Identity: Youth and crisis*. New York: Norton.

Eveleth, P., and Tanner, J. (1976). *Worldwide variation in human growth*. New York: Cambridge University Press.

Farel, A. (1982). *Early adolescence and religion: A status study*. Carrboro, N.C.: Center for Early Adolescence.

Farrell, M., and Rosenberg, S. (1981). *Men at midlife*. Boston: Auburn House.

Farrington, D. (1986). Parenting and delinquency: Parent training and delinquency prevention. *Today's Delinquent*, 5, 51–66.

Featherman, D. (1980). Schooling and occupational careers: Constancy and change in worldly success. In O. Brim, Jr., and J. Kagan (Eds.), *Constancy and change in human development*. Cambridge, Mass.: Harvard University Press.

Federal Bureau of Investigation. (1983). *Uniform crime reports for the United States*. Washington, D.C.: U.S. Government Printing Office.

Feld, S. (1967). Longitudinal study of the origins of achievement strivings. *Journal of Personality and Social Psychology*, 7, 408–414.

Feldstein, M., and Ellwood, D. (1982). Teenage unemployment: What is the problem? In R. Freeman and D. Wise (Eds.), *The youth labor market problem: Its nature, causes, and consequences*. Chicago: University of Chicago Press.

Fennema, E., and Peterson, P. (1985). Autonomous learning behavior: A possible explanation of gender-related differences in mathematics. In P. Peterson, L. Wilkinson, and M. Hallinan, *The social context of instruction*. Orlando: Academic Press.

Fennema, E., and Sherman, J. (1977). Sex-related differences in mathematics achievement, spatial visualization, and affective factors. *American Educational Research Journal*, 14, 51–71.

Ferrell, M., Tolone, W., and Walsh, R. (1977). Maturational and societal changes in the sexual double-standard: A panel analysis (1967–1971; 1970–1974). *Journal of Marriage and the Family*, 39, 255–271.

Fine, G. (1981). Friends, impression management, and preadolescent behavior. In S. Asher and J. Gottman (Eds.), *The development of children's friendships*. Cambridge: Cambridge University Press.

Fischer, K. (1983). Illuminating the processes of moral development. In A. Colby, L. Kohlberg, J. Gibbs, and M. Lieberman, *A longitudinal study of moral judgment*. *Monographs of the Society for Research in Child Development*, 48 (Serial No. 200).

Fiske, E. (November 12, 1987). Colleges open new minority drive. *The New York Times*, p. 12.

Flavell, J. (1977). *Cognitive development*. Englewood Cliffs, N.J.: Prentice-Hall.

Ford, C., and Beach, F. (1951). *Patterns of sexual behavior*. New York: Harper & Row.

Ford, M. (1982). Social cognition and social competence in adolescence. *Developmental Psychology*, 18, 323–340.

Ford, M., and Lowery, C. (1986). Gender differences in moral reasoning: A comparison of the use of justice and care orientations. *Journal of Personality and Social Psychology*, 50, 777–783.

Fordham, C., and Ogbu, J. (1986). Black students' school success: Coping with the burden of "acting white." *Urban Review*, 18, 176–206.

Foster-Clark, F. & Blyth, D. (1987). Predicting adolescents' drug use: The role of personal and social network characteristics. Paper presented at the biennial meetings of the Society for Research in Child Development, Baltimore.

Freeman, R., and Wise, D. (Eds.). (1982). *The youth labor market problem: Its nature, causes, and consequences*. Chicago: University of Chicago Press.

Freud, A. (1958). Adolescence. *Psychoanalytic Study of the Child*, 13, 255–278.

Freud, A. (1969). Adolescence as a developmental disturbance. In G. Caplan and S. Lebovici (Eds.), *Adolescence: Psychosocial perspectives* (pp. 5–10). New York: Basic Books.

Freudenberg, W. (1984). Boomtown's youth: The differential impacts of rapid community growth on adolescents and adults. *American Sociological Review*, 49, 697–705.

Fried, M., and Fried, M. (1980). *Transitions: Four rituals in eight cultures*. New York: Norton.

Friedenberg, E. (1967). *Coming of age in America*. New York: Vintage Books.

Friedenberg, E. (1959). *The vanishing adolescent*. Boston: Beacon Press.

Frisch, R. (1983). Fatness, puberty, and fertility: The effects of nutrition and physical training on menarche and ovulation. In J. Brooks-Gunn and A. Petersen (Eds.), *Girls at puberty*. New York: Plenum.

Furman, W., and Buhrmester, D. (1985). Children's perceptions of the personal relationships in their social networks. *Developmental Psychology*, 21, 1016–1024.

Furstenberg, F., Jr. (1976). *Unplanned parenthood*. New York: Free Press.

Furstenberg, F., Jr., Brooks-Gunn, J., and Morgan, S. (1987). *Adolescent mothers in later life*. New York: Cambridge University Press.

Furstenberg, F., Jr., Moore, K., and Peterson, J. (1985). Sex education and sexual experience among adolescents. *American Journal of Public Health*, 75, 1331–1332.

Furstenberg, F., Peterson, J., Nord, C., and Zill, N. (1983). The life course of children of divorce: Marital disruption and parental contact. *American Sociological Review*, 48, 125–129.

Gaddis, A., and Brooks-Gunn, J. (1985). The male experience of pubertal change. *Journal of Youth and Adolescence*, 14, 61–70.

Gagne, E. (1985). *The cognitive psychology of school learning*. Boston: Little Brown.

Gagnon, J. (1972). The creation of the sexual in early adolescence. In J. Kagan and R. Coles (Eds.), *Twelve to sixteen: Early adolescence*. New York: Norton.

Gallagher, J. (1979). Issues in education for the gifted. In A. Passow (Ed.), *The gifted and the talented: Their education and development* (Seventy-eighth yearbook of the National Society for the Study of Education). Chicago: University of Chicago Press.

Gallatin, J. (1975). *Adolescence and individuality*. New York: Harper & Row.

Gallatin, J. (1980). Political thinking in adolescence. In J. Adelson (Ed.), *Handbook of adolescent psychology*. New York: Wiley.

Garbarino, J., and Asp, C. (1981). *Successful schools and competent students*. Lexington, Mass.: Lexington Books.

Garbarino, J., and Bronfenbrenner, U. (1976). The socialization of moral judgment and behavior in cross-cultural perspective. In T. Lickona (Ed.), *Moral development and behavior*. New York: Holt, Rinehart and Winston.

Garbarino, J., Burston, N., Raber, S., Russell, R., and Crouter, A. (1978). The social maps of children approaching adolescence: Studying the ecology of youth development. *Journal of Youth and Adolescence*, 7, 417–428.

Garbarino, J., Sebes, J., and Schellenbach, C. (1984). Families at risk for destructive parent-child relations in adolescence. *Child Development*, 55, 174–183.

Gerrard, M. (1987). Sex, sex guilt, and contraceptive use revisited: The 1980s. *Journal of Personality and Social Psychology*, 52, 975–980.

Gilbert, J. (1985). Mass culture and the fear of delinquency: The 1950s. *Journal of Early Adolescence*, 5, 505–516.

Gilligan, C. (1982). *In a different voice*. Cambridge: Harvard University Press.

Gilligan, C. (1986). *Adolescent development reconsidered*. Paper presented at the Invitational Conference on Health Futures of Adolescents, Daytona Beach, Florida.

Ginzberg, E. (1977). The job problem. *Scientific American*, 237, 43–51.

Glueck, S., and Glueck, E. (1950). *Unraveling juvenile delinquency*. New York: Commonwealth Fund.

Gold, M., and Petronio, R. (1980). Delinquent behavior in adolescence. In J. Adelson (Ed.), *Handbook of adolescent psychology*. New York: Wiley.

Gold, M., and Yanof, D. (1985). Mothers, daughters, and girlfriends. *Journal of Personality and Social Psychology*, 49, 654–659.

Good, T., and Brophy, J. (1984). *Looking in classrooms*. New York: Harper & Row.

Goodlad, J. (1984). *A place called school*. New York: McGraw-Hill.

Gottfredson, D. (1985). Youth employment, crime, and schooling: A longitudinal study of a national sample. *Developmental Psychology*, 21, 419–432.

Gould, M., and Shaffer, D. (1986). The impact of suicide in television movies. *New England Journal of Medicine*, 351, 690–694.

Gould, R. (1972). The phases of adult life. *American Journal of Psychiatry*, 129, 521–531.

Gove, W. (1972). The relationships between sex roles, marital status, and mental illness. *Social Forces*, 51, 34–44.

Gray, W., and Hudson, L. (1984). Formal operations and the imaginary audience. *Developmental Psychology*, 20, 619–627.

Green, R. (1980). Homosexuality. In H. Kaplan, A. Freedman, and B. Sadock (Eds.), *Comprehensive textbook of psychiatry* (Vol 2.) (3rd Edition). Baltimore: Williams & Wilkins.

Green, R. (1987). *The 'Sissy Boy' syndrome and the development of homosexuality*. New Haven: Yale University Press.

Greenberg, M., Siegel, J., and Leitch, C. (1983). The nature and importance of attachment relationships to parents and peers during adolescence. *Journal of Youth and Adolescence*, 12, 373–386.

Greenberger, E. (1982). Education and the acquisition of psychosocial maturity. In D. McClelland (Ed.), *The development of social maturity*. New York: Irvington Publishers.

Greenberger, E., and Steinberg, L. (1981). The workplace as a context for the socialization of youth. *Journal of Youth and Adolescence*, 10, 185–210.

Greenberger, E., and Steinberg, L. (1983). Sex differences in early work experience: Harbinger of things to come? *Social Forces*, 62, 467–486.

Greenberger, E., and Steinberg, L. (1986). *When teenagers work: The psychological and social costs of adolescent employment*. New York: Basic Books.

Greenberger, E., Steinberg, L., and Ruggiero, M. (1982). A job is a job is a job . . . Or is it? Behavioral observations in the adolescent workplace. *Work and Occupations*, 9, 79–96.

Greenberger, E., Steinberg, L., and Vaux, A. (1981). Adolescents who work: Health and behavioral consequences of job stress. *Developmental psychology*, 17, 691–703.

Greenberger, E., Steinberg, L., Vaux, A., and McAuliffe, S. (1980). Adolescents who work: Effects of part-time employment on family and peer relations. *Journal of Youth and Adolescence*, 9, 189–202.

Grief, E., and Ulman, K. (1982). The psychological impact of menarche on early adolescent females: A review of the literature. *Child Development*, 53, 1413–1430.

Grotevant, H., and Adams, G. (1984). Development of an objective measure to assess ego identity in adolescence: Validation and replication. *Journal of Youth and Adolescence*, 13, 419–438.

Grotevant, H., and Cooper, C. (1985). Patterns of interaction in family relationships and the development of identity exploration in adolescence. *Child Development*, 56, 415–428.

Grotevant, H., and Cooper, C. (1986). Individuation in family relationships: A perspective on individual differences in the development of identity and role-taking skill in adolescence. *Human Development*, 29, 82–100.

Grotevant, H., and Cooper, C. (1988). The role of family experience in career exploration during adolescence. In P. Baltes, D. Featherman, and R. Lerner (Eds.), *Life-Span Development and Behavior* (vol. 8). Hillsdale, NJ: Erlbaum.

Grotevant, H., and Durrett, M. (1980). Occupational knowledge and career development in adolescence. *Journal of Vocational Behavior*, 17, 171–182.

Grotevant, H., and Thorbecke, W. (1982). Sex differences in styles of occupational identity formation in late adolescence. *Developmental Psychology*, 18, 396–405.

Grumbach, M., Roth, J., Kaplan, S., and Kelch, R. (1974). Hypothalamic-pituitary regulation of puberty in man: Evidence and concepts derived from clinical research. In M. Grumbach, G. Grave, and F. Mayer (Eds.), *Control of the onset of puberty*. New York: Wiley.

Haan, N., Smith, M., and Block, J. (1968). Moral reasoning of young adults: Political-social behavior, family background, and personality correlates. *Journal of Personality and Social Psychology*, 10, 183–201.

Hafetz, E. (1976). Parameters of sexual maturity in man. In E. Hafetz (Ed.), *Perspectives in human reproduction*, Vol. 3: *Sexual maturity: Physiological and clinical parameters*. Ann Arbor, Mich.: Ann Arbor Science Publishers.

Hall, G. S. (1904). *Adolescence*. New York: Appleton.

Hallinan, M. (1981). Recent advances in sociometry. In S. Asher and J. Gottman (Eds.), *The development of children's friendships*. New York: Cambridge University Press.

Hallinan, M., and Sorensen, A. (1987). Ability grouping and sex differences in mathematics achievement. *Sociology of Education*, 60, 63–72.

Hallinan, M., and Teixeira, R. (1987). Opportunities and constraints: Black-white differences in the formation of interracial friendships. *Child Development*, 58, 1358–1371.

Hamburg, D. (1986). *Preparing for life: The critical transition of adolescence*. New York: Carnegie Corporation of New York.

Hamilton, S. (1981). Adolescents in community settings: What is to be learned? *Theory and Research in Social Education*, 9, 23–38.

Hanson, S., Myers, D., and Ginsburg, A. (1987). The role of responsibility and knowledge in reducing teenage out-of-wedlock childbearing. *Journal of Marriage and the Family*, 49, 241–256.

Harter, S. (1983). Developmental perspectives on the self-system. In E. M. Hetherington (Ed.), *Handbook of child psychology; Socialization, personality, and social development* (Vol. 4). New York: Wiley.

Hartup, W. (1977). Adolescent peer relations: A look to the future. In J. Hill and F. Monks (Eds.), *Adolescence and youth in prospect*. Guildford, England: IPC Press.

Hartup, W. (1983). Peer relations. In E.M. Hetherington (Ed.), *Handbook of child psychology; Socialization, personality, and social development* (Vol. 4). New York: Wiley.

Hauser, S., Book, B., Houlihan, J., Powers, S., Weiss-Perry, B., Follansbee, D., Jacobson, A., and Noam, G. (1987). Sex differences within the family: Studies of adolescent and parent family interactions. *Journal of Youth and Adolescence*, 16, 199–220.

Hauser, S., Powers, S., Jacobson, A., Noam, G., Weiss, B., Follansbee, D. (1984). Family contexts of adolescent ego development. *Child Development*, 55, 195–213.

Hayes, C. (Ed.) (1987). *Risking the future: Adolescent sexuality, pregnancy, and childbearing* (Volume 1). Washington: National Academy Press.

Hetherington, E. (1972). Effects of father absence on personality development in adolescent daughters. *Developmental Psychology*, 7, 313–326.

Hetherington, E. (1981). Children and divorce. In R. Henderson (Ed.), *Parent-child interaction: Theory, research, and prospects*. New York: Academic Press.

Hetherington, E., Cox, M., and Cox, R. (1978). The aftermath of divorce. In J. Stevens, Jr., and M. Matthews (Eds.), *Mother-child, father-child relations*. Washington, D.C.: National Association for the Education of Young Children.

Hetherington, E. M., and Camara, K. (1984). Families in transition: The processes of dissolution and reconstitution. In R. Parke (Ed.), *Review of child development research* (Vol. 7). Chicago: University of Chicago Press.

Heyns, B. (1982). *Summer learning and the effects of schooling*. New York: Academic Press.

Hill, C., Rubin, Z., and Peplau, L. (1979). Breakups before marriage: The end of 103 affairs. In G. Levinger and O. Moles (Eds.), *Divorce and separation*. New York: Basic Books.

Hill, J. (June 1978). *Secondary schools, socialization, and social development during adolescence*. Position paper prepared for the National Institute of Education, U.S. Department of Health, Education, and Welfare.

Hill, J. (1980). The family. In M. Johnson (Ed.), *Toward adolescence: The middle school years* (Seventy-ninth yearbook of the National Society for the Study of Education). Chicago: University of Chicago Press.

Hill, J. (1983). Early adolescence: A framework. *Journal of Early Adolescence*, 3, 1–21.

Hill, J., and Holmbeck, G. (1986). Attachment and autonomy during adolescence. In G. Whitehurst (Ed.), *Annals of child development*. Greenwich: JAI Press.

Hill, J., and Holmbeck, G. (1987). Disagreements about rules in families with seventh-grade girls and boys. *Journal of Youth and Adolescence*, 16, 221–246.

Hill, J., Holmbeck, G., Marlow, L., Green, T., and Lynch, M. (1985a). Pubertal status and parent-child relations in families of seventh-grade boys. *Journal of Early Adolescence*, 5, 31–44.

Hill, J., Holmbeck, G., Marlow, L., Green, T., and Lynch, M. (1985b). Menarcheal status and parent-child relations in families of seventh-grade boys. *Journal of Youth and Adolescence*, 14, 301–316.

Hill, J., and Lynch, M. (1983). The intensification of gender-related role expectations during early adolescence. In J. Brooks-Gunn and A. Petersen (Eds.), *Female puberty*. New York: Plenum Press.

Hill, J., and Palmquist, W. (1978). Social cognition and social relations in early adolescence. *International Journal of Behavioral Development, 1*, 1–36.

Hill, J., and Steinberg, L. (1976). The development of autonomy during adolescence. Paper presented at the Symposium on Research on Youth Problems Today, Fundacion Faustino Orbegoza Eizaguirre, Madrid.

Hill, K., and Sarason, S. (1966). The relation of test anxiety and defensiveness to test and school performance over the elementary school years: A further longitudinal study. *Monographs of the Society for Research in Child Development, 31* (Serial No. 104).

Hirschi, T. (1969). *Causes of delinquency*. Berkeley, CA: University of California Press.

Hodgkinson, H. (1985). *All one system: Demographics of education, kindergarten through graduate school*. Washington: Institute for Educational Leadership.

Hoffman, L. (1974). Effects of maternal employment on the child: A review of the research. *Developmental Psychology, 10*, 204–228.

Hoffman, L. (1977). Fear of success in 1965 and 1974: A follow-up study. *Journal of Consulting and Clinical Psychology, 45*, 310–321.

Hoffman, M. (1980). Moral development in adolescence. In J. Adelson (Ed.), *Handbook of adolescent psychology*. New York: Wiley.

Holland, J. (1973). *Making vocational choice: A theory of careers*. Englewood Cliffs, N.J.: Prentice-Hall.

Hollingshead, A. (1975). *Elmtown's youth and Elmtown revisited*. New York: Wiley. (Orig. pub. 1949.)

Holmbeck, G., and Hill, J. (March 1986). Storm and stress beliefs about adolescence: Prevalence, antecedents, and effects of an undergraduate course. Paper presented at the biennial meetings of the Society for Research on Adolescence, Madison.

Holstein, C. (1972). The relation of children's moral judgment level to that of their parents and to communication patterns in the family. In R. Smart and M. Smart (Eds.), *Readings in child development and relationships*. New York: Macmillan.

Horner, M. (1970). Femininity and successful achievement: A basic inconsistency. In J. Bardwick, E. Douvan, M. Horner, and D. Gutmann (Eds.), *Feminine personality and conflict*. Belmont, Calif.: Brooks-Cole.

Huizinga, D., and Elliot, D. (1985). *Juvenile offenders prevalence, offender incidence, and arrest rates by race*. Boulder, CO: Institute of Behavioral Science.

Hunt, M. (1974). *Sexual behavior in the 1970s*. Chicago: Playboy Press.

Hunter, F. (1984). Socializing procedures in parent-child and friendship relations during adolescence. *Developmental Psychology, 18*, 806–811.

Hunter, F., and Youniss, J. (1982). Changes in functions of three relations during adolescence. *Developmental Psychology, 18*, 806–811.

Hyde, J. (1981). How large are cognitive gender differences? *American Psychologist, 36*, 892–901.

Inhelder, B., and Piaget, J. (1958). *The growth of logical thinking from childhood to adolescence*. New York: Basic Books.

Irwin, C. (1986). Biopsychosocial correlates of risk-taking behaviors during adolescence: Can the physician intervene? *Journal of Adolescent Health Care, 7*, 82–96.

Ishiyama, I., and Chabassol, D. (1985). Adolescents' fear of social consequences of academic success as a function of age and sex. *Journal of Youth and Adolescence, 14*, 37–46.

Jacob, T. (1974). Patterns of family conflict and dominance as a function of child age and social class. *Developmental Psychology, 10*, 1–12.

Jessor, R., Costa, F., Jessor, L., and Donovan, J. (1983). Time of first intercourse: A prospective study. *Journal of Personality and Social Psychology, 44*, 608–626.

Jessor, R., and Jessor, S. (1977). *Problem behavior and psychosocial development: A longitudinal study of youth*. New York: Academic Press.

Johnson, S. (1975). *Update on education: A digest of the National Assessment of Education Progress*. Denver: The Education Commission of the States.

Johnston, L., Bachman, J., and O'Malley, P. (1982). *Monitoring the future: Questionnaire responses from the nation's high school seniors, 1981*. Ann Arbor, MI: Institute for Social Research.

Johnston, L., O'Malley, P., and Bachman, J. (1986). *Drug use among American high school students, college students, and other young adults: National trends through 1985*. Washington: National Institute on Drug Abuse.

Jones, E., Forrest, J., Goldman, N., Henshaw, S., Lincoln, R., Rosoff, J., Westhoff, C., and Wulf, D. (1985). Teenage pregnancy in developed countries: Determinants and policy implications. *Family Planning Perspectives, 17*, 53–63.

Jones, H. (1949). Adolescence in our society. In *The family in a democratic society* (Anniversary papers of the Community Service Society of New York). New York: Columbia University Press.

Jones, M. C. (1957). The later careers of boys who were early- or late-maturing. *Child Development, 28*, 113–128.

Jones, M. C. (1965). Psychological correlates of somatic development. *Child Development, 36*, 899–911.

Jones, M. C., and Bayley, N. (1950). Physical maturing among boys as related to behavior. *Journal of Educational Psychology, 41*, 129–148.

Jones, M. C., and Mussen, P. (1958). Self-conceptions, motivations, and inter-personal attitudes of early- and late-maturing girls. *Child Development, 29*, 491–501.

Josselson, R. (1980). Ego development in adolescence. In J.

Adelson (Ed.), *Handbook of adolescent psychology*. New York: Wiley.

Josselson, R., Greenberger, E., and McConochie, D. (1977a). Phenomenological aspects of psychosocial maturity in adolescence. Part I: Boys. *Journal of Youth and Adolescence*, 6, 25–56.

Josselson, R., Greenberger, E., and McConochie, D. (1977b). Phenomenological aspects of psychosocial maturity in adolescence. Part II: Girls. *Journal of Youth and Adolescence*, 6, 145–167.

Junod, H. (1927). *The life of a South African tribe*. London: Macmillan.

Kagan, J. (1958). The concept of identification. *Psychological Review*, 65, 296–305.

Kagan, J., and Coles, R. (Eds.). (1972). *Twelve to sixteen: Early adolescence*. New York: Norton.

Kahn, S., Zimmerman, G., Csikszentmihalyi, M., and Getzels, J. (1985). Relations between identity in young adulthood and intimacy at midlife. *Journal of Personality and Social Psychology*, 49, 1316–1322.

Kallen, D., and Stephenson, J. (1982). Talking about sex revisited. *Journal of Youth and Adolescence*, 11, 11–24.

Kandel, D. (1978). Homophily, selection, and socialization in adolescent friendships. *American Journal of Sociology*, 84, 427–436.

Kandel, D. (1980). Drug and drinking behavior among youth. *Annual review of sociology*, 6, 235–285.

Kandel, D., and Lesser, G. (1972). *Youth in two worlds*. San Francisco: Jossey-Bass.

Kandel, D., and Logan (1984). Patterns of drug use from adolescence to young adulthood: I. Periods of risk for initiation, continued use, and discontinuation. *American Journal of Public Health*, 74, 660–666.

Kaplan, L. (1983). *Coping with peer pressure*. New York: Rosen.

Katz, M. (1975). *The people of Hamilton, Canada West: Family and class in a mid-nineteenth-century city*. Cambridge, Mass.: Harvard University Press.

Kavrell, A., and Petersen, A. (1984). Patterns of achievement in early adolescence. *Advances in Motivation and Achievement*, 2, 1–35.

Kaye, E. (April 1982). Growing up stoned. *California*, p. 80 and ff.

Keating, D. (1979). Secondary-school programs. In A. Passow (Ed.), *The gifted and the talented: Their education and development* (Seventy-eighth yearbook of the National Society for the Study of Education). Chicago: University of Chicago Press.

Keating, D. (1980). Thinking processes in adolescence. In J. Adelson (Ed.), *Handbook of adolescent psychology*. New York: Wiley.

Keating, D., and Bobbitt, B. (1978). Individual and developmental differences in cognitive processing components of ability. *Child Development*, 49, 155–167.

Keating, D., and Clark, L. (1980). Development of physical and social reasoning in adolescence. *Developmental Psychology*, 16, 23–30.

Keniston, K. (1970). Youth: A "new" stage of life. *American Scholar*, 39, 631–641.

Kessen, W. (Ed.). (1975). *Childhood in China*. New Haven: Yale University Press.

Kett, J. (1977). *Rites of passage: Adolescence in America, 1790 to the present*. New York: Basic Books.

King, K., Balswick, J., and Robinson, I. (1977). The continuing premarital sexual revolution among college females. *Journal of Marriage and the Family*, 39, 455–459.

Kinsey, A., Pomeroy, W., and Martin, C. (1948). *Sexual behavior in the human male*. Philadelphia: Saunders.

Kirkendall, L. (1981). Sex education in the United States: A historical perspective. In L. Brown (Ed.), *Sex education in the eighties*. New York: Plenum.

Kite, M. (1984). Sex differences in attitudes towards homosexuals: A meta-analytic review. *Journal of Homosexuality*, 10, 69–81.

Kneisel, P. (1987). Social support preferences of female adolescents in the context of interpersonal stress. Paper presented at the biennial meetings of the Society for Research in Child Development, Baltimore.

Kohlberg, L. (1969). Stage and sequence: The cognitive-developmental approach to socialization. In D. Goslin (Ed.), *Handbook of socialization theory and research*. Chicago: Rand McNally.

Kohlberg, L., and Gilligan, C. (1972). The adolescent as philosopher: The discovery of the self in a post-conventional world. In J. Kagan and R. Coles (Eds.), *Twelve to sixteen: Early adolescence*. New York: Norton.

Kohn, M. (1977). *Class and conformity* (2nd ed.). Chicago: University of Chicago Press.

Krisberg, B., Schwartz, I., Fishman, G., Eisikovits, Z., and Guttman, E. (1986). *The incarceration of minority youth*. Minneapolis: Hubert H. Humphrey Institute of Public Affairs, National Council on Crime and Delinquency.

Krosnick, J., and Judd, C. (1982). Transitions in social influence at adolescence: Who induces cigarette smoking? *Developmental Psychology*, 18, 359–368.

Kuhn, D., and Angelev, J. (1976). An experimental study of the development of formal operational thought. *Child Development*, 47, 697–706.

Kuhn, D., Ho, V., and Adams, C. (1979). Formal reasoning among pre- and late adolescents. *Child Development*, 50, 1128–1135.

Kuhn, D., Langer, J., Kohlberg, L., and Haan, N. (1977). The development of formal operations in logical and moral judgment. *Genetic Psychology Monographs*, 95, 97–188.

Kurdek, L., and Krile, D. (1982). A developmental analysis of the relation between peer acceptance and both interpersonal understanding and perceived social competence. *Child Development*, 53, 1485–1491.

Langway, L., Abramson, P., and Foote, D. (February 16, 1981). The latchkey children. *Newsweek*, pp. 96–97.

Lapsley, D., Enright, R., and Serlin, R. (1985). Toward a theoretical perspective on the legislation of adolescence. *Journal of Early Adolescence*, 5, 441–466.

Lapsley, D., and Murphy, M. (1985). Another look at the theoretical assumptions of adolescent egocentrism. *Developmental Review*, 5, 201–217.

Larson, R. (November 1983). Adolescents' daily experience with family and friends: Contrasting opportunity systems. *Journal of Marriage and the Family*, 739–750.

Leslie, L. (1986). The impact of adolescent females' assessments of parenthood and employment on plans for the future. *Journal of Youth and Adolescence*, 15, 29–49.

Levinson, D. (1978). *The seasons of a man's life*. New York: Knopf.

Levitz-Jones, E., and Orlofsky, J. (1985). Separation-individuation and intimacy capacity in college women. *Journal of Personality and Social Psychology*, 49, 156–169.

Lewin, K. (1948). *Resolving social conflict*. New York: Harper.

Lewin-Epstein, N. (1981). *Youth employment during high school*. Washington, D.C.: National Center for Education Statistics.

Lewinsohn, P. (1975). The behavioral study and treatment of depression. In M. Herson, R. Eisler, and P. Miller (Eds.). *Progress in behavior modifications*. New York: Academic Press.

Lewis, C. (1981a). The effects of parental firm control. *Psychological Bulletin*, 90, 547–563.

Lewis, C. (1981b). How adolescents approach decisions: Changes over grades seven to twelve and policy implications. *Child Development*, 52, 538–544.

Lewis, R., and Spanier, G. (1979). Theorizing about the quality and stability of marriage. In W. Burr, R. Hill, I. Nye, and I. Reiss (Eds.), *Contemporary theories about the family*. Glencoe, Ill.: Free Press.

Lightfoot, S. (1983). *The good high school*. New York: Basic Books.

Lipsitz, J. (1977). *Growing up forgotten*. Lexington, Mass.: Lexington Books.

Litovsky, V., and Dusek, J. (1985). Perceptions of child rearing and self-concept development during the early adolescent years. *Journal of Youth and Adolescence*, 14, 373–388.

Livesley, W., and Bromley, D. (1973). *Person perception in childhood and adolescence*. New York: Wiley.

Livson, N., and Peskin, H. (1980). Perspectives on adolescence from longitudinal research. In J. Adelson (Ed.), *Handbook of adolescent psychology*. New York: Wiley.

Lloyd, D. (1978). Prediction of school failure from third-grade data. *Educational and Psychological Measurement*, 38, 1193–1200.

Loeber, R., and Stouthamer-Loeber, M. (1986). Family factors as correlates and predictors of juvenile conduct problems and delinquency. In M. Tonry and N. Morris (Eds.), *Crime and justice* (Vol. 7). Chicago: University of Chicago Press.

Lynn, D. (November 1966). The process of learning parental and sex-role identification. *Journal of Marriage and the Family*, 446–470.

McCall, R., Applebaum, M., and Hogarty, P. (1973). Developmental changes in mental performance. *Monographs of the Society for Research in Child Development*, 38 (Serial No. 150).

McClelland, D. (1961). *The achieving society*. Princeton, N.J.: Van Nostrand.

McClelland, D., Atkinson, J., Clark, R., and Lowell, E. (1953). *The achievement motive*. New York: Appleton-Century-Crofts.

McClintock, M. (1980). Major gaps in menstrual cycle research: Behavioral and physiological controls in a biological context. In P. Komenich, M. McSweeney, J. Noack, and N. Elder (Eds.), *The menstrual cycle*, Volume 2 (pp. 7–23). New York: Springer.

McGanity, W. (1976). Problems of nutritional evaluation of the adolescent. In J. McKigney and H. Munro (Eds.), *Nutrient requirements in adolescence*. Cambridge, Mass.: MIT Press.

McGovern, K., Arkowitz, H., and Gilmore, S. (1975). Evaluation of social skill training programs for college dating inhibitions. *Journal of Counseling Psychology*, 22, 505–512.

McGuire, K., and Weisz, J. (1982). Social cognition and behavior correlates of preadolescent chumship. *Child Development*, 53, 1478–1484.

McNeil, L. (1984). *Lowering Expectations: The Impact of Student Employment on Classroom Knowledge*. Madison, WI: Wisconsin Center for Education Research.

Maccoby, E., and Jacklin, C. (1974). *The psychology of sex differences*. Stanford, Calif.: Stanford University Press.

Maccoby, E., and Martin, J. (1983). Socialization in the context of the family: Parent-child interaction. In E. M. Hetherington (Ed.), *Handbook of child psychology; Socialization, personality, and social development* (Vol. 4). New York: Wiley.

Macklin, E. (1978). Review of research on nonmarital cohabitation in the United States. In B. Murstein (Ed.), *Exploring intimate life styles*. New York: Springer.

Magnusson, D., Stattin, H., and Allen, V. (1986). Differential maturation among girls and its relation to social adjustment in a longitudinal perspective. In P. Baltes, D. Featherman, and R. Lerner (Eds.) *Life span development and behavior* (Volume 7), Hillsdale, NJ: Erlbaum.

Mahoney, E. (1983). *Human sexuality*. New York: McGraw-Hill.

Marcia, J. (1966). Development and validation of ego identity status. *Journal of Personality and Social Psychology*, 3, 551–558.

Marcia, J. (1976). Identity six years after: A follow-up study. *Journal of Youth and Adolescence*, 5, 145–150.

Marcia, J. (1980). Identity in adolescence. In J. Adelson

(Ed.), *Handbook of adolescent psychology*. New York: Wiley.

Mare, R., Winship, C., and Kubitschek, W. (1984). The transition from youth to adult: Understanding the age pattern of employment. *American Journal of Sociology*, *90*, 326–358.

Marini, M. (1978). The transition to adulthood: Sex differences on educational attainment and age at marriage. *American Sociological Review*, *43*, 483–507.

Marini, M. (1980). Sex differences in the process of occupational attainment: A closer look. *Social Science Research*, *9*, 307–361.

Marini, M. (1984). The order of events in the transition to adulthood. *Sociology of Education*, *57*, 63–84.

Marshall, W. (1978). Puberty. In F. Falkner and J. Tanner (Eds.), *Human growth* (Vol. 2). New York: Plenum Press.

Masnick, G., and Bane, M. (1980). *The nation's families: 1960–1990*. Boston: Auburn House.

Massad, C. (1981). Sex role identity and adjustment during adolescence. *Child Development*, *52*, 1290–1298.

Mayer, J. (1968). *Overweight: Causes, cost, and control*. Englewood Cliffs, N.J.: Prentice-Hall.

Mead, M. (1928). *Coming of age in Samoa*. New York: Morrow.

Mead, M. (1978). *Culture and commitment*. Garden City, N.Y.: Anchor.

Medrich, E., Roizen, J., Rubin, V., and Buckley, S. (1982). *The serious business of growing up*. Berkeley: University of California Press.

Miller, N. (1928). *The child in primitive society*. New York: Brentano.

Miller, P., and Simon, W. (1980). The development of sexuality in adolescence. In J. Adelson (Ed.), *Handbook of adolescent psychology*. New York: Wiley.

Miller, W. (1958). Lower-class culture as a generating milieu of gang delinquency. *Journal of Social Issues*, *14*, 5–19.

Minuchin, S. (1974). *Families and family therapy*. Cambridge, Mass.: Harvard University Press.

Minuchin, S., Rosman, B., and Baker, L. (1978). *Psychosomatic families: Anorexia nervosa in context*. Cambridge: Harvard University Press.

Modell, J., Furstenberg, F., Jr., and Hershberg, T. (1976). Social change and transitions to adulthood in historical perspective. *Journal of Family History*, *1*, 7–32.

Monahan, L., Kuhn, D., and Shaver, P. (1974). Intrapsychic versus cultural explanations of the "fear of success" motive. *Journal of Personality and Social Psychology*, *29*, 60–64.

Montemayor, R. (1982). The relationship between parent-adolescent conflict and the amount of time adolescents spend alone and with parents and peers. *Child Development*, *53*, 1512–1519.

Montemayor, R. (1983). Parents and adolescents in conflict: All families some of the time and some families most of the time. *Journal of Early Adolescence*, *3*, 83–103.

Montemayor, R. (1986). Family variation in parent-adoles-

cent storm and stress. *Journal of Adolescent Research*, *1*, 15–31.

Montemayor, R., and Brownlee, J. (1987). Fathers, mothers, and adolescents: Gender-based differences in parental roles during adolescence. *Journal of Youth and Adolescence*, *16*, 281–292.

Montemayor, R., Brown, B., and Adams, G. (1985). Changes in identity status and psychological adjustment after leaving home and entering college. Paper presented at the biennial meetings of the Society for Research in Child Development, Toronto.

Montemayor, R., and Eisen, M. (1977). The development of self-conceptions from childhood to adolescence. *Developmental Psychology*, *13*, 314–319.

Moore, K., Peterson, J., and Furstenberg, F., Jr. (1986). Parental attitudes and the occurrence of early sexual activity. *Journal of Marriage and the Family*, *48*, 777–782.

Moos, R. (1978). A typology of junior high and high school classrooms. *American Educational Research Journal*, *15*, 53–66.

Moos, R., and Trickett, E. (1974). *Classroom environment scale manual*. Palo Alto, Calif.: Consulting Psychologists Press.

Mortimer, J., and Finch, M. (1986). The effects of part-time work on adolescent self-concept and achievement. In P. Borman and J. Reisman (Eds.), *Becoming a worker*. Norwood: Ablex.

Mortimer, J., and Lorence, J. (1979). Work experience and occupational value socialization: A longitudinal study. *American Journal of Sociology*, *84*, 1361–1385.

Moschis, G. (1982). Advertising to adolescents. In M. Schwartz (Ed.), *TV and teens*. Reading, Mass.: Addison-Wesley.

Mounger, J. (1970). Nutrition. In W. Daniel, Jr. (Ed.), *The adolescent patient*. Saint Louis: Mosby.

Mueller, J. (1976). Current recommended dietary allowances for adolescents. In J. McKigney and H. Munro (Eds.), *Nutrient requirements in adolescence*. Cambridge, Mass.: MIT Press.

Munro, G., and Adams, G. (1977). Ego-identity formation in college students and working youth. *Developmental Psychology*, *13*, 523–524.

Mussen, P., and Jones, M. C. (1957). Self-conceptions, motivations, and interpersonal attitudes of late- and early-maturing boys. *Child Development*, *28*, 243–256.

Mussen, P., and Jones, M. C. (1958). The behavior-inferred motivations of late- and early-maturing boys. *Child Development*, *29*, 61–67.

Myers, J., Lindenthal, J., and Pepper, M. (1975). Life events, social integration, and psychiatric symptomatology. *Journal of Health and Social Behavior*, *16*, 421–429.

National Center for Health Statistics. (1982). *Vital Statistics of the United States*. Washington, D.C.: U.S. Government Printing Office.

National Commission on Excellence in Education. (1983).

A nation at risk: The imperative for educational reform. Washington, D.C.: U.S. Department of Education.

National Commission on Youth. (1980). *The transition of youth to adulthood: A bridge too long.* Boulder, Colo.: Westview Press.

National Panel on High School and Adolescent Education. (1976). *The education of adolescents.* Washington, D.C.: U.S. Government Printing Office.

Neilsen, L. (1987). *Adolescent psychology.* New York: Holt, Rinehart & Winston.

Neimark, E. (1975). Intellectual development during adolescence. In F. Horowitz (Ed.), *Review of child development research* (Vol. 4). Chicago: University of Chicago Press.

Neugarten, B. (1975). The psychology of aging: An overview. *Master Lectures on Developmental Psychology.* Washington, D.C.: American Psychological Association.

Neugarten, B., and Datan, N. (1974). The middle years. In S. Arieti (Ed.), *American Handbook of Psychiatry* (2nd ed.), Vol. 1, Part 3. New York: Basic Books.

Newcomb, M., Huba, G., and Bentler, P. (1981). A multidimensional assessment of stressful life events among adolescents: Derivation and correlates. *Journal of Health and Social Behavior, 22,* 400–415.

Newcomb, M., Huba, G., and Bentler, P. (1983). Mothers' influence on the drug use of their children: Confirmatory tests of direct modeling and mediational theories. *Developmental Psychology, 19,* 714–726.

Newcomb, M., Maddahain, E., and Bentler, P. (1986). Risk factors for drug use among adolescents: Concurrent and longitudinal analyses. *American Journal of Public Health, 76,* 525–531.

Newcombe, N., and Dubas, J. (1987). Individual differences in cognitive ability: Are they related to timing of puberty? In R. Lerner and T. Foch (Eds.), *Biological-psychosocial interactions in early adolescence* (pp. 249–302). Hillsdale, NJ: Erlbaum.

Newcomer, S., and Udry, J. (1984). Mothers' influence on the sexual behavior of their teenage children. *Journal of Marriage and the Family, May,* 477–485.

Newcomer, S., and Udry, J. (1987). Parental marital status effects on adolescent sexual behavior. *Journal of Marriage and the Family, 49,* 235–240.

Nottelmann, E. (1987). Competence and self-esteem during transition from childhood to adolescence. *Developmental Psychology, 23,* 441–450.

Nottelmann, E., Susman, E., Inhoff-Germain, G., and Chrousos, G. (1987). Concurrent and predictive relations between hormone levels and social-emotional functioning in early adolescence. Paper presented at the biennial meetings of the Society for Research in Child Development, Baltimore.

Offer, D. (1969). *The psychological world of the teenager.* New York: Basic Books.

Offer, D., Ostrov, E., and Howard, K. (1981). *The adolescent: A psychological self-portrait.* New York: Basic Books.

Ogbu, J. (1974). *The next generation: An ethnography of education in an urban neighborhood.* New York: Academic Press.

Ogbu, J. (1978). *Minority education and caste.* New York: Academic Press.

O'Malley, P., and Bachman, J. (1983). Self-esteem: Change and stability between ages 13 and 23. *Developmental Psychology, 19,* 257–268.

Orlofsky, J., Marcia, J., and Lesser, I. (1973). Ego identity status and the intimacy versus isolation crisis of young adulthood. *Journal of Personality and Social Psychology, 27,* 211–219.

Osipow, S. (1973). *Theories of career development* (2nd ed.). New York: Appleton-Century-Crofts.

Owens, T. (1982). Experience-based career education: Summary and implications of research and evaluation findings. *Child and Youth Services Journal, 4,* 77–91.

Paige, K. (1983). A bargaining theory of menarcheal responses in preindustrialized cultures. In J. Brooks-Gunn and A. Petersen (Eds.), *Girls at puberty.* New York: Plenum.

Pantages, T., and Creedon, C. (1978). Studies of college attrition: 1950–1975. *Review of Educational Research, 48,* 49–101.

Papini, D., and Sebby, R. (1987). Adolescent pubertal status and affective family relationships: A multivariate assessment. *Journal of Youth and Adolescence, 16,* 1–15.

Parke, R. (Ed.). (1984). *Review of child development research* (Volume 7). Chicago: University of Chicago Press.

Parsons, J. Eccles, Adler, T., and Kaczala, C. (1982). Socialization of achievement attitudes and beliefs: Parental influences. *Child Development, 53,* 310–321.

Parsons, T. (1949). The social structure of the family. In R. Anshen (Ed.), *The family: Its function and destiny.* New York: Harper.

Patterson, G., and Stouthamer-Loeber, M. (1984). The correlation of family management practices and delinquency. *Child Development, 55,* 1299–1307.

Paulsen, E. (1972). Obesity in children and adolescents. In H. Barnett and A. Einhorn (Eds.), *Pediatrics.* New York: Appleton-Century-Crofts.

Paulsen, K., and Johnson, M. (1983). Sex role attitudes and mathematical ability in 4th-, 8th-, and 11th-grade students from a high socioeconomic area. *Developmental Psychology, 19,* 210–214.

Peel, E. (1971). *The nature of adolescent judgment.* London: Staples Press.

Peplau, L., Rubin, Z., and Hill, C. (1977). Sexual intimacy in dating relationships. *Journal of Social Issues, 33,* 86–109.

Peskin, H. (1967). Pubertal onset and ego functioning: A psychoanalytic approach. *Journal of Abnormal Psychology, 72,* 1–15.

Peskin, H. (1973). Influence of the developmental schedule of puberty on learning and ego functioning. *Journal of Youth and Adolescence, 2*, 273–290.

Petersen, A. (1979). Differential cognitive development in adolescent girls. In M. Sugar (Ed.), *Female adolescent development*. New York: Brunner/Mazel.

Petersen, A. (1985). Pubertal development as a cause of disturbance: Myths, realities, and unanswered questions. *Genetic, Social, and General Psychology Monographs, 111*, 205–232.

Petersen, A. (1988). Adolescent development. *Annual review of psychology, 39*, 583–607.

Petersen, A., and Taylor, B. (1980). The biological approach to adolescence: Biological change and psychological adaptation. In J. Adelson (Ed.), *Handbook of adolescent psychology*. New York: Wiley.

Peterson, J., and Zill, N. (1986). Marital disruption, parent-child relationships, and behavior problems in children. *Journal of Marriage and the Family, 48*, 295–307.

Phillips, D., and Carstensen, L. (1986). Clustering of teen-age suicides after television news stories about suicide. *New England Journal of Medicine, 315*, 685–689.

Phinney, J., and Alipuria, L. (1987). Ethnic identity in older adolescents from four ethnic groups. Paper presented at the biennial meetings of the Society for Research in Child Development, Baltimore.

Piaget, J. (1932). *The moral judgment of the child*. New York: Harcourt.

Piaget, J. (1972). Intellectual evolution from adolescence to adulthood. *Human Development, 15*, 1–12.

Pincus, F. (1980). The false promises of community colleges: Class conflict and vocational education. *Harvard Educational Review, 50*, 332–361.

Pitt, R. (1976). Toward a comprehensive model of problem-solving: Application to solutions of chemistry problems in high-school and college students. Unpublished doctoral dissertation, University of California, San Diego.

Plomin, R., and Daniels, D. (1987). Why are children in the same family so different from one another? *Behavioral and Brain Sciences, 10*, 1–60.

Powell, A., Farrar, E., and Cohen, D. (1985). *The shopping mall high school*. Boston: Houghton Mifflin.

Powers, O., and Wagner, M. (1984). Attributions for school achievement of middle school students. *Journal of Early Adolescence, 4*, 215–222.

President's Science Advisory Committee. (1974). *Youth: Transition to adulthood*. Chicago: University of Chicago Press.

Pulkkinen, L. (1982). Self-control and continuity from childhood to adolescence. In P. Baltes and O. Brim (Eds.), *Life-span development and behavior* (Vol. 4). New York: Academic Press.

Raffaelli, M., and Larson, R. (1987). Sibling interactions in late childhood and early adolescence. Paper presented at the Biennial meetings of the Society for Research in Child Development, Baltimore.

Reiss, I. (1960). *Premarital sexual standards in America*. New York: Free Press.

Religion in America: The Gallup report. (1984). Princeton, NJ: Princeton Religious Research Center.

Rest, J. (1983). Morality. In J. Flavell and E. Markman (Eds.), *Handbook of child psychology; Volume III: Cognitive development*. New York: Wiley.

Rest, J., Davison, M., and Robbins, S. (1978). Age trends in judging moral issues: A review of cross-sectional, longitudinal, and sequential studies of the Defining Issues Test. *Child Development, 49*, 263–279.

Reubens, B., Harrison, J., and Rupp, K. (1981). *The youth labor force, 1945–1995: A cross-national analysis*. Totowa, N.J.: Allanheld, Osmun, and Co.

Riesman, D. (1950). *The lonely crowd*. New Haven: Yale University Press.

Riley, T., Adams, G., and Neilsen, E. (1984). Adolescent egocentrism: The association among imaginary audience behavior, cognitive development, and parental support and rejection. *Journal of Youth and Adolescence, 13*, 401–438.

Robbins, C., Kaplan, H., and Martin, S. (1985). Antecedents of pregnancy among unmarried adolescents. *Journal of Marriage and the Family, August*, 567–583.

Robinson, I., and Jedlicka, D. (February 1982). Change in sexual attitudes and behavior of college students from 1965 to 1980: A research note. *Journal of Marriage and the Family*, 237–240.

Rodgers, R. (1973). *Family interaction and transaction: A developmental approach*. Englewood Cliffs, N.J.: Prentice-Hall.

Rodman, H., Pratto, D., and Nelson, R. (1985). Child care arrangements and children's functioning: A comparison of self-care and adult-care children. *Developmental Psychology, 21*, 413–418.

Rosen, B. (1956). The achievement syndrome: A psychocultural dimension of social stratification. *American Sociological Review, 21*, 203–211.

Rosen, B., and Aneshensel, C. (1975). The chameleon syndrome. *Journal of Marriage and the Family, 38*, 605–617.

Rosen, B., and D'Andrade, R. (1959). The psychosocial origins of achievement motivation. *Sociometry, 22*, 185–218.

Rosenbaum, J. (1976). *Making inequality: The hidden curriculum of high school tracking*. New York: Wiley.

Rosenbaum, J. (1978). Structure of opportunity in schools. *Social Forces, 57*, 236–256.

Rosenberg, M. (1975). The dissonant context and the adolescent self-concept. In S. Dragastin and G. Elder, Jr. (Eds.), *Adolescence in the life cycle*. Washington, D.C.: Hemisphere.

Rosenberg, M. (1986). Self concept from middle childhood through adolescence. In J. Suls and A. Greenwald (Eds.),

Psychological perspectives on the self (Vol. 3). Hillsdale, NJ: Erlbaum.

Rosenberg, M., and Simmons, R. (1972). *Black and white self-esteem: The urban school child.* Washington, D.C.: American Sociological Association.

Rosenthal, R., and Jacobson, E. (1968). *Pygmalion in the classroom.* New York: Holt, Rinehart & Winston.

Rotbart, D. (March 2, 1981). Allowances stay flat, candy rises—And kids lose their innocence. *Wall Street Journal*, p. 1 and ff.

Rousseau, J. (1911). *Emile* (B. Foxley, trans.). London: Dent. (Originally published 1762.)

Ruble, D., and Brooks-Gunn, J. (1982). The experience of menarche. *Child Development, 53*, 1557–1566.

Ruggiero, M., Greenberger, E., and Steinberg, L. (1982). Occupational deviance among first-time workers. *Youth and Society, 13*, 423–448.

Rumberger, R. (1983). Dropping out of high school: The influence of race, sex, and family background. *American Educational Research Journal, 20*, 199–220.

Rutter, M. (1978). Protective factors in children's responses to stress and disadvantage. In M. Kent and J. Rolf (Eds.), *Primary prevention of psychopathology*, Vol. 3: *Promoting social competence and coping in children.* Hanover, N.J.: University Press of New England.

Rutter, M. (1983). School effects on pupil progress: Research findings and policy implications. *Child Development, 54*, 1–29.

Rutter, M., and Garmezy, N. (1983). Developmental psychopathology. In E. M. Hetherington (Ed.), *Handbook of child psychology, Volume IV: Socialization, personality, and social development.* New York: Wiley.

Rutter, M., Graham, P., Chadwick, F., and Yule, W. (1976). Adolescent turmoil: Fact or fiction? *Journal of Child Psychology and Psychiatry, 17*, 35–56.

Rutter, M., Maugham, B., Mortimore, P., and Ouston, J. (1979). *Fifteen thousand hours: Secondary schools and their effects on children.* London: Open Books.

Safer, D. (1986). The stress of secondary school for vulnerable students. *Journal of Youth and Adolescence, 15*, 405–417.

Sagar, H., Schofield, J., and Snyder, H. (1983). Race and gender barriers: Preadolescent peer behavior in academic classrooms. *Child Development, 54*, 1032–1040.

St. John, N. (1975). *School desegregation outcomes for children.* New York: Wiley.

Salinger, J. D. (1964). *The catcher in the rye.* New York: Bantam.

Santrock, J., and Warshak, R. (1979). Father custody and social development in boys and girls. *Journal of Social Issues, 35*(4), 112–125.

Savin-Williams, R. (1976). An ethological study of dominance formation and maintenance in a group of human adolescents. *Child Development, 47*, 972–979.

Savin-Williams, R. (1979). Dominance hierarchies in groups of adolescents. *Child Development, 50*, 923–935.

Savin-Williams, R., and Demo, D. (1983). Situational and transituational determinants of adolescent self-feelings. *Journal of Personality and Social Psychology, 44*, 824–833.

Savin-Williams, R., and Demo, D. (1984). Developmental change and stability in adolescent self-concept. *Developmental Psychology, 20*, 1100–1110.

Schiff, A., and Knopf, I. (1985). The effects of task demands on attention allocation in children of different ages. *Child Development, 56*, 621–630.

Schofield, J. (1981). Complementary and conflicting identities: Images and interaction in an interracial school. In S. Asher and J. Gottman (Eds.), *The development of children's friendships.* Cambridge: Cambridge University Press.

Schofield, J. (1982). *Black and white in school: Trust, tension, or tolerance?* New York: Praeger.

Schwartz, P., and Blumstein, P. (1983). *American couples: Money, work, and sex.* New York: William Morrow.

Sebald, H. (1986). Adolescents' shifting orientation toward parents and peers: A curvilinear trend over recent decades. *Journal of Marriage and the Family, 48*, 5–13.

Seligman M., and Peterson, C. (1986). A learned helplessness perspective on childhood depression. Theory and research. In M. Rutter, C. Izard, and P. Read (Eds.), *Depression in childhood: Developmental perspectives.* New York: Guilford Press.

Selman, R. (1976). Toward a structural analysis of developing interpersonal relations concepts: Research with normal and disturbed preadolescent boys. In A. Pick (Ed.), *Minnesota Symposia on Child Psychology* (Vol. 10). Minneapolis: University of Minnesota Press.

Selman, R. (1980). *The growth of interpersonal understanding: Developmental and clinical analyses.* New York: Academic Press.

Shapiro, B., and O'Brien, T. (1970). Logical thinking in children ages six through thirteen. *Child Development, 41*, 823–829.

Sharabany, R., Gershoni, R., and Hofman, J. (1981). Girlfriend, boyfriend: Age and sex differences in intimate friendship. *Developmental Psychology, 17*, 800–808.

Shaw, M., and White, D. (1965). The relationship between child-parent identification and academic underachievement. *Journal of Clinical Psychology, 21*, 10–13.

Shelton, L. (1974). Personal communication. College of Human Development, University of Vermont, Burlington, VT.

Sherif, M., and Sherif, C. (1969). Adolescent attitudes and behavior in their reference groups within differing sociocultural settings. In J. Hill (Ed.), *Minnesota Symposia on Child Psychology* (Vol. 3). Minneapolis: University of Minnesota Press.

Shipman, G. (1971). The psychodynamics of sex education. In R. E. Muuss (Ed.), *Adolescent behavior and society.* New York: Random House.

Shuttleworth, F. (1951). The adolescent period: A pictorial atlas. *Monographs of the Society for Research in Child Development*, *14*, (Serial No. 50).

Siegler, R., Liebert, D., and Liebert, R. (1973). Inhelder and Piaget's pendulum problem: Teaching adolescents to act as scientists. *Developmental Psychology*, *9*, 97–101.

Silverberg, S. (1986). Psychological well-being of parents with early adolescent children. Unpublished doctoral dissertation. Department of Child and Family Studies, University of Wisconsin—Madison.

Silverberg, S., and Steinberg, L. (1987). Adolescent autonomy, parent-adolescent conflict, and parental well-being. *Journal of Youth and Adolescence*, *16*, 293–312.

Silverberg, S., and Steinberg, L. (in press). Psychological well-being of parents at midlife: The impact of early adolescent children. *Developmental Psychology*.

Simmons, R., and Blyth, D. (1987). *Moving into adolescence*. New York: Aldine de Gruyter.

Simmons, R., Blyth, D., and McKinney, K. (1983). The social and psychological effects of puberty on white females. In J. Brooks-Gunn and A. Petersen (Eds.), *Girls at puberty*. New York: Plenum Press.

Simmons, R., Blyth, D., Van Cleave, E., and Bush, D. (1979). Entry into early adolescence: The impact of school structure, puberty, and early dating on self-esteem. *American Sociological Review*, *44*, 948–967.

Simmons, R., Brown, L., Bush, D., and Blyth, D. (1978). Self-esteem and achievement of black and white adolescents. *Social Problems*, *26*, 86–96.

Simmons, R., Burgeson, R., Carlton-Ford, S., and Blyth, D. (1987). The impact of cumulative change in early adolescence. *Child Development*, *58*, 1220–1234.

Simmons, R., and Rosenberg, F. (1975). Sex, sex roles, and self-image. *Journal of Youth and Adolescence*, *4*, 229–258.

Simmons, R., Rosenberg, F., and Rosenberg, M. (1973). Disturbance in the self-image at adolescence. *American Sociological Review*, *38*, 553–568.

Simon, W., Berger, A., and Gagnon, J. (1972). Beyond anxiety and fantasy: The coital experience of college youth. *Journal of Youth and Adolescence*, *1*, 203–222.

Simon, W., and Gagnon, J. (1969). On psychosexual development. In D. Goslin (Ed.), *Handbook of socialization theory and research*. Chicago: Rand McNally.

Simpson, R. (1962). Parental influence, anticipatory socialization, and social mobility. *American Sociological Review*, *27*, 517–522.

Sizer, T. (1984). *Horace's compromise*. Boston: Houghton Mifflin.

Small, S., Eastman, G., and Cornelius, S. (in press). Adolescent autonomy and parental stress. *Journal of Youth and Adolescence*.

Smetana, J. (1988). Concepts of self and social convention: Adolescents' and parents' reasoning about hypothetical and actual family conflicts. In M. Gunnar (Ed.), *21st Minnesota symposium on child psychology*. Hillsdale, NJ: Erlbaum.

Smith, E., and Udry, J. (1985). Coital and non-coital sexual behaviors of white and black adolescents. *American Journal of Public Health*, *75*, 1200–1203.

Smith, E., Udry, J., and Morris, N. (1985). Pubertal development and friends: A biosocial explanation of adolescent sexual behavior. *Journal of Health and Social Behavior*, *26*, 183–192.

Smollar, J., and Youniss, J. (1985). Transformation in adolescents' perceptions of parents. Paper presented at the biennial meetings of the Society for Research in Child Development, Baltimore.

Sobesky, W. (1983). The effects of situational factors on moral judgments. *Child Development*, *54*, 575–584.

Sorensen, R. (1973). *Adolescent sexuality in contemporary society*. New York: World Book.

Spanier, G. (1976). Formal and informal sex education as determinants of premarital sexual behavior. *Archives of Sexual Behavior*, *5*, 39–67.

Spence, J., and Helmreich, R. (1978). *Masculinity and femininity: Their psychological dimensions, correlates, and antecedents*. Austin: University of Texas Press.

Spenner, K., and Featherman, D. (1978). Achievement ambitions. *Annual review of sociology* (Vol. 4). Palo Alto, Calif.: Annual Reviews.

Spielberger, C. (1966). The effects of anxiety on complex learning and academic achievement. In C. Spielberger (Ed.), *Anxiety and behavior*. New York: Academic Press.

Steinberg, L. (1981). Transformations in family relations at puberty. *Developmental Psychology*, *17*, 833–840.

Steinberg, L. (1982). Jumping off the work experience bandwagon. *Journal of Youth and Adolescence*, *11*, 183–205.

Steinberg, L. (1986). Latchkey children and susceptibility to peer pressure: An ecological analysis. *Developmental Psychology*, *22*, 433–439.

Steinberg, L. (1987a). The impact of puberty on family relations: Effects of pubertal status and pubertal timing. *Developmental Psychology*, *23*, 451–460.

Steinberg, L. (1987b). Bound to bicker: Pubescent primates leave home for good reasons. Our teens stay with us and squabble. *Psychology Today*, September, 36–39.

Steinberg, L. (1987c). Single parents, stepparents, and the susceptibility of adolescents to antisocial peer pressure. *Child Development*, *58*, 269–275.

Steinberg, L. (1988). Reciprocal relation between parent-child distance and pubertal maturation. *Developmental Psychology*, in press.

Steinberg, L., Blinn, P., and Chan, K. (1984). Dropping out among language minority youth. *Review of Educational Research*, *54*, 113–132.

Steinberg, L., Greenberger, E., Garduque, L., and McAuliffe, S. (1982). Adolescents in the labor force: Some costs and benefits to schooling and learning. *Educational Evaluation and Policy Analysis*, *4*, 363–372.

Steinberg, L., Greenberger, E., Garduque, L., Ruggiero,

M., and Vaux, A. (1982). Effects of working on adolescent development. *Developmental Psychology, 18,* 385–395.

Steinberg, L., and Silverberg, S. (1986). The vicissitudes of autonomy in early adolescence. *Child Development, 57,* 841–851.

Steinberg, L., and Silverberg, S. (1987). Influences on marital satisfaction during the middle stages of the family life cycle. *Journal of Marriage and the Family, 49,* 751–760.

Sternberg, R. (1977). *Intelligence, information, processing, and analogical reasoning: The componential analysis of human abilities.* Hillsdale, N.J.: Erlbaum.

Sternberg, R., and Nigro, G. (1980). Developmental patterns in the solution of verbal analogies. *Child Development, 51,* 27–38.

Sternberg, R., and Rifkin, B. (1979). The development of analogical reasoning processes. *Journal of Experimental Child Psychology, 27,* 195–232.

Stevenson, D., and Baker, D. (1987). The family-school relation and the child's school performance. *Child Development, 58,* 1348–1357.

Stevenson, W. (1978). The relationship between early work experience and future employability. In A. Adams and G. Mangum (Eds.), *The lingering crisis of youth unemployment.* Kalamazoo, Mich.: Upjohn Institute for Employment Research.

Stipek, D. (1981). Adolescents—Too young to earn, too old to learn? Compulsory school attendance and intellectual development. *Journal of Youth and Adolescence, 10,* 113–139.

Stipek, D., and Weisz, J. (1981). Perceived personal control and academic achievement. *Review of Educational Research, 51,* 101–137.

Sullivan, H. S. (1953a). *The interpersonal theory of psychiatry.* New York: Norton.

Sullivan, H. S. (1953b). *Conceptions of modern psychiatry.* New York: Norton.

Sullivan, K., and Sullivan, A. (1980). Adolescent-parent separation. *Developmental Psychology, 16,* 93–99.

Super, D. (1967). *The psychology of careers.* New York: Harper & Row.

Susman, E., Inhoff-Germain, G., Nottelmann, E., Loriaux, D., Cutler, G., Jr., and Chrousos, G. (1987). Hormones, emotional dispositions, and aggressive attributes in young adolescents. *Child Development, 58,* 1114–1134.

Tanner, D. (1972). *Secondary education.* New York: Macmillan.

Tanner, J. (1972). Sequence, tempo, and individual variation in growth and development of boys and girls aged twelve to sixteen. In J. Kagan and R. Coles (Eds.), *Twelve to sixteen: Early adolescence.* New York: Norton.

Tobin-Richards, M. (1985). Sex differences and similarities in heterosexual activity in early adolescence. Paper presented at the biennial meetings of the Society for Research in Child Development, Toronto.

Trickett, E. (1978). Toward a social-ecological conception of adolescent socialization: Normative data on contrasting types of public school classrooms. *Child Development, 49,* 408–414.

Trickett, E., and Moos, R. (1973). Social environment of junior high and high school classrooms. *Journal of Educational Psychology, 65,* 93–102.

Troll, L. (1975). *Early and middle adulthood.* Monterey, Calif.: Brooks/Cole.

Turiel, E. (1978). The development of concepts of social structure: Social convention. In J. Glick and K. A. Clarke-Stewart (Eds.), *The development of social understanding.* New York: Gardner.

Turnbull, A., and Schultz, J. (1979). *Mainstreaming handicapped students.* Boston: Allyn & Bacon.

Udry, J. (1987). Hormonal and social determinants of adolescent sexual initiation. In J. Bancroft (Ed.), *Adolescence and puberty.* New York: Oxford University Press.

Udry, J., Billy, J., Morris, N., Gruff, T., and Raj, M. (1985). Serum androgenic hormones motivate sexual behavior in boys. *Fertility and Sterility, 43,* 90–94.

Udry, J., Talbert, L., and Morris, N. (1986). Biosocial foundations for adolescent female sexuality. *Demography, 23,* 217–230.

United Nations Population Division. (1976). *Population by sex and age for regions and countries, 1950–2000, as assessed in 1973: Medium variant.* New York: United Nations, Department of Economic and Social Affairs.

U.S. Bureau of the Census. (May 1980). *American families and living arrangements, 1978.* Washington, D.C.: U.S. Department of Commerce.

U.S. Bureau of the Census. (1981). *Statistical abstract of the United States (102nd Edition).* Washington, D.C.: U.S. Government Printing Office.

U.S. Bureau of the Census. (June 1982). *Marital status and living arrangements: March 1981.* Washington, D.C.: U.S. Department of Commerce.

U.S. Bureau of the Census. (1985). *Statistical abstract of the United States.* Washington: U.S. Government Printing Office.

U.S. Bureau of the Census. (1986). *Statistical abstract of the United States.* Washington: U.S. Government Printing Office.

U.S. Department of Commerce, Bureau of the Census. (1940). *Characteristics of the population.* Washington, D.C.: U.S. Government Printing Office.

Vanfossen, B., Jones, J., and Spade, J. (1987). Curriculum tracking and status maintenance. *Sociology of Education, 60,* 104–122.

Vener, A., and Stewart, C. (1974). Adolescent sexual behavior in Middle America revisited: 1970–1973. *Journal of Marriage and the Family, 36,* 728–735.

Ventura, S. (1984). Trends in teenage child bearing, United States, 1970–81. *Vital and Health Statistics Series,* (Vol. 21). Washington: U.S. Government Printing Office.

Vigersky, R. (Ed.). (1977). *Anorexia nervosa.* New York: Raven Press.

Waber, D. (1977). Sex differences in mental abilities, hemispheric lateralization, and rate of physical growth at adolescence. *Developmental Psychology, 13,* 29–38.

Waite, L., Goldscheider, F., and Witsberger, C. (1986). Nonfamily living and the erosion of traditional family orientations among young adults. *American Sociological Review, 51,* 541–554.

Walker, L., de Vries, B., and Trevethan, S. (1987). Moral stages and moral orientations in real-life and hypothetical dilemmas. *Child Development, 58,* 842–858.

Wallerstein, J., and Kelley, J. (1974). The effects of parental divorce: The adolescent experience. In E. Anthony and A. Koupernik (Eds.), *The child in his family: Children as a psychiatric risk* (Vol. 3). New York: Wiley.

Wallerstein, J., and Kelley, J. (1980). *Surviving the breakup: How children and parents cope with divorce.* New York: Basic Books.

Walster, E., Aronson, V., Abrahams, D., and Rottman, L. (1966). Importance of physical attractiveness in dating behavior. *Journal of Personality and Social Psychology, 4,* 508–516.

Walters, H., and Kranzler, G. (1970). Early identification of the school dropout. *School Counselor, 18,* 97–104.

Waterman, A. (1982). Identity development from adolescence to adulthood: An extension of theory and a review of research. *Developmental Psychology, 18,* 341–358.

Waterman, A., Geary, P., and Waterman, A. (1974). A longitudinal study of changes in ego identity status from the freshman to the senior year at college. *Developmental Psychology, 10,* 387–392.

Waterman, A., and Goldman, J. (1976). A longitudinal study of ego identity development at a liberal arts college. *Journal of Youth and Adolescence, 5,* 361–369.

Waterman, A., and Waterman, M. (1971). A longitudinal study of changes in ego identity status during the freshman year at college. *Developmental Psychology, 5,* 167–173.

Watson, R. (1983). Premarital cohabitation versus traditional courtship: Their effects on subsequent marital adjustment. *Family Relations, 32,* 139–147.

Weideger, P. (1976). *Menstruation and menopause.* New York: Knopf.

Weiner, I. (1980). Psychopathology in adolescence. In J. Adelson (Ed.), *Handbook of adolescent psychology.* New York: Wiley.

Weiss, R. (1974). The provisions of social relationships. In Z. Rubin (Ed.), *Doing unto others.* Englewood Cliffs, N.J.: Prentice-Hall.

Wetzel, J. (1987). *American youth: A statistical snapshot.* New York: William T. Grant Foundation Commission on Work, Family, and Citizenship.

White, K., Speisman, J., and Costos, D. (1983). Young adults and their parents. In H. Grotevant and C. Cooper (Eds.), *Adolescent development in the family.* San Francisco: Jossey-Bass.

White, K., Speisman, J., Costos, D., and Smith, A. (1987). Relationship maturity: A conceptual and empirical approach. In J. Meacham (Ed.), *Contributions to human development* (Vol. 18). New York: Karger.

White, L., and Brinkerhoff, D. (1981). The sexual division of labor: Evidence from childhood. *Social Forces, 60,* 170–181.

Whiting, B., and Whiting, J. (1975). *Children of six cultures.* Cambridge, Mass.: Harvard University Press.

Wilms, W. (1975). *Public and proprietary vocational training: A study of effectiveness.* Lexington, Mass.: Lexington Books.

Wilson, F. (1985). The impact of school desegregation programs on white public-school enrollment, 1968–1976. *Sociology of Education, 58,* 137–153.

Wilson, T., and Linville, P. (1985). Improving the performance of college freshmen with attributional techniques. *Journal of Personality and Social Psychology, 49,* 287–293.

Winterbottem, M. (1958). The relation of need for achievement to learning experiences in independence and mastery. In J. Atkinson (Ed.), *Motives in fantasy, action, and society.* Princeton, N.J.: Van Nostrand.

Wintre, M., Hicks, R., McVey, G., and Fox, J. (in press). Age and sex differences in choice of consultant for various types of problems. *Child Development.*

Wirtz, P., Rohrbeck, C., Charner, I., and Fraser, B. (1987). Intense employment while in high school: Are teachers, guidance counselors, and parents misguiding academically-oriented adolescents? Paper available from the Graduate Institute for Policy Education and Research, The George Washington University, Washington, DC.

Wolfe, T. (August 23, 1976) The "me" decade and the third great awakening. *New York,* pp. 26–40.

Wuthnow, R., and Glock, C. (1973). Religious loyalty, defection, and experimentation among college youth. *Journal for the Scientific Study of Religion, 12,* 157–180.

Wyatt, K., and Geis, M. (1978). Level of formal thought and organizational memory strategies. *Developmental Psychology, 14,* 433–434.

Yamaguichi, K., and Kandel, D. (1987). Drug use and other determinants of premarital pregnancy and its outcome: A dynamic analysis of competing life events. *Journal of Marriage and the Family, 49,* 257–270.

Yankelovich, D. (1974). *The new morality: A profile of American youth in the 1970s.* New York: McGraw-Hill.

Young, H., and Ferguson, L. (1979). Developmental changes through adolescence in the spontaneous nomination of reference groups as a function of decision context. *Journal of Youth and Adolescence, 8,* 239–252.

Youniss, J., and Ketterlinus, R. (1987). Communication and connectedness in mother- and father-adolescent relationships. *Journal of Youth and Adolescence, 16,* 265–292.

Youniss, J., and Smollar, J. (1985). *Adolescent relations with mothers, fathers, and friends.* Chicago: University of Chicago Press.

Youth and America's Future. (1988). *The forgotten half: Non-college youth in America.* Washington: William T. Grant Foundation Commission on Work, Family, and Citizenship.

Yussen, S. (1976). Moral reasoning from the perspective of others. *Child Development, 47,* 551–555.

Zabin, L., Hirsch, M., Smith, E., Streett, R., and Hardy, J. (1986). Evaluation of a pregnancy prevention program for urban teenagers. *Family Planning Perspectives, 16,* 119–126.

Zajonc, R. (1976). Family configuration and intelligence. *Science, 192,* 227–236.

Zeldin, R., Small, S., and Savin-Williams, R. (1982). Pro-social interactions in two mixed-sex adolescent groups. *Child Development, 53,* 1492–1498.

Zelnick, M., and Kantner, J. (1973). Sex and contraception among unmarried teenagers. In C. Westoff et al. (Eds.), *Toward the end of growth: Population in America.* Englewood Cliffs, N.J.: Prentice-Hall.

Zelnick, M., Kantner, J., and Ford, K. (1981). *Sex and pregnancy in adolescence.* Beverly Hills, Calif.: Sage.

Zill, N. (1984). *Happy, healthy and insecure.* New York: Doubleday.

Zimring, F. (1982). *The changing legal world of adolescence.* New York: Free Press.

Zucker, R. (1979). Developmental aspects of drinking through the young adult years. In H. Blane and M. Chafetz (Eds.), *Youth, alcohol, and social policy.* New York: Plenum Press.

Name Index

Subject Index

PERMISSIONS ACKNOWLEDGMENTS

Text

23, 29: Fig. 1.1, 1.4 from Grumbach, M., et al. "Hypothalamic-pituitary regulation of puberty in man: Evidence and concepts derived from clinical research." In M. Grumbach, G. Grave, and F. Mayer (Eds.), *Control of the Onset of Puberty.* New York: Wiley.

26: Fig. 1.3 adapted from Marshall, W., "Puberty." In F. Falkner and J. Tanner (Eds.), *Human Growth*, Vol. 2. New York: Plenum, 1978.

30: Fig. 1.5, 1.6 adapted from Tanner, J. "Sequence, tempo, and individual variation in growth and development of boys and girls aged twelve to sixteen." In J. Kagan and R. Coles (Eds.), *Twelve to Sixteen: Early Adolescence.* New York: Norton, 1972.

31: Excerpt copyright © 1972 by Nora Ephron. Reprinted by permission of Alfred A. Knopf, Inc.

38, 39, 40: Figs. 1.11, 1.12, 1.13 adapted from Eveleth, P., and Tanner, J. *World-wide Variation in Human Growth.* New York: Cambridge University Press, 1976.

44, 45: Fig. 1.14 from *Being Adolescent: Conflict and Growth in the Teenage Years*, by Mihaly Csikszentmihalyi and Reed Larson. Copyright © 1984 by Basic Books, Inc. Reprinted by permission of Basic Books, Inc., Publishers.

60: Fig. 2.1 from *The Growth of Logical Thinking from Childhood to Adolescence.* New York: Basic Books, 1958.

61, 270, 329: Excerpts copyright © 1981 by Delia Ephron. Reprinted by permission of Viking Penguin, Inc.

77: Fig. 2.3 copyright © by The Society for Research in Child Development, Inc.

83: The "Hornybird" dialogue from Berkowitz, M.W. "The role of discussion in moral education." In M.W. Berkowitz and F. Oser (Eds.), *Moral Education: Theory and Application* (pp. 197–218). Hillsdale, NJ: Lawrence Erlbaum Associates, 1985.

105: Excerpt reprinted from *Transitions: Four Rituals in Eight Cultures*, by Martha Nemes Fried and Morton H. Fried, by permission of W. W. Norton & Company, Inc. Copyright © 1980 by Martha Nemes Fried and Morton H. Fried.

146: Fig. 4.6 from Furman, W., and Buhrmester, D. (1985). "Children's perceptions of the personal relationships in their social networks." *Developmental Psychology*, *21*, 1016–1024.

159: Fig. 5.3 adapted from *The Adolescent Society*, by James C. Coleman. Copyright © 1961 by The Free Press. Adapted with permission of The Free Press, a division of Macmillan, Inc.

161: Fig. 5.4 reprinted from the *Journal of Early Adolescence*, 1984, *4*, 155–181. By permission of the publisher, H.E.L.P. Books, Inc., Tucson, AZ.

190: Fig. 6.2 adapted from Barker, R., and Gump, P. *Big School, Small School: High School Size and Student Behavior.* Stanford, CA: Stanford University Press, 1964.

201: Fig. 6.4 copyright © The Society for Research in Child Development, Inc.

218: Excerpt reprinted by permission of the *Wall Street Journal*. Copyright © 1981 Dow Jones & Company, Inc. All rights reserved.

225: Excerpt reprinted by permission of the *Wall Street Journal*. Copyright © 1979 Dow Jones & Company, Inc. All rights reserved.

229: Table 7.2 reprinted from *Economic Outlook USA*, Summer 1983, by special permission. Copyright © 1983 by the University of Michigan.

245: Fig. 8.1 from Simmons, R., et al. "Disturbance in the self-image at adolescence," *American Sociological Review*, 1973, Vol. 38.

255: Excerpt from *The Member of the Wedding*, by Carson McCullers. Copyright © 1946 by Carson McCullers. Copyright © renewed 1974 by Floria V. Lasky. Reprinted by permission of Houghton Mifflin Company.

318: Fig. 10.2 from Hunter, F., and Youniss, J. "Changes in functions of three relations during adolescence." *Developmental Psychology*, 1982, *18*, 806–811. Copyright © 1982 by the American Psychological Association. Reprinted by permission of the author.

325: Box figure adapted from Sharabany, R., et al. (1981). "Girlfriend, boyfriend: Age and sex difference in intimate friendship." *Developmental Psychology*, *17*, 800–808. Copyright © 1981 by the American Psychological Association. Reprinted by permission of the author.

383: Fig. 12.1 from the article by E. Fiske, "Colleges open new minority drive," *New York Times*, November 12, 1987. Copyright © 1987 by The New York Times Company. Reprinted by permission.